New Sweden:
1638   1655

Scale
Miles

5   10   15   20   25   30   35   40   45   50

SWEDES IN AMERICA

JOHAN PRINTZ

GOVERNOR OF NEW SWEDEN, 1643–53

SWEDES

IN

AMERICA

1638-1938

EDITED BY ADOLPH B. BENSON

AND

NABOTH HEDIN

PUBLISHED FOR THE
SWEDISH AMERICAN TERCENTENARY
ASSOCIATION

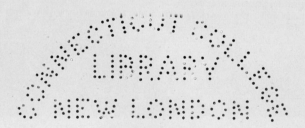
NEW HAVEN
YALE UNIVERSITY PRESS
LONDON · HUMPHREY MILFORD · OXFORD UNIVERSITY PRESS
1938

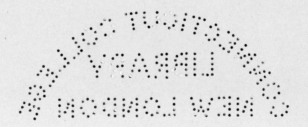

I must needs commend the Swedes respect to Authority, and Kind behaviour to the English; they do not degenerate from the old Friendship between both Kingdoms. As they are People proper and strong of Body, so they have fine children, and almost every house full; rare to find one of them without three or four Boys, and as many Girls; some six, seven and eight Sons: And I must do them that right, I see few young men more sober and laborious.

WILLIAM PENN

in

The Present State of His Majesty's Isles and Territories in America, London, 1687.

First Honorary Patron

HIS ROYAL HIGHNESS
THE CROWN PRINCE OF SWEDEN

Honorary Patron

HONORABLE WOLLMAR F. BOSTRÖM,
SWEDISH MINISTER TO U. S.

SPONSOR PATRONS

ALBERT I. APPLETON
WILLIAM L. BATT
MRS. WILLIAM L. BATT
FOLKE BECKER
J. G. BERGQUIST
GEORGE F. BERKANDER
JOHN S. BIOREN
NILS BJORK
H. BJORNSTROM-STEFFANSON
ROBERT WOODS BLISS
WILLIS H. BOOTH
CARL OSCAR BORG
CARL R. CHINDBLOM
J. F. A. COMSTEDT
BROR G. DAHLBERG
EMIL O. J. DANIELSON
OLAV J. S. DE BRUN
FREDERICK ENDERS
RICHARD ENGSTROM
K. O. ERICKSON
E. WALFRID ERICSSON
DR. CARL H. ERNLUND
FRITZ O. FERNSTROM
WALTER W. FREEMAN
COLIN G. HOYLAND
GEORGE N. JEPPSON
NILS R. JOHANESON
MRS. NILS R. JOHANESON
OSCAR A. LENNA

MRS. OSCAR A. LENNA
DAVID L. LINDQUIST
G. HILMER LUNDBECK
EDWARD MAGNUSON
H. EDWARD MANVILLE
J. KEARSLEY MITCHELL
JOHN M. MOREHEAD
IRA NELSON MORRIS
FRANK MOSSBERG
ERIK H. NELSON
ELIS OLSON
A. J. PAGEL
FRANCIS J. PLYM
ORMOND RAMBO, JR.
MRS. ORMOND RAMBO, JR.
JUSTUS P. SEEBURG
COUNT PEHR SPARRE
DR. F. J. SWANSON
W. O. LILJENSTOLPE-SWANSON
N. K. G. THOLAND
WOLFGANG THOMAS
MAJ. GEN. I. THORD-GRAY
MRS. I. THORD-GRAY
CHARLES H. THORLING
EMIL TYDEN
THOMAS J. WATSON
SAMUEL P. WETHERILL
C. E. WICKMAN

SWEDISH AMERICAN TERCENTENARY ASSOCIATION

O. N. SOLBERT
Chairman, Board of Directors and Executive Committee

FRANCIS J. PLYM
President

GEORGE N. JEPPSON
1st Vice-President

WILLIS H. BOOTH
Treasurer

NILS R. JOHANESON
Chairman Finance Committee

DR. AMANDUS JOHNSON
Corresponding Secretary

DR. JULIUS LINCOLN
Recording Secretary

NABOTH HEDIN
Chairman Publicity Committee

HARRY C. HALLBERG
Executive Secretary

DIRECTORS

SOLBERT, O. N., *Chairman*
BERGQUIST, J. G., *V. Ch.*
ANDERSON, REV. THEO. W.
APPLETON, ALBERT I.
BENSON, PROF. A. B.
BERKANDER, GEORGE F.
BERSELL, REV. P. O.
CHINDBLOM, HON. CARL R.
DANIELSON, HON. E. O. J.
ERICSSON, HENRY
FERNSTROM, F. O.
GUSTAFSON, C. A.
GUSTAVSON, MARK
HEDIN, NABOTH
HEDMAN, HERBERT
HOLM, HON. MIKE
JACOBSON, E. R.
JEPPSON, GEORGE N.

JOHANESON, NILS R.
JOHNSON, DR. AMANDUS
JOHNSON, BERNARD
KLINGBERG, REV. J. E.
KRAFFT, BERNHARD
LINCOLN, REV. JULIUS
LUNDBECK, G. HILMER
MARELL, O. G.
PAGEL, A. J.
PLYM, FRANCIS J.
RAMBO, ORMOND, JR.
RYDEN, PROF. GEORGE H.
SKOGLUND, AUGUST H.
THULIN, ERIK
TYDEN, EMIL
WALLENIUS, REV. CARL G.
WESTERLIN, J. M.
WICKMAN, C. E.

EXECUTIVE COMMITTEE

Editors' Preface

THE purpose of this volume, the publication of which is a part of the New Sweden Tercentenary celebration, is to recall by summaries and representative examples the rôles played by Swedes as American pioneers and citizens. It is a review of deeds and influences in many fields of endeavor, the value of which we shall leave to the judgment of the reader. Some of the material has long been known in a general way, but it has been widely scattered and often of an indiscriminate character. In the following pages the alert student will discover, we trust, many new and interesting details. Obviously, SWEDES IN AMERICA makes no claim to completeness—not every deserving name could even be mentioned. Our collection of articles, though written by the best authorities available, constitutes only a beginning which we hope will prove an incentive to further research and evaluation.

Under the limiting circumstances of time and space, the literary and historical *modus operandi* has been one of selection and condensation, each author being generally responsible for the contents of his own chapter. For the final form of the book as a whole, however, the Editors alone are accountable. Since each article is intended to be a unit by itself, and since several people have merited recognition in two or more fields of activity, some names will appear in more than one chapter; but an attempt has been made to reduce unavoidable duplications to a minimum. Painstaking efforts have been made, also, to check all important facts and to bring these up to date, but in a compilation of this kind mistakes are bound to creep in. We hope they are few and minor ones. At all events, the Editors will welcome corrections and notices of serious omissions, for, if the work meets with sufficient encouragement, it will be followed immediately by a revised edition and, in the not too distant future, perhaps by an enlarged one.

The Swedish American Tercentenary Association hereby wishes to express its appreciation to the contributors and editors of this book and to Mrs. Hannah Nicholson Benson of New Haven, Connecticut, for compiling the index.

ADOLPH B. BENSON
NABOTH HEDIN

New Haven, Conn.,
  May, 1938.

CONTENTS

PREFACE · · · · · · · · · · · · *The Editors* · · · · · · · · · · xi
LIST OF ILLUSTRATIONS · xv
INTRODUCTION · · · · · · · · *Henry Goddard Leach* · · · · · 1
COLONISTS · · · · · · · · · · *Amandus Johnson* · · · · · · · 5
COLONIAL LANDMARKS · · · · · *George H. Ryden* · · · · · · · 35
THE SWEDISH LANGUAGE IN
   AMERICA · · · · · · · · · · *Axel Johan Uppvall* · · · · · 52
FARMERS · · · · · · · · · · · *Eric Englund* · · · · · · · · · 75
PIONEERS OF THE NORTH-
   WEST · · · · · · · · · · · · *Andrew A. Stomberg* · · · · · 92
GEOGRAPHICAL DISTRIBUTION · · *W. Elmer Ekblaw* · · · · · · 107
SWEDISH PLACE NAMES IN
   AMERICA · · · · · · · · · · *Vilhelm Berger* · · · · · · · 123
RELIGION · · · · · · · · · · · *George M. Stephenson* · · · · 126
CHARITIES AND SELF-HELP · · · *Julius Lincoln* · · · · · · · · 140
COLLEGES · · · · · · · · · · · *Ernst W. Olson* · · · · · · · 154
NEWSPAPERS · · · · · · · · · · *Oliver A. Linder* · · · · · · 181
WRITERS IN SWEDISH · · · · · · *Joseph E. A. Alexis* · · · · · 191
MAGAZINES · · · · · · · · · · *Adolph B. Benson* · · · · · · 206
AUTHORS · · · · · · · · · · · *Anna Olsson* · · · · · · · · · 209
JOURNALISTS · · · · · · · · · *Roy W. Swanson* · · · · · · · 219
TRANSLATIONS OF SWEDISH
   LITERATURE · · · · · · · · · *Adolph B. Benson* · · · · · · 237
FOUR REPRESENTATIVES OF
   THE INTELLECT · · · · · · · *David F. Swenson* · · · · · · 253
THE NEW CHURCH · · · · · · · *Marguerite Beck Block* · · · · 279
PROFESSORS · · · · · · · · · · *Adolph B. Benson* · · · · · · 282
PUBLIC SCHOOL EDUCATORS · · · *O. Fritiof Ander* · · · · · · 300
LAWYERS · · · · · · · · · · · *G. Aaron Youngquist* · · · · · 315
PUBLIC OFFICIALS · · · · · · · *O. Fritiof Ander* · · · · · · 321
DOCTORS · · · · · · · · · · · *Selma Giving* and
    · · · · · · · · · · · · · · *David L. Tilderquist, M.D.* · 338
GYMNASTICS · · · · · · · · · · *Theodor A. Melander* · · · · · 357
SPORTS AND SPORTSMEN · · · · · *Gerhard T. Rooth* · · · · · · 366
INVENTORS · · · · · · · · · · *Johan Liljencrants* · · · · · 382

ENGINEERS	*Lawrence E. Widmark*	407
ARCHITECTS AND BUILDERS	*C. Theodore Larson*	416
COMPOSERS	*Victor Nilsson*	435
OPERA SINGERS	*Marie Sundelius*	453
THE AMERICAN UNION OF SWEDISH SINGERS	*Charles K. Johansen*	469
MOVING PICTURE ACTORS	*Leonard Clairmont*	473
STAGE AND RADIO PERFORMERS	*Holger Lundbergh*	482
PAINTERS AND SCULPTORS	*Oliver A. Linder*	488
SOLDIERS AND SAILORS	*Nils G. Sahlin*	506
AVIATION	*John Goldstrom*	532
MANUFACTURERS	*Bernard Peterson*	551
BUSINESSMEN	*Gustaf Sundelius*	572
IMPORTS AND IMPORTERS	*Victor O. Freeburg*	584
INDEX	*Hannah N. Benson*	599

ILLUSTRATIONS

JOHAN PRINTZ *Frontispiece*
Courtesy of the Swedish Colonial Society

HOLY TRINITY (OLD SWEDES) CHURCH, WILMINGTON, DELA-
WARE 40
Courtesy of the American Swedish Historical Museum

WHERE SKY AND GRAIN MEET 82
Courtesy of the U. S. Department of Agriculture

MILK AND MEAT 82
Courtesy of the U. S. Department of Agriculture

JOHANNES HULT, PIONEER 102
Courtesy of Prof. A. A. Stomberg, University of Minnesota

TUVE NILSSON HASSELQUIST 132
Courtesy of the Denkmann Memorial Library, Augustana College

CARL AARON SWENSSON 168
Courtesy of Bethany College, Kansas

ERNST TEOFIL SKARSTEDT 198
Courtesy of *Nordstjernan*, New York

CARL SANDBURG 210
Photograph by Eugene Hutchinson

SELMA LAGERLÖF 250
Courtesy of the American Swedish News Exchange, Inc.

EMANUEL SWEDENBORG 262

CARL EMIL SEASHORE 204
Courtesy of The State University of Iowa

JOHAN AUGUST UDDEN 296
Courtesy of The University of Texas

AGNES SAMUELSON 310
Photograph by Peter Berkeley, Denver, Colorado

JOHN LIND 324
Courtesy of *The American Swedish Monthly*

THE LINDBERGHS 330
Courtesy of Mrs. Eva Lindbergh Christie

CARL ARTHUR HEDBLOM, M.D. 346
Courtesy of The University of Illinois

JOHN ERICSSON   382
    Courtesy of the American Swedish Historical Museum

VINCENT BENDIX   398
    Photograph by Fernand De Gueldre, Chicago

ERNST FREDERIK WERNER ALEXANDERSON   400

HOWARD HANSON   448
    Courtesy of the American Swedish News Exchange, Inc.

JENNY LIND   454
    Courtesy of the American Swedish Historical Museum

WARNER OLAND   474

GRETA GARBO   476

DOROTHY PETERSON   480

CARL MILLES   504
    Courtesy of the American Swedish News Exchange, Inc.

CAPTAIN GEORGE FRIED   530
    Courtesy of *The American Swedish Monthly*

MAJOR ERIK H. NELSON   534

COLONEL CHARLES A. LINDBERGH   542
    Courtesy of Wide World Photos

COMMANDER CHARLES E. ROSENDAHL   546
    Courtesy of *The New York Times* Studio

FRANCIS J. PLYM   554

GEORGE N. JEPPSON   558

G. HILMER LUNDBECK   596

SWEDES IN AMERICA

Introduction

HENRY GODDARD LEACH

A native of Philadelphia, a member of the Society of Mayflower Descendants, and holder of academic degrees from both Princeton and Harvard, Dr. Leach has for twenty-five years served the American Scandinavian Foundation, first as Secretary and then as President. In this capacity he has done pioneering work for a better appreciation of Northern culture in the United States and for more friendly international relations. He lives in New York and is Editor of the *Forum*.

HIS Royal Highness Crown Prince Gustaf Adolf of Sweden will be very welcome when he returns to New Sweden this Tercentenary year. He is a worthy successor to Gustavus Adolphus the Great, who conceived the dream of a Swedish colony in the New World. The earlier monarch was a leader of Europe in the arts of war; his namesake is a leader in the still more difficult strategy of peace. Now, for more than a century, Sweden has kept the peace and demonstrated her right to be called one of the most civilized of modern nations. The Crown Prince is a distinguished spokesman for a race that three hundred years ago, and again more recently, has vitalized the blood stream of America and given us many of our most impressive symbols of progress.

The earliest contribution of the Swedes to America was the log cabin. The Swedes came from a land of great forests to another land of vast woodlands. In New Sweden, on the banks of the Delaware in 1638, they rejected the wigwams of the Indians and erected, instead, by applying their inborn engineering skill, strong dwellings made out of roughhewn timber. From New Sweden the log cabin design spread wherever American colonists moved into virgin country.

Ever since 1638 the Swedes have continued to make signal contributions to the New World in research and in the applied sciences, in construction, engineering, and mechanical wonders. The *Monitor* which, more than any other single "miracle" except Gettysburg, helped to preserve the Union is, of course, the outstanding symbol of Swedish mechanical genius in America. But today no great bridge is planned, no important dam constructed, no skyscraper erected, no aeroplane factory completed in the United States without somewhere in the process the employment of Swedish brains.

Today Swedish inventions radiate from our lighthouses and highway beacons. Swedish separators prepare the cream for our butter. Swedish "controlled heat" stoves cook our food. Silent Swedish chemical refrigerators cool our drinks. Swedish ball bearings reduce the friction of our modern living.

Swedish inventions add not only to the efficiency but also to the beauty of our mechanical life. Did anyone ever see a Swedish separator or highway beacon that did not look graceful and streamlined? This is the characteristic of the Swedish mind that makes Sweden one of the most intelligent of modern nations: the equilibrium between the æsthetic and the mechanical, between the ideal and the real, between happiness and achievement. *Mens sana in corpore sano*—with a flower in the workingman's buttonhole!

Of all words in the Swedish dictionary, the one that appeals most to Americans is *levnadslust*—"joy of life." This word, made famous by the Swedish poet Tegnér, expresses to us Americans the poise, the joyousness, the smiling intelligence, the rhythm of Swedish personality and living.

A person of English descent, meeting a group of typical Swedes, is impressed with four characteristics: their love of physical culture, their appreciation of art, their facility in science, their coöperative instinct. In the home country practically every Swede is proficient in some form of athletics, and it was Swedish gymnastics which first made us Americans conscious nationally of the culture of the human body.

What William Penn said of the Swedes whom he found on the Delaware is true of our Swedish population today. "They have fine children and almost every house full; rare to find one of them without three or four boys and as many girls; some six, seven and eight sons. And I must do them right—I see few young men more sober and laborious."

Penn took over the Swedish courts and system of law which he found planted on the Delaware. A century later it was a

Pennsylvanian of Swedish descent, John Morton, it is reputed, who cast the deciding vote in his own delegation for the Declaration of Independence; and another Swede, John Hanson of Maryland, presided over Congress for one year after the Revolution. This tradition of statesmanship has been followed by the leaders of our more recent Swedish immigration. The roll of Swedish governors of our states, of Swedes in the Senate and Congress, is impressive.

In politics the American of Swedish descent is likely to be a conservative. In Sweden the typical Conservative is not a reactionary, but one who feels a high responsibility for the country and is ready to legislate, if it be proved good, any reform, no matter how radical its source. Like the American, the Swede is an individualist; but he has a high appreciation of economic and social balance, and for this reason labor unions are a matter of course in Sweden, and the consumers' coöperatives prosper. Some of their coöperative principles have been transplanted satisfactorily in American farm districts where Swedes have settled.

Swedish-Americans have distinguished themselves in science and in the learned professions, and our universities appreciate the contemporary progress of science in Sweden, as evidenced by the honorary degrees bestowed on Swedes at the recent Tercentenary of Harvard University. Two hundred of our institutions of learning, this year of the Tercentenary of New Sweden, are inviting some of the leading scientists of Sweden to lecture here. The first of these lecturers was Nobelprizeman The Svedberg, inventor of the ultracentrifuge, who distinguished the dedication of the new Chemistry Building of the University of Delaware. Among these lecturers are architects, economists, and physicians. A close relation exists today between the great surgeons and medical scientists of Sweden and America.

In the arts, the contribution of Sweden to modern literature has been reflected, not only by the circulation of translations of Swedish authors, but by American authors of Swedish ancestry emerging from Swedish-American farms and industrial centers. Some of our leading American painters are proud of their Swedish ancestry. Swedish song has enriched the æsthetic life of our nation. Choral societies of Swedish-Americans are welcome everywhere. Visiting prima donnas from Sweden contribute fully as much as Italians to raise American opera to its present high level of quality as well as popularity.

The magnificent debt of the United States to the Swedes is reviewed in detail by the eminent writers who have contributed in this book to a symposium on the Swedes in the United States.

May the New Sweden Tercentenary turn the attention of America in the future, even more than in the past, to the success of the experiments of that smaller friendly country in northern Europe which, in its imaginative realism, is solving so many matters essential to progress and to civilization, that can be translated for use in our larger, but more inchoate nation.

Colonists

AMANDUS JOHNSON

Dr. Johnson, born in Sweden, was educated at Gustavus Adolphus College, the University of Colorado, and the University of Pennsylvania, where he received the Ph.D. degree in 1908. He also holds honorary doctorates from his Alma Mater, Gustavus Adolphus College, from Augustana College, and the University of Gothenburg. For a number of years he taught Scandinavian languages at the University of Pennsylvania; for two years was director of an educational expedition to Africa; and, since his return, has devoted his time to the study of the Swedes in America. He is now President of the American Swedish Historical Foundation, Philadelphia. His work, *The Swedish Settlements on the Delaware,* in two volumes, is the authoritative publication on the subject, while *The Swedes on the Delaware, 1638–1664* is a more popular version in one volume. He is also the author of *Instruction for Johan Printz* and has translated and edited Peter Lindeström's *Geographia Americæ* and *The Journal and Biography of Nicholas Collin.* Besides writing other books, he has contributed numerous articles and reviews to various newspapers and journals.

IN the early seventeenth century Holland established far-flung settlements in North and South America, and soon England founded colonies on the James River and at other places on the North American coast. Denmark likewise aspired to a share in the colonial enterprise, and sent an expedition to the Hudson Bay district in 1619, but nothing came of it. Somewhat later Sweden decided to join in the movement that was now becoming general.

The first impetus toward Swedish transatlantic trade and colonization came from Holland. Willem Usselinx, the great Dutch promoter of the seventeenth century, persuaded Gustavus Adolphus to found, in 1626, a commercial company called the South Sea Company, for trade and colonization in Asia and America. Shares in the corporation were bought by the King and the nobility, and even by the people at large. Many of the cities in the Kingdom also subscribed relatively large sums; an American trading company was considered a sure road to wealth. Capital was scarce in Sweden at this time, however, and the sums gathered from all sources were insufficient for the great plans conceived by Usselinx.

In 1634–35, Samuel Blommaert, a Dutchman in Swedish service, proposed a new scheme for a Swedish colony in the Delaware region of North America. He knew a man well acquainted with these parts, Peter Minuit, for some years Governor of New Amsterdam. Minuit was now without employment, having been dismissed by his Dutch employers, and he was looking for a new sponsor. Through Blommaert he was introduced to the Swedish Chancellor, Axel Oxenstierna, and after considerable discussion a practical plan was evolved. A company was to be formed of Swedish and Dutch stockholders. Two ships were to be sent to the Delaware region, where land should be bought from the Indians. The colony should be called New Sweden. Forts were to be erected and trade carried on with the Delaware Indians, largely in beaver skins.

Large cargoes were purchased in Holland and sent to Gothenburg where two ships, the *Kalmar Nyckel* ("Key of Kalmar") and the *Fogel Grip* ("Bird Griffon"), were prepared for the journey. The *Kalmar Nyckel*, furnished by the old South Sea Company, corresponded somewhat to the auxiliary cruiser of our day. The *Griffon* was supplied by the Government. It was a fast-sailing warship, corresponding somewhat to a light cruiser of today.

The two ships, with Peter Minuit as director of the expedition, left the harbor of Gothenburg about November 20, 1637. Encountering terrible storms in the North Sea, they were obliged to put in at Texel in Holland for repairs and more supplies. Contrary winds delayed their departure from there, but at last, on December 31, the two little vessels left the shores of Europe on their historic voyage across the Atlantic. Almost three months more elapsed before they reached Delaware Bay, and, sailing up the Delaware River to the mouth of the Christina River on the left and up the latter stream for a distance of about two miles, they finally cast anchor before a ledge of rocks at the site of present Wilmington, Delaware, about March 25, 1638. Presently Peter Minuit explored the land for some miles along the Christina River—then called Minquas Kill—to establish the fact that no white people were then in possession.

In the meantime Indian chiefs with their retainers appeared at the "Rocks," and on the twenty-ninth of March (N.S. April 8) five sachems, Mattahorn, Mitatsimint, Erupacken, Mahomen, and Chiton, entered the cabin of the *Kalmar Nyckel* and sold as much "of the land in all parts and places of the river, up the river and on both sides, as Minuit desired." The deeds, drawn up and explained to the Indians, recited that for "value received in merchandise the Indians ceded and transferred the title of the land with its jurisdictions and rights to the Swedish Florida Company under the protection of the Great Princess, Virgin and Elected Queen of the Swedes, Goths and Wends." The Indians traced their sprawling totem marks on the documents; Peter Minuit, Måns Kling, Hendrick Huygen, Andreas Lucassen, and Jacob Evertssen Sandelin signed their names below, and thus the western shore of the Delaware River from Bombay Hook to the Schuylkill River, extending westward indefinitely as far "as Minuit desired," became the legal possession of the Swedish Crown. The Swedish coat of arms was erected on a pole "and with the report of cannon, followed by other solemn ceremonies, the land was called New Sweden." The river was called Christina in honor of the young Queen, and the fort, which was erected back of the rocks about thirty or forty feet from the water's edge, was also called Christina.

Some dwellings were built within the fort as a shelter for the garrison. Small tracts in the neighborhood were planted with vegetables, and patches were sown with rye and barley and perhaps with some wheat and other grain, for "two barrels of wheat and two barrels of seed corn" were brought over on the ships. Twenty-one men were stationed in the fort as a garrison, under the command of Måns Nilsson Kling. Hendrick Huygen was put in charge of the storehouse, and William Laury was provost marshal.

About the middle of June, Minuit left the colony in charge of Kling—who thus became the first acting Governor of New Sweden—and departed on the *Kalmar Nyckel*. The ship put into Vlie in Holland for repairs in October, but without Minuit, who had been drowned during a storm in the West Indies while visiting the captain of a Dutch vessel at the island of St. Christopher.

In May of 1638 the *Griffon* left New Sweden in search of Spanish treasure ships, but practically nothing is known about this expedition. In the early part of 1639 the vessel returned to Fort Christina, and near the end of April set sail for Sweden with a cargo of skins, arriving at Gothenburg about the beginning of June, a record journey for those early days.

The first expedition was a financial failure. The total value of the cargoes—pelts and tobacco—was 23,849 florins, while the expenses amounted to more than 46,000 florins.

In the spring of 1638, Klas Fleming, an admiral in the Swedish Navy who had become enthusiastic about the colonial venture, proposed that several ships should be prepared for a new voyage. When, therefore, the reports, the Indian deeds to the land, and other papers arrived on the *Kalmar Nyckel*, Fleming's enthusiasm was increased, and preparations for a second expedition to the Delaware were begun in earnest. The trusty *Kalmar Nyckel* was again fitted out. Fleming and the other Swedish stockholders apparently decided that the colony should be not only a trading post, as the Dutch stockholders had conceived it, but an agricultural establishment as well. Accordingly, laborers, colonists, horses, cattle, fodder and provisions, farming implements, ammunition, as well as supplies for the Indian trade, were taken on board. Peter Hollender Ridder went on the ship as the second governor of the colony. The Reverend Reorus Torkillus was appointed pastor in New Sweden, and Gregorius van Dyck, a Dutchman, but a faithful servant of the Swedish Crown, was sent out as assistant commissary.

On its second voyage to New Sweden, the *Kalmar Nyckel* left Gothenburg in the beginning of September, 1639, but on the way encountered all manner of difficulties—crew trouble, storms, and prolonged repairs—so that the people and cattle suffered severely, and the vessel did not arrive at Fort Christina until April 17, 1640.

Governor Ridder now took charge of the colony. The keys of the storehouse were delivered to Joost von Langdonk. Gregorius van Dyck became assistant commissary, and Göran Olsson was made provost marshal, while Per Anderson was guard and skipper on the yacht. The *Kalmar Nyckel* set sail for Europe about the middle of May. Måns Kling and Hendrick Huygen returned to Sweden on the vessel.

The financial losses of the second expedition were even greater than those of the first, and the Dutch shareholders were thoroughly dissatisfied. The Government at Stockholm therefore "found it expedient to release the Dutch participants in the New Indian or Florida Company, as they are a hinderance . . ." and in February, 1641, 18,000 riksdalers were paid for their shares. From now on the New Sweden Company was operated entirely by Swedish money. The Company was reorganized and several new officers were appointed.

At this time a plan was on foot to establish a group of Dutch settlers in New Sweden. A ship was chartered for the purpose, and in the autumn of 1640 the emigrants, fifty in number, established themselves a few miles above Fort Christina. The colony, however, soon disappeared, and we do not know what became of it.

A fourth expedition of two ships, the faithful *Kalmar Nyckel* and a new vessel, the *Charitas*, was prepared in the spring and summer of 1641. The *Kalmar Nyckel* carried most of the settlers, who now consisted of Swedes and a few Finns from the northern part of the Kingdom. Horses, goats, cattle, sheep, and farming implements, as well as seed corn of every kind, were loaded onto the *Charitas*. The two vessels sailed in July. The voyage was unusually stormy. Some cattle and two passengers died on the journey, and when the ships finally cast anchor at Fort Christina on November 7, 1641, "the . . . people were very weak and powerless."

A new clergyman, Pastor Christopher, came on this expedition. Måns Kling returned as commander of the fort, and a tailor, a millwright, a blacksmith, and other skilled laborers, as well as some freemen or colonists, arrived on the vessel. Five horses, eight cows, five sheep, and two goats were landed alive, but two horses and one cow died soon after they had been brought ashore. New Sweden was now firmly established as a colony.

The ships departed from New Sweden about the end of November, carrying a detailed report from Governor Ridder and one or two returning soldiers, but no cargo. Before the ships

reached Sweden, Admiral Fleming had begun preparations on
a large scale for a new expedition—three ships were to be sent.
The arrival of Ridder's report at Stockholm in the late spring
or early summer of 1642 stimulated the preparations, and it
was decided to dispatch the vessels at the earliest possible moment, even though supplies for the Indian trade could not be
procured.

It was resolved to establish Swedish authority on the Delaware even more firmly. A new governor was to be appointed and
the civil as well as military authority was to be placed on a
stable and more businesslike basis. Lieutenant Colonel Johan
Printz, who had gained success in the Thirty Years' War, but
who for some time had been in retirement, was appointed governor. Printz had had a varied career. In his youth he studied
theology, expecting to follow in the footsteps of his paternal
ancestors, who had been pastors in the Swedish church for generations. However, circumstances made him a soldier of fortune
and he served under many masters, in many armies, and in many
countries before he entered the Swedish ranks.

Printz, as stated above, was recalled from his retirement and
appointed Governor of New Sweden at a salary of 800 riksdalers a year. A famous "Instruction," which has been called
the "First Constitution or Fundamental Law of Delaware and
Pennsylvania," was issued to him. The "Instruction," dated
August 15, 1642, contained twenty-eight articles regulating
the religious, civic, legal, military, commercial, agricultural,
and manufacturing activities of the settlement, and defining
the powers of the governor and his relation to the natives and
the neighboring colonies.

As in the case of previous expeditions, emphasis was placed
on the development of the colony and the settlement of the
country. No cargo was purchased for the Indian trade. Great
efforts were made to obtain settlers. Soldiers were engaged to
persuade people to migrate, and governors of the northern provinces were instructed to prevail upon their subjects to go to
America, those of good standing to take their families with
them. But persuasive methods failed to arouse enthusiasm for
a journey to the New World. Even in those days news traveled
fast, especially bad news, and the voyages to New Sweden were

in bad repute. The Council of State decided that soldiers guilty of desertion and poachers should be sent to the colony for some years as a punishment, but even these measures proved inadequate. It was then resolved that Finns, who had settled in the northern and central provinces of Sweden and were reputed to have destroyed valuable forests, should be sent to the Delaware with their families. It was also ordered that citizens unable to pay their debts, but suitable as colonists or workers, should be taken to the Delaware. At no time, however, were criminals who had committed grave offenses deported to New Sweden.

A mining expert was engaged to look for minerals, and skilled laborers and workmen were hired to serve on the plantations and in the forts. Additional soldiers and officers were enlisted for garrison duty, and two new pastors, the Reverend Johan Campanius and the Reverend Israel Fluviander, accompanied the expedition.

The Company was reorganized in August, 1642, and "the Royal Government and their respective participants resolved to furnish a capital stock of 36,000 riksdalers in the New Sweden Company," the various entries being made in the Journal of the Corporation on August 28, 1642.

The preparations dragged on throughout the summer, and not until the end of October were the ships ready to depart. On the first of November, 1642, the *Swan* and the *Fama*, the two ships selected for the expedition, left Gothenburg harbor, and by the end of January, 1643, arrived in Delaware Bay. As they were about to enter the river, a terrible storm broke. The *Fama* tore away from her three anchors and was cast ashore with heavy damage, losing her mainmast and spritsail. The anchors of the *Swan* held, but the ship suffered heavily and part of her cargo was ruined. The *Fama* was refloated with the rising tide and temporary repairs were made. On February 15, the ships arrived before the Rocks at Fort Christina.

The ships left the colony about the middle of April, 1643, with large cargoes of pelts. Peter Ridder, Johan Papegoja, and some soldiers and workmen departed on the vessels, which reached Gothenburg about the end of July. Johan Papegoja, and perhaps Ridder and the others, went overland to Stockholm, bringing letters and the first report of Governor Printz from New Sweden. The documents arrived in the Swedish capital on August 1, the ships with their cargoes making their appearance some weeks later.

Even before the ships reached Stockholm, preparations had begun for another expedition. Two ships were fitted out, and this time trade with the aborigines and commerce in the West Indies were to be the main purposes of the voyage. Large supplies of merchandise were procured in Holland and in Sweden. Colonists, however, were not forgotten. In the autumn Papegoja enlisted some soldiers and, as emigrants did not appear voluntarily, the Government decreed that timber thieves and game poachers should be sent to New Sweden. Two or three colonists came from Finland, and two noblemen, Knut and Per Lilliehöök, were among the passengers. Johan Papegoja also made arrangements to return to his new home.

The *Fama*, which had just returned from the fifth of the Company's expeditions, and the *Kalmar Nyckel* were selected for the voyage. The *Kalmar Nyckel* made a trading voyage to the Caribbean Islands, and only the *Fama* went to Fort Christina on the Delaware, arriving there on March 11, 1644. In her cargo were, among other supplies, the following: three large saws for a sawmill; eight grindstones; one pair of stones for a hand mill; one pair of large millstones for a gristmill; five anchors; five pumps with necessary repairs and a hide of pump leather; twelve small and eight large augers; four compasses; thirty-six blocks; two hundred and fifty copper kettles; several barrels of lime and pitch; a few thousand bricks; two hundred barrels of flour; twenty barrels of "Spanish salt;" ten hogsheads of French wine; one hogshead of brandy; several hundred yards of cloth; ten gilded flagpole knobs; three hundred pairs of shoes; and two hundred pairs of stockings.

About June 20, 1644, the *Fama* set her course for Europe with a large cargo of skins and tobacco. She and the *Kalmar Nyckel* (the latter returning from the Caribbean Islands), having put into Harlingen on their homeward journey, were seized by order of the Dutch West India Company, but were finally released through the efforts of Peter Spiring, the Swedish Ambassador to Holland.

The *Fama* brought an earnest request from Printz and Papegoja for more colonists and more supplies. But Admiral Klas Fleming, the driving force in the New Sweden Company, was at this time engaged in a task of far more importance to Sweden than the fortunes of the little settlements along the Delaware. A war with Denmark was in progress and Admiral Fleming pressed every ship into service. The *Swan* and the *Charitas*, which had made journeys to New Sweden, fought in the battle of Femern, and when the *Kalmar Nyckel* and the *Fama* arrived at Gothenburg, they were refitted and added to the fleet. The war not only prevented the dispatching of aid to Governor Printz at this time, but inflicted an irreparable loss on the Company and the colony. In July, 1644, Fleming was killed by a stray bullet from a Danish battery. Axel Oxenstierna, the Swedish Chancellor, became the head of the New Sweden Company, but since he was deeply engrossed in peace negotiations with Denmark, he did not find time even to peruse the letters and reports which Governor Printz dispatched to Sweden. Eventually the documents were sent to Hans Kramer and Johan Beier, officers of the Company, who made every effort possible to comply with the requests of Printz; but nothing was, nor could be, accomplished, since final decisions in the matter had to be made by the Government.

On August 13, 1645, the Danish war came to an end, and now ships could be spared for commercial voyages. A new expedition on a large scale was to be sent as soon as ships could be prepared. Four hundred women, four hundred men (half of them soldiers), and two hundred children were to be dispatched to Governor Printz. So large a project, however, could not be realized. It was found that but two vessels could be sent. A new ship, the *Golden Shark*, fully rigged, was purchased in Holland for the journey, and the official documents state that the *Fama* was to sail also.

For some unknown reason, however, the *Golden Shark* sailed alone in May, 1646. She had a perilous and stormy voyage and did not reach Fort Christina until October 1, lacking most of her sails and her topmast. "The master of the ship, the mate and all the crew, except one man, were ill, so that according to their reports, they would all have perished, if they had not reached land when they did." The sailors recovered but slowly, and the repairs on the ship were not completed until December. As the winter was hard, the river froze over and the ship could not begin its homeward journey until March. She arrived safely at Gothenburg in June, 1647, with a cargo of tobacco, and reached Stockholm in the autumn.

In the meantime a new expedition was prepared. Provisions for the needs of New Sweden and merchandise for the Indian trade were loaded into the holds of the *Swan*, a veteran in the colonial service, and in September she was ready to sail. Johan Papegoja, the great traveler to and from New Sweden, endeavored to obtain passengers. He was but moderately successful and few colonists came to the Delaware on the vessel. This was probably the most successful and most fortunate expedition to New Sweden during the existence of the colony. The *Swan* left Gothenburg harbor on September 25, 1647, and arrived at Fort Christina in the late autumn without casualties and without mishap, an unusual experience for a ship in those days. On May 16, 1648, the *Swan* spread her white sails for the return voyage. She was a lucky ship, as mariners would say. On the nineteenth she rounded Cape Henlopen for the open sea and on the thirteenth of June she was off Plymouth, having crossed the Atlantic in twenty-five days! On June 17 the ship was approaching the Scandinavian shores and, without touching at Gothenburg, proceeded directly to Stockholm, where she arrived on July 3. The Reverend Johan Campanius, Måns Nilsson Kling, and other officers and men were passengers on the vessel.

Preparations for a new expedition were on foot at the Swedish capital before the *Swan* returned, but these made little progress, and not until the following summer was a ship, the *Cat* (*Kattan*), ready to sail. By now, rumors of fabulous opportunities for colonists in New Sweden were abroad in old Sweden, circulated by letters and reports, and after 1648 emigrants in abundance were willing to brave the dangers of the long voyage to the Delaware; but soldiers and officers still had "a great dread of New Sweden" and looked upon it almost as a penal colony. It was, therefore, necessary to draft some soldiers needed for service in the forts along the river.

Hundreds of prospective colonists apparently applied for

passage on the ship. About seventy of these were selected, including many women and some children—not counted, however. Joachim Lycke and Hans Amundsson were sent as aides to Governor Printz. In accordance with the request of Printz, cannon and a large quantity of ammunition were loaded on the ship and provisions for twelve months were taken on board. After long delays the *Cat* finally got under sail on Monday, July 3, 1649. But it was the ship's fate never to reach her destination. Wrecked on a reef near the island of Puerto Rico in the West Indies, over one hundred of the passengers and crew succumbed from subsequent exposures and ill treatment by Spaniards and Frenchmen on Puerto Rico and the neighboring island of Santa Cruz. Only nineteen of the passengers and a few soldiers and sailors, including the clergyman, Matthias Nertunius, the barber-surgeon, Timon Stidden, and Johan Rudberus, who wrote an interesting journal of the voyage, made their way back to their native land. The cargo and provisions of the *Cat* were confiscated by the Spaniards and the vessel was ordered burned by the Spanish Governor of Puerto Rico.

The shipwreck was an irreparable blow to Printz and his colony. It was one of the links in a chain of misfortunes which finally overwhelmed the colony and forever put an end to Swedish power on the Delaware. Had the cannon and other munitions of war, as well as the soldiers and colonists, reached New Sweden, it is quite likely that the Dutch would have sat quietly on the Hudson in 1651 and later, and left New Sweden alone for years to come.

As soon as the officers of the Company in Stockholm heard of the shipwreck, they decided to send aid to the colony from Holland, and money was assigned to Peter Spiring, Swedish diplomatic agent at The Hague, for the purchase of a cargo. But the activity of the Company was hampered by the inactivity of the Government, and the resolutions and orders of the Council of State, necessary as a stamp of approval of anything the officers of the Company decided, were not forthcoming.

Preparations were also begun for a new expedition from Sweden. The *Golden Shark*, which had been riding at anchor for months and months, was repainted and generally repaired, but for some unknown reason the activities subsided. The officers of

the Company, who realized the condition in the colony, must have been desperate, but they lacked authority to do anything. Oxenstierna was old, and Queen Christina was more interested at this time in pageants, court festivals, and philosophical discussions than in matters of State and colonial affairs.

In the autumn of 1651, however, the Government seemed to bestir itself about its colony on the South River. On March 16 the following year (1652), the Queen was actually present in the Council Chamber to discuss the requirements of New Sweden. It seems that the reports of Governor Printz about the invasion of the colony by the Dutch, the "outrages" of Governor Stuyvesant, and his disrespect of Her Royal Majesty's authority finally awakened the Swedish Government to a realization of its obligation to its forsaken settlement on the Delaware. A second meeting was held on March 18. Again the Queen was present. It appears that some member of the Council advised that a sufficient force be dispatched to New Sweden to drive the Dutch from the river, but "Her Majesty's idea was that the States General [of Holland] should be approached for a settlement."

A few days later the Queen ordered the Admiralty to make the *Swan* ready for "a new journey to the West Indies." It was found, however, that the ship was unseaworthy, and the Company made new repairs on its own vessel, the *Golden Shark*. But the summer and fall of 1652 came and went and nothing was done. The winter of 1652–53 and the summer of 1653 followed, and still nothing was done. Queen Christina had important personal matters to consider at this time—she was planning her abdication.

In the late summer of 1653, new letters from Printz were received by Per Brahe and Axel Oxenstierna. New life was put into the preparations. The Commercial College, or Board of Trade, which had previously been instructed to manage the affairs of the New Sweden Company, was ordered by Queen Christina to take charge of the situation. This was fortunate for the colony. Eric Oxenstierna, son of the great Chancellor, was Chairman of the College, and he possessed much of his father's ability. Intensely interested in the colonial enterprise, he assumed the direction of the preparations in 1653, and they im-

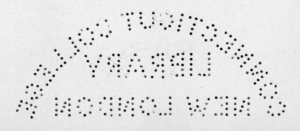

mediately began to take definite shape. As the Government was in arrears to the Company for several thousand riksdalers, the Queen ordered the Admiralty "to fit out a ship for a voyage to New Sweden." Three hundred colonists and a large cargo, including munitions of war, were to be sent to the South River "in order that New Sweden should not go to ruin."

The *Örn* ("Eagle"), a Government vessel, was selected for the journey, and Jan Bockhorn, first mate on the shipwrecked *Cat*, was made captain of the ship. Great efforts were made to enlist soldiers and to find colonists and skilled workmen. The soldiers and passengers from central Sweden—many came from Västerås—boarded the ship at Stockholm. The *Örn* left the capital on October 8, 1653. She had a rough journey from Stockholm to Gothenburg, ran on banks in the Sound "through the negligence of the sailors," and encountered other misfortunes, but after a month of sailing arrived safely at Gothenburg. Admiral Anckerhielm, who was in charge of the preparations at Gothenburg, built cabins for the passengers and made other arrangements for their comfort. New supplies were also loaded on the ship.

The various requests of Printz were now to be granted. Johan Rising, the Secretary of the newly established Commercial College, was appointed assistant to Printz and director of the colony, in case Printz should leave. Johan Rising was a man of outstanding ability and of wide training, the first economist of note in Sweden, a generation or more ahead of his time. He had traveled widely on the Continent and in England, and had studied at first hand the economic and commercial theories and activities of the great mercantile nations of Europe. Like all educated Swedes of his day, he was intensely patriotic and devoted his energies to the furtherance of Swedish interests.

Peter Lindeström, a young nobleman who had specialized in "mathematics and the art of fortification," was appointed for service in New Sweden as a military engineer; and Sven Skute, an officer who had returned to Sweden in 1650 bringing reports from Governor Printz, was now sent back to the colony as "Captain of the landspeople."

Lindeström has left us a detailed account of the preparations at Gothenburg and the voyage of the *Örn* to New Sweden. No criminals, other malefactors, or people of generally evil report, he informs us, were permitted to sail. Moreover,

about one hundred families, good honest people, who had fine recommendations and a splendid reputation, had to remain [behind] in the [old] country with their wives and children, unable to get on the ship for want of room for such a great number, and [these] increased more and more daily. These people were very much to be pitied because they had sold all their household articles, cattle, and all their [real] property, and all that they possessed, turned it into money and necessary commodities [for the voyage], supposing it could not by any means fail them to go along on the ship.

On January 27, 1654, all of the people who had been fortunate enough to secure passage on the *Örn* took the oath of allegiance to their Queen, their Fatherland, and the "Royal South Company," and on February 2 the ship weighed anchor and sailed for New Sweden.

The expedition encountered storms, contrary winds, and other misfortunes of many kinds. The vessel was searched by English warships and attacked by Turkish corsairs. The passengers and sailors, for lack of fresh water and food, were tormented by various diseases, particularly dysentery and intermittent fevers, and many died at the Canaries and on the crossing of the Atlantic to the West Indies. And, as if not enough afflictions had tried the souls of the brave voyagers, violent storms off the American coast almost sent the battered ship with the remaining passengers and sailors to the bottom of the sea. With a great deal of difficulty, and only after the mainmast had been cut loose so as to right the ship in one storm, did the *Örn* finally reach "New Sweden Bay" (Delaware Bay) and cast anchor before the ruins of Fort Elfsborg on the evening of May 20, 1654.

It may be explained at this point that the Dutch, in 1651, had erected a post on the site of present New Castle, Delaware, which they had named Fort Casimir. This post made the Swedish post, Fort Elfsborg, across the river, untenable, and hence it was abandoned by Printz in the same year. Now Rising, having learned that Governor Printz had left New Sweden, resolved to capture Fort Casimir forthwith. Consequently, on

Trinity Sunday, May 21, he sailed from the vicinity of old Fort Elfsborg across and up the Delaware River a short distance and, without any difficulty, dispossessed the Dutch of their post, renaming it Fort Trefaldighet (Trinity). The *Örn* then proceeded to Fort Christina, where it arrived the next day, May 22.

The *Örn* left New Sweden on July 15. Its return voyage was long and dangerous and it did not reach Stockholm until late September.

The *Golden Shark*, which was to have sailed in company with the *Örn*, was greatly delayed by repairs and by the incompetence of its crew. Captain Amundsson, a survivor of the unfortunate *Cat* expedition, was placed in command of the vessel, but was removed, and Swen Höök appointed in his stead. Some of the emigrants who could not find room on the *Örn* went on the *Shark*, and a few soldiers and laborers also took passage on the ship. "But some of the people were bad," and the mate was incompetent and "a rascal"—not a good omen for a successful journey. The ship was to go by way of Puerto Rico to collect damages from the Spaniards for the *Cat* and its cargo, and lengthy instructions were given to Hendrick von Elswick, who was appointed to succeed Hendrick Huygen as commissary of the colony, and to the other officers in New Sweden.

On April 15, after three months of delay, the ship finally set sail "with a good wind." It encountered the usual storms, the usual hardships and dangers. The water supply and the provisions became exhausted long before it reached its destination, making it necessary to touch at the Azores as well as the Caribbean Islands, and the vessel did not reach Puerto Rico until June 20. Elswick, who had been especially charged with the task of collecting the *Cat* damages, was unsuccessful. After a month and a half of almost constant effort, he found the case hopeless and Swen Höök ordered the ship to proceed to New Sweden.

The *Golden Shark* left Puerto Rico on August 15 for the South River. By mistake she passed Delaware Bay and, probably through the treachery of the mate, she was run in "behind Staten Island," where she was seized by the Dutch. The majority of the colonists and the crew were persuaded to remain in New Amsterdam. The name of the ship was changed to *Diemen* and it was used "for the West Indian trade." The addition in men and material which Rising was expecting thus miscarried. This was the last expedition sent from Gothenburg during the existence of the Delaware colony as a Swedish possession.

The officers of the Company planned to send another expedition shortly after the sailing of the *Golden Shark* in April, 1654, but the treasury was empty and the money which the Government owed the Company could not be collected. In June, Queen Christina delivered her scepter into the hands of her cousin, the more forceful Charles X. Immediately new life began to animate the various departments of State. The New Sweden Company was reorganized and its capital stock increased. Several of the old stockholders paid up their subscriptions, and the tobacco monopoly of the Kingdom was assigned to the Company by royal proclamation. The reorganized corporation was officially called the American Company, but the old name was retained in the journals and account books.

In the beginning of 1655 it was decided to buy a new ship in Holland for a journey to the Delaware, but no new ship answering the requirements could be purchased. Therefore an old one, the *Mercurius*, was bought instead, and was "rebuilt anew entirely." A cargo was also procured in Holland and sent to Gothenburg on the vessel.

The usual difficulties—contrary winds, nonarrival of supplies and ammunition, deserting sailors—delayed the expedition. Some efforts were made to obtain colonists, but this was unnecessary. When the *Mercurius* was ready to sail, only 110 passengers were taken on board (making 130 souls, including the crew, on the ship) :

A hundred persons or more were left behind [writes Papegoja] . . . it is a pity and shame that they cannot all go along. Here was seen such a lamentation and weeping, for the unfortunate ones have sold all they possessed, yea [they have] done away with home and ground for half of the value, journeyed such a long way at their own expense and are now compelled to take up the beggar's staff, the one going here, the other there.

After two or three futile starts, the *Mercurius* finally got under sail on November 25. She was nearly four months at sea, but apparently she had a rather pleasant voyage, and about the middle of March, 1656, sailed up the Delaware River.

In the meantime the colony had been captured by the Dutch (1655), and the *Mercurius* was ordered to New Amsterdam without disembarking her passengers or unloading her cargo in former New Sweden. When the Indians heard about it, they went down to the vessel in great numbers and threatened to destroy all the white people in the river, Swedes and Dutch alike, unless the ship remained. Accordingly the *Mercurius*, with some savages on board, sailed up to Tinicum Island, where the passengers and cargo were taken ashore. The ship returned to Sweden some time during the summer.

It is proper, at this point, to transfer our story to the settlement which was founded on March 29 (N.S. April 8), 1638: the present Wilmington, Delaware. When Peter Minuit left the colony in the summer of 1638, the soldiers and workmen continued their daily routine, clearing ground for future farms, improving the fort, building new houses near the river, trading with the Indians, fishing, and hunting to provide fresh provision for the table.

The primitive dwellings which they erected here were, according to archeologists, the first log cabins of their type ever constructed in the United States. From the Swedes on the Delaware, according to these authorities, came this important contribution to early American life.

Måns Kling with his little garrison expected a ship from Sweden in 1639, but none came. The visit of the *Griffon* in the late winter and early spring of that year, before her return to Europe, broke the monotony of their isolated lives, and we may assume that the commander of the vessel promised to hurry reinforcements.

The Swedes, under the leadership of Hendrick Huygen, carried on a brisk traffic with the Indians, and Governor Kieft of New Amsterdam complained bitterly that the Dutch-Indian trade "had fallen short fully thirty thousand [florins], because the Swedes, by underselling, depressed the market."

We know nothing about the internal life of New Sweden during the first two years, except a report from Dutch sources

that the garrison of Fort Christina was about to desert on
April 17, 1640, and repair to the Dutch, having been invited
to do so by the Dutch governor. The report seems improbable.
At any rate the *Kalmar Nyckel* cast anchor before Fort Christina on April 16, bringing new supplies, additional colonists, a
pastor, the Reverend Reorus Torkillus, and a new Governor,
Peter Hollender Ridder.

Ridder was a man of great energy. He had been employed
in Swedish services for many years and had proven himself a
faithful and dependable officer. When he arrived in the colony
he found much to improve, but his first concern was to mend
the walls of the fort, which were dilapidated, to build new
houses, and repair the old ones. He cleared new tracts and had
fences erected for the "two horses and a colt." Some of the pigs
which had been brought on the first expedition, or purchased
from the neighbors, escaped into the woods, where they increased rapidly "and became wild."

Ridder made several proposals for betterments in the settlement and sent detailed reports to Stockholm. Huygen, assisted
by Van Dyck, continued the Indian trade with splendid results,
making it possible to dispatch the *Kalmar Nyckel* to Sweden on
May 14, 1640, with a large cargo.

The Dutch, who had a fort (Nassau) on the eastern bank of
the Delaware River, on Big Timber Creek opposite Philadelphia, had protested vigorously to Minuit, and now protested to
Ridder, about the presence of the Swedes on the land that the
Dutch claimed by first discovery and purchase from the Indians. When the Swedes sailed up the Delaware above the
Dutch stronghold, the commander tried to stop them, and did
what he could with his limited means to keep the Swedes in
check.

Shortly after his arrival, Ridder increased the limits of New
Sweden considerably by purchases from the Indians. One tract
was bought on the western side of the river from the Schuylkill
up to the Falls (present Trenton), a second tract on the same
side of the river from Bombay Hook southward to beyond Cape
Henlopen, and a third tract on the Jersey side, extending north
and south from the present Salem.

The English from New Haven came into the Delaware in

1641, and bought land, first on the eastern side above and below Varkens Kill, and second, on the western shore at the Schuyl-kill River. Several English settled at Varkens Kill (now Salem, New Jersey), where they built their dwellings in the English fashion and cleared land for plantations. Ridder reported their presence to Stockholm, but did not interfere with them.

From English sources we learn that "sickness and mortality befell the Swedes in 1642," but Swedish records are silent on the subject.

There were two pastors in New Sweden before the coming of Printz: the Reverend Reorus Torkillus, arriving in 1640, and the Reverend Mr. Christopher, who arrived in November, 1641, but we know little about their labors. A chapel was probably erected near or inside Fort Christina in 1640. It is likely that Torkillus served in the fort and that Mr. Christopher minis-tered to the Swedes on the near-by plantations.

Reorus Torkillus became the pioneer of Lutheranism in the New World, and the first Lutheran clergyman to serve within the present territory of the United States. He learned the In-dian language and tried to instruct the aborigines in the truths of Christianity, thus becoming the first Lutheran missionary among the American Indians, and the first Protestant clergy-man in the Delaware River Valley. Torkillus died on September 7, 1643, at the age of thirty-five.

Johan Printz, as we have seen above, arrived at Fort Chris-tina on February 15, 1643, and assumed the management of the colony. He took his duties seriously and entered upon his work with all the energy at his command. In a letter to Oxen-stierna, the Swedish Chancellor, written on April 14, 1643, about two months after his arrival, he says:

And I cannot humbly withold from Y[our] Excell[ency] in what manner I, with utmost diligence, have passed through the country New Sweden, firstly from Godin's Bay, from Cape Henlopen unto Bomshuuk [Bombay Hook], and then from there way up to San-kikan [Trenton].

He found that it was "a remarkably beautiful country, with all the glories that any human being on earth at any time can de-

sire. . . . And this I wish to repeat," he exclaims in a letter
to Per Brahe, April 12, 1643, "that such a splendid country
as this, which is endowed with all kinds of wonderful things, I
have never seen, and nothing is wanting except means, diligence
and seriousness to continue this work." He found it fertile and
well suited for agriculture, and he was certain that in time it
would develop into one of the jewels of the Swedish Crown.

We may be certain that the Swedish settlers were also impressed with the country. The climate was very different from
that of their native land. The summers were long and extremely
hot and the winters were short—or there was no winter at all—
compared to those in Sweden. The settlers were undoubtedly
impressed with the long days in the fall and winter. From November until early spring they had been used to only a few
hours of sunlight, while here more than half of the twenty-four
hours were light, even on the shortest days.

In his "Instruction" Printz was ordered to fortify the country against the neighbors of New Sweden. Fort Christina was
located far from the Delaware and could not command the
river. Printz therefore selected a more convenient spot on the
eastern shore, on an island (at present Elsenburg Fort Point,
New Jersey), as the location for a new stronghold, which would
be "the key to the Delaware River," and would "keep out all
intruders." When this stronghold was ready, some time in the
autumn of 1643, Printz had complete control of the Delaware,
as the cannon of Fort Elfsborg could prevent any ship from
sailing past. Printz also selected a place for his residence at
Tinicum Island, and established another stronghold here, which
he called Fort New Gothenburg. On the Island he erected a
mansion for himself, beautiful and well built, says a contemporary, with orchards and pleasure gardens. This was the first
Statehouse of Pennsylvania, and from 1643 to the autumn of
1653 Tinicum Island was the capital of New Sweden.

During his administration in New Sweden (1643–53),
Printz erected three forts—the two mentioned above, and "New
Korsholm" in 1647, on Province Island in the Schuylkill; and
six blockhouses: "Upland," 1643 (at present Chester); "New
Vasa," 1643, at Kingsessing (West Philadelphia); a block-
house on Province Island in the Schuylkill, 1643; "Mölndal,"

1645 (at present Blue Bell Tavern, where Woodland Avenue crosses Cobb's Creek in West Philadelphia) ; "Torne," in 1647; and a blockhouse on the east bank of the Schuylkill within present Philadelphia.

Printz assigned plantations to the colonists who arrived with him, and during 1643 several new tracts were cleared along the river and creek. Printz had been advised to plant corn on most of the land, as it was said that corn would yield the largest crops; but the planting did not turn out according to expectations. Besides, it was found that Indian corn could be bought cheaply from the aborigines. Printz, therefore, planted tobacco and sowed grain on the new lands the following year. The Indian trade in New Sweden was lively at certain periods, when a ship came in or when merchandise had been bought from the English or Dutch traders; but New Sweden soon developed into an agricultural community rather than a trading colony, and the beaver trade was never large. Some years, the crops in New Sweden were so plentiful that large quantities of grain could be sold, but other years there were crop failures and provisions had to be purchased from the neighbors. Several trading expeditions were sent from New Sweden to New Amsterdam, to New England, and to Virginia. Cattle, horses, and other domestic animals were purchased on these journeys, as well as merchandise of various kinds. The Swedes also sold to their neighbors considerable quantities of goods manufactured in Sweden, such as brushes, and tools made of Swedish steel and iron.

Printz was greatly handicapped, not only by lack of supplies but by the absence of skilled laborers and sufficient colonists. The work at first was slow and tedious on account of the few workmen, but Printz was a hard taskmaster and kept the people constantly at their jobs.

Printz purchased two or three vessels from the English and Dutch and also built his own boats. He asked for a warship from Sweden to remain in the river as a protection against intruders and, as such a ship was not furnished, he built a vessel himself of about two hundred tons burden, a very large ship for those days. It was completely ready in 1652, except for tackle, cannon, and other equipment. The equipment never arrived from Sweden, and the ship finally decayed and fell to pieces.

The first flour mill in New Sweden was erected on the Rocks in the present Wilmington. It was a windmill that ground the flour for the colonists for several years. In 1645 the mill became inadequate to serve the increased population. Accordingly, Printz erected a water mill on Cobb's Creek near present Blue Bell Tavern, about two hundred feet above the bridge on Woodland Avenue that crosses the creek. The place was called Mölndal, "as the mill was there," and a miller had charge of "the factory" and ground the flour of the colonists for a certain toll. This mill served for generations and is often mentioned in the records throughout the seventeenth century. It was the first "factory" in the Commonwealth of Pennsylvania.

After the arrival of the large expedition in 1643, the total male population of New Sweden was 135, but 26 officers and men died during the year and 4 returned to Europe, leaving only 105 adult male inhabitants in the colony in June, 1644. We do not know how many women and children there were, but the total population of the settlement at this time could not have been over two hundred souls.

Most of these were Swedes. At least nine were English. One of the settlers, Lars Andersson, came from Åland. There were at least two Germans, Röther Tyck and Johan Hartman, both from Hamburg. There were very few Finns in the colony at this early date (1644). Only two are definitely mentioned in the lists, although there were undoubtedly a few more: "Martin Tomasson, the Finn from Österbotten," and "the freeman, called Johan the Finn, [who was] drowned at Upland."[1]

Finns came here on later expeditions, but at no time did they make up a predominant element in New Sweden. A district south of Upland (present Chester) is actually called Finland on Lindeström's map. This place was first settled in 1641, but apparently it was not called Finland until the arrival of Rising in 1654. Governor Printz does not call the place Finland in his list of cultivated districts in 1644, nor in his inventory of 1653. The fact that he called the blockhouse at Kingsessing (present

1. See Amandus Johnson, *Swedish Settlements*, II, 699 ff.; *Instruction for Johan Printz*, 42–44.

Philadelphia) Vasa, after a town in Finland, may indicate that the place was settled by "Swedish Finns."

In 1648, the total adult male population was only about ninety. These were also mostly Swedes. There was at least one Dane, one Negro slave, three or four Dutchmen, about four Germans, and probably a dozen Finns (only six, however, are definitely mentioned on the list of this year[2] as Finns). The fact that some were singled out and called "Henrik, the Finn," "Måns, the Finn," etc., proves conclusively that the Finns were in the minority; that they were very few in number. It is likely, however, that no distinction was made between Swedish Finns and citizens from Sweden proper. Most of the 110 colonists that arrived here on the *Mercurius* in 1656 were Finns from Värmland, who in some cases spoke no Swedish, but all of whom had Swedish names.[3]

The first dwellings erected here by the Swedes and Finns were primitive, one-room log cabins, probably about 12 feet by 14 feet in size, and this room served as workshop, dining room, bedroom, and everything else. A primitive fireplace was set up in one of the corners. These earliest dwellings were built of round logs laid close together, with their ends cut into each other. Log cabins of this character are still found in the Delaware Valley. As time went on, more pretentious dwellings were erected. Some of these were built of square logs with flush corners. At least one dwelling of this type still survives in New Jersey.

The diet of the people was greatly changed after coming to New Sweden. They could not always obtain the provisions to which they had been accustomed and were often compelled to adopt new dishes from the Indians. Indian corn bread was one of these adaptations which the Swedes seem to have relished. Fish and venison were at times plentiful. The Swedes used nets and fishhooks for catching fish, and fowling pieces, as well as snares, for larger game. It is also quite likely that in hunting,

2. Johnson, *Swedish Settlements,* II, 710 ff. In the *Förklaring* we find "Clemet" and Lars called Finns, and we may take for granted that Johan and Anders mentioned in connection with "Clemet" and Lars are also Finns. See *idem,* I, 462 ff.

3. *Idem,* II, 634, 724 ff.

many of the settlers used crossbows, which were common in
Sweden at this time and were very efficient in the hands of a
skilled marksman.

The relations between the Indians and the Swedes were
nearly always friendly. Only one or two minor incidents occurred. In the "Instruction" for Governor Printz it was stated
that the Governor must treat the Indians in a friendly manner,
never do them any injustice, and try to convert them to Christianity. This policy was followed throughout the history of
New Sweden. As a result, the Indians called the Swedes *Ne-
tappi;* i.e., "our kind," or "our people." The English and
Dutch were foreigners, an entirely strange race, but the Swedes
were different. This friendship continued for many generations; and long after New Sweden had been absorbed by the
Dutch, and later by the English, the Indians looked upon the
Swedes as their particular friends.

On June 8, 1654, ten Indian chiefs came to Tinicum Island
to renew the friendship with the Swedes. Governor Rising, who
was in charge, has given us an interesting account of this convention. After presents had been delivered to the Indians the
leading chief spoke somewhat as follows:

See how good friends these are who have given us these gifts. We
shall be as one body and one soul. If in the time of Governor
Printz, the big belly, we were friendly, we shall now be as a cala-
bash without a crack or crevice and we want to make a pact of
perpetual friendship with you. If someone should attack you,
though it were in the middle of the night, we will come to your aid,
and if someone should attack us, though it were in the middle of
the night, you must come to our aid.´

William Penn has been praised for his peaceful relations
with the Indians and he deserves this commendation. But if it
had not been for the attitude of the Swedes long before William Penn came to America, it would not have been possible for
him to carry out his policies. The Indians would not have had
confidence in the white man, had they been treated by the
Swedes as they were treated by the English and the Dutch.
William Penn's interpreters were Swedes, and the Indians re-

lied on their word when they assured them that William Penn was honest and would treat them justly.

Johan Printz has been called the first judge in the Delaware Valley. That is not true. Law courts were held here before Johan Printz arrived, but it is a fact that justice and order were more firmly established after his arrival. We have several records of law courts held within the present limits of Pennsylvania during the existence of New Sweden. It is also an interesting fact that the jury was first introduced into this territory by the Swedes and not by the English, as is usually stated. The jury system had been prevalent in Sweden from time immemorial, and Johan Printz was instructed to follow the customs and usages that obtained in the mother country.

The seventeenth century was a religious age. Prayers and religious exercises were conducted on all occasions, and religion, although not regarded in the same way as it is today, occupied a very important place in the daily lives of the people of Sweden. Special paragraphs in the various instructions to the governors of New Sweden are devoted to religion and religious exercises, and Printz was especially enjoined to see to it that churches were erected, and that the strict Lutheran doctrine was taught according to Swedish church laws and usage.

During the governorship of Printz, four pastors served in the colony. These clergymen were also farmers, and raised domestic animals for their own needs. The most important of these was Johan Campanius who came here, as we have seen, with the Governor, and served until 1648. He was a man of unusual attainments, a scientist and scholar as well as a theologian, and has been called the first meteorologist in America. He translated Luther's small catechism into the Indian language (1644–48) and did considerable missionary work among the aborigines.

Printz erected a chapel on Tinicum Island in 1643, but this was destroyed in the great fire two years later. In the spring of 1646, Printz made plans for the erection of a church at Tinicum Island. It was built of logs with a roof of clapboards bought from the English. It was fitted out and decorated in Swedish fashion and a burial place was laid out near the church. "The Handsome Church," as it was called, was ready in the autumn, and was dedicated on September 4 by Johan Campanius and Israel Fluviander.

The Swedish Lutheran order of services was followed closely in New Sweden and the three principal holidays, Christmas, Easter, and Pentecost, were strictly observed. The services on these holidays began very early in the morning—about four or five—and lasted until eight or nine. Sometimes services were conducted in the afternoon also. Other holidays, such as New Year's, Epiphany, and Candlemas Day, were likewise observed, as well as two or three solemn prayer days during the week. Services were conducted on Wednesdays and Fridays, probably alternately at New Gothenburg and Christina. Prayers were offered every morning and evening, accompanied with psalm singing, in the forts as well as in the private dwellings of the settlers.

During the first few years of the governorship of Printz, peaceful relations existed with the Dutch, but there was much trouble with the English. Several people from the New England colonies came into the river to trade, and especially one George Lamberton, from the colony of New Haven, trucked with the aborigines without respect for the Swedes and without paying any attention to Swedish protests. As a consequence, Lamberton was arrested by Governor Printz, tried at Fort Christina, and fined heavily. On Lamberton's return to New Haven, he complained bitterly of the treatment he had received in New Sweden. Out of this grew an interesting correspondence between Governor Winthrop and Governor Printz. Finally, the matter was settled amicably. Other attempts were made by the English to establish themselves along the Delaware, but these efforts were frustrated by the Dutch and the Swedes. The small English colony, now Salem, New Jersey, was allowed to remain, however, for there the English swore allegiance to the Swedish Crown. They raised tobacco and probably corn and other grains, and they were able to sell several thousand pounds of tobacco to the New Sweden Company for one of the cargoes.

The relations with the Dutch took a turn for the worse in 1645, when Andreas Hudde replaced Jan Janssen as commandant at the Dutch post of Fort Nassau. From now on, we read of constant disputes, protests, and counterprotests between the two peoples. Finally, in 1651, Peter Stuyvesant himself came to the South River, since none of his inferiors could make an impression on Governor Printz. Stuyvesant arrived with a strong force against which Printz could do nothing. He bought from the Indians large tracts of land, which the Swedes had purchased years before, and finally erected, as has already been noted, a fortress at Sandhook (now New Castle, Delaware), calling it Fort Casimir. This fort commanded the river and made the Dutch masters of the valley. Printz wrote often to Sweden asking for aid, new supplies, new colonists, and more soldiers; but Queen Christina was, as noted above, more interested at this time in philosophy, pageants, and balls than in the little settlement on the Delaware, and Printz was left more or less to himself. The *Cat* expedition, which would have relieved the distress, was wrecked, as we have seen.

Printz also had internal troubles to contend with. An insurrection arose against the Governor, and some of his people deserted him. "The rebels," as the Governor called them, presented a written supplication of eleven articles, signed by twenty-two settlers. The Governor was accused of avarice and brutality, and of ill-treating the settlers on many occasions, making it almost impossible for them "to find their sustenance." The petition kindled the wrath of the Governor, who used strong measures. He had the ringleader, Anders Jönsson, arrested and, after trial, executed on a charge of treason. A few days after the execution, which took place on August 1, 1653, the Governor made a written reply to the charges, denying everything he had been accused of and explaining the various points of difference. Printz was now finding his position untenable, however, and made preparations to return to Europe to hurry the dispatching of ships and aid to the sorely tried Swedish settlement. Delivering the government of the colony into the hands of Johan Papegoja, Printz left New Sweden with his family about the beginning of October, 1653, and reached old Sweden shortly after Rising's expedition had left Gothenburg.

When Rising arrived in the Delaware in May, 1654, and took over the management of the colony, he settled at Fort Christina, which thus again became the capital of New Sweden. Rising was a man of great energy and much learning, but he was undiplomatic; and by his unwise capture of Fort Casimir on Trinity Sunday, 1654, he called forth the storm which finally destroyed Swedish power in the New World.

Shortly after his arrival, Rising assembled the settlers, first at Fort Christina, and later at Tinicum Island. He admonished them to be true and faithful citizens and to live up to the laws and regulations of the Swedish Government and of the Swedish Company. The old difficulties with Printz were aired and discussed; but not even a compromise could be effected—the feelings ran too high.

The new arrivals were given farms and plantations to cultivate, most of them between Fort Christina and Fort Trefaldighet, and by fall a great many new dwellings had been erected. Rising paid much attention to agriculture, cattle raising, and even forestry. He drew up rules and regulations for every form of activity, and the outlook for a prosperous period was bright. By the summer of 1655 the tillable area of New Sweden had increased greatly, and the settlers were prosperous and contented. There was activity everywhere, and a new spirit animated the people. But in the autumn the merchandise in the storehouse at Fort Christina became low. The *Golden Shark*, whose cargo would have supplied every want, ran into New Amsterdam and was captured by Stuyvesant. Soon the entire stock of cloth for undergarments and other clothes was consumed. It became necessary to sew shirts out of sailcloth for the soldiers and servants. But this material also gave out, and the plight of the people was great.

In August the Dutch Governor came to New Sweden with a large force of ships and soldiers, ravaged the farms, and seized the Swedish posts. On September 15, Rising signed articles of capitulation.

When this had been done, Governor Stuyvesant made a generous proposal to his defeated foe. He offered to return the colony and the forts (except Fort Casimir) to the Swedes and let bygones be bygones, on condition that the Swedes and the Dutch would live together as friends and work for their mutual benefit. Rising could not accept this offer, as he felt that the matter was too grave and could be passed on only by his superiors at Stockholm. Stuyvesant, of course, did not make this surprising offer out of the goodness of his heart. The fact was that the Indians, true to their treaty with the Swedes, had fallen upon the Dutch and threatened to destroy the settlement of New Amsterdam. Those in authority there frantically called upon Stuyvesant to return as quickly as possible and defend his own colony against the savage foes. In Stuyvesant's opinion, it was dangerous to leave the Swedish farmers as enemies in the Delaware River Valley.

Thus New Sweden as a political unit came to an end. Rising and about thirty other officers and soldiers returned to the fatherland, but the rest remained. According to the articles of surrender, the Swedes were allowed to keep a pastor of their own confession among them. The Reverend Lars Lock, who had come to New Sweden in 1648, remained, but the other pastors returned to Sweden.

After 1655, the Swedes and Finns began to clear lands and to build homes on the Jersey shore, and by 1682 (the coming of Penn) the eastern side of the Delaware was dotted with homesteads for a considerable distance from Salem northward. One of the settlements was called Stockholm, indicating that the colonists came from the Swedish capital—the date of the settlement, however, is uncertain; and another place became known as Sveaborg (present Swedesboro). On the western side of the Delaware River, the Swedish settlements at the time of Penn's arrival were, of course, greater in number and larger in area. They extended roughly from a point between New Castle and Wilmington, on both sides of the Christina River, in the present State of Delaware, northward beyond Philadelphia, almost as far as Bristol in the present State of Pennsylvania.

The Swedish colony as a social unit did not disappear with the capture of its forts. The Swedes dominated the Delaware Valley until the coming of Penn. Several new additions arrived from Sweden and Finland, and a few Dutch and English who came to live here were compelled to learn Swedish in order to be able to trade with their neighbors. As a result, Swedish was the everyday language along the Delaware for more than a generation.

With the coming of William Penn in 1682, the situation changed. The Swedes lost their ascendancy and English be-

came the dominant language. It has been said that William
Penn founded Pennsylvania. When he came here, he found a
fully established community with churches and schools and law
courts, and all the other elements of civilization. He changed
the name of the colony, as well as the name of some of the cities
that existed before he came—as, for instance, Upland to Chester. He did found the city of Philadelphia and some other
places, but not the colony as such—he merely changed its name.

Colonial Landmarks

GEORGE H. RYDEN

As chairman of the Department of History and Political Science at the
University of Delaware, Professor Ryden has been one of the prime
movers back of the New Sweden Tercentenary celebration. Since 1935
he has been Secretary of the Delaware Tercentenary Commission. He is
also State Archivist of Delaware and the compiler and editor of *Letters
to and from Caesar Rodney* (a signer of the Declaration of Independence), as well as the author of *The Foreign Policy of the United States
in Relation to Samoa,* published in 1933. Professor Ryden is a native of
Kansas City, Missouri, and was educated at Augustana College and
Yale University, where he received his doctor's degree as well as the
John Addison Porter Prize. He has contributed to both the *Encyclopædia Britannica* (article on "Delaware") and the *Dictionary of American Biography* (biographical sketches of ten Delawareans). During
the World War he served as Educational Secretary of the Y.M.C.A.
in Texas camps, and in Italy and in France. During the civil war in
Russia (1919–20) he was the Director of the South Russian Mission
of the American Red Cross, and in 1920 was elected an honorary member of both the Kuban and the Don Cossacks.

ALL aboard," cries the guide, as eager groups of tourists
from the East, the Middle West, and the Far West, as
well as from Sweden itself, hurriedly enter gaily be-
flagged omnibuses to be off on a tour of northern Delaware,
southeastern Pennsylvania, and southwestern New Jersey—a
territorial area which once upon a time comprised the ancient
colony of New Sweden.

The occasion of all the commotion, of course, is the celebration of the three-hundredth anniversary, in 1938, of the landing
of the Swedes at the "Rocks," located in what is now Wilmington, Delaware; for, naturally enough, people of Swedish birth
and descent throughout the United States, as well as people in
Sweden, are much interested in the place where the representatives of their race first set foot upon American soil. They are
also eager to see the other places in the Delaware River Valley
where the Swedes of the seventeenth century once settled, and,
so, the tour of New Sweden is herewith presented.

The "Rocks" at Fort Christina State Park

BEGINNING our tour at Rodney Square, the civic center of Wilmington, and proceeding southward on Market Street to Seventh Street, we turn east at that intersection, and continue on our course directly past "Old Swedes" Church (to be described later) until we reach the entrance to Fort Christina State Park, the site of which was recently acquired by the State of Delaware. Here we are treading upon sacred soil; for here, at the farther end of a walk bordered by trees, we come upon the famous landing place; a ledge of rock jutting out upon the Christina River and forming a natural wharf for the seventeenth-century Swedish pioneers.

Beside the Rocks the Swedes built a fort which they named "Fort Christina," after their youthful Queen. They also named the river "Christina River," and the hamlet, which eventually was built beside the fort, they called "Christinehamn." There are no remains of these human habitations, to be sure, but there will soon stand near the Rocks a magnificent monument, executed by the world-famous Swedish sculptor, Carl Milles. This monument, which will be unveiled on June 27, 1938, will depict in Swedish black granite the arrival of the *Kalmar Nyckel,* the ship that brought the first Swedish settlers. It will consist of a column twenty-one feet high, with a representation of the ship at its top, and will be a gift from the people of Sweden to the people of America, expressing the good will of the Swedish people toward the people of our country.

The fort which the Swedes built at the Rocks was not only a military stronghold but also a trading post. Here the Swedes purchased furs from the Indians, and here the furs were stored in a warehouse until such time as they could be transported to Sweden to be sold. As more Swedish settlements were established to the north, in what is now Pennsylvania, and across the Delaware River, in what is today New Jersey, Fort Christina assumed the greater dignity of being the capital of the little colony of New Sweden. It retained this dignity until the arrival, in 1643, of Governor Johan Printz, who transferred the seat of government to the island of Tinicum near present-day Philadelphia. Fort Christina, in point of fact, was the first permanent settlement, not only in the State of Delaware, but in the whole Delaware River Valley as well. Here, too, were conducted the first religious services (the Swedish Lutheran), the Reverend Reorus Torkillus, who came in 1640, being the first ordained clergyman in the valley to preach the Christian Gospel and to administer the Christian sacraments.

Fortunately, the plan of Fort Christina was preserved for posterity by a Swedish military engineer, Peter Lindeström by name, who arrived in this country in the company of the last Swedish Governor of New Sweden, Johan Rising. The original drawing is deposited in the Royal Archives in Stockholm, Sweden, but it has been reproduced in several publications, notably in Dr. Amandus Johnson's work entitled *The Swedish Settlements on the Delaware*. Lindeström assisted Governor Rising in the defense of Fort Christina in September, 1655, and described in detail in his *Geographia Americæ* its investment by the Dutch and its surrender to Peter Stuyvesant, the Governor of the colony of New Netherland.

Back in 1903, the Delaware Society of Colonial Dames of America erected a large fragment of the Rocks, with one side highly polished, and with an inscription that reads as follows:

This stone is a portion of the Rocks on which landed the first Swedish Colonists in America, 29 March, 1638. On this spot stood Fort Christina. Here the Swedes held their first Civil Courts and in the Chapel of the Fort celebrated their first Christian Worship in the New World.

When Peter Kalm, the Swedish naturalist, visited Wilmington in the fall of 1748, the local Swedish pastor, the Reverend Peter Tranberg, informed him that during the previous summer, when Wilmington residents built a fort to guard the town against French and Spanish privateers, they erected it on the site of Fort Christina, and in making excavations had come upon old iron tools such as axes and shovels, and a Swedish silver coin which had been minted in 1633 or during the reign of Queen Christina.

Not very far from Fort Christina Governor Rising built a governor's mansion where he entertained many visitors, English and Dutch as well as Swedes.

Swedish farmsteads were to be seen on both sides of the Christina River, tobacco and Indian corn being important staples. Orchard trees were likewise planted, and cattle and hogs were raised. The present Brandywine River, which empties into the Christina River, the Swedes named "Fiske Kill" or Fish River, and a creek that flows into the Brandywine near its confluence with the Christina they named "Sköldpaddekill," or Turtle Creek. With the coming of the English, this name, like so many other Swedish and Dutch place and family names in Delaware, was corrupted. Nowadays Sköldpaddekill is known as Shellpot Creek, giving no indication of its first Swedish form.

Site of Tranhook (Cranehook) Church

ALTHOUGH the Swedes in all probability built a chapel within the walls of Fort Christina during the days when Torkillus was chaplain, and continued to worship there after the capture of the fort by the Dutch in 1655, as well as before that event, they decided in 1667, after the establishment of English authority which followed the fall of New Netherland in 1664, to build a house of worship at "Tranhook" (Cranehook), on the south side of the Christina River, near its confluence with the Delaware River. This was to accommodate the Swedish farmers living southward along the Delaware as far as Sandhook (called by the English, New Castle), the Swedish farmers in New Jersey on the east side of the Delaware River, and those living north of the Christina River in the direction of Upland (Chester) and Tinicum—settlements now within the boundaries of Pennsylvania. This church was evidently of modest dimensions and built of logs. To reach the site in these modern days one can go down the Christina River by boat a distance of two miles or so, debark at the modern Marine Terminal, and then walk a half-mile to the south; or one can drive over the bridge which crosses the Christina River just above the Wilson Boat Line wharf at Fourth Street and Christina Avenue, go thence along Christina Avenue to the vicinity of the Marine Terminal, and turn southward to the site. Although this site is marked by a modest stone erected by the Historical Society of Delaware in 1896, nothing remains of the church building. Even the farm lands are now deserted, only abandoned roads indicating that formerly a population lived here large enough to support a church and a preacher of the Christian Gospel.

Site of Fort Trefaldighet at New Castle

By driving from the site of Cranehook Church about five miles to the south, one reaches the quaint old town of New Castle. This place was founded by Peter Stuyvesant, the Dutch Governor of New Amsterdam, when, in 1651, he built Fort Casimir in an attempt to secure from the Swedes the control of the Delaware River. Although, before his return to Sweden in 1653, Governor Printz took no steps to dislodge the Dutch, his successor, Johan Rising, with the aid of his military engineer, Peter Lindeström, seized Fort Casimir on Trinity Sunday, 1654, and renamed it "Fort Trefaldighet," or Fort Trinity. The site of the fort is at the shore of the Delaware River, immediately beside the present New Castle ferry landing. Lindeström said, in his *Geographia Americæ*, that the Dutch had permitted the fort to decay and that he rebuilt it from its foundations. The Swedes, however, held the fort only until September, 1655, when Peter Stuyvesant came into the Delaware River with a large force and conquered New Sweden by taking both Fort Trinity and Fort Christina. The Dutch hamlet that grew up beside Fort Casimir was called New Amstel, and when the English seized control of the place in 1664, they renamed it New Castle.

Heliga Trefaldighets Kyrka (Old Swedes Church) in Wilmington

Retracing our route to Wilmington, we shall stop at the intersection of Seventh and Church Streets, to visit the far-famed Swedish church which was dedicated on Trinity Sunday, June 4, 1699, and called by the Swedes "Heliga Trefaldighets Kyrka" (Holy Trinity Church). Our attention is immediately attracted to the beautiful bronze tablet which the Historic Markers Commission of Delaware placed on the wall beside the entrance to the churchyard in the year 1933. The inscription on its reads as follows:

Holy Trinity Church

(*Heliga Trefaldighets Kyrka*)

In 1638 a colony from Sweden landed at "The Rocks" nearby. There they built Fort Christina, worshiped therein until 1667, and then built a log church at Cranehook on South side of Christina River.

In 1698, inspired by their pastor, Erik Björk, they erected Holy Trinity Church. The tower was added in 1802. The Church of Sweden withdrew in 1791 and was thenceforth succeeded by the Protestant Episcopal Church.

When Swedish sovereignty over the colony of New Sweden came to an end in 1655, the Swedish settlers were left for a period of forty-two years without any supervision of their spiritual needs by the State Church of Sweden. To be sure, one of the Swedish pastors, the Reverend Lars Lock, who had arrived in 1648, remained in the country until his death in 1688. At first he served the Swedes on Tinicum Island and at Fort Christina, and, when the church at Cranehook was built in 1667, he preached there as well.

In the year 1697, however, three new Lutheran clergymen arrived from Sweden, with instructions from the Swedish church authorities to revive the church work among the Swedes in America. These ministers were Andreas Rudman, Erik Björk, and Jonas Aurén. Since Rudman elected to serve the people in what is now Philadelphia and its vicinity, Björk entered upon his duties as pastor of the Cranehook church.

Very soon Björk perceived that the thirty-year-old log church would not accommodate an expanding congregation, if success should attend his efforts. Moreover, he regarded its location as rather disadvantageous. Consequently, he lost no time in suggesting that a better site be obtained and a new church building erected.

The old Swedish graveyard, only a stone's throw from old Fort Christina, was fixed upon as the site of the new building, and to accommodate the members on the New Jersey side, in what is now called Pennsneck, as well as the people living south of the Christina River, a ferry service was arranged for.

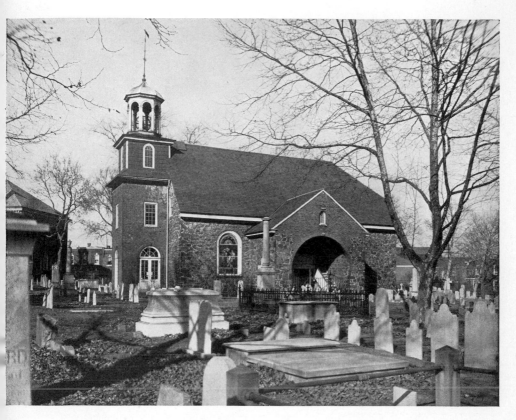

HOLY TRINITY (OLD SWEDES) CHURCH
WILMINGTON, DELAWARE. DEDICATED JUNE 4, 1699

The most precious historical document belonging to Holy Trinity Church is the church book begun by Björk. In this book the pastor recounts in great detail the building operations and also the dedication services, which occurred on Trinity Sunday, June 4, 1699. The dimensions of the building, as finally determined upon, were sixty feet in length, thirty-six feet in width, and twenty feet in height to the eaves. The material used was granite, easily obtained in the northern part of Delaware, and the floor was of brick. That the Swedes built well is evident, for the Holy Trinity Church or, as it is popularly called, "Old Swedes" Church, is the oldest Protestant church still in use in America. Small wonder that, when the Delaware Tercentenary Commission was confronted with the task of selecting the most outstanding building in the State to be shown on the United States commemorative half dollar, it chose Holy Trinity Church of Wilmington.

When one enters the Church, one is most impressed by its simplicity and dignity. The old pulpit, from which many sermons were preached in Swedish, stands at its original place. To be sure, the old altar is not to be seen, but it is, nevertheless, in its place; only, it is covered by a new altar to preserve it from too much usage. On the right side of the new altar are engraved the names of all the Swedish pastors from Björk to Girelius—nine in all. The most outstanding of these clergymen, aside from Björk and Girelius, was the Reverend Israel Acrelius who served the parish from 1749 to 1756, and who wrote a history of the colony of New Sweden and of the Swedish churches in America, which was published in Stockholm in 1759. The present vicar of Holy Trinity Church is the Reverend Robert Bell.

The Church cherishes a communion set which was presented to it by the Falun Mining Company of Sweden in 1718. Once a year this set is taken out of a bank vault and used at a communion service. On the floor, in the aisle near the altar railing, is to be seen the tombstone of the Reverend Peter Tranberg, who died in 1748, and it is said that the remains of Torkillus, the first clergyman to come over with the Swedes, are under one of the walls of the Church.

"Old Swedes" at Wilmington holds a secure place in the traditions of Delaware, and in the hearts of the Swedish people throughout the land. It stands as a symbol of permanent settlement, as well as of the highest aspirations of those who have worshiped there. Swedish psalms have been sung there and the Swedish liturgy has been intoned there. Swedish sermons for the edification of thousands have been preached there, and baptisms and marriages of untold numbers of Swedes have been celebrated there. Swedish services for the dead have likewise been held through many a year. In short, "Old Swedes" stands as a reminder of an age that is gone, an age that was in the beginning of this great land of America.

Governor Printz Boulevard

BUT we must be on our way to see other places that are hallowed by their associations with the Swedish pioneers in the Delaware River Valley. In leaving "Old Swedes" of Wilmington, we proceed northward on Church Street until we reach a new bridge spanning the Brandywine River. The broad new pavement on the other side of the river is the beginning of a heavy-traffic highway which, when completed, will extend to the northern boundary of Delaware, near Naaman's Creek. At the 1937 session of the Delaware General Assembly, this highway was officially named "Governor Printz Boulevard," in memory of the Swedish Governor who directed the affairs of the colony of New Sweden for ten years, from 1643 to 1653. Although the new boulevard does not retrace the old Indian and Swedish trail which connected Fort Christina with Governor Printz's governmental establishment on Tinicum Island, it certainly is not far away, and it passes all the way through lands which once belonged to the Swedish farmers in northern Delaware.

Governor Rising's Blockhouse

IMMEDIATELY after crossing Naaman's Creek, we descry, on the left, the famous Robinson House, which nowadays is used as a tea house. Connected with the Robinson House is a blockhouse made of logs which, tradition says, was built in the days of Governor Rising; i.e., either in 1654 or 1655. The blockhouse, at all events, is the only building remaining of a small ancient settlement on Naaman's Creek. Two Swedish artists,

Gustavus Hesselius and Adolph Ulric Wertmüller, are said to have lived on plantations bordering on the creek.

Immediately after passing the Swedish blockhouse, we reach the northern circular boundary of Delaware and enter the State of Pennsylvania. But let us be reminded of the fact that this political boundary was established as late as 1681, when, in the royal charter to William Penn, the southern boundary of the province of Pennsylvania near the Delaware River was described as an arc of a circle, with New Castle, Delaware—twelve miles away—as the center. Hence, in the days of the colony of New Sweden, the Swedish pioneers crossed no boundary near Naaman's Creek. In fact, they continued to be within the domain of their colony as far north as the falls of Trenton.

Finland and Upland (*Marcus Hook and Chester*)

VERY soon after entering Pennsylvania, we reach the industrial cities of Marcus Hook and Chester—both located on the Delaware River. These two places were the first permanent settlements in the State of Pennsylvania. The former was known as Finland in the old days, and the latter was named Upland, in honor of a province in Old Sweden. Both settlements were made in the year 1641, three years after Fort Christina was founded. Upland became an important center and retained its Swedish character for many years, due to its greater distance from the Dutch settlement at New Amstel, which, during the Dutch regime, was the government headquarters on the Delaware River. When the English came in 1664, Upland became a court seat for the enforcement of English law, but, nevertheless, most of the magistrates were former Swedish settlers. However, when William Penn arrived in 1682, accompanied and followed by thousands of Quakers and other colonists, the importance of Upland declined. The newer city of Philadelphia, founded by Penn, became the center of government for the Swedish communities in Pennsylvania as well as for the later English, Welsh, German, and Scotch-Irish settlements.

Tequirassy

IN order to pass through the Swedish villages which were started immediately after Finland and Upland, it will be necessary to follow State highway No. 420 from Chester (Upland)—the highway nearest to the Delaware River. The year 1643 was important, not only because Governor Printz arrived to take over the government of the colony of New Sweden, but also because in that year three new settlements were made between Upland and the Schuylkill River, and one new settlement, Printztorp, between Upland and Finland. Moreover, Upland and Finland received more inhabitants. Driving northeastward on State highway No. 420 from Chester, after crossing Ridley Creek—called by the Swedes "Kyrke" (Church) Kill—we pass over land referred to in the records as "Tequirassy." This land lies between Ridley Creek and Crum Creek—called by the Swedes "Kroke" (Crooked) Kill—and on a detailed road map it can be identified northeast of the town of Eddystone on the way to Essington.

Tinicum Island

AFTER crossing Darby Creek—called by the Indians Tenakon—one reaches the town of Essington and the so-called island of Tinicum. Here, in 1643, Governor Printz established his capital of the colony of New Sweden, when he decided that Fort Christina in Delaware was too far inland from the Delaware River for him to maintain control of that important waterway. In this year he built a fort which he named Fort Göteborg, and a mansion which was known as Printzhof. Three years later (1646) the Tinicum Swedish Lutheran Church was dedicated by the Reverend Johan Campanius who had come to America with Governor Printz. The executive mansion, Printzhof, stood on the site of the present Corinthian Yacht Club, and in 1923, under the auspices of the Swedish Colonial Society, near the entrance to the Club grounds, a beautiful monolith was dedicated with the following inscription: "On this site Governor Johan Printz established and maintained the Government of New Sweden, 1643–1653."

A small bronze tablet is to be seen on one of the porch posts of the clubhouse entrance of the Corinthian Yacht Club, bearing an inscription which definitely locates the sites of Swedish buildings on Tinicum Island.

It is interesting to note here that during the past year excavations have been made on the site of Printzhof on Tinicum Island, and not only has its exact location been determined but some remains of the building recovered.

Province Island

By continuing along State highway No. 420, locally called Tinicum Island Road and then Penrose Ferry Road, one traverses Province Island just before reaching the Penrose Ferry bridge over the Schuylkill River. On this so-called island the Swedes made another settlement in 1643 and built a blockhouse there the same year.

Fort Nya Korsholm

On the left-hand side of the road on the south side of the bridge, where it joins the road to Fort Mifflin, stood from 1647 to 1653 a Swedish fort named Fort Nya Korsholm, or Fort Manayunk —Manayunk being the Indian name of the Schuylkill.

Passyunk

We are now in Philadelphia, and on both banks of the Schuylkill is to be found land which was taken up from time to time by Swedish pioneers, one of the largest landholders being Capt. Lasse Cock, official agent and interpreter to the Indians for William Penn. Cock's one thousand-acre plantation—confirmed to him by deed in 1667 by Richard Nicolls, the English Governor in New York—was in all probability acquired before the end of the period of the Swedish sovereignty. Two brick houses and a barn belonging to Captain Cock are to be seen at the junction of Penrose Ferry Road and Magazine, or Beggartown, Road, just west of the aviation field and the old Sesquicentennial fairgrounds.

American Swedish Historical Museum

By continuing along Penrose Ferry Road to its junction with Packer Avenue at Twentieth Street, one reaches the northwest corner of the Sesquicentennial fairgrounds, and, in order to come to the American Swedish Historical Museum, it is then only necessary to drive east on Packer Avenue to Broad Street, south on Broad Street to Pattison Avenue, and west on Pattison Avenue to Nineteenth Street.

Gloria Dei Church (Old Swedes) of Philadelphia

BUT we must be on our way to the Gloria Dei Church (Old Swedes) of Philadelphia, located at the intersection of Swanson and Christian Streets. To reach the Church one drives along Broad Street until it intersects Christian Street and then east on Christian to Swanson Street. Gloria Dei Church, next to Holy Trinity in Wilmington, is the oldest Protestant church in the United States, having been dedicated on the Sunday after Trinity Sunday in the year 1700. The old Wicaco Blockhouse had stood on the site of the Church since 1669, but, although it had been erected for defense against robber Indians in the vicinity, from 1677 onward it had also been used for Lutheran services. The Reverend Jacob Fabritius preached in the Wicaco Blockhouse from that year until his death in 1692. He also preached in the old church on Tinicum Island. When in 1693 Carl Springer of the Cranehook church, near the Christina River in Delaware, wrote to Sweden, requesting that two Lutheran clergymen be sent to America, the church authorities there determined to grant the request. As a matter of fact, three clergymen were sent over in 1697, as we have already noted, and Andreas Rudman elected to labor among the Swedes who had settled on both sides of the Schuylkill River, especially among those living in the districts known as Wicaco, Passyunk, Tinicum, and Kingsessing. Rudman, like his colleague Björk, in Delaware, immediately upon his arrival determined to build a new church. After considerable discussion concerning the proper location of a church for the widely scattered membership of his parish, it was decided to erect the building on the site of the Wicaco Blockhouse. The largest Swedish landowners in the Wicaco district were the Swenson brothers, Swen, Ole, and Andreas. Back in 1681 they had sold to William Penn's agent, William Markham, a considerable portion of land on which old Philadelphia now stands, and now they gave some of their land for the new church. The masons and carpenters who built Björk's church at Christina also built Rudman's church. Some of the materials, as well as the bell and baptismal font, were taken from the abandoned church at Tinicum. Whereas the Christina church was built of stone, the Wicaco church was built of brick. When it was dedicated, the Reverend Mr. Björk of the Christina church assisted in the ceremony. The Reverend Mr. Rudman continued as pastor until 1702, expecting at that time to return to Sweden. However, he later served the Christ Episcopal Church in Philadelphia until his death in 1708. His remains were buried beneath the chancel of the Gloria Dei Church.

Ten clergymen from Sweden served the Gloria Dei congregation after the resignation of Rudman, the two outstanding ones being Dr. Carl Magnus von Wrangel (1759–68) and Dr. Nicholas Collin (1786–1831). Upon the death of Collin, the Swedish Lutheran mission in America came to a close.

In the course of time two branch churches of the Gloria Dei were erected, but remained under the control of the vestry of the Gloria Dei Church until after the death of Dr. Collin. These churches were the St. James at Kingsessing and Christ Church at Upper Merion. The corporate name of the three churches from 1765 onward was "The Rector, Church Wardens and Vestrymen of the United Swedish Lutheran Churches of Wicaco, Kingsessing, and Upper Merion." The present rector of Gloria Dei Church is the Reverend John Roak.

St. James Church (Old Swedes) of Kingsessing

To reach St. James's Church of Kingsessing from the Gloria Dei of Wicaco, one drives west to Passyunk Avenue, and along this avenue across the Schuylkill River to Sixty-third Street; thence northwest along Sixty-third Street to Woodland Avenue, and southwest on Woodland Avenue to Sixty-ninth Street. Built of stone, St. James's stands in a large yard quite apart from other buildings, and is the most imposing of all five of the "Old Swedes" churches now remaining. The St. James branch of the Gloria Dei Church was founded in 1760, and the cornerstone of the Church was laid in 1762 by Dr. Wrangel, Provost of the Swedish churches in America. As originally built, St.

James's Church had no transepts nor tower. When it was rebuilt in 1854, these were added. The present rector of St.
James's Church is the Reverend William Roberts.

Christ Church (Old Swedes) in Upper Merion
(now Bridgeport, Pennsylvania)

To reach the other branch of the Gloria Dei Church, namely,
Christ Church in Upper Merion, one may drive from St.
James's in Kingsessing along Woodland Avenue across Cobb's
Creek to the center of Darby, and thence follow the alternate
routes of U.S. highways Nos. 1 and 13, through Lansdowne,
and along City Line Avenue, until the Schuylkill River is
crossed just below the mouth of the Wissahickon River in Fair-
mount Park, where Ridge Avenue is joined. At this point one
drives in a northwesterly direction along the Ridge Pike to
DeKalb Street in Norristown. One then turns south on DeKalb
Street and, driving through Norristown, crosses the Schuylkill
River into Bridgeport, turning left on route No. 123. At the
eastern end of Bridgeport, on route No. 123, stands the Church.
The congregation was organized in 1758, and in the same year
a plot of ground upon which to build a church was purchased
from Ezekiel Rambo for eleven pounds ($55). On June 25,
1760, the Church building was dedicated by Dr. Wrangel. Like
the St. James, Christ Church originally had no transepts, chancel, and tower, and was enlarged by the addition of these in
1837. Since then, several other changes within the Church have
been made. In 1886 a baptismal font was presented to the
Church by Prince Oscar of Sweden, a younger brother of King
Gustaf, in memory of his visit to the Church on July 2, 1876.

When the writer recently called upon Reverend James Hart
Lamb, Jr., the rector of Christ Church, he confirmed the statement that has so often been made about Christ Church; namely,
that it was the only one of five "Old Swedes" churches that had
not formally entered the Protestant Episcopal Church. When
the corporate union of the three churches—the Gloria Dei of
Wicaco, St. James of Kingsessing, and Christ Church of Upper Merion—was dissolved in 1842, the first two by formal act
entered the Protestant Episcopal diocese of Pennsylvania, but

Christ Church failed to take such action. It has been argued, therefore, that Christ Church is still under the jurisdiction of the State church of Sweden; but, to all intents and purposes it is a member of the diocese of Pennsylvania, since its rector recognizes the bishop of that diocese as his superior, and since the parish pays its regular annual dues to the diocese and the general church, and is represented by clerical and lay delegates in the annual diocesan conventions. It is interesting to note, however, that the charter of incorporation, dated February 25, 1842, gives the corporation the name of "The Church Wardens and Vestrymen of the Swedish Lutheran Congregation of Christ Church, Upper Merion." The charter further states that "the affairs of the said Congregation shall be managed and super-intended by nine Vestrymen, members of said corporation, of whom seven shall be descendants, or intermarried with descend-ants of those ancient Swedes who contributed to the purchase of the property belonging to the church." The vestrymen can choose as rector of the parish only one who "shall be in the ministry of the Lutheran or Episcopal churches, and hold his faith in the doctrine of the same."

Fort Elfsborg (near Salem) in New Jersey

WHILE the Swedish settlers in Upper Merion were the farthest removed from the center of the colony of New Sweden on the northwest, the Swedish settlers in New Jersey occupied the op-posite frontier of the colony. When Governor Printz arrived in 1643, he determined to secure full control of the Delaware River by building a fort on the eastern shore south of the mouth of Salem Creek. The fort was built in 1643 and continued to be held until 1651, when the erection of Fort Casimir by the Dutch below Fort Christina made Fort Elfsborg untenable. Fort Elfs-borg was popularly known as Mosquito Fort, and no doubt the soldiers stationed there were happy to leave an extremely un-healthy post. Of course, nothing remains of Fort Elfsborg, but, if one wishes to see the site of a Swedish stronghold of former days that defied for a number of years Englishmen and Dutchmen trying to wrest the Indian trade from the Swedes, one can take the ferry from New Castle, Delaware, to Penns-ville, New Jersey, and drive about seven miles on State highway No. 409 to Salem and then about three miles southwest from Salem to the shore of the Delaware River.

St. George's Church of Pennsville, New Jersey

IMMEDIATELY after the building of Holy Trinity Church in Wilmington and the Gloria Dei Church in Philadelphia, the Swedish settlers, in the upper part of what was later called Pennsneck in New Jersey, began an agitation for the building of a church in their midst, also. Ever since 1667 they had crossed the Delaware River and worshiped at Cranehook Church near the mouth of the Christina River, but Holy Trinity, two miles inland, near the site of old Fort Christina, seemed too far for them to go. Consequently, they built their first church (of logs) in 1702–04 on the south bank of Raccoon Creek, in what is now Swedesboro, New Jersey.

This church in time came to be regarded as too far distant from the settlers living immediately on or near the Jersey shore of the Delaware River. Therefore, they built in 1717 a chapel of logs in what is now the northern outskirts of Pennsville, New Jersey, and named it St. George's Chapel. Four or five buildings have succeeded the first log church, the present chapel of brick having been erected since St. George's entered the Episcopal diocese of New Jersey. During the Swedish Lutheran period, Trinity Church of Swedesboro and St. George's Chapel of Pennsville were served by the same pastors, the glebe being situated about midway between the two places. Nothing remains at St. George's to indicate its Swedish origin, except some fallen tombstones with Swedish names engraved thereon.

Trinity Church (Old Swedes), Swedesboro, New Jersey

THE fifth of the old Swedish churches still standing is Trinity at Swedesboro. This town may be reached by several routes, depending upon the direction from which one is driving. From Philadelphia one crosses the bridge to Camden, and by driving southward through Gloucester one reaches State highway No. 45, which brings one to Woodbury. From Woodbury one travels in a southwesterly direction to Swedesboro. One can also reach Swedesboro easily by taking a ferry from Wilmington to Pennsgrove, or from New Castle to Pennsville, and by driving from either place in a northeasterly direction to Swedesboro.

The first church (of logs) was dedicated about 1704 on the south bank of Raccoon Creek, in what is now Swedesboro. The present brick church, except for the steeple, was erected during the pastorate of the last resident Swedish clergyman, Dr. Nicholas Collin, and was dedicated in 1784. The Swedish records of the parish go back to 1713, and the charter was secured in 1735. With the steeple, which was added in 1838, and which curiously enough was erected at the rear of the original building, the church is the most imposing structure in Swedesboro. An interesting fact, told to the writer by the present rector, Reverend Joseph T. Urban, is that the parish has continued down to the present time to collect quitrents from all the property owners in the town of Swedesboro, an indication that all the land on which the town stands was once the property of the parish. The church building is two stories high and has a gallery on three sides supported by columns.

The Swedish Language in America

AXEL JOHAN UPPVALL

For biographical notes on the Author, see the chapter on "Professors."

THE history of the Swedish settlements on the Delaware, from the time they passed definitely from the control of the Swedish Crown, is yet to be written. In the meantime, it may be assumed that in so far as the Swedes were concerned, the time between the fall of the colony (1655) and the arrival of the clergymen from Sweden (1697) was one of hardship and disappointment.

Relatively little is known about the domestic, social, and religious life of the settlers prior to the arrival of Governor Printz, and, even during the latter's governorship and that of Director Rising, much that the historian would like to learn can only be surmised. From the "Instruction" furnished Governor Printz we know, however, that the Swedish Government was most anxious that "all persons, especially the young, [should] be well instructed in the articles of their Christian faith, and besides [that] all good church discipline be [duly] held and exercised."[1]

But more than that, the Swedish Government was also concerned about the instruction and salvation of the aborigines of the region: "The wild nations, bordering upon the other sides, the Governor shall know how to treat with all humanity and respect, that no violence or wrong be done to them . . . that the same wild people may gradually be instructed in the true Christian religion and worship and in other ways be brought to civility and good public manner as though led by the hand."[2]

On these grounds we may feel assured that the spiritual welfare of the settlers was at no time wilfully neglected by the authorities. The Reverend Reorus Torkillus arrived in 1639. He was the first preacher of the Gospel and teacher of the young in the colony, and remained so until his death in 1643. During the

1. Amandus Johnson: *Instruction for Johan Printz*, pp. 94 ff.
2. *Ibid.*, pp. 78 ff.

governorship of Printz (1642–53) there were three or four
spiritual guardians in the colony, all active in the dual capacity
of preacher and teacher of their people. Apparently the educational outlook was promising, for, according to a report of July
13, 1654, the next governor, Johan Rising, was making plans
"for meeting the expenses of the church [at Tinicum] and for
building of schools and houses of worship." To this end he recommended "that tithes of grain and cattle be paid 'willingly
by the people,' the half part of it to be used for the salaries of
the preachers and the other half part for the erection and support of a school-building and a church."[3] But the realization of
Rising's project was prevented by the falling of the colony into
the hands of the Dutch (1655).

While the educational work, carried on in close connection
with the religious services, was very elementary, it no doubt
helped to a considerable extent in preserving Swedish speech
and Swedish traditions. When, however, the relatively few colonists came under Dutch rule (1655–64), their mode of living
became radically changed in some respects, in spite of the fact
that they were permitted for a time to live under a kind of
"home rule" at Tinicum. Religious services were presumably
conducted regularly, but the instruction of the young was probably neglected. Pastor Lock was, it seems, the only clergyman
in the large and growing parish, and although he could have
had the assistance of a schoolteacher, he opposed the engaging
of him.

That the Swedish language suffered under such circumstances is self-evident. To the further detriment of the language it was, according to historians, spoken to some extent by
the Germans, the Dutch, and the English people dwelling in
and about the Swedish centers. The effect that such conditions
must have had on the quality of the Swedish language can
easily be imagined. When, finally, the British drove the Dutch
from the Delaware and took over the erstwhile Swedish colony
(1664), the degeneration of the Swedish language continued.
The Swedish settlers had by this time become completely isolated from the mother country. For the most part, they were
poor in respect to worldly possessions, and lived scattered over

3. Amandus Johnson: *Settlements,* p. 546.

a relatively vast area, but little better than a wilderness. But the worst of all was that they were without leaders, spiritual or otherwise. The Nestor of their teachers, the Reverend Reorus Torkillus, had died in 1646, and the Reverend Mr. Campanius had returned to Sweden in 1648. Of the remaining clergymen, two were still alive, but both of them were too old to administer to the people.

In 1682, the Swedes beheld the coming of William Penn to the shores of the Delaware. In the year 1693, a census was taken of the settlers of New Sweden. It revealed that there were on both sides of the river 188 families, comprising 924 individuals, who were reckoned as Swedes or Swedish descendants. The former colonists and their descendants, watching the progress of the numerous, resourceful, and energetic English newcomers, must of necessity have realized that the time of their complete disappearance as a racial group was fast approaching. But the lingering love of the mother tongue, and a deepseated desire to worship after the manner of their forefathers, still lived within them.

It is significant that in the same year in which the census was taken, i.e., 1693, a letter, formulated by a certain Carl Springer and signed by thirty persons, was forwarded to Sweden. In due time it was submitted to the then ruling monarch, Charles XI. The petitioners asked for books and two pious and learned ministers to preach the Word of God and break the Bread of Life among them. The good King was touched by the appeal and granted the request. In 1697 three clergymen arrived; Andreas Rudman, Erik Björk, and Jonas Aurén, and along with them the desired books.

The arrival of the ministers marked the beginning of a new era for the Swedes on the Delaware. The newcomers lost no time in erecting houses of worship—Holy Trinity (Old Swedes), Wilmington, and the Gloria Dei (Old Swedes), Philadelphia, in 1699 and 1700, respectively. Around these spiritual fastnesses and others built later, the Swedes rallied, struggling against great odds, in an effort to preserve their identity. And they actually succeeded in doing so, from the time of the coming of Penn to that of the Revolution. But during that century of momentous events, the thinning out of the Swedish blood, the cessation of practically all emigration from Sweden to America, the intermarriages with the English, and the natural inclination on the part of the younger generation to adopt the manner of thinking and the official language of the land—all meant an acceleration of the decline of Swedish customs, ideals, and Swedish speech which had begun during the pre-Penn period.

Thus, gradually and unavoidably, as the Swedish language became replaced more and more by English, the third and fourth generations of the old settlers drifted away from their ancestral anchorage and became English. It was but natural that, under the circumstances, the Swedish churches should eventually pass from the control of the vanishing congregations and fall into the hands of the English (Anglican) church. After lengthy negotiations between the congregations and the Swedish ecclesiastical authorities, Archbishop Uno von Troil, on the twenty-fifth day of June, 1789, bade a touching farewell to the Swedish congregations in the name of his sovereign Lord, King Gustavus III.

Thus ended the saga of the spiritual mission on the Delaware, for although the Reverend Nicholas Collin remained rector of the United Swedish Lutheran churches until his death in 1831, Archbishop von Troil's communication technically severed all ties between the Swedish element in America and Sweden—with one exception, perhaps, the dormant Swedish language, which was often referred to during the latter part of the eighteenth century as "nearly extinct."

But the language, which was threatened with ultimate extinction from the early days of its appearance on the Delaware, did not meet its hostile forces without a struggle. To picture this struggle in detail is not within the scope of this survey. However, an excerpt from a letter written at Christina Kill (Wilmington), October 29, 1697, by the Reverend Erik Björk, addressed to Dr. Collmodin (Gotland), and a few additional remarks relative to the language question on the Delaware, may not be without interest to the reader. Reverend Mr. Björk writes:

. . . Not without wonder I can tell to the praise of this people that when there were scarcely three Swedish books here, they were nevertheless so anxious about their children that although they borrowed them [the books] from one another, all can nevertheless read a book fairly well, so that not a single one of the books His Royal Majesty favored them with is lying without use, and they are furthermore distributed, according to the number of grown-ups and youths in the houses and their ability to read, in such a way that whosoever would make the best use of this or that [book] received it, another [received] another, in such a manner that each one may enjoy the gift of the King and this they do with rejoicing and much gratitude.

But [I] hope that if God spares me, there will be, by the Grace of God, more and better churches, parsonages, regulations, cate-chizing, and other discipline, so that the young folks shall not come into the presence of their spiritual adviser with pipes in their mouths and hats on their heads, and those who are destined to follow us may find that road cleared, which we took over un-cleared. . . .[4]

The hopes of Reverend Mr. Björk and of his contemporary fellow clergymen, as well as those of later teachers in the field, were realized only in part. As already indicated, and for rea-sons given or implied, the Swedish language did not prosper, in spite of the devoted services of some thirty well-trained clergymen and a dozen schoolteachers, all Swedish-born and educated. During the time between the return of Pastor Björk to Sweden (1711) and the arrival of the Reverend Israel Acre-lius (1749), the parochial schools seem not to have functioned satisfactorily. Provost Acrelius labored hard to remedy the lacking educational facilities. He bewailed the lack of efficient teachers, chided the young for staying away from divine serv-ices, and endeavored to impress upon the parishioners the vital importance of keeping the Swedish language alive, but to no avail. Similar conditions seem to have obtained in Wicaco (Gloria Dei) parish and at the missions of the Jersey side. Illiteracy was widespread in the land.

The fears entertained by Acrelius for the future of the Swed-ish language in America were fully shared by Peter Kalm, the

4. English translation of original Swedish in the archives of the American Swedish Historical Museum, Philadelphia.

Finlander, who sojourned in New Jersey and Pennsylvania in 1748–50. On page 683 of his work entitled *Travels in North America*,[5] we read, under the caption, *Swedish vs. English:*

In the morning we continued our journey from near Maurice River down to Cape May. We had a Swedish guide along who was probably born of Swedish parents, and was married to a Swedish woman, but who could not, himself, speak Swedish. There are many such here of both sexes; for since English is the principal language in the land all people gradually get to speak that, and they become ashamed to talk in their own tongue, because they fear they may not in such a case be real English. Consequently many Swedish women are married to Englishmen, and although they can speak Swedish very well it is impossible to make them do so, and when they are spoken to in Swedish, they always answer in English. The same condition obtains among the men; so that it is easy to see that the Swedish language is doomed to extinction in America; and in fifty or sixty years' time there will not be many left who can understand Swedish, and still less of those who can converse in it [May 7, 1750].

That, like so many prophets before and after him, Professor Kalm could see nothing but complete extinction of the Swedish language "in a short time," as he puts it in another statement, we must accept as a *bona fide* conviction, for as Professor Benson remarks: "Kalm did not dream that a century later there would commence an immigration tide from Scandinavia that was ultimately to bring hundreds of thousands of Swedes to America, and perpetuate the Swedish language in North America for several generations at least."[6]

Kalm's statement is extremely significant, for it shows clearly that descendants of Swedish parentage behaved in 1748, and perhaps earlier, in the very same manner as do present-day American boys and girls of Swedish descent. They are ashamed of talking in their mother tongue because they fear that they may not in such a case be "real Americans." To confirm his statement, Kalm gathered concrete evidence of the degenera-

5. *The America of 1750: Peter Kalm's Travels in North America,* by Adolph B. Benson, New York, Wilson-Erickson, Inc., 1937.
6. *Op. cit.,* p. 687, n. 12.

tion of the Swedish language in the form of borrowings of single terms, the introduction of Anglicisms, and general misuse of the Swedish language. Owing to the limited space no examples of the language and its usages can be given here. The interested reader is, therefore, referred to pages 687 and following of the work already indicated. A brief list of works dealing with various developmental aspects, use, and nature of the Swedish language in America is added at the end of this chapter for the convenience of the reader.

To enter into a further discussion of the uphill work of the ministers and schoolmasters in attempting to cultivate and preserve the Swedish language on the Delaware is unnecessary. It became dormant in a measure as the Swedish Lutheran culture declined. That culture reached its highest level between 1749 and 1768, the last mentioned year being that of the departure for Sweden of the Reverend Dr. Carl Magnus Wrangel, the most distinguished Swedish schoolman on the Delaware. For years—as far back as 1756—both the Christina parish and that of Wicaco seem to have been preponderantly English. The Swedes, as already indicated, were becoming Anglicized in language:

The Revolution [says Professor Conrad Peterson] hastened matters. The colonists had become English subjects, but many had never liked England. They had preferred to lean on Sweden, and this had reacted in favor of the Swedish language which the pastors were instructed to favor, and which they could speak most fluently. To be independent Americans was a different matter, and it was felt in both Sweden and America that they must no longer lean on foreign support.[7]

The Reverend Dr. Nicholas Collin was the last minister sent by the Swedish Government to America. Having arrived in 1770, he lived and labored for the most part in Gloria Dei Church to the end of his days. He was entirely Americanized, but never relinquished his hold on the vernacular which he is

7. Conrad Peterson: "The Beginning of Swedish American Education" (prior to 1860). *Year-Book,* The Swedish Historical Society of America. St. Paul, Minn. 1922–23, pp. 26–55.

reported to have used in the pulpit once a month as long as he preached. His incumbency of sixty-one years coincides with what we may call the dormant period, linguistically speaking. At the time of the death of Dr. Collin in 1831, the Swedish language in America was at its lowest ebb. About a decade later, ships arrived in the harbor of New York, bringing the vanguard of those friendly armies of Swedish immigrants who were destined to play such an important part in the upbuilding of the country of their adoption. A new era had begun.

The chief forces that have been instrumental in maintaining and fostering the Swedish language in the United States since the middle of the nineteenth century are: 1, the Swedish-American churches of various denominations, and their parochial schools; 2, the Swedish-American secondary schools and colleges; 3, the Swedish-American press; 4, Swedish-American fraternal organizations; 5, American colleges and universities, and American secondary schools.

"The story of the founding and the growth of the Swedish-American educational institutions," says Dr. Julius Lincoln,[8] "is a stirring epic of idealism, sacrifice, and most arduous work. The first concern of the Swedish settlers, after having built their own primitive dwellings," he continues, "was the erection of a church. . . . As congregations were organized, it became the general practice to conduct a summer school for the children, where the courses of study consisted of instruction in catechism, Bible History, and the Swedish language."

As early as 1846, only fifteen years after the death of Reverend Mr. Collin, a Swedish school, he continues, "was organized in the Bishop Hill [Illinois] colony, with a few women as teachers. At Christmas time, the same year, an English class for the young children was started in a sod-house." This modest beginning of a parochial school has now only an historical interest. Here we need merely point out that a single religious denomination, that of The Augustana Synod, is represented at the present time in thirty-four states of the Union, and that its 1,216 congregations have more than one third of a million

8. Julius Lincoln: "Swedish-American Educational Institutions," in *The Swedish Element in America*, Chicago, 1931.

members. When we take this into consideration and realize, furthermore, that other denominational bodies such as the Baptists, the Methodists, the Swedish Mission Covenant, the Swedish Free Church, and the Swedish Adventists, are engaged in similar pursuits on a nation-wide scale, and that thirty educational institutions of college or academy grade have been founded during the past seventy or eighty years—if we take this into consideration, we realize to a certain degree the extensive use of the Swedish language in the United States at the present time.

It is true that for the past two decades the Swedish-American churches have been forced to curtail the use of Swedish, or, in most cases, perhaps, to replace Swedish with English, in order to reach and to attract the younger generations whose language is now exclusively English. But whether this is a permanent or temporary adjustment remains to be seen.

The second important force for the maintenance and cultivation of the Swedish language and the dissemination of Swedish culture in America is found in the Swedish academies and colleges. Like practically all educational institutions the world over, the Swedish-American higher schools have, as already indicated, had their origin and development under the aegis of the Cross. As in the case of the oldest American colleges, the purpose of the early Swedish-American schools was primarily to prepare pastors for the churches. In the course of time, all these higher schools expanded their curricula and became standardized academic institutions for the cultivation of the arts and sciences.

The third powerful instrument for the preservation of the Swedish language in America is the Swedish-American press. It has been pronounced a "cultural phenomenon," and justly so, because from its very inception one of its missions has been, on the one hand to help the immigrant preserve and appreciate the racial and cultural inheritance inseparably bound up with his mother tongue, and, on the other hand, so to guide him as to make it possible for him to become a good American citizen. The full significance of the constructive cultural work achieved by the Swedish language press—this mighty and faithful auxiliary of church, school, college, and university, has never been fully appreciated by the general public, either at home or abroad, and probably never will be. (See article on this subject by O. A. Linder, in this volume.)

A factor of no small importance in the conscious and unconscious endeavor of Swedish-Americans to guard and perpetuate their racial inheritance is found in the numerous societies, lodges, unions, and fraternal orders existing in all parts of the United States. Swedish is probably no longer the official language of all of these groups, but the foundation of the organizations and their *raison d'être* is rooted in the concept of race and nationality. The chief purpose of some of these societies is to promote the cultivation of the Swedish language, literature, and Swedish culture in general. Such are, among others: Svenska Kulturförbundet; The American-Scandinavian Foundation; the Society for the Advancement of Scandinavian Study, whose secretary is Dr. Joseph Alexis, University of Nebraska; and the Swedish American Council, whose chairman is Karl G. Fredin, Worcester, Massachusetts.

In spite of the splendid work performed by the aforementioned agencies, and the Swedish-American population in the United States where Swedish is still a living language, a warning is occasionally sounded that the time is approaching when the Swedish language is bound to become extinct in the United States. When this becomes an actual fact it will be due, not to the lack of love of and interest in the language by Swedish-Americans, but to the lack of sufficient new blood from the mother country.

The term "extinct" is here used in a limited sense; i.e., a period is visualized in which the language shall not be heard in public places (churches, in particular), and where *Requiescat in Pace* shall be engraved on the tombstone of the last Swedish-American newspaper editor. Some of us will not be present at that ceremony. Hence we are not fearful of it. But when the day comes, and long before that time, those who keep abreast with the times will learn, perhaps to their surprise, that a language is not dead simply because it is not spoken in the marketplace, or printed in newspapers. Any country, the cultured manifestations of which are genuine, need fear no extinction of its language. Swedish may and probably will become extinct in a limited sense in the United States, but there are many indications that, long before the coming of this linguistic Fimbul-winter, the language will have entrenched itself as a discipline in our higher secondary schools, colleges, and universities. In fact, this has already taken place on a modest scale.

In 1906 Professor George T. Flom of the University of Illinois published an essay entitled: "Nordiske Studier ved Amerikanske Universiteter" (*Symra*, pp. 151–180, Decorah, Iowa). It was expanded and published in "Iowa Studies in Language and Literature," No. 11, May, 1907, under the title, *A History of Scandinavian Studies in American Universities together with a Bibliography*. This work was published in condensed form in Swedish in *Svea*, Worcester, Massachusetts, on the thirteenth and twenty-seventh of December, 1933, under the title: "Historik över studiet av nordiska språk vid amerikanska lärosäten under åren 1858–1907." According to this source, courses in Scandinavian languages and literature were offered in some thirty institutions between the years 1869 and 1906.

Since 1907 no survey similar to that by Professor Flom has been made. But, in 1911, at the first meeting of the Society for the Advancement of Scandinavian Study, held at the University of Chicago, he read a paper on the subject of "Scandinavian Study in American Universities."[9] It was, in substance, a restatement in condensed form of his study of 1906, with certain additions which brought the survey up to date. According to his findings, thirty-seven institutions of college and university rank offered instruction in one or more of the Scandinavian languages in 1911. Of these institutions, ten were located in the East, twenty-one in the Central States, and six on the Pacific coast. In 1858, the first professorship in Scandinavian languages and literature was founded in New York University. But, as the instruction was limited to a private class, the introduction of the study of Scandinavian began properly with the establishment of a department of Scandinavian languages in the University of Wisconsin in 1869, and the

9. George T. Flom: "A Sketch of Scandinavian Study in American Universities," *Publications of the Society for the Advancement of Scandinavian Study*, I, 12 ff.

appointment of a professor in North European languages in Cornell University in the same year.

Until the year 1880, the two universities mentioned were alone in the Scandinavian field. But, in that year, Columbia University introduced Danish, Swedish, and Old Icelandic. Then followed two other institutions; namely, the University of Minnesota, where a department of Scandinavian was established in 1883, and Northwestern University, where courses in Swedish and Dano-Norwegian were introduced in 1882 in the Swedish and Norwegian Theological seminaries, which at that time were affiliated with the University. During the 'eighties and the 'nineties, Old Icelandic was introduced in eleven institutions. A department of Scandinavian languages and literature was created in the University of North Dakota, and a lecturer was appointed in Scandinavian in the University of Chicago in 1893. Instruction in modern languages was also provided in the following institutions: University of Indiana, 1885; Nebraska, Swedish first taught by Hjalmar A. Edgren, 1885; University of Michigan, Swedish, 1888, introduced by Calvin Thomas; Yale, 1889, Swedish and Norwegian.

During the first decade of the twentieth century, several Scandinavian departments were created in universities in the West and Far West, and Scandinavian courses were introduced in a number of other institutions. Thus, new departments of modern Scandinavian languages began to function in the University of Iowa, 1900; the University of South Dakota, 1902; departments or chairs of modern Scandinavian languages in Wittenberg College, Ohio, 1906; University of Illinois, 1909; University of Kansas, 1909; University of Nebraska, 1910; Washington State University, 1910; Willamette College, Portland, Oregon, 1910; California University, 1910; and the University of Oregon, 1911. Institutions where instruction had been provided prior to 1911 include: Princeton University; Ohio University; Cincinnati University; Washington Agricultural College; Missouri University; Washington University (St. Louis); Drake University (Des Moines); Texas University; the University of Pennsylvania, 1910; and Wellesley College, 1905. While there were but three institutions offering

Scandinavian courses in 1880, and eleven in 1890, there were twenty-one in 1900. The number in 1911 was thirty-seven. The total number of courses actually given at the different periods was estimated as follows: seven in 1880; twenty-seven in 1890; thirty-eight in 1900; and seventy in 1911.

As regards the subjects taught, the demand for Old Icelandic was the largest, the subject having been given in all but seven of the institutions named. Of the modern languages, Norwegian led, the larger demand being due, supposedly, to the general interest in Ibsen and Björnson. Swedish held second place, the courses offered having been taken in about one-half of the total number of institutions. The authors read in the Swedish courses were, as a rule, Tegnér, Runeberg, Strindberg, and Selma Lagerlöf.

For the twenty-six years that have elapsed since Professor Flom's résumé was made, no reliable statistics are available. But, in order to bridge this gap temporarily and to ascertain to some extent the present status of the teaching of Scandinavian languages and literature, a letter, requesting information relative to the number and nature of courses offered within the field in question, was sent by the writer to several representative institutions. The desired information is now available from the following universities:

The University of Chicago, Professor Chester N. Gould
Harvard University, Professor F. Stanton Cawley
University of Illinois, Dr. W. G. Johnson
University of Minnesota, Professor A. A. Stomberg
University of Michigan, Dr. Karl Litzenberg
University of Nebraska, Professor Joseph Alexis and Dr. A. Louis
    Elmquist
University of Pennsylvania, Professor Axel Johan Uppvall
University of Washington (Seattle), Professor Edwin J. Vickner
    and Dr. Sverre Arestad
University of Wisconsin, Professor Einar Haugen
Yale University, Professor Adolph B. Benson

As the letter soliciting the information was not drawn up in the form of a questionnaire, only a brief general summary of the reports can be given here.

Geographically, Harvard, Yale, and the University of Pennsylvania represent the interest of Scandinavian languages in the Atlantic States; the Universities of Chicago, Illinois, Michigan, Kansas, and Nebraska are the banner bearers of the Central States; the University of Washington (Seattle) represents the interests in the Western States. Historically speaking, the institutions fall into three classes. Wisconsin represents the pioneer period, having established a department of Scandinavian languages in 1869. While the Swedish language as such seems not to have been cultivated there, Swedish literature has received some attention in the past. The present head of the department, Professor Einar Haugen, is now planning two classes in Scandinavian literature (in translation) which will include several Swedish novelists, poets, and dramatists, particularly Selma Lagerlöf, Fröding, Karlfeldt, and Strindberg. Professor Haugen has already given courses in Scandinavian mythology and, in connection with it, Swedish folklore.

The universities of Illinois and Washington (Seattle) represent the youngest group in the field; i.e., institutions which introduced Scandinavian languages after 1900. The seven remaining universities in the list are representative of institutions that entered the Scandinavian field during the 'eighties and the 'nineties. The institutions concerned are either private, endowed, universities; i.e., Harvard, Yale, University of Chicago, University of Pennsylvania, or State institutions; i.e., universities of Minnesota, Michigan, Nebraska, Illinois, and Washington (Seattle). They may, furthermore, be grouped as institutions with an independent Scandinavian department (universities of Minnesota and Washington [Seattle], and institutions in which the Scandinavian interests constitute a subdivision of the German department (Harvard, Yale, the universities of Chicago, Pennsylvania, Michigan). They may also be characterized as institutions offering work in Scandinavian subjects "occasionally" and only in literature (Wisconsin, Michigan) ; such as have a permanent and systematically constructed program and actually give courses from year to year (all institutions named with the exceptions noted) ; and finally, such as have the facilities for instruction in modern Scandinavian languages and offer courses but do not have any applicants. There are not many institutions of the last-named category in the United States.

So far as Swedish is concerned, regular courses, elementary, intermediate, and advanced, are given in all the institutions named, with the exceptions and limitations already noted (Wisconsin and Michigan). Generally speaking, all are interested in Swedish culture as such, and particularly in Swedish literature of the modern era. Beyond this, no characterization or comparison of the linguistic courses in the different institutions is possible, because, as already indicated, some of the statements furnished no specifications. It is to be assumed, however, that the time allotment, for instance, is the same as that which characterizes the instruction in other modern languages.

In reference to the intermediate and advanced courses, the reading material was indicated in a few cases and showed a striking uniformity. The favorite authors are still Geijerstam, Lagerlöf, Tegnér, Runeberg, and Strindberg. This is naturally due to the fact that the choice of annotated texts is somewhat limited.[10] Only one report made mention of a course in composition. Courses in literature and lecture courses on a variety of subjects were indicated by two institutions.

Several universities have made important statements relative to the purpose of the teaching of Swedish. *At Yale, Harvard, and Chicago, the emphasis is not so much on the ability of the student to make oral use of the language; it is the intelligent reading of it for cultural, diplomatic, and scientific purposes that counts.*

The following statements are very significant:

"The reason for studying Swedish here," one report reads, "is that it is required for the doctorate in Germanics. Some years ago students of biology took Swedish. Their real desire, however, was to read Danish on account of the works of certain Danish botanists and geneticists. Just now [1937] students of economics desire Swedish. With few exceptions the students taking Swedish are graduate students. The entire purpose of the instruction is to enable them to read Swedish." (Chicago.)

10. A partial list of textbooks used in the study of Swedish at educational institutions in the United States will be found at the end of this chapter.

"Candidates for the degree of Ph.D. in Germanic Languages must have a reading knowledge of one modern Germanic language exclusive of German, i.e., either Dutch or one of the Scandinavian languages. No courses in Dutch are at present offered, so that Scandinavian is practically required in most cases." (Harvard.)

"Swedish at this institution is taken seriously, *because a reading knowledge of a Scandinavian language is required for the Ph.D. in Germanics;* graduate students in forestry may elect Swedish in place of French for the doctor's degree. Students of architecture have also taken Swedish and received full credit for it. Most of the students of Swedish at this University are non-Scandinavian."[11] (Yale.)

"The future of Swedish at this University is not promising *quantitatively,* but *qualitatively* it is bright. It is so on account of the encouragement and interest of the members of the Department of Germanics, all of whom can read Swedish, and the quality of the students." (Chicago.)

The last-quoted statement expresses the sentiment of more than one institution at the present time. Most of the statements report comparatively limited attendance in linguistic courses. Literary courses and lecture courses are more popular, the attendance often being twenty-five to thirty.

The universities of Minnesota and Washington may legitimately claim high standards in addition to the distinction of having the largest student bodies in the country centering about Scandinavian studies. "Taking the fall term of 1936–1937 as a basis," Professor Stomberg writes, "we had 106 students in Swedish at Minnesota. They were distributed over seven classes. With the exception of a few of them, all studied the Swedish language or its literature. About 20% were in classes primarily for seniors and graduates." Incidentally, Professor Stomberg points to the fact that if it were not for the strong departments of Swedish and Norwegian at Gustavus

11. The importance of Swedish for the science of forestry is demonstrated by the fact that *The Swedish-English Vocabulary for Foresters* by Deen, Dannfelt, and Benson, which was published by the Yale School of Forestry in 1935, was sold out (500 copies) in about a year.

Adolphus College, St. Olaf College, Concordia and Augsburg colleges, the enrollment in the Scandinavian department of the University of Minnesota would be considerably larger than it is at present. "The further fact," he continues, "that about 500 students take Swedish in the high schools of Minneapolis, undoubtedly helps reduce the number in our department."

At the University of Washington (Seattle), the attendance during the last quarter (1936–37) was 300. This included the summer school. Some 115 students were registered in Swedish (linguistic courses), and 95 in courses dealing with literature, Scandinavian culture and social institutions, and comparative philology.

The future of the study of the Swedish language and its literature, and Swedish culture in general, is particularly bright at the two great state universities because of the large Scandinavian populations supporting them, and, in particular, because of the splendid coöperation of all the students in attendance, regardless of nationality or descent. The permanency of Scandinavian study is assured, thanks to State control and to the sympathetic university administrations. Professor Stomberg closes his statement as follows:

I am decidedly optimistic regarding the future of Swedish as a university study here. Interest is evidently growing. Scientists and economists particularly are beginning more and more to recognize the study of Swedish as valuable. In an interesting number of cases Swedish is submitted and accepted as one of the language requirements for the Ph.D. degree.

While Scandinavian studies in the higher American institutions cannot be traced back to their origins along a line of consecutive years, statistical information for the study of Scandinavian languages in American secondary schools is available, thanks to the aforementioned Society for the Advancement of Scandinavian Study. The significance of this Society and its internationally well-known and highly rated organ *Scandinavian Studies and Notes* would deserve its own chapter, but, for want of space, a brief account of its work during the last twenty-six years will have to suffice. Summarizing the contents of this journal we may say that in addition to the large number

of philological and literary critical papers contributed by
scholars of Scandinavian birth or lineage, and others, American
and foreign, and in addition also to publications, domestic and
foreign, noted, announced, and reviewed in it between 1911 and
1937, all bearing the stamp of genuine scholarship, the Society
which publishes it has also found time to render services of such
significance to the modern Scandinavian languages that they
could not easily be overestimated.

The outstanding facts are: that the Society, from its very
first meeting in the spring of 1911, sponsored by such outstanding scholars as Professors G. T. Flom, Julius E. Olson,
A. A. Stomberg, Chester N. Gould, A. Louis Elmquist, and
A. M. Sturtevant, received a most hearty support from the
various regions of the country; that the Society immediately
became deeply concerned with the introduction of Scandinavian languages in American high schools and the status of these
languages; that in less than two years Professor Flom reported
the introduction of Scandinavian languages into many high
schools in the Northwest; that in the spring of 1910 a petition
to the school board in Minneapolis resulted in the introduction
of the languages in question into some of the city high schools;
that, in 1911–12, the languages had found their way into
schools in the State of New York (Jamestown and Brooklyn),
North Dakota, and Washington, and that in 1912 Minneapolis
high schools had an enrollment of 352 pupils.

The Society had also inquired into the status of Scandinavian languages in colleges and universities, and found that,
with or without qualifications, a number of Middle West institutions, mainly state universities, granted the Scandinavian
languages college-entrance credit. In one institution (the College of the University of Minnesota), the languages were "absolutely on par with other modern foreign languages."

At the fifth annual meeting of the Society in May, 1915,
Professor Stomberg's committee reported 1,965 students in
Scandinavian languages in fifty-four high schools in the United
States. In *Scandinavian Studies* (III [1916], 213), Miss
Maren Michelet[12] pleaded for more support, praised the Scan-

12. Educational Secretary of the Society for the Advancement of Scandinavian Study.

dinavian-American press for its support, and called for better
equipment (textbooks, dictionaries, etc.). Miss Michelet's report (May, 1917) on the enrollment in Scandinavian classes
was most encouraging. There were at the time 2,228 students
in eight states and sixty-three high schools. This was the greatest attendance reported. There were at that time ninety-five
teachers actively engaged in teaching Swedish and Norwegian.

But as early as 1919 discordant notes began to be heard in
the reports of Miss Michelet. "The war and a hostile feeling
against modern foreign languages, except French," she writes,
"has caused the Scandinavian languages to suffer severe defeat. . . ." In 1920 Professor K. A. Kilander of Gustavus
Adolphus College deplored the indifference of the Scandinavian
population to the advancement of the Scandinavian languages,
even in communities where the voters of Scandinavian origin
constituted a majority. In May, 1926, Miss Michelet reported
that the number of students of Scandinavian languages in the
Minneapolis high schools had decreased to 477.

Since the death of Miss Michelet in 1932, the reports on the
progress of the study of Scandinavian languages have been
brief. The blow dealt the modern-language instruction in the
United States by the World War is still felt. The financial depression has also added its share to the setback. In no way must
this temporary decline be construed as a lack of interest on the
part of the leading men. A revival of increasing popular interest has been discernible during the last two years. The enrollment has risen steadily in the Middle West. Unusual things
have happened in the East: Swedish as a curricular subject in
high schools has made its debut in Massachusetts. This is
chiefly due to the untiring efforts of Karl G. Fredin, Editor-
in-chief of the Swedish weekly, *Svea*. For years he has pleaded
with the school authorities to make provisions for the study of
the Swedish language in high schools in cities and towns where
there is an actual demand for such courses. In the spring of
1937, the school authorities in the city of Worcester decided
that a course in Swedish should be introduced in the Commercial High School. On the first day of registration, one hundred students elected the subject. This course in Swedish en-

joys the distinction of being the first one ever offered in a high school in the State of Massachusetts.

In 1937 the Swedish American Council sponsored a summer course in Swedish, with a view to providing instruction for prospective teachers of Swedish. The course was conducted by the writer. Through the courtesy of President Atwood of Clark University, Worcester, Massachusetts, it was given at that institution.

The aim of the teaching of Swedish in American secondary school naturally differs from that of the universities. But even on the high-school level, the purpose of the study is, in the final analysis, a utilitarian one; namely, to increase the capacities of the student, over and above those of his fellow student who has not had the opportunity of enriching his life through the acquisition of a language not hitherto offered in the secondary schools of the country. In so far as the rising generations of Swedish descent in the United States are concerned, no opportunity should be lost of urging them to cultivate the language of their ancestors. They need not be timid about it; it does not endanger good citizenship, but rather strengthens it.

The question naturally presents itself: What is the future of the Swedish language, its literature, and Swedish culture in the United States? This query is difficult to answer, but one thing is almost certain: Without a vital interest on the part of the Swedish-American population, the progress in the study of the language cannot be great. It is the writer's firm conviction, too, that it cannot prosper without more official recognition by our secondary schools and colleges. The recognition of Swedish by the College Entrance Examination Board, for instance, would be an ideal goal of united Swedish-American endeavors. This Board, which covers the entire United States, already recognizes Greek, Latin, German, French, Spanish, and Italian, and the writer feels that Swedish should be granted the same privilege as these languages.

To assist the Scandinavian languages in obtaining the rightful official recognition among the higher institutions of learning in the United States—more particularly in parts of the country and in centers where citizens of Scandinavian birth or descent have made their homes in great numbers—will require far-reaching and united efforts, not only on the part of the leading men in Scandinavian-American colleges, of the teaching profession, the clergy, The Cultural Society (Kulturförbundet), The National Society (Nationalförbundet), The Order of Vasa, The American Sons and Daughters of Sweden, the Society for the Advancement of Scandinavian Study, the Modern Language Association of America, The American-Scandinavian Foundation, and of the entire Scandinavian-American press, but also on the part of the private individual, and of the parents and guardians wherever the Scandinavian languages are spoken and the heritage, which the Scandinavian-Americans have received from their ancestors, is being cherished and shared with the people of the country.

The submitting of this proposition to State and local educational authorities as well as to the College Entrance Examination Board, and the Modern Language Association of America, for an open-minded and serious consideration, calls for no discussion here. But, in the opinion of the writer, the matter ought to be taken in hand without delay by a representative central committee of national scope, with subcommittees in the Eastern, Central, and Western States. Only in this manner can we look forward to a satisfactory solution of the question of the future status of the Swedish language and the other Scandinavian language within the educational system of the United States.

Bibliography

ACRELIUS, ISRAEL. Beskrifning om de Swenska Församlingars Forna och Närwarande Tilstånd, etc. Stockholm, 1759. In the Archives of the American Swedish Historical Museum, Philadelphia.

BENSON, ADOLPH B. The America of 1750. Peter Kalm's Travels in North America. Wilson-Erickson, Inc., 1937.

FLOM, G. T. "Nordiske Studier ved Amerikanske Universiteter," in *Symra,* pp. 151 ff. Decorah, Iowa.

—— A History of Scandinavian Studies in American Universities together with a Bibliography. In: *Iowa Studies in Language and Literature,* No. II. May, 1907.

JOHNSON, AMANDUS. The Swedish Settlements on the Delaware . . ., 1638–1664.

LINCOLN, JULIUS. "Swedish American Educational Institutions," in *The Swedish Element in America,* Chicago, 1931.

LINDER, OLIVER A. "Svensk-Amerikanska tidningspressen," in *Svenskarna i Amerika,* II, by Hildebrand och Fredenholm. Stockholm, 1924–25.

PAXON, HENRY D. Where Pennsylvania History Began, 1926.

PETERSON, C. "The Beginning of Swedish-American Education," in *Year-Book* of the Swedish Historical Society of America, 1922–23.

UPPVALL, AXEL JOHAN. "Den svenska kulturen i Amerika till mitten av 1800-talet, in *Svenskarna i Amerika* by Hildebrand och Fredenholm. Stockholm, 1925–26. Band I, II.

WICKERSHAM, J. P. History of Education in Pennsylvania. Lancaster, Pa., 1886.

Some of the textbooks for students of Swedish, published by the Augustana Book Concern, Rock Island, Illinois, and by Albert Bonnier, Stockholm, and distributed by the Albert Bonnier Publishing House, New York City.

By the Augustana Concern:

VICKNER, EDW. J. Simplified Swedish Grammar.
—— Swedish Composition and Word Study.
ELMQUIST, A. LOUIS. Elementary Swedish Grammar.
—— Swedish Phonology.
SWEDISH READER. Notes and vocabulary by A. Louis Elmquist. For graded schools, high schools, and colleges.

College and High School Series of Swedish Authors:

GEIJERSTAM, GUSTAV AF. Mina Pojkar. With introduction notes and vocabulary. Edited by Joseph Alexis.

LAGERLÖF, SELMA. Valda Berättelser. With notes and vocabulary. Edited by Prof. Jules Mauritzson.

TEGNÉR, ESAIAS. Fritiofs Saga. With introduction, bibliography, notes, and vocabulary. Edited by A. A. Stomberg.

RUNEBERG, JOHAN LUDVIG. Fänrik Ståls Sägner. With introduction, notes, and vocabulary. Edited by A. Louis Elmquist.

GRADED READER (Tredje Läseboken), for classes in Swedish, compiled by Jules Mauritzson.

GLOSSARY, for Graded Reader.

SVENSK DIKTNING, selections from Swedish poets, with brief monographs, notes, and vocabulary, by J. Mauritzson and E. Olson.

By Albert Bonnier:

LAGERLÖF, SELMA. En Herrgårdssägen.

—— Nils Holgerssons underbara resa genom Sverige.

NYBLOM, HELENA. Det Ringer, all three with notes and vocabulary by A. Louis Elmquist.

STRINDBERG, AUGUST. Lycko-Pers resa, with notes and vocabulary by J. Thorsten Sellin.

—— Master Olof, with notes and vocabulary by Joseph E. A. Alexis.

—— Påsk, with notes and vocabulary by Joseph E. A. Alexis.

—— Stories and Poems, with notes and vocabulary by Joseph E. A. Alexis.

UPPVALL, AXEL JOHAN. Manual of Swedish Phonology with International Phonetic Transcription.

Farmers

ERIC ENGLUND

The Author of this chapter was born on a farm at Trehörningsjö, northern Ångermanland, Sweden. In 1907, as a boy, he migrated to America, and, after spending a few years among Swedish farmers in southern Texas, moved to western Oregon. After preparing for college at Portland, he studied at the Oregon State Agricultural College, receiving his B.S. degree in agriculture in 1918, and at the University of Oregon, where he obtained his A.B. During the World War he served as lieutenant of infantry. He holds a degree of Master of Science from the University of Wisconsin, and a Ph.D. from Harvard. For a period of years, he was a member of the staff of the Kansas State Agricultural College. Since coming to the U. S. Department of Agriculture in 1926, he has served as economist for the Office of Experiment Stations; as special assistant to the Secretary of Agriculture; in charge of the division of agricultural finance in the Bureau of Agricultural Economics; and as assistant chief in charge of research in that Bureau, which position he now holds. Special credit is due Everett E. Edwards, Agricultural Economist, United States Department of Agriculture, for extensive contributions, both in compiling the facts and in writing the chapter.

THE story of Sweden's contributions to American agriculture begins in the seventeenth century, with the establishment of New Sweden on the Delaware River.[1] As a colony under Swedish auspices, its history is relatively brief. The first settlers—some fifty in number—arrived in 1638, and the entire colony, consisting of about five hundred Swedes, Finns, and Dutch, passed under Dutch control in 1655. However, this brief attempt on the part of Swedish leaders to rival England and Holland in the development of commercial outposts and overseas dominions was not without constructive consequences for America.

The Swedes established trading communities at Fort Christina, now Wilmington, Delaware, at Tinicum and Wicaco, now

1. This essay is based on wide reading in the historical studies of the subject, as well as on personal observations. Special acknowledgment is due two scholarly works: Florence E. Janson, *The Background of Swedish Immigration, 1840–1930* (Chicago, 1931), and George M. Stephenson, *The Religious Aspects of Swedish Immigration* (Minneapolis, 1932).

parts of Philadelphia, and at Raccoon Creek and Penn's Neck, now in Gloucester County, New Jersey.[2] From these three centers, they gradually dispersed, following the natural lines of expansion. From the first center they spread into what is now New Castle County, Delaware, and into adjacent Maryland; from the second, inland along the Schuylkill Valley, and southward on the banks of the Delaware; and from the third, along the eastern shore of the Delaware River and Bay, into the present counties of Burlington, Cumberland, Salem, and Cape May in New Jersey. Swedish emigration to the Delaware region practically ceased by the end of the seventeenth century. Yet it has been estimated that there were 21,500 persons of Swedish descent in the United States in 1790.[3] Of this number 15,-000 lived in the region of the original Swedish settlements along the Delaware, and in the hinterland populated from that base.

It was soon realized by the Swedish leaders that the success of their colony in America was dependent on the establishment of agriculture. Large tracts of land were purchased from the Indians, and these transactions were duly executed by signed agreements. The friendly relations with the Indians furnished an example for William Penn when he undertook the settlement of his vast commonwealth.

The first expeditions included "cattle and implements of husbandry," and Johan Printz, who served as Governor from 1643 to 1653, was directed to "arrange and urge forward agriculture and the improvement of the land, setting and urging the people thereto with zeal and energy." Printz was also instructed to arrange for the production of a good breed of cattle, to direct his attention to sheep, to encourage the cultivation of tobacco as an export crop, and to investigate the possibilities of producing wine and silk.[4] He pursued his instructions with diligence, and his successor, Johan Rising, followed his example.

2. The most comprehensive treatment of this phase of the subject is in Amandus Johnson's *The Swedish Settlements on the Delaware* (New York, 1911).

3. Marcus L. Hansen, in *Report of Committee on Linguistic and National Stocks in the Population of the United States,* pp. 391–396, published in the American Historical Association Annual Report for 1931.

4. Printz's instructions are quoted in C. R. Woodward, *The Development of Agriculture in New Jersey, 1640–1880,* p. 6 (New Brunswick, 1927).

These settlers of Swedish origin succeeded better as farmers than as traders and colonizers. After their colony passed to Dutch and, later, to English rule, they continued to clear fields, plant crops, and tend their livestock.[5] The agriculture of these sturdy husbandmen was similar to that of the neighboring settlements of other European powers. There were few wants which could not be satisfied locally. The large meadows along the river furnished grazing grounds and hay for the livestock, and foodstuffs were grown in abundance. Hemp, flax, and wool constituted the raw materials from which textiles for clothing were made. Rye became a basic grain crop, taking precedence over wheat, because the colonists were used to rye bread in the homeland. Tobacco was the staple crop grown for export, and Indian corn and barley were also raised. The abundant use of buckwheat in the three English colonies of the Delaware region may be traced to the early Swedish settlers.

Near the end of the seventeenth century, 1693, an appeal for a minister of their faith to be sent from the homeland was made by the Swedes along the Delaware. Their life was described in the following words:

Almost all of us are husbandmen; we plough, and sow, and cultivate the land; and as to our meat and drink, we live according to the old Swedish custom. This country is very rich and fruitful; it produces, God be praised, all sorts of grain, all that we plant and sow gives us plentiful returns, so that we are richly supplied with meat and drink, and we send out yearly to our neighbours on this continent and neighbouring islands, bread, grain, flour. . . . Our wives and daughters employ themselves in spinning wool and flax, and many of them in weaving, so that we have good reason to thank the Almighty for daily support.[6]

The Reverend Erik Björk, one of the ministers who came to America in response to this appeal, wrote home in 1697: "There are no poor in this country but they all provide for themselves;

5. Amandus Johnson, "History of the Swedes in the Eastern States from the Earliest Times until 1782," in *The Swedish Element in America*, II, 16–17, 27 (Chicago, 1931).

6. Quoted in Lyman Carrier, *The Beginnings of Agriculture in America*, p. 173 (New York, 1923).

for the land is rich and fruitful, and no man who will labour can suffer want." His colleague, the Reverend Andreas Rudman, further reported that "the houses are built after the Swedish manner; the women brew excellent drink as in Sweden; they have also a liquor made of apples or peaches which they call cider; it is very pleasant to the taste, and very wholesome."[7]

As agricultural pioneers in the Delaware region, the Swedes created a secure source of agricultural supplies for the colonizing efforts of the English in Delaware, New Jersey, and Pennsylvania. Traces of Swedish influence linger, even to the present day, in the type of local building used and in the red cattle of eastern Pennsylvania.[8]

The modern movement of Swedes to America began in 1841 with the settlement of a small group under the leadership of Gustaf Unonius, at Pine Lake, Wisconsin. Two years later, Thure Ludvig Kumlien, noted frontier botanist and ornithologist, established a similar colony at Koshkonong Lake in the same State. The settlement of the Jansenists at Bishop Hill, Illinois, followed in 1846. These pioneering efforts of intellectuals and idealists helped clear the way for the mass movement which followed. During the 1850's, the number of Swedish immigrants averaged 1,690 annually. In the 'sixties, the average was 12,245, and it was during this decade that Sweden first came to be regarded as an important source of hardy, thrifty, and persevering immigrants, by the Federal and State governments, and by steamship, railroad, and land companies, which were interested in securing settlers. Disastrous crop failures in Sweden from 1867 to 1869, preceded by overspeculation in agricultural lands, caused many to heed the promises of economic betterment in America. Letters from the early arrivals to relatives and friends in the homeland accentuated the movement, and the activities of the agents of transportation companies helped to spread the contagion of "America fever."

As news concerning the opportunities in the United States filtered through the Swedish countrysides, America became a veritable Land of Canaan. It ceased to be a place and became

7. Quoted in Carrier, *The Beginnings of Agriculture in America*, p. 173.
8. J. T. Adams, *Provincial Society, 1690–1763*, p. 5 (New York, 1928).

an ideal; it lost in reality, and became a symbol. Those who contemplated emigration

visualized America as a land where the dignity of the human soul was recognized, where work was honorable, where class distinctions were levelled, and where the future beckoned on to a status of economic independence. The equality that the law gives is not the equality of custom. . . . In America there existed no scorn for the common man, no rejoicing over seeing him sweat while others were idle; there were no haughty gentlemen, no uniforms, and no privileged classes.[9]

The average annual number of emigrants increased slightly during the 'seventies, in spite of better economic conditions in Sweden. The total for the decade averaged 15,000 a year. In the 'eighties, the acute agricultural depression in Europe, precipitated by the ever-increasing flow of American surpluses into the world markets, fell with full force upon the agricultural classes of northern and western Europe, including Sweden. During this decade the annual average of Swedish emigration was 37,000, the number being 44,000 for 1882, 46,000 for 1887, and 45,000 in 1888—the highest ever attained.

The exodus from Sweden continued, at the average rate of 25,000 a year from 1891 to 1910, in spite of the financial depression of 1893 in the United States and better economic conditions in Europe. Because of the hazards of travel and the high wages in neutral countries during the World War, Swedish emigration fell to an annual average of 11,000 during the second decade of the present century. Since 1921, the American quota laws have gradually decreased the number of Swedes that may enter the United States.[10]

The age of the immigrants also changed during the course of the nineteenth century. In the 'forties, 'fifties, and 'sixties, the majority of those arriving were families with young children, usually traveling with others—often relatives—as a group. As railroads were built to facilitate rapid transporta-

9. Stephenson, *Religious Aspects of Swedish Immigration*, pp. 400–401.
10. Janson, *The Background of Swedish Immigration, 1840–1930*, pp. 9–12, 497–498.

tion, the family units tended to travel by themselves. Throughout the movement there was a steady increase in the proportionate number of single men and women. By the end of the century, three fourths of the Swedish immigrants were single persons.

Sweden, a country with only a little over six million inhabitants today, has contributed over one million immigrants to the United States since 1850. The economic life of some of the provinces was adversely affected by the devastating loss of population. This contributed to the formation, in Sweden, of associations against emigration, whose principal means of discouraging the outflow of population was for a time an extensive propaganda designed to show that life in America, "the land of the future" (*framtidslandet*), was far from being all that had been claimed for it, and that the Swedes, for reasons of both patriotism and self-interest, should remain at home.

Taking the Kingdom as a whole, one out of every seven has emigrated during the last seventy-five years, and most of this number have come to the United States. Although the total number of Swedish stock in America can be estimated only in a general way, it must be well over two million. Even the United States Census of 1930 gives the number born in Sweden and those of Swedish or mixed parentage, classified according to the country of birth of the father, except where the father was native and the mother Swedish-born, as 1,562,703. However, this total does not give cognizance to second and later generations of Swedish-Americans. Through their fusion with the main stream of American citizenry, the Swedish element has exerted wide influence on American life.

The main factors causing this vast *Volkswanderung* have already been indicated. The basic reason was the desire on the part of the emigrants to better their economic status. Most of the desirable land of Sweden had been appropriated for many centuries and the land values were high. The Kingdom had areas of unoccupied land in the north, but the rigorous climate of that region precluded settlement until the opportunities in America were gone. The millions of acres of cheap land across the Atlantic drew like a gigantic magnet, and especially after the Homestead Act of 1862 made it possible for anyone who had declared his intention of becoming a citizen to acquire 160 acres, simply by occupation and cultivation.

Since estates in Sweden usually passed to the eldest son, it was always necessary for most of the younger sons and the daughters of landholders to leave the home farm, and go out into the world. As the opportunities in America became known, this surplus turned westward. Even today, the emigration consists largely of the surplus population from the peasant homes, together with crofters and cotters. By 1870, the young peasant girls had come to prefer domestic service in America to the routine on farms in the homeland, which the custom of centuries had allotted to them.

The relatively high wages in America were an additional reason for emigration. Prior to its industrialization in the late nineteenth century, the wages in Sweden were low. In the United States it was easier to accumulate the cash needed to start a farm or a profession. Economic depressions and the agricultural crisis already referred to also precipitated wholesale exoduses.

News of opportunities in America was also a great stimulus to emigration from Sweden. Emigrant travel and land companies began to advertise in the rural press of Sweden in the late 'sixties. Steamship and railroad companies, also, did everything within their power to encourage the movement to America, including the sending of agents throughout the rural districts of Sweden. The States, especially Iowa, Wisconsin, Minnesota, Kansas, Nebraska, and the Dakotas, actively bid for the attention of the Swedes. They, as well as the railroad companies, flooded the rural districts of Sweden with illustrated pamphlets about farming opportunities in America. The numerous letters from friends and relatives, the so-called "America letters," were without doubt the most subtle and effective kind of publicity. The stream of these letters began in the early 'forties and continued unabated throughout the decades. Often they contained tickets and promises of jobs. The sums of money sent back across the Atlantic to care for aging parents furnished concrete evidence of American prosperity.

Factors in Swedish social and political life may also have contributed to the movement. Until the achievement of uni-

versal manhood and womanhood suffrage in 1909 and 1919, the
limited franchise was especially galling to the lower classes.
Social inequalities were probably more irritating, and the introduction of compulsory military training made many who
intended to migrate for economic reasons decide to leave by the
time they were twenty. A free social order, an apparently un-
limited supply of cheap land, and the possibility of a poor man
rising to an independent and respected position, beckoned the
Swedish emigrants toward America.

These immigrants and their descendants have played an important part in the development of the United States, and especially is this true of the agricultural communities of the Middle
West and the Pacific coast. In order of their Swedish population, the ten leading States in 1880 were: Illinois (42,415);
Minnesota (39,176); Iowa (17,559); Kansas (11,207); New
York (11,164); Nebraska (10,164); Michigan (9,412); Wisconsin (8,138); Pennsylvania (7,576); and Massachusetts
(4,756). By 1910 Minnesota outranked Illinois, New York
was third, Massachusetts fourth, Michigan fifth, California
sixth, Washington seventh, Iowa eighth, Wisconsin ninth, and
Nebraska tenth.

In 1920 the order was the same for the first four, and Washington, California, Michigan, Wisconsin, Iowa, and Pennsylvania followed in the order given. According to the Census of
1930 the ten States having over fifty thousand Swedes were:
Minnesota (270,773); Illinois (261,374); New York (121,-
503); California (103,603); Massachusetts (81,106); Washington (76,843); Michigan (68,577); Iowa (57,365); Wisconsin (56,915); and Nebraska (50,087).

An overwhelming majority of the Swedish emigrants were
farmers or persons familiar with rural life. Until quite recently,
most of the people of Sweden were dependent on agriculture for
a living. In 1870, as many as 72.4 per cent were still engaged
in farming and related occupations, and only since 1880 has
the rural population declined rapidly. By 1900 the percentage
had fallen to 52.4, and now only about 34 per cent derive their
income from agriculture, although it has undergone vast improvements during the last century.

At first this rural exodus was from the agricultural districts

WHERE SKY AND GRAIN MEET
PHILIP LINDSTROM'S WHEAT FIELD, COLORADO

MILK AND MEAT
PURE BRED CATTLE OWNED BY IVAR PETERSON, KANSAS

where the soil was less fertile, and where distance from market and poor communications tended toward isolation. After 1880, it even came from districts where the landholdings were of fair size. The crisis, which proved so disastrous to all of European agriculture during the 'eighties, compelled many to emigrate who might never otherwise have done so. The number of farms and farm laborers remained almost stationary, and, in practically all of the purely agricultural districts, the population decreased after 1880, in spite of better wages and working conditions. The number of crofters and cotters also declined rapidly. Yet the rural population practically doubled during the last century, and it was this vast surplus, especially the younger sons and daughters from the farms, which turned to America.

Considering these facts, it was only natural that many thousands of the Swedish immigrants and their descendants should become farmers in America. They have created thousands of frontier homes from the virgin lands of the Middle and Far West. In 1930, the rural-farm population included 98,589 persons of Swedish birth and 215,221 persons, one, or both, of whose parents were Swedish. This made a total of 313,810 or 7.1 per cent of the entire so-called "foreign white stock," and ranked next to the Norwegians and Germans in this respect. The corresponding figures for the rural-nonfarm population are 88,629 and 150,139, or a total of 238,768 or 4.8 per cent. There was, therefore, a total of 552,578 Swedish immigrants and their children, living in the rural communities in the United States in 1930. This number does not include the many Americans of Swedish descent whose parents were also born in the United States.

The States having the largest Swedish rural-farm population, as indicated by the Census, were: Minnesota (88,041); Nebraska (23,099); Wisconsin (22,706); Iowa (21,196); Illinois (18,311); Washington (14,648); Michigan (11,863); California (10,852); New York (4,610); and Massachusetts (2,013). When the figures for the rural-nonfarm population are added, the ranking is as follows: Minnesota (124,908); Illinois (36,244); Nebraska (34,176); Wisconsin (33,233); Iowa (32,269); Washington (31,495); California (25,231);

Michigan (23,484); New York (17,412); and Massachusetts (8,574).

In the beginning, the Swedish immigrants who turned to farming in America, and especially those who were pioneers in the communities where they settled, had to be content with the barest necessities. As practically all of the immigrants were determined to make their permanent home in America, their first main objective was a piece of land which could be developed into a farm. Their hopes and aspirations thus became fixed in America.

The early homeseekers secured land by preëmption, the usual price being $1.25 per acre. It remained, however, for the Homestead Act, passed in 1862, to provide the chief means by which they acquired land. The opportunities offered by this act sustained the spirits of many an immigrant, both before and after his arrival in America. The future came to hold for him the possibility of his owning his own farm—not just a small holding similar to those in Sweden, but 160 acres—and the possibility of his being economically independent, as well. This feeling of independence and self-confidence, actual as well as potential, was further stimulated by the vision and reality of the vast distances of the Middle West, with its large farms and cities that sprang forth as if by magic. With a background of small farms and tiny hamlets, the Swedish farmers in America came to feel that they were part of a vast empire whose possibilities were just beginning.

With few exceptions, they were without means when they reached their ultimate destination in America. Many were in debt for at least part of their passage. In the earlier days it was necessary, in addition to paying the fare, to lay in a store of provisions for the trip, which took as much as three or four months. The outlay for an entire family was therefore considerable, and even the young unmarried people had not had time to accumulate much money before leaving Sweden. The result was that many of the immigrants were unable to turn to farming immediately upon their arrival, because they lacked the necessary capital. They worked at railroad construction, in factories, and as farmhands, before acquiring the land and equipment needed for a farm. Working as hired men on farms acquainted them with the American language, customs, and farming methods.

Opportune time of opening up a region to settlement was probably the main factor which determined where the Swedish farm communities of America were to be. In some instances, the particular choice of a group was probably influenced also by the opinion of someone in whose judgment they had faith. The lands of Minnesota were being thrown open to settlement, just at the time when the flood of Swedish immigrants was assuming large proportions. This coincidence, together with the wide circulation of Fredrika Bremer's discerning comments on the opportunities in this portion of the upper Mississippi Valley, and her enthusiasm at the possibility of Minnesota's becoming "a glorious new Scandinavia," did much to make her dream a reality.

The general similarity of the nature of the upper Mississippi Valley, especially the forests and almost countless lakes, to the homeland, also seems to have influenced the location of Swedish settlements. There are many examples of the natives of different provinces in Sweden choosing similar countrysides in America in which to settle. The immigrants from Småland did not feel at home on the open prairies, but those from Skåne moved there without hesitation; those from Värmland often cleared and broke new land in the forests, only to turn it over to people from Västergötland to develop into permanent agricultural communities. The immigrants also tended to gravitate to communities where relatives and friends had already begun to develop farmsteads. In this way many settlements came to have a preponderance of settlers from the same parishes and provinces of the homeland.

In the early Swedish settlements of Minnesota, the first arrivals selected wooded land as the sites for their farm settlements. The choice was due at least in part to familiarity with this sort of land in Sweden, and possibly also to the traditional belief that this was the only kind of virgin land which was worth developing into farms. The necessity of having timber for fuel and building material was likewise a factor. The result was that the clearing of the fields for farm crops was exceedingly slow and laborious. Eventually the Swedes, like their

American neighbors, found that the open prairies waited only the breaking, to turn them into rich agricultural lands.

In the pioneering efforts of the Swedes on the frontier, their background of frugality and subsistence farming stood them in good stead. All were used to hard incessant labor. The men knew enough of carpentering, blacksmithing, and masonry to do the work of this kind, either individually or in coöperation with neighbors, on their farms. Chests of tools were brought from Sweden for this purpose. Many of the immigrants had learned trades in the homeland, and these skills were utilized to great advantage. Few of the homes of the settlers who arrived before 1870 could boast of any bought furniture; the bedsteads, tables, and chairs were generally homemade. It has been said that the older Swedish rural communities of the Middle West were almost as self-sufficient as the feudal manors of medieval Europe.

In many communities, individuals put their knowledge of the trades to profitable use by making implements for their neighbors. Sometimes they made farm tools considered indispensable because of long usage in Sweden, or, at other times, they may have devised adaptations designed to meet the new needs. In some communities this practice became a business. With the development of the farm-machinery manufacturing plants, and large-scale production of standard machines, these small concerns which had served the immigrant communities were forced to close their shops.

The Swedish women made homes in the log cabins and sod houses on the frontier. They spun, and knitted, and wove, and made the clothing for their families. They cared for the livestock and cultivated the fields while the menfolks were away earning cash to tide the family over until the farm was producing a cash income. Their devotion to their homes and communities, like that of their American sisters, constitutes an epic theme.

The details of the ways in which the farming practices, inherited from the Old World, were gradually adjusted to meet the urgent realities of the New, are largely lost. In matters of making a living and in economic organization, adjustment to American conditions was most rapid. The Swedes, like their

American-born neighbors, were always confronted with actualities. In the earlier years of their communities, they were without adequate roads and markets. As soon as practicable, however, the log cabins, sod houses, and straw-covered stables, typical of a quasi self-sufficient economy, were displaced by comfortable and commodious dwellings and large barns and granaries. With the mechanization of agriculture, the cradle and the flail gave place to the binder and the steam thresher.

The manner of farming in Sweden was entirely unadapted to the Great Plains, where the climate and physiography dictated the operation of large acreages. Like their neighbors of native stock, the Swedes had to experiment and devise agricultural methods suited to this Western region. It is difficult to delineate any essential differences in the economic organization of the Swedish communities, from other pioneer American settlements on the plains. In the matter of shelter, the Swedes were quick to adopt the dugouts and sod houses developed by the Americans.

A similar statement may be made with reference to the rapidity of their general Americanization. The Swedes, more than any other group, became naturalized as soon as it was legally possible for them to do so, and practically 100 per cent of them became citizens of their adopted country. These facts are an indication of the rapidity with which the Swedes merged themselves into the mass of the American people. Using the church as the main medium, their leaders fought to preserve a distinctive Swedish culture in Swedish America. However, it was as if the Swedes, transplanted to American soil, were placed in an inexorable environment. Had their particular culture lingered somewhat longer as a distinct element, it might well have served as an even more constructive and enriching leaven in American civilization generally, as well as in the lives of the later generations of Swedish-Americans.

The members of the Swedish farm communities were imbued with a fine neighborly spirit, and they sought on every occasion to aid, comfort, and cheer each other. This spirit manifested itself especially in times of sickness and misfortune, and when new arrivals from the homeland needed shelter and food until they could start homes of their own. The traditional sociability and hospitality of the Swedes have been handed on to later generations, and America is the richer for these gifts. Neighborly coöperation was necessary, as the early settlers of a community seldom had all of the draft power and equipment needed to break the fields and plant them for crops. Often three or four yoke of oxen were needed, and the teams and their drivers were freely loaned on such occasions. At harvesting and threshing times, neighbors also exchanged work.

Commentators have emphasized the industry, thrift, and frugality of the Swedish-American farmers—characteristics inherited from the centuries of struggle with necessity, in the homeland. They have worked and saved to own their farms, and to improve them with good buildings and equipment. As a generalization, it may be said that the Swedish farmers have tended to follow a more diversified program of production, and produce more of the necessities of life on their farms, than their neighbors of native stock. Especially is this statement true of those who immigrated. This has contributed toward a somewhat greater economic security in Swedish farm communities. The Swedes have aided in the development of producer and consumer coöperatives, as the occasion justified or permitted. As agrarian liberals, they have contributed their strength to progressive political movements which looked to the solution of agricultural problems. They have thought in terms of free farmers and free farms, privately owned.

By general consent, the American farmers of Swedish extraction are recognized as among the better farmers of their respective communities. The testimony of county agents, in regions where Swedish stock constitutes a substantial part of the rural population, amply confirms this point. Of the forty-six Master-Farmer awards, made by the *Farmer* of St. Paul, Minnesota, to farmers of that State during the years from 1926 to 1932, nine, or practically one fifth, were to farmers of Swedish descent; whereas the Swedes, as listed by the Census of 1930, constituted only one tenth of the rural-farm population of Minnesota.

Sweden has also made contributions other than sturdy tillers of the soil to American agriculture. Alsike clover, long an important forage crop in the northeastern United States and as far west as the Great Plains, was originally cultivated in Sweden, its name being derived from the parish of Alsike in Uppland.[11] It was introduced into England about 1834, and five years later the editors of the *New Genesee Farmer* of Rochester, New York, distributed alsike-clover seed among its readers. In 1854, a distribution was made by the agricultural division of the United States Patent Office, and probably there were other importations. The immigrants from northern Europe also brought alsike clover with them.

The cream separator, invented by Carl Gustaf Patrik De Laval of Sweden, in 1877, proved to be one of the epoch-making events in the history of dairying.[12] The idea of separating the cream by whirling the whole milk did not originate with De Laval, but it remained for him to devise a machine which accomplished that objective in a practical way. His first machines were power driven, but he also invented the first hand separator, and a number of the latter machines were imported into the United States in 1885. De Laval also invented the lactocrite, which was the first practical milk tester. It led to the development, by Stephen M. Babcock, of the simple Babcock milk tester, which is now used throughout America for the determination of the butterfat content of milk. De Laval also invented the centrifugal churn, to churn continuously the cream delivered from the bowl of a separator, and an emulsifier, designed to emulsify with skim milk, substitutes for the butterfat which had been removed from it. The latter device was later used in making various chemical emulsions. He also invented one of the first mechanical milkers. The cream separator and the milk tester, both conceived by De Laval, though further developed by others, have meant billions in money to dairying, and have contributed greatly to the wide use of dairy products as we know them today.

Sweden was among the first countries to develop scientific

11. U. S. Department of Agriculture, *Annual Report* for 1865, p. 352, and *Farmers' Bulletin* 1151, pp. 3–4.

12. J. C. McDowell, "Carl Gustaf Patrik De Laval," *The Ten Master Minds of Dairying* (Des Moines, Iowa, 1930), pp. 29–33; L. S. Ivins and A. E. Winship, *Fifty Famous Farmers* (New York, 1924), pp. 13–20; S. R. Guard, "A Saga of the Soil," *Breeder's Gazette,* XCIII, 12: pp. 30–31, 35 (December, 1928).

forestry. A number of America's forestry specialists received training as exchange students in Sweden. The Swedes were pioneers in the study of forest soils, and their knowledge and inspiration in this field have passed to America. The methods of taking inventory of the forest resources in the United States were influenced and evolved from those developed in Sweden. The increment borer, used to ascertain tree growth without felling the tree, is a Swedish invention.

In more recent years, contributions have also come from the plant-breeding station at Svalöf, a small village in southern Sweden. Possibly no other single institution of a foreign country has contributed more to American agriculture. The chief practical contributions of this station are Victory oats and Hannchen barley.[13] American oat breeders regard Victory oats as the high-water mark in oat improvement by pure-line selection in Europe. The variety is popular in many of the agricultural districts of Europe, and is recommended in many parts of the United States, particularly in the Northwest. The Victory oat is a midseason variety, fairly plump, and adapted primarily to regions of cool climate. Its high-yielding ability, excellent quality, and great uniformity, mark it as one of the most valuable varieties ever developed. Other oats, which were developed at Svalöf and have gained recognition, are the Swedish Select, the Golden Rain, the Star, and the Eagle.

Hannchen barley was introduced into the United States from Svalöf in 1904. It is a two-row type which has given better yields and exhibited much wider range than most any other barley of this type grown in America. It is now grown on over sixty thousand acres, mostly in Oregon, and there are indications that it may prove valuable in the upper Mississippi Valley.

The foregoing discussion of the Swedes and of American agriculture has of necessity been general in character. It would be possible to expand the chapter indefinitely, by citing examples of individual Swedish immigrants and their descendants who, from small beginnings, have developed successful farms in various parts of the United States, and whose activities, as

13. U. S. Department of Agriculture, *Yearbook* for 1936, pp. 321, 358, 362–363, 369.

farmers and as citizens rooted in the soil, have exerted a strong influence upon their communities. The same could be done with numerous neighborhoods in which the Swedish people have been the leading element. It would be possible, if space permitted, to develop an interesting and instructive story of these Swedish settlements.

Any attempt to write such a story, however, whether based upon individuals or communities, would soon lead into generalizations with respect to the communities themselves, as a part of the progress of American agriculture and of our national life, in which the contribution of the Swedish people has become merged with those of citizens of other national origins. Such a record would illustrate functioning of the American "melting pot," in which individuals and groups merged their efforts, and were themselves influenced by pioneer conditions and by the economic and social institutions that have emerged into a more mature rural life of America.

As pointed out earlier in this chapter, the Swedes have been notably adaptable to the life and institutions of their adopted country. With the passage of years after the arrival of particular immigrants, their distinctly Swedish attributes have become increasingly difficult to differentiate, because of the rapid fusion of their influence into American life and institutions. Their industry, thrift, and standard of values, merged with those of other groups, have influenced the community as a whole. While this merging of influences makes it difficult to draw distinct demarcations between the Swedish achievements and those of other nationality groups, the attribute of ready and influential adaptability must be counted among the principal contributions of the Swedes to American agriculture and rural life.[14]

14. A careful study of the geography of the United States, various phases of its agriculture, and the Swedish share in the development of the same, may be found in Professor Helge Nelson's work, *Nordamerika: bygd och svenskbygd* (Stockholm, 1926).

Pioneers of the Northwest

ANDREW A. STOMBERG

For biographical notes on the Author, see the chapter on "Professors."

THE first Swedish colony in the New World was founded in the period when the Swedish domain was being greatly extended in Europe by military conquests. By superiority in military efficiency and diplomatic sagacity, Sweden had gained possession of large areas, east and south of the Baltic, stretching from Lake Ladoga to the Elbe. These areas were so advantageously located that the country held control of the lands at the mouths of nearly all the rivers flowing into the Baltic. The brilliant military leadership and diplomatic skill of the Swedish kings and their aides, and the unexpected magnitude of the victories, have given the title, the "Age of Sweden's Greatness," to the period. Swedish and non-Swedish historians and poets have exalted the achievements of this heroic age in which a hitherto almost obscure country of a million people, by heavy sacrifices and a remarkable national unity, and under masterly leadership, not only made great territorial gains, but struck a decisive blow in defense of one of the most precious of human rights; namely, religious liberty.

A Swedish achievement which, until quite recently, has been little noted and still less acclaimed by historians and poets, but which, in fact, won for the Swedes almost as much land as did wars and diplomacy in the seventeenth century, is the settlement of Swedish immigrants in the American Northwest in the nineteenth century. Aside from the actual amount of land wrested from the wilderness, and made into fertile fields by Swedish colonists, this nineteenth-century movement has had great economic and cultural significance. One of the ablest and most thoughtful among the Swedish-American writers, Ernst Skarstedt, once wrote: "The Swedes at home ought to feel proud of the new realm which their kinsmen on the other side of the Atlantic have won for themselves. Swedish-America is the most important conquest ever made by Swedes." And the late Archbishop Nathan Söderblom said that what the Swedes had done as colonists and immigrants in America in the nineteenth century was the greatest contribution of the race to the world, since the Thirty Years' War.

Dr. Helge Nelson, professor of geography at the University of Lund, Sweden, who, no doubt, is better informed than anyone else regarding the Swedish settlements in America, estimates that Swedish immigrants to the United States, and their descendants, cultivate greater areas of land than their kinsmen in the homeland. The total area under cultivation in Sweden is approximately nine and one half million acres. According to Nelson's careful researches, there were, in 1920, in the United States, 60,461 farmers who were born in Sweden, and of these about 85 per cent owned their farms. According to Government reports, about 10,000 more Swedish-born citizens operated farms of which they were not the owners. In Minnesota alone, there were 16,634 farmers born in Sweden. This number equaled the number of owners of manorial estates, farmers, and fruit growers in the populous Swedish *läns* or counties, such as those of Stockholm, Uppsala, and Södermanland. If the citizens of Swedish extraction in the second, third, and fourth generations were also included, the figures would, of course, be much higher. In Minnesota the number of farmers who were born in Sweden, or count their descent from this country, constitutes about 20 per cent of the rural population of the State.

Since from 70 to 80 per cent of the Swedish immigrants, coming to the United States in the decades after 1850, were classed as farmers, farm laborers, or simply laborers, it was natural that most of them settled on farms. Their desire for land was an important factor in building up the populous Swedish rural communities in Minnesota, Iowa, Wisconsin, and the Dakotas, which States are generally included under the designation, "the Northwest."

The Swedish immigrants, who came to the United States in large groups after the middle of the nineteenth century, were land-conscious; no immigrant people have believed more firmly than they that land is the unfailing guarantee of a high standard of living and of social prestige. The history of Sweden since time immemorial and the traditions of the Swedes had helped to fix the idea firmly in their minds that he who has land has wealth. The reports, therefore, which began to trickle through to the hard-working folk in Sweden, that in the United States large and fertile tracts could be had almost for the asking, had an especially strong appeal. True, the tales seemed at first utterly fantastic, but evidence of their creditability soon became so strong that doubts melted away. The author of this chapter, the son of a Swedish father and mother who left Sweden in 1852, could, in his youth, never understand how strong the lure of America had been for the *bönder, torpare,* and day laborers of Sweden; how these steady-going and far from reckless folk, whom he knew as neighbors in the parental home, had been able to resolve to leave the old home, emigrate to America, and, despite almost incredible hardships and anxieties, travel far into the interior where Indians still roamed at will. On his first visit, at the age of twenty-six, to the community in Sweden whence parents and neighbors had emigrated, the whole phenomenon became quite understandable. The region seemed like a hopeless conglomeration of granite-strewn patches of ground, moorland, shallow lakes, stunted trees, and only here and there small plots of arable land. This, it should be noted, was before reforestation, drainage, dairy farming, and the application of modern methods of agriculture had made the same neighborhood the fair and beautiful place it is today. A relative had on his land a particularly fine fifteen-acre field, set like a garden amidst projecting rocks and sand ridges, but this field he had made himself by digging deep and wide trenches, rolling the rocks into these, and then hauling soil from a distance, for surfacing. It had required the expenditure of an enormous amount of muscular strength by both man and beast, and the field had been about thirty years in the making. The thoughts of the visitor from the United States went back to the story told by his parents of how they, soon after arriving in Minnesota in 1854, had acquired title to several hundred acres of land as fine and as fertile as may be found anywhere for $1.25 an acre. It now became easier to understand how it had happened that, in this particular section of Sweden, there could hardly be found a family that did not have one or more of its members in America, most of these living in Minnesota. In a distressingly large number of homes only the parents remained.

In his valuable monogram, *The Scandinavian Element in the United States*, Kendrick C. Babcock points to the strong appeal of America for the people of the North, because of the contrast in nature between the homeland and the land of plenty beyond the seas.

To speak to a Norwegian from Telemarken, to a Swede from Småland, or to a Dane from the misty, sandy coast of Jutland about rich, rolling prairies stretching away for miles upon miles, about land which was neither rocky, nor swampy, nor pure sand, nor set at an angle of forty-five degrees, about land which could be had almost for the asking in fee simple, and not by some semi-manorial title—this was to speak to his imagination rather than to his understanding.

On the same point Babcock writes in another place,

The broad rich prairies of the Northwest had from the first an Eden-like attractiveness to these North folk, coming as they did from land where mountains, marshes, thin soil, and short summers made life a continual struggle for existence. It was the vision of level fields, of marvellous fertility that could be had almost for the asking that in the early days cheered their tedious way across the Atlantic, up the Erie Canal and around the Great Lakes.

When the tide of Swedish immigration began to assume large proportions, the arable land in the States bordering on the Atlantic and along the Ohio River was already held by farmers or speculators, and commanded prices which the immigrants could not pay, even had they wanted to settle in the older sections of the country. The economic factor was, however, only one of the influences which brought the Swedish immigrants in preponderating numbers to the Northwest, and especially to Minnesota. In her book, *Homes in the New World*, published in 1853–57, the famous Swedish novelist, Fredrika Bremer, wrote in connection with her visit to St. Paul in 1850,

What a glorious new Scandinavia might not Minnesota become. Here would the Swede find his clear romantic lakes, the plains of

Skåne, rich in corn, and the valleys of Norrland—the climate, the situation, the character of the scenery agrees with our people better than any other of the American states, and none of them appear to me to have a greater or more beautiful future before them than Minnesota.

Fredrika Bremer's glowing account was probably more a prophecy than a potent influence in bringing Swedish immigrants to Minnesota and neighboring States; for she wrote for a public that was not greatly interested in the question of new homes in the United States. She had, however, with surprising accuracy, appraised the factors which were to induce hundreds of thousands of poor and hard-working Swedes to push their way to the Northwest. It was with them, not merely a question of cheap land, but of an invigorating climate, lakes, forests, snow. Letters of immigrants who had happened to come to the Northwest, to friends in Sweden; accounts sent to newspapers in Sweden, and published by them; the glowing and often fantastic tales of returning emigrants, were perhaps the principal influences in directing the stream of Swedish immigrants westward.

A tremendous impetus to Swedish settlement of the Northwest was soon given by an organized and well-financed propaganda. States like Minnesota and Wisconsin, railroads which had secured grants of vast areas of land on which they were naturally anxious to place bona fide settlers, colonization companies—all began intensive campaigns in Sweden to induce her people to emigrate and settle in the particular State of the respective agents. These agents were active in practically every part of rural Sweden—addressing public meetings or speaking to smaller gatherings in homes; distributing literature giving most alluring pictures of the life that awaited the able and ambitious in the New World; and providing guides for almost any kind of group that set sail for the United States.

The effects of these organized and lavishly financed campaigns, as well as of the swelling flood of "America letters" to Sweden, are graphically told in the Census reports of States and of the Federal Government. Thus, the report of 1850 gives the number of Swedish-born persons in the United States as 3,559, and ten years later, as 18,625. By 1870, the number had

grown to 97,332, and after another decade had swelled to 194,-
337. The largest increase came in the decade from 1880 to 1890.
The Census report of the latter year listed 478,041 persons in
the United States, born in Sweden. To the factors which encouraged emigration from Sweden, discussed above, had been
added: the Homestead Act, which gave lands free to settlers;
cheap transportation rates from Sweden; and the common practice that men, after being established here, would arrange to
have kinsfolk or friends join them, offering them jobs and ad-
vancing money for their trips.

Census reports reveal that, in 1890, no less than 73 per cent
of the Scandinavians in the United States lived in the Northwestern group of States. In Minnesota alone, there were in that
year 99,913 persons born in Sweden, but ten years later the
number was 225,990, including both persons born in Sweden
and those with one or both parents born there. Illinois ranked
next, with 200,032; Iowa, 64,579; Nebraska, 54,380; Michigan, 49,780; and Wisconsin, 48,382. As late as the turn of the
century, about one fourth of the people living in the typical
Swedish Minnesota counties, Chisago and Isanti, had been born
in Sweden, and if all persons of Swedish extraction in those
counties had been counted, they would have constituted approximately 87 per cent of the total population. North and
northwest from Minneapolis, one may travel for a hundred to
a hundred and fifty miles past farms owned or operated by
Swedish immigrants or their descendants.

The Swedes' desire for land, and the easy terms on which it
could be secured, were factors in enlarging the areas held by
them, but other factors tended in the same direction. Farm
laborers were not plentiful, as most of the able-bodied men
could themselves become landowners, and so farmers, in most
instances, had to depend upon their own brawn and muscles,
and on the help of wife and children, to run the farm. Especially in regions where lands could be cleared with comparative
ease, large areas were put under cultivation, as it was temporarily more profitable to work large fields, after a fashion, than
smaller tracts by intensive methods. Naturally, grain raising
became the first industry, as it required less capital, and gave
promise of quicker returns, than diversified farming. Large

farms, therefore, became the rule wherever the Swedes made settlements.

Farming was the chief occupation of the Swedish immigrants, and, while their children in the course of the years have migrated in large numbers to industrial centers, the majority of citizens of Swedish extraction in the Northwest are still to be found on farms. In 1890, approximately one out of every four Swedes or Norwegians in the United States was engaged in farming. For the Northwestern States the percentage was much higher, while, in the country as a whole, one out of every five Englishmen or descendants of the colonial stocks was thus engaged; one out of every six Germans; and one out of every twelve Irish. The percentage would have been considerably higher for the Swedish group, had there not been a later large Swedish immigration to the industrial centers, mainly in the Eastern States.

The Swedes had certain qualifications for succeeding as farmers in the Northwest where others, including Yankees, had failed. Life in the homeland had accustomed them to hardships, giving them strong, untiring bodies. Stern experience had also taught them to be frugal and patient.

Nature is no spendthrift in any part of the Scandinavian Peninsula [says Babcock]. Small economies are the alphabet of her teaching, and their lessons once learned, are rarely forgotten. Her children of the North, therefore, down to the stolidest laborer, mountaineer and fisherman are generally frugal and when they emigrate to the American West to enter upon the work of pioneering with the stern requirements of endurance, patience, persistent endeavor and thrift, they start out in the new life with decided temperamental advantages over most other immigrants and even over most native-born Americans.

An agent of the British Government, sent to this country to study immigration, adds Babcock, wrote concerning the Scandinavians: "It is generally admitted that physically, morally, and socially no better class of immigrants enters the United States. In some respects they are the most desirable of them all."

The Swedish immigrants who settled on farms have contributed enormously to the increase of wealth in the Northwestern

States. Some statistics from Chisago County, which is, as stated above, about 87 per cent Swedish, may be cited as proof. In the twenty-year period from 1870 to 1890, the number of acres put under cultivation in this county increased from 8,004 to 43,-476, and the value of farms from $477,720 to $2,563,630. By 1900 the cultivated area had increased to 85,277 acres, and the value of the farms was placed at $3,419,310. This was typical of the ceaseless labors and steady increase of wealth in hundreds of Swedish communities.

One of the pressing needs of the Northwest at the time when Swedish immigrants began to settle there was transportation facilities. Distances were great, and getting to market was generally very difficult. The navigable streams were not many. The years following the Civil War was an era of railroad building on an unprecedented scale. Almost every community soon became linked with the rest of the country by steel rails. Gigantic labor-saving machinery had not yet been invented and clearing the right of way, building roadbeds, and laying rails required strong muscles and steady patience, and these elements the Swedes contributed abundantly. The story of the Swedes' part in building railroads in the Northwest is a tale no less heroic and economically important than their part in the agricultural development of the region. The newcomers from Sweden were to be found in almost every construction gang, and large stretches of road were built by Swedish contractors and Swedish crews.

When the Swedish railroad workers had earned and saved some money, they generally bought land, became permanent settlers in a farm community, and thus added still further to the economic development of the region. A traveler in the 'eighties and 'nineties who visited Swedish communities, especially in the Red River Valley, was constantly reminded that a large proportion of the landowners had worked as railroad laborers before becoming farmers. It was faith in the Swedes, and in their kinsmen, the Norwegians, which greatly encouraged the railroad executives to extend their lines further and further into new sections; they felt certain that these people would settle along the newly laid lines and build prosperous communities. This faith was fully justified, and was frequently attested by

James J. Hill, the famous railroad builder and executive. In a notable address, in 1902, he pointed to the splendid revenue his company was annually reaping from typical Swedish and Norwegian communities.

Agriculture and railroad construction were by no means the only important occupations which attracted the Swedish immigrant. Wherever hard work was required, and economic development was the aim, there the Swedes were to be found in preponderating numbers. One of these occupations was lumbering, which perhaps required even greater physical strength and endurance, and was linked with more hardships, than either farming or railroad building. No statistics reveal with any accuracy the number of Swedes who, in the decades during which the vast pine regions of northern Michigan, Wisconsin, and Minnesota were cut down and converted into lumber, were busy in the lumber camps, but anyone who, in those days, saw and heard the lumberjacks in places like Minneapolis and Duluth, and who talked with scores and scores of the laborers, foremen, and contractors, must be convinced that the Swedish contingent in this army of loggers was very large. The biggest sawmill in operation in the Middle West, during part of the era in which the lumber industry flourished, was built and managed by C. A. Smith, a native of Sweden. His employees were nearly all Swedes. Nowadays one is likely to think first of the ruthless spoliation which the lumber industry wrought, but naturally it had its great economic importance in the building of the Northwest. Lumber in large quantities was necessary for the hundreds of thousands of homes, barns, granaries, and office buildings erected in town and country, and in helping to supply this need, the Swedish immigrant again played an important part in the economic development of the country.

From railroad building and lumbering, the Swedes soon turned by the tens of thousands to more profitable but less fatiguing work; they became skilled workers in the building trades and in furniture manufacturing. Wherever they have settled in large numbers, the Swedes have practically dominated these industries, as a study of cities such as Chicago, Minneapolis, Rockford, Illinois, and Jamestown, New York, will show. A former building commissioner of the first-named place once asserted—and the claim was not contested—that about one third of the building-construction work in his city had been done by Swedish workingmen, and under the supervision of Swedish contractors. The interior work of the world's largest business structure, the Merchandise Mart in Chicago, was done by a Swedish firm in Minneapolis, employing mainly Swedish skilled labor. The same firm likewise did the interior finishing work in some of Detroit's famous buildings, such as the Ford Company headquarters. It has been claimed, and the claim seems well substantiated, that about 80 per cent of the finer interior work in office structures, public buildings, churches, and private homes in Minneapolis has been done by Swedes.

The story of life among the Swedish pioneers in the Northwest is an epic of toil, sacrifice, endurance, unending hope, and great achievement, amidst every kind of discouragement. If their expectation of material well-being rose high, when they found themselves possessors of quantities of land such as in their wildest dreams in "old Sweden" they had never hoped to own, their fond hopes were soon considerably crimped, or entirely crushed, in the testing process of stern realities. The ones who settled on forest land soon discovered that the clearing of only a few acres meant backbreaking labor, and settlers on prairie lands experienced great trouble in getting building material and fuel. Houses were often poorly built and inadequately heated. Many harrowing tales of suffering and death in early Swedish prairie communities, as terrible blizzards swept over the land, have come down to a later generation.

Whether they had settled on forest land or prairie, most of the early pioneers found themselves far from markets, and transportation by land had to be carried on over rough and miry roads. The writer remembers his father telling of his first trip to St. Anthony, now a part of Minneapolis, to get some flour. With a half-filled grain sack over his shoulders, he walked thirty-five miles through thickets, lowlands, and sandy paths to the nearest mill, then built near St. Anthony Falls, got his wheat ground, and then trudged the weary way home again with his load. Not only was the trip fatiguing, but also hazardous, because Indians still inhabited the region. The trip required two nights and a day. Later he thought himself well on the way to comfort when he had procured a pair of oxen and built a crude wagon with wheels made from sawed-off logs; soon he could take several sacks to the mill at one time and could himself ride, as well as be relieved of heavy loads upon his own shoulders. In his *Memoirs of an Immigrant*, Col. Hans Mattson, the well-known founder of the Vasa community, relates how he carried on his back along an Indian trail nearly seventy pounds of provisions for his household from Red Wing to Vasa, a distance of about twenty miles, the latter part of his trip, he says, being speeded up considerably by the ominous howling of wolves on the trail behind him.

Judge Andrew Holt relates another story, which vividly illustrates the hardships which the pioneers had to endure and the fortitude they displayed. Living in a community about thirty-five miles from St. Paul, as the crow flies, but about fifty miles by the meandering Minnesota River, a young man and the lady of his choice wanted to get married, but inasmuch as there was no clergyman to be found nearer than St. Paul, the young couple, accompanied by Judge Holt's parents, set out for the pastor's house by boat. Downstream the trip was, of course, easy, although they first had to walk several miles through thickets before they reached the river. On the return trip there was a strenuous fifty-mile pull against the current.

"On the return, when Carver was reached about the third or fourth day," to quote Judge Holt's own words, "the bridegroom suggested that he, the bride, and my mother walk home from there, as that was a shorter walk than from the Rapids where the boat had been rented, and that my father row the boat back to the owner at the Rapids alone. Father complied, but all night he worked against the swift current without being able to get past the Rapids and mother was in agony at home thinking that because of his failure to arrive within a reasonable time, he must have been drowned."

All pioneers in the Northwest, whether of New England descent or immigrants from Europe, suffered great privations, and the Swedes, generally speaking, suffered no more than the others. As compared with the Yankees, however, they were at first handicapped by their ignorance of the language of the

JOHANNES HULT

PIONEER AND FATHER OF JUDGE ANDREW HOLT
OF THE SUPREME COURT OF MINNESOTA

land, but this they overcame in a surprisingly short time. Common observation, supported after investigation by the United States Immigration Commission, proves that no immigrant race has learned English more rapidly than the Swedes. The process was made easier for them by the fact that practically all adults among them could read and write their own language when they arrived, and they had had at least an elementary-school education. They were ambitious to succeed in the new land and, knowing that a knowledge of English was indispensable, the acquisition of the new tongue became a most urgent task.

To the hardships of backbreaking work and frequent disappointments was added the anguish of homesickness and disturbing doubts as to the wisdom of having left the homeland. Time had a way of relieving this anguish, but that it was terribly real in the early years no one can doubt who has heard the pioneers speak frankly of early experiences. The days of the Civil War were for them especially distressing. While still strangers in a new land, most of them unfamiliar with English, and barely started on the work of building homes in the wilderness, the men were called upon to leave their wives and children, and fight for the Union cause on Southern battlefields. They did not shirk their duty, and statistics bear witness to the fact that the Swedes in the Northwestern States furnished more than their proportionate number of volunteers to the Union armies. Tragic, indeed, was also the fate that befell some of the Swedish settlements in Minnesota in the Sioux Indian uprising.

Any account of the hard, patient, and intelligent work done by most of the Swedish immigrants who helped so largely to convert the wilderness of the Northwest into a land of fair and productive fields, and to dot the forest and prairie region with attractive homes and gardens—impressive as it is in itself— would be lacking its most important feature, did it not include a reference to the spiritual and ethical values preserved and augmented in the early Swedish communities. Felling trees and plowing land, planting and harvesting wheat, oats, corn, potatoes, raising horses and cattle, building granaries and barns; founding banks and creameries, building roads and bridges— these, and other enterprises, were vastly important. But their real worth was derived from the fact that they formed the material basis for a life in which ethical and æsthetic values are dominant.

A higher standard of living than that to which they had been accustomed in the homeland became the first desideratum of the Swedish colonists, after the arduous labor of the first years of pioneering had been completed. The sod house or the one-room log cabin was replaced as soon as possible by a more spacious dwelling and greater comfort. As a rule they built good dwelling houses, in which wives and children would find comfort, before they built better barns for their cattle or granaries for their crops. Seldom was a well-cared-for garden missing from the pioneer homes of the Swedes.

Unbiased writers who visited early Swedish communities testify that the standard of living was by no means lower among them than among the native-born in both rural and urban communities. They set as good a table as the Yankees, to say the least; their homes were as clean and attractive as any. Interesting investigations by the United States Immigration Commission in the early part of the present century show that among all immigrant peoples, the Swedes held first rank in point of room space per family and individual, in cleanliness and sanitation of living quarters, and attractiveness of grounds surrounding the homes. As home owners, they ranked second. The study was made mainly in an industrial community, and from a limited number of cases, but the findings did undoubtedly, in the main, express the true situation in all Swedish communities, whether rural or urban.

To every Swedish settlement came preachers of the Gospel; congregations were organized and churches built. In view of the poverty and privation of the early pioneers, their liberality in support of religious work seems especially praiseworthy. Only a genuine interest in spiritual matters could have prompted this liberality. While the clergymen who labored among them were not, as a rule, men of learning, they were fearless teachers of righteousness, and became real leaders of their people. Incidentally, it may be noted here that one of the pioneer Swedish Lutheran ministers, Reverend P. A. Cederstam, was a member of the convention which framed the constitution of Minnesota.

The compelling zeal, ceaseless labors, and undying devotion to a holy cause of these men wrote a fine chapter in the history of early Swedish settlements. Men like Eric Norelius, Peter Carlson, P. A. Hedenstam, S. J. Kronberg, E. A. Skogsbergh, Nils Frykman, A. W. Franklin, F. O. Nilsson, Frank Peterson, Olof Bodien, Jonas Hedstrom, and others have left an indelible impress upon the culture and spiritual life of the Swedish people of the Northwest.

The self-denial and sacrifices of the Swedish pioneers are well exemplified by some personal experiences related by the Reverend Peter Carlson, who for many years served as pastor of Union settlement, about thirty miles southwest of Minneapolis. For many years no salary was paid him, and his only material rewards were gifts, mostly *in natura,* which his parishioners brought him. Besides serving two congregations, to which he had been called, he frequently visited other Swedish settlements. To one of these he went regularly once a month for eighteen months, traveling fifty miles each trip, often on foot, and his total monetary compensation for all his labor was one dollar. A second community, about twenty-five miles from his home, which he visited quite regularly for a long time, also paid him a meager dollar for all his time and sacrifice. But he was never heard to complain. His faith was of the kind which can move mountains. On one trip, so he relates, his horse sank so deep in the mire that he could not get up. Carlson stood up to his knees in water, urging his horse on, only to find that the animal sank deeper and deeper into the mudhole. As no deliverance from his plight seemed possible, Carlson folded his hands over the reins and whip, and spoke to God:

Yes, dear God, now I have done all that can be done and human help and animal strength is not here; a meeting has been announced and I am on time and have neglected nothing. If I cannot get there and the people complain of me, Thy honor must suffer thereby. Thou must take the blame, for I will not be responsible. Hence the matter is Thine. If Thou wilt, Thou canst help, otherwise it remaineth as it is. Therefore, Lord, fulfill Thy promise.

And then, Carlson continues his account, the horse made one more mighty effort and succeeded in getting out of the mire and on to firm ground. The pastor was two hours late in arriving at the meeting, but the people had waited patiently. After washing his face and hands, and making himself more presentable, he preached a sermon of two hours, the entire congregation remaining to the end and listening attentively.

Education was close to the heart of the early Swedish pioneers. Especially were they anxious that their children should enjoy good instruction, and, from the beginning, they were staunch supporters of the public schools. The annual reports of the superintendents of schools in the 'sixties and 'seventies, for counties in which the Swedish element predominated, often contain significant statements that the people of the respective counties gave the public schools their loyal support. As early as 1862, the school which now is known as Gustavus Adolphus College was founded by the Swedish Lutherans, and since its first class in the collegiate department in 1890, it has been a fully accredited college. The Swedish Covenanters founded a school of academy rank in Minneapolis in 1885. This was the forerunner of the present Minnehaha Academy. The Swedish Baptists founded and maintain the Bethel Seminary and Junior College in St. Paul, but its beginning belongs to a period subsequent to the pioneer era. The Swedish Lutherans also established Hope Academy in Moorehead, Minnesota; Emanuel Academy and Minnesota College, Minneapolis; Northwestern College, Fergus Falls; and North Star College, Warren, Minnesota—all of academy rank, but with the development of the public high schools, support failed them, and now they have all been discontinued.

It is almost a commonplace to say that the Swedes were and are law-abiding citizens. Criminal statistics in Minnesota, which can be taken as typical, give ample evidence that this reputation rests on a solid basis of fact. Thus, in 1882, one out of every 2,835 persons in the State was a convict in confinement, while the Scandinavian-born had a proportion of only one to 4,145. No separate statistics are given for the Swedes, but it can be taken for granted that they did not fall below the average of the Scandinavians as a whole.

Geographical Distribution

W. ELMER EKBLAW

For biographical notes on the Author, see the chapter on "Professors."

THE distribution of the Swedish element in the population and culture of the United States intrigues the interest of all Americans, but naturally engages more effectively the attention of those who are of Swedish birth or ancestry. The Swedish element in American population which first made itself felt in the settlement along the Delaware in 1638, the Tercentenary celebration of which in 1938 is the occasion of this study, has since then played a more or less significant rôle in the development of the American nation.

The chronicle of that early colony and its influence upon the activities of its pioneer neighbors, its part in the affairs of the whole American colonial domain, and its relation to the development of an incipient nation, has been set down elsewhere, parts of it exhaustively and authoritatively. Unfortunately, all too little of the historical material, which might have aided in tracing the spread and further distribution of those early Scandinavians, has been preserved; and many records, which might have contributed to a better knowledge of their activities and attributes, have been irrevocably lost.

The records and vital statistics of the early colonial settlements were hopelessly inadequate and everywhere incomplete for any satisfactory record of Swedish, or other Scandinavian, immigration, elsewhere than into Delaware; or for a record of any attempt by Scandinavians to make their homes in the new land. Except for a few fragmentary references, scattered far and wide in literature generally not germane to vital records, practically nothing has been uncovered in America that indicates any other Scandinavian immigration in the seventeenth century. One such reference is contained in the early records of Scituate and Cohasset, Massachusetts, which relates that one "James Bowker, from Sweden, came to Scituate in 1680, and was one of the earliest settlers to take up lands in the outlying sections, the pioneer settler on land around what has been known as Bryant's Corner. . . . The house built by James Bowker is said to be one still standing a short distance west of the corner." One of James Bowker's sons was a partner in a sawmill enterprise established on Groundsell Brook in 1752, but sold out his interest when he moved to Georgetown, Maine, in 1764. "Parse" Bowker, called "Parsie" by the boys with whom he was a great favorite, drove a small mail and passenger coach from Duxbury to Boston, about the middle of the eighteenth century.

During the seventeenth and eighteenth centuries, the Swedes who had settled in the Delaware country gradually lost their distinctive European attributes, and became essentially Americans, practically indistinguishable in ethnic type and culture from their neighbors, who had become equally Americanized.

Miss Florence E. Janson, in her monographic *The Background of Swedish Immigration*, is authority for the statement that emigration from Sweden during the sixteenth and seventeenth centuries, when the Baltic had become substantially a Swedish sea, was chiefly to Finland, Esthonia, Pomerania, and Stralsund; it was in this period of political strength and economic expansion that the Swedes planted their colony in Delaware. This period of emigration continued well into the eighteenth century, but was appreciably checked by agitation against it, consequent upon the shortage of labor that resulted, and practically terminated by the emigration law passed in 1739 at the instance of the House of Peasants in the Riksdag. The loss of Finland to Russia, in 1809, concluded the considerable exchange of population between Sweden and Finland that had continued significant for the three previous centuries, and reduced emigration from Sweden to the minimum.

From Gustav Sundbärg's *Den svenska och europeiska folköknings och omflyttningsstatistiken* Miss Janson takes the statement that only 9,561 Swedes emigrated to America during the thirty-five years between 1816 and 1850. Assuming that of even this small number, which averaged 273 annually, very few came in the first years of the period, and that the number increased as order, prosperity, and power accrued to the new United States, the growing attraction of America for the Scandinavians who sought freer religious, economic, and political conditions, is nevertheless indicated.

Emigration from Sweden to the United States was rapidly accelerated during the 1850's, when it averaged 1,486 annually. It rose to an average of 8,873 for each of the years of the next decade, to 10,117 a year during the 'seventies, and to the peak of 32,500 average for the 'eighties, the highest record being more than 37,000 in 1887. (Figures have been published indicating an immigration of more than 54,000 for the year 1888.) For the two decades, 1890–1910, the average annual movement from Sweden to the United States was 21,000; but since the passage of the first law-restricting immigration to a quota basis in 1921, the number of Swedish immigrants has steadily declined.

The background against which emigration from Sweden stands out—religious restrictions, compulsory military training, agricultural and industrial limitations, crop failures, and foreign competition in manufactures, and many others—has been fully discussed in Miss Janson's admirable work. The conditions in America which attracted Swedish immigrants, as so many others—religious tolerance, political equality, economic opportunity, advantageous laws encouraging ownership of land and rise of industry, unsurpassed wealth of unexploited natural resources, fertile soils easily tilled, hospitable, stimulating climate, protective location, and a multitude of others—are common knowledge. To dwell further upon the past would be superfluous.

Distribution of Swedes in the United States in 1930

THE present distribution of the Swedish element in American population and culture must be based upon the decennial Census of 1930, the latest which furnishes authoritative statistics for the survey. The attributes of Swedish character, which affect the culture of the communities wherein they reside, are intangible and imponderable, but the extent of their influence, in general, is a function of the number and concentration of Swedes within the community. Hence a survey of the distribution of Swedes in the United States should reveal the centers of

Swedish influence, and provide some measure of their relative importance in the economy and culture of the land. It is true that the census statistics include only Swedish-born citizens and their offspring, the second generation designated in the census reports as "Native Whites of Foreign or Mixed Parentage." They furnish no direct clue to the number and distribution of the third and subsequent generations, which unquestionably retain some of their Swedish attributes as they preserve, more or less unblended, their blood, or ethnic stock.

Any distinctive qualities or attributes, racial or cultural, which an ethnic group possesses, affect the community of which it is a part, not only in proportion to the number which it comprises, but to the concentration of the group; i.e., the ratio of its number to the total composition of the group, or to other parts of the group. When the number is large enough to enable the group to organize and to maintain solidarity in church, fraternal, or social organization, or some other social or economic institution, its cultural and ethnic integrity is better maintained, and its influence more effectively and permanently exerted, than when the number is too small or too widely scattered for successful organization and integration.

Thus there are vast sections of the United States where the number of Swedes is so small that any ethnic or cultural influence they may have is submerged in the overwhelming preponderance of other peoples, other cultures. There are other great areas where the Swedes, though relatively numerous, are so widely scattered that they cannot achieve any community of interest or influence. There are a few localities where the Swedes are numerous enough, concentrated enough, to preserve Swedish cultural values, and to exert salutary Swedish influence upon the body social and politic, but where their interests or their loyalties are so divided that any cultural or ethnic effect is dissipated. There are, however, a goodly number of sections of the United States where the Swedish population has been, and still is, numerous enough, concentrated enough, united and homogeneous enough in interest and activity, to maintain a distinct Swedish culture, to exert a significant Swedish influence in promoting superior American citizenship, and in otherwise making itself a power for progress and good in the land.

The Swedish element in the United States, restricted for the purposes of this paper to the two groups distinguished in the decennial censuses,—those born in Sweden, and those born of Swedish parents or a single Swedish parent, and not including any of the third or subsequent generations (counting the immigrant parents as the first)—thus number 1,562,703, of whom 595,250, or slightly more than one third, were born in Sweden, and 967,453, or not quite two thirds, were born in the United States of Swedish parents, or at least of a Swedish father or mother. They constitute 4 per cent of the total similar foreign stock, and 1¼ per cent of the total white population of the United States. Of the total Swedish element, 819,215 are males and 743,488 females, or 110.2 males for every 100 females. Of the Swedish-born group, 333,623 are males and 261,627 are females, a sex ratio of 127.5 males to 100 females; and of the second generation, those born in America of Swedish-born parents or parent, 485,592 are males, and 481,861 are females, or 100.8 males to every 100 females. Thus the preponderance of males, which characterizes the immigrants from Sweden, is practically lost in the first generation of their offspring.

The Swedish stock is spread extremely thin when the whole land area of the United States, 2,973,776 square miles, is included, less than .53 to the square mile; but when the area of improved land, only 786,000 square miles, is considered, a density of two to the square mile makes a much better showing. Since most of the population of the United States is resident upon the improved land, it is proper to take only improved land as the areal basis. The density of the total population of the United States is 41.3 to the square mile of total area, 156.1 to the square mile of improved land. As will be explained later, the density of the Swedish element—just as does its proportion of the whole population—varies widely from section to section.

More than half the Swedes of the United States live in the eleven North Central States—Ohio, Indiana, Illinois, Michigan, and Wisconsin, which constitute the eastern division of the section, and Minnesota, Iowa, Missouri, North Dakota, South Dakota, Nebraska, and Kansas, which form the western division. In the latter, or western division, the six western North Central States, 473,252 Swedes are resident and in the former,

or eastern division, 420,553 are resident. The North Central
States thus aggregate 893,805 Swedes. The industrial north-
east, which embraces the six New England States—Maine,
New Hampshire, Vermont, Massachusetts, Connecticut, Rhode
Island—and the three Middle Atlantic States—New York,
New Jersey, and Pennsylvania—supports 346,042 folk of
Swedish stock, 147,920 in New England and 198,122 in the
Middle Atlantic States. All the other States, twenty-seven in
number, and the District of Columbia, aggregate only 320,856
Swedes, of which the three States of the Pacific coast, California, Oregon, and Washington, furnish homes for 207,224, or
two thirds; the eight mountain States—Montana, Idaho, Wyoming, Colorado, New Mexico, Arizona, Utah, and Nevada,
77,907, or one fourth; and the sixteen Southern States and
the District of Columbia, embracing the South Atlantic, east
South Central, and the western South Central sections, 37,725,
or less than half as many as the mountain States.

Swedes in New England

In the six New England States, where 147,920 Swedes of the
first and second generations are resident, the density of the
Swedish stock is 2.36 to the square mile, somewhat more than
four times the density of the United States as a whole. Of the
total population of the New England section the Swedish stock
forms 1.8 per cent, or roughly one Swede to every fifty persons; and of the total foreign stock of the area 3.0 per cent or
one Swede to every thirty-three persons of foreign stock.

Of the total Swedish stock of New England, 118,842, or 80
per cent, are urban in residence; only 7,104, or 4 per cent, live
on farms; and 21,974, or 16 per cent, are rural nonfarm; i.e.,
live in small villages and farms without deriving any large part
of their own income directly from farming. Almost exactly the
same percentages hold for the immigrant Swedes and the
American-born Swedes of the first generation, indicating little
variation in place of residence, and probably in character of
occupation, of the American-born portion of the Swedish stock
from that of its Swedish-born parents.

With such definite urban concentration of Swedes in New
England, it is to be expected that the cities constitute the chief

centers of distribution, and Boston, with its satellite cities, aggregates 23,000 Swedes; Worcester, with its suburban towns, affords homes for about 20,000; Providence and its environs about 7,000; the Hartford community embraces, in round numbers, 9,500 Swedes; Springfield, 3,500; Bridgeport, 3,300; New Britain, 4,800; and New Haven, 2,500. Practically all the industrial cities are distinguished by considerable numbers of Swedes, in addition to those already named: Brockton, 4,651; Lynn, 2,048; and the two Warwicks (Rhode Island), 2,000; Manchester, 1,170; Pawtucket, 1,026; Lowell, 823; Meriden, 700.

In New England, as in all the seaboard States, the Swedes, probably like all Scandinavians, show a definite concentration above normal along the coast, revealing the seafaring interests and activities of their ancestral homelands. Metal-working cities like Worcester and Bridgeport, with their iron and steel and other heavy industries; Providence, Hartford, and Meriden with their copper, brass, and silver manufactories, reflect in both the number and provincial origin of their Swedish populations the skilled craftsmanship of definite Swedish provinces.

New England presents several centers of concentration of Swedish population. A general concentration in the southern industrial half of New England is distinguished by major centers of density in Worcester and Providence; secondary centers of density in the Boston metropolitan area, the Connecticut Valley of Connecticut, and the Connecticut portion of the New York conurbation. The western uplands of Connecticut and Massachusetts, the Cape Cod area of Massachusetts, and eastern Connecticut and upland Rhode Island are relatively sparsely occupied by Swedes. The three northern New England States afford no centers of major concentration, though there are definite centers of denser Swedish occupancy in Aroostook County (definitely an agricultural center), in Portland and Bangor, Maine; in the lower Merrimac Valley of New Hampshire; and in Rutland County, Vermont.

Swedes of the Middle Atlantic States

In the three Middle Atlantic States—New York, New Jersey, and Pennsylvania—the Swedish population numbers 198,122, very nearly 50,000 more than in the six New England States. Nearly two thirds, or more accurately, 62 per cent of that number, 121,503, are resident in New York alone; only 29,849, about 15 per cent, or a little less than one sixth, live in New Jersey; and 46,770, 24 per cent, or nearly one fourth, are spread rather thinly over Pennsylvania. In other words, New York has four times as many Swedes as New Jersey, and almost three times as many as Pennsylvania. The three States together have one fourth more Swedes than the six New England States, though, because they are nearly twice as large in aggregate area, their density of Swedes is only 1.98 to the square mile, while New England's is 2.36. The percentage of Swedes in the total population of the Middle Atlantic States is only 0.8 as compared with 1.8 in that of New England; and the percentage of Swedes in the total foreign population is 1.6 compared with 3.0 in New England. The density of the Swedish population in the Middle Atlantic States, 1.98 to the square mile, is not quite four times the density of the whole United States, which is, as already stated, 0.53 to the square mile.

The percentage of Swedish stock, urban in residence in the Middle Atlantic States, is 80, exactly the same as in the New England States; of the Swedish-born, or immigrant Swedes, 5 per cent live on farms, only 1 per cent more than in New England, and 15 per cent live in villages, as compared with 16 per cent in villages in New England, indicating a remarkable similarity in residence and occupation of the Swedes in the two sections, both dominantly industrial. Of the 198,122 Swedish folk in the Middle Atlantic States, 159,092 live in cities; 9,310, are farmers; and 29,720 live in small villages and on farms, but do not farm.

Greater New York, with its 50,000 of Swedish stock, and Pittsburgh and its industrial satellites of western Pennsylvania with 7,000 Swedish folk, constitute major concentrations of Swedish stock in this section. Philadelphia with its 3,000 Swedes, Buffalo with its 2,700, Rochester with its 1,100, Syracuse with its 600, and the Albany-Troy-Schenectady conurbation with 1,100, constitute secondary urban concentrations chiefly related to metallic crafts or technical skills. An important center, not wholly or definitely urban in its relationships, is the concentration of Swedes in Chautauqua County in extreme western New York, and the adjoining counties, Erie and Warren, in northwestern Pennsylvania, a concentration of which Jamestown, New York, is the center.

The same tendency of the American-born Swedes to leave the cities for smaller villages and the country reveals itself in all three of the Middle Atlantic States, as in every New England State. It is evident that the concentration of immigrant Swedes in the cities of the industrial Northeast is abnormal, and contrary to Swedish disposition, for during the years when general movement of American folk led from country to city, the movement of Swedes in America led from city to country, in rather significant tempo. Metal-working or other technical industries and seafaring interests tend to attract Swedes in seaboard and industrial cities, as in New England.

Swedes of the North Central States

THE North Central States, with their total Swedish population of 893,805, 57 per cent of all the Swedes in the United States, form the substantial mass of Swedish influence in the United States, not only in number but in proportion of total population and of total foreign stock as well.

Except for Illinois with a density of 4.66 Swedes to the square mile, and Minnesota with a density of 3.35, none of the North Central States, with densities ranging from 0.33 in South Dakota, where Norwegians have monopolized the land, to 1.19 in Michigan, where industries have attracted the Swedes, approaches the density of New England with its 2.36, or the Middle Atlantic section with its 1.98, and not even the relatively high densities of Illinois or Minnesota can compare with Connecticut's density of 8.58, Massachusetts', of 10.09, or Rhode Island's, of 13.23.

But Minnesota surpasses all other States in its proportion of Swedes—10½ per cent of the total population, and 19 per cent of the total foreign stock; i.e., one of every ten of all the folk of Minnesota, and one of every five of foreign stock, is Swedish, by birth or parentage. North Dakota has 4.3 per cent Swedes in its total population, 7.2 per cent in its foreign stock; Nebraska has 3.6 per cent in its total population and 10.5

per cent in its foreign stock; South Dakota and Illinois have each 3.4 per cent Swedes in their total population, and 8 per cent and 7.5 per cent, respectively, in their foreign stock. Only Washington, on the Pacific coast, with 4.9 per cent Swedes in its total population and 11.9 per cent Swedes in its foreign stock, shows such large percentage of Swedes.

Ohio's Swedes constitute only 0.3 per cent of its total population, 1.0 per cent of its foreign stock; Indiana's and Missouri's 0.4 per cent of their total folk, and 2.7 and 2.1 per cent, respectively, of their foreign stock; Michigan's 1.4 per cent of its total population, and 3 per cent of its foreign stock; Kansas' 1.5 per cent of all its folk, and 8.3 per cent of its foreign stock; Wisconsin's 1.9 per cent of its population and 3.8 per cent of its foreign stock; and Iowa's 2.2 per cent of its whole folk, and 7.7 per cent of its foreign stock.

Indiana and Missouri reveal the smallest number of Swedes for the States of the North Central section, with 13,823, or a density of 0.4 to the square mile, and 13,371, or a density of 0.24, respectively, with Ohio not far behind with only 19,864, or a density of 0.49. South Dakota with 23,563 Swedes, a density of 0.33; Kansas, with 28,200, a density of 0.35; and North Dakota with 29,893, a density of 0.43, constitute a second group of thin Swedish population. A third group with somewhat higher number and density of Swedish stock includes: Nebraska, 50,087 Swedes, a density of 0.66; Wisconsin, 56,915, a density of 1.03; Iowa, 57,365, a density of 1.03; and Michigan, 68,577, a density of 1.19. As already stated, Minnesota and Illinois lead the section with 270,773 and 261,374 Swedes respectively, and densities of 3.35 and 4.66 respectively.

The percentage of urban Swedes in the population of the North Central section is 86 in Illinois; 85 in Ohio; 72 in Missouri; 68 in Indiana; and 66 in Michigan. The urban concentration of Swedes is appreciably lower in Minnesota, 54 per cent; in Iowa, 44 per cent; and in Wisconsin, 41 per cent. The Swedes of Nebraska and Kansas are more than two-thirds rural, only 31 per cent and 30 per cent, respectively, living in cities; and the Dakotas are, most of all, strictly rural, with only 18 per cent in North Dakota urban, and 17 per cent in South Dakota. Like the northeast industrial sections already discussed, the North Central States have considerable development of technological industries to which the Swedes are attracted.

In the North Central States a host of cities include more than a thousand Swedes, but fewer than two thousand. More than twenty cities have over two thousand. Chicago, as is well known, is the principal Swedish city of America, with 130,913 immigrant and second-generation Swedes, but the whole Chicago community or conurbation approaches an aggregate of 200,000 Swedes, or more. Minneapolis with 70,463 and St. Paul with 25,430 Swedes, an aggregate of 95,893, form the second largest urban center, the center of a conurbation of 135,000 Swedes, or more. Rockford, Illinois, with 22,331 Swedes, Duluth with 16,968, and Detroit with 11,603, form another group with more than 10,000 Swedes. Moline and Rock Island, Illinois, a continuous city, approach 10,000 with 9,552 Swedes; and Omaha, Nebraska, with 8,886 belongs in the same class. Ohio has two fairly important Swedish cities, both centers of the iron and steel industry—Cleveland with 4,422 and Youngstown with 2,059 Swedes. Kansas City with 5,290 Swedes, Des Moines with 5,203, and Superior, Wisconsin, with 5,351, all stand well above 5,000. North Central cities not already named, with between 5,000 and 2,000 Swedes, are Milwaukee with 4,321; Evanston and Galesburg, Illinois, with 4,909, and 4,260, respectively; Sioux City, Iowa, with 3,805; Grand Rapids and Muskegon, Michigan, with 2,896, and 2,774, respectively; and St. Louis with 2,051. Fargo, North Dakota, comes very close with 1,958. North Dakota, South Dakota, Indiana, and Kansas have no cities with 2,000 or more Swedes.

In no State are the Swedes so uniformly distributed throughout all the counties as in Iowa, with Wisconsin, Minnesota, Kansas, Nebraska, and the Dakotas also exhibiting a fair degree of uniformity. The southern parts of Ohio, Indiana, and Illinois, and the whole of Missouri reveal a very sparse Swedish occupancy, many counties having no Swedes among their folk. A number of the States, notably Illinois, Wisconsin, Minnesota, and Kansas, are characterized by distinctive historical, religious, or educational communities of Swedes, like Paxton and Bishop Hill, Illinois, and Lindsborg, Kansas.

Swedes of the Mountain Section

THE Swedes of the eight States of the mountain section aggregate 77,907, varying in number from 885 in New Mexico to 23,753 in Colorado. Montana with 16,226 Swedes, Utah with 15,838, and Idaho with 12,328, constitute a group that ranks considerably below Colorado; and Nevada with 1,238 Swedes, Arizona with 2,505, and Wyoming with 5,157 form a second group with very small Swedish population.

In none of the mountain states is the density of Swedes high, varying from 0.007 in New Mexico to 0.23 in Colorado; i.e., from 7 to 1,000 square miles in New Mexico, to 230 to 1,000 square miles in Colorado. The percentage of Swedes in the total population varies from 0.1 in New Mexico to 0.6 in Arizona, and to 3.0 in Montana and 3.1 in Utah; in the foreign stock from 3.0 per cent in New Mexico and 3.7 in Nevada to 10.5 in Idaho and 9.0 in Utah.

The Swedes of the mountain section are dominantly rural, the proportion living in cities exceeding 50 per cent only in Utah, 57 per cent, and Colorado, 58 per cent, and running as low as 27 per cent in Idaho. The percentage of farmers varies from a maximum of 42 in Idaho to a minimum of 11 in Arizona and 12 in Nevada. Three counties in the forested northern part of Idaho probably serve to illustrate the attraction the lumber industry has for the Swedes: Bonner with 278 Swedes, Kootenai with 562, and Shoshone with 418.

Denver, Colorado, and Salt Lake City, Utah, with 9,429 and 5,614 Swedes, respectively, are the chief urban concentrations of Swedes in the mountain states. The Butte-Anaconda of Montana conurbation has 1,874 Swedes. Great Falls with 1,239 is the only other city of Montana, or for that matter, of the whole mountain section, with more than 1,000 Swedes.

Swedes of the Pacific Coast

OF the Pacific coast States, with an aggregate Swedish stock of 207,224, California leads with almost exactly 50 per cent, or 103,603 Swedes; Washington follows with 37 per cent or 76,-843 Swedes; and Oregon falls to 13 per cent or 26,778. The areal density of the Swedish stock is far the highest in Washington, 1.19, or 119 to the hundred square miles; only half as high in California, 0.66, or 66 to the hundred square miles; and lowest of all in Oregon with only 0.135, or 13½ to the hundred square miles. Likewise Washington leads in proportion of Swedes to total population, 4.9 per cent, and also to foreign stock, 11.9 per cent; Oregon follows with a proportion of 2.8 per cent of the total population and 8.7 of the foreign stock; and California comes last with 1.8 per cent of the total population, and 4.8 per cent of the foreign stock.

The percentage of urban, farm, and village Swedes in Washington and Oregon is the same—59 per cent of the Swedes live in cities; 19 per cent are farmers; and 22 per cent live on farms and in villages, but do not farm. In California the percentage of urban Swedes is much higher, 76 per cent, and the percentages on farms and in villages, appreciably lower, 11 per cent and 13 per cent respectively.

The Los Angeles community includes more than 50,000 of California's Swedes, the San Francisco district 30,000, or, together, more than four fifths the Swedes of the States. Most of them live in the larger cities of those communities: 23,126 in Los Angeles; 4,272 in Pasadena and Long Beach; 14,416 in San Francisco; and 7,787 in Oakland. Portland with 11,559 Swedes is by far the largest, and most important, Swedish city in Oregon. In Washington, Seattle, with 21,001 Swedes, leads; Spokane with 7,802, Takoma with 6,498, Everett with 2,073, and Bellingham with 1,852 follow.

Swedes of the Southern States

BECAUSE it has always been so, it is a well-known fact that the so-called Southern States, sixteen in number, have not attracted the Swedes in large numbers. Except for the early and influential settlement about Austin, Texas, which has exercised a great deal of influence in the economic and cultural development of that imperial State, and small centers elsewhere unimportant, except historically, the Swedes have played no significant rôle in that whole section.

The aggregate number of Swedes in the whole South is but 37,725, of whom 13,399 live in the eight States of the South Atlantic section—Delaware, Maryland, Virginia, West Vir-

ginia, North Carolina, South Carolina, Georgia, and Florida—
and the District of Columbia; only 3,912 live in the four States
of the east South Central section—Kentucky, Tennessee, Alabama, and Mississippi; and 20,414 in the four States of the
west South Central section—Arkansas, Louisiana, Oklahoma,
and Texas. Of all these States only Texas, with 14,365 Swedes,
exceeds 10,000, and Florida, with 5,238, barely exceeds 5,000.
Oklahoma, with 3,777, ranks third, and Maryland with 2,088,
fourth. The District of Columbia with 1,358 Swedes, all urban,
of course, and Virginia with 1,359, only 50 per cent urban, are
very nearly comparable in number. Alabama, with its 1,690
Swedes, is fifth in rank, chiefly because of its iron and steel industries to which they have been attracted. Louisiana with 1,341,
chiefly in the New Orleans community, constitutes the only
other Southern State with more than 1,000 Swedes. Arkansas
with 931, and West Virginia with 924, approach a thousand;
Tennessee with 875, and Georgia, with 835, come fairly close;
Delaware with 718, Mississippi with 716, and Kentucky with
631 lag behind considerably; and the Carolinas, North Carolina with 515 and South Carolina with 364, represent the smallest numbers of Swedish folk of all the States.

Nowhere else in the United States are the Swedes spread so
thin. The density of Swedes in the several Southern States
varies from 0.37, or 370 to the 1,000 square miles, in Delaware,
and 0.23, or 230 to the 1,000 square miles, in Maryland, to
0.013, or 13 to the 1,000 square miles, in North Carolina. Seven
States—Arkansas, Tennessee, Mississippi, Kentucky, Georgia,
South Carolina, and North Carolina—have 15 Swedes to the
1,000 square miles, or fewer; Virginia, West Virginia, Alabama, Louisiana, Oklahoma, Texas, and Florida vary from 30
to the 1,000 square miles to 100 to the 1,000 square miles. Despite the large number of Swedes in Texas, they form a density
of only 65 to the 1,000 square miles, considerably lower than
Florida with 100 to the 1,000 square miles. In the District of
Columbia the Swedes are concentrated 22.0 to the square mile.

In not one of the Southern States does the percentage of
Swedes in the total population attain 1 per cent. In Delaware,
Florida, and the District of Columbia the percentage is three
tenths of one per cent, and very nearly attains that percentage

in Texas; in Maryland and Oklahoma the percentage exceeds one tenth of one per cent, but in all the rest it drops significantly below; and in South Carolina, the lowest, to 0.014 per cent, or fourteen thousandths of 1 per cent.

The following two tables are reproduced from the Jubilee Number of *Svea*, of Worcester, Massachusetts, for October 28, 1936. Permission to reprint them is here gratefully acknowledged.

Immigration from Sweden, 1870–1935

Year		Year		Year	
1870	13,443	1892	41,845	1914	14,800
1871	10,669	1893	35,710	1915	6,585
1872	13,464	1894	18,286	1916	6,248
1873	14,303	1895	15,361	1917	6,368
1874	5,712	1896	21,177	1918	2,298
1875	5,573	1897	13,162	1919	2,243
1876	5,603	1898	12,398	1920	5,862
1877	4,991	1899	12,797	1921	9,171
1878	5,390	1900	18,650	1922	6,624
1879	11,001	1901	23,331	1923	17,916
1880	39,186	1902	30,894	1924	18,310
1881	49,760	1903	46,028	1925	8,365
1882	64,607	1904	27,763	1926	8,513
1883	38,277	1905	26,591	1927	8,287
1884	26,552	1906	23,310	1928	8,051
1885	22,248	1907	20,589	1929	8,877
1886	27,751	1908	12,809	1930	3,109
1887	42,836	1909	14,474	1931	1,298
1888	54,698	1910	23,745	1932	328
1889	35,415	1911	20,780	1933	105
1890	29,632	1912	12,688	1934	153
1891	36,880	1913	17,202	1935	160

Distribution of Swedish-born residents in the United States

	1850	1860	1870	1880	1890	1900	1910	1920	1930
Ala.	51	155	105	119	294	488	766	748	638
Ariz.	1		7	106	168	342	928	859	778
Ark.		25	134	211	338	355	395	331	249
Calif.	162	1,405	1,944	4,209	10,923	14,549	27,980	31,925	41,734
Colo.		27	180	2,172	9,659	10,765	12,855	10,112	8,328
Conn.	13	42	323	2,086	10,021	16,164	18,726	17,697	18,453
Dak. Ter.			380	3,177					
Del.	2	8	9	71	246	302	332	316	294
D. C.	5	16	22	51	128	234	361	481	435
Fla.	33	31	30	231	529	561	732	1,399	2,145
Ga.	11	37	35	138	191	204	285	209	266
Idaho			91	323	1,524	2,822	5,126	5,112	4,200
Ill.	1,123	6,470	29,979	42,415	86,514	99,147	116,127	105,577	111,016
Ind.	16	329	2,180	3,121	4,512	4,673	5,128	4,942	4,666
Iowa	231	1,465	10,796	17,559	30,276	29,875	26,793	22,493	16,810
Kans.		122	4,954	11,207	17,096	15,144	13,351	10,337	7,315
Ky.	29	43	112	95	184	222	191	214	170
La.	249	193	358	270	328	359	359	522	433
Maine	55	74	91	988	1,704	1,935	2,247	2,026	1,182
Md.	57	48	100	177	305	347	431	630	764
Mass.	253	685	1,384	2,756	18,624	32,192	41,261	38,012	36,810
Mich.	16	266	2,406	9,412	27,306	26,956	28,667	24,707	23,905
Minn.	4	3,178	20,987	39,176	99,913	115,476	124,443	112,117	90,623
Miss.	14	21	970	302	305	303	293	247	206
Mo.	37	239	2,302	3,174	5,602	5,692	5,706	4,741	3,895
Mont.			141	280	3,771	5,346	6,712	7,179	5,655
Nebr.		70	2,332	10,164	28,364	24,693	23,287	18,821	14,335
Nev.		41	217	317	314	278	765	545	443
N. H.	12	20	42	131	1,210	2,032	2,081	1,886	1,608
N. J.	34	88	554	1,622	4,159	7,337	10,909	10,675	13,360
N. M.		3	6	39	149	244	374	310	268
N. Y.	753	1,678	5,522	11,164	28,430	42,708	55,739	53,025	61,233
N. C.	9	9	38	24	51	68	113	170	160
N. D.					5,583	8,419	12,236	10,543	8,470
Ohio	55	117	252	1,186	2,712	3,951	5,504	7,266	7,390
Okla.					138	494	1,033	931	835
Ore.	2	56	205	983	3,774	4,555	10,982	10,532	11,032
Pa.	133	448	2,266	7,575	19,346	24,130	23,787	19,847	16,452
R. I.	17	33	106	776	3,392	6,072	7,508	6,542	6,181
S. C.	29	38	60	63	60	65	96	133	106
S. D.					7,746	8,647	10,039	8,573	6,540
Tenn.	8	82	349	251	332	337	367	305	232
Tex.	48	153	364	1,293	2,806	4,388	4,747	4,536	4,017
Utah	1	196	1,790	3,750	5,986	7,025	7,721	6,073	4,389
Vt.		1	83	68	870	1,020	1,380	1,123	1,089
Va.	16	57	30	49	215	218	372	664	467
Wash.		33	158	648	10,272	12,737	34,179	34,793	34,084
W. Va.			5	21	72	132	283	326	86
Wis.	88	673	2,799	8,138	20,157	26,196	26,942	28,896	18,808
Wyo.			109	249	1,357	1,727	2,519	2,042	1,783
Total	3,567	18,625	97,307	192,337	477,956	571,926	683,158	631,490	594,333

Swedish Place Names in America

VILHELM BERGER

A Summary by the Editors

For biographical information on the Author, see the chapter on "Writers in Swedish."

VALUABLE confirmatory information about the distribution of Swedish pioneers in this country may be obtained by a study of American place names, many of which, naturally, are of Swedish origin. In the fiftieth anniversary number of *Svea*, 1936, Vilhelm Berger, who had long been interested in this subject, published the results of his investigation of Swedish place names in the United States and Canada. Though admittedly incomplete, as yet, the findings are already of sufficient importance to deserve a brief résumé here. We refer to the Swedish original for the details.

In twenty-five states and Canada, Mr. Berger found almost three hundred place names of obviously Swedish origin. More than a third of these are in Minnesota, an illuminating, though not wholly surprising, fact which needs no further comment. None of the communities having Swedish names is very large, so far as population is concerned. Occasionally a bridge, park, mountain peak, boulevard, or body of water has received a Swedish name. That some denominational churches, colleges, and charitable institutions established by Swedes should receive and retain names reminiscent of the race of the founders need not be emphasized. Here we are most interested in names of post offices, townships, and counties; for these not only indicate, generally, in some way or other, the racial and geographical origin of the settlers, but have a more general public interest and historical value.

Of course, a large number of place names have just "Swede" in them—Swede Bend, Swede Lane, Swede Point, and Swede Valley, all in Iowa; Swede Grove, Swede Lake, and Swede Prairie, in Minnesota; and Swede Home, in Nebraska. Missouri has a Swedeborg, and Swedesburg is found in Pennsylvania,

Iowa, Kansas, and Nebraska. To these might be added Swedesboro, New Jersey. Stockholm is found in at least six states, and in one province of Canada. New Sweden graces the map of four states; West Sweden appears in at least two; Falun, or Fahlun, is found in three; and Fridhem in three. Both Illinois and Minnesota have named communities after Admiral J. A. Dahlgren, and Alaska has a Dahlgren Peak.

Minneapolis has a Jenny Lind School as well as a Bremer School, named after Fredrika Bremer. That there should be a Lind, Minnesota (after Governor John Lind), is only natural, and that we have a Lindbergh Drive in Minnesota, and a Lindbergh State Park, in the same State, is now well known. John Ericsson has been honored in Ericsson Peak, Alaska, and in the names of three schools, in Chicago, Minneapolis, and New York City. Lund, Texas, indicates that its first settlers came from Skåne; Illinois has a forest preserve called Linné Woods. There is also a Linne, California, and New York has a Linnæus Bridge. A township in Michigan is named Carlson, after Conrad Carlson, who for twenty years was its trusted town clerk. The late Swedish merchant, Sven J. Benson, has been immortalized in Benson, Wisconsin; a pioneer settler, Peter Holmquist from Småland, has provided a name for Holmquist, South Dakota; Vasa turns up in at least three states; and Lake Oscar, Minnesota, was named in the 'fifties after King Oscar I. Lindsborg, Kansas, is probably the best-known Swedish community with a Swedish name in the Middle West. Formerly there was a Hedin in Minnesota, named after Axel Hedin, but the settlement was literally and completely blown off the map by a cyclone, about 1907, and the name apparently disappeared with it.

Berger found six or more Swedish place names in Alaska, Canada, Illinois, Iowa, Kansas, Michigan, Nebraska, New York, South Dakota, Texas, Washington, and Wisconsin. An appreciable number were also found in California, Colorado, Maine, Florida, and Pennsylvania. Minnesota, as intimated above, tops the list with over a hundred names. Here are a few more examples chosen at random: Dalbo and Dalstorp, Minnesota; Dannemora, New York; Gothenburg, Nebraska; Hornell (from Höör, Hörnell), New York; Jemtland, Maine; Norbeck, South Dakota; Nordenskjöld River, Alaska; Skansen, Wisconsin; Stromburg, Nebraska; Thorsby, Alabama; Upsala, Florida; and Yalmar (from "Hjalmar"), Michigan. Andre, Minnesota, is named after the unfortunate Swedish explorer, S. A. Andrée; and Klinckowstrom, Alaska, recalls the name of the scientist, Martin Klinckowström, who, in the beginning of the last century, made extensive oceanographic investigations near the Aleutian Islands, and especially Amchitka Island, Alaska.

Let these names suffice as illustrations.

Religion

GEORGE M. STEPHENSON

The Author of this chapter is the grandson of an American pioneer who emigrated from Småland and settled in Iowa in 1849. He holds academic degrees from Augustana College, the University of Chicago, and Harvard University, where he earned his doctor's degree. He has been a member of the faculties of De Pauw University and Dartmouth College, and is at present professor of history at the University of Minnesota. He was John Simon Guggenheim Memorial Fellow in Sweden, 1927–28, and has recently been made a Knight of the Royal Swedish Order of the North Star. Professor Stephenson has been a member of the Board of Directors of Augustana College; has contributed numerous articles to historical publications, including the *Dictionary of American Biography* and *Svenskt Biografiskt Lexicon;* and has written six notable books, among which are *A History of American Immigration* (1926); *The Founding of the Augustana Synod* (1927); *The Religious Aspects of Swedish Immigration* (1932); and *John Lind of Minnesota* (1935).

THE seeds of religion in Swedish America were planted in frontier soil. The plants that sprang up and flourished were nurtured by husbandmen who knew at first hand the hardships, trials, hopes, and aspirations of men and women who raised log cabins and built sod houses. Eric Janson, the founder of a "New Jerusalem"; Gustaf Unonius, the Episcopalian; Lars Paul Esbjörn, the Lutheran; Gustaf Palmquist, the Baptist; Jonas J. Hedstrom, the Methodist; and Carl August Björk, the Mission Friend, were pioneers among pioneers. These leaders and their co-laborers, whether clergymen or laymen, laid the foundations of churches whose mission it was to furnish spiritual homes, not only for the poor in spirit, but also for those poor in the goods of this world.

It is significant that, after the colonial period was over, it was in the Mississippi Valley that the first congregations were founded, the first churches erected, and the first conferences and synods organized. The frontier was not fruitful soil for planting stiff, formal, liturgical churches. Neither were the clergymen who ministered to the pioneers suitable instruments for the establishment of such churches, nor were there sharp distinctions between pioneer farmers and pioneer ministers, in birth, education, or cultural attainments. The chronologies of the several Swedish-American churches are contemporaneous; the founders of the respective denominations labored as competitors within the same regions. Proselyters crossed paths, not infrequently exchanged greetings, and more frequently engaged in polemics, in the pulpit and on the printed page.

The Swedish immigrant pastors received encouragement, and some financial assistance, from the mother country, and from individuals and organizations in the United States; but they charted their courses and steered their ecclesiastical ships with but little assistance, financial or otherwise, from sources outside of the Swedish population. The indifference of the ecclesiastical authorities in Sweden—with the notable exception of a few men like Peter Wieselgren and Peter Fjellstedt—to the religious fate of their countrymen in a remote continent was natural and, in a way, fortunate for the Swedish-American leaders. The indifference of the church of Sweden, the remoteness of America, and the elixir of the free religious atmosphere of the frontier transformed the Swedish-American churches into democratic organizations in polity, spirit, and outlook. With a perspective of three quarters of a century, the historian marvels at the speed with which the immigrants from Sweden, of whatever faith, became a part of a nation with common ideals, language, traditions, and institutions. Within a half-century the Swedish churches were woven into the fabric of American society. The immigrants and their churches became a part of a unique pattern.

The founders of the Swedish-American churches were children of the pietistic reformation in Sweden. This movement came from below, not from above. The impulse that drove thousands across the Atlantic from Sweden is inextricably bound up with the movement for democracy in both church and State. It is by no means purely accidental that the confluence of various forms of dissatisfaction with conditions in church and State coincides with the beginnings of emigration. To the historian the parallel between the English Puritans of the seventeenth century and the Swedish pietists of the nineteenth century is obvious.

The letters that crossed the Atlantic, written by Swedish Puritans to friends and relatives in the old country, breathe the spirit of the American frontier. These letters from the "Land of Canaan" praise the respect of the American people for the Sabbath; the unbelievable temperance of the Americans; the stern moral code; the fervent religious spirit; the zeal and democracy of the American clergy. "America is a great light in Christendom; there is a ceaseless striving to spread the healing salvation of the Gospel. The pastors are not lords in their profession, neither are they rich in the goods of this world," wrote an immigrant in 1851. Another letter describes the situation in America as follows: "It is not unusual for men of meager education to witness for the truth with much greater blessing than the most learned preacher who has no religious experience." And still another wrote: "There are also Swedish preachers here who are so well versed in the Bible and in the correct interpretation that they seek the lost sheep and receive them again into their embrace and do not conduct themselves after the manner of Sweden, where the sheep must seek the shepherd and address him with high-sounding titles."

The hyperevangelicals who formed the vanguard of the Mission Friends, immediately after the close of the American Civil War, found a utopia just as real as did the Lutherans, Baptists, Methodists, and Eric-Jansonists who preceded them. The Mission Friends—the true disciples of the Rosenian revival—were the extreme Puritans among the immigrants. Their conception of the church was that it was composed exclusively of "believers." They would pluck the tares before the harvest. Like the English Puritans, they would eliminate everything from the church edifice, and from the service, that suggested the "world." They believed that spiritual experience was superior to formal education and to the rite of ordination; they even questioned the scriptural soundness of paying the pastor a salary. Some of them went to the extreme of banning choir singing and instrumental music from their churches.

The intensely Protestant sons and daughters of Sweden, who founded churches in America, added to the pietistic and puritanical leaven that leavened the whole lump of American Protestantism. In everything except language and certain customs, they conformed to the American pattern. The American Sunday school was speedily adopted by Swedish congregations; the constitutions of congregations and synods were American in form and spirit; methods of recruiting members were copied from American churches; churches became "meetinghouses" from which social activity radiated; and even the Lutheran liturgy was modified.

In the nature of the case, the Swedish-American churches took their conception in laymen's missionary movements. There was a spontaneity about them that suggests the conditions that prevailed among the Christians in the Apostolic age. In many Swedish communities, laymen took the initiative in calling their countrymen together, in homes, for devotional meetings. Out of these informal gatherings emerged congregations organized through the instrumentality of "circuit riding" clergymen, whose parishes were as numerous as the fervent appeals from settlements made them. Consultations among pastors evolved into "missionary conferences"; and the final stage was reached when these germs of institutionalism became synods and conferences. The first generations of immigrants were eyewitnesses of every one of these stages of institutional development.

After the beginning, in the 1840's, of the great Swedish emigration to America, the first Swedish pastor to minister to his countrymen was Gustaf Unonius, if exception is made of Peter Böckman, whose stay in America was short and unfruitful. After a few years of effort to eke out a living as a pioneer farmer in Wisconsin, Unonius was admitted to holy orders in the Protestant Episcopal church, in 1845. Unonius' choice of the Episcopal church in preference to the Lutheran was dictated, partly by personal considerations, and partly by the chaotic conditions that prevailed within American Lutheranism. In spite of a letter from the archbishop of Uppsala, emphasizing three major points of disagreement between the church of Sweden and the Protestant Episcopal church, Unonius adhered to his conviction that, as a Lutheran, he could take orders in the Episcopal church and still keep his Lutheranism unblemished. His efforts to minister to a handful of his scattered countrymen in the Mississippi Valley were not fruitful, if the results are measured by the yardstick of communicant members; and, in 1858, he returned to Sweden, with the feeling that he had failed to attract his countrymen into a church with a constitution subscribing to the "apostolic faith and communion, under episcopal jurisdiction, as it is sanctioned and preserved in our native land." All there was to show for his labor was a church edifice in Chicago and the St. Ansgarius congregation, with a fluctuating membership. However, he was among the first of many Swedish-American pastors who played the part of the good Samaritan, to immigrants who stood in need of spiritual comfort and practical assistance, in the midst of sickness and death and misfortune. Throughout the years of immigration, thousands had reason to remember the healing effect of advice and assistance, rendered by individual pastors or through the instrumentality of immigrant homes in New York, Boston, and Chicago, established and maintained by churches. From 1845 to 1875, the Bethel ship in New York harbor, of which the Methodist missionary, Olof Gustaf Hedstrom, was the pastor, furnished a haven of rest, shelter, and solace.

Unonius emigrated in 1841, and the Hedstrom brothers preceded him by several years. These men came under the influence of ministers who served English-speaking congregations, and urged them to take up the high calling of preaching the Gospel to their countrymen, who, already, in the decade of the 'forties, were settling in and around Chicago, Galesburg, Bishop Hill, Rock Island, Moline, and Andover in Illinois, and New Sweden in Iowa. It was not until the summer of 1849 that Esbjörn arrived at Andover.

Esbjörn was trained in the doctrine, polity, and practice of the church of Sweden. For seventeen years, he had served as a pastor in Norrland—a province strongly infected with pietism —from which some fifteen hundred disciples of the prophet, Eric Janson, migrated in the decade of the 'forties, to establish a "New Jerusalem" at Bishop Hill, Illinois. The establishment of a theocratic communistic colony on the prairies of Illinois constitutes an interesting and tragic chapter in the history of Swedish immigration, even though the experiment soon ran its course and appears, in the pages of history, among similar ill-fated utopias on American soil.

When Esbjörn took his departure from Sweden, the exponents of Methodism, Baptism, Mormonism, Eric-Jansonism, and other shades of nonconformity and sectarianism, were already hacking at the roots of Lutheranism; and, in the New World, he found that his countrymen had already become the prey of missionaries in the service of several ecclesiastical organizations. However, Lutheranism soon claimed the center of the stage; and the organization of the Swedish Lutheran church preceded that of the other churches, with the exception of the Eric-Jansonist.

Within seven years after Esbjörn's arrival, the Lutheran forces were recruited by four additional pastors who had been ordained in the church of Sweden, the ablest of whom were Tuve Nilsson Hasselquist and Erland Carlsson. For four decades, Hasselquist and Carlsson steered Lutheranism in the channels that, in the main, have been followed ever since. These men, like Esbjörn, had been closely associated with men known for their piety and free-church tendencies. They had been very active in the temperance movement, and it was largely through the influence of two distinguished temperance agitators, Wieselgren and Fjellstedt, that they reached the decision to emigrate. Hasselquist was the most versatile and the ablest leader in the annals of Swedish-American Lutheranism. In accounting for any major policy adopted by the Swedish Lutheran church in the first four decades of its existence, the historian must reckon with this God-fearing son of Skåne, who gained the reputation of preaching sermons that soothed his hearers like a fresh breeze, and of chanting like an angel. He was the first president of the Augustana Synod, the second president of Augustana College and Theological Seminary, the editor of the first Swedish religious paper published in the United States, and the pastor of congregations. He wielded an influence that placed the stamp of pietism and Low-Church form so indelibly on the Augustana Synod, that it occupied a unique place among Lutheran synods. He knew the problems and limitations of a church that depended for its support upon a transplanted population, and he anticipated the day when the propagation of the Gospel in America, through the medium of a foreign language, would be over. As educator and ecclesiastical statesman, his orientation in the American environment was remarkably rapid. His contacts with influential men in Sweden, and in other American Lutheran synods, were invaluable to the church he served.

After a sojourn of nine years in the Synod of Northern Illinois, a district synod of the General Synod, the Swedish Lutheran congregations, together with a few Norwegian congregations, seceded, and organized the Augustana Synod, in 1860. With the separation of the Norwegians, in 1870, the Augustana Synod became exclusively Swedish, and has had an enduring existence. Although from 1870 to 1918 the Synod was affiliated with the General Council, it functioned in all respects as an independent body; and, after 1930, when it became a member of the American Lutheran Conference, it still retained its autonomy. Its affiliation with the two larger confederations was prompted by the desire to coöperate in common enterprises, such as foreign and home missions.

The other religious groups among the Swedish immigrants also aspired to effect organizations that would nurture their heritage from the mother country, though, in this respect, the numerical superiority of the Augustana Synod gave it the advantage, especially in the earlier years. There were more real and potential Lutherans among the immigrants than there were adherents to other faiths. However, the zeal and loyalty of the Lutheran leaders was matched by that of leaders in other churches.

The first meeting of the Swedish Baptist Conference was held in 1856, three years after the first meeting of the Mississippi Conference, which was a constituent member of the Lutheran Synod of Northern Illinois. Until the organization of the Swedish Baptist General Conference in 1879, the congregations were distributed within regional Swedish conferences. Likewise, prior to 1877, the Swedish Methodist congregations had been included with American congregations in district conferences; but, in that year, permission was obtained to organize a separate body, which took the name, Northwestern Swedish Methodist Conference. At present this organization is designated as the Central Northwest Swedish Methodist Conference.

The institutional history of the Mission Friends is somewhat different from that of the other denominations. In 1873, one

TUVE NILSSON HASSELQUIST, 1816–91

FIRST PRESIDENT OF THE AUGUSTANA SYNOD, 1867

element among the Mission Friends organized the Swedish
Evangelical Lutheran Mission Synod; and, the following year,
a competing organization took the name, Swedish Evangelical
Lutheran Ansgarius Synod, and functioned as a constituent
member of the General Synod until 1882. Regardless of serious
differences, both Synods subscribed to the unaltered Augsburg
Confession, and recruited members from the same constituency.
The Mission Synod attached less importance to organization
than did the sister Synod. The strength of the "leftist wing"
was concentrated in the older body. However, the two bodies
had things in common, more fundamental than otherwise. A
common faith and common problems steadily drew clergy and
laity together, until, in 1885, the two Synods, and a number
of independent congregations, joined forces in organizing the
Swedish Evangelical Mission Covenant in America, under the
presidency of Carl August Björk. Among orthodox and conservative churches in the United States, the Mission Covenant
enjoys the distinction of having no formal creed. It contents itself with the statement in its constitution that it accepts the
Word of God and the Old and New Testaments as the only rule
of faith, doctrine, and conduct. Its acceptance of the doctrine
of the atonement, expounded by Paul Peter Waldenström, the
great leader of the Mission Friends in Sweden, gives the Mission Covenant a special doctrinal position among churches calling themselves Lutheran.

A number of individuals and congregations that followed the
lead of John G. Princell, and could not subscribe to the constitution of the Mission Covenant, remained aloof, and carried
on their activity under various names until, in 1908, the Swedish Evangelical Free Church was incorporated.

With the exception of the Protestant Episcopal church, the
Swedish congregations in the United States have functioned as
constituent members of exclusively Swedish conferences or synods, though affiliated with brethren of the same faith in larger
and more comprehensive organizations, for the facilitation of
certain activities of mutual benefit. In 1856, the Protestant
Episcopal church appointed a Joint Committee on Friendly
Relations with the Church of Sweden, with the primary purpose of persuading the archbishop of Uppsala to consecrate a

bishop for the Swedes in the United States. It was the dream
and hope of prelates of the Episcopal church to include the
Augustana Synod within the scope of this plan. Negotiations
and diplomatic gestures in both Sweden and the United States,
over a long term of years, have not brought the dream to fulfillment, despite the steady progress of High-Church tendencies
in the Augustana Synod, and increasingly cordial relations between that synod and the church of Sweden, a *rapprochement*
for which credit, in no small measure, must be awarded to the
liberal, versatile, and ecumenical Archbishop Nathan Söderblom.

During the last thirty years, the number and membership of
Swedish Episcopal churches has steadily declined. In 1893, the
appointment of a general missionary and superintendent of
Swedish work was authorized; and, in 1920, a dean and associate dean of Scandinavian work were appointed; but the
churches are hastening toward the exclusive use of English, as
are the other congregations composed of members of Swedish
birth and descent.

From the time of the organization of the first congregations
in the 1840's, down to the enactment of drastic immigration
restriction legislation by Congress in the years immediately following the World War, the problem of the Swedish-American
churches was to adjust their agencies, in order to minister to
successive waves of immigrants and to follow the march of
population across the continent. The mission fields extended
from ocean to ocean, and into the Dominion of Canada. Moreover, to fail to make mention of missionary and educational activity in India, China, Africa, and Latin America, would be to
ignore a large chapter in Swedish-American church history.

The magnitude of the problem that confronted the earliest
pastors, when of necessity the only medium of worship was the
Swedish language, convinced some of them that the only solution, or at least the key to the solution, was the importation of
ministers educated and ordained in Sweden. The educational
opportunities available to the early immigrants were severely
restricted, and recruits for the ministry were, consequently, few
in number. On the other hand, conditions in the old country
were such that, in the aggregate, relatively few ordained min-

isters in Sweden hearkened to the Macedonian cry from across the water: "Come over and help us!" Not a few of the Swedish ministers, ordained in the United States, had served as school-teachers in Sweden, and had profited by their work as students, in such institutions as the schools maintained by Fjellstedt and Ahlberg, and the academies and seminaries supported by the free churches.

Notwithstanding the services rendered by these institutions, the sustenance for the ministeriums of Swedish-American churches came largely from their own educational organizations. The establishment of these schools solved the gravest and most immediate problem—and in a way that determined that the clerical estate in Swedish America was to be *sui generis*. Moreover, as the churches crossed the threshold of the twentieth century, to approach new problems that rushed in with the mingling of the second generation with the first, the educational institutions had already made adjustments in their curricula designed to train men and women to cope with them.

The Swedish-American educational establishments were conceived in the idea of establishing "nurseries in the kingdom." It is significant that no enduring institutions of higher learning have been formed apart from the churches. Whatever contributions to education have been made by the Swedish immigrants as a group must be credited to their ecclesiastical organizations. Libraries, museums, archives, and lectures pertaining to the contributions of the Swedes to American civilization, have, until recently, been founded and supported by churches. To the foresight and industry of men like President Tuve Nilsson Hasselquist and Professor Claude William Foss must be credited the unique collection of manuscripts, newspapers, pamphlets, and other fugitive material in the Denkmann Memorial Library at Augustana College, which will become the mecca of scholars engaged in writing an important chapter in the history of the American people.

The first stage of Swedish-American educational activity is marked by the birth of institutions that combined the curricula of academies and theological seminaries; and, for some years, the line of demarcation that divided theological studies from those purely secular was scarcely perceptible. At a time when congregations were pleading for leaders, it was neither feasible nor wise to detain men preparing to serve them, for eight or ten years, in order to enable them to qualify for academic degrees. Moreover, nearly all of the students in the early history of these institutions craved and needed instruction in subjects ordinarily confined to the conventional academy. It was only after the Swedish immigrants and their children had risen to a higher economic level that it was possible to require the completion of a certain course of study as a prerequisite to admission to the theological seminary. Before the close of the nineteenth century, however, the Lutheran institutions—Augustana, Gustavus Adolphus, Bethany, and Upsala—had attained to the stature of colleges; and by the first decade of the present century, their student bodies included only a small minority preparing themselves for the ministry. The first generation of immigrants witnessed the transformation of these institutions from the status of shaky academies and seminaries to the rank of colleges, whose alumni were distributed among the professions, of which the ministry was only a single field. The smaller numerical strength of the Baptists and Mission Friends has as yet prevented their institutions from rising above the rank of junior colleges. (See the chapter on "Colleges.")

The pioneer Swedish-American educational institution is Augustana Seminary, whose inception may be traced to the establishment, in 1855, of a Scandinavian professorship at Illinois State University at Springfield, an institution owned jointly by district synods within the Lutheran General Synod. A series of misunderstandings resulted in the withdrawal of the Scandinavian professor, Lars Paul Esbjörn, and his seven Swedish students, an event that precipitated the secession of the Swedish congregations from the Synod of Northern Illinois, and the establishment of Augustana Seminary at Chicago in 1860. When this precarious institution, with only a handful of students, migrated to Paxton, Illinois, in 1863, its future was still uncertain; and only the herculean efforts and indefatigable spirit of Hasselquist, ably assisted by Erland Carlsson, brought it through a Civil War and financial depression, to its present location at Rock Island, Illinois, in 1875, where it is known as Augustana College and Theological Seminary. The history of this oldest and most distinguished Swedish-American educational institution is the prototype of the story of its sister institutions—small beginnings, financial difficulties, uncertainty of location, and expansion. The dynamic personality of Carl Aaron Swensson, the founder and President of Bethany College, Lindsborg, Kansas, projected itself into the educational world during the last two decades of the nineteenth century.

The Swedish Baptist theological seminary operated for a time as a department of the Baptist Union Theological Seminary, when John A. Edgren, the founder of educational work among the Baptists, taught practically every subject in the curriculum, in addition to his duties as pastor of a congregation, editor of periodicals, and author of books. After a series of migrations, the seminary was finally located at St. Paul, Minnesota, in 1905, where it shares the campus with Bethel Institute, which rose from an academy to a junior college in 1931. Carl G. Lagergren shares with Edgren the honor of having brought the educational aspirations of the Baptists to a measure of realization.

The Methodist educational institution experienced the same difficulty of finding a permanent home as did the other institutions. From 1870 to 1872, it sojourned at Galesburg, Illinois, and from 1872 to 1875 at Galva (from the Swedish *Gävle*), in the same State. Upon the invitation of Northwestern University, it migrated to Evanston, where it was known as Wesley Academy and Seminary, under the presidencies of William Henschen and Carl G. Wallenius, until the fourth decade of the present century, when, for lack of support, the Swedish Methodists lost their only educational institution.

The educational work among the Mission Friends was hampered by doctrinal differences among themselves, and by conflicting opinions with respect to the function of educational institutions maintained by the church. On the eve of the organization of the Mission Covenant, in 1885, the Mission Friends lost their only academy and theological seminary, Ansgarius College and Lutheran Ansgarius Theological Seminary, located at Knoxville, Illinois. Years of uncertainty and experimentation followed, until, in 1894, North Park College in Chicago, under the presidency of David Nyvall, became the educational capital of the Mission Covenant. The desire of the followers of Waldenström in the Twin Cities of Minnesota, under the spur of their distinguished leader, E. August Skogsbergh, the "Swedish Moody," to have an educational institution in their midst, brought Minnehaha Academy into the world.

The rôle of the educational institutions in stimulating and keeping alive Swedish, as a spoken language, was in a sense forced upon them by the necessity of training pastors for congregations that worshiped in the language of Sweden. In a sense, this is also true of the publication houses maintained by the churches. The leaders of the churches supplied what their members desired or demanded. Without the unifying influence of the churches, their academies, colleges, theological seminaries, Sunday schools, parochial schools, and publishing houses, the children of the immigrants would shortly have lost contact with the customs, language, and culture of an older civilization. It is true that the pietistic slant of pioneer clergymen and laymen deprived their children of certain cultural advantages enjoyed by their cousins in Sweden; but it is equally true that, through no other agency, was the contact between Sweden and her American children maintained so successfully, as it was through the instrumentality of the church.

Although the number of people of Swedish blood, who have elected to affiliate with churches bearing the Swedish name, has been small in comparison with the total Swedish population in the United States, the influence of the church, spiritually and culturally, extended into homes where the parents were not communicant members. The church, as a factor in the life of a community, directly and indirectly came into the lives of individuals. The immigrant church as a social institution kept the individual on an even keel, by bridging a difficult transitional stage in his life. Through the church, he made wholesome contacts with men and women who spoke his language and understood his background.

In the early years of Swedish immigration, before the landscape was dotted with plain and unpretentious Swedish churches, the first Christmas in America was the most lonesome and dreary day of which the immigrant had recollection. The Puritan horror of "Romanism" had eliminated Christmas as a holy day in many American communities; but to the Swedish puritan it was the most festive, and joyous, and sacred of all days. The forest, the snow, the long winter nights, and the culinary skill of the housewife all conspired to make Christmas Eve in Sweden the inauguration of twenty days of feasting, fellowship, and worship. Christmas matins brought the aged and the infirm, the young and the strong, the pietist and the reveler, to the parish church, where all joined in singing Wallin's beautiful Christmas hymn, "All hail to thee, O blessed morn!"

The home of the Swedish immigrant, whether it was a log cabin, a sod house, or a "residence," celebrated Christmas Eve in the spirit of the home in the red cottage that nestled among the pine-clad hills of Sweden. And on Christmas morning in the Swedish church, whether its spire broke the monotony of the Iowa prairies or measured its height with the structures in the city, the candles, the Christmas tree, Wallin's hymn, and the service reproduced the spirit of Christmas in the Land of the Midnight Sun. And in these latter days the Olsons, Johnsons, Petersons, Swensons, and Andersons in Minnesota can dial their radios to stations in New England and New York and hear *julotta*, while brewing coffee before departing for the identical service in the Swedish church of their neighborhood or community.

The American Christmas is richer for the exodus of hundreds of thousands of sons and daughters of Svea. A festive week, elaborate decorations that adorn homes and streets, the music that comes over the air, and the *smörgåsbord* are among the contributions brought to America by the men and women who founded Swedish churches in the Mississippi Valley.

It seems hardly possible that the Swedish churches will in the future be called upon to adjust their agencies in order to minister to hosts of immigrants, as they did during the first seventy-five years of their existence. Congregation after congregation has yielded to the invasion of the English language; but the churches, theological seminaries, colleges, hospitals, orphan homes, and homes for the aged stand as monuments to commemorate the faith of the pioneers.

Charities and Self-Help

JULIUS LINCOLN

Dr. Lincoln, noted Lutheran clergyman, organizer, speaker, and administrator, is a native of Kansas, and was educated at Bethany College, Augustana Theological Seminary, and at Yale University. After serving as pastor in Jamestown, New York and Los Angeles, California, he became associated with the Swedish National Sanatorium for Tuberculosis in Denver, Colorado. Later he accepted the executive secretaryship of the Brotherhood of the Augustana Synod, and is now Secretary of the American Swedish Historical Foundation. He has been in close touch with various charitable organizations; has been President of the Board of Education in Jamestown (New York); and a member of the New York Assembly.

THE purpose of the first Swedish expeditions to North America, beginning in 1638, was the honorable acquisition of territory for colonization, cultivation, and trade. The monuments and records of "New Sweden" tell an incontrovertible story of the high aspirations of a race that were realized by intelligent, concurrent effort. Entirely dependent on their own initiative and resources, in constructing houses of worship as well as in earning their daily bread and the building of homes, they set about the work themselves. In Sweden they had been accustomed to see churches built by either the State or local governments. In Wilmington, Delaware, a record—a list of donors of either materials or labor—is preserved in regard to the building of the "Old Swedes" church, now two hundred and thirty-nine years old. Some of these items consist of logs, boards, tools, and nails. Much of the material was transported on sledges in the wintertime from Brandywine Hundred, and it is written in the books of Holy Trinity Church that Swedish women carried stone chips to the building in their ample aprons.

Two hundred years later, another exodus of much larger proportions started from Sweden; and the controlling motive of these new emigrants was, likewise, a desire to share in the abundant possibilities for earning a living in the New World. Their fatherland was not then the highly industrialized and socialized nation that it has since become. The impetus to general employment and prosperity, held in the natural resources of Sweden, was still awaiting the signal of release. Intermittent failures of crops and other discouragements were in sharp contrast with the reports of plenty, enjoyed by countrymen who had already gone to America. Authentic statistics place the number of Swedes who have emigrated to the United States within the past hundred years at 1,200,000—a considerable percentage of a nation's population which was never much above 6,000,000. (For details, see the chapter, "Geographical Distribution," in this volume.)

Most of these Swedes came to America empty-handed, but neither empty-headed nor empty-hearted. In material resources their heritage was meager, but it was rich in courage, love of adventure, health, physical strength, and a sound philosophy of life, founded on a creed of fundamental virtues. Their filial relations with their former homeland have been revealed by a generous thoughtfulness of the comfort and happiness of their kinsmen and friends across the sea, and by manifestations of gratitude and legitimate pride in the advancement of the mother country, to her present exemplary and honored position among nations.

Rural in experience, and by inclination, the vanguard of Swedish immigrants settled in the then undeveloped agricultural sections of the United States. (See the chapters on "Pioneers" and "Farmers.") Some of the later arrivals veered to the industrial centers, but they, too, tended toward constructive, creative occupations. Few have been parasites. Whatever their jobs, these strangers in a new land felt the need of one another; hence their gregariousness, and the resultant Swedish organizations for mutual help and for the promotion of common interests. A few years ago, "Svenska Societeten" ("The Swedish Society") in New York—the oldest Swedish organization in the United States, and one of the oldest of any nationality in the city—celebrated its one-hundredth anniversary. The brief declaration of its aim is a definition and practical exemplification of Swedish solidarity, fellowship, discussion of community welfare, and lifting of the burden of the weaker members.

Unacquaintance with the new language, coupled with an inherent rural shyness that even, at times, doubted the cordiality of welcome, made entrance into existing American organizations out of the question for the early Swedish immigrants. The gulf was too wide to be bridged immediately. These Swedes could not feel at home, or enjoy worship, in churches where every word was unintelligible, and the forms utterly different from the ones to which they had been accustomed. Nor could they feel at ease in fraternal or social groups where the indispensable basis was lacking for immediate congenial association. And yet, there is no record of a single Swedish society for fostering and perpetuating any doctrines or ideas inconsonant with American institutions. Whether religious, social, fraternal, or professional, all these organizations founded by Swedish-Americans have justified their existence, as the natural ground for the healthful exercise of an inherited idealism, and for the absorption of the true spirit of the new homeland. By mutual self-help they have forestalled, in numerous instances, recourse to public, tax-supported agencies.

The American Swedes have expressed their philosophy of life and idealism in over 3,500 variously organized units, through which, by combined effort, they are conserving the priceless heritage of the fatherland, and enriching our national life. The types of these organizations are an index to the versatile character of the racial membership, and are, also, testimonials to an appreciation of cultural, social, and moral values. Churches, leading in number and in membership, have founded, and are adequately maintaining, sixteen colleges, junior colleges, theological seminaries, schools of music and art, and publishing houses. In addition, the churches are engaged in a diversified eleemosynary and social program that covers many phases of human needs—from the care of orphaned or abandoned children (including nurseries) to friendly ports for weather-beaten seamen and robust loggers; pleasant dormitories for young women seeking livelihoods and careers in metropolitan centers; an asylum for epileptics; a sanatorium for the victims of tuberculosis; a system of pensions for disabled or superannuated clergymen and other church servants; hospitals for the sick; and homes for the aged.

The fraternal orders translate their sense of personal obligations to afflicted countrymen into the practical helpfulness of financial aid, in times of sickness and of death. They also provide shelter for aged countrymen and countrywomen in regional homes and in a magnificent central institution at Evanston, Illinois. Willingly, they all do their part in supporting the one institution that has been built by the united spirit and strength of Swedish-Americans, irrespective of religious affiliations, a marvelous achievement that concretely exemplifies Swedish solidarity—the Swedish National Sanatorium for tuberculosis patients at Englewood, Colorado.

The responsiveness of the collective, merciful heart of Swedish-Americans is clearly demonstrated by the history of the Swedish National Sanatorium. When it became evident that the resources of the Swedish residents of Denver, Colorado, would be insufficient to care for the increasing number of tubercular health seekers, mostly without means, who were constantly coming to the Rocky Mountain region, hopeful of recovery in that climate, an appeal for help was broadcast to countrymen throughout the nation, with most gratifying results. The religious denominations joined hands in pledging moral and financial support. Fraternal orders took similar action. An enthusiastic group of Swedish men and women in Providence, Rhode Island—more than two thousand miles away from Denver—undertook the manufacture, distribution, and annual sale, without commission or other remuneration, of a small token, "The Mayflower," at a price of ten cents each. The response to this happy idea became so general among Swedish-Americans that the net proceeds have mounted in a few years to an amazing sum in excess of $200,000. The Swedish National Sanatorium has thereby been enabled to erect the largest pavilion for patients on its campus. The tidy yearly income from this source is used for the free care of needy sick in the institution. By united coöperative efforts, the Swedish National Sanatorium has developed into one of the model institutions of its kind in the United States; and so well supported by its gener-

ous constituency has it been that, while only one half of the
number of patients can contribute to their own maintenance,
the Sanatorium has been able to perform its mission of mercy
without financial embarrassment. Buildings, grounds, and
equipment are valued at $250,000; and upon this property
there is no indebtedness—another testimonial to the solidarity
of a race that has expressed itself in shouldering a common responsibility, rather than delegating it to others.

Aside from national federations, a large number of local and
special organizations have knit Swedish-Americans together in
units for laudable aims, thus strengthening the bond of kinship and sympathy. In them power is generated and stored,
ready for release whenever a call comes for action in behalf of
the public good. Social clubs for the preservation of quaint,
colorful customs and old-time memories—singers' unions, orchestras, art clubs, athletic associations, historical societies,
literary guilds, political leagues, engineering societies, crafts
circles, press associations—cover almost the entire range of
physical and mental exercise. Without these diversified bodies
and societies, federated and local, there would not now be the
story to tell, of a people in America that, in per capita support
of educational and charitable institutions, stand close to the top.

The philanthropic program of Swedish-Americans has been
unfolded gradually to meet needs, as they arose and grew, beyond the bounds of willing, individual succor. There is ample
material for a chapter on the Swedish-American heart of pity,
in the years before a single institution of mercy had been
founded. Indeed, prior to the day when any of these immigrants
could afford to pledge a small donation of money to a general
cause, their humble log cabins in the north, huts of sod on the
prairies, or cramped quarters in the cities, were open to homeless, poor, or sick countrymen on the "share everything with
us" basis, until a better day would come. In the glamour that
time and fancy have laid upon the pioneer period, later generations lose the true perspective. It must not be lost sight of that
those days were hard, filled with tremendous, discouraging
struggles for the preservation of life itself, amid discomforts
and difficulties beyond the power of the imagination of children's children. Sickness and death struck swiftly and often,

sometimes at the head of the household himself, before the first week's or month's wage had been received—a poor prospect, in a strange land, for the family that had been brought over here on money borrowed, even for the passage. Burdened down with cares for the barest existence of their own families, those who were spared would seem helpless in such tragic circumstances, but in that garden of tears and sorrows the flower of altruism bloomed. Years before a home for children was planned, motherless or fatherless boys and girls were tenderly housed in already crowded dugouts or cabins or tenements, by kindhearted countrymen. Long before a hospital had been built by Swedish-Americans, their habitations were open to the sick countryman-stranger, no matter what the disease. The strong truly bore the burdens of the weak—a community of interests, where every exigency was met and eased by voluntary ministration. In the agricultural sections, the coöperative habits of the Swedish settlers were put into practice by alternating loans of farm implements and even of kitchen and laundry utensils, until improved conditions permitted the purchase of individual equipment. In this general practice of sharing, and of mutual helpfulness until a foothold had been secured, a spirit of cautious planning and racial self-reliance was fostered; and this fact explains why a mere minimum of Swedes and their descendants in America have become public charges. Two innate traits, a strong desire to own their homes and a frugality that has put this goal within reach, characterize Swedish-Americans as a class, and have helped them to become productive, self-supporting citizens.

The earliest Swedish-American organized charity was a children's home in Minnesota, started in 1865. In the basement of his church at Red Wing, Minnesota, the Reverend Eric Norelius prepared rooms to shelter four suddenly orphaned children, of a family by the name of Eriksson, who had recently arrived at St. Paul from Sweden. He engaged a woman to care for them. This was the beginning of an imposing charity, and it was followed by a similar institution in Illinois in 1867. Temporary homes, in scattered houses, for these unfortunate children, the number of whom increased with the growing immigration, did not solve the problem. The alternative, of making public charges of children of their own blood or of placing them in institutions where their ancestral, religious, and cultural background and their sense of relationship would be obliterated, did not appeal to their Swedish neighbors and friends. There are now throughout the United States seventeen such homes and nurseries, and it may be safely asserted that no homeless child of Swedish lineage in America needs to be without shelter. The marked decrease in the number of purely Swedish wards in these homes may be accounted for by the improved economic situations of the descendants of the Swedish immigrants. In granting admittances, the racial line is not now drawn, and these Swedish institutions have become hospitable homes for children of other nationalities—another indication of social development among the Swedish-Americans. Carrying this observation out still further, it is no reflection upon the later comers, who may be passing through experiences similar to those of the early Swedish settlers, to point out that during the current financial crisis, even in hospitals of Swedish founding, the ratio of charity and "relief" patients of Swedish origin is small, in comparison with those of other nationalities.

The next step in the philanthropic activities of Swedish-Americans was in the formation of hospitals, the first of which was founded in St. Paul, Minnesota, in 1882, followed by a second in Chicago in 1884. In a little over a half-century, this number has increased to twenty-one, and some of these houses of healing have won national and international reputations. The capital investment of millions of dollars in these plants is another index of the solidarity of the Swedish promoters and builders. These institutions are, without exception, voluntary hospitals, by which is understood nonprofit corporations, and so chartered by their respective states. In no instance are there stockholders to reap private gain. Net proceeds from operation are used to purchase replacements in equipment and for the care of needy patients—the latter, a considerable sum, is a reflection of the Swedish spirit of mercy. The majority of these hospitals also maintain standard schools of nursing, in which young women are educated for their honorable profession. In this group of hospitals is, in addition, an institute for the care of the feeble-minded and of epileptics, an imposing complex of buildings erected, and entirely supported, by a thoughtful and generous public.

Twenty to thirty years after the second migration to the United States from Sweden had started, another type of social service claimed the attention of the new citizens—homes for the aged. Time had taken its toll from the pioneer settlers, who were compelled, by age or feebleness, to retire from active work. Again the collective considerateness of the race asserted itself, now in behalf of battle-scarred veterans in life's heroic struggle. In some cases these elders had been victimized by unfortunate circumstances, but others, by careful planning, had set aside a savings fund for old age. For these countrymen and women, pleasant retreats are now provided, in thirty-five comfortable homes with all modern improvements. These homes are so well distributed geographically that the guests are not far removed from their accustomed surroundings. Within these walls there is a congenial atmosphere, created by common memories, similar tastes and customs—most desirable elements for peace of mind in the closing years of life. The motive that actuated the founders of the Swedish homes for the aged in the United States was that their elderly countrymen should not be forced to spend their declining years as public charges, or in public institutions.

The solidarity of the Swedish-American family—no term can better describe the nationality—is evidenced, not only by this program of mercy, but also by its provisions for the able-bodied, whose careers call them away from their hearthstone. Twenty sailors' and loggers' havens, hospices for wayfarers, and homes for young women in industrial and commercial centers, complete a series of activities for the physical well-being of blood relations, dating back only sixty-eight years in the annals of America. Elsewhere in this volume, the story is told of the colleges founded and maintained by Swedish-Americans. Paralleling the performance of erecting and supporting the seventy-three social-service institutions, outlined above, is the heavy financial investment in education by Swedish-Americans, a logical action for the sons and daughters of a country that has one of the lowest percentages of illiteracy in the world, or practically none.

In the pursuit of these idealistic activities, Swedish-Americans have also become well grounded in the cardinal virtues of good citizenship. The racial characteristics, embodied in these agencies of mercy and education, are clearly discernible in the Federal statistical tables, setting forth the Scandinavians as the smallest contributors to crime of any race, and with a minimum of dependents upon public funds.

Protection against loss from raging elements, as well as sick-benefit and life insurance, engaged the early attention of Swedish-Americans. The Scandinavian Mutual Aid Association of Galesburg, Illinois, was a pioneer life-insurance venture that developed into the Mutual Trust Life Insurance Company of Illinois, a strong corporation with $150,135,799 insurance in force, and admitted assets of $37,741,576.70. Scandinavians are also a strong factor in the successful management and clientele of the Lutheran Brotherhood Life Insurance of Minnesota.

Mutual fire-, hail-, and storm-insurance companies have become popular and flourishing in Swedish-American centers, and have established enviable records of economically conducted service. The character of their constituency is revealed by the official statement at the fiftieth anniversary of the Swedish-American Fire Insurance of Kansas that, in the entire period of its existence, there had not been a single suspected case of arson.

Coöperative societies among Swedish-American agriculturists, building and loan, and savings associations have been, and still are, favored mediums for reaching a stable status.

The current massing of the spiritual and physical resources of Swedish-Americans, in view of the three-hundredth anniversary, is a further demonstration of an undying collective idealism. Among the leaders in this movement are descendants of the first colonists, who greatly prize their lineage, as well as men and women of the second migration—either born in Sweden themselves, or belonging to the second and third generations of sons and daughters of the pioneers of the 'forties, 'fifties, or 'sixties—some of whom, though unacquainted with the language of their forefathers, nevertheless, are uniting with their kinsmen in celebrating the anniversary of 1638, as a tribute to their forebears.

Twelve years ago, in 1926, at the Sesquicentennial of the Declaration of Independence, a group of representative Swedish-Americans met in Chicago, to discuss plans for honoring and preserving the names and rôles of their colonial countrymen, in the drama of the Revolution that made America free. These deliberations resulted in a unanimous decision to invite the coöperation of Swedish compatriots in the United States, in the erection of a National Museum in Philadelphia on ground that formerly was a part and parcel of "New Sweden." The original name given this monument was "The John Morton Memorial Museum," in honor of John Morton of Pennsylvania, a signer of the Declaration of Independence, a great-grandson of a Swedish colonist. Later this name was changed to "The American Swedish Historical Museum"; this more clearly defines the aims and purposes of the institution, while still conveying the original idea of the founders, of a memorial to Swedish-American builders of the Republic.

This project crowns the solidarity of Swedish-Americans. The appeal of it leaped over denominational walls and the response was instantaneous. This unique institution will be dedicated at the Tercentenary celebration, and, in itself, will be a witness to the idealism and generosity of a race whose patriotic fervor and freewill gifts have made it possible. In the sixteen Museum halls, the records and exhibits of the contributions in as many different fields, by Swedish-Americans to American history, will be kept. It will naturally be the archives of Swedish-Americans—a repository of source material, to which researchers will turn. Children of the founders and promoters will enlarge its usefulness and secure its future by the needed endowments and other funds. On the purpose of the American-Swedish Historical Museum, Swedish-Americans will always be united. The name will be a bond to hold them together in all time to come.

Through these three hundred years of Swedish-American life runs a golden thread of devotion to the genius of the new homeland. From colonial days to the founding of the Republic, through wars that threatened its existence, and in peaceful, constructive pursuits, the Americans of Swedish blood have been a dependable, ready unit in the ranks of the citizenry that forms the bulwark of the nation.

For more details in regard to the Swedish-American charitable organizations and fraternal orders, see *The Swedish Element in America* (II).

The following table gives a fair idea of the annual contribution of Swedish-American organizations for idealistic purposes. It is based on reports for 1936 or 1937. If close inspection should discover duplications, the difference would be offset by returns from activities not herein included, as, for instance, the book concerns and publishing houses of the several religious denominations.

Religious Organizations

	Churches	Members	Expenditures (1936) for local work, education, charity, etc.
Augustana Synod	1,203	254,677	$ 6,497,434.64
Baptist	300	36,820	1,146,378.34
Evangelical Free	150	9,000	260,000.00
Methodist	175	19,441	380,088.00
Mission Covenant	441	45,000	2,366,865.00
Total			$10,650,765.98

Fraternal Organizations

	Lodges	Members	Expenditures including institutional work
Vasa	463	56,292	$ 270,392.46
Svithiod	73	12,139	273,336.77
Scandinavian Fraternity	237	30,000	150,000.00
Vikings	105	12,000	236,668.65
Total			$ 930,397.88
Grand total			$11,581,163.86

The following list of Swedish-American charitable institutions has been compiled by the late Vilhelm Berger of Brooklyn, New York.

Children's Homes

Vasa Children's Home, Red Wing, Minnesota
Lutheran Home for Children, Andover, Illinois
Iowa Lutheran Children's Home, Stanton, Iowa
Gustavus Adolphus Children's Home, Jamestown, New York
Lutheran Home for Children, Joliet, Illinois
Immanuel Children's Home, Omaha, Nebraska
Lutheran Children's Home, Avon, Massachusetts
Augustana Children's Home, Minneapolis, Minnesota
Bethany Children's Home, Duluth, Minnesota
Bethany Children's Home, Alexandria, Minnesota
Augustana Nursery, Chicago, Illinois
Mariadahl Receiving Home, Cleburne, Kansas
Receiving Home, St. Paul, Minnesota
Swedish Christian Orphanage, Cromwell, Connecticut
Covenant Children's Home, Princeton, Illinois
The Children's Home, New Britain, Connecticut
The Klingberg Children's Home, Chicago, Illinois
Swedish Christian Children's Home, Phelp, Nebraska
Kallman Home for Children, Brooklyn, New York

Homes for the Aged

Immanuel Home for the Aged, Omaha, Nebraska
Bethesda Old People's Home, Chisago City, Minnesota
Iowa Lutheran Home for the Aged, Madrid, Iowa
Salem Home for the Aged, Joliet, Illinois
Swedish Augustana Home for the Aged, Brooklyn, New York
Bethany Home for the Aged, Lindsborg, Kansas
Augustana Home for the Aged, Chicago, Illinois
Bethany Home, Alexandria, Minnesota
Luther Home, Marinette, Wisconsin
Augustana Home for the Aged, Minneapolis, Minnesota
Swedish Lutheran Old People's Home, Worcester, Massachusetts
Home for the Aged, Seattle, Washington
Salem Lutheran Home for the Aged, Kansas City, Missouri
Lutheran Home for the Aged, Grand Rapids, Michigan
Lake Shore Lutheran Home, Duluth, Minnesota
Lutheran Home for the Aged, Jamestown, New York

Salem Lutheran Home for the Aged, Oakland, California
Old People's Home, Mankato, Minnesota
The Covenant Home for the Aged, Chicago, Illinois
Bethany Home, Turlock, California
The Middle East Old People's Home, Frewsburg, New York
The Old People's Home of the Eastern Missionary Association,
   Bronx, New York
Covenant Bethany Home for the Aged, Minneapolis, Minnesota
The Ebenezer Home, Buffalo, Minnesota
Bethany Old People's Home, Spokane, Washington
Elim Park, Shelton, Connecticut
Fridhem, Chicago, Illinois
Sunset Home, Concordia, Kansas
Pacific Home, Los Angeles, California
Bethany Home for the Aged, Chicago, Illinois
Bethel Home for the Aged, Ossining, New York
Swedish Old People's Home, Boone, Iowa
Elim Old People's Home, Princeton, Minnesota
Viking's Valhalla, Gurnee, Illinois
Old People's Home, Birch Bluff, Minnesota
Swedish Old People's Home, Evanston, Illinois
Swedish Old People's Home, Staten Island, New York
Swedish Old People's Home, West Newton, Massachusetts
Scandinavian Old People's Home, Cranston, Rhode Island
Linnea Home for the Aged, St. Paul, Minnesota
Scandinavian Union Relief, Minneapolis, Minnesota

Hospitals

Bethesda Hospital, St. Paul, Minnesota
Augustana Hospital, Chicago, Illinois
Immanuel Hospital, Omaha, Nebraska
Warren Hospital, Warren, Minnesota
Trinity Lutheran Hospital, Kansas City, Missouri
Emanuel Hospital, Portland, Oregon
Iowa Lutheran Hospital, Des Moines, Iowa
Lutheran Hospital, Moline, Illinois
Columbia Hospital, Astoria, Oregon
Immanuel Home for Invalids, Omaha, Nebraska
Bethesda Invalid Home, St. Paul, Minnesota

Bethphage Mission for Epileptics and Incurables, Axtell, Nebraska
Immanuel Deaconess Institute, Omaha, Nebraska
Swedish Covenant Hospital, Chicago, Illinois
Emanuel Hospital, Turlock, California
Covenant Hospital, Omaha, Nebraska
Swedish Baptist Hospital, Concordia, Kansas
Mounds Park Sanatorium, St. Paul, Minnesota
Bethany Hospital, Chicago, Illinois
Swedish National Sanatorium, Denver, Colorado
Swedish Hospital, Minneapolis, Minnesota
Swedish Hospital, Brooklyn, New York
Fairlawn Hospital, Worcester, Massachusetts

Hospices

Swedish Lutheran Immigrant and Seamen's Home, New York City
Lutheran Immigrant and Seamen's Home, East Boston, Massachusetts
Lutheran Compass Mission, Seattle, Washington
Lutheran Compass Mission, Tacoma, Washington
Augustana Central Home, Chicago, Illinois
Immanuel Women's Home, Chicago, Illinois
Augustana Young Women's Home, Minneapolis, Minnesota
Augustana Lutheran Home, Denver, Colorado
Lutheran Young Women's Home, St. Paul, Minnesota
Augustana Lutheran Mission Home, Chicago, Illinois
Lutheran Home for Women, New York
Lutheran Home for Girls, Vancouver, B.C., Canada
Lutheran Hospice, Colorado Springs, Colorado
Augustana Lutheran Women's Home, Omaha, Nebraska
Lutheran Hospice, Seattle, Washington
Scandinavian Sailors' Home, East Boston, Massachusetts
Scandinavian Sailors' Home, San Francisco, California
Fridhem, Brooklyn, New York
Freedhem, Chicago, Illinois
Fridhem, Boston, Massachusetts
Susanna Wesley Home for Young Women, Chicago, Illinois
Scandinavian Home of Shelter, Minneapolis, Minnesota
Colony of Mercy, Bartlett, Illinois

Colleges

ERNST W. OLSON

All cultured Swedish-American Lutherans and all Swedish journalists in America know the name and work of E. W. Olson. Born in Sweden, he was brought to the United States in 1878, and was educated at Luther Academy in Nebraska and Augustana College in Illinois. Later his Alma Mater honored him with a degree of Doctor of Letters. He is so well known among the Swedes as editor, translator, poet, general author, historian, and writer of cantatas (with music), that we need only refer to *Who's Who* for the details of his activities. Perhaps his most outstanding publication is *History of the Swedes of Illinois,* in two volumes, which appeared in 1908. He has known the Swedish-American colleges from childhood. He is now literary editor for the Augustana Book Concern.

ALL the schools of higher learning founded by the Swedish element in America—and there has been a score or more—have been of churchly origin, although the religious bodies, taken together, make up much less than half of that element in our nation. This tells us one of the two chief reasons for their existence; i.e., to serve the needs of the church. The second reason may be stated in the words of Dr. Nicholas Murray Butler: "There comes from these northern people a certain sturdiness of character, simplicity, and dignity of life, *an interest in and contribution to music, art, literature, and to the science of the world that causes them to take a place in the van of civilization.*"

Out of the many schools started, ostensibly with a view to their development into complete colleges, only six have attained to college status, and are now maintaining themselves as standard American colleges. The high rate of mortality is accounted for by a number of causes. Some schools were begun with more zeal than foresight and in too small fields from which to draw students and pecuniary support. The constituency back of them all was restricted, first by the bounds of nationality, and then further hemmed in by denominational confines. A school might have its few friends and supporters scattered throughout so large an area that it stood practically alone, with no chance of survival.

In more recent times, these privately supported schools have had their field greatly reduced by the enormous growth and great inner development of tax-supported institutions of learning. The academies were gradually crowded out by the high schools, and, in the rivalry with the state colleges and those of the independent universities, the church college was hard put to it to hold its own. Leaving out of the reckoning the four theological seminaries of the respective churches of Swedish origin—the Lutheran, the Methodist, the Baptist, and the Mission Covenant—we have left, after this final process of elimination, the following Christian colleges founded by Swedish immigrants, and maintained by their descendants; namely, Augustana College, at Rock Island, Illinois; Gustavus Adolphus College, at St. Peter, Minnesota; Bethany College, at Lindsborg, Kansas; Upsala College, at East Orange, New Jersey; Luther College, at Wahoo, Nebraska, and North Park College, at Chicago, Illinois—the last two being junior colleges. The first five are supported by the Augustana Lutheran Synod, the last by the Mission Covenant. Suomi College, at Hancock, Michigan, was founded as a Swedish-Finnish institution, and it is proper to add here that the Swedenborgian institutions, including the academy at Bryn Athyn, Pennsylvania, have a Swedish cultural background and are founded on a religious system of purely Swedish origin. While the schools have grown fewer, students of Swedish extraction at other colleges have so greatly increased in number that, at best, only a fractional part could have been accommodated in these church colleges—a compensating fact of high importance in the history of Swedish-American education and culture.

Augustana College

A LUTHERAN school was established in 1851, at Springfield, Illinois, by joint action of several bodies, including the Synod of Northern Illinois. To this Synod belonged the Swedish and Norwegian newcomers who had settled in the Middle West and had formed two small church bodies of their own, the Swedish Mississippi Conference and the Norwegian Chicago Conference. The need of pastors for the Scandinavian churches, urged on the Synod by the two conferences, brought about a decision in 1855 to found a Scandinavian professorship at the new seminary in Springfield, too ambitiously named Illinois State University. To that Scandinavian chair, definitely established two years later, and first occupied by Reverend Lars Paul Esbjörn in 1858, Augustana College and Theological Seminary traces its origin.

Divergent Lutheran views and strained personal relations in the faculty at Springfield soon caused a rupture, and in March, 1860, Esbjörn abandoned his position, his score of Scandinavian students leaving at the same time. His action precipitated a breach in the Synod, the Swedish and Norwegian conferences withdrawing and organizing the Scandinavian Augustana Synod, in June of the same year. Expressly on the basis of the Scandinavian professorship, the new Synod at once founded its own institution of learning, and named it Augustana Seminary.

Headed by Esbjörn, the little school was maintained in Chicago for three years, provisional quarters being furnished by the Immanuel congregation. No permanent school building was contemplated, owing to a plan, pending from the outset, to purchase and cultivate land for its maintenance, and move the school out into the country. When, in 1862, it was decided to remove it to Paxton, Illinois, a mere railway station on the open prairie, Esbjörn resigned his position, and, after completing an ingathering of funds in Sweden, he remained there. The support from the churches was inadequate from the start, and the urgent need of means for the maintenance of the school had compelled its sponsors to turn to the mother church for help. Reverend O. C. T. Andrén was sent over to Sweden as emissary, with a petition to the Crown, asking for the right to solicit funds. King Charles XV granted the privilege of soliciting and receiving collections from the churches of the realm. A total of almost $11,000 was raised. As a personal gift, the King himself donated five thousand volumes from his private collections as a nucleus for the library of the new school.

Esbjörn had at first been engaged to solicit funds among the Lutherans of the Eastern States. He went on a special mission to Columbus, Ohio, to secure the transfer to the Seminary of

$1,500, given by Jenny Lind to the Capital University, to endow a Scandinavian chair. The chair was never established there, and the endowment could not now be retrieved for its specified purpose, no record of the fund having been kept.

In 1861, the Synod instructed the board to call to a teaching position P. P. Waldenström of Uppsala, who years afterward dissented from the church of Sweden and became the leader of the movement which crystallized in the Mission Covenant in Sweden, and in a church body of the same name in the United States. Both Waldenström and Andrén declined calls to become Esbjörn's successor, and Reverend T. N. Hasselquist was chosen to teach provisionally. After having failed, also, to secure Reverend S. L. Bring from Sweden, the Synod made Hasselquist the incumbent of the chair of theology until further action. No change was made, and Hasselquist remained, serving both as theological professor and as president of the institution until his death in 1891. Not only as an educator, but in his capacity of publisher and editor, preacher, religious writer, and church leader, he rendered, during four decades, such services as to make him one of the chief figures of his time in the Lutheran church of America.

After looking about in various rural localities for a suitable site for the school, the board finally came to an agreement with the Illinois Central Railway Company, and in June, 1863, the Synod ratified the action and decided to move the Seminary to Paxton. One thousand acres of land were purchased at $6 per acre, and the Directors were given the agency for the sale of a large tract at the modest commission of from $1 down to 50c. per acre. As buyers moved in, a congregation was organized, with Hasselquist as pastor. School opened in September without available quarters, and Hasselquist accommodated the first few students for two months in his own house. After renovation, an old schoolhouse was then used for class instruction, ten students attending during the first year. Up to 1870, the yearly average was thirty-five.

Instruction was given in college subjects as early as 1866. A charter was granted in 1865, and altered in 1869, changing the name to read Augustana College and Theological Seminary. A new plan of instruction was drawn up in 1870, providing for a preparatory department and a complete college in addition to the theological course comprising two years of studies. The Norwegian constituency withdrew from the Synod that year, entailing some loss of support for the school.

The institution made but slow progress during its twelve years at Paxton. The plan to surround it with populous rural settlements miscarried when the stream of Swedish immigration bore mainly to the west and northwest from Chicago. The desirability of a better location grew more apparent year by year. This matter was first broached publicly in the Synod in 1869, a tender of land and money having been made by Geneseo, Illinois, the year before. The Synod accepted the offer in good faith, but the city officials failed to carry out their part of the contract, and no further steps were taken for another five years. Then Rock Island was agreed upon as the most favorable location, and in 1873 a tract of nineteen acres of high ground overlooking the Mississippi was purchased in that city. The erection of the first main building was begun that fall, the cornerstone being laid November 7. The panic of 1873, coupled with other causes, delayed the completion of the structure until 1875, when the removal actually took place, and the school opened in the new building in the fall. Thereby, after practically three removals, the institution was permanently established in Rock Island.

The plan to establish complete college courses now received added impetus from the ambition of the members of the highest class to acquire the Bachelor's degree at their own school. In 1877 the first college class was graduated, including Constantin M. Esbjörn, later a teacher at Augustana, Carl J. Petri, a noted pastor, and two college presidents, Matthias Wahlstrom of Gustavus Adolphus College, and Carl Swensson, who built his own institution, Bethany College, at Lindsborg, Kansas, from the ground up. Up to 1880, the classical was the only college course.

A botanizing expedition in the fall of 1877, under the direction of Dr. A. R. Cervin, is said to have marked the beginning of the study of the natural sciences at Augustana. Out of love for the subject, Cervin taught botany for a year or two, besides his other subjects. There was no regular teaching of the sciences until Dr. Josua Lindahl arrived in 1878 as professor of natural science. This acquisition was a stroke of rare good fortune for the young college. Lindahl, who had earned his degree of Ph.D. at the University of Lund, had been the official botanist of a deep-sea expedition fitted out by the British Government, the first of its kind. He was afterward sent to Philadelphia by the Swedish Government, as assistant to the commissioner-general of the Centennial Exposition, in 1876. In him the institution found at once an enthusiastic scientist and an authority of high rank. The museum was practically created by him, and interest in scientific studies struck deep roots at Augustana during the decade he taught there. He was succeeded by John A. Udden, a member of Dr. Cervin's first botany class, who later made a name for himself in geology, first at Augustana, and later at the University of Texas. His researches and discoveries were of inestimable value to that State. He himself was an Augustana graduate, class of '81. (See the chapter on "Professors.")

Among the graduates who have made their mark in science are also the following: Dr. O. W. Oestlund ('79), head of the Department of Entomology at the University of Minnesota, and State Entomologist; Philip Dowell ('85), head of the Department of Biology, in the school system of New York City; J. A. Edquist ('86), head of the Department of Natural History at Gustavus Adolphus College, and discoverer of a fine saurian specimen in Wyoming; Dr. J. E. Wallin ('97), distinguished psychologist; and Dr. Anton J. Carlson ('98), professor of Physiology at the University of Chicago, whose investigations and experiments have compelled the rewriting of the physiology relating to the heart. (See "Professors.")

For twenty years the Swedish language was the medium of instruction in almost all subjects. Hasselquist, however, sensed the trend and consistently urged the transformation of the school into a fully American institution of learning. Begun about 1880, the transition to the English medium was practically completed in the College during the next ten years, and in the Seminary somewhat later. The same process has taken place in all the Swedish-American colleges. The schools early accepted this obligation to become thoroughly American, while in the churches the bilingual period is not yet at an end.

Two new departments were added in the middle 'eighties, first a conservatory of music, then a commercial school. Professor Olof Olsson, of the Seminary, first built up a chorus and an orchestra for the rendition of *The Messiah* of Händel, and of other oratorios. The next step was the engagement of Gustav Stolpe as college instructor in music, Hasselquist holding that "the cultivation of the art of song ought to be a required subject throughout the institution." Due to the efforts of the two theologians and music lovers, a conservatory of music was privately established in 1886, incorporated with the institution the next year, and Dr. Stolpe was placed at its head. This great organist and composer served at Augustana from 1882 to 1893. After 1910, J. Victor Bergquist, noted teacher, conductor, and composer, was in charge for a term of years. National recognition of Augustana as a musical center has been gained in recent years by the Augustana choir and Henry Veld, its creator and director.

After more than twenty-seven years of service as president, Dr. Hasselquist died in 1891. His mantle fell on Dr. Olof Olsson, his colleague in the divinity school for twelve years (1876–88). Olsson's administration, cut short by his death in 1900, was marked by uniform progress. He was the outstanding theological scholar of the Augustana Synod, noted alike as preacher, teacher, and writer. Ericson Park, of about twelve acres and costing $25,000, was added to the campus in 1893, as the gift of C. J. A. Ericson of Boone, Iowa, and the University Association.

The normal department, opened in 1891, gradually merged with the college courses in Education and other divisions of teaching. From 1897, the subjects of drawing and painting were taught by Olof Grafström. This led to the establishment of the School of Art, conducted by him for two decades, and then the Division of Fine Arts in the College. Grafström, who excelled as a landscape painter, later took up church art, and his altarpieces adorn the chancel and reredos of many a church.

Since the erection of a new main building, begun in 1885 and completed in 1888, there had been little development of the physical plant. The administration of Gustav Andreen as president (1901–35) presents a different picture. He has had more to do with the economic development of the institution than any other man. The endowment of the Oscar II chair of science (100,000 kronor) was the fruit of his solicitation while studying in Sweden, on leave of absence from Yale University. The raising of an endowment fund of $250,000 was left largely in his charge, and was completed as a jubilee fund at the time of the fiftieth anniversary of the School and the Synod. The Denkmann Memorial Library, the munificent gift of the heirs of Frederick C. A. Denkmann, valued at $210,000, was erected on the campus at this time, and with funds furnished mainly by local businessmen a gymnasium with auditorium was built some time after. Next followed a women's dormitory, the cost of which was mainly defrayed by the Woman's Missionary Society of the Synod. The block of ground surrounding the Woman's Building is the gift of Dr. and Mrs. John H. Hauberg of Rock Island—and not the only gift from that source. A unit of two buildings for the theological seminary was erected by synod-wide subscription, and completed in 1923. The Most Reverend Nathan Söderblom, Archbishop of Sweden, participated in the dedication of the new home of the Theological Seminary. In 1928 a project was started to raise a new endowment of a million and a half, and the amount was covered by general subscription, but, due to the financial crisis, only about $900,000 has been realized from pledges made. The Wallberg Hall of Science was completed in 1935, erected with money accruing from bequests by Emil and Marie Wallberg. Reverend Dr. C. A. Lindvall of Chicago, through his affiliation with the family, was chiefly instrumental in securing these legacies. At first valued at $150,000, these bequests, after a rise in the value of the securities involved, now bid fair to yield over half a million dollars.

Both College and Seminary were maintained by the Synod at large until about ten years ago, when three of the thirteen conferences were made responsible for the support of the college proper, but with control remaining in the hands of the Synod as a whole.

In 1935 Dr. Andreen retired on a pension, as president emeritus, and the Reverend Conrad Bergendoff, Ph.D. (Chicago), Dean of the Seminary, succeeded him. In his first year, the oldest college building was removed, as no longer usable as a men's dormitory, and, in his second, a modern building for the men students was erected at a cost of more than $130,000, and named Andreen Hall, in honor of his predecessor.

The college library has in the course of years come to be an important historical depository. Through the efforts of Dr. Hasselquist, Dr. Claude W. Foss, Dr. Andreen, and others, a wealth of material on the Lutheran church and the Swedish element in the United States has been accumulated, from 1863 on, and in recent years a number of private collections have been added by gift or legacy. Thus collections or entire libraries have been given by Eric Norelius, the Esbjörn and Hasselquist families; the Right Reverend Gezelius von Schéele, Bishop of Gottland; Nils Forsander, Conrad E. Lindberg, and Sven Gustaf Youngert, professors of the Seminary; Gustaf N. Swan of Sioux City, Iowa; Oliver A. Linder of Chicago; Vilhelm Berger of Brooklyn; and A. Theodore Ekblad, former president of the board. The Augustana Historical Society was formed in 1930 to aid in archival research, acquiring and publishing historical material, and collecting objects for the museum connected with the library. While general in scope, it makes the Swedish element and the Lutheran church in America its specific field. The college library now contains approximately 65,000 volumes, bound and catalogued, and 53,000 pamphlets.

Not a few men of more than ordinary capacity—now deceased—have taught at this institution in the past. Working with those already spoken of, were: In the Seminary, Dr. Revere F. Weidner, Biblical scholar and author of many published texts and commentaries; in the College, Dr. C. W. Foss, who taught history for almost fifty years; Dr. A. W. Williamson, professor of higher mathematics; Dr. C. M. Esbjörn, professor of Swedish and Christianity; Dr. Anders O. Bersell, who occupied the Greek chair; Dr. Jules Mauritzson, professor of Swedish and Dean of the College.

The present teaching staff averages fifty regular professors and instructors, divided into three faculties. The student enrollment approached 1,000 in the year 1937; 517 in the college of liberal arts, 103 of whom were graduated. Endowments total

$975,000, and fund assets aggregate $1,368,000, while $1,-354,000 represents the total investment in buildings, grounds, and equipment. Augustana is a member of the North Central Association of Colleges and Secondary Schools; it is on the accredited list of the American Association of University Professors, and its women graduates are eligible to membership in the American Association of University Women.

Dr. Bergendoff, the new President, has spoken not only for Augustana, but on behalf of all the Swedish-American colleges, when characterizing their common function in these words: "Very briefly stated, my belief is that the Christian college does most for American citizenship when it remains true to the purpose for which it exists, namely, the interpretation of all knowledge in the light of the Word of God."

Gustavus Adolphus College

Newcomers from Sweden came to the territory of Minnesota and established their first settlements there, in 1850 at Scandia, and in 1851 at Chisago Lake. Those who located at the latter place remained, making that the first permanent Swedish settlement. Others of their countrymen followed, and in the next few years they formed communities and founded churches of their own in a number of localities, including Vasa, Red Wing, St. Paul, East and West Union, and St. Peter. In 1858 these churches, through their eight delegates, organized themselves into a Lutheran body named the Minnesota Conference. Other churches were added, and within four years the Conference realized the need of a school to train young men "to teach school in both the Swedish and the English language." Eric Norelius, pastor at Red Wing, taught one pupil in the fall of 1862, and eleven in the spring term. This was the modest beginning of the Lutheran institution known as Gustavus Adolphus College. After a year, the school was located at East Union (Carver), called Minnesota Elementary School, and placed in charge of Pastor A. Jackson, who had been driven from his mission field in Kandiyohi County by the Indian uprising of 1862. The School was incorporated in 1865 and then named St. Ansgar's Academy, in commemoration of the Apostle of the North, who died in the year 865.

The institution remained at East Union for thirteen years, Pastor Jackson serving as principal, except for an interval of two years. But the location in a distant country settlement had its drawbacks. In 1873 it was proposed to move the school to Minneapolis and connect it with the University of Minnesota; Swedish and Christianity alone were to be taught, while the general curriculum would be left to the University. The plan, favored by both parties, was adopted; yet it miscarried, owing, in part, to the panic of 1873. At that juncture the people of St. Peter, headed by Andrew Thorson, offered to subscribe $10,000 and provide a site for the school in their city. A new corporation, the Swedish Lutheran Board of Education, acting for the Minnesota Conference, accepted the offer in 1874, and the school was permanently established at St. Peter under a new name, Gustavus Adolphus College. The first college building, erected in 1875, was dedicated October 31, 1876.

The institution was headed by Pastor J. P. Nyquist until 1881, when the Reverend Dr. Matthias Wahlstrom assumed the presidency. He served for twenty-three years, being succeeded in 1904 by the Reverend Dr. P. A. Mattson. He resigned in 1911, and, after an interim of two years, Dr. O. J. Johnson, the present President of the College, assumed charge.

The development of the physical plant is marked by the following building projects: in 1904, a building containing auditorium and classrooms; in 1910, the erection of the women's dormitory, named Johnson Hall, in recognition of the fact that Governor John A. Johnson of Minnesota secured $41,000 toward the enterprise (including $32,500 from Andrew Carnegie) ; in 1922, a gymnasium erected at a cost of $141,000. In 1928 a boys' dormitory costing $165,000, and accommodating 150 students, was built; also a stadium at a cost of $15,000.

The work of building up an endowment fund for the support of the College began with the administration of Dr. O. J. Johnson. Spurred by conditional pledges of $50,000 each from C. A. Smith, the Swedish-American "timber king," and James J. Hill of railway fame, he and his staff of solicitors raised $200,-000 by May 1, 1914, a fund of $300,000 thereby having been completed. In 1920 a like endeavor was made, aiming to bring the endowment up to and past the half-million mark. Overtures were made to the General Education Board of the Rockefeller Foundation, which brought a promise of $100,000, on condition that twice that sum be raised by the College constituency. After several years of effort, the condition was met in 1925, yielding an additional $300,000 to the endowment fund.

In 1889, the institution attained its full stature as a college, and its first Senior class was graduated in May the following year. The courses are those of the standard American college, to which are added required instruction in Christianity and a course in Swedish, both of which were part of the curriculum from the earliest days. The college graduates have long had access to the universities on the credits earned, and for more than fifteen years Gustavus Adolphus has had its place on the accredited list of colleges and secondary schools in the North Central Association.

The first department established was the Academy, a department of four classes, preparatory to college. In 1887 a commercial school was added, which was maintained for thirty-five years and discontinued in 1922. The same year was added a school of music, which is still part of the institution. Teacher training was a function of the school from the beginning, but a standardized normal department was not established until 1893. Through its various departments, the institution at St. Peter offers opportunities for study afforded only by the best equipped of the independent colleges.

The student attendance had a very conservative growth. The school was coeducational from the first. Beginning with eleven students, it had only 57 in 1874, and not until 1880 were there 100 students. In 1887, the number reached 200; in 1899, it exceeded 300, and in 1922 it was 455, a number not exceeded until recent years.

When, at its seventy-fifth anniversary in 1937, Gustavus Adolphus looked over its records, it found 3,488 names on its roll of graduates. Included were 1,791 from the College, 882 from the Academy, 731 from the commercial school, and 84 from the school of music. As a church college for the education of pastors and teachers, the school had kept faith with its founders as evidenced, in the first place, by the fact that, of its alumni, 250 had become ministers of the Gospel and missionaries, and 479 teachers in our public schools. During the seventy-five years a total of 10,228 had been enrolled. The highest enrollment, 692, was in 1930–31, when the college department had 487 students, and the Senior class numbered 108 graduates.

The seventy-fifth anniversary celebrated in connection with the convocation in June, 1937, was the occasion for a roll call of former students and of alumni of note, a number of whom were guests of honor at their Alma Mater. Among them were Col. J. A. Lundeen of Washington, D.C., now eighty-nine, who studied at St. Ansgar's in East Union in 1864, and whose service in the United States Army dates back sixty-nine years. Another distinguished visitor, and early student, was Andrew Holt, now eighty-five, and senior Judge of the Supreme Court of Minnesota. One of the alumni present was Dr. Carl E. Seashore, noted psychologist and Dean-emeritus at the Graduate College of the University of Iowa. Another Gustavian alumnus, Henry N. Benson, former attorney-general of Minnesota, made one of the historical addresses of the occasion. In a way, the College honored its first student, Reverend J. Magny, in conferring the degree of LL.D. on his son, Judge Clarence R. Magney. It should be noted further that two governors of the State of Minnesota were educated at this institution. John Lind was a student during the Carver period, and A. Olson Eberhart was graduated with the class of 1895.

The veteran of the faculty is Dr. J. P. Uhler, who came to the institution fifty-five years ago, and has taught more than ten student generations.

The nucleus of the college library was a little collection of books bequeathed by A. Engholm, a student. H. L. Smith of Columbia College, New York City, in 1889 donated 1,700 volumes, and in 1909 the book collections of two pastors, Dr. P. J. Swärd and Dr. P. Sjöblom, were obtained as gifts. By 1920, the library contained 15,000 bound volumes and 7,000 pamphlets. More recent additions, by gift and by purchase, have greatly enlarged these collections, so that new housing facilities are needed. A fund of $600,000 for the erection and endowment of a new library building is sought by the Alumni Association. The student body of Gustavus Adolphus College averages 80 per cent of Swedish descent and 90 per cent Lutherans, giving it the highest Swedish Lutheran constituency of the five colleges of the Augustana Synod.

Bethany College

WHILE all the other Swedish-American colleges came into being by decision of church bodies or groups, Bethany College was virtually founded by one man—the young and enterprising pastor of Bethany Church at Lindsborg, Kansas, Carl Aaron Swensson. When the proposition was first put by him, in 1881, to pastors of the Smoky Hill District of the Kansas Conference, they wished him God's blessing in the undertaking, but assumed no responsibility. The only material support in sight was a decision of December 30, 1879, by his congregation, setting aside the proceeds from the sale of lots "one half as a fund for a local Lutheran school, the other half as a church building fund."

The day set for opening the new school was October 15, and J. A. Udden, a recent graduate from Augustana, was on hand as an instructor, but when Swensson appeared in the schoolroom of the church, prepared to welcome them, no students had arrived. In spite of the discouraging start, the first year's attendance reached twenty-seven. Swensson taught Christianity, Udden all the rest of the curriculum, and the school managed on less than $300 the first year.

A tract of land was turned over by the Church in 1882 as a site for "the Bethany high school, provided it be located there when duly organized," and a renovated schoolhouse, moved to this site, was in readiness for the second year. Seeing the enterprise thus launched as Bethany Academy, the Smoky Hill churches that summer pledged their united support, and chose a board of directors, who later, by incorporation under charter, formally adopted the institution as their own. The year brought the number of students up to ninety-two, necessitating two additional instructors. One of these was Reverend E. Nelander, who was made head of the school and served as such for seven

years. Larger quarters were needed, and a new building was
erected, which was dedicated at a Luther festival held in October, 1883, commemorating the quadricentenary of the birth of
Martin Luther.

In 1884, the Kansas Conference adopted, as its own, two new
schools, Bethany Academy and Luther Academy. The latter,
just founded at Wahoo, Nebraska, was taken over by the Nebraska Conference, while the former has, to the present time,
remained the educational institution of the Kansas Conference.

The function of the school from its inception was largely to
train parish schoolteachers, and when, in 1885, four-year
courses for public schoolteachers were added, the name Bethany
Normal Institute was adopted. The housing then proved inadequate, but the matter was remedied the same year, and in
January, 1886, the school moved into its newly erected main
building.

The growth of Bethany into a complete college began when,
in the fall of that year, a Freshman class was added. The school
was then chartered as Bethany College and Normal Institute,
and in 1891 its first college class was graduated with the degrees of Bachelor of Arts. One of its members, Ernst F. Pihlblad, was destined to succeed the founder, Dr. Swensson, as
head of the institution. An educational plan of wide scope was
Swensson's ideal, and by 1888 Bethany was offering instruction in six general departments, academy, normal, college, music, business, and sloyd.

While Bethany was gaining a place of importance among
educational institutions in the Middle West, its musical activities gave the school its national reputation, and carried its name
abroad. This high repute is sustained by three factors, the
Messiah Chorus, the large conservatory of music, and the college orchestra. From a small beginning in 1882, when *The Messiah* of Händel was first sung on the Kansas prairies, at the
instance of Swensson and by the inspiration and aid of Professor Olof Olsson and an orchestra from Augustana College,
the Messiah Chorus of Lindsborg grew into a permanent community organization of some five hundred singers. People come
from near and far to attend the annual Easter-week music fes-

CARL AARON SWENSSON, 1857–1904

FOUNDER OF BETHANY COLLEGE, KANSAS

tivals, at which the foremost singers deem it a privilege to appear in the solo parts. Conductors have been teachers of the conservatory, Mrs. Carl Swensson directing during the first years, and more recently Professor Hagbard Brase. Recitals by visiting artists, orchestra concerts, and tournaments of highschool glee clubs and bands are features of this music festival.

A school of art was established in 1890, headed by Olof Grafström, landscape painter, who took charge of a similar department at Augustana College in 1897. Grafström was succeeded by other artists, chief of whom is Birger Sandzén, who found his theme in the Rockies, the Grand Canyon, and other scenes of the Great West. All these motifs he has done with titanic power and gorgeous color, in a manner all his own. His canvases have found their way into the principal galleries of America and Europe. His name now attracts other American artists to the art exhibits, arranged by him annually, at Bethany. Dr. Sandzén succeeds the late Lorado Taft as honorary president of Delta Phi Delta, the national art fraternity.

Swensson had implicit faith in the future of the institution he had founded. To maintain it and carry it through difficult periods, now of drought and crop failure in the area from which it drew its support, now of general financial crises, called for all the energy, resourcefulness, faith, and vision that characterized this man. As chairman of the board from the outset, and as President of the school from 1889, when Nelander resigned, until his death in 1904, Swensson was at all times the driving force back of the institution. The enrollment would often exceed its capacity, running close to a thousand, but he would somehow find ways and means. His great friend, C. A. Smith, timber magnate, helped him build an auditorium to hold the great *Messiah* concert audiences, and befriended the institution in other ways. W. W. Thomas, American Envoy to Sweden, was another good friend of his, and, as a gift from him, the Swedish pavilion, at the Louisiana Purchase Exposition in St. Louis, was removed to Bethany College in 1905.

Swensson was a man of brilliant mind and dynamic personality. As educator, preacher, forensic speaker, and author, he did a prodigious amount of work in a brief span of life—less than forty-seven years. Both as a churchman and as a citizen, he fought in the vanguard. Born and bred in America, the son of a pioneer pastor, he has been considered by many Swedish-Americans the foremost man in their second generation.

After Swensson's death, Reverend Ernst F. Pihlblad, assistant pastor of Bethany Church and Vice-President of the College, was chosen President of the institution which he still directs, faithful to the progressive policy of the man to whose memory Bethany College stands as an enduring monument. Following up preparatory work by Swensson, Mr. Pihlblad, in 1907, obtained a donation of $20,000 from Andrew Carnegie toward the erection of the college library. By persistent efforts, a substantial endowment fund has been built up. This work began in 1905, when Mr. Smith gave the impetus by promising to give to the school 100,000,000 feet of lumber, on condition that its other friends raise $100,000. The Kansas Conference began the work by wiping out a debt of more than $32,000. The value of Mr. Smith's contribution has been estimated at $25,000. The year 1906 yielded a total of more than $85,000 in donations.

The largest single gift that has come to Bethany College was a fund of $75,000 from the Presser Foundation, for the erection of a building dedicated to the musical art. This made it possible to build Presser Hall, which contains music studios and an auditorium for the *Messiah* concerts, said to hold about three thousand persons. This structure, completed in 1929, is looked upon as high recognition and fine encouragement of Bethany and Lindsborg as a musical center.

The first notable donation to the college library was made by P. T. Berg, a Swedish engineer of Pittsburgh, who gave a collection of Swedish literature, numbering one thousand volumes. The Carnegie Library at Bethany is now a well-stocked college library. The museum was started by the first teacher, J. A. Udden, who early became interested in scientific investigation. His first valuable contribution to science was a discovery made in the Equus beds of McPherson County, Kansas—the skull of a prehistoric animal differing from any other of which remains had been unearthed. Two similar skulls have since been found, neither one in so good a state of preservation. It was named *Megalonyx leidyi,* by Dr. Josua Lindahl. The specimen remains the prized treasure of the museum. Among Udden's ethnographic finds were numerous Indian relics from an old Indian village at Paint Creek, five miles from Lindsborg, several of its fifteen burial mounds having been explored by him. In one of the graves was found a section of steel-chain mail, supposedly taken from one of the fallen warriors of Coronado, the Spanish conquistador.

Bethany is classed with the fully accredited American colleges.

Upsala College

THE people of the Augustana Synod scattered throughout the Eastern States were too far removed to take advantage of the synodical schools in the Middle West. About 1887 they began to sense the need of a Christian college in their own territory, and five years later definite action was taken. A committee was then authorized by the New York Conference to set a time and place for opening a school of higher learning. This they did in 1893, locating it in Brooklyn, fixing the time for October, and naming the institution Upsala College. These decisions were made by the committee while at Rock Island, Illinois, attending a tercentenary celebration of the Council of Uppsala in 1593, and the name chosen seemed appropriate, both to the occasion and to the purpose the school was to serve, as a Lutheran institution of learning.

On October 3, 1893, the school opened in temporary quarters, room being provided in the Bethlehem Church of Brooklyn. Pastor Lars H. Beck, Ph.D. (Yale), was chosen as first instructor and headmaster. From the first, instruction was given in an academic and a music department, a commercial school being added after the fall term. There was an enrollment of thirty-six students the first year. A Freshman class was added the second year, and from 1902 the other college classes were added in regular order, completing the college department in 1905, when the Bachelor's degree was awarded to the first graduates—a class of four.

Founded in a time of general financial distress, the school was without a home for the first five years. After being housed one year in the Bethlehem Church, and the next four in a rented building belonging to St. Paul's Church, it was moved to New Orange (Kenilworth), New Jersey, in 1898, the Conference having accepted a fourteen-acre site, and the promise of a bonus of $8,000 from the New Orange Industrial Association. An old building was put into shape and used until 1900, when a proper school building was finally erected. Later, two other old buildings, purchased from the association, were remodeled into dormitories for the women and the men students. The whole transaction proved to be a real-estate promotion scheme, pure and simple. There was no community where the school was located, New Orange consisting of only a few houses and some buildings put up as decoys by the association, which purported to start a new industrial city. The board had not taken care to have the contract signed by the "donors" before the school was moved there, and soon found itself involved with a concern that did not respect its agreements. When a new realty company succeeded the former concern and changed the name of the place to Kenilworth, conditions only grew worse. The school lost its meager income from the sale of lots, and the support derived from the churches was small. As early as 1904, the search for a new home for the school was begun again, but for twenty years it remained in its unfortunate location. While the board struggled with financial difficulties, and the Conference debated, Dr. Beck and his coworkers kept the school going. It was largely by private efforts that means and equipment for carrying on regular college work were obtained.

Dr. Beck resigned his position in 1910, resuming pastoral work, and in 1912 Reverend Peter Froeberg was elected. That same year part of the churches organized themselves into the New England Conference, which has continued in support and control of the school conjointly with the mother conference. The new president set out to wipe out a debt of $30,000 and succeeded in raising $23,000 in two years.

We read in a report on the College, made in 1898, that

"Providence had evidently decreed that it should be located in New Orange." Despite the high hopes of its sponsors, the school did not prosper there. In its twentieth year it had eighty-nine students—a small enough gain over the first year. In 1917, overtures were made to induce removal to Worcester, Massachusetts, and other localities, also, were proposed as more favorable. After six strenuous years of effort at building up the school, Froeberg gave up the attempt, resigning in 1918 and leaving shortly after the opening of the fall term. The administration was left to Dean Frans Ericsson for the next two scholastic years.

In 1920 Reverend C. G. Erickson, Ph.D. (Yale), was elected President. He found a school plant with equipment valued at $62,000. In Kenilworth the school had no future, and he prevailed on the two conferences to authorize its location elsewhere. In a campaign for funds, carried on for two years, more than $445,000 was pledged. A favorable location was found in East Orange, a prosperous community, where properties, aggregating twenty-eight acres and comprising three large adjacent residences, were purchased for $228,000 out of the development fund. In the fall of 1924, the school opened in its new location. The buildings were remodeled for their new uses, and others were added. The first year in East Orange showed an enrollment of 203, more than double that of the year before. Readjustments were made; the curriculum was arranged to conform to the best educational standards, and, in 1925, the academy was separated from the College, which added one class each year in accordance with demands placed on colleges that expect full recognition. In another year the student attendance reached 300, almost the limit of the school's capacity. In 1926 Upsala was admitted to membership in the Middle States Association, the accrediting agency of that area, while the American Association of Colleges and Universities gave it qualified recognition, the conditions to be removed, when a better library and more scientific equipment should be acquired and the debts wiped out. In 1928 the enrollment reached 300 in the College alone, and the academic department was discontinued.

A proposal to erect a $300,000 classroom building fell through when, in 1930, the conferences refused to underwrite bonds for financing the project. Although the income from churches shrank, and fewer students were sent to their church college than before, the institution went through the depression years without retrenching or curtailing its work, due to the influx of students from neighboring communities. For $25,000 several acres were added to the campus in 1934, and a large building on the premises was remodeled into a library and administration quarters. The pressure on classroom facilities was thereby relieved, so that 344 students were accommodated that year, and 400 the next—the record enrollment.

The library now had 15,000 bound volumes, having been augmented by purchases and a number of donated collections, 1,000 volumes from Dr. Sven Gustaf Youngert of Augustana Seminary being among those of greatest value.

A new feature at Upsala is the adult school, opened in the fall of 1936, offering short noncredit courses in a great variety of subjects. In the first year, no less than 600 persons from near-by communities, enrolled in fifteen courses, availed themselves of this opportunity for selective study.

Dr. Erickson died in 1936, his energy and interest in behalf of Upsala College having in no way abated, although some of his aims had not been attained. The institution made remarkable progress under his direction. In 1935, an investigation for the Middle States Association of Colleges found the teaching force at Upsala well qualified, even above the average, for colleges of its size; the courses up to a fair standard; laboratories adequate; library ample and well arranged; and full approval was granted with the understanding that the college would be reëxamined two years later when its financial position was expected to have been strengthened. Dr. Erickson's ambition was to remove the handicap resulting from lack of funds and to win for his school unqualified accreditation as a Christian college of standard American type. Again Dean Frans Ericsson was made acting President, and he still serves.

For the year 1936–37, the College had an enrollment of 402, the school of music, 38. Upsala has no other regular department. The faculty numbered 29 professors and instructors, 18 of whom are full-time teachers. The College plant is valued at $450,000.

Luther College

THREE early pastors of Swedish Lutheran churches in Nebraska, E. A. Fogelström, J. Torell, and J. E. Nordling, discussed the project of a religious elementary school as early as 1880, little more than ten years after the first church of the group had been established at Omaha. This led to action in 1883, when subscriptions were solicited at public meetings in the various churches. The first was at Swedeburg, where about $2,000 was pledged—John Olson, a farmer, subscribing the first $200. The Mead and Malmo churches each raised a somewhat smaller amount, and the citizens of Wahoo pledged $3,400 and ten acres of land, the gift of a Mrs. DeFoe of Utica, New York, to the school, if located there. Of three towns contending for the school, Wahoo was selected. Articles of incorporation were signed March 28. Work was shortly begun on a building, and the school was opened in October, 1883, with Reverend Martin Noyd as principal. The name chosen was Luther Academy, and the first building was dedicated November 10, the four hundredth anniversary of Luther's birth. Five students were present at the first recitation, but the number grew to thirty-five during the first term.

In 1886 the first graduation took place, the class numbering nine members. After serving three years as rector of the school, Noyd resigned at the end of that year, and was succeeded by Professor S. M. Hill, who had taught under him since 1884. Hill served as President until 1902, when he was succeeded by Reverend O. J. Johnson; but he remained to teach another sixteen years.

The first building was designed as the south wing of a larger structure, which was never completed, and for almost twenty years the school was crowded for room. A combined ladies' hall and rectory (now serving as music hall) was built in 1885. With President Johnson in charge, it entered on a period of outward expansion and inner development. A new building was decided upon by the Nebraska Conference, and in 1903 the present main building was erected at a cost of $25,000, the funds having been solicited by the President. The West Hall, built in 1892 as a girls' dormitory, was much enlarged in 1905, and then served as a boys' dormitory and refectory.

A business course, started in 1886, developed into a school of business in the course of years. Music was taught by Professor Hill as the beginning of the departments of music and art, established about 1893. The normal department was enlarged in 1910 by the addition of a model school for observation and practical teaching. Domestic science courses were introduced the following year.

The school was accredited by the University of Nebraska in 1905. Its name was changed to Luther College in 1909, and it was admitted to membership in the North Central Association ten years later. In 1908 its normal department was authorized to grant elementary State certificates to teachers. An advanced normal course, with two years of college work for first-grade certificates, was added in 1911. After eleven years of service, Dr. Johnson left Luther College a better school than he had found it and assumed the presidency of Gustavus Adolphus College. Reverend A. T. Seashore succeeded him in 1915, Professor L. Bonander having served in the interim.

The development of the school continued under its new head. A gymnasium was built the year he came, and a rectory the year after. East Hall (girls' dormitory) and a central heating plant were completed in 1923 at a cost of approximately $100,-000. This, the costliest structure on the campus, was dedicated in September, in connection with the commemoration of the fortieth anniversary of the college.

The institution was made a complete junior college in 1925 and now includes premedical, predental, prenursing, prelaw, business administration, and arts and science courses, besides the several teachers' courses.

One of the early teachers was the late Dr. P. A. Rydberg, widely known as a botanist, later Curator of New York Botanical Gardens, and author of several scientific treatises, including one on the flora of the Rocky Mountains. A former music student at Luther College is Dr. Howard Hanson, noted composer, who has conducted symphony orchestras here and in Europe, including his own works in the repertory. He is engaged on his third symphony for the Columbia Broadcasting System, and, in 1937, was commissioned to compose a musical work to be rendered as a part of the New Sweden Tercentenary commemoration. Dr. Hanson now heads the Eastman School of Music at Rochester, New York. (See "Composers.")

Luther College has sought to safeguard its future by raising an adequate endowment, but with indifferent success. A twenty-fifth anniversary fund of $50,000 was to have been raised, but failed of completion, and as late as 1930 the endowment still fell short of that amount.

For the fiftieth anniversary in 1933 statistics were compiled, showing that 4,560 had been enrolled and 1,305 graduated. With an average communicant membership of 6,460, the Nebraska Conference had contributed $235,000 toward the maintenance of its school, and raised $211,000 for buildings and development. The attendance in recent years has been somewhat below the average enrollment of 186.

Dr. Seashore, under whom the college advanced in scholastic standing through a well ordered variety of courses, was given the honorary degree of D.D., in 1924, by both Augustana and his Alma Mater, Gustavus Adolphus College. He was taken by death February 26, 1934. Reverend Paul M. Lindberg was chosen his successor and assumed the duties of his office in 1935.

North Park College

THE Mission Covenant was organized in 1885 by congregational groups formed by followers of P. P. Waldenström about ten years before and known as Mission Friends. The idea of establishing an institution of learning for the denomination was born at its organization. The first opportunity to realize this purpose presented itself the same year, when the Chicago Theological Seminary (Congregational) agreed to open a Swedish department, to be partly under the control of the Covenant. This was done, but the arrangement did not prove entirely satisfactory, and the idea of founding a school of its own was never abandoned by the Covenant. The first step toward its realization was taken in 1891. The Covenant then resolved to take over a school conducted in Minneapolis by Reverend E. A. Skogsbergh and David Nyvall, combining theological subjects with general courses of instruction. For the next two years the school, maintained in its original location, enjoyed a measure of success, the attendance reaching 125, a number not equaled again until much later.

The affairs of the school were in sound condition; but buildings and equipment were lacking, and, when people in Chicago offered substantial means for expansion, conditioned upon removal, the school was located at North Park, Chicago, in 1894, and named North Park College, with Nyvall at the head. The institution enjoyed material development during the next few years, but meanwhile the attendance fell. In 1899, the low mark of 51 was reached, but, from that point on, there was a uniform average increase, the enrollment exceeding 200 in 1907. At that time the school comprised, besides the theological department, a complete academy, a school of music, and a commercial department.

Professor Nyvall served as President for eleven years, resigning in 1905 to head Walden College at McPherson, Kansas, and, later, to occupy the chair of Scandinavian at the University of Washington. After a seven-year administration by Professor A. W. Fredrickson, Nyvall resumed the presidency and served until 1923, when he relinquished the office, but continued to teach in the divinity school, where he still serves. Nyvall is a New Testament scholar, known also as a preacher, lecturer, poet, and prose writer. Chief among the thirty-odd books and pamphlets from his hand, published in this country and in Sweden, are: *My Father's Testament* (life of Karl Johan Nyvall) ; *Seek Ye the Kingdom;* a trilogy entitled *Via Dolorosa —Via Vitalis—Via Regia;* and *Woodland Trills*, a book of collected poems.

The junior-college classes were added in 1902, but later discontinued, not to be reëstablished until 1919. That year marks the beginning of a new period of development. A campaign for funds, completed in 1924, brought in $300,000 for endowment purposes, and additional funds for buildings and equipment. In its fortieth year the institution enjoyed an annual revenue of about $50,000, approximately half of which was in freewill contributions from the 324 churches then comprising the Covenant. The physical property of the institution is now valued at half a million dollars, and is free of encumbrance. It comprises a campus of eight acres and seven buildings, including the original building erected in 1893, the men's dormitory (1901), the gymnasium (auditorium) building (1916), the conservatory of music, and the women's dormitory, known as Caroline Hall (1925). Twenty acres of leased ground are used as an athletic field. During the present scholastic year a new classroom and auditorium building is to be erected. This will vacate rooms needed for the extension of the library—in both contents and facilities. It now contains 11,000 bound volumes, 1,500 pamphlets, and about 100 files of periodicals.

At the head of the institution stands Reverend Algoth Ohlson, elected in 1924 when Nyvall retired and was made President-emeritus. The teaching staff numbers more than seventy, forty-five being regular teachers and members of the faculties. Notable among its teachers in the past were Reverend Axel Mellander, who taught Old Testament for twenty-seven years; J. A. Hultman, Gospel singer; and Gustaf Holmquist, distinguished baritone and oratorio singer. Both Hultman and Holmquist taught in the school of music, which now has on its faculty Ebba Sundstrom, directress of the Woman's Symphony Orchestra of Chicago. Among the alumni are: Dr. Knute E. Carlson, economist with the Department of the Interior, for more than twenty years; Dr. William Fredrickson, professor of physics at Syracuse University; J. A. Liljengren and Frithiof Peterson (Röl Gording), novelists and short-story writers; and Reverend Fredrich E. Pamp, translator of works by Nathan Söderblom.

At the present time the institution comprises four main divisions: the junior college; the academy, corresponding to four-year high school; the divinity school, including seminary and Bible institute, and the school of music. The academy, which in most other places has had to yield to the public high school, has stood its ground at North Park. A department not common to colleges is a two-year terminal course in the graphic arts, acquainting students with the art of printing in all its branches. The college has also just introduced the so-called work-study plan, a coöperative system of education originated at the University of Cincinnati in 1906, and now followed in upwards of fifty universities and colleges. It bridges over the gap between school and work, allowing the student half the year to put into practice, in actual employment, the knowledge and skill acquired during the previous term, the workers and the students changing places in February and August.

During the past year the attendance by sessions, including evening and summer schools, was 1,568. The teaching staff numbered 73, of whom 45 were full-time professors and instructors. The enrollment by departments was: junior college, 901; academy, 444; seminary and Bible institute, 153; school of music, 355; making North Park proportionately the best attended of the six Swedish-American colleges.

Bibliography

THE AUGUSTANA SYNOD, 1860–1910. Rock Island, 1910.

AUGUSTANA, 1873.

AUGUSTANA ALUMNI REGISTER. Rock Island, 1924.

MINNEN FRÅN JUBELFESTEN, 1910. Rock Island, 1911.

MINNESSKRIFT. Rock Island, 1910.

LUND, EMIL. Minnesota-konferensens och dess församlingars historia. Rock Island, 1926.

SANDAHL, CHARLES FREDRICK. The Nebraska Conference: Survey of Its Work. Rock Island, 1931.

OLSON, ERNST W. History of the Swedes of Illinois. Chicago, 1908.

BERGIN, ALFRED. Lindsborg. Lindsborg, Kansas, 1909.

SVENSKARNA I AMERIKA, II. Stockholm, 1925.

NELSON, A. P. Svenska Missionsvännernas i Amerika historia. Minneapolis, 1905.

COLLEGE CATALOGS and BULLETINS.

MINUTES OF THE AUGUSTANA SYNOD AND ITS CONFERENCES.

Newspapers

OLIVER A. LINDER

Mr. Linder is one of the veterans of the Swedish-American press. Born in Skåne in 1862, he came to America in 1880, and served as city editor of *Svenska Amerikanaren,* Chicago, from 1892 to 1908, when he was appointed Editor-in-chief. He is the author of poems, short stories, and humorous essays in Swedish, and has contributed many articles to the Swedish encyclopædia, *Nordisk familjebok,* on Swedish-American subjects. He retired from his newspaper work in 1936.

IT has been said by someone who has studied deeply the complex social phenomena that, in the process of lifting civilization the world over, during the last century, to its present status, one of the mightiest levers has been the press. It has not only furnished the impetus, but it has ever been the steadying force. Without its help, much of the efforts of other forces would have been of small avail.

If this be true anywhere, it must be particularly acknowledged as a gratifying fact in relation to this country. The newspapers of the United States have, from the earliest date, exerted a tremendous influence for good. The few exceptions count for little. The blessings of a free press cannot be overestimated. Even more, it can be said, in all truth, that its activities have in the greatest measure been praiseworthily motivated.

In a country like America, where the population is not racially homogeneous, there was bound to appear in it certain foreign characteristics which, if left alone, might have become more or less disturbing. That this danger—if we call it so—has been reduced to a minimum, causing no real worries, is to a great extent due to the good influence of the foreign-language press; for the English-language newspapers could hardly have reached the danger spots, if aware of them at all. It is, therefore, something to be concerned about, when this good influence of the foreign-language press is belittled, as has been done occasionally, and even blindly accused of fostering un-American tendencies.

As a general proposition, the existence of a foreign-language press within the borders of a nation seems somewhat of an anomaly, or even worse—at all events, something to be resented. But, in the case of the United States of America, it takes on the nature of a highly beneficent auxiliary to the English-language newspapers; inasmuch as the foreign-language press steps in and does the work which the English-language medium, for obvious reasons, is kept from doing. On this account, there have never been any conflicts between the two; and they have all the while lived in peace and agreement, side by side. There is not an analogous situation to be found anywhere else on this globe.

Among the many foreign nationalities in America, there is not one that can point to a press more able and more honest than the Swedish-American. Its influence for the betterment of the Swedish-born population in the United States has been of the most wholesome character. With two or three insignificant exceptions, there have been among the many Swedish-American publications, from the earliest time to the present date, no dirt-slinging scandalmongers, no brazen radicals, and no one exercising a demoralizing influence. It is a record of which the Swedish-Americans have good reasons to be proud.

On every occasion, when it was of consequence to take sides, the Swedish-American press has wholeheartedly espoused the welfare of the country. This was particularly the case during the World War. The press was, above all, American-minded. Indeed, from its modest beginning, it has ever been one of the outstanding factors in furthering those racial modes, manners of thinking, and other traditions, which are regarded as a rightfully beneficial heritage, and which, at the same time, prepare the newcomer for his duties as an American citizen. In other words, the press has consistently, with an educative purpose in view, kept up a program of instructing its readers, both as Swedes and as Americans. This may at first seem a hopeless task, beset with a thousand troubles and conflicting aims—one which it is difficult to evade and difficult to accomplish. But it is generally acknowledged that the efforts of the press have been very successful. It has intended to make the young immigrant as good a citizen as possible—as soon as possible. These ends must be looked upon as imperative conditions for reaching the goal he had set up for himself, in coming to the new country. In doing this, it has not been deemed at all necessary to exclude everything that reminded him of the old country. The Swedish-American press has, at all times, urged its readers to place the highest value on their cultural heritage. The aim has been, as the great editor, Johan A. Enander, most happily formulated it, to foster, in the soul of the Swedish-American, the right love for America as the chosen bride, while not crushing out the natural love for Sweden as the dear old mother.

In passing, it will not be amiss to cite here a few lines written by the well-known journalist and author, Johan Person: "When one wishes to measure the cultural standing of a people, the best measuring-sticks are the schools and the newspapers. The Swedish-Americans, mostly poor immigrants in the beginning, without higher education, have made themselves possessors of both." It can also be pointed out, statistically, that there is only one other of the many groups of foreign nationalities in America which has proportionately as many naturalized citizens as the Swedish-Americans. And to the press, certainly, we owe due acknowledgment for the invaluable help rendered in obtaining this result.

As has been the case with all the foreign nationalities in this country, the earliest attempts to foster a Swedish-American press were, in general, inspired by some form of denominational fervor. There were psychological as well as sociological reasons for this. The earliest Swedish-American papers, therefore, were not newspapers in the commonly accepted meaning of the term. They were, far into the 'sixties, out and out denominational organs. Their influence for good, however, was much wider than is ordinarily expected in strictly religious publications.

But the *very* first newspaper in the Swedish language had no religious color; rather, the opposite. The name of it was *Skandinaven*, and it was issued weekly from New York City, during the years 1851–53—not regularly, but only when the publisher was able to scrape together enough money to pay for printing, paper, etc. It contained four pages, 13.8 by 8.8 inches in size. The publisher's name was A. G. Öbom, and he was also the editor and typesetter. He was considered a very erratic person, who really did not prove any good intentions by his publication.

He certainly did not exert himself much in behalf of his countrymen. His irate temper and whimsical vanity were, more often than not, the only incentive for him to write about them or their interests.

The real beginning of the press was the establishing of *Det Gamla och det Nya Hemlandet*, 1855, in Galesburg, Illinois. It was a small affair of only four pages, 10 by 14 inches in size, and the subscription price was $2 a year. *Hemlandet*, as the paper was generally called for short, through the sixty years of its existence, had for a time no secular program, but contained, mostly, family reading matter of a devotional nature. The Editor for a time was Reverend T. N. Hasselquist, a man with a noble but, at the same time, aggressive character, who was later to become perhaps the most important figure among the Swedish-Americans of the Lutheran confession, being one of the founders of the Augustana Synod, and builder-up of the Augustana College and Theological Seminary.

At the end of the first six months *Hemlandet* counted 400 subscribers, and, after a year's time, the number had grown to over 1,000, which we must consider a remarkable success, in view of the fact that, in those days, there were no facilities whatever for subscription campaigns. The members of the Swedish Lutheran congregations, then organized in Illinois and Iowa, were practically the only potential subscribers. As the entire Swedish-born population in the States mentioned at this time was not above 1,500, it can readily be seen that the job of circulation manager was not an easy one, and that only a conjurer could succeed at it. Also, on account of its Lutheran proclivities, *Hemlandet* could not count on getting readers among the Jansonists, the Methodists, or the Baptists, but was compelled to depend solely on the Swedish Lutherans for support. After the removal of the paper to Chicago, in 1859, it had a hard struggle to make both ends meet. There were many secular, as well as religious, competitors started from time to time in the constantly widening field.

In 1869, Johan Alfred Enander became Editor of *Hemlandet*. He was a man of strong convictions, well educated and high-spirited. Under his leadership, the paper grew amazingly in popularity, and it was, undoubtedly, for many years the most ably edited Swedish paper in America. It was later to meet strong competitors under adverse conditions, and finally, in 1914, was merged with one of them. As an organ for the Lutheran Synod, *Hemlandet* had, in 1868, been followed by *Augustana*, which still exists and is published in Rock Island, Illinois.

Sändebudet, the organ of the Swedish Methodists, was started in 1862, and is still issued. These two publications—*Augustana* and *Sändebudet*—are now the only survivors from the early days in the religious field. The Swedish Baptists did not get a regular publication until 1871, when *Zions Väktare* was started. Eventually it changed its name to *Nya Veckoposten*, now out of the race. The present official organ is *Svenska Standaret*, published in Chicago. The Mission Covenant has two journalistic organs, *Missionsvännen*, founded in 1874, and *Chicago-Bladet*, which started publication three years later.

Ever since the middle of the nineteenth century, when Swedish immigrants began to flock to this country, Chicago has been looked upon as a kind of metropolis for them, being centrally located, in regard to most of the Swedish settlements then existing. Also, there have always been more Swedish-born residents in Chicago than in any other city in America. Therefore, it was only to be expected that Chicago should be picked as the publication place of a newspaper that would pay attention to something more than local affairs. And Chicago naturally became the center, so to speak, of the Swedish-American newspaper-publishing business—a position it holds to this day.

It would serve no purpose to give a detailed list of the many publications in the Swedish language, that have sprung up in Chicago since 1860. But we shall give a few figures to prove that it has been the favorite city of Swedish-American publishers. About twenty-five weekly political newspapers have been started there, some hardly more than started. Of all these, only one remains. As late as 1914, Chicago had four Swedish weeklies with a secular program: *Hemlandet, Svenska Tribunen Nyheter, Svenska Kuriren,* and *Svenska Amerikanaren,* all of them seemingly doing well, with an aggregate of about 100,000 subscribers. The four papers named are now merged into one, *Svenska Amerikanaren Tribunen*, which has thus acquired the largest subscription list ever attained by a Swedish-American paper.

Chicago has had not less than ten humorous papers, all of which have succumbed. Two dailies were started in the 'nineties. One of these continued for nine months, in vain attempts to gain a foothold; the other one lasted only two weeks.

Below, we give a list of cities, from which at one time or another a newspaper in the Swedish language was published before the year 1910. This list possesses a certain amount of interest, because it shows that well-to-do Swedish settlements had sprung up all over the country. Each city on this list must necessarily have had a good many Swedish residents in order to give support to a newspaper, for most of these papers were local. One may also gather, from this list, that the Central States were best provided with Swedish papers, while, naturally, the fewest were found in the South. The total number, small and big, weekly and monthly, exceeded 1,000, which would be unbelievable, if proofs could not be produced. The majority consisted of small denominational monthlies. The number of weeklies with a secular program, most of them published for short periods, was about 250. The list of cities looks like this:

MICHIGAN: Ishpeming, Grand Rapids, Manistique, Manistee, Muskegon, Ironwood, Escanaba, Iron Mountain, Cadillac, Menominee, Calumet.

MINNESOTA: Red Wing, Cambridge, St. Paul, Duluth, Grove City, Minneapolis, Litchfield, Lindstrom, Stillwater, St. Peter.

ILLINOIS: Chicago, Rockford, Rock Island, Batavia, Moline, Galesburg, Galva, Paxton.

NEBRASKA: Kearney, Stromsburg, Omaha, Wahoo, Lincoln, Oakland, Holdredge.

IOWA: Sioux City, Burlington, Boone, Des Moines, Cedar Rapids, Sheldon.

CONNECTICUT: New Haven, Hartford, New Britain, Bridgeport.

WISCONSIN: Superior, Ashland, Marinette, Rhinelander, Grantsburg.

CALIFORNIA: San Francisco, Oakland, Los Angeles, Eureka.

NEW YORK: New York City, Brooklyn, Jamestown.

PENNSYLVANIA: Braddock, McKeesport, Philadelphia.

WASHINGTON: Seattle, Tacoma, Spokane, Bellingham.
MASSACHUSETTS: Boston, Worcester.
KANSAS: Lindsborg, Topeka, Salina.
TEXAS: Austin, Hutto, Georgetown.
MISSOURI: Kansas City.
UTAH: Salt Lake City.
COLORADO: Denver.
OREGON: Portland, Astoria.
MONTANA: Helena.
OHIO: Cleveland.
NEW JERSEY: Passaic.
INDIANA: South Bend.
IDAHO: Idaho Falls.
ALABAMA: Silver Hill.
RHODE ISLAND: Providence.
SOUTH DAKOTA: Sioux Falls.
NORTH DAKOTA: Fargo.

It is generally admitted that the Swedish-American press enjoyed its heyday of success during the first twenty-five years of the present century. The Swedes, being a hardworking and thrifty class, earned good incomes, and to their number were yearly added, roughly, 15,000 newcomers. Any great falling off in the total Swedish-born population, by deaths among the earlier settlers, had not as yet appeared. And the newcomer could, of course, always be counted on to subscribe to one or two papers in his own language.

It was conceded at one time that out of the nearly 650,000 Swedish-born inhabitants in America, about 250,000 were subscribers to a Swedish-language paper. The largest subscription list ever attained by a Swedish-American paper was 80,000. The nearest competitor had about 70,000 subscribers. It may also be of interest to know that each one of these two topnotchers sent from 10,000 to 12,000 copies to subscribers in Sweden.

A decrease in the number of immigrants was caused by the quota law; and then came the depression years. With the influx of immigrants nearly shut off, the total number of Swedish-born residents has naturally fallen off somewhat from deaths, and the result is apparent in the discontinuance of many papers, and in the reduced sizes of the subscribers' lists of those remaining. Between 1920 and 1930, the number of Swedish-born in the United States fell from 625,000 to 595,000.

In regard to its political affiliations, the Swedish-American press has never consisted of slavish organs, while it must be conceded that the papers have been more often Republican than Democratic. They were predominantly progressive with Theodore Roosevelt. Very few of them have proclaimed Socialistic views, and then only of a mild sort.

The fact that the immigrant Swede, perhaps of all newcomers, is the first one to Americanize himself, and acquire a knowledge of the English language, relieves the Swedish-American newspaper of having to serve their readers with all the news of the world; for they get this from the English-language papers, which they are eager to read. But what they get in their own paper is what they can get nowhere else; namely, a summary of events in the old country. Each province gets its own quota of news. And then there is a page or two devoted to the Swedish-Americans—news gathered from all sources—thus putting the reader in a sort of contact with his countrymen here. Therefore, when he reads about their successes, their commendable deeds in one field or another, their patriotism and rise in the estimation of their neighbors, it acts upon him as an urge: Go thou and do likewise.

A detailed story of the development of the Swedish-American press, with its successes and its failures, would perhaps be interesting enough, but it would take up too much space in a volume of this kind. So we have to forego the pleasure of writing it. Of each one of the larger papers, a vivid story could be told. This is especially true of such veteran publications as *Nordstjernan, Svea, Svenska Amerikanaren Tribunen, Svenska Amerikanska Posten,* and *Vestkusten.*

In the service of the Swedish-American press, there have been engaged from the earliest time to the present a great many gifted and sturdy men, who have given their best in fulfilling their duties. Some of these have been fine writers who have acquired a lasting reputation, as authors and poets as well as journalists. Of those that have passed on, we may name a few:

A. A. Anderson; Vilhelm Berger; Aron Edström; Magnus Elmblad; Carlos Goldhuhl; Leonard Gyllenhaal; C. G. Linderborg; F. W. Lönegren; Magnus Lunnow; C. F. Peterson; Herman Roos; Anders Schön; Herman Stockenström; and Ernst Skarstedt. And among those who are still working, with a will to serve their papers, we may mention L. G. Abrahamson; E. Einar Andersson; J. O. Backlund; Daniel Birgers; Jakob Bonggren; Nils F-son Brown; Einar O. Enard; C. George Ericson; Harry F-son Fabbe; K. G. Fredin; O. Gullmes; Alfred Haij; Axel Hedberg; G. F. Hedstrand; Otto Hogfeldt; Charles K. Johansen; Otto Knape; Karl Knudson; C. J. Larson; F. A. Larson; C. E. Lindstone; Esse W. Ljungh; Frithiof Malmquist; Emil Meurling; Alexander Olson; E. V. Olson; Enoch Peterson; Ivar Peterson; Gerhard T. Rooth; Edgar Swenson; Andrew Tofft; Nelson T. Thorson; Anton M. Trulson; and Gunnar Wickman.

American Publications in Swedish, 1938

Augustana, 639 Thirty-eighth Street, Rock Island, Ill.

Missionstidningen California, 247 West Main Street, Turlock, Calif.

California Veckoblad, 1421 West Pico Street, Los Angeles, Calif.

Chicago Bladet, 4211 North Hermitage Avenue, Chicago, Ill.

Förbundets Veckotidning, 1005 Belmont Avenue, Chicago, Ill.

Kvinnan och Hemmet, 400 South First Street East, Cedar Rapids, Iowa.

Ledstjärnan, 234 East Ash Street, Ironwood, Mich.

Minnesota Stats Tidning, Fourth Street and Broadway, St. Paul, Minn.

Missionsposten, 915 North Lavergne Avenue, Chicago, Ill.

Missions Tidning, 3906 Seventh Avenue, Rock Island, Ill.

Missions-Vännen, 365 West Chicago Avenue, Chicago, Ill.

Monitor, 6 West Second Street, Jamestown, N.Y.

Musiktidning, 216 Institute Place, Chicago, Ill.

Norden, 4314 Eighth Avenue, Brooklyn, N.Y.

Nordstjernan, 108 Park Row, New York City.

Omaha Posten, 306 South Nineteenth Street, Omaha, Neb.

Sions Väktare, Brookfield, Ill.

Skandia, 16 West Second Street, Jamestown, N.Y.

Svea, 311 Main Street, Worcester, Mass.

Svenska Amerikanaren Tribunen, 208 North Wells Street, Chicago, Ill.

Svenska Amerikanska Posten, 309 South Sixth Street, Minneapolis, Minn.

Svenska Monitoren, 420 Jones Street, Sioux City, Iowa.

Svenska Pacific Tribunen, 1213 First Avenue, Seattle, Wash.

Svenska Posten, 1632 Eighth Avenue, Seattle, Wash.

Svenska Pressen, 130 Second Avenue, Spokane, Wash.

Svenska Standaret, 912 Belmont Avenue, Chicago, Ill.

Sändebudet, 740 Rush Street, Chicago, Ill.

Texas Posten, 910 Brazos Street, Austin, Texas.

Vasastjärnan, 1661 Hollywood Avenue, Chicago, Ill.

Vestkusten, 253 Church Street, San Francisco, Calif.

Vikingen, 404 North Wesley Avenue, Mount Morris, Ill.

Westerns Nyheter, 1405 Lawrence Street, Denver, Colo.

Canadian Publications in Swedish

Canada Posten, 396 Logan Avenue, Winnipeg, Man.

Canada Tidningen, 325 Logan Avenue, Winnipeg, Man.

Nya Svenska Pressen, 144 W. Hastings Street, Vancouver, B.C.

Writers in Swedish

JOSEPH E. A. ALEXIS

For biographical notes on the Author, see the chapter on "Professors."

WHEN, at the middle of the nineteenth century, an ever-increasing stream of Swedes turned to the opportunities of the New World, the literary heritage from Sweden found expression in a new type of writing, sometimes called Swedish-American. As early as the 'eighties, the noted Swedish author, Victor Rydberg, recognized the existence of this literature. Fundamentally, it is a transplanted product, whose rapid development, from the middle of the century, was due to the fact that the authors carried with them to the New World the traditional molds, into which they poured the content of new experiences. Almost without exception, the Swedish-American authors of note were born in the Old World, and their average age, on arriving in America, was about twenty-two; so that one might well call this literary outburst, Swedish literature in America, instead of Swedish-American literature. The cultural tendencies in Sweden, as well as the trends of the American authors writing in English, all exerted their influence on the generation of writers trained in Sweden and practicing their art in the United States.

While both America and Sweden were realistic in their literary expression, the Swedish-American authors were more of the idealistic order, differing, therefore, from the general tendencies, both in Sweden and in the United States. Before the Swede left the Old World, he had been a part of the very nature of the country. His poems had been portrayals of Nature as it was. But, when this realist came to America, he found the atmosphere here to be different. He had the feeling, at times, that he was a stranger in the new land. He began to think idealistically about the old home, which he painted in glowing colors—thus getting away from reality. He lauded, even more than did the writers of Sweden, the charm of the ancestral home.

This struggle in the mind and heart of the newcomer, between the attachment to the old and the interest for the new, has been exemplified again and again in the lives of Swedish-American poets. Some there were who could not endure the separation from the old soil, and who finally returned to the fatherland. The greater number, however, remained here, finally becoming an integral part of the new nation. Still, while owing full allegiance to the land of his adoption, the newcomer could not forget old conditions; and this knowledge of two countries, and the acquaintance he had with their cultures, made him a cosmopolitan.

The literary tendencies of the Swedish-American authors were determined largely by their profession or occupation. As Swedish literature in America kept no pot boiling, the writers had to seek employment at tasks other than belles-lettres, to secure a livelihood. A large number were journalists, a fact which makes it necessary in this article to refer often to the Swedish-American press; another group was made up of clergymen; still another consisted of educators. Certain writers might well be called simply "Swedes in America," preserving, in great measure, the Swedish point of view; others, particularly of a later day, were American in their outlook on life. Incidentally, among the immigrants of the middle of the nineteenth century, only a few had enjoyed the privileges of a higher education. Persons of college training were mostly in the service of the church, under the auspices of which they founded schools, primarily for the purpose of preparing young men for the ministry, but also with a view to giving the layman a general education.

Swedish-American literature is an expression of the thoughts and aspirations of a people in the process of adaptation and assimilation, and furnishes an interesting chapter in the history of our nation. Efforts of such expression found their first outlet in the newspapers that were founded soon after the Swedish settlements had been established; and it will be the first purpose of this article to provide a few details about the writers who were actively connected with journalistic ventures. Of course, many of these authors are naturally mentioned, and some treated more fully, in other chapters of this volume, such as in those on the Swedish-American press, and on the denominational colleges and scholars. So far as the journalists are concerned, this account, therefore, will serve as a descriptive and biographical continuation of Mr. Linder's summary on the press. Obviously, it has proved impossible, even to mention all authors—Skarstedt's *Pennfäktare* speaks of several hundred of them—or all writings. Additional names will be found elsewhere in this work. The author's own selection of writers follows.

Johan Alfred Enander (1842–1910), who was on the staff of *Hemlandet* for almost four decades, was born in Skinmoen, Härja Parish, Västergötland, and came to America in 1869. During a break in his connection with *Hemlandet*, 1890–96, he was, first, professor of the Swedish language and literature at Augustana College, and, then, Editor of *Svenska Journalen* of Omaha. Enander is a good example of the journalist who contributes to Swedish-American literature. Many of his best lyrics are dedicated to the land of his adoption, but his heart always beats warmly for the old homeland. His short stories and sketches are characterized by a pure and dignified style. His mind turns with fondness to themes of the past. In his *Förenta staternas historia*, his enthusiasm for the Scandinavian contribution causes him to give more attention than they deserve to the Viking voyages. It was typical of Enander, as a public speaker, to thrill his listeners with vivid accounts of the accomplishments of his race.

Anders Schön (1864–1932), who was born at Rengsjö, in Gävleborgs län, emigrated to this country in 1889, and Aron Edström (1847–1923), born at Edstorp, Dalsland, were both associated with *Hemlandet*. For several years Schön edited the literary annual, *Prärieblomman*, to which he contributed many excellent biographies of prominent Swedish-Americans. He collaborated with Ernst W. Olson on the first eight chapters of the colossal work, *History of the Swedes of Illinois*. Aron Edström came to America at the age of twenty-two. He graduated from Augustana College in 1879 and, the following year, joined the staff of *Skaffaren*. To *Hemlandet* he gave thirty-one years of his life. Edström wrote excellent accounts of the early days of the Swedish-American settlements, which were published in *Prärieblomman* and *Ungdomsvännen*. It was in *Hemlandet*, too, that Gustaf Sjöström (1855–1912) published his amusing account of Jan Olson, which later appeared in book form. He describes the experiences of a *Värmlänning* in the New World. As a humorous lecturer, he was outstanding. Sjöström was born at Umeå and emigrated in 1887. After having been connected with *Svenska Tribunen, Vårt Land*, and *Österns Härold*, he became pastor of a Swedish Episcopal church in Chicago. He finally returned to Sweden, to hold a position in the State church.

Three editors of denominational publications deserve a passing notice. Laurentius G. Abrahamson, since 1908 the Editor of *Augustana*, was born in Västmanland in 1856, and came to America in 1868. In coöperation with Carl A. Swensson, he published, in 1893, a magnificent volume entitled *Jubelalbum*, containing numerous biographies of pastors of the Augustana Synod. William Henschen (1842–1925), a native of Uppsala, where he earned the Ph.D. degree, came to America in 1870. After working on the staff of other papers, he joined the Methodist church in 1875, and became the Editor of its organ, *Sändebudet*, which he served for a quarter of a century. His editorials were characterized by an unusual tolerance and understanding. Henschen's successor was John Emanuel Hillberg, born 1873 in Malmköping, who emigrated in 1892. He wrote a number of books on travel and religious subjects.

Eric Johnson (1838–1919), the son of the founder of the Bishop Hill colony, was born in Österunda Parish, Västmanland, and came to America with his parents, in 1846. In 1869 he started a newspaper, called the *Illinois Swede*. The following year, this name was changed to *Nya Världen*, in 1876 to *Svenska Tribunen*, in 1906 to *Svenska Tribunen-Nyheter*, and has since been absorbed by *Svenska Amerikanaren-Tribunen*. P. A. Sundelius was one of the first editors; and, among the literary men of note who have served on the staff at different times, we find C. F. Peterson, Ernst Lindblom, Konni Zilliacus, C. G. Norman, E. W. Olson, and Johan Person.

Carl Fredrik Peterson (1843–1901) was born at Fittja, Södermanland, and came to America at the beginning of the Civil War. Due to nearsightedness, he was rejected as a soldier. He worked successively at various jobs, improving every opportunity to educate himself. He joined the *Illinois Swede* in 1870, and remained with it through various vicissitudes until 1884, when he was attracted to *Svenska Amerikanaren.* He edited *Svea* in 1888–89, and, from 1890 to 1891, the Swedish daily newspaper, *Aftonbladet Skandia.* When the latter failed, Peterson turned to independent work on literary, historical, and political subjects, and wrote several books. He was of a speculative bent and ready to modify his opinions. Thus he championed at different times the principles of the Republicans, the Democrats, and the Populists.

Ernst Lindblom (1865–1925) was a native of Stockholm and emigrated in 1884. He first secured a position with *Svenska Folkets Tidning* in Minneapolis, and from 1885 to 1891 was on the staff of *Svenska Tribunen,* after which he was Editor of *Humoristen,* for a year. It was in this humorous sheet that he published every week his amusing sketches. His play, *Pelle Pihlqvists Amerika-resa,* was very successfully performed at Chicago. *På försök* is the title of a collection of his verse. Lindblom returned to Sweden and spent his last years in Stockholm.

Carl Gustaf Norman (1861–1916) was born at Tävelsås, Småland, and emigrated to America in 1879. He was in the Lutheran ministry from 1890 to 1897, when he went into newspaper work, serving *Svea,* in Worcester, Massachusetts, and *Svenska Tribunen.* His collection of poems is called *Emigrantens sånger,* a title which indicates something of the pathos characteristic of them. Konni Zilliacus (1855–1924) was born in Finland and came to Chicago in 1889. In this country he published *Amerika, Amerikas Förenta Stater,* and *Chicago.* But, as almost his whole life belonged to Finland, to which he returned, the greater number of his works appeared there.

Ernst W. Olson was born in Finja Parish, Skåne, in 1870, and came to America at the age of eight. He has been Editor of *Fosterlandet, The Young Observer* in Rock Island, *Nya Pressen* in Moline, and *Svenska Tribunen* in Chicago. From 1906 to 1911, he was editor of publications for the Engberg-Holmberg Publishing Company of Chicago; and, since then, he has served in a similar capacity for the Augustana Book Concern in Rock Island. During this latter period, he was, for a time, Editor of *Ungdomsvännen,* and of *Lutheran Companion.*

Good specimens of his poetic work are *Kantat vid Augustana-synodens 50-årsjubileum* and *Reformationskantat 1917*. Olson translates Swedish poems into English and English into Swedish with apparently equal ease. In the English language, he has written two gigantic works: *History of the Swedes of Illinois* and *The Swedish Element in Illinois*.

Connected with the newspaper, *Nordstjernan*, in New York City, at different periods, was the late Vilhelm Berger, a novelist, short-story writer, historian, and biographer. Born in Värmland in 1867, he came to America in 1896. Berger portrayed the life of the Swedish-Americans in clear outline. His accurate knowledge of his subject was seen particularly in *Svensk-amerikanska meditationer*. He died in January, 1938.

The first editor of the original *Svenska Amerikanaren* was Hans Mattson (1832–93), who was born at Önnestad, Skåne, and came to America in 1851. When the Civil War broke out, he raised a Scandinavian company and rose to the rank of colonel. Mattson wrote an autobiography entitled *Minnen*, the title of the English version being *The Story of an Emigrant*. He was Editor of *Svenska Amerikanaren* from 1866 to 1867, and was succeeded by Måns Herman Roos (1831–80), who had emigrated to America in 1864 and had, like Mattson, served in the Union Army. Roos edited the paper from 1867 to the end of 1869, when he went into different work. In 1876 he became one of the founders of *Svenska Posten*, which was changed in the following year to *Nya Svenska Amerikanaren*. Roos was the representative of the liberal Swedish press and opposed the conservative editors of the religious papers. He led the attack on the growing power of the clergy.

One of the most brilliant members of the staff of *Svenska Amerikanaren* was Magnus Henrik Elmblad (1848–88), who was born at Herrestad, Småland. Before his departure from Sweden in 1871, he had translated Ibsen's *Brand* into Swedish and had done other literary work. Elmblad was also in the service of *Hemlandet*, *Vårt Nya Hem* at Kearney, Nebraska, and *Skandia*, at Moline, Illinois. *Azilla*, in which he portrays the Indians and their desire for vengeance on the whites who had taken their land, is typical of his art. The clarity of Elmblad's style and the sublimity of his thought are always evident.

For over fifty years, Olof Jakob Bonggren has been connected with *Svenska Amerikanaren.* Born in Håbol Parish, Dalsland, in 1854, Bonggren came to America in 1882. He joined *Svenska Amerikanaren* in 1883, and his service of more than half a century on one paper is a record that no other Swedish-American has excelled. Bonggren is a poet of a high class, a literary critic, and a scholar. In 1882 he published *Förstlingar. Sånger och sagor* appeared in 1902. While his love for the land of his fathers, and for the language of his childhood, often finds expression in his poetry, he furthers, among his countrymen, a spirit faithful to American institutions.

Ernst Teofil Skarstedt (1857–1929), who was born in Solberga, Bohuslän, and emigrated to America in 1878, was also on the staff of *Svenska Amerikanaren* for a time. Employed in many different capacities during his eventful life, he was not only an editor of various newspapers but also a photographer; musician; farmer; always a collector of books; a contributor to *Valkyrian* and *Prärieblomman;* and the author of numerous volumes of poetry and prose. Through all these publications, particularly *Våra pennfäktare* and *Svensk-amerikanska folket i helg och söcken,* Skarstedt has done more than any other one man to make known, and evaluate, Swedish-American literature. His wide sympathies and thorough honesty pervade his literary work. Sincerity and impartiality are characteristic of Skarstedt the critic.

In 1888 Frans Albin Lindstrand bought *Svenska Amerikanaren.* Born at Blixthult, Östergötland, in 1847, he left for America in 1871. Lindstrand had been in the jewelry business for a number of years before he entered the journalistic field, and he soon became one of the most productive writers. He had such a simple and easy style that the masses read his articles with delight, and his *Brev från onkel Ola* made him widely known. In 1898, he published *Pennteckningar och reseskildringar,* and the following year *I öster- och vesterland.* He died in 1913. Among the prominent writers that he had on his staff were Olof Jakob Bonggren, Edwin Björkman, Oliver A. Linder, and Ninian Waerner.

Edwin Björkman was born in Stockholm in 1866. In 1891

he left for America and joined the staff of *Svenska Ameri-kanaren*, later becoming the Editor of *Minnesota-Posten* in St. Paul, and of the monthly *Freja*. As early as 1894 he began to write for the Minneapolis *Times*, and, since then, his literary work has been mainly in the English language. He has written several books of high value, and his translations of plays and novels by different authors are excellent. (See the article by Miss Olson.)

Oliver A. Linder was born in Gylle, Skåne, in 1862, and came to America in 1880. After service on different newspapers, he joined, in 1892, the staff of *Svenska Amerikanaren* for which he still writes. In 1891, Linder published *Glada grin, vers och prosa*, and in 1914 *I västerland, stycken på vers och prosa*. Linder is an optimist and a humorist, able to perceive in the distance the beginning of a better day. Fully conscious of the value of the Swedish heritage, Linder would make it serve the purpose of developing a truly American civilization.

Ninian Waerner (1856–1905) was born in Norrköping. After having studied law in Sweden, and æsthetics and violoncello in Germany, he came to America in 1884. His journalistic career in America began with the humorous paper, *Kurre*. Later he served other papers, and finally returned to Sweden, where he published *Mina hundår i Amerika*. Previously, in America, he had written *I höst- och vinterkväll, svensk-ameri-kanska dikter*, and *Pennstreck, humoresker, skizzer och berät-telser*. Waerner was by nature a humorist.

Frithiof Malmquist was born in Landskrona in 1866 and left for America in 1888. After having been Associate Editor of *Forskaren*, he secured a post with *Svenska Tribunen*, then with *Svenska Nyheter*, and finally with *Svenska Amerikanaren*. He has published a volume of poems, entitled *Törnen och tistlar*.

Svenska Folkets Tidning, in Minneapolis, was founded by Alfred Söderström in 1881. Born in Stockholm in 1848, Söderström came to America in 1869. He was an indefatigable collector of historical material and published *Minneapolis min-nen* and *Blixtar på tidningshorisonten*, works that reveal the tireless investigator. Söderström died in 1928.

Gustaf Wicklund (1852–1905) was born in Gävle and left

ERNST TEOFIL SKARSTEDT, 1857–1929

AUTHOR AND JOURNALIST

for America in 1878. In 1884, with Ninian Waerner, he became editor of *Kurre*. Four years later he obtained a position with *Svenska Folkets Tidning*. In 1891 he was again associated with Waerner on *Friskytten*, and two years later, he was the Editor of *Humoristen*, in Chicago. At the time of his death, he was on the staff of *Svenska Amerikanska Posten*. Wicklund wrote a number of successful plays, performed repeatedly, both in America and in Sweden. The humorous paper, *Kurre*, founded in 1884, came, through purchase, into the hands of Alexander J. Johnson (1850–1930), who changed the name to *Svenska Kuriren*. Johnson was born at Stockholm. After studying at the University of Uppsala, and spending a few years in Germany and France, he emigrated to America in 1882. He published *Svenska Kuriren* from 1888 until 1929, when he sold it to *Svenska Amerikanaren*. As an editorial writer Johnson was unexcelled. Not only did he possess uncommonly good grasp of the problems of the day, but discussed them with such vigor and charming style, that friend and foe alike enjoyed reading his articles.

Johan Person (1864–1921) was born at Asarum, Blekinge, and came to America in 1887. At various times he served on the staffs of *Svenska Tribunen*, *Svea*, *Skandinavia*, and *Svenska Folkets Tidning*. He was with *Svenska Kuriren* from 1904 to 1910, later with *Vestkusten*, and with *Svenska Amerikanska Posten*. From 1914 until his death, he was again with *Kuriren*. *I Svensk-Amerika* and *Svensk-amerikanska studier* show his intimate understanding of the Swedish element in the United States, and his ability to evaluate the people and the prevailing conditions. Person was an excellent columnist, a keen critic, and a sympathetic biographer.

In 1877 the Swedish Baptists founded *Evangelisk Tidskrift*, which name was changed, in 1884, to *Nya Veckoposten*. Johan Alexis Edgren (1839–1908), the brother of August Hjalmar Edgren, was the Editor from 1877 to 1879. Born at Östanå, Edgren emigrated to America during the Civil War, and became a lieutenant in the Union fleet. After the war, he served the Baptist denomination, both in Sweden and in America, as editor of church papers, and as a teacher in theological schools, writing many volumes on religious questions. Emanuel Schmidt

(1868–1921), another leader among the Baptists, was born at Hudiksvall, Sweden, and came to America in 1886. For two years he edited *Hemmets Vän* in Chicago. He was President of Adelphia College at Seattle and, later, professor in the Swedish Baptist Theological Seminary (Bethel) at St. Paul. He wrote biographies, historical sketches, and numerous articles on Biblical subjects, besides contributing, in English and in Swedish, to the press.

A poet, with much experience on Swedish-American newspapers, is Axel Fredenholm, who was born in Anderstorps Parish, Jönköpings län, in 1881, and came to America in 1902. He returned to Sweden in 1920, and was appointed president of a college at Karlskoga. Besides *Purpur och hemspunnet*, and other collections of poetry, he edited, in coöperation with K. Hildebrand, a large two-volume work, *Svenskarna i Amerika*.

The reason for giving so much attention to the Swedish-American newspapers is the fact—as indicated before—that it would have been impossible for most of our leading authors to exist, if they had not been connected with these weekly publications. Another class of professional men, who have contributed a large number of good writers, is the clergy. Some of them were, as we have already seen, journalists. Writing was an avocation with them, to which they could devote only a part of their time.

Axel August Swärd (1854–91) was born at Snavlunda, Närke, and came to America in 1883. After his ordination to the ministry in 1887, he served congregations in Marshfield, Oregon, and Templeton, California. His two collections of poetry, *Vilda blommor från prärien* and *Från vestanskog*, are among the best that have been published in Swedish in this country. The sincerity of his sentiments, his noble idealism, and his exceptional mastery of the language, are characteristic traits.

Another outstanding Augustana poet was Ludvig Holmes (1858–1910), who was born at Strövelstorp, Skåne, and left for America in 1879. His two collections of poems, *Dikter* and *Nya dikter*, express thoughts that often arise in the mind of one who has left the old homeland, to establish himself in a new country. Like Enander, Holmes loves Sweden as his mother, but has confidence in the Swedish youth of America, and awaits a happy future here. There is a strain of good humor that runs through his poetry, which is characterized by clarity and originality. He avoids bombastic phrases and flowery figures of speech. In clear, melodious language, he gives expression to noble idealism and deep feeling.

Carl Adolf Lönnquist was also a poet of the Lutheran ministry. Born at Fröderyd, Jönköpings län, in 1869, he came to this country in 1891. From 1893 until his death in 1937, he was a resident of Nebraska, serving pastorates and the Bethphage institution, founded by Reverend K. G. William Dahl. He wrote several volumes of verse, expressing a profound feeling as well as a practical sense. Trained in Sweden, Lönnquist has an impeccable style, and his use of the Swedish language is flawless. His *Dikter, Sundet vid Treskär och andra dikter,* and *Vildros, ett nytt knippe,* are collections of poetry of as high an order as any ever written in America in the Swedish tongue.

K. G. W. Dahl (1883–1917) was born in Sweden and came to America in 1902. He entered the ministry, and his name will always be associated with the institution of mercy at Axtell, Nebraska, known as Bethphage. *Hedens barn, bilder ur nybyggarelivet,* published in 1913, is a collection of stories that not only reveal the literary genius that Dahl possessed, but also his sympathetic heart, which led him to dedicate his life to the afflicted.

Edward Schuch (1871–1904) was born at Jönköping, and emigrated to America in 1889. He was another Swedish Lutheran pastor with literary interests. In 1917 appeared *Emigranterna,* a novel of pioneer days, which shows the author's knowledge of the background of emigration, and his ability to characterize individuals and to portray the economic situation.

Carl William Andeer was born in 1870 at Stigtomta in Södermanland, and came to America in 1891. He served as pastor in the Lutheran church in the United States, and wrote three collections of stories, dealing with Swedish-American life: *I brytningstid, skisser ur det svensk-amerikanska folklivet; Augustana-folk; Augustana-folk, andra samlingen.* Andeer returned to Sweden in 1912 and entered the State church.

Carl A. Swensson (1857–1904) was one of the very few

Swedish-American authors born in this country. As his father was one of the pioneer Swedish Lutheran pastors, the son was as well at home in the Swedish language as he was in the English. He was not only the pastor of the Lindsborg congregation, but also the President of Bethany College. He appeared frequently on the lecture platform, being considered the most brilliant orator among the Swedish people of this country. He wrote regularly for the press, and published books that appealed to all, among them *I Sverige, minnen och bilder från mina fäders land*, and *Åter i Sverige, minnen och bilder från mina fäders land*.

Alfred Bergin, the successor of Carl A. Swensson in the church work, was born in Vester Bitterna, Västergötland, in 1866. He arrived in America in 1883, and, since 1904, has served a congregation in Lindsborg, Kansas. He has written historical books, particularly about Lindsborg and other Swedish settlements in Kansas, and *Under furor och palmer, reseintryck från Europa vid världskrigets början*.

Carl Axel Lindvall was born at Kila, Värmland, in 1868, and departed for America in 1886. He is pastor of one of the older Lutheran churches of Chicago. Besides his contributions to various publications in America and in Sweden, he has edited the annual *Korsbaneret* for many years and *Svenska historiska sällskapets årbok*, 1916–17. He was a contributor to *Svenskt biografiskt lexikon*.

Another clergyman is Walter Lindberg, who was born at Vasa, Finland, in 1876, and came to America in 1893. After devoting several years to the study of voice and to concert tours, he took up the study of theology and entered the Lutheran ministry. *Mot det hägrande landet* is the title of a collection of poems. He has also written an interesting autobiographical novel. A contributor to the history of the pioneer settlers was Sven Kronberg (1840–1925), an Augustana pastor who was born at Kyrkhult, Halland, and departed for America in 1868. *Banbrytaren* is the title of a book in which he gives an autobiography and an account of pioneering in church work.

Among the writers of the Mission Covenant, David Nyvall is the most prominent. Born in Karlskoga, Värmland, he studied at Gävle, Uppsala, and Stockholm, before he left for America in 1886. He has devoted his best energies to the educational institutions of the Mission Covenant, serving for many years as the President of North Park College at Chicago. An excellent lecturer, he has been in much demand for speaking on cultural and religious subjects. Among his many books one might particularly mention *Vers och saga, Medsols, tre fosterländska tal, Skogsdrillar,* and *Min faders testamente,* in which he gives a well-written account of the life of his father. Nyvall is a master of the Swedish language. His writings inspire his countrymen to enrich American civilization, by adding to it the best elements of Swedish culture.

In the Swedish Methodist church is found the prolific writer, Oscar Leonard Strömberg, who was born at Arboga, Sweden, in 1871. He arrived in America in 1895 and has spent most of his time, since then, in Nebraska. While Strömberg has written poetry of a high order, it is particularly in the field of the novel that he has distinguished himself, and he has written, on the average, about one book a year for the last four decades. His descriptions are vivid, and the movement of the story is rapid, so that the interest of the reader is maintained from beginning to end.

Finally, there is the group of writers who are not members of a newspaper staff, or clergymen, but followers of some other profession which allows some leisure for literary labors. The famous scholar, August Hjalmar Edgren (1840–1903), who was born at Östanå bruk, Värmland, left for America in 1861, and here became an officer in the Union Army. After the war, he studied philology in Germany, France, and the United States. He taught at Yale University, at the University of Nebraska, later at the University of Gothenburg, and, again, at the University of Nebraska. Frequent changes in the life of Edgren typify the struggle that went on in the heart of many a newcomer, after he had left the old home to build a new one in a distant land.

Gustaf Nathanael Malm (1869–1928) was born at Svarttorp, Jönköpings län, and came to America in 1889. On the advice of Carl Swensson, he settled down at Lindsborg in 1894. Like Anna Olsson, Malm has succeeded in presenting the Swedish-Americans in the mixed language prevalent in this country.

His *Charli Johnson, svensk-amerikan, verklighetsbild ur folk-livet bland svenskarne i Vestern på 1890-talet*, which appeared in 1909, is taken from life. *Härute, verklighetsbild ur svensk-amerikanarnes vardagsliv i fyra akter* treats the relation between the immigrants and their new country in the period of assimilation.

Anna Olsson (Aina) was born in Värmland in 1866, and accompanied her parents to Kansas three years later. Aina possesses unusual talent in reconstructing the conversation of the first generation, and in repeating the mixed idioms and phrases often heard on the lips of the newcomers. *Från solsidan* is the title of one of her humorous books. The importance of Anna Olsson's works lies in the truthfulness of the picture they afford of a passing epoch. She has described a generation that has now practically disappeared, but which will be remembered through her writings.

Johan Gustaf R. Banér was born in Moheda, Småland, in 1862, and emigrated to America in 1884. He has served on the staff of *Svenska Romanbladet* in Minneapolis and edited *Frihet* at Ashland, Wisconsin; but, for the most part, he has lived at Ironwood, Michigan, writing poems and sketches for numerous periodicals, and publishing collections of poetry in English as well as in Swedish. His themes are often taken from Scandinavian or from Indian mythology. O. N. Nelson (1859–1917), a native of Vittskövle, Skåne, reached America in 1881. In 1893 appeared the first part of his *History of the Scandinavians and Successful Scandinavians in the United States*. The second volume was printed in 1897. His accounts of Scandinavian institutions, and the bibliography of books and articles on Scandinavian-American subjects, are of great value. Dr. Johannes W. W. Hoving, formerly of New York City but now of Stockholm, Sweden, was born of Swedish stock at Viborg, Finland, in 1868, and arrived in America in 1903. Hoving has published some articles and books in the field of medicine, but his wide interests have attracted him to many fields of literary endeavor. His memoirs, entitled *60 år*, appeared in 1928. Oscar Magnus Benzon was born in Moline in 1870, and died in 1893. During this short span of life, Benzon gave evidence of great poetic ability and wrote masterly poems in

Swedish, German, and English. *Illusions* is a poem of great power and beauty. His poems in the Swedish language are characterized by noble thought and faultless form.

Victor Nilsson was born in Östra Torp, Skåne, in 1867, and emigrated to this country in 1885. He has been connected with *Skaffaren; Svenska Folkets Tidning;* and *Minnesota-Posten.* A music critic, he has written numerous articles for the Minneapolis *Journal.* Among his books are *Förenta staternas presidenter; History of Sweden;* and *Strindberg's Treatment of Swedish History.*

Gustaf N. Swan is the foremost scholar and historian in the field of Swedish-American literature, and during his life has collected the most valuable library in the country, for this study. Swan was born at Tjärstad, Östergötland, in 1856, and accompanied his parents to America in 1870. He began to write poetry at an early age, but it is in the domain of literary history and criticism that he especially excels. His work is based on the best source material and on a just evaluation of men and events.

From this brief survey of Swedish-American authors, it is apparent that their contribution concerns itself chiefly with the period of Americanization. The study of their writings reveals the fact that the Swedes were easily acclimated in America, in spite of the difficulties and hardships connected with pioneering. The similarity between the two languages facilitated the acquisition of the English tongue, and the long experience Sweden has had with free institutions made the Swedish immigrant an excellent prospect for citizenship. To understand this period of intimate contact between Sweden and the United States, one should study Swedish-American literature. The books that have been written during this time will constitute an illuminating record of the Swedish contribution to the cultural development of the New World.[1]

1. Since this article was written, Bonggren and Linder have retired, as regular members of the newspaper staffs to which they formerly belonged, but are still active as free-lance writers.

Magazines

ADOLPH B. BENSON

For biographical information on the compiler, see the chapter on "Professors."

A T least sixteen attempts have been made, in America, to publish magazines in Swedish. Two of these lived a healthy life for several years, though none has survived. The first periodical seems to have been *Vårt Nya Hem*, an illustrated monthly, which made its appearance in 1873. It lived about a year. It was followed by *Närr och Fjerran* (1874–77), and then, in 1879, by *Ungdomsvännen*. The latter started, like so many other literary ventures, in Chicago, but, later, a second magazine of the same name appeared in St. Paul, and this one, having many excellent contributors, survived in Rock Island—to which it had finally moved—until 1918. *Nutiden* was born in New York, 1882, was "profusely and beautifully illustrated," and flourished until 1885. *Skandia*, intended for all Scandinavians, though printed in Swedish, was started in New York in April, 1886, but succumbed after a couple of months. Then there followed *Vega* (Boston, 1889–90), which, like the others, soon perished for lack of encouragement, though the contents are said to have been of good variety and quality. *Ungdomens Tidning*, Chicago, gave up the ghost in 1892, after only three numbers; and *Freja*, the "Northwest's first Swedish literary monthly," appeared in ten issues during the years 1893–94. About 1896 or 1897, *Nornan*, a magazine for women, was printed in Boston; *Svenska Revyen* was published in Michigan, 1897; *Broder Lustig* made its, or *his*, debut in Chicago about the same time, and, apparently changing its sex, was continued as *Iduna* until 1899. Other periodicals were *Förgät-Mig-Ej*, which died in May, 1898, after a life of little over a year; and *Land och Folk*, which had about the same span of life, from December, 1898 to August, 1900. A splendid magazine was *Valkyrian*, which lasted from

January, 1897, to December, 1909. *Fylgia* had already perished in September of the same year. *Kvinnan och Hemmet*, also published in Norwegian, was started at Cedar Rapids, Iowa, in 1888, and has therefore lasted fifty years. For details about editors, contributors, and contents see the article on "Swedish-American Literary Periodicals," by G. N. Swan, in *Augustana Historical Publications* (VI, 35–87). Some of the best writings that Swedes in America ever produced first appeared in some of these magazines.

Among the annuals in Swedish, the best undoubtedly was *Prärieblomman*, which was published for several years, at the beginning of the century, by the Augustana Book Concern. It contained articles and biographies of great historical value for Swedish-Americans.

That there are, in English, denominational periodicals like the *Augustana Quarterly* and the *Lutheran Companion*, is well known. The latter, with twenty thousand subscribers, is still going strong, and its future is promising. It is well edited by Ernest Edwin Ryden, D.D., an authority on hymnology. But there have been, also, some undenominational magazines in English, intended for all Scandinavian-Americans. Among these was an ambitious literary and historical undertaking, *Scandinavia*, which was published in Chicago by the learned Dane, N. C. Frederiksen, and which ran, with one long interruption, from November, 1883, to May, 1886. Works of some of the best classical writers of Scandinavia appeared in its pages. The *Northland Magazine*, also catering to Scandinavians in general, lived a promising, but brief, life near the close of the century, and several learned articles and able translations first made their appearance in this periodical. Still another journal for all Northerners in America took the name of a predecessor, *Scandinavia*. It was started by a Norwegian-American, P. O. Thorson, in June, 1924, but six months later, when the patron died, the venture died with him. In September, 1935, "a monthly magazine for the Swedes, Danes and Norwegians" was established in Los Angeles, California. It is edited and published by Harry Lorenzen, born near Kristianstad, Sweden, and is called the *Pacific Coast Viking*. Its Associate

Editor is A. W. Dellquest, well-known American writer, and author of several successful books, published by Burt & Company.

Today the specifically Swedish-American magazine is *The American Swedish Monthly*, published in New York, since 1934, by The Swedish Chamber of Commerce of the United States of America, as a successor to *The Swedish American Trade Journal*, started in 1915, and *The Bulletin*, begun in 1907. It has exclusively English text, contains a large variety of information and illustrations, and is carefully edited by Victor O. Freeburg. Its present success is fully merited, and its immediate future seems secure. It has many thousand subscribers.

The oldest and best-known American journal in English, which deals with all northern countries, and Scandinavians everywhere, is *The American-Scandinavian Review*, published by The American-Scandinavian Foundation. In the beginning it was edited by Henry Goddard Leach, first Secretary, later President, and now Trustee of the Foundation, but, for many years, the editorial work has been ably done by Miss Hanna Astrup Larsen, well-known Norwegian-American literary critic and translator. The magazine, formerly a bimonthly, then a monthly, and now a quarterly, has had a commendable record for over twenty-five years. The literary and intellectual qualities of its pages have always been high, and among its Scandinavian contributors are some of the most outstanding Swedes of the day. The present Editor holds an honorary doctorate from Augustana College.

Authors

ANNA OLSSON

Miss Olsson is a resident of Boston, where, during the last few years, she has been a literary consultant in Swedish for American publishers. She was educated in Stockholm, Uppsala, and Heidelberg.

THIS informal survey of writers with Swedish forebears in American literature, presents a list of men and women, who, in English, have contributed to some field of writing: poetry, fiction, science, biography, religion, and travelogue.

It is amazing, indeed, to find so many able authors who, in the course of a generation or two, have not only mastered the English language, but also grasped the complicated spirit of the mixed and adventurous race in this young and bewildering land. The country itself, with its numerous stimulating possibilities may, in many instances, have been the inspiration of their achievement. On the other hand, the writers have done their part to immortalize each period of its history, step by step; and it is gratifying to find so many Swedes among the group of workers who are gradually erecting to America a monument of letters. At best, the list included here is incomplete, but it serves, at least, as an indication of the Swedish contribution to American literature.

Carl Sandburg belongs, not only to Sweden and America, but to the world at large, by virtue of his outstanding accomplishment in the literary field. His father, August Johnson, was a poor, hard-working immigrant from Sweden, who settled in Illinois in the 'seventies, during the hectic railroad construction through the West. He soon changed his name to Sandburg, because of the great number of Johnsons living in the same community. Carl was but one of the many children born to strife and struggle, which seemed to be the birthright of the first generation of immigrants of that period. His early life was marked with the usual diversity of occupations. He was a milk-driver, barber, farmhand, dishwasher, working at anything and everything that would yield a living, until he enlisted in the Spanish War. Then he attended college for a time, and, while there, his first poems began to appear. From then on, his art of writing developed with gigantic strides, and today he occupies a niche all his own in the Hall of Fame.

Mr. Sandburg has given to the world several volumes of matchless poetry, both of biting satire and pure, enchanting lyric. Apparently he has liberated himself from any set rules in writing; but there is always present a certain quantitative syllable rhythm, which greatly enhances his free verse, such as in his almost tragic, but descriptive, composition in "Smoke and Steel":

> Smoke of the fields in the spring is one,
> Smoke of the leaves in the autumn another.
> Smoke of a steel mill roof or a battleship funnel
> They all go up in a line with a smokestack.
> Or they twist—in the slow twist—of the wind.

Another strange feature in Carl Sandburg's writing is his subtle way of addressing people from every walk of life. He flings a warning at a reporter here: "Speak softly—the sacred cows may hear . . ." and, shortly after, he turns smilingly to a Negro: "I am a nigger—singer of songs, dancer—softer than fluff of cotton . . ." With the minister he prays solemnly: "Lay me an anvil, O God. Beat me and hammer me into a crowbar . . ." And thus he continues through the social strata, always changing his meter from playful mirth to a slow, somber mood, thereby achieving the desired effect.

His social satire is probably never more apparent than in the following poem:

> The sins of Kalamazoo are neither scarlet nor crimson.
> The sins of Kalamazoo are convict grey and dishwater drab.
> And the people, who sin the sins of Kalamazoo
> Are neither scarlet nor crimson.
> They run to drabs and greys—and some of them sing
> They shall be washed whiter than snow—and some:
> We should worry!

CARL SANDBURG
POET, SINGER AND HISTORIAN

The titles of his books are indicative of their contents: *The People, Yes; Good Morning, America; Slabs of the Sunburnt West; Cornhuskers,* etc., all emanating an astringent, male quality in every line of every poem. It is really not surprising at all to find, in this superb collection, a translation of one of Gustaf Fröding's poems, as there is a decided kinship between the soaring spirits of these two artists.

Poetry, magnificent as it is, is not Mr. Sandburg's only contribution to American literature. There are his two books: *Abe Lincoln Grows Up* and *Abraham Lincoln: The Prairie Years,* comprising an immortal ode to America's great emancipator. Whole pages of these books read like poetry, captivating and intangible, almost, in their sensitive combinations of words. The birth of Lincoln, for instance, is told in the following stanza: "And into this world of battle and blood, of whispering dreams and wistful dust—a new child, a boy . . ." His description of the basic characteristic in Lincoln's nature is expressed in one sentence: "Silence found him, he met silence. In the making of him, as he was, the element of silence was immense."

Typical of Mr. Sandburg's conception of his own creations is a story, told about an interview between him and a critic, who had heard of the impending publication of another book. The latter asked whether it was prose or poetry. "I hope there will be some poetry in it," was the reply. The book was the biography of Lincoln.

Rootabaga Stories and *Rootabaga Pigeons* are fairy tales, whimsical and fascinating, the background of which is the conglomeration of the American people. There is a glowing thread of love—especially love for children—running throughout these stories, abundant with old folk sayings, primitive life on this continent, and priceless bits of wisdom.

Speaking of his own countrymen, Mr. Sandburg makes the following statement: "We are afraid of nothing—only—the sky may fall on us." He has also lingered long enough by the numerous statues in Stockholm to express his reaction in his poem, "Savoir Faire": "If the young men will read five lines of one of my poems, I will let the kings have all the bronze . . ."

We could go on indefinitely, selecting passages of arresting beauty from this poetry and prose—one gliding into the other, from one meter to another, rhymeless—and yet, poetry unique and supreme, prose unsurpassed.

Neil H. Swanson was born in Minneapolis in 1896 of Swedish parents—his father an immigrant. He was brought up on a farm, and attended school until the War broke out; then he joined the Army. Returning from France with distinction for bravery, he went into newspaper work, in which field he advanced steadily, until he is now the Assistant Managing Editor of the Baltimore *Evening Sun.* An ardent student of history, he made extensive soundings in to the olden times and discovered many heretofore untold episodes of American life, which he has published in his narratives: *The Judas Tree* and *The Phantom Emperor.* His latest book, *The First Rebel*, is an excellent account of pre-Revolutionary American history, where he has given new life and bright hues to the events of that period. It is both biography and fiction, merged into a completed chronicle of virile and inspiring entertainment.

Another historian of a somewhat different caliber is Mauritz A. Hallgren, hailing from Chicago, where he was born of Swedish parents. He has been a prolific contributor to newspapers and magazines here, in London, Paris, Berlin, and even in Japan. With his book, *Seeds of Revolt*, he made his debut in book circles, following closely with his portrait of President Roosevelt, in *The Gay Reformer.* Far more important, however, is his last novel, *The Tragic Fallacy.* All through it, we are horribly aware of the ominous rumblings of war. It is a timely study of America's war preparations, despite all the vociferous propaganda for peace. He offers a scathing analysis of our present war politics, and draws a terrifying chart of the future.

Stuart David Engstrand is a youthful and promising novelist, whose parents came from Blekinge. He followed the same circuitous route of hardship which writers have had to tread before winning recognition. After a year as a dirt-farmer in the Southwest, Mr. Engstrand counted $2.80 in profit, and decided that farming was not worth anybody's while. During that time, however, he had gathered material for his eminently successful novel, *The Invaders*—a crystallized patch of everyday life, as he had seen it—seething with strong emotions, crushed hopes, struggle, pain, and very little happiness. It is simply and comprehensibly presented, with the sort of intimacy that only a keenly observing person could ever achieve. Another novel is expected in the near future.

In the history of journalism, 1936 was a remarkable year, as it produced two biographies of Hearst, both signed by Swedish-Americans. Ferdinand Lundberg, with his daring and devastating analysis, *Imperial Hearst*—which the critics considered authentic enough to serve as a textbook in every recognized school of journalism. The other, *Hearst: Lord of San Simeon*, written by Oliver Carlson and Ernest Sutherland Bates, deals primarily with the personal life of the American newspaper tycoon.

Ferdinand Lundberg was born in this country, of a Swedish father and a Norwegian mother. He has been a newspaperman most of his life—an ace reporter, covering many outstanding events of recent times. But, lately, he has withdrawn from the whirl to write books instead. He has the fast-moving, vital style of a journalist, challenging in his statement, and penetrating in his analysis. His closing chapter of *Imperial Hearst* is typical of his powerful descriptions: "Hearst at seventy-three is the weakest strong man and the strongest weak man in the world to-day. His power stems from the ignorance of his audience, which, in turn, is fostered by fundamental economic forces in American society . . ." Mr. Lundberg's book, *America's Sixty Families*, is a study of the contemporary use and influences of wealth.

Oliver Carlson was born in Sweden, but has lived in this country since childhood. There are few men here today so well versed in labor and labor politics, as Mr. Carlson. He has traveled extensively, been at the ringside of revolutions of various nature, interviewed the leaders in contemporary history, and learned their aims and programs at first hand. He has lectured throughout the country, and written of his experiences, in magazines and newspapers, in a forceful, vivid style. His book on Hearst was not quite as sharp and venomous as Mr. Lundberg's; but the two authors have in no way failed to expose the degradation and iniquity of their leading character. Mr. Carlson's next book was *Brisbane*, another unauthorized biography published in the fall of 1937. In the near future, he has promised *The South in Transition*, and *What Makes You Think So?*—the latter, a study in the technique of molding public opinion.

Our Daily Bread flashed across the book market a couple of years ago, creating quite a stir among the reading public. Gösta Larsson, the author, was a young and studious immigrant, who had struggled in vain, for years, to have some manuscripts published in Sweden. With the usual, undaunted Viking persistence, he resolved to master the English language instead, and try his luck among the American publishers. This brought him success far beyond his expectation. Mr. Larsson writes with remarkable ease, depicting the rather cheerless and colorless, but interesting, everyday people, with a glowing enthusiasm that lends light and luster to the drab background of workingmen's life. His publications in our leading magazines are appearing frequently and another book, *Fatherland, Farewell!* was published during the past winter.

Very few of our countrymen are endowed with the enviable versatility of Charlton Lawrence Edholm, whose father was born in Sweden. He is an excellent artist, having had several one-man exhibits, with enthusiastic reception both in New York and elsewhere; a vigorous poet; and a light and amusing fiction writer. The background of his novels is generally the romantic West, wild and unruly as the mountain ranges of the region itself. *Doomed Cowboy, Reckless Road,* and *Wildcat* are some of his titles. He is also a frequent contributor to the radio, magazines, and newspapers.

Charles Telford Ericson, American educator abroad, is in a class by himself among the authors of Swedish origin. He has journeyed far and wide to gather his material. His contribution to literature is unique: *Albania; Asia Minor; Classical Greece;* and many other books, built on years of diligent and conscientious observation, and careful study.

The Swedes seem to have been particularly attracted by the strenuous life of newspaper work, as so many of them have sharpened their wits and writing ability by their journalistic experiences. Edwin Björkman belongs in this group, also, for, although born and educated in Sweden, he has spent the better part of his life covering the news world from the angles of reporter, dramatic critic, editor, and director. He has a definite standing as a poet of note, and has several books to his credit, such as *Gates of Life; Is There Anything New under the Sun; The Soul of a Child*—to select a few of his publications. His greatest service to literature, however, is probably his exceptional translations of Scandinavian plays and novels.

Herman Landon is another novelist, born in Sweden, but now a true son of America. He has given the public a delightful selection of detective and mystery stories of varying nature: *The Gray Phantom; Human Pawn; Silver Chest; Knight Errant*, are some of his books, which have been eagerly absorbed by a wide and appreciative audience.

Across the Years is an inspiring and beautifully composed autobiography by Charles Stedman MacFarland, a very able author and prominent churchman, whose father was born in Härnösand, Sweden, of Scotch and Swedish ancestry. The story of his life is a stirring tale of hardship, strong faith, and an indomitable iron will, which urged him on to ever greater deeds. He has written several books on religious subjects: *The Conflict of Church and State; Chaos in Mexico; Contemporary Christian Thoughts*, and others in the genre. The world today seems in sad need of more men like Dr. MacFarland.

The magazine, *Better Homes and Gardens*, an invaluable instrument in the beautification of the American home, was until 1938 skillfully edited by Elmer T. Peterson, son of Swedish immigrants. His artistic talent was at first seeking its expression in painting, but soon found its channel in letters. His excellent editorials have been included in several school-books, on account of their high educational quality. His *Trumpets West*, when it was published a few years ago, won wide acclaim, as the best book on pioneer life in Iowa and Kansas. (See the chapter on "Journalists.")

It is difficult to know what to write about Dr. Frederick

Peterson, who is an eminent physician, professor, poet, and author, all in one. He sees beauty enough, even in a cactus, to inspire an ode to it.

> You might have been a tree in a more gracious land,
> But deserts overwhelmed you with their hot blown sand.
> Ages of thirst have made you, what you are,
> Grossly misshapen, odd, grotesque, bizarre. . . .

His contribution to the medical field is well recognized. *Creative Re-education,* his latest book on medical science, has won him international fame. His *Chinese Lyrics,* with a distinct Oriental coloring, were published under a pseudonym, and it was a long time before the identity of the author was revealed. Some of his lyrics have been set to music. And, what is more, Dr. Peterson is also a collector and connoisseur of art. He was born in Minnesota of Swedish parents.

Nelson Algren belongs to the younger set of reckless and impetuous writers. He has walked the tightrope of misery and trouble, as he traveled aimlessly about the country in a boxcar, or by any other available means of transportation. Out of his experience, thus gathered, sprang his book: *Somebody in Boots* —a compelling story about the wandering boys in America. The critics called it a boxcar odyssey. Most of our leading magazines carry frequent publications by Mr. Algren, whose grandfather was Swedish.

Stepping from one age to another, from one field of activity to its opposite, we find Gustavus A. Eisen, a celebrated sociologist and biologist, as well as a prominent author. He was born in Stockholm in 1847, and has devoted all his life to assiduous research on strange and utilitarian subjects, such as amœbas, earthworms, and Sequoia trees. He has to his literary credit a great number of books, of which *The Fig; The Raisin Industry; The Legend of the Holy Grail and the Great Chalice* belong to those understandable by the laymen. His scientific records are as invaluable as they are extensive.

From Stockholm also comes Olof Hall, who yielded to the temptation of going West. Like many of his fellowmen, he joined the ranks of itinerant labor, and had a good chance of studying intimately the life of those who lived on the frayed edges of society. During an exciting trip down the entire length of the Yukon River in Alaska, he assembled data for his novel, *Youth North*, which was published in the fall of 1936. It is a human tale, wavering between deeds good and bad, with the frozen Bering Sea and the wild beauty of British Columbia as a background.

Samuel A. Carlson is, perhaps, better known for his honest and upright political career as a mayor of Jamestown, New York, than as an author. He has contributed *Saga of the City* and *New Concept of Government*.

A dramatic writer of considerable ability is Hans Folke Alin, who has a good command of both Swedish and English. Among his numerous works in English are *Closing Up; The Final Curtain; Poverty; Who Shall Judge?* and *Enchanted Cairo*.

Margaret Lee Runbeck boasts of her Swedish grandparents, and introduced her grandmother, Magnold Lauren, as the leading character in her novel, *People Will Talk*. Miss Runbeck is a captivating storyteller who keeps her readers in constant, breathless suspense all through her numerous short stories, which appear as the leading features in several of our best magazines. There is a blithe and happy spirit behind all her sketches, so delightfully drawn by her colorful pen. She is at present working on her second novel, whenever she can bear to tear herself away from her country house that "hugs a hillside."

Another novelist, probably better known to the English audience, is Flora Sandström, whose entertaining novel, *Thelma Svane*, has given so much pleasure to its many readers. Nora Burglon is a prolific writer of juvenile stories. She is a true daughter of Sweden, and maintains her relationship by frequent trips to, and prolonged sojourns in, her fatherland. Her narratives possess the kind of charm which appeals to children and grownups alike. P. H. Pearson and Victor Folke Nelson are both Swedes who have contributed *Prairie Vikings* and *Prison Days and Nights*, respectively. Edith and Warner Oland are far better known as actors than as writers. Warner Oland, however, with the able coöperation of his wife, has found time, in addition to his screen work, to translate several plays by Strindberg.

In this list should be mentioned, also, the unforgettable trans-

lator of Selma Lagerlöf's books: Velma Swanston Howard—
born in Sweden in 1868. Her death occurred in 1937. She
endeared herself to the entire English-reading public by her
magnificent accomplishment in translating Selma Lagerlöf's
poetic and descriptive language into equally beautiful and expressive English. Her shadings of words and delicate treatment
of superstitions, myths, and unreal personalities made real in
these immortal tales, bespeak a very sensitive spirit merged
with a keen intellect. It is a noble deed, nobly done, and posterity will be forever grateful to Mrs. Howard for her unselfish
and conscientious contribution to the Lagerlöf literature.

Charles A. Lindbergh and his *We* need no further introduction, as they both live, like precious possessions, in the memory
of us all.

Last, but by no means least, there is David Edström, internationally known as a sculptor and philosopher. His book, *The
Testament of Caliban*, is a rapturous, at times fairly flaming,
account of a tempestuous life—vibrant with awesome contrasts
from abject poverty to royal luxury, from an infinitely peaceful and docile existence beneath the crackling aurora borealis
in Northern Sweden, to the whirling, restless, exciting life
among the artists in Florence. Through this most extraordinary autobiography, Mr. Edström reviews a parade of Sweden's
celebrities in art and letter, from Ellen Key and Anders Zorn
down to Prince Eugen and Selma Lagerlöf of our own time. He
knew them intimately. He introduces his astounded audience to
kings and coal stokers with the same careless, gallant gestures.
It seems to be all in a day for this unfathomable personality,
who has known poverty and tasted plenty. This book has laid
violent hands on the imagination of the readers, and whatever
other virtue it may have, it will always be a record of Sweden's
artists and writers during the last half-century.

Sweden has reason to be proud of her enterprising descendants on American soil. No doubt there are many more who have
worked industriously with paper and pen to spread the good
will between two nations, so closely related in spirit and general
characteristics as Sweden and America.

Journalists

ROY W. SWANSON

Mr. Swanson, who has been an editorial writer on the St. Paul *Pioneer Press and Dispatch* since 1930, is a native of Duluth, Minnesota. He attended the University of Minnesota, from which he holds two degrees, having done graduate work in American history, with special attention to Swedish immigration and the West. He contributed to the most recent edition of H. L. Mencken's *American Language,* and has published several articles on the Swedes in America, in such historical and language-study publications as *Minnesota History, Iowa Journal of History and Politics, The Swedish American Historical Bulletin,* and *American Speech.*

YAH, I bane a Svenska poik!" This was the ebullient reply received from an Associated Press man to whom I had addressed a discreet letter of inquiry to verify the Swedish look of his name. I have decided to use it as an opener for this article about Swedes in American journalism because, to me, it suggests so many things that are typical.

The writer of that sentence is a third-generation Swede, thoroughly American in training and outlook, only meagerly acquainted with the mother tongue of his immigrant grandparents, as the above quotation shows, but taking a wholesome pride in his origin. I have taken him as a typical representative of the present generation of Swedish-Americans in American journalism today. This type was born on a mid-Western farm at the turn of the century, was educated in the public schools and the university of his home State, and, upon completion of his schooling, started on a newspaper career which has taken him to all parts of the United States and, sometimes, abroad. Just now he occupies a responsible post in a great newsgathering agency. He is married to a non-Swede. Although his surname may or may not still be Swedish, his baptismal names are usually non-Swedish, as are the names of his children. His church affiliations are not always Lutheran, and his political preferences are, decidedly, not always Republican.

I think this is a fairly accurate portrait of the 1938 edition of the American newspaperman of Swedish blood. He is aware that there is a Tercentenary celebration, commemorating three hundred years of his forebears in America, and he wholeheartedly approves the idea; but he is not boasting unduly, because he realizes that several other nationalities have helped make the United States. Meanwhile, he is busy at his job of furthering American journalism.

It would serve no valid purpose to list all the newspapermen of Swedish ancestry. Indeed, the task would be well-nigh impossible, if only for the reason that, in the second and third generations, many Swedish family names, in this country of many nationalities, are lost through intermarriages with other stocks. Suffice it to say, however, that their number must be large, and, as one sympathetic colleague put it, "You've got yourself a job, trying to line up all the Swedish boys who are doing things in journalism." Swedish-looking names appear constantly in such publications as the *Associated Press Directory*, the *Editor and Publisher* annual, *Who's Who in Journalism*, the roster of the press gallery in the Capitol at Washington, and the membership lists of the various State editorial associations. So large is the number of Swedes in American journalism, and so widely scattered from New York to Alaska, that it must be admitted at the outset that only a few outstanding individuals, and those known or suggested to me, can be mentioned here. It is expected that many deserving of notice will be missed.

Since a start must be made somewhere, let us first consider one of the outstanding newspapermen of Swedish extraction in contemporary New York City. Inquiries in this field invariably brought forth the name, "Ted" Wallen of the *Herald Tribune*, who died in 1936. He was called by his superiors, "the best political reporter developed in this country in the last quarter of a century," and his untimely death deprived the American newspaper profession of one of its most prominent younger members.

Theodore Clifford Wallen was born in New Britain, Connecticut, in 1894, of Swedish parents. In 1915 he joined the staff of the *Hartford Courant*, where his talent for political reporting was soon discovered, and he was assigned to the capitol "beat." During his career, he covered New York State politics at Albany, having joined the *Herald Tribune* in 1927, several national party conventions, and then accompanied presidential candidates on campaign tours; reported the Naval Disarmament Conference in London; and made frequent trips throughout the country for political surveys. In 1929, Mr. Wallen was assigned to the Washington bureau of the *Herald Tribune*, and the following year became its chief. He was occupying this post at the time of his death.

He was widely known and respected among public men of all political affiliations, who admired in him his gift of being able to write political and governmental news free from partisanship. Mr. Wallen's reportorial work was of a caliber that also earned for him the distinction of academic recognition. In 1935 the George Washington University conferred on him the honorary degree of Doctor of Laws. The quality of his dispatches was praised in the citation, which read: "Clear-minded student, able in reporting public action, a good citizen who tempers judgment with high loyalties. The mould of his life bespeaks strength dedicated to right thinking."

The passing of Mr. Wallen was a real loss to the American newspaper-reading public. How great this loss was, is indicated in the obituary editorial that appeared in the journal on which he began his newspaper career:

The task he performed with outstanding ability—recording and interpreting governmental and political activities—has seldom, if ever, been of more importance to all citizens than it is today. The task will be carried on and will take on even more importance as citizens realize their responsibilities in government and the necessity of bringing knowledge and understanding to bear upon its problems.

There are few newspapermen in America better known than "Baron" Warn of the New York *Times*. William Axel Warn is dean of the legislative correspondents at Albany, and is highly thought of in journalistic circles as a political reporter of spotless character and a credit to the profession.

The "Baron" is a native of Sweden, having been born in Linköping in 1868, and he was schooled preparatory to matriculating at the university, but, instead, he set off for America when a youth under twenty. He did not remain here long the first time, however, for New York became the starting point for wanderings in many lands, and on the seven seas. Looking back on this period, Mr. Warn says that it brought him small return in money, but a wealth of experience, "undoubtedly useful and certainly delightful in retrospect." His wanderings took him to Costa Rica and to Central America, where he spent three years. Then followed more years of seafaring, including a voyage on one of the last American clipper ships. At last he gave up the sea and, in 1895, was back in the United States, this time to stay. The day after he landed, he declared his intention to become a citizen before a commissioner of the United States Court.

For some years, the young man depended mainly on the hard work of his hands for a livelihood, but, in addition, contributed articles to newspapers in Sweden and to Swedish-language publications here, "always with the hope and ambition," he recalls, "that some time I might find a place in American journalism." This wish was fulfilled around the turn of the century by an offer to become a regular contributor, to the Brooklyn *Daily Eagle*, of articles dealing with Scandinavian topics. Next we find him a reporter for the New York City News Association, in which service he remained until he received a call from the *Times* in 1902. He was assigned to cover the Criminal Courts Building, at that time the most productive news center in the city. He was in the thick of things in the hectic 1905 mayoralty campaign of William Randolph Hearst, which still stands out unique in the political annals of Manhattan. Since 1906, he has represented the *Times* at the state and national conventions of major political parties, and, in 1912, was appointed legislative correspondent at Albany, the position he now holds.

Mr. Warn's years of service at the New York State capitol have afforded him unrivaled opportunity to observe at close range, and to write an extensive correspondence about, a great era in the political and administrative history of the Empire State—an era which included the eventful terms of such leaders as Governors Charles Evans Hughes, Alfred E. Smith, Franklin D. Roosevelt, and Herbert H. Lehman. A tragic development at the capitol, which he reported, was the impeachment, and ousting from office of Governor William Sulzer in 1913. He also witnessed the first appearance in public of Mr. Franklin Roosevelt when, in 1911, he took his seat in the State Senate. The "Baron," from his vantage point of twenty-five years at Albany, has had close-up views of the beginning of two illustrious public careers which culminated in the presidency for Mr. Roosevelt and the chief justiceship of the United States Supreme Court for Mr. Hughes.

A political writer whose newspaper experience led to high public office was the late George E. Akerson, who was born of Swedish parentage in Minneapolis, and who became secretary to President Hoover in 1928, serving until 1930. He had attended Allegheny College, and was graduated from Harvard University in 1912. After working on the Minneapolis *Tribune*, he was sent to Washington in 1921, to help cover the Naval Arms Conference. In 1922 he served as publicity manager for Frank B. Kellogg, later Secretary of State, in his senatorial campaign against Charles A. Lindbergh, father of the aviator, and later became closely connected with the publicity phase of Hoover's campaign for the Presidential nomination. His reward was the secretaryship. In 1930, he resigned to join the Paramount-Publix Moving Picture Corporation, but at the time of his death in December, 1937, he was in the bond business in New York.

Before entering on special publicity work of a varied nature, including radio, Eric Palmer, who represented the famous American Committee on Public Information in the Scandinavian countries during the latter part of the War, also had a wide experience as political correspondent. As a reporter for the now defunct Brooklyn *Standard Union*, he covered over fifty State and national conventions, and also wrote articles on baseball. Palmer was born in Östergötland, and came to the United States with his parents, when but five years old. He is a brother of George M. Palmer, who is still in the sports department of the New York *Times*.

Several of the younger generation of Swedes in American

journalism have made their mark in various fields of writing. Neil Harmon Swanson, at present Assistant Managing Editor of the Baltimore *Evening Sun*, and formerly of the Minneapolis *Journal*, has several historical novels to his credit. (See the chapter on "Authors.") Ferdinand Lundberg, after ten years on Chicago and New York papers, gave up journalism a few years ago, to carry on independent literary work, and is the author of *Imperial Hearst* and *America's Sixty Families*. The former book is described as an "unauthorized" biography of William Randolph Hearst, the American newspaper magnate, and is regarded as a significant contribution to the history of American journalism, while the latter has recently been used as a text in a most heated political controversy.

The same year, 1936, Mr. Hearst was the target of another young Swedish critic, Oliver Carlson, who is joint-author of *Hearst: Lord of San Simeon*. Mr. Carlson, who was born in Sweden and grew up in Michigan, where he got his newspaper training, is in free-lance work. Although he has not been on the staff of a paper for a number of years, he continues to write an occasional feature article for the New York *Post* and the Philadelphia *Record*. Chiefly, however, he contributes to leading magazines on political and economic subjects; some of his articles, especially on the agricultural and industrial situation in the South, have been widely quoted and reprinted. Mr. Carlson divides his time between writing and lecturing. At the time of the writing of this chapter, he was touring the country as a public-forum leader, under the sponsorship of the Federal Office of Education, and also preparing two books—a biography of Arthur Brisbane, which has since been published, and a study of the South in transition, scheduled to be brought out shortly.

Prominent in this group of young journalist-authors of Swedish stock is Mauritz A. Hallgren, now well established, by his numerous writings, as one of America's leading commentators on politics and economics. He was born in Chicago in 1899, of Södermanland parentage, and spent his early boyhood years in the then thoroughgoing Swedish community of Englewood, Illinois. Mr. Hallgren worked on newspapers in Chicago and other cities, and was, for several years, a Washington and European correspondent for the United Press. Until recently, he was Associate Editor of the *Nation*, and is now on the editorial staff of the Baltimore *Sun*. The latest book from his pen is *The Tragic Fallacy: a Study of America's War Policies*, published in 1937. Mr. Hallgren is also the author of two previous works, *Seeds of Revolt* and *The Gay Reformer*. He has likewise contributed numerous articles to leading magazines in this country and abroad.

The career of Mr. Hallgren shows that the road of journalism can sometimes lead to an editorial post on a national magazine. This has also been the experience of Elmer T. Peterson who, until 1938, was the Editor of the *Better Homes and Gardens* magazine, the circulation of which approaches the two million mark. This Iowa-born farm boy, son of Swedish parents, arrived at this post in 1927 after twenty years of Kansas journalism, which ranged from proprietorship of a rural weekly in the western part of that State, to the editorship of the Wichita *Beacon*. During his Kansas newspaper period, Mr. Peterson took an active part in civic affairs, and is credited with being one of the founders of "The New Santa Fe Trail," which was the first transcontinental automobile highway. Articles by Mr. Peterson frequently appear in national periodicals, and he is also the author of a novel, *Trumpets West*, dealing with Swedish pioneering in Iowa and Kansas. It was while on the Wichita *Beacon*, during the War years, that Mr. Peterson won the Editor & Publisher gold medal for the best editorial in relation to the Fourth Liberty Loan. He is now a free-lance writer, living in California.

Another nationally known magazine with an editor of Swedish antecedents is *Machinery*, a trade monthly of impressive proportions, published in New York, and edited by Erik Oberg, a native of Värnamo in Småland. In Sweden, Oberg had both an academic and an engineering education, before coming to the United States in 1901. For the next five years he worked as a designer of machine tools and shop-manufacturing equipment for the Pratt and Whitney concern in Hartford, and, later, for a brief period, for a similar plant in Cincinnati, Ohio. In 1906 he joined the publishers of *Machinery*, and in 1918 became Editor-in-chief. In addition to his engineering journalism, Mr. Oberg is also the author of numerous technical books in the machine-building field. Thus he was the editor and principal author of *Machinery's Engineering Handbook*, first published in 1914, and now distributed to the extent of over 260,000 copies throughout the English-reading world. He is also the editor and principal author of the same magazine's *Engineering Encyclopedia*, a large work in seven volumes, published in 1917. He has been chairman of the Editorial Conference of the New York Business Publishers Association and, during the War period, served as one of three members of a special Government Commission to adjust American industries to the needs of war and demobilization.

Dr. Victor O. Freeburg, Editor of *The American Swedish Monthly*, which also enjoys nation-wide circulation, is a native of Iowa, and was first educated in Kansas, and later at Yale University. Author of several books and numerous magazine articles, he began his professional career as a teacher of English at the United States Naval Academy, and continued this work at other institutions, including Columbia University. He was at one time Editor of *The Swedish-American Trade Journal*, and later served as the assistant director of the American-Swedish News Exchange; after this, he spent several years in publicity work. He is of old Swedish stock on both sides of his family, the surname having originally been "Fredberg."

The press in this country has followed closely the dramatic development of American flying. Among the early observers of this new form of transportation was John Gustaf Goldstrom, who was born fifty years ago in Pittsburgh, to which city his paternal grandfather had immigrated, shortly after the Civil War, to lend his skill as a Värmland ironworker to the rising New World industry of steel.

Almost from the beginning of his newspaper career, which started in Pittsburgh in 1908, Mr. Goldstrom has been reporting the events of pioneer aviation in the United States. He was reporting flying exhibitions as early as 1910, his first flight being made at that time, with Glenn M. Curtiss. Since then he has witnessed many "firsts" in our aviation history. He participated in the first through-delivery of the newly organized air-mail service in 1919. He was an observer on the first U. S. Navy torpedo-plane maneuvers in 1922; traveled with the Army Air Corps' dirigible, C–2, in the first all-night airship flight made in the United States; and did the first aerial reporting of a total eclipse, in 1925. Accordingly, Mr. Goldstrom was well qualified to write *A Narrative History of Aviation*, which is extensively used by educational institutions teaching aeronautics, and has a secure place in the bibliography of aviation. Mr. Goldstrom was at one time aeronautical editor of the New York *Evening World*, and has contributed frequent articles on aviation to leading magazines. He has the distinction of having a street in Pittsburgh named after him, as the first Pittsburgher to fly over that city. (See also the chapter on "Aviation.")

Several American newspapermen of Swedish descent have won high executive positions. Among these are Everett Kallgren, a brother of Dean Carl Alfred Kallgren of Colgate University, who is now night editor of the New York *Herald Tribune*; J. Harold Swanson, Editor of the Jamestown (N.Y.) *Post*, and Harvey Ellsworth Newbranch, Editor of the Omaha *World Herald*. Mr. Kallgren was born in New Haven in 1900, rose to city editor of the New Haven *Journal Courier*, and joined the old New York *Herald*, before the merger with the *Tribune*, as proofreader. When the paper was absorbed by the *Tribune*, he was retained and, in 1927, became foreign editor. He has held his present position since 1935.

J. Harold Swanson is a third-generation Swede whose grandparents were among the pioneer settlers of Jamestown, New York, and Chandler's Valley, Pennsylvania. He has been connected with the Jamestown *Post* since 1902 and is now not only Editor, but also Secretary of the Corporation, and General Manager. He attended Cornell University and, for several years, has been President of the Municipal Service Commission. In both 1934 and 1936 he was a delegate to the Republican Convention of the State of New York.

H. E. Newbranch rose from the ranks to become Editor and

Vice-President of the newspaper he joined as a reporter nearly forty years ago. He was born in Henry County, Iowa, both his parents being natives of Sweden. He attended the University of Nebraska, and joined the staff of the Omaha *World-Herald* in 1899, becoming successively editorial writer, Associate Editor, and Editor, attaining the last position in 1910. Mr. Newbranch was awarded the Pulitzer Prize for the best editorial written in 1919.

By common consent, the most glamorous career that journalism affords is that of foreign, or war, correspondent. Swedish-American newspapermen have had a share in these coveted assignments abroad. The late Theodore Wallen of the New York *Herald Tribune* covered the Naval Disarmament Conference in London, and "Baron" Warn's quarter-century record as the *Times* legislative correspondent at Albany was interrupted briefly during the War years by an assignment in Europe. A more extended experience has been that of Naboth Hedin, now manager of the American-Swedish News Exchange in New York. Mr. Hedin, who is Swedish-born and Harvard-educated, was for ten years (1908–18) a member of the editorial staff of the Brooklyn *Daily Eagle*, of which he spent the last five years as its Paris correspondent. During the World War he was an accredited correspondent with the French, Belgian, British, and American armies, and in this capacity made frequent visits to the fronts in France, the munition plants, and the French naval establishments, about all of which he wrote an extensive correspondence. Just before the Armistice he transferred to the Universal Service Syndicate, for which he covered the Peace Conference and the founding of the League of Nations. Returning to the United States, Mr. Hedin worked for a few years as free-lance translator and editorial writer in Boston, before making his present connection in 1925. Mr. Hedin has written numerous magazine articles and collaborated on several books about Sweden. Together with his wife, born Florence Benedict, he has translated a collection of short stories by Selma Lagerlöf, published in 1935 under the title of *Harvest*.

Postwar European newspaper experience has been the lot of two mid-Western journalists of Swedish descent, Albin E. Johnson and Elmer W. Peterson. Of these, the former was born in Kansas in 1890 and, after graduating from both Ottawa and Kansas universities, served in the United States Navy during the War, and worked for the United Press in both New York and Washington. Between 1919 and 1922, he covered the Turko-Greek War in Asia Minor, the Wrangel refugee invasion of Constantinople, the Irish rebellion, and various sessions of the League of Nations. Between 1922 and 1924 he was foreign editor of the Philadelphia *Public Ledger*, and then of the New York *Evening World*. Next he returned to Europe and, between 1924 and 1935, covered—for such papers as the New York *World;* the Kansas City *Star;* the Washington *Star;* the Los Angeles *Times;* and several Canadian organs—practically every session of the League of Nations at Geneva and elsewhere, including the Locarno and other "disarmament" conferences. He likewise reported the overthrow of the monarchy in Spain; the rise of Hitler in Germany; and, in 1933, witnessed the Japanese invasion of Manchuria. For the past year or so, he has been the Foreign Commissioner of the New York World's Fair, being accredited to twenty-four countries, most of which he has visited.

At the time of this writing, Elmer W. Peterson has just joined the Washington staff of the Associated Press, after five years of covering some of Europe's greatest news stories. He was in Spain when the recent revolution broke out, and followed General Franco's army through the fall of Alcazar. As a member of the Berlin bureau of the Associated Press, he had reported Hitler's famous blood purge of 1934. In Belgium, he pictured the sorrow of the nation at the time of Queen Astrid's tragic death. At Stockholm, he described the pomp and ceremony of Princess Ingrid's marriage, and at London he wrote of the coronation of King George VI.

It is interesting to note that Mr. Peterson's career as a foreign correspondent began in Stockholm, where he arrived in 1932, after a few years of reportorial work on Duluth and Minneapolis papers. The following year, after a period of freelance writing, he joined the Associated Press, as full member of the foreign staff, and subsequently held posts for that or-

ganization in Berlin, London, and Stockholm. In the Swedish
city he served as chief of the Associated Press bureau. Altogether, Mr. Peterson resided about two and a half years in
Sweden, which is something of a record for an American correspondent. He was born in Duluth, Minnesota, and is a graduate
of Carleton College.

Swedish newspapermen have also made their mark in the
musical and literary fields of American journalism. A few of
them have functioned as influential emissaries of Swedish culture in this country, notably Dr. Victor Nilsson, Edwin August
Björkman, and Johan Ludwig Wallin.

The first of this trio, who recently completed thirty years as
music critic on the Minneapolis *Journal,* is perhaps as well
known to Sweden as he is to Minnesota, having received recognition from the Swedish Government for his work in the promotion of Swedish culture in the United States. In 1937, musical organizations in Minneapolis gave a testimonial dinner to
Dr. Nilsson, honoring him for fifty years of service to music in
that city. As a young man Dr. Nilsson came to Minnesota from
Sweden, and literally grew up with the cultural flowering of
that mid-Western community, a development which he recorded
faithfully in his columns. He is coeval with the rise of musical
interest in Minneapolis, an interest which he nurtured at every
stage by his enthusiasm and understanding. Today he has the
pleasure of seeing his adopted city one of the musical centers
of the United States, boasting a nationally known symphony
orchestra and numerous musical organizations. Through the
medium of the press, Dr. Nilsson has done valuable work in
interpreting Scandinavian music and drama to American audiences, while his countrymen are particularly grateful to him
for fostering among them the art of the Swedish song. No one
realizes better than Dr. Nilsson the importance of keeping alive
the transplanted culture of the immigrant, and incorporating
it into the cultural life of America.

Besides Dr. Nilsson, Minneapolis journalistic circles of the
1890's contained another culture-minded young Swede, who was
to make his mark chiefly in the domain of literature. This was
Edwin August Björkman, best known to present-day readers

as translator and novelist, and who, at this writing, is State Director of the North Carolina Federal Writers' Project. Mr. Björkman was born in Stockholm and came to the United States in 1891. He served for a time on a local Swedish-language paper, and then became reporter and music critic on the Minneapolis *Times*. Next he joined, in turn, the staffs of several New York papers, the *Sun*, the *Times*, and the *Evening Post*. Later he appeared as one of the directors of the League of Nations News Bureau and, after that, as literary editor of the Asheville *Times*. During his journalistic career, Mr. Björkman has made a lasting contribution to the cultural relations between Scandinavia and his adopted country in his numerous translations, including some of Strindberg's plays, his literary essays, and his novels of Swedish life. His latest translation is that of *Memory of Youth* by Vilhelm Moberg, published in the spring of 1938. (See the chapter on "Authors.")

Closely paralleling the career of Dr. Nilsson is that of the late Johan Ludwig Wallin of Portland, who died in 1936, after thirty years of service on the *Oregon Journal*. "Count" Wallin, as he was called, was veteran music critic of that paper, and had a wide influence in musical circles in the Pacific Northwest. As a music reporter and music leader, he was highly esteemed by his colleagues and the citizens of Portland. Throughout his life he championed, fostered, organized, and publicized local musical endeavors of all kinds, giving advisory and promotional assistance to the old Portland Opera Association, and acting as organizer and guiding influence of the Portland Junior Symphony Orchestra, which has won national recognition. Mr. Wallin was an earnest worker for the musical education of youth, and was responsible for the development of many outstanding artists in the field of music. His death was a distinct loss to the cause of Swedish culture in America, since he was its foremost exponent in the press of the Pacific Northwest. Mr. Wallin was born in Helsingborg in 1875, and came to Portland with his parents when a boy. For that Western city it was a fortunate migration, since it gave her a citizen who was to be a force in directing the humanistic development of the whole Oregon country.

Some of the older Swedish-American newspapermen have served the press of both languages in America. A young immigrant of good education would join the staff of a Swedish-language paper, and, later, transfer his allegiance to the local American press. This was the procedure of Dr. Nilsson and Mr. Björkman; and Mr. Wallin, also, had an experience in Swedish-language publications. It seems fitting in this connection to mention a figure of the last century, Col. Hans Mattson, whose varied career also included ventures in both fields of journalism. In addition to owning and editing Swedish papers in Minneapolis and Chicago, the Colonel also made a sally in the English-language press. In 1889 he formed a company in Minneapolis for the publication of a weekly called the *North*, his name appearing on the masthead, first as President, and later as Editor. This publication had an interesting purpose. According to the opening editorial, the *North* was "a business enterprise established in response to a demand for a newspaper that shall meet the wants of the young generation of Scandinavian-Americans more fully than can the newspapers now printed in the languages of the Scandinavian races." Although an idealistic conception, it seems at this distance to have missed the fact that the English-speaking second generation would naturally find its reading in the English-language press. However, it continued publication for a half-dozen years, which indicates that it was not so hopeless a "business enterprise" as one might think. In content, the *North* was less a newspaper than a weekly magazine of comment and literature, and in that respect was rather unique in Northwestern journalism. Its columns were filled with translations from Scandinavian authors, and interpretations of current events in the three Northern countries, and thus deserves to be remembered as an early effort in the promotion of cultural relations between the United States and the Scandinavian countries. Certainly, in evaluating the influence of Colonel Mattson as an outstanding Swedish-American citizen of the last century, this particular contribution of his to American journalism should not be overlooked.

A conspicuous example of a Swedish-American who mixes journalism with education is Kenneth E. Olson, now Director of the Medill School of Journalism at Northwestern University, Evanston, Illinois. Mr. Olson was born in Sioux Falls, South Dakota, and is a graduate of the University of Wisconsin. He taught journalism at his Alma Mater, and at the University of Minnesota, and was for a while chairman of the Rutgers University department of journalism. Mr. Olson has been executive secretary of the New Jersey Press Association, and has had active newspaper experience in Milwaukee, Madison, and Ashland, Wisconsin.

The country press in the United States has its quota of journalists of Swedish blood, and more especially so, of course, in communities such as Minnesota. As a matter of fact, that State drew one of its governors from the Swedish ranks of its fourth estate, John A. Johnson, who served three terms, dying in office in 1909. Before entering politics, Governor Johnson was Editor of the St. Peter *Herald*, and took an active part in the Minnesota Editors' and Publishers' Association, serving at one time as its President. He had a wide reputation for putting out a very creditable country newspaper and, when Governor, wrote an article for the *Youth's Companion*, in which he brought out fully his ideas of the duties and responsibilities of the country editor.

The oldest active editor in Minnesota today is a Swede, N. P. Olson, of the Red Wing *Daily Eagle*. Now a veteran in his eighties, Mr. Olson can look back on more than sixty years in the publication business in that State. Beginning in 1876, he has operated and founded newspapers in a half-dozen Minnesota communities—all of which can claim him as a builder and civic leader. Mr. Olson was born in Christianstad in Skåne, and came to the United States with his parents when ten years old. The name of his first paper, at Hutchinson, was the *Enterprise*, which quality, by the way, seems to have characterized throughout the career of the Swedish immigrant boy who chose to make journalism the field of his endeavors in his adopted country.

While Mr. Olson is a native of Sweden, Victor Emanuel Lawson, publisher of the Willmar *Daily Tribune*, is American-born, but of Swedish stock. A generation of Mr. Lawson's editorship has made this rural journal not only a successful business enterprise but also an important factor in the life and affairs of Kandiyohi County. Mr. Lawson is a prominent figure in Minnesota publishing circles, and in 1937 was elected president of the Associated Press of that State. When Governor Johnson extolled the country editor, he could easily have had in mind these two Swedish newspapermen of rural Minnesota.

Chicago journalism has had many Swedes—including Carl Sandburg—in all sorts of capacities, as would be expected in this large center of the Swedish population in America. But I should like to dwell, particularly, on one whose career has contributed to, and perpetuated, the literary myth of the hard-boiled American newspaperman. This was the late Hilding Johnson, whose personality furnished the basis for the popular newspaper melodrama and motion picture, "The Front Page" (1928). "Hildy," as he was called, was for twenty years Criminal Courts Building reporter for the Chicago *Herald & Examiner*, and was acknowledged one of the most picturesque characters of the profession. Upon his death in 1931, he was described in the press as "knowing everybody worth knowing in the political and criminal world of Chicago." According to obituary accounts, Mr. Johnson was born in Sweden and evidently was brought to this country by his parents when a child. He began his newspaper career as a copy boy and, at his death at the age of forty, was regarded as one of the top-notch crime reporters of the country. Out of respect for his memory, all activities ceased in the Criminal Courts Building on the day of his funeral, and his chair and telephone in the pressroom were draped in black.

Newsroom legends grew up about the figure of "Hildy" Johnson, among them, that he played poker with condemned murderers the night before they were to hang. It is not surprising, therefore, that the Chicago playwrights, Ben Hecht and Charles McArthur, quite frankly used Johnson, even to his name, as their protagonist in "The Front Page," and thus we have the appearance of a Swede in a central journalistic rôle in one of the best-known plays in recent American drama. He is portrayed as "a happy-go-lucky Swede with a pants-kicking sense of humor. . . . Hildy is of the vanishing type—the lusty, hoodlumesque, half drunken caballero that was the newspaper man of our youth. Schools of journalism and the advertising business have nearly extirpated the species. Now and then one of these boys still pops up in the profession and is hailed by his editor as a survival of a golden age." Although his character was, of course, greatly distorted, Johnson himself always referred to "The Front Page" as "that play those guys wrote about me."

There is a representative number of Swedes in the art and cartooning end of American journalism, and the most widely known of them is, undoubtedly, Abian Anders Wallgren, creator of "The Saluting Demon" of World War fame. "Wally," as he is called by thousands of admiring veterans, was official cartoonist for the *Stars and Stripes*, wartime newspaper of the American Expeditionary Forces in France, and is now official cartoonist for the *American Legion Monthly*.

Wally was born in Philadelphia in 1892 of Swedish parents. He entered newspaper work at an early age and was, indeed, something of a youthful prodigy in the art department of the old Philadelphia *North American*, for by the time he was sixteen he had two Sunday comic strips running; "Inbad, the Sailor" and "Ruff and Reddy." In the years that followed, Wally drew sports cartoons and Sunday comics for various papers in Philadelphia and Washington. When the United States entered the War, he was drawing for the sports page of the Philadelphia *Evening Ledger*. Immediately he enlisted in the Marine Corps, and was among the first to see service in France as a buck private and regimental sign painter, a post which army logic assigned him on his "professional" record. According to his own account, for nine months he painted "Latrine" and "Officers Only" signs up and down France, from St. Nazaire, through Menaucourt, to Damblaine in the Vosges. Private Wallgren's light, however, was being kept under a bushel. His great opportunity came when the *Stars and Stripes* was started as the official newspaper of the A.E.F., and Wally was placed on the staff as cartoonist. In February, 1918, he was transferred to Paris and drew cartoons for this doughboy newspaper throughout the War, until the final issue in June, 1919.

Wally's cartoons and comic strips made an instantaneous hit

with the doughboys, especially with the combat divisions. He had lived their life and possessed their point of view. Above all, he knew how deeply the man in the ranks of this Yankee army hated discipline, and with this valuable knowledge Private Wallgren set to work to ridicule those two luckless individuals, the top sergeant and the second lieutenant, who, together, personified discipline, in the eyes of the men. It was precisely the line to take to win the approval and delight of the doughboys. Wally's pen delineated the real history of their war in the way they could feel and understand. He knew the private soldier's disillusion of war; the mud, the cooties, the trench rats, and the "slum." But he accepted it all philosophically, saw the funny side, and laughed it off. For this achievement Wally was singled out by General Pershing for high praise. His rollicking cartoons and comic strips were fulfilling the purpose of the *Stars and Stripes* to uphold the morale of the Army. That he succeeded to a gratifying degree was attested by the great popularity and affection gained by him among the men of the A.E.F.

Since the War, Wally has been living in Philadelphia, and working as a free-lance artist. Although he is not, and does not want to be known as, a one-subject artist, his name will always be associated with the hard-boiled doughboy caricatures in the *Stars and Stripes* that did so much to bolster the spirit of an American Army overseas. His was a service which deserves the recognition of a grateful nation, as it already has the hearty indorsement of several thousand veterans who were "over there."

Another widely known newspaper artist of Swedish extraction is Robert Edgren, former Sports Editor of the New York *Evening World*. His drawings of famous boxers in action were real gems. In his younger days he was one of the best hammer and discus throwers in the United States and as such he is supposed to have taken part in the Olympic Games at Athens in 1906. (See the chapter on "Sports and Sportsmen.") Since the beginning of the century he covered most of the championship prize fights, and for years his drawings were popular features in the New York newspapers. He now lives in retirement in California, but has served as a member of the California State Boxing Commission.

Translations of Swedish Literature

ADOLPH B. BENSON

For biographical information on the Author, see the chapter on "Professors."

ENGLISH and American readers have long had abundant opportunity to get acquainted, in their own language, not only with Swedish literature itself, but with its social, political, and geographical background. In fact, Englishmen and Americans, through sources in English, knew, logically enough, not a little about Sweden long before they had heard of its literary products. Ever since the seventeenth century, when the Swedish Protestant champion, Gustavus Adolphus—for obvious reasons—became for a time the national hero of England, English-speaking peoples have maintained a certain interest in outstanding Swedish historical periods and characters, and, especially, in such sensational rulers as Queen Christina and Charles XII. Consequently, English translations of Swedish historical writings began to appear relatively early. An English version of Olaus Magnus' highly popular, but uncritical, *A Compendious History of the Goths, Swedes, and Vandals*—the original of which had been written in Latin —was published in London, 1658. Other historical works, both originals and translations, appeared in the eighteenth century, and, in 1844 and 1845, respectively, the English renderings of Anders Fryxell's *The History of Sweden* (edited by Mary Howitt), and E. G. Geijer's *The History of the Swedes* (in a translation by J. H. Turner), made their appearance. The latest translations to come out in this field are *A Short History of Sweden*, by R. Svanström and C. F. Palmstierna (Oxford, 1934), and *A History of Sweden* by C. Grimberg, "translated and adapted for the American teacher, student, and reader," by C. W. Foss (Rock Island, 1935). *The Sweden Year-Book* for 1936 lists sixty-four general and specific works in English, which deal either wholly or in part with Swedish historical subjects, not counting Swedish-American relations; and this list is selective only. Next to the royal personages just mentioned, the greatest foreign interest in Swedish historical figures has, naturally, centered about Gustavus Vasa, Gustavus III, and Bernadotte.

The same *Year-Book* lists a hundred and twenty-five travel books in English, in which information about Sweden may be obtained. They were published between 1698 and 1934, and many deal exclusively with Swedish territory. Conspicuous among the travel publications are *Northern Travel* (1858), by Bayard Taylor, which required at least three editions; *A Scandinavian Summer*, by H. A. Franck (1930); and the well-known *Sweden, the Land and the People*, by Agnes Rothery (1934). Also, especially during the last thirty-five years, numerous English and American publications have dealt wholly and extensively with the social, economic, industrial, and commercial conditions of Sweden. I refer to the *Year-Book* for a selected list, to which should now be added *Sweden, the Middle Way*, by Marquis W. Childs, an American venture which has had an amazingly large sale in this country. At the time of writing, about 25,000 copies have been sold.

Works in English, on Swedish music, art, and religion, have helped contribute the necessary background for an understanding of Swedish literature in its broadest sense. Jenny Lind has been the subject of several biographies, including one by N. P. Willis, which appeared in Philadelphia in 1851, and in 1931, the well-written, illustrated volume by E. Wagenknecht, which was published in Boston and New York. Swedish architecture, peasant art, embroideries, and textiles have been treated in English; a "Survey of Swedish Art," by C. G. Laurin, was translated by the present writer from the original manuscript, and published in *Scandinavian Art* (1922) by the American-Scandinavian Foundation. The *Kahn Lectures on Swedish Art* (1929) by Professor J. Roosval are now available in the series of "Princeton Monographs in Art and Archæology" (No. 18). Separate publications in English deal with Christina Nilsson, the pioneer Metropolitan soprano of the 'seventies; Anders Zorn, the versatile artist of Dalecarlia; and Bruno Liljefors, painter of animals. The *Hale Lectures* in America on "The National Church of Sweden," by the Bishop of Salisbury (J.

Wordsworth), appeared both in Milwaukee and London in 1911; two works on St. Birgitta of Sweden were published in London, 1909 and 1934, respectively; and there have, of course, been innumerable monographs and popular volumes on Swedenborg, the Swedish scientist and seer, whose enormous legacy of religious and spiritualistic writings are probably better known in English-speaking lands than in his own country. With the possible exception of some of his early minor scientific works, it is safe to say that everything Swedenborg wrote, which is decipherable—for it is, we are told, notoriously difficult to read his manuscripts—has been translated into English. His *Divine Love and Wisdom*, for instance, and *Heaven and Its Wonders, and Hell* may be read in "Everyman's Library." No Swede during the nineteenth century exerted a greater influence on American thought, religion, and letters, than Emanuel Swedenborg. He was the acknowledged master of Emerson; and Walt Whitman seems to have been deeply impressed by him. The translations of Swedenborg accomplished two or three generations ago in America what those of Strindberg seem to have done in our own day. But what a difference in kind!

Swedish scientists and explorers have indirectly done much to stimulate interest in all things Swedish. By their universally important inventions and discoveries, they have, time and again, consciously or unconsciously, directed attention to their native land and its culture; and they have thereby prepared the way for a more favorable reception of all its cultural productions. For example, Peter Kalm's scientific *Travels in North America* were translated in England, 1770–71; Olof Torbern Bergman's *Outlines of Mineralogy* appeared at Birmingham in an English translation in 1783; *A Tour of Lapland*, by Carl von Linné (Linnæus), pioneer naturalist, was translated from the original manuscript journal by J. E. Smith, and published in two volumes (London, 1811); *The Kidneys and Urine*, by the noted chemist, Jöns Jacob Berzelius, appeared in Philadelphia, 1843; and his *Use of the Blowpipe in Chemistry and Mineralogy*, in a translation by J. D. Whitney, came out two years later, in Boston. More recently, in 1934, appeared, in Baltimore, the *Autobiographical Notes* of Berzelius, in a translation by Professor Olof Larsell. English versions of archæological works on Sweden by Sven Nilson (*The Primitive Inhabitants of Scandinavia*) and Oscar Montelius (*The Civilization of Sweden in Heathen Times*) were published in England, 1868 and 1888, respectively. Several scientific volumes by Svante Arrhenius, Nobel Prize winner, have appeared in English translation, and, notably, *Life of the Universe* (I, II), which was, in 1909, added to Harper's "Library of Living Thought," and *The Destinies of the Stars*, which was published in a translation by J. E. Fries, in 1918. There are others. Numerous original works, translations, and adaptations from the Swedish, of a biographical nature, have made their appearance from time to time. Most of these treat of Linné, John Ericsson, Alfred Nobel, P. H. Ling, the "father of Swedish gymnastics," and S. A. Andrée, who, forty years ago, with two companions, tried unsuccessfully to reach the North Pole in a balloon. That the travel and exploration records of such eminent explorers as Adolf and Otto Nordenskjöld, J. G. Andersson, Prince Wilhelm, and, particularly, Sven Hedin, are available in English, every intelligent American reader knows. They need not be enumerated here. For details, consult the card catalogue of any fair-sized library.

It is about a century since translations in book form, of specifically Swedish belles-lettres of any consequence, appeared in an English translation; unless, perchance, we include the *Works* of Queen Christina (1626–89), which were translated from the French, and published in London, 1753, or the two series of *Letters . . . to a Young Prince*, by Carl Gustaf Tessin (1695–1770), which appeared in London during the years 1755 to 1759. In 1833, however, appeared the first complete English translation by William Strong, of *Frithiofs Saga*, by Esaias Tegnér (1782–1846); and by 1841 four more, distinct English versions of this romantic epic had been published. Altogether, there have been fifteen different complete renderings of this poetic cycle into English, the last, centennial version, so-called, by C. D. Locock of England, appearing in 1924. Among the fifteen, four were American, including the relatively popular versions by Martha A. L. and Thomas A. E. Holcomb, 1877, and the elaborately illustrated and annotated translation by Clement B. Shaw, 1908. The first American edition, however, was a reprint of an English version by the Reverend W. Lewery Blackley, 1857, which was edited by Bayard Taylor and published in New York, 1867. This same translation was reproduced in 1914 in the series of "Scandinavian Classics," published by the American-Scandinavian Foundation. In addition to these complete—or nearly complete—versions, there have been numerous partial translations of *Frithiofs Saga,* by Longfellow and others. Tegnér's *Axel,* a narrative romantic poem, has been done into English at least seven different times; though the total number of renderings is probably much larger. English forms of the shorter lyric poems by Tegnér may be found in the various anthologies of English translations from the Swedish, to which we shall refer again, later. That Longfellow translated Tegnér's "The Children of the Lord's Supper," and incorporated it among his works, is tolerably well known.

Despite the many translations of his poems, however, the general fame of Tegnér among English-reading peoples has been limited, in part, because of the form in which he wrote. Barring certain notable exceptions, it is infinitely more difficult, of course, to translate and popularize verse in foreign lands than prose, no matter how popular the original may be to its readers. This is particularly true, perhaps, of English reproductions of Swedish poetry. At all events, it was fated that a woman novelist, Fredrika Bremer (1801–65), should become the most noted Swedish writer of the nineteenth century in England and America. For almost three decades, beginning in 1842—when *The Neighbors* appeared in London in an English translation (from the German) by that untiring enthusiast, Mary Howitt—Fredrika Bremer enjoyed on both sides of the Atlantic an almost incredible literary reputation and prestige. Thorvald Solberg, of the Library of Congress, in his *Bibliography* of Scandinavia compiled a generation ago, lists seventy-nine translation items or editions under Miss Bremer's name, which had appeared by the year 1868; and several of these had contained two or more volumes, with numerous extra printings. Her domestic novels appealed to the peculiarly effeminate and sentimental taste of the midcentury period, and, occasionally, her work was considered a wholesome, moral antidote to the more traditional, sensational, and "objectionable" novels of other lands. Nor did Fredrika Bremer's household tales appeal only to women. Longfellow had, upon his return from Sweden in 1835, brought her early works to the Harvard Library; James Russell Lowell published, in 1844, an extensive review of her later novels in the *North American Review;* and on August 18, 1846, Walt Whitman declared in the Brooklyn *Daily Eagle,* of which he was Editor, that "If we ever have children, the first book after the New Testament . . . that shall be their household companion . . . shall be Miss Bremer's novels." Translations of these appeared in rapid succession: *The H— Family; The President's Daughters; Morning Watches; Strife and Peace;* and *The Home*—all appeared in 1843, and several others, later. One excellent translation of *Trälinnan* ("The Bondmaid") was executed in 1844, from the original Swedish, by Mary Lowell (Putnam), elder sister of the poet. *The Neighbors* had been published at the translator's expense, but Mary Howitt found no difficulty in finding publishers for her subsequent translations. Several other translators appeared on the scene, such as E. A. Friedländer and at least two anonymous aspirants; and Mary Howitt felt not a little peeved when Americans, like Mary Lowell, began to encroach upon what she considered her own private domain, by right of discovery. However, it was pointed out that Miss Bremer had been known in Boston for five years before her first work appeared in an English translation, and that all American versions of her writings had been made from the original Swedish, while the first ones by the English translator had obviously been made from the German. Mary Howitt had, however, begun the study of Swedish, as soon as she had made an acquaintance with the Bremer novels. The author's extensive travels in America, 1849–51, resulted in another, voluminous work, *The Homes of the New World* (1853), which required several editions and printings. A selection of the letters comprising this diary was edited by the present writer and published in the "Scandinavian Classics" (XXIII, 1924), under the title, *America of the Fifties.*

In the English-speaking countries, Swedish women writers have always been more popular than the men. At least, this seems a fair conclusion when seeking a meaning of the number of English translations from the Swedish. With the exception of Selma Lagerlöf, in whom the divine spark of genius plays such a conspicuous rôle, this is due in part, as we have already intimated, to the fact that most Swedish women have confined their literary work to the more popular genre of the short story, fairy tale, or novel; in other words, to more translatable *prose*. But the type, workmanship, and localization of the novels have also played a part. This is the case with Emelie Flygare-Carlén (1807–92), whose novels—happily localized among the Swedish skerries, and of a romantic, exotic, and often sensational character—enjoyed a popularity in America during the 'forties and 'fifties, second only to those by Fredrika Bremer. *The Professor and His Favorites* appeared in New York, 1843; two different translations of another novel, *The Rose of Thistle Island*, were published the following year—one in London, by Mary Howitt (*The Rose of Tistelön*), and the other in New York, by G. C. Hebbe and H. C. Deming; *The Magic Goblet* followed, in 1845; *The Temptation of Wealth*, 1846; and several others in 1851, 1852, 1853, etc. Solberg, in the abovementioned bibliography, lists thirty-nine English and American items under Carlén. There were several editions. Among the translators were Alexander L. Krause, Elbert Perce, and "F. E. D."

The indefatigable (but hasty and, therefore, sometimes inaccurate) Mary Howitt published, in 1848, an English version of the principal work of still another Swedish woman novelist, Sophie Knorring (1797–1848). It was *The Peasant and His Landlord* (*Torparen och hans omgivning*), of which a new edition was required within the year. In the period from 1868 to 1874, appeared the translations of at least eleven of the mediocre, but popular, novels by Marie Sophie Schwartz (1819–94). They were published in Boston, Hartford, New York, Philadelphia, and London—nine of them, in translations by Selma Borg and Marie A. Brown, of which five bear the imprint of 1871, including *Birth and Education* and *Guilt and Innocence*. The best one, *The Son of the Organ Grinder*, came out in 1873. *The Man of Birth and the Woman of the People*, in three volumes, had appeared in London, 1868, and there, also, in a translation by A. Wood, was published *Elvira, Lady*

Casterton, 1874. Other women writers of Sweden, who have found translators, are: Victoria Benedictsson (1850–88), whose *Truls Jonasson* appeared in 1895; Hildur Dixelius (1879–), whose novels, including *The Minister's Daughter* (1926), have been translated by Anna C. Settergren; Sophie Elkan (1853–1921), who lived to see an English version of her two-volume historical novel, *An Exiled King, Gustaf Adolf IV of Sweden* (1913); Laura Fitinghoff (1848–1908), whose *Children of the Moor* appeared at Boston, 1927, in an illustrated edition, translated by Siri Andrews; and the less-known Christina J. A. von Hofsten (1832–1913), who made her debut in America with a translation, *The Stark Family* (1876), followed in 1889 by *A Visit to the Björkheda Parsonage*, both done into English by C. Larsen, and published in Cincinnati and New York.

Readers interested in modern family problems know that the internationally famed feminist and writer, Ellen Key (1849–1926), found willing publishers for her essays and books on social subjects. We need but mention *Love and Marriage*, which appeared in a translation by A. G. Chater, 1913, and *The Renaissance of Motherhood*, translated by Anna E. B. Fries, 1914; but since she does not properly belong in the field of polite literature, we shall here refrain from enumerating the other works by this courageous and influential modern crusader. A list of the books translated will be found in the *Sweden Year-Book* (1936). Anne-Charlotte Leffler (1849–92) is represented in this same source by the translation of a play, *True Women*, published about fifty years ago. Mathilda Malling (1864–) has attracted translators for three of her books, the first one, *A Romance of the First Consul*, appearing in 1898. E. W. Olson has translated several works by Emily Nonnen (1812–1905), all published between 1908 and "*c.* 1925" in Chicago or Rock Island, Illinois; Swedish fairy tales by Helena Nyblom (1843–1926) have appeared simultaneously in London and New York (1912); Mathilda Roos (1852–1908) has, in C. A. Wendell, E. W. Olson, and C. W. Foss, found translators for her children's stories; *Two Women*, by Margareta Suber (1892–) has been published in London, 1934; the Swedish fairy tales, collected and translated by Anna Wahlenberg (1858–1933), have proved popular with publishers in London, Chicago, and Philadelphia; and a selection of short stories, in two volumes, entitled *Queer People*, by Josefina Wettergrund (1830–1903), appeared in England, 1882. We shall discuss Selma Lagerlöf later. Lack of space forbids the mentioning by name of all deserving writers, men or women, and several names will be found only in our anthologies and magazines. Now we must return to the men authors.

Besides those mentioned, translations of a great variety of Swedish writers made their appearance in the 'seventies. Gustaf Henrik Mellin (1803–76) was represented by *The Nomads of the North, A Tale of Lapland* (London, 1871); the royal orator, Gustavus III (1746–92), was given a small niche in American translation literature by his conventionally eloquent *Eulogy of Lennart Torstenson*, the noted Swedish general of the Thirty Years' War (New York, 1872); the popular, humorous August Blanche (1811–68) made his literary debut in New York, the same year, in *The Bandit*, in a translation by Selma Borg and Marie A. Brown; and in St. Louis, Missouri, 1876, appeared *Envy*, a drama by the eighteenth-century rationalist, Olof von Dalin (1708–63). Both Dalin and Gustavus III had, in their own day, been cultural leaders, whose names for all time have been attached to the respective literary periods which they represent. Here, too, we might recall that *The Angel of Death*, an outstanding religious poem by the Swedish Archbishop, Johan Olof Wallin (1779–1839), had, by 1920, been translated at least four times into English, including once by Clement B. Shaw, with illustrations by Carl Larsson (Chicago, 1910).

Among the foremost authors in the history of Swedish literature, are Viktor Rydberg (1828–95), and the two Finns, Johan Ludvig Runeberg (1804–77) and Zacharias Topelius (1818–98), both of whom wrote in Swedish. Eight different translators essayed to interpret Rydberg in English. This liberal poet, novelist, and scholarly classicist first found a sympathetic, conscientious translator in W. W. Thomas, Jr., later United States Minister to Sweden, who Englified *The Last Athenian* (Philadelphia, 1869; 2d ed., 1879), a historical novel of large and noble proportions. It was followed, in 1879, by *The Magic of the Middle Ages*, in a translation by the poet and professor,

A. Hjalmar Edgren; and Rydberg's *Roman Legends*, and the medieval tale of *Singoalla*, each found two translators. Another interesting historical novel, *The Freebooter of the Baltic*, appeared in Media, Pennsylvania, in 1891; and a part of his gigantic and authoritative work on *Teutonic Mythology* was translated by R. B. Anderson (1889) and required two subsequent editions, the one of 1906 appearing in three volumes, in London, Stockholm, and New York. Runeberg's *Lyrical Songs, Idylls and Epigrams*, 1878, was the first collection of his poems to appear in English; *Nadeschda*, a poem in nine cantos by the same author, was published in Boston, 1879, in a translation by Marie A. Brown. Other works by Runeberg, and notably *King Fjalar*, came out at various times in English form; and in 1925, in New York, appeared the first complete English translation of Runeberg's masterpiece, *The Songs of Ensign Stål*, a cycle of remarkable poems which glorify the exploits and sufferings of his countrymen in the Finnish War. The translation was executed by Clement B. Shaw, and provided with all the essential editorial, musical, and illustrative material that an American reader would need. (Mr. Shaw was an American music teacher whose Swedish pupils, in Chicago, first inspired him with a desire to learn Swedish.) A second complete translation of this classic is now being prepared by another well-known translator. The children's stories by Topelius have been done into English, both in England and America, by Albert Alberg, appearing in 1881. The first cycle of Topelius' *The Surgeon's Stories*, picturing various phases of Swedish history, was published in New York, 1872, in a joint translation by Selma Borg and Marie A. Brown—whom we have met before—and, in 1883–91, appeared the complete six cycles, in Chicago, in a version by Miss Brown (Mrs. J. B. Shipley). *Canute Thistlewinks and Other Stories*, by Topelius, was published in New York, in 1927, in a translation by C. W. Foss.

That a large proportion of the novels, stories, and plays by August Strindberg (1849–1912), Sweden's greatest dramatist, are accessible in English translations, is known by most readers. Several of his plays have appeared on the American stage. The *Sweden Year-Book* lists forty-one Strindberg publication units in English, some of them including several volumes. There may be even more. Some of his dramas have been translated several times, and have required many editions. Edwin Björkman alone has translated twenty-four of Strindberg's plays. Other translators are Velma Swanston Howard, C. Field, C. D. Locock, H. B. Samuel, F. J. Ziegler, and Edith and Warner Oland (the Swedish Hollywood actor of Chinese characters). Those who have limited their translating to the novels include Ellie Schleussner and Elizabeth Clarke Westergren. Most of the English and American versions have appeared since the author's death, though a few had been published before, and during, the year 1912. It is unnecessary to enumerate the many individual items here, since this information can readily be obtained elsewhere. Incidentally, the writer cannot help wondering whether it is not a waste of time, money, and energy, and an evidence of conceit, for the recently established Anglo-Swedish Literary Foundation in London to duplicate translations of Strindberg plays, which were long ago available in good American translations. I am now thinking, for example, of *Master Olof*, which was published in a translation by Björkman (1915), by the American-Scandinavian Foundation ("Scandinavian Classics," IV). Sixteen years later a new translation appeared in England by the Anglo-Swedish Foundation. Even *Lucky Pehr*, in the sensitive rendering by Mrs. Howard, was later retranslated in England. Was this imperative? I doubt whether an unbiased microscopic comparison of the two versions would show any substantial improvement. In fact, I suspect the opposite may be true. Next to Swedenborg, the Swedish author to exert the greatest influence abroad is probably Strindberg. In the United States Eugene O'Neill, the recent Nobel Prize winner, has acknowledged Strindberg as his model and master.

A Swedish Nobel Prize winner in literature, Verner von Heidenstam (1859–), artist, poet, patriot, and novelist, has, of course, been made available in English, in translations by A. Tegnier, Karoline M. Knudsen, and Charles Wharton Stork. Mr. Stork, for example, published, in 1919, in New Haven, a volume of Heidenstam's selected poems under the title *Sweden's Laureate*, followed in 1920 and 1925, respectively, by renderings of *The Charles Men* (*Karolinerna*) and *The Swedes and their Chieftains*, the latter two appearing in the "Scandinavian

Classics" (XV–XVI, and XXV). A new edition of *The Charles Men* came out in 1933, in England. Dr. Stork, able and prolific interpreter of Swedish literature in English, has also translated (1916) a volume of poems by Gustaf Fröding (1860–1911) ; *The Motherless* (1922) by Bengt Berg (1885–) ; *Martin Birck's Youth* (1930), and *Selected Short Stories* (1935), by Hjalmar Söderberg (1869–) ; and three anthologies— *Modern Swedish Masterpieces*, a selection of short stories (1923) ; *Anthology of Swedish Lyrics from 1750 to 1915* (1917, revised and enlarged edition to 1925, 1930) ; and *Sweden's Best Stories*, edited by Hanna Astrup Larsen (1928). The last two appeared in the "Scandinavian Classics" (IX and XXX), and contain selections from practically all the outstanding Swedish poets and short-story writers.

It is of curious interest to note that anthologies of Swedish literature in English have appeared, not only in many cities of the United States, from Brownfield, Maine, to San Francisco, California, but also in Bergen, Stockholm, London, and Helsingfors. In America the Misses Borg and Brown translated a number of Swedish and Finnish stories which appeared in 1873, under the caption of *Northern Lights*. Two volumes of *Masterpieces from Swedish Literature in English Form*, edited by C. W. Foss, came out during 1906–08; the New York poet and psychiatrist, Dr. Frederick Peterson, published, in 1883, *Poems and Swedish Translations;* R. Ahléen filled in a gap by publishing, in 1932, *Swedish Poets of the Seventeenth Century;* and *Songs of Sweden*, with music—but highly unsatisfactory translations by H. G. Chapman—was published in the series of *Songs of the People* (New York, 1909). Four anthologies of Swedish polite letters have appeared in England, one of modern poetry, by Locock (1929), and a volume of *Modern Swedish Short Stories*, published by the Anglo-Swedish Literary Foundation (1934). *Under the Swedish Colours. A Short Anthology of Modern Swedish Poets Done into English Verse*, by F. A. Judd, with a Preface by Edmund Gosse, had already appeared (1911). It contained, among others, selected poems by Oscar II, Carl Snoilsky, Oscar Levertin, Per Hallström, and Erik Axel Karlfeldt (formerly Secretary of the Swedish Academy and posthumous Nobel Prize winner).

Other Swedish authors, whose works have broken through
the barriers of language into English—to mention a few more
miscellaneous names alphabetically—are: Carl J. L. Almquist
(1793–1866), a bizarre combination of romanticist and realist, whose *Gabriele Mimanso* had attracted a translator, G. C.
Hebbe, in 1846, and whose revolutionary *Sara Videbeck* (*Det
går an*) and *The Chapel*, in an effort by the present writer,
formed No. XII of the "Scandinavian Classics," 1919; Hjalmar
Bergman (1833–1931), represented by *God's Orchid*, 1924;
Herman Bjursten (1825–66), who could not foresee that his
The Play of Fate would appear in English twenty-six years
after his death; Gustaf af Geijerstam (1858–1909), two of
whose products, *The Book about Little Brother*, and *Woman
Power*, have appeared in the "Classics" (XVIII and XXVIII,
in 1921 and 1927, respectively) ; and another, *My Boys*, 1933,
in a translation by Alfhild Huebsch; Richard Gustafson
(1840–1918), whose tales for young folk have won many readers, especially in England; Per Hallström (1866–), who, in
the short story, has found enviable favor, both in England and
the United States, in translations by F. J. Fielden ("Scandinavian Classics," XX) ; Ola Hansson (1860–1925), whose *Young
Ofeg's Ditties* were translated in 1895; Gustaf Hellström
(1882–), whose *Lacemaker Lekholm has an Idea* appeared in
New York, 1930; and Jarl Hemmer, a Finn (1893–), found
a publisher in New York for his *A Fool of Faith*, in a
translation by F. H. Lyon, 1935. Gustaf Jansson (1866–
1913), Richert von Koch (1838–1913), Henry Martinson
(1904–), and Harald Molander (1858–1900) have also appeared in English dress; and, that *The Story of San Michele*
by Axel Munthe (1857–) long ago became a best seller in
America is now common knowledge. An illustrated novel, *The
Moonlight Sonata*, by Johan Nordling (1863–) made its debut
in England, 1912. Several novels by Martin Gunnar Serner
(Frank Heller, 1886–) have been translated, by Björkman,
Pauline de Chary, and R. E. Lee. *Downstream*, by Sigfrid
Siwertz (1882–) was welcomed with some enthusiasm, 1922;
and *Roaring Bones*, by Prince Wilhelm (1884–), found appreciative readers in 1927. Then, also, in addition to those already
mentioned, a number of books on Swedish folklore have been

translated and published. Swedish fairy tales, like those from the other Scandinavian countries, have been very popular in America.

The above list is, obviously, not complete, with respect to either authors or works; nor can we, for obvious reasons, make it complete in this article. But a good majority of the important writers have been named. About seventy Swedish authors of belles-lettres have had one or more volumes of their writings appear in English form, under their own names; and in some cases, as we have seen, a dozen or more different items by the same author have been translated. Many additional names of poets and short-story writers, like C. M. Bellman, Anna Maria Lenngren, C. M. Franzén, Anders Österling, Bo Bergman, Pelle Molin, and Anna Lenah Elgström, will be found in the anthologies mentioned and in our periodicals. But there is one more Swedish writer to whom we must devote a special paragraph—Selma Lagerlöf.

I have stated that the Swedish women writers, as a rule, have been more popular in America than the men. This is still the case. Miss Lagerlöf seems to retain her hold upon the English-speaking public, in all circles. As Hanna Astrup Larsen, in her book, *Selma Lagerlöf*, has already pointed out, the only Scandinavian writer who can compare with Miss Lagerlöf in popularity abroad is Hans Christian Andersen. She is more beloved, and her writings give consistently more pure æsthetic delight to readers of all grades of maturity and intellect, than those of any other Scandinavian author I have ever known. And no writer of any land has more completely fulfilled the original provisions of the Nobel Prize in Literature, which she received, than she. This prize stipulated that the works submitted in competition; i.e., the ones to be considered in the award of that prize, should be of an "idealistic tendency." In Selma Lagerlöf we find this idealism, tolerance, humanity, realism, steeped in an atmosphere of fairyland, imagination, legend, and religion, and a subtle, profound, nonoffensive didacticism, all combined. The universal appeal of her numerous stories, novels, addresses, and autobiographical material has attracted, and challenged, many translators all over the world, including, of course, America and the British Isles. Over a dozen translators have endeavored,

SELMA LAGERLÖF

more or less successfully, to reproduce her works in English, the most successful in word and spirit being, undoubtedly, those studied and meticulous re-creations by Velma Swanston Howard. Works like *Gösta Berling's Saga, Jerusalem,* and *The Miracles of Antichrist* have been translated more than once, and the *Wonderful Adventures of Nils* has not only, like some others, required several editions, but has, in extracts or condensations, been introduced as reading material for children in our public schools. Among the recent Lagerlöf publications in New York are *Harvest* (1935), a collection of short stories and reminiscences, translated by Florence and Naboth Hedin, and *The Diary of Selma Lagerlöf* (1936), in a distinctive version by Mrs. Howard. We need not give further details here.

Despite the number and variety of translations of Swedish masterpieces and products of more ordinary quality, it can hardly be said that there existed, during the last century, any widespread or deep knowledge of Swedish literature in America or England, even in intellectual circles, before the advent of Strindberg and Lagerlöf—and not always, then. Except for the novels of Miss Bremer, and possibly those of Mrs. Carlén, many translations appeared only in small editions. Sometimes they were published in obscure places, from which the distribution was small, difficult, and ineffective; and often they were made by relatively obscure translators of only mediocre ability, or less. Many versions in English, of course, never passed beyond the first printing. With the exception of some Germans, few non-Scandinavian people today know Tegnér well, if at all, the many translations of his *Frithiofs Saga* notwithstanding. And, unless a work has been translated within the last generation, it is simply not available any more, except in some local or large library, or in some private collection like that of Consul G. N. Swan of Sioux City. Most copies of the early translations are lost for all time, and the few remaining are exceedingly rare.

Nevertheless, with the translating of more recent writers like Fröding, Heidenstam, Hallström, Söderberg, Strindberg, and particularly Lagerlöf, the development of more able translators, and the increasing knowledge of Sweden as a whole, the situation has visibly improved. The more commercial interest

of certain publishing houses in the younger Swedish writers
has also helped the matter, from a publicity viewpoint at least.
In the interim, the American-Scandinavian Foundation, a
strictly noncommercial institution, has, during its quarter-
century of activity and its scrupulous editorship by Hanna
Astrup Larsen, published fifty volumes of Scandinavian monographs and classics, especially such as would not generally appeal to a purely business concern. Among these volumes, to
date, fourteen have been specifically Swedish, not counting
translated material in common with all Scandinavian countries,
such as *Scandinavian Art, Scandinavian Mythology*, etc. Other
volumes are in preparation. What we need most of all, and what
the Foundation is very desirous of publishing in the near future, is a history of Swedish literature in English, which is
especially adapted to Americans. But, in the meantime, we may
be reasonably proud of both the magnitude and quality of the
Swedish literature in English translation. The list given is impressive; it contains a sufficient number of translations of distinction to be really valuable; and we know quite definitely
that some Swedish writers have exerted an influence, however
small or intangible, on certain American authors. What the
influence has been on the American public as a whole, we can
never fully know, but we believe it has been extensive and wholesome. However, this is a problem that future students may
determine.

Four Representatives of the Intellect
Arrhenius, Berzelius, Linné, and Swedenborg

DAVID F. SWENSON

For biographical notes on the Author, see the chapter on "Professors."

IN a time which displays, in many quarters, a febrile intensification of the deep-seated human passion to dominate
others, it is an observation that might be cooling to this
passion, if any passion could be moderated by mere knowledge,
that the nationals of the smaller civilized countries of the world
apparently occupy as high a plane of intellectual and moral
culture as do the citizens of states that exercise a world-wide
dominion. The smaller countries have contributed their full
quota to the intellectual and spiritual riches of the world. They
do, indeed, share in the culture of their larger neighbors; and it
is an edifying and inspiring thought that the higher goods of
life, just in proportion as they really are higher, are communi-
cable without diminution. They refuse to be stamped with a
particular and exclusive ownership; the richer any man or nation is in them, the richer all others are also. The treasures of
science and thought cannot be monopolized in the long run,
either by a privileged caste, a favored nation, or a supposedly
superior race.

The intellect of man is, when rightly used, a weapon of eman-
cipation. As it liberates the human being from the dominance
of the present moment, so it frees him from exclusive subjection
to his local and contextual relativity. A man of science has, by
virtue of his occupation, a certain universality impressed upon
his nature. I remember a remark made by Svante Arrhenius,
the Swedish cosmographer and Nobel Prize winner, upon the
occasion of his last visit to America. It was at one of those
public receptions where the privilege of clasping the hand, and
addressing some banal remark to the guest of honor, is the
reward of taking the trouble to be present. This particular
questioner asked Arrhenius how he liked America. He replied
a little coolly: "My friend, you see my kind of people are

the same all over the world." The reply was indeed true and
apposite, and the implied rebuke no doubt deserved. One is
tempted to make a single qualifying reservation, which the
casual and impromptu character of the remark forbids one to
press: in tearing down one type of barrier we sometimes set up
another, not essentially more tolerable; as *in casu*, the barrier
between the scientist and other men.

It is in this spirit that I approach the task of describing the
services that four representative men of Swedish birth, essentially members of the kingdom of the spirit, have directly or
indirectly rendered to the country of our adoption. Of none of
them could it truly be said that to mention his name is like running up his country's flag; they loved their country and their
countrymen, but none was inflamed with an exaggerated nationalism. They were "men of Europe," and wrote for an international public; they achieved, while still living, an international fame.

The men whose contribution to the world's heritage of culture it is here proposed to sketch are two chemists, Svante
Arrhenius and Jöns Jakob Berzelius; the great botanist and
taxonomist, Carl von Linné; and Emanuel Swedenborg. If we
were choosing a typical philosopher to represent the Swedish
genius, we might perhaps let our choice fall upon some other
than Swedenborg—notably, Christopher Jakob Boström. But
none has had so great an influence upon the culture of America
as the vast and manifold personality whom Emerson calls "the
Swede Emanuel." The lives of these men form an almost unbroken chain, stretching across more than two centuries. Indeed, as in 1938, we celebrate the Tercentenary of the Swedish
settlements on the Delaware, so we also celebrate, in the same
year, the two hundred and fiftieth anniversary of the birth of
Emanuel Swedenborg.

Svante Arrhenius (1859–1927)

To the American public, Arrhenius is known chiefly for his
speculations in the field of cosmic physics. Two popular scientific works of his dealing with this subject have been translated
into English. His special contacts with American scientists in-

clude two visits to this country: by invitation of the University of California in 1904, when he lectured on general theories of chemistry and upon the special problem of immunity in physiological chemistry; by invitation of Yale University in 1911, when he lectured on the theory of solutions.

In his doctoral dissertation of 1884, dealing with the electrolytic solutions, the first hints were given of that dissociation theory with which his name is inseparably linked. He noted then the increase in the number of conducting molecules, at the expense of the rest, which takes place with increased dilution, and explains the increased electrical conductivity. But at that time he did not indicate the nature of the difference between the conducting and the nonconducting molecules. After four years spent in research and reflection, including work at several foreign laboratories, Arrhenius transmitted to the Stockholm Academy of Sciences on June 8, 1887, the brief paper of only ten pages, which established his fame securely as a chemist of great distinction. This essay is marked by originality, simplicity, and clearness in argument; it has been described as one of the finest essays in all scientific literature. Here he establishes the principle that electrolytic solutions are characterized by the formation of a large number of free ions; i.e., a high degree of dissociation in the molecular constituents. He shows how this principle explains a number of collateral phenomena, as, for example, the electrical conductivity and the osmotic pressures. The next ten years of his life were devoted to a further elaboration of the theory, and to the discovery and exhibition of confirmatory evidence.

After 1895 Arrhenius turned his attention to new fields: meteorology, geophysics, and cosmic physics. Among other things, he attacked the problem of entropy, the apparent probability of an eventual running down of the universe through an inevitable decrease in the availability of its energy for work. He suggested that the nebulae could be regarded as energy-improvers; he called attention to the rôle of radiation pressure upon the smaller and lighter particles in the peripheral portions of the suns, effecting a redistribution of matter which would tend to restore an energy-balance; he noted how energy might be replenished to our sun, through chemical action in its interior. In short, Arrhenius was fertile in the suggestion of ways in which the energy-balance of the universe might have been maintained in the past, and might continue to be maintained in the future.

His most arresting idea in this connection is that, in the absence of what is called "spontaneous generation" on our own planet through the failure here of favorable circumstances, germs of life may have come to our earth by the action of radiation pressure—the pressure of light, from centers of life scattered through the vast material universe. The low temperatures obtaining in the interstellar spaces, and the experimental evidence of the effect of cold in slowing down the life processes, make the maintenance of vitality in living germs, for as much as millions of years, not utterly improbable. On such foundations Arrhenius worked out the conception of a cyclic development of the universe, not unlike Herbert Spencer's notion of an alternation of evolution and dissolution, or that of ancient Hindu sages; though he was not contending, as does Nietzsche, for a precise and literal repetition of the past in each stage, since the occasional collisions between celestial bodies, on which the rhythm is in part conditioned, "must involve an element of the accidental." Thus he pictures the universe, not as destined for death, but rather as living an everlasting life, past as well as future being without limits.

The later years of his life Arrhenius devoted to biochemical and physiological studies, investigating especially the action of toxins and antitoxins, and the processes of digestion and absorption. In 1905, after having declined the offer of a professorship at the Berlin Academy of Sciences, he was made the first Director of the newly established Nobel Institute for Physical Chemistry in Stockholm, retaining this position until his death. He was the recipient of the Nobel Prize in Chemistry in 1903, and held honorary doctorates from many foreign institutions, including Leipzig, Cambridge, Oxford, Birmingham, and Heidelberg. His many courses of lectures delivered abroad were marked by great breadth of view, objectivity of treatment, and a thought unusually clear and precise.

Jöns Jakob Berzelius (1779–1848)

CHEMISTRY owes to Berzelius a debt even more fundamental. His contributions to its progress have reference to its nomenclature, the unification within it of organic and inorganic points of view, the radicle conception of the constitution of organic compounds, and the law of multiple proportions, the primary empirical basis of modern atomic theory. During his lifetime, he was recognized as one of the greatest chemists of his age, an age which included such men as Dalton, Davy, Ampère, Örsted, Bertholet, Tennant, and Guy Lussac. Besides his original researches, described in more than 250 monographs, he unfolded an extraordinary productivity relating to the general progress of the science. His *Lehrbuch der Chemie* was widely accepted as the best handbook of its time, being in general use for half a century. In his capacity as Secretary of the Academy of Sciences in Stockholm, he prepared twenty-seven volumes of "Annual Reports," in which he dealt with the world progress of physical and chemical research, reports which furnish the original pattern for the system of scientific reference literature in vogue today. A man of genial insight and sober judgment, he succeeded in achieving remarkable accuracy with primitive laboratory resources, displaying a phenomenal capacity for fruitful, detailed work. His is one of the great names in the annals of natural science.

His natural bent led him, at Uppsala, to pursue medical studies, as being at that time the only way open to satisfy the powerful attraction that physics and chemistry exerted upon him, from his first introduction to these sciences. Circumstances compelled him to become chiefly his own teacher. In a student room, rented for the purpose, he started a private laboratory while still in residence at the University. He continued independent chemical research, while practicing medicine in Stockholm, and here, in 1803, he discovered cerium, a rare metallic element found in samples of a mineral from Bastnäs, Sweden. In 1806 he was appointed to a professorship in the Stockholm Medical School, and the next ten years saw him plunged into intensive scientific labor, the experiments undertaken giving him world-wide renown. His earlier work had been in the field of physiological chemistry; but in 1807 he began the stoichiometric investigations which were to provide the first comprehensive and accurate determination of atomic weights. He ascertained the constant basic combining weights for no less than two thousand simple and compound substances, a substantial majority of those then known to science. This work was accomplished under great difficulties. When he began, the methods of quantitative analysis were still largely undeveloped; and laboratory resources, as compared with those available in our day, were limited in the extreme. Working quite alone, and in the face of these handicaps, Berzelius made a major contribution toward the establishment of chemistry as a quantitative science. The theoretical result of his measurements was to give to Dalton's atomic theory the support of a mass of evidence hitherto lacking.

In the course of his investigations Berzelius discovered, or isolated for the first time, a considerable number of elements: cerium (1803); selenium (1817); silicon (1823); zirconium (1824); thorium (1828). His reform of chemical nomenclature, carrying forward the work initiated by Lavoisier, consisted of using the initial letters of the Latin names of the elements, and furnishing them with numerical subscripts to indicate the number of atoms of each, present in a compound. This is the system in use today. Berzelius can thus be said to have left his mark indelibly upon the science of chemistry. "Berzelius Hall" at Yale University is named after him.

Carl von Linné (1707–78)

A RECENT American textbook of zoology tells how Linnæus (ennobled as Linné; many Swedes love to call him *blomsterkungen*) was the son of a Swedish clergyman; that as a student he was adjudged good-for-nothing and was apprenticed to a cobbler; that he came under the influence of a physician who enlisted his interest in biology; that he grew to be a man of high attainments in medicine, but finally devoted himself to problems of pure biology. This account is about as accurate as most anecdotal biographies, except that he was never apprenticed to a cobbler, and that his interest in plants was manifest from a very early age. His failure to apply himself to classical studies led his teachers at the gymnasium to suggest to his father that he apprentice his son to a tailor or a shoemaker. It is not known how great the danger was that this advice might be followed, nor how seriously it was meant. But a friend of the family, a physician, did give the boy instruction in physiology, and predicted distinction for him in medicine or natural history. Linnæus' father had a passion for gardening, and gave his son, when he was but eight years old, a plot of ground to cultivate, which the boy soon converted into a miniature botanical garden. At twenty, while a student at Lund, his interest in botany was already so marked as to prompt him to collect and arrange an herbarium. The following years were spent at Uppsala, where the botanizing theologian, Olaus Celsius, took note of the boy's talent and need, giving him a home with him, while at the same time engaging his coöperation in preparing his own *Hierobotanicon* for publication.

There are one or two interesting links between Linnæus and American life. He described 780 species of North American plants. For example, he gave our mountain laurel its scientific classification and name. Specimens were collected for him by a naturalist trained under his direction at Uppsala—Peter Kalm, who was sent over, in 1748, to bring back such plants and seeds as might be useful to Sweden, now that its dreams of empire were over. To this plant, as well as to its relative, the sheep laurel, Linnæus gave the name of the collector: the mountain laurel he called *Kalmia latifolia;* the sheep laurel *Kalmia angustifolia*, making the width of the leaf the distinguishing mark. Peter Kalm was not only a naturalist, but a man interested in all things human. He kept a journal of his travels, known and appreciated by Thoreau, which he filled with interesting observations relating to the country and its social customs. He had relations of friendship with Benjamin Franklin and others; he traveled through the Hudson River country and reached Canada on the north; he ventured as far west as Niagara Falls, of which he gives the first description written in English from firsthand information. There is a valuable account of the Delaware River region, the place of the Swedish settlements. He reports in detail how the farmers lived; what they ate and drank; how they dressed; what they learned from the Indians; what weeds troubled them; how they managed to get through the winter. This diary, which is a valuable source book for the student of eighteenth-century American colonial life, has recently been brought out in an improved translation by Professor Adolph B. Benson of Yale.

A genus of some twenty American species belonging to the aster family was named, by Linnæus, *Rudbeckia*, from his predecessor in the chair of Botany at Uppsala, and the latter's still more distinguished father. He also identified and classified our now nearly extinct white whooping crane, *Grus americana*, a magnificent bird standing five feet tall when erect. Previously, all three American species had been lumped together as cranes of different sizes. The whooping crane was by far the largest specimen, when in flight making a tremendous impression on the beholder. Nuttall, describing a great migration of these birds up the Mississippi Valley in 1811, says that "the passage of their mighty armies fills the mind with wonder."

Linnæus' great work was to lay the foundations for modern taxonomic methods in biology. In 1735, after having conceived and worked out his system of classification, he began his great and triumphant journey through the centers of scientific studies in Europe. He had with him his manuscript of *Systema Naturae*.[1] When Professor Gronovius of Leyden saw it, he was so much impressed that he undertook to print it at his own expense. In 1736, he was elected to membership in the Academy of Sciences at Vienna, under the fanciful title of Dioscorides the Second. The following year he visited England, making contacts with its outstanding scientists, and being received with especial enthusiasm by the younger men. The Chelsea gardens were the first in England to be arranged on the Linnean system.

1. It is of interest in this connection to recall the enthusiasm and reverence for Linnæus of the American poet, linguist, and geologist, Dr. James Gates Percival (1795–1856). While a student at Yale, Percival made a full extract of the *Systema Naturae,* lauded Linnæus at every opportunity, and, later, wrote in his honor an appreciative birthday poem, wherein he publicly acknowledged the Swedish scientist as his guide and master. Incidentally, Percival learned privately, over a century ago, to read all the modern Scandinavian languages.

Upon his return to Sweden, he at first practiced medicine in Stockholm; after three years he was elected to the chair of physics and anatomy at Uppsala, but, in the subsequent year, the more suitable chair of botany was made available to him through an exchange. His lectures and courses attracted to Uppsala a phenomenal number of students from every country in Europe. When the sixth edition of *Systema Naturae* was published in 1748, his fame was secure and world-wide, and his death in 1778 was marked by universal mourning. There is in Edinburgh a monument to Linnæus, in the Botanical Garden; a Linnean society was established at Paris in 1787; at London in 1788; and at Leipzig in 1790. New York has a Linnean society, and many botanical organizations throughout the world make use of his name to indicate the spirit and purpose that animate their activities.

Before Linnæus' day no scientific system of classification was in general use in botany, though some slight attempts in that direction had been made, notably by the Florentine, Andreas Cæsalpinus, whom Linnæus calls the first true systematician. Botanical studies had been, for the most part, subordinated to medicine; and descriptions and classifications were based on external appearance or, from the point of view of use to man, chiefly medical. The system of Linnæus was derived from observation of the stamens and pistils, the so-called sexual organs; it was in so far an "artificial" system, recognized as such by the author. It had the great virtue of giving the scientist a convenient arrangement of his materials, replacing the reigning confusion. It served as a sort of index to the book of nature—of almost indispensable assistance in deeper inquiries. The standard set by Linnæus for clear definition and precise diagnosis was of the highest; his descriptions were models of compression. In his system of classification and nomenclature, he gave to each species a Latin name consisting of two parts: first a noun indicating the genus, and second an adjective descriptive of the particular species.

Linnæus combined a collector's passion with a logician's zeal for systematic arrangement; he even drew up a scheme for the classification of diseases. Due to the opening up of new trade routes and consequent increased contact with all parts of the world, new plants and animals were in his time being discovered daily. It was thus an age calling for such a genius; he was a man born in due time. He had an immense enthusiasm for teaching and training naturalists, impressing his own character forcibly upon them. His students were reared in an atmosphere of almost exalted enthusiasm, his influence being in this respect outstanding, even in an age when scientific enthusiasm was the order of the day.

Emanuel Swedenborg (1688–1772)

THE men of science, whose careers have been lightly sketched in the preceding pages, have trodden the safe and, in our days, well-beaten path of intellectual specialization. Their enduring contributions to science were the fruits of an energetic concentration on particular problems. Swedenborg's intellect was cast in a different mold. No mere specialization could satisfy his ambition; he aimed to comprehend in his thought both the finite and the infinite, both time and eternity, both man and the world, both Nature and God.

The circumstances of his life mirror the universality of his interests. He was an engineer, and, also, financial adviser to kings; he was metallurgist and mathematician; geologist and physicist and astronomer; biologist and brain anatomist; psychologist and moralist; pursuer of dialectical subtleties and metaphysical poet in the grand style of a Lucretius or a Milton. As if this were not enough, he rounded out his career as mystic and spirit seer, theosophist and theologian, the founder of a new religion; or, rather, the revealer of the hitherto hidden meaning of an old religion, as such giving the impulse to the foundation of a New Church—having in this country at present some ten thousand formal adherents—to supplant the decadent sects of Christendom. Verily an arresting phenomenon, a riddle to read and solve; unless, indeed, one is disposed to dismiss him at once with Plato's ironical remark: "The promise is so vast, that a feeling of incredulity will creep in."

Swedenborg was by no means neglected by his contemporaries. His work in all its chief phases was known to European scholars, and his theosophical writings attracted the attention

EMANUEL SWEDENBORG, 1688–1772
SCIENTIST AND RELIGIOUS LEADER

of no less a thinker than Immanuel Kant, who published, in 1766, an essay on Swedenborg's spirit visions. Some sixty years after his death, partly through the publication of previously inaccessible writings and the translation of many of his works from the Latin to the vernacular, there was evoked in Germany, England, and America a more popular and widely spread interest in his thought. When Emerson wrote *Nature*, he was profoundly influenced by Swedenborg's doctrine of microcosm and macrocosm; the idea that a single plan is everywhere repeated, so that the innermost essence of the greatest is the same with that of the least, the whole present in every part—a translation into terms of imaginative intuition of the thought of the omnipresence of God. "Who guesseth one of my meanings," says the Sphinx, "is master of all that I am." The lecture on Swedenborg, which Emerson included in *Representative Men*, published in 1850, and during the preceding five years repeatedly gave before American audiences, was but a symptom of the prevalent American interest in Swedenborg. Among the eager reforming spirits of New England, revolving about the "transcendentalist" group, Swedenborg was for a time the official theologian, ministering to the needs of the inner man, just as Fourier was the official social scientist, providing a program for the community life. Included in this group, or hovering sympathetically about it, were such well-known men as Charles A. Dana, Albert Brisbane, Horace Greeley, George W. Curtis, John G. Whittier, Nathaniel Hawthorne, Thomas Wentworth Higginson, William Ellery Channing, James Freeman Clarke, James Russell Lowell, and Theodore Parker.

Henry James the elder—father of two distinguished sons, William James, the psychologist and pragmatist-philosopher, and Henry James, the novelist—published in 1869 a book called *The Secret of Swedenborg*. He had been interested in Swedenborg since 1841, and an emotional crisis, a depressed state of mind, dating from 1844 when he was residing in England, was resolved when two years later, at the suggestion of a friend, he began reading Swedenborg in real earnest. He says he felt at once, as by a divination of the heart, "the unequalled amount of truth to be found in these writings." The common interest in Swedenborg led to a lifelong intimacy between James and J. J. Garth Wilkinson, the English physician who was Swedenborg's translator and editor. Nevertheless, Wilkinson would not acknowledge in James's version a faithful Swedenborgianism, just as James in his turn regarded himself as holding to the master while repudiating the disciples. In a letter written upon the publication of his book, Wilkinson tells James that he has only the *phrase*, "Divine Natural Humanity," in common with Swedenborg. The latter means by it "God in Jesus Christ triumphant over his own infirm humanity," while James signifies by it a deification of humanity or society in the abstract, as is indeed suggested by the title of one of James's books: *Society the Redeemed Form of Man.* C. S. Pierce, the original thinker whom William James called "the father of American pragmatism," wrote in 1897 of his memories of Henry James the elder, and says in this connection that the experiences of his later life have been calculated to bring Swedenborg home to him often.

Walt Whitman, while editor of the Brooklyn *Daily Eagle*, wrote and published, in 1858, an informative article on Swedenborg, the occasion being the annual Swedenborgian celebration in New York. He stresses the "revolutionary" character of Swedenborg's thought; speaks of him as one of the very few to whom the spiritual world has been opened; and notes the sober and balanced form, free from all hysterics, in which these astonishing spiritual discoveries are by him communicated. He says that Swedenborg's followers, "among whom are some of the leading minds of the nation, boldly claim that no man of any age is now making more significant marks upon American thought, theology and literature." On his own account, Whitman ventures to prophesy that "of any man that ever walked the earth, Swedenborg will probably make the deepest mark upon the religion of future ages." What deeper mark Swedenborg may have set on Walt Whitman himself or his poetry, has not yet been fully determined.

In the collected works of the poet Whittier, there is included a little essay on Swedenborg, dating from the year 1844. He compares him with Fox, and notes the points of resemblance: a

mystic inwardness and a revolt against institutionalized orthodoxy. He notes that Swedenborg aspires to revelations, whose
truth Whittier does not question; while the inner light of the
Quakers is a universal, and not an exceptional, form of religious guidance, reserved for the few or for one. He is puzzled
that Swedenborg should have spoken so sharply of Fox, and
wonders what Fox would have said of Swedenborg if he had
been contemporary or later. As a poet he is naturally impressed
by Swedenborg's systematic schematization of the idea that all
objects in the world of sense are but types and symbols of the
world of spirit, or, as Goethe puts it, *"Alles Vergängliches ist
nur ein Gleichnis."* He finds in Swedenborg a poetic power to
make abstractions wonderfully beautiful. Swedenborg has
"unmasked the universe"; he has laid bare "the profoundest
mysteries of life." In general, Whittier tends to read the spirit
conversations as poetry, and from this point of view he regards
Swedenborg's angels and devils as inferior to those of Milton
and Dante, being of the earth earthy.

Of all the American writers who felt the influence of Swedenborg, Emerson, certainly, was by far the most significant. The
essay in *Representative Men* is familiar to almost every high-
school student. A poem published in 1861 gives an exalted estimate of "the Swede Emanuel." He trod spirit paths alone; his
air-sown words of one generation become, in the next, "flaming
swords." In the *Journals* Emerson speaks of Swedenborg as
having set his mark on ages and millions. To be a reader of his
works is to be receptive of an influence from a "genius still
unmeasured." He is one of five immortal poets, with Homer,
Dante, Shakespeare, and Goethe. This estimate recalls what the
Swedish romantic poet, Atterbom, said of Swedenborg's creation epic, *De Cultu et Amore Dei;* namely, that it "was written
with a poetic inspiration such that if divided among a dozen
poets, it would suffice to fix them in the firmament of song as
stars of the first magnitude." Swedenborg does indeed exhibit,
both in scientific-philosophical and theological writings, as well
as in the prose poem referred to, flashes of imagination and
feeling that reveal a poetic power of distinction; had not the
poet in him and the thinker, due to a misdirection of energies,

come to hamper one another mutually, precisely through that systematization of imagery which the thinker sought to effect, for purposes irrelevant to both poetry and thought.

In connection with the following brief summary, I am greatly indebted to Martin Lamm's judicious essay (Stockholm, 1915). This writer has put every student of Swedenborg under large obligations, by the care with which he has traced the development of his thought, showing the continuity which the dramatic rupture, initiated by the crisis of 1743–45, tends to conceal. This rupture concerned much more the outer form of his life and writings than the inner spirit of his thought, which remains essentially the same before and after the crisis.

Swedenborg's childhood was enveloped in an atmosphere of warm and simple piety. His father was Jesper Swedberg, parish priest, bishop, hymn writer, and author of a voluminous sermonic literature with a homely and practical appeal. He was a man of force and character, of a sturdy practical intelligence, though tinged with the superstitions of his age. The mystical element in his favorite writers, Arndt and Scriver, found an echo in his soul. In the autobiography of one thousand manuscript pages, which he presented to each of his seven children, the only reference to Emanuel is a comment upon his name; he notes that it means *God with us*, and says, "May he always remind himself of God's presence, and of that intimate, secret, and sacred union in which we stand through faith with our good and gracious God."

The boy Emanuel was undoubtedly precocious. That he was looked upon somewhat as a "wonder child," and encouraged to express himself, may be gathered from the following note about his early childhood, which Swedenborg himself communicated to a friend in 1769:

From the fourth to the tenth year, my thoughts were constantly occupied with God, eternal bliss, and the spiritual passions of men. Several times I was able to discover things which my father and mother had long puzzled over; they said that angels must be speaking through me. From the sixth to the tenth year it was my pleasure ever to be arguing with clergymen about faith, setting forth that the life of faith is love, and that the love which gives life is the love of our neighbor; and that God gives faith to each and every one on the sole condition of their receiving it, and practicing this kind of love. I knew of no other faith than this, that God is the author and sustainer of nature and that He gives wisdom and understanding to men, together with what is immediately consequent upon this. The learned kind of faith, that God the Father imputes the righteousness of His Son to whom He wills, and when He wills, even to those who have neither repented nor made amends, I knew nothing about; had I known about it, it would then as now have been far above my comprehension.

One other childhood trait must be mentioned, since it came to have significance for his entire life. During morning and evening devotions, the boy fell into the habit of partially suspending his breathing, thus bringing on a mild sort of trance. Swedenborg later calls this checked breathing "inner respiration," and says that intensive speculation on the truth is impossible without it. Still later he describes it as his gateway to the spirit world. It is a familiar bit of mystical technique, and Swedenborg develops a theory of it which makes it the breathing of the higher part of the soul, *anima*, while the ordinary breathing ministers to the bodily and lower conscious life, *mens* and *animus*. It is a curious fact that this lifelong habit was, in its origin, so casual and innocent of any special purpose; and it is also a curious fact that it led Swedenborg to one of his famous physiological anticipations; namely, that the pulse of activity in the cerebral hemispheres synchronizes with the breathing.

During his student years Swedenborg had the guidance of his kinsman, Eric Benzelius, a humanist intensely interested in the progress of the newer science. At Uppsala he studied Cartesian philosophy, natural science, and mathematics, besides steeping himself pretty thoroughly in the poetry and mythology of the ancients, as all his earlier writings bear witness. Later he prevailed upon his father to finance a four-years' study-journey abroad, including a prolonged stay in England, then the center of physical and mechanical science in Europe. He studied Newton and had frequent intercourse with such men as Halley and Flamsteed. His enthusiasm for mechanical

problems was roused to highest pitch; in letters to Benzelius
he confesses to an "immoderate desire" for such learning. His
busy brain and lively fancy begin to conceive a multitude of
theories, projects, and inventions; among them a submarine
boat, a steam engine, and a flying machine. His writings show
an acquaintance with the empiricist philosophy of John Locke,
probably acquired at this time. To Locke's account of the
growth of knowledge from the senses, and his denial of innate
ideas, he ever after yields his assent; though he develops Locke's
notion of an *intuition*, by which we compare with one another
the logical content of our ideas in a direction that would doubtless have astonished that sober and cautious thinker.

In 1715, at the age of twenty-seven, he returns to Stockholm,
and the following year he is made "Assessor" in the Bureau of
Mines. This position he held for thirty-two years, until his voluntary retirement in 1747, when he accepted, as pension, half his
salary. In that office he proved himself a man diligent in business; his services were varied and important. His scientific
productivity was distinguished by an unusually keen sense for
practical applications, combined with breadth of view and speculative interests. He wrote on the finances of Sweden; on the
tides, canals, docks; on the development of the salt industry.
He made beginnings in paleontology; is credited with the first
attempt to establish a system of crystallography; devised a
method for determining longitude at sea; invented an ear
trumpet for the deaf; and was the first to use mercury to produce a vacuum.

In 1719 the family received a patent of nobility, and the
name Swedberg was changed to Swedenborg. At one time the
young man was engaged to be married to a daughter of his
patron, Christopher Polhem, in coöperation with whom he established Sweden's first scientific periodical. The arrangement
was broken off because of the girl's own unwillingness, and
Swedenborg never married. He was cut to the quick by this
unfortunate affair, and broke off all relations with Polhem.

In an objective-intellectual sense, Swedenborg never broke
with religion. His philosophy of nature is, under all changes
of thought and attitude, theistic, and his view of life envisages

a union between the human and the divine. It is, nevertheless, evident from scattered utterances and from the tone of his writing, that during these decades of busy scientific activity, until, perhaps, close upon the period of the crisis, his subjectively personal religious consciousness had been held in abeyance. His striving is worldly, concentrated upon the achievement of fame; and his habits of life were probably to some degree irregular, or at least such as his own awakened conscience did not approve of. His sexual instincts were strong; and he sets down in his diary, at the inception of the crisis in 1743, that a weakness for women had been his chief passion all his life. He was then approaching sixty. An effort to control the expression of this impulse brought on vivid and detailed sexual dreams during the crisis, which he records in his notes, together with other experiences. I mention this here because it would be difficult to grasp the central features of the great and prolonged crisis without some knowledge of this fact.

In the decade between 1734 and 1744 Swedenborg reaches the highest level of scientific-philosophical productivity. Four important publications mark the period: an *Introduction to a Philosophy of the Infinite* (1734); three volumes of mineralogical and philosophical essays, the first of which deals with underlying principles, and sketches a cosmology which anticipates the so-called nebular hypothesis (1734); and, toward the end of the decade, two comprehensive biological-psychological works. Of these latter the first, *Œconomia Regni Animalis,* is in three parts, of which two were published in 1740 and 1741, respectively, while the third was published posthumously by Wilkinson in 1847; the second, *Regnum Animale,* is also in three parts, and was revised and published during the crisis, in 1744 and 1745.

It is impossible to give here any impression of the detail of fact and wealth of thought that these works contain. They constitute a review and restatement of the physical and biological knowledge of the time, with not insignificant contributions of genial hypothesis original with Swedenborg himself. The whole is organized from a single point of view, and given a philosophical orientation. In the physical-cosmological works, Swe-

denborg formulates the theory that the planets have originated
by ejection from the sun, thus antedating Kant and Laplace.
But he rejects Newton's conception of action at a distance,
because it seems to him to establish an exception to the general
order of nature, and reverts, instead, to the vortex theory of
Descartes, according to which the planets float in a sort of ether
sea, and are carried along by its motion. And he generalizes the
vortex-motion idea so as to conceive the smallest particles as
also miniature solar systems, in vortex motion. In the biological
works, which lean heavily on the new microscopic and anatomi-
cal knowledge of the human body, he propounds a theory of the
localization of conscious functions in the cortex of the cerebral
hemispheres, thus here, also, anticipating later knowledge.

But the most remarkable and significant feature of these
works is the complete shift in point of view that takes place
between the earlier and the later. Swedenborg begins with a
mechanistic world view of radical consistency. Everything is
motion, even the soul and its activities; the universe is a vast
machine. God is its infinite ground; between Him and ordinary
matter, Swedenborg introduces the mathematical point as a
mediating conception. Its motion gives rise to matter of varying degrees of fineness; all physics is geometry. The soul is
spatial, and is made up of the finest particles. Its immortality
is assured by the fact that their fineness does not permit the
coarser matter of the universe to act upon it destructively; it
escapes between the meshes. By 1736, when he began writing
Œconomia, Swedenborg had become a vitalist. He now under-
stands the world within the framework of the Aristotelian categories of form and matter; motion has become secondary. He
assumes a formative energy teleologically directed, *vis formatrix;* such a conception is found in Renaissance mystical philosophies of nature; and it is analogous to what Bergson calls *élan
vital*, and Hans Driesch, *entelechies.* He works out in great
detail a theory of series and discrete degrees, intended to give
to nature an hierarchical organization, with hierarchies within
hierarchies. He assigns to forms and final ends a subordinate
creative efficiency in the Neoplatonic manner; and his theory
of God and the soul is developed in a Neoplatonic spirit. Now

the world is a single huge organism, ensouled, composed of minor organisms *ad infinitum.*

An underlying motive for all this restless research and speculation has come into being during the period, but receives, as yet, only partial expression in the writings. This is to understand the nature of the soul, and *its life after death.* The method was to be empirical; anatomy was to be the guide; in his letter asking for leave to revise and publish *Regnum Animale,* he says proudly that he is the first to have attacked this problem in a thoroughly empirical manner. But Swedenborg is by no means entirely satisfied with his achievements, and thoughts of a different order disturb his restless mind, even now. In a passage which begins with an eloquent statement of the pitfalls that wait for the mind which does not take experience for its guide, in the search for truth, he leads finally up to a description of the true scientist. He is born rather than made; he must have an active memory, a strong imagination, and *intuition.* When such a born thinker, after long and intense reflection, finds a truth, he feels a vitalizing light, a happy confirmatory flash. It is a mysterious radiant energy that passes through some sacred temple of his brain. It is as if he receives a sign that the soul is called to inner communion with the entire universe, and that, in this moment, it has been *restored to the golden age of its integrity.* The soul that has once known this deep joy will ever afterwards occupy itself in striving for its renewal; in comparison, it will hold all bodily pleasures in contempt.

The impossibility of a deduction from principles without a previous induction, and the uncertainty which this introduces into our knowledge, have, from his first formulation of a theory of knowledge, been for Swedenborg a melancholy necessity, an evidence of disorder in our mental machinery, due ultimately to man's loss of moral integrity in the fall. Before this loss, man was capable of an intuition of first principles; and there hovers before Swedenborg's mind the possibility of regaining this power, as the above reference to the golden age indicates. Not only so, but such intuition is connected in Swedenborg's mind with the photisms he has already experienced—"confirmatory

flashes." Flames are a sign of confirmation, he teaches in the
theosophical period; and a manuscript note in the margin of an
exposition of his corpuscular theory, dating from 1741, reads:
Haec verae sunt, quia signum habeo (These things are true,
because I have a sign).

We thus have a sensory automatism taken as evidence for
scientific truth, and the whole connected with the restoration of
moral integrity, yielding an intuition that constitutes a higher
way of knowledge than the empirical. In his essay on Swedenborg, Emerson speaks of the privilege of the caste of saints "to
have access to the secrets and structure of nature by some
higher method than experience," so that a good man *divines*
what another slowly learns; and affirms that the holy soul
mixes with all things, and is sympathetic with their structure
and law. This thought of a connection between moral integrity
and scientific insight is one that often recurs in mystical philosophies; but it is a confusion of values and categories, an
attempt to enhance the significance of the ethical, as if this were
needed, by attaching to it a fantastic intellectual power that
no man ever had or could have.

But Swedenborg has still another method in reserve for attaining insight into the spiritual and transempirical: the doctrine of correspondences. In the 'forties, or still earlier, he was
engaged in effecting an allegorical interpretation of certain
Scripture passages. Casting about for principles to guide him,
he had recourse, among other things, to the mystic, cabalistic,
and Neoplatonic tradition, a tradition that reaches back to
Philo Judæus and the Stoic interpretation of the Homeric
myths. As Swedenborg finally conceives the system, it is based
upon a division of all realities into three realms: the divine, the
spiritual, and the natural—the relation between them being
that of pattern, copy, shadow. Thus, every natural object is a
copy or shadow of something spiritual, and this, again, a representation of something divine. The correspondence attaches
also to the words denoting these different realities, so that if one
sets down in natural phraseology some law of physical things,
and then translates by correspondence, one will have found a
spiritual truth. When we know that the sun is the source of
all light and life in its own cosmos, we may conclude by corre-

spondences that God, as the spiritual sun, is the source of all
wisdom and love in the spiritual world, light meaning wisdom,
and heat being love.

The point of departure for such a view is partly in the fact
of expression, that the inner life of thought and feeling finds
an immediately natural expression in sound, gesture, and physi-
ognomy; and partly in the existence of an element of the meta-
phorical in language. When the consciousness of the psychological becomes sufficiently well defined to demand and receive
expression on its own account, it does not create for itself a
separate language, but uses old words in a new meaning; and
so with the moral and spiritual consciousness. To *perceive* is to
take hold of something thoroughly; to *conceive* is to grasp
many things together; to *edify* is to build up from the foundations. Continued use tends to strip such terms of their original
meaning. A poetic temperament, however, will be especially
sensitive to the æsthetic values inherent in the *metaphor* as such.
But the thinker and the poet have, in this connection, opposite
interests. A metaphor is an unanalyzed resemblance; when the
identity at the bottom of it has been brought to light, the
thinker as such loses interest in the analogy; his task is to
think each thing and law through itself and not through something else loosely corresponding with it.

Emerson objects to the preponderantly Hebraic cast of Swedenborg's dictionary of metaphor; he wants a universal system,
the poetry of all nature and all history, and objects to having
another man's rhetoric crammed down his throat. But there is a
deeper objection. A *system*, to be of value for thought, and not
a mere convenience for reference, must be a conceptual system;
it is an interconnection of thoughts, and not a juxtaposition of
images and symbols. Poetic metaphor, on the other hand, needs
to be free and spontaneous, like Plato's myths, the improvisa-
tion of the moment and the man, alive and sprattling, like a fish
just out of water. A *system* of metaphor is an attempt to stereo-
type poetic genius, and means nothing to the dialectician unless, indeed, the latter is unfortunately obsessed with the notion
that spiritual insight is to be gained through the discovery of
a dictionary and a dream book.

Already then, in 1743, while Swedenborg was at the height

of his scientific-philosophical productivity, the elements of a mystical way of life were present to his consciousness. He had a technique for bringing on trances, learned as a boy; he was in the habit of noting his dreams, and interpreting them symbolically, chiefly through the correspondence theory; he had for some time been subject to visual and other sensory automatisms; he had had experience of ecstasies and longed for their reinstatement; he had worked out a developed Neoplatonic philosophy of an individual coloring; and he had the beginnings of a system of correspondences.

Then came the religious awakening. It seems to have begun in the fall of 1743, while he was in Holland on behalf of *Regnum Animale,* and it did not end until the spring of 1745 or later. The diary, which is our chief source of information, ends abruptly before that time and gives no certain clue as to the basis on which the crisis is finally resolved. All the elements enumerated above were factors in the prolonged state of spiritual tension, but the apparently controlling factor is a new one: a moral-religious anxiety about the conquest of temptation, worldly vanity, and sensuous desire, and the search of an aroused conscience for peace of mind in commitment to the divine grace. What had hitherto been present in an objective manner in his thought, now becomes a problem for his subjective inwardness; namely, the harmonious union between the human and the divine. The form that this subjectivity predominantly takes is the simplest possible form of an orthodox Christianity; it is an attempt to come to rest in the consciousness of the forgiveness of sins through Jesus Christ. The Neoplatonism is quite forgotten in the culminating moments, just as the spirit and form of these climactic emotions are quite absent from his later theological writings. Among the many visions, there are three of Christ; one of them in 1743, and another at Easter in the following year. The third vision (April, 1745) follows upon an hallucination of seeing creeping things on the floor while eating his supper in a London restaurant, which terrifies Swedenborg profoundly so that he goes home shaken. That night he has an ecstatic state, and thereupon he begins to see into the spirit world and to hear the spirits speak audibly.

The visions are taken as real appearances, tokens of an exceptional divine grace; and this last vision of Christ is always, because of the circumstances, regarded by Swedenborg as the beginning of his new mission and call.

During the period of tension and unrest, with its intensification of every pathological factor already present in his experience, Swedenborg sometimes so conducted himself as to suggest insanity to some of his associates. But he was, nevertheless, sane enough to write in this period a great prose poem, an epic of creation, a paraphrase of the story in Genesis, in which he introduces in stately poetic form such relevant parts of his philosophy as he can use, notably the cosmology from the physical treatises and the psychology from the biological ones. It resembles in many things Milton's *Paradise Lost;* its spirit is more Greek than Hebrew, more Neoplatonic than Christian. In the theosophical period, Swedenborg speaks of this work as transitional; it makes a "playful use of the Latin language."

In so far as this spiritual crisis consists of a transition from objectivity to subjectivity, it is a normal religious phenomenon, the first step in the direction of an inward, that is, real religiosity. The experience has been shared by thousands upon thousands, simple and cultured, nonmystical individuals, as well as those of mystical tendencies. But in his reflections, Swedenborg seems almost to lose sight of the universal element of what he experiences simply as a human being, essentially like all other human beings. He fixes an inordinate amount of attention on what seems special and exclusive to himself. There are other abnormal features besides the physiological-pathological ones. He is, from the beginning of the crisis, strongly expectant of a release from temptation once for all, a permanent purification, and, at times, believes this to have taken place. When this shows itself to be an illusion, he is plunged into despair. This is a sign of religious inexperience; the tried and tested religious personality knows that the most exalted state, when faith seems almost to have become one with sight, and peace reigns supreme, may be only a signal for the conflict to begin again, perhaps in a still more acute form; and he also knows that to believe one's self finished is death.

As for the accompanying "psychic" abnormalities, visions and voices, hallucinations and pseudohallucinations, it must be remembered that Swedenborg was a trained physiologist, conversant with such phenomena in an objective-scientific manner, and author of a physiological interpretation of them as abnormalities. It would seem to have been open to him to interpret them as due to a constitutional weakness, and to have humbled himself under the consciousness that, with all his genius, he still had this imperfection: *nullum ingenium sine dementia*. He takes, instead, the road of regarding them as revelations, exceptional divine favors, endowing him with a mission to humanity at large, and one of no mean dimensions. Indeed, there was some hesitation at first, and he frequently complains of how hard it is to distinguish between true inspirations and false ones; it is well known that Satan can disguise himself as an angel of light. But he soon comes to believe in his revelations and his mission, with a simple fixity that knows no doubt.

The outcome of the crisis in its outward aspects is well known. Swedenborg resigned his position in the Bureau of Mines, discontinued all further technical-scientific activity, and settled down to a retired life of Spartan simplicity in Stockholm, though not giving up his habit of frequent journeys abroad. Almost daily he cultivated the trance state in which he conversed with the spirits and learned of their world and mode of life. On the basis of these experiences, and on the basis of a free allegorical interpretation of Scripture by means of correspondences, he wrote and published an extraordinary number of theosophical-theological works, his productivity and his capacity for connected thought remaining unimpaired to the end more than two decades later.

It is not always so well understood as it needs to be, that the essential content of these works, as distinguished from their form, is an elaboration and development of the Neoplatonic philosophy he had sketched in the pretheosophical period, with such added features as a doctrine of spiritual marriages and a Last Judgment witnessed by him in the spirit world. The spirits even take an interest in his old differences with Newton about the absence of matter in the interstellar spaces, and in a

conversation with them, overheard by Swedenborg, Newton
has to confess his conversion. The spirits also tell Swedenborg
that our sun is the largest in the universe, thus sharing the
limited knowledge of the times; and they say that a certain
planet is the smallest of all, though the astronomers have since
that time discovered about six hundred smaller ones. In short,
the spirit-world inhabitants, from whom he learns, are an unconscious and involuntary objectification, through auditory
and visual pseudohallucinations occurring in trances induced
by suspension of breathing, of Swedenborg's own knowledge,
opinions, and reflections. The spirit world is a *replica* of this
world, with a spiritual sun, and spiritual atmospheres, waters,
and lands; what marks it as spiritual is that it obeys at all
times the poet's cherished dream, the æsthetic principle that the
external is completely commensurable with the internal, so that
even spatial and temporal relations are but a reflection of states
of mind.

The Neoplatonic revision of Christianity, which Swedenborg
effects in his theological writings, cannot here be described. Its
essential feature is a substitution for the sharp qualitative an-
titheses and transitions characteristic of Christian teaching, of
a series of quantitative gradations through the interpolation of
intermediaries, much as, in the mechanistic period, he so inter-
polated between the infinite and the finite the Janus-faced
mathematical point, or, in the vitalistic period, a subordinate
creative energy, the *vis formatrix*. Nothing whatever is included which could figure as a representation of Swedenborg's
own culminating emotional attitude in the religious crisis; all
is pretty much as it was before the crisis, only more profes-
sorially calm and authoritative. There is, to be sure, a dramatic
change in the outward form of his life and an obvious altera-
tion in the form of his writings. It is a great pity that the diary
does not explain precisely how he finally attained to his later
state of spiritual equilibrium.

While on a visit to London in 1772, Swedenborg died of an
apoplectic stroke, and was interred in the Swedish church there,
but, since 1908, his remains rest in Uppsala Cathedral in Sweden. The previous year he had published a summary of his doc-

trine, *Vera Christiana Religio*, which is deemed by Lamm to be superior, in clarity and abstract-intellectual grasp, to the exposition given similar thoughts in the scientific-philosophical works of middle life. Much can be learned from the life and thought of this man of such gigantic proportions, both in his insights and his errors, provided one has ears to hear and eyes to see.[2]

2. No serious attempt to evaluate Swedenborg can avoid touching upon what is controversial. In so far as the above sketch contains comment of this character, it is a matter of course that the responsibility rests upon the writer as an individual. A disciple of Swedenborg would wish to interpret the phenomena differently; a naturalistic thinker, whose view of life excludes religion, would urge a radically divergent type of criticism. The attentive reader will not fail to perceive that the standpoint of the writer is a religious standpoint, albeit, one which cannot find universal significance for man's religious life, either in the Swedenborgian revelations or in his revision of Christianity. He finds for his own part more essential religious truth in the unassuming piety of Jesper Swedberg than in the ambitious and ingenious philosophy of his gifted son, although this is not to say that he has not learned from Swedenborg, or that he denies the presence of important elements of insight in his thought.

The New Church

MARGUERITE BECK BLOCK

The author of this chapter is Curator of the Bush Collection of Religion and Culture at Columbia University, and Secretary of the *Review of Religion,* published by the same university. In 1932 she received a degree of Doctor of Philosophy from Columbia, and her thesis was published by Henry Holt in 1932, under the title, *The New Church in the New World.*

O NE of the important contributions which Sweden has made to the religious life of America is embodied in the writings of Emanuel Swedenborg, which form the doctrinal foundation of the New Church, or the Church of the New Jerusalem. Although the Church itself is small in numbers, it has exerted an influence on American thought out of all proportion to its size, and there are thousands who, though keeping aloof from Church membership, still call themselves Swedenborgians. The New Church consists of two separate bodies, the General Convention and the General Church, a split having occurred in 1890 as a result of disagreements in the matter of doctrine, and of ecclesiastical organization. The former, the parent body, maintains its original Congregational form, while the latter has adopted an Episcopal form of church government. A deeper difference, however, lies in the attitude toward the writings of Swedenborg. The General Convention believes them to be a divinely revealed interpretation of the Scriptures and the Christian dogmas; the General Church goes further, and maintains that they are actually a third canon of the Word of God, coequal with the Old and New Testaments.

The history of the New Church in America goes back to the early days of our national life. It was not in Sweden, but in England, that the New Church was founded—a fact due to the religious toleration of which the English are so justly proud. As early as 1750, an English translation of the first volume of *Arcana Coelestia* was brought out at Swedenborg's own expense, indicating that he considered England suitable soil for the propagation of his doctrines. By 1783, there were enough disciples in London to form a society and conduct public meetings. It happened that a plantation owner from Demerara, James Glen, who was in London on business, saw an advertisement of one of these meetings, and, after attending it, became a convert. The following year he returned home by way of Philadelphia, as a missionary of the new faith. At Bell's Bookstore in that city, on the fifth of June, 1784, Glen delivered "A Discourse on the extraordinary Science of Celestial and Terrestrial Connections and Correspondences, recently revived by the late honorable and learned Emanuel Swedenborg." And thus the New Church was born in the New World, only twelve years after the death of its founder.

In estimating the influence which the New Church has had on American religious thought, one may well quote the words of an Episcopal clergyman, Heber Newton (in *Mind*, August, 1900) :

Swedenborg's thought has been slowly leavening the great churches of Christianity in the Western world; and under its influence, the traditional conception of immortality has been unconsciously changing. . . . The first really new conception of the character of immortality given to the world for eighteen centuries, came through the great savant and philosopher and theologian of Sweden, Emanuel Swedenborg. . . . Whatever the nature and sources of this thought, its character was revolutionary,—he reconstructed the whole idea of the hereafter. For the first time in eighteen centuries, one might almost say for the first time in the history of humanity,—it took on sane and sensible forms, and became rational and conceivable, natural and necessary.

And, indeed, it is true that Swedenborg's teaching that the life-after-death is merely a continuation and fulfillment of our earthly life on a spiritual plane, has very largely supplanted the old orthodox belief that the dead are sleeping in their graves, until the Last Trump shall call them to a bodily resurrection. This revolution has taken place, not only through the wide dissemination of Swedenborg's *Heaven and Hell*, but, also, due to the fact that the early Spiritualists adopted his teachings as the theological framework for their own psychic investigations. And thousands in the orthodox churches, who consciously repudiate Spiritualism and all its works, have nevertheless unconsciously been deeply influenced by the new immortality.

"Among prominent Americans familiar with Swedenborg's teachings," says a booklet, *The Testimony of Genius*, issued by the General Convention of the New Church, "are Henry W. Longfellow, Nathaniel and Julian Hawthorne, Charles A. Dana, Joseph Jefferson, Henry D. Thoreau, Margaret Fuller, Francis Millet, Frances E. Willard, William D. Howells, Louis F. Post, Vachel Lindsay. The name of John Chapman (Johnny Appleseed), America's pioneer orchardist must not be overlooked.

"George Washington's acquaintance with Swedenborg's teaching probably dates back to his employment as a surveyor by the famous Swedenborgian, Lord Thomas Fairfax. Washington's copies of some of Swedenborg's theological works are in the Boston Athenaeum Library.

"Of perhaps equal interest is the likelihood that Lincoln was influenced by Swedenborg. In 1842, a set of Swedenborg's writings was presented to the great Emancipator by the Hon. I. S. Britten, superintendent of Common Schools in Springfield, Ill. Lincoln as a young lawyer, was a friend of J. Young Scammon, a pioneer Illinois New-Churchman. It is on record that Benjamin Franklin and Robert Morris were among the subscribers to the first American edition of Swedenborg's *True Christian Religion*. There is evidence of Thomas Jefferson's acquaintance with Swedenborg's teachings."

Appreciative expressions about Swedenborg's writings are quoted from the following: Joseph G. Cannon, former Speaker of the House of Representatives; Dr. Wilfred T. Grenfell; Calvin Coolidge; William Lyon Phelps; Amelita Galli-Curci; Judge Ben B. Lindsey; Phillips Brooks; Henry Ward Beecher; John Greenleaf Whittier; Luther Burbank; Edgar Guest; Clarence Walker Barron; Ella Wheeler Wilcox; John Bigelow; Elbert Hubbard; Helen Keller; Ralph Waldo Emerson; David Starr Jordan; Lyman Abbott, D.D.; Edward Everett Hale; Basil King; Theodore Parker; S. Parkes Cadman, D.D.; Dr. Frank Crane; Henry James, the Elder; Joseph Fort Newton; Garrett P. Serviss, B.S., LL.B.; James Freeman Clarke; Edwin Markham; and Howard Pyle.

Professors

ADOLPH B. BENSON

The writer of this chapter was brought to America from Skåne at the age of eleven and was educated at Wesleyan and Columbia universities. For three years he taught German at Dartmouth College, and came to Yale University in 1914, where he is now professor of German and Scandinavian, and chairman of the Department of Germanics. He has written, edited, or translated a number of books and articles on primarily Swedish subjects, and has contributed to Webster's *Dictionary* and the *Dictionary of American Biography*.

MORE Americans of Swedish birth or extraction have advanced technical and university training than is generally supposed. We find an impressive number of them, not only in the industrial laboratories and in our State and Federal experiment stations, or in the more practical forestry, medical, and legal professions, but in our higher institutions of learning, as teachers and administrators. Professors of Swedish lineage are found in all parts of the United States, teaching not only science and engineering, for which the Swede has a special predilection, but also language, literature, history, and philosophy. Many Swedish-Americans have specialized in psychology and education. Not a small number have won distinction in our botanical gardens, our museums of natural history, and our observatories, and at least one Swedish scholar gained, seventy years ago, an immortality in America through the private study of insects. From 1868 to 1873, the educational repositories of London, Stockholm, Cambridge, Brussels, St. Petersburg, and Boston, all acquired valuable collections of insects made by the Swedish nobleman, Gustaf Wilhelm Belfrage (born, 1834, in Stockholm; died, 1882, in Texas), a real "naturalist of the frontier," who, at his death, left over 36,000 "pinned specimens in good order," besides many others preserved in paper, sawdust, and alcohol. Recently—to give another example—an official bulletin (No. 3201) of the University of Texas declares that "no other geologist has contributed more to making possible the utilization of the wealth, partly realized but mostly still unexploited of Texas than has Dr. Johan August Udden." We shall discuss him later.

Probably the first Swede to hold an official position in an outstanding American university was Maximilian Scheele De Vere (1820–98), the son of a Swedish *friherre*, von Scheele, and a French mother, De Vere, and born near Växjö, Småland. He came to the United States in 1843, and the following year, upon the recommendation of Longfellow and others, was appointed professor of modern languages at the University of Virginia, a position which he held for fifty-one years. Fredrika Bremer, who visited his home in Virginia in the early 'fifties, mentions him in her *Homes of the New World*. Educated at Bonn, Berlin, Greifswald, and Harvard, he early mastered all the important European dialects, including Slavic, and at Virginia taught French, German, Spanish, and Italian. He inaugurated the systematic study of Anglo-Saxon, and was one of the founders of the American Philological Society. His *Outlines of Comparative Philology* appeared in 1853. Other scholarly works followed. Besides, he wrote numerous articles for magazines and encyclopedias, both here and abroad, and translated many European authors into English. His productive scholarship included a French and a Spanish grammar. (For details, see the *Dictionary of American Biography*.)

For obvious reasons, the total number of American professors of Swedish blood can probably never be ascertained, and this investigation could not hope to be exhaustive, even if space permitted; but we can obtain an idea of the relative proportion of such teachers from the results summarized or tabulated below. From a reasonably careful examination of college and university catalogues, reference works, and private correspondence, the writer has identified, he believes, between 400 and 500 men and women faculty members of Swedish extraction—there are about 100 at the University of Minnesota alone—including, in all parts of America, about 180 full professors. Teachers of music and art and scholars in our own denominational institutions will be treated elsewhere in this volume. Because of enforced brevity, we can mention here only a fraction of those identified, so that omission implies neither neglect on the part of the compiler nor lack of distinction on the part of those unnamed. Regarding relative merit there will, of course, be a difference of opinion. My own barometer of values, naturally, has first been the academic position held by the teacher in question, and the size and rank of the institution involved. With two or three exceptions—and one of these is a Nobel Prize winner—only professors of full academic rank have been included, and only about half of these. Other factors which figured in the selection were the productive scholarship, general fame, historical importance, age, subject taught, and, to some slight extent, the personal acquaintance and geographic distribution of the educators. Although the writer alone is responsible for the selection in its final form, the following alphabetical list of fifty administrators and professors was compiled from the returns of a longer list, checked and augmented by educators in various parts of the country. Their opinions have been carefully considered in the conclusion. The list includes both living and deceased scholars. More detailed information about them may in most instances be found in *Who's Who in America*, in *Vem är det?* in *Svenskar i utlandet*, and in *American Men of Science*. Many are members of the American Academy of Sciences, and six—Carlson, Dahlgren, Folin, Lind, Lindgren, and Seashore—have won elections to the National Academy of Sciences.

Joseph Emanuel Alexander Alexis, born in Nebraska, 1885, and educated at Augustana and at the universities of Michigan and Chicago, has also studied in Lund, Paris, and Madrid. He holds the degree of Docteur d'Université from Paris. He is the author or editor of a number of textbooks in Swedish, German, Spanish, and French. Formerly professor of Romance languages, he is now chairman of the department of Germanic languages at the University of Nebraska.

Carl David Anderson, a native of New York City, is a young man of about thirty years of age. His parents came from Östergötland and moved, in 1911, to Los Angeles, California. The son, educated at the California Institute of Technology, was in 1930 appointed assistant professor of physics at his Alma Mater, and received, in 1936, half of the Nobel Prize in Physics for his discovery of the positron, the only Swedish-American so far to win a Nobel award.

Charles Joseph Anderson, Dean of the School of Education at the University of Wisconsin, was born in Minnesota, 1880, and educated at the State Normal School in Superior, and at the universities of Wisconsin and Chicago. After serving as principal of a high school in Wisconsin and Superintendent of Schools in Stoughton (Wis.), he became Assistant State Superintendent of Public Instruction in the same State, 1921–26, and was in the latter year called to the University of Wisconsin, where in 1928 he became Director of the Department of Education. He was elevated to the deanship in 1930. He is the author or co-author of several volumes in the field of education.

Rudolph John Anderson, born in Sweden, 1879, came to the United States in 1893, and was educated at the New Orleans College of Pharmacy, at Tulane University, and in Uppsala, Berlin, and London, later obtaining his doctorate at Cornell in the field of biochemistry. Formerly a professor in that subject at Cornell, he became, in 1927, professor of chemistry in the Graduate School of Yale University, where he specializes in "chemical problems dealing with plant products having biological significance and in the chemistry of bacteria." Professor Anderson has contributed many articles to scientific journals.

Nels August Bengtson, geologist and geographer, is also a native of Sweden, where he was born, 1879. Educated at Cornell, Nebraska, and Clark universities, he has served as professor of geography at the University of Nebraska since 1908. He has also taught at summer sessions in the universities of Columbia, Cornell, Virginia, and Wisconsin. Professor Bengtson was geologist in Honduras, 1920; Ecuador, 1922; and Venezuela, 1927–28. One of his latest publications is *Fundamentals of Economic Geography*, 1935.

Ernst Julius Berg, electrical engineer, was born in Östersund, Sweden, 1871. After graduating from the Royal Polytecknicum in Stockholm, 1892, he emigrated to the United States. Having served as consulting engineer to The General Electric Company, he was in 1910 chosen professor of his subject at the University of Illinois, but accepted, in 1913, a similar position at Union College, Schenectady, New York. In 1932 he became Dean of the School of Engineering there. He is the author of numerous textbooks in his chosen field.

Abraham Berglund is a native of California. Born in 1875, he received his education at the universities of Chicago and Columbia. For a time he taught economics in Washington State College and the University of Washington, served from 1918 to 1922 as special expert to the United States Tariff Commission, and became, in the latter year, associate professor at the University of Virginia. He was made full professor of commerce in 1926. His first published work was *The United States Steel Corporation*, 1907, followed in 1931 by *The Principles of Ocean Transportation*. He is also the joint author of other publications in his field, and has contributed articles to several economic journals.

Anton Julius Carlson, noted physiologist, was born in Bohuslän, 1875, and came to America in 1891. A graduate of Augustana, he won his doctorate at the Leland Stanford Jr. University, 1902. Gaining teaching experience at Stanford, the Carnegie Institution, and Wood's Hole laboratories, he was called to the University of Chicago in 1904 and became professor of physiology there in 1909. He has contributed numerous scientific articles to both American and German journals of physiology. At the time of writing, Dr. Carlson is President of the American Association of University Professors.

Ulric Dahlgren, professor of biology at Princeton University, where he received his higher education, is a native of Brooklyn, New York, born 1870. He has served as assistant director of the laboratories in Wood's Hole, Massachusetts; as trustee of the Harpswell (Me.) Biological Laboratory; and as director of Mount Desert Island Biological Laboratory at Bar Harbor. He has written a series of publications on the production of light by organisms, and contributed to German and home journals a number of zoölogical memoirs on the production of light and electricity by animals. He secured his present position in 1911.

August Hjalmar Edgren (1840–1903), well known on two continents, was a Swedish-born poet, grammarian, and lexicographer. The first Swede, apparently, to receive his doctorate at Yale, 1874, he wrote grammars and dictionaries for French, German, Spanish, Italian, and Sanskrit, being probably the most distinguished Swedish scholar in America half a century ago. He taught languages in several institutions, both here and in Sweden, and some of his dictionaries are still regarded as standard works. He was a graduate of Cornell, taught French at Yale from 1874 to 1880, and later became professor of Sanskrit and comparative philology, and Dean of the Graduate School, at the University of Nebraska.

Walter Elmer Ekblaw, geographer, was born in Illinois, 1882. A graduate of the University of Illinois, he won his doctorate at Clark University, Worcester, Massachusetts. From 1913 to 1917 he served as geologist and botanist of the Crocker Land Arctic Expedition, and for a number of years was research associate in the American Museum of Natural History. He has explored large areas of Grant Land and Ellesmere Land, and is the Editor of the *Home Geographical Monthly*. Since 1926, he has been professor of geography at Clark University.

John Bernard Ekeley, chemist, is a native of Sweden, being born in Örebro, 1869. For thirty-five years he served as professor and head of the Department of Chemistry at the University of Colorado, having only recently resigned from that position. He was educated at Colgate, and in France and Germany. He has also filled the post of State chemist and was, in 1911, appointed collaborating chemist in the U. S. Bureau of Chemistry. He is a contributor to both American and foreign scientific magazines, has written books and text manuals, and, together with W. B. Stoddard, is the inventor of a process for extracting tungsten from its ores.

Otto Knut Olof Folin (1867–1935) came to America from Småland in 1882, graduated from the University of Minnesota, 1892, and six years later earned his doctor's degree at the University of Chicago. "His special domain was biological chemistry, in which he won international renown. He was appointed professor in that subject in the Harvard Medical School, 1907, a position which he held until his death." He held many honorary degrees from Sweden, Germany, and the United States; and published an unusually large number of scientific treatises on urinalysis, metabolism, and blood analysis.

Tenney Frank, a native of Kansas, born in 1876, has, since 1919, served as professor of Latin at Johns Hopkins University. Educated at the universities of Kansas and Chicago, he later studied at Berlin and Göttingen, Germany. He first taught at Chicago and Bryn Mawr. He has lectured widely, both at home and abroad; he is a Fellow of the British Academy, a member of the American Academy of Arts and Sciences, and of the Swedish Royal Society of Letters. He is the author of a dozen scholarly volumes in the classical field, including *Virgil, A Biography*, 1922, and *A History of Rome*, 1923. He is also editor of the *American Journal of Philology*. Professor Frank is listed in the British *Who's Who* as well as in similar American books of reference.

William Anthony Granville, mathematician, born in Minnesota, 1863, was educated at Gustavus Adolphus College and at Yale University. He taught for a number of years at Yale and was for thirteen years President of Gettysburg College in Pennsylvania. He has designed various devices for use by students in mathematics and has written textbooks on integral calculus and trigonometry. Since 1920 Dr. Granville has been director of publications for the Washington National Insurance Company of Chicago.

Reuben Gilbert Gustafson, chemist, born in Denver, 1892, took his doctorate at the University of Chicago, 1925. First professor of chemistry at the Colorado Agricultural College, he has recently completed a ten-year service as professor of the same subject at the University of Denver. He has now been appointed successor to Professor Ekeley at the State University at Boulder, Colorado.

Carl Arthur Hedblom (1879–1934): see the chapter on "Doctors."

Vivian Allen Charles Henmon, born in Wisconsin, 1877, received his higher education at Bethany College (Kans.) and Columbia. He has taught pedagogy at his Alma Mater; has lectured on psychology at Columbia; has been professor of psychology and education and acting Dean of the College of Liberal Arts in the University of Colorado; professor of educational psychology at Yale for a year; and, since 1927, has served as professor of psychology at the University of Wisconsin. His advice in matters pertaining to his field of study has been widely sought. From 1919 to 1931 he held a major's commission in the Aviation Section, Signal ORC.

Einar Hille, mathematician, though born in New York, 1894, of Swedish parents, was educated in Stockholm, where he received the Mittag-Leffler Prize, and for a time taught in Stockholms Högskola. He has taught his subject in Harvard, Princeton, Stanford, and Chicago. Since 1933 he has held an endowed professorship in mathematics in the Graduate School of Yale University. Professor Hille is a member of the London Mathematical Society and the Circulo Matematico di Palermo. He has published numerous articles in the field of higher mathematics.

Gottfried Emanuel Hult, born in Chicago, 1869, has since 1916 been professor of classical languages and literatures at the University of North Dakota. A graduate of the University of Minnesota, he later studied in Germany, Italy, and Greece. He published *Reveries and Other Poems*, 1909, and has translated and edited, with critical introductions and notes, five of Ibsen's dramas.

Carl Edward Johnson, plant pathologist and administrator, a graduate of the University of Minnesota, was born in 1880. He has served as plant pathologist in the U. S. Department of Agriculture, and as dean of the division of college extension at the Kansas State Agricultural College. Since 1919 he has been Dean and Director of the College of Agriculture and Experiment Station in the State College of Washington.

Henry Johnson, born 1867, in Sweden, has since 1906 been professor of history in Teachers College of Columbia University. He received his training at Minnesota and Columbia, and in Berlin and Paris. He has been connected academically with secondary schools, has been superintendent of city schools, and has taught history in normal schools and summer schools. He is the author of three textbooks on the teaching of history. (See next article, by Ander.)

Olof Larsell was born in Rättvik, Dalarne, 1886. He attended Linfield College (Oregon) and Northwestern University and taught biology in these institutions. He has served as assisant professor of anatomy at the University of Wisconsin and as associate professor in zoölogy at Northwestern. Since 1921 he has held the professorship of anatomy in the University of Oregon Medical School. He has also lectured on neuro-anatomy at the University of California. In 1928 Dr. Larsell was awarded the Casselberry Prize by the American Laryngological Association.

Samuel Colville Lind, now Dean of the Institute of Technology at the University of Minnesota, and Editor of the *Journal of Physical Chemistry*, was born, 1879, in Tennessee, and was educated at Washington and Lee University, the Massachusetts Institute of Technology, and in Leipzig and Paris. He was, in 1923–25, chief chemist in the U. S. Bureau of Mines, and from 1926 to 1935 director of the School of Chemistry in the University of Minnesota. He has written abundantly on chemical and radioactive subjects and is the inventor of the Lind interchangeable electroscope for radium measurements.

Valdemar Lindgren, born in Kalmar, Sweden, 1860, was educated in Sweden and Germany. He was for many years—part of the time as chief geologist—associated with the U. S. Geological Survey. From 1912 to 1933 he served as William Barton Rogers professor of economic geology at the Massachusetts Institute of Technology. He retired in 1933 as professor-emeritus. He is the author of numerous reports in Government publications and technical journals on mining geology.

Axel Leonard Melander, zoölogist, born 1878 in Chicago, was educated at the universities of Texas, Chicago, and Harvard (Sc.D.). From 1907 to 1926 he was head of the Department of Zoölogy at Washington State College, and in the latter year was appointed professor and head of the Department of Biology in the College of the City of New York. He has contributed to scientific journals about one hundred articles on systematic and economic entomology.

Victor Emanuel Nelson is a product of Wisconsin, where he was born, 1888. He was educated at the University of Wisconsin;

taught for a time at his Alma Mater and Johns Hopkins University; and was then called to a position in the chemical department of the Iowa State College of Agriculture and Mechanic Arts, Ames, Iowa, where since 1923 he has held a professorship in chemistry. Like so many of the Swedish-American teachers he is a Fellow of the American Association for the Advancement of Science.

George Norlin, President of the University of Colorado, was born in Kansas, 1871. Educated at Hastings College (Nebr.), at the University of Chicago and the Sorbonne, Paris, Dr. Norlin first became professor of Greek at Hastings and later at the University of Colorado. In 1917 he was appointed acting President of the latter institution, and President two years later. He was Visiting Roosevelt Professor of American History and Institutions in the University of Berlin, 1932–33, and Weil Lecturer at the University of North Carolina, 1934. He became an elector of the Hall of Fame, 1930, and is a member of the board of trustees of the Carnegie Foundation. Among his writings are *Integrity in Education and Other Papers* and *Fascism and Citizenship*.

Paul Henry Nystrom, economist, is professor of marketing at Columbia University. He was born in 1878 and educated in Wisconsin. He has taught political economy at the University of Wisconsin and economics at the University of Minnesota; has served as director of trade research for the United States Rubber Company; has been sales manager for the International Magazine Company; and became professor at Columbia in 1926. *Who's Who* lists eight volumes of publications under his name, of which *Economics of Retailing* had required three editions by 1930.

Emery Evans Olson is now Dean of The School of Government in the University of Southern California. Born in Illinois, 1892, he acquired his higher education at the universities of Southern California, Cornell, and Wisconsin. For a time he was Assistant Director of the College of Commerce and Business Administration at the University of Wisconsin, and has since 1924 served the University of Southern California in various administrative capacities. He became Dean in 1931. In 1935–36, while on leave of absence, he directed service training at the American University in Washington, D.C.

Dr. John A. Ouchterlony (1838–1905), physician, author, and teacher, was born in Småland; came to America at the age of twenty-one; served in the Medical Corps in our Civil War; became in 1869 a founder of Louisville Medical College, in which he was professor until 1876; was two years later appointed professor of practical medicine in the Kentucky School of Medicine; and in 1882 professor in the same subject at the University of Louisville, a position that he held until his death. From Sweden he had received knighthood in the Order of the North Star and the Linné medal in gold; from the University of Notre Dame, an LL.D.; and, being a loyal Roman Catholic, the Order of St. Gregory the Great, from Pope Leo XIII.

Alfred John Pearson, a native of Landskrona, Sweden, 1869, received his B.A. at Bethany College and his Ph.D. from Yale. In 1926 he was honored with an LL.D. from Drake University, Des Moines, Iowa, where, in 1930, he became Dean of the College of Liberal Arts. He had previously served as professor of German at the same institution. In 1924 he was appointed United States Minister to Poland by President Coolidge, and in 1925 was transferred to the same post in Finland, where he represented the United States Government for five years. He was decorated by both countries.

Frederick Peterson, M.D., veteran poet, translator, and neurologist, born 1859, came from Minnesota. He received his medical education at the University of Buffalo and holds honorary degrees from Niagara University and the University of Pennsylvania. He was professor of insanity at the Woman's Medical College of the New York Infirmary, 1890–95, and has since 1903 been active, or emeritus, clinical professor of psychiatry at Columbia University. His publication, *Mental Diseases*, had in 1920 gone through nine editions. A textbook on legal medicine and toxology has seen two editions. Five volumes of poems and translations have appeared from his pen, including the famous *Chinese Lyrics*, 1916. *Poems and Swedish Translations* was published in 1883. Several of his lyrics have been set to music.

William Harold Peterson, professor of agricultural chemistry at the University of Wisconsin, was born in New York State, 1880, and was educated at Wesleyan University (Conn.), at Columbia, and the University of Wisconsin. He has been a member of the faculty at Wisconsin since 1909, attaining full professorial rank in 1925. Dr. Peterson, a classmate of the present writer, has published more than 175 articles in his domain, and visited "nearly every research laboratory in Europe, including many in Russia."

Carl-Gustaf Arvid Rossby, meteorologist, was born in Stockholm, Sweden, 1898, and received his technical training in the Swedish capital, Bergen, Norway, and Leipzig, Germany. He served first as Government meteorologist of Norway, 1919; and of Sweden, 1922–25; coming to the United States and accepting a position with the U. S. Weather Bureau in 1926. He was called to an associate professorship in his subject at the Massachusetts Institute of Technology, 1928, and was three years later promoted to a full professorship. In 1934 he received jointly with H. C. Willett the Sylvanus Albert Reed award from the Institute of Aeronautical Sciences. He has written many meteorological papers.

Per Axel Rydberg (1860–1931), botanist, born in Sweden, was educated at Skara Gymnasium, at the University of Nebraska, and took his doctorate at Columbia. For a time he taught at Luther Academy (Wahoo, Nebr.) and at Upsala College, but became in 1899 curator of the New York Botanical Gardens, Bronx Park. He was the author of innumerable botanical reports, books, and monographs, such as *Catalogue of Flora of Rocky Mountains and Yellowstone Park*, 1900; *Flora of Colorado*, 1906; and *Flora of Rocky Mountains and Adjacent Plains*, 1917.

George Herbert Ryden, historian, acquired his academic training at Augustana and Yale. (For details of his career see the introduction to the chapter on "Colonial Landmarks.")

Nathaniel [Anderson] Schmidt, born 1862 in Hudiksvall, Sweden, received his education in Stockholms Högskola, Colgate University, and in Berlin. In 1931 he was honored with a D.H.L. by the Jewish Institute of Religion. Professor of Semitic languages and literatures at Colgate from 1888 to 1896, he became, in the latter year, professor in the same subjects at Cornell University and retired as professor-emeritus in 1932. He has served as director of the American School of Archæology in Jerusalem, and is now a member of the board of trustees of the American School of Oriental Research in Jerusalem and Baghdad. Besides being the author or editor of eleven volumes in his chosen field, he has contributed "more than 1500 articles in the *New International Encyclopædia*," not counting the contributions to other reference works and many theological papers. In 1931–32 he was President of the American Oriental Society.

Carl Emil Seashore, Dean (to 1936) of the Graduate School of the State University of Iowa and, in a sense, dean of all Scandinavian-American professors, was born in Sweden, 1866. Educationally he is a product of Gustavus Adolphus College and Yale, and holds three honorary degrees, including an Sc.D. from the latter university. For a number of years he was professor of psychology at the institution where he later became Dean, 1908. A very eminent and productive scholar, he has written scores of research papers on work and fatigue, mental work, illusions, gifted students, and the psychology of music. Among his publications in book form we note particularly *The Psychology of Musical Talent*, 1919. In 1911 he was President of the American Psychological Association. (See the chapter on "Composers.")

Johan Thorsten Sellin, a graduate of Augustana, is also a native of Sweden, born 1896, and is now professor of sociology at the University of Pennsylvania, where he won his doctor's degree. He has done much study and research in Europe. He is a member of several sociological societies, both here and in Europe, and has served on various civic bureaus as consultant on sociological questions. He is Editor-in-chief of *Annals of the American Academy of Political and Social Science*, contributor to encyclopædias, other reference works, and scientific journals, and is the author of *Marriage and Divorce Legislation in Sweden*, 1922.

Andrew Adin Stomberg was born in Minnesota, 1871, and was educated at Gustavus Adolphus College and at the University of Minnesota. He was first a professor of history at his Alma Mater, but has for thirty years been professor of Scandinavian at the University of Minnesota. He has lectured at the University of Uppsala and is a Knight of the Royal Swedish Order of the North

CARL EMIL SEASHORE
PSYCHOLOGIST AND EDUCATOR

Star. Professor Stomberg has, among other works, edited the *Fritiofs Saga* for school and college use and written *A History of Sweden,* 1931.

John Sundwall is a native of Utah. Born 1880, he holds a Ph.D. from Chicago and an M.D. from Johns Hopkins University. He has taught anatomy and health subjects in three universities, has served as hygiene expert in the U. S. Public Health Service at Washington, and since 1921 has been professor of hygiene and public health and director of the division of hygiene, public health, and physical education at the University of Michigan.

David Ferdinand Swenson, professor of philosophy, was born in Sweden, 1876, received his education at the University of Minnesota and Columbia, and has taught his subject at the University of Minnesota since 1901. He became full professor in 1917. He recently translated and edited a volume on the philosophy of the Dane Kirkegaard for the "Scandinavian Classics."

Louis Leon Thurstone, psychologist, first saw the light of day in Chicago, 1887. His universities were Cornell and Chicago. First teaching psychology at the Carnegie Institute of Technology, he has since 1924 served as professor of psychology at the University of Chicago. Among his writings are *The Nature of Intelligence,* 1924, and *The Measurement of Attitude,* 1929.

Johan August Udden (1859–1932), native of Sweden and noted geologist, was a graduate of Augustana, and later won several honorary degrees. He taught at Bethany College; was Oscar II professor of geology at his Alma Mater; and held various important State and Federal positions in geology. Professor Udden held the Order of the North Star, was a Fellow of the Geological Society of America, and the author of several geological treatises. It was he who first suggested the likelihood of finding petroleum on the State university land of West Texas. From 1915 to his death he served as professor of geology and Director of the Bureau of Economic Geology and Technology at the University of Texas.

Axel Johan Uppvall, professor of Scandinavian at the University of Pennsylvania, was born in Värmland, 1872, and studied at Göttingen, the University of Nancy, Colby College, Harvard, and

Clark University, where he obtained his doctorate with a dissertation on *August Strindberg, A Psychoanalytic Study*. He taught at the universities of New Brunswick and Clark, and has since 1924 held his present position, attaining full professorial rank in 1930. He has traveled extensively in Germany and Iceland, and published books, translations, and articles, principally on Karlfeldt and Strindberg. He has just completed the manuscript of a Swedish grammar in English.

Axel Ebenezer Vestling, born in Kansas, 1879, was educated at Bethany College and Yale, and studied at the foreign universities of Marburg and Berlin. He has taught German at Dartmouth and Yale, and became professor of that subject at Carleton College in 1912, dean of men there, 1921, and Dean, 1925. After serving four years as President of Olivet College (Mich.), he returned to Carleton in 1930 as professor of German.

Edwin Johan Vallentin Vickner is a native of Stockholm, born 1879, and came to the United States in 1895. Receiving his doctorate at Minnesota, he first held the chair of modern languages at Gustavus Adolphus College, and became, in 1912, professor of Scandinavian at the University of Washington, in Seattle. He has pursued studies at the Sorbonne, and in Leipzig, Brussels, and Oslo. He is the author of the well-known *Simplified Swedish Grammar*, 1934.

Ivan E. Wallin, anatomist, born in Iowa, 1883, received his training in Iowa and Nebraska, and earned an Sc.D. from New York University. After teaching biology and anatomy at Upsala College and other institutions, he became in 1918 professor and head of the Department of Anatomy at the University of Colorado School of Medicine. Details of his scientific work may be found in *American Men of Science*.

John Edward Wallace Wallin, psychologist, born in Iowa, 1876, was educated at Augustana, and at Yale and Clark universities. He has taught his subject in several normal schools and universities, including Johns Hopkins. Since 1932 he has been the director of the division of special education and mental hygiene in the Delaware State Department of Public Instruction and in the Wilming-

JOHAN AUGUST UDDEN, 1859–1932

GEOLOGIST AND EDUCATOR

ton public schools. He has been a very prolific writer in his chosen specialty.

Scores of other scholars and university educators, including, no doubt, many of outstanding order, deserve fuller biographical treatment than we can give them here. Among these are Eugene Ewald Agger, professor and head of the Department of Economics at Rutgers University; Elam J. Anderson, President of Linfield College, McMinnville, Oregon; Paul A. Anderson, professor and head of the Department of Physics at the State College of Washington; Dr. Hilding Berglund, formerly chief of the Division of Medicine at the University of Minnesota, who has returned to Sweden; John Andrew Bexell, late Dean of the School of Commerce in the Oregon State Agricultural College; Hugo Leander Blomquist, professor of botany at Duke University, North Carolina; E. S. Borgquist, professor of civil engineering at the University of Arizona; Axel Brett, a native of Sweden, who is head of the Department of Psychology and Philosophy at the University of Tennessee; Harry G. Carlson, dean of men at the University of Colorado; C. Emanuel Ekstrom, professor and chairman of the Department of Education at Brown University, Providence, Rhode Island; A. Louis Elmquist, author of textbooks for the study of Swedish, and now member of the Germanic department at the University of Nebraska; Carl Christian Engberg (1872–1929), a native of Sweden, who was for many years professor of mathematics and Executive Dean of the University of Nebraska; Hasse Octavius Enwall, professor of philosophy at the University of Florida; E. E. Erickson, professor of English at the University of North Carolina; and Franklin C. Erickson, head of the Department of Geography at the University of South Carolina. Further, we have Gustaf Freden, Dean of the School of Education in Louisiana Polytechnic Institute; Bror Leonard Gröndahl, professor of forest products at the University of Washington; Thomas Hakon Gronwall (1877–1932), born in Sweden, formerly of Princeton University, who, at his death, left over a hundred published and unpublished mathematical papers; Axel Ferdinand Gustafson, professor of soil technology in Cornell University; Signe Hagelthorn, Dean of Adelphi College; Bengt Leopold Knutsson Hamilton, professor of pediatrics in the University of Chicago; Dr. Axel Magnus Hjort, formerly professor of pharmacology at Dartmouth College; Clarence Hylander, professor of botany at Colgate University; Florence Edith Janson, professor of government in Rockford College, and author of *The Background of Swedish Immigration 1840–1930;* Einar Jöranson, associate professor of medieval history at the University of Chicago; Carl Alfred Kallgren, dean of Colgate University; Emil Leonard Larson, professor of education at the University of Arizona; Gustus Ludwig Larson, native of Sweden, who is professor and chairman of the Department of Steam and Gas Engineering at the University of Wisconsin; Leonard A. Lawson, chairman of the Department of History and Politics, Hobart College; Dr. Carl C. Lindgren, chairman of the Department of Bacteriology at the University of Southern California; Oscar Helge Lundholm, associate professor of psychology at Duke University; Laura M. Lundin, professor of physics and mathematics at Russell Sage College of Troy, New York, whose father, a native of Vänersborg, Sweden, was an eminent telescope-maker of Cambridge, Massachusetts; Gustaf Adolph Lundquist, professor of sociology at Hamline University; Carl Edward Magnusson, electrical engineer, and formerly Dean of the College of Engineering in the University of Washington; Luther Ansgarius Malmberg, professor of psychology and philosophy, and Dean of Thiel College; Milton Nels Nelson, head of the Department of Agricultural Economics at the Oregon State Agricultural College; Dr. Victor Theodore Nylander, professor of operative dentistry and head of the department and director of the infirmary in the University of Illinois (at Chicago); Axel Ragnar Olson, born in Sweden, professor of chemistry at the University of California at Berkeley; Roy V. Peel, professor of government in New York University; Olof August Peterson (1865–1933), paleontologist in the American Museum of Natural History; Arvid Reuterdahl (1876–1933), a native of Sweden, and graduate of Brown University, who later became professor of physics at Colby College and, in 1922, President of the Ramsey Institute of Technology; Lars Gunnar Torgny Romell, formerly research professor in forest soils at Cornell University, who is now living in Sweden; Oscar Waldemar Rosewall, professor of entomology in Louisiana State University at Baton Rouge; Dr. Thor Christian Rothstein, born and educated in Sweden, who died, in 1937, as professor-emeritus of neurology at Rush Medical College, Chicago; Robert H. Seashore, professor of psychology at the University of Southern California; Karl W. Stenstrom, professor of biophysics at the University of Minnesota; Gustaf Benjamin Stromberg, astronomer, Mount Wilson Observatory, Pasadena, California; Bengt Strömgren, associate professor of theoretical astrophysics at the Yerkes Observatory; Gustaf Eric Wahlin, professor of mathematics at the University of Missouri; and Hugo Bernard Wahlin, specialist in electricity and magnetism, who is professor of physics at the University of Wisconsin.

Finally, we must recall that the eminent veteran educator, Professor Albert Bushnell Hart of Harvard University, is of Swedish ancestry on the distaff side; and among the descendants of the Delaware Swedes we are equally proud to mention Charles Janeway Stillé (1819–99) who, from 1868 to 1880, was President of the University of Pennsylvania.

We regret we cannot mention more; but these examples will suffice to show that the Swedish element is contributing its part to the higher education of Americans. (See also, chapters on the "Public School Educators" and "Colleges.")

Public School Educators

O. FRITIOF ANDER

Professor Ander is head of the Department of History at Augustana College. He is the author of *T. N. Hasselquist* (1931), and from 1931 to 1937 served as Editor of the Augustana Historical Society *Publications*. He has contributed frequently to historical journals and has prepared a bibliographical guide, both for Swedish history in general, and for Swedish-American newspapers in particular. A member of several historical associations, he is especially interested in the subject of immigration. He was born in Sweden, arriving in the United States in 1921. In 1938 he was awarded a Guggenheim fellowship for the preparation of a history of Sweden since 1815.

WHEN immigration from Sweden to the United States increased after the Civil War, the American system of free, public education was regarded as a well-established institution. Though this system could trace its origin to colonial New England, Horace Mann and Henry Barnard were largely responsible for the growth and extension of the public schools. The principle of free public instruction was accepted in all the Northern States before the Civil War. It was looked upon as a thoroughly American system, and intimately connected with the idea of better citizenship. When strikes and riots expressed a spirit of social and economic unrest after the war between the States, the importance of the public-school system, as a bulwark against anarchy and "alien influences" of socialism, increased. Therefore, efforts on the part of certain immigrant groups, to secure a division of the public-school funds between parochial and public schools, stimulated a wave of Americanism.

As the wave was essentially anti-Catholic, and directed as well against the spread of socialism and radical ideas, the Swedish-Americans, who were uninfluenced by the Catholics, and were safely within the conservative fold of the Republican party, readily joined the movement in defense of the public schools. A Swede in the Illinois legislature, shortly before the

election of 1892, was responsible for the framing of the Illinois
Compulsory Education Act, which became a political issue in
that State. Throughout the Union, where Swedes were to be
found in large numbers, they supported educational legislation
to further the growth of public schools, and to retard the
spread of parochial schools. When the Bennett Law of Wisconsin, a law directed against parochial schools, was declared un-
constitutional, and repealed, the Swedish-Americans lent their
support in a voice of protest.

The public-school question in the early 'nineties was a "burning" issue in many states, and stimulated the growth of a
fanatical organization called the American Protective Association. This group distributed fantastic propaganda in its efforts "to save the public schools," and to prevent the parochial
schools from sharing any tax money. It was essentially anti-
Catholic, and thousands of Swedes joined the association. Other
patriotic groups and secret anti-Catholic organizations joined
in the movement, and were so successful in spreading their
propaganda that the Swedes were convinced that the public
schools faced a real danger. The Augustana Synod, which had
maintained what might resemble a parochial school in the various congregations, was forced by this intensive move of Americanism, to attest to its belief in free, compulsory public education. Anti-Augustana forces, however, insisted that the Synod
was un-American, in maintaining its summer schools for the
purpose of teaching Swedish and propagating the Lutheran
faith, which was associated with the State religion of Sweden.
These attacks were answered by the Synod in its pleas for the
support of the public schools and educational legislation, which
would permanently create these schools as a bulwark against
anarchy, and a safeguard of American liberties.

Throughout this period American educators received inspiration from abroad, and if Sweden had no Froebel or Her-
bart, such Swedish schoolmen as N. G. W. Lagerstedt, Carl
Lidman, and C. J. Mejerberg had contributed articles to
American journals of education. America, therefore, prior to
1900, was not entirely ignorant of the Swedish system of public
education. This knowledge was widened and broadened immedi-

ately before and after the World War by the expression of a greater interest in Swedish gymnastics and *slöjd*, or manual training.

It is difficult to state, however, the extent of Swedish influence along these lines. A very large number of Swedish-Americans are found directing the program of physical education throughout the nation's public schools. It is probable that many of these directors are only college and university "star athletes" and, therefore, have little or no knowledge of Swedish gymnastics. Professor William Skarstrom of Wellesley College has undoubtedly done more than anyone else to encourage Swedish gymnastics. (See the chapter on "Gymnastics.") In his work, he has been aided by John Sundwall and O. Holmberg, who have contributed articles to such magazines as *Health and Physical Education* and *Mind and Body*. The best presentation of the virtues of the Swedish system is found in Skarstrom's *Gymnastic Teaching*, which has been published in two editions. Though held in high esteem by American leaders in physical education, the Swedish system has not been generally adopted, except as "corrective exercises." This failure is due to the fact that the Swedish system does not make allowance for "the play and competitive" instincts.

The system of Swedish *slöjd* has long interested the Americans. But it is impossible to determine the relationship of this interest to the number of Swedish descendants in America, engaged as directors of manual training in the public schools. The directories of education, published by the various states, indicate that in certain sections as many as one out of fifteen heads of manual training may be of Swedish descent. Probably, the children of Swedish-Americans have received from their parents an interest in manual and industrial arts. Certainly, the contributions of the Swedes in building and furniture industries are widely recognized. (See the chapter on "Architects and Builders.")

Only a few of these sons of Swedish-Americans, who have made definite contributions, can be mentioned. Dr. Leonard Lundgren has secured an enviable reputation as Director of Adult and Vocational Education of the public schools of San

Francisco. The same is true of Albin V. Larson, Supervisor of Industrial Arts, Peru, Nebraska; of L. W. Wahlstrom of the Francis W. Parker School, Chicago, Illinois; of G. A. Glyer, Supervisor of Distributive Trades, Department of Public Instruction of the State of Delaware; and of Carl E. Karlstrom, Supervisor of Vocational Education, Detroit, Michigan. Probably the best-known Swedish-Americans in this field are J. H. Trybom, Director of Vocational Education, Wayne University, and his associate, Verne Charles Frycklund, who was connected with the University of Minnesota during the period 1930–37. They have contributed articles to *Industrial Education Magazine, Popular Homecraft, Industrial Arts, Vocational Education, Occupation, School Review, Everyday Art,* and many other journals. Frycklund is a prolific writer, and, in addition to some thirty or more articles, he has written several books and bulletins.

Interest in Swedish cookery is manifested in American household journals, and, undoubtedly, Swedish-Americans have made important contributions in the field of home economics. From a study of names, it appears that a large percentage of the teachers of this subject are Swedes. It is not at all certain, however, that this is due to a general acceptance of Swedish excellency in this field. It is probable that many of these teachers of Swedish parentage have had no closer acquaintance with Swedish cooking than digestive troubles from a *smörgåsbord*. Frequent radio talks, many dealing with Swedish cooking, by Swedish-American and American experts in home economics, and articles and books dealing with Sweden and Swedish cooking, can hardly explain the large number of home-economics teachers of Swedish descent. Many psychologists would undoubtedly ridicule any effort to explain this situation by attributing it to influences of the home.

Probably the greatest direct contribution to the public schools by Swedish-Americans is, and will be, in the field of music. The reasons for this are more easily explained than the influx of Swedish-American teachers in the field of home economics and of vocational training. No "supernatural causes" need to be used in explaining the contributions of the Swedes to public-school music. Swedish-American colleges, such as Bethany, Augustana, Gustavus Adolphus, Upsala, and others, have well-established and recognized schools of music. Long before Händel's oratorio, *The Messiah*, was extensively rendered in the United States, these schools had received attention of the public for their presentation of it. Soon they were to compete with the Norwegian college, St. Olaf, in choral music, and today these schools of music cannot meet the demands for public-school music teachers. Jenny Lind's and Christina Nilsson's visits to the United States, and their interest in furthering the growth of the Swedish-American institutions, undoubtedly played a part in developing these interests. One of the greatest—if not the greatest—American composers and directors, Howard Hanson, a former student of the small Swedish-American college, Luther College (Wahoo, Nebr.), as head of the Eastman School of Music at Rochester, New York, is exerting a direct influence on teachers of music throughout the nation. (See the chapter on "Composers.") Hanson is more than a musician; he is definitely an educator.

Though he has not attained the fame of Hanson, Edgar Andrew Nelson, President of the Chicago Conservatory of Music, has exerted influence far beyond the city of Chicago. Throughout the country, Swedish-Americans have won recognition as instructors of music. Many of them are associated with teachers' colleges, and have secured general acclaim as authors of articles in journals of public-school music.

There is no question that, in the fields of physical education, vocational training, home economics, and music, the Swedes have made a real contribution to the American public school. But Swedes have also found their way to executive positions within the public schools, as county superintendents, city superintendents, and principals. They have played an important rôle in formulating the educational policies of states and large cities. In the capacity of educational reformers associated with colleges, universities, and teachers' colleges, they have had a part in planning the present and the future public schools.

In Minnesota alone, approximately seventeen of the county superintendents are of Swedish origin. A lesser number are found in such States as Michigan, Wisconsin, Iowa, Illinois, Kansas, Nebraska, Colorado, Arizona, California, Oregon, and Washington. Since this office is an elective or a political one, ability and an understanding of the problems of the public schools are not always a prerequisite. Few county superintendents may, therefore, be classified as true leaders in the public-school system. It is an unfortunate situation, and in many of the Eastern States the office of county superintendent has been eliminated. Because of lack of leadership, and because of inadequate and poor training, superintendents of city schools and principals have been forced to look for guidance to the normal schools, colleges, and universities. Therefore, most of the reforms in the public-school system have come from graduate schools of education.

It would be foolish to list hundreds of Swedish-American county superintendents, superintendents of city schools, and principals, as leaders in American education. They represent merely a cross section of the entire nation, and are, presumably, neither poorer nor better qualified to fill the positions of trust they hold, than any other group. The folly of listing even the names of these Swedish-Americans is apparent, when they number nearly three hundred superintendents and principals, in Minnesota and Illinois alone.

A few, however, because of their length of service in the public schools, or because of definite contributions, might be mentioned. Among these we find a progressive leader in Irving F. Pearson, Superintendent of Schools of Winnebago County, Illinois. Pearson has sought to extend the system of individualized instruction to the rural schools, and to introduce rural-school-music supervision. He has contributed important articles to *School Executives Magazine*, the *Illinois Teacher*, and *School Life*. He has frequently been requested to address the Department of Rural Education of the National Education Association. He has been engaged, also, in the writing of textbooks, and is at present completing a textbook in civics for the junior high school.

W. H. Eliason, the Superintendent of Decatur County Schools, Iowa, has made an excellent record as a progressive leader; and James A. Sheldon, Superintendent of Schools, Garden Grove, Iowa, has recently published an article on "Student Government" in a leading educational journal. Paul E. Exstrom, since 1934 County Superintendent of Schools, Lincoln County, Nebraska, has made extensive studies in "Proper Assignment of the Lesson," and has published a special bulletin dealing with this subject. Arthur E. Erikson is Superintendent of Schools in Ironwood, Michigan. During the last eighteen years, Miss Vera C. Rehnstrand has made a remarkable record as Superintendent of Douglas County Schools, Wisconsin. She has organized forty parent-teacher associations, and was the founder of the first 4-H Club in her county. She is responsible for the establishment of the dental and corrective clinics for children in Douglas County. George V. Larson is President of the Larson Junior College in Hamden, Connecticut.

Clarence Ostlund, a progressive leader of the Wasatch County School district (Utah), has had an interesting educational career. He has been superintendent of schools in three States; namely, Idaho, Wyoming, and Utah. Joseph Waldemar Wicklund, County Superintendent of Schools and clerk of the Board of Education for Unorganized Territory, Minnesota, has achieved notable economies through the consolidation of school agencies. He has sought to improve the efficiency of the schools of Cass County, by raising the qualifications for teachers and improving "the learning conditions." Miss Elna E. Nelson, Commissioner of Education, Baraga County Schools, Wisconsin, has decreased the number of one-room schools in her county, from forty-eight to fifteen. She is planning further consolidations in the near future, and hopes to be able to eliminate all her one-room schools. Miss Alice M. Aronson has been reëlected for a fourth term, as County Superintendent of Schools in Oberlin, Kansas. Miss Agnes Engstrand, also a Kansas "county superintendent," has been a member of the board of directors of Kansas State Teachers' Association, and is at present a member of Kansas State Board of Directors of County Superintendents, and of the State Reading Circle Committee. During summer vacations, she has taught at Kansas State College of Agriculture. Albert A. Anderson, Superintendent of

Wright County Schools (Minn.), was elected Secretary of the Minnesota Association of County Superintendents in 1934, and founded the first completely organized School Officers' Association, in the State of Minnesota. He introduced rural-school music, rural-school declamatory, and rural-school spelling contests, in Wright County. Wallace Olson, another Minnesota county superintendent, has done much to develop interest in music and choral singing in his county, and Superintendents E. T. Jacobson of Cokato, and Gilbert Palmer of Delano, have made noteworthy contributions in the field of public-school education. Undoubtedly, many others should be mentioned, but those listed are among the leaders.

The influence of these superintendents has, however, been hardly more than local, and, only occasionally, state-wide. Other Swedes have exerted a wider influence in the public-school system, and have played a part in shaping various state educational policies. Among these, probably no one has done more for his own State than C. G. Schulz of Minnesota. As Assistant State Superintendent of Public Instruction during 1901–09, and as State Superintendent from 1909 to 1919, Schulz was responsible for the extension of the public-school system into the "newer" regions of Minnesota. He advocated successfully a longer school year, practical school consolidations, and established the agricultural departments in the State high schools. In 1919, Schulz was appointed specialist in charge of the Extension Service of the United States Bureau of Education, and later became district director of the rehabilitation work under the Federal Board of Vocational Education. For sixteen years, until ill-health forced his resignation in 1936, Schulz continued to exert a great influence on the State of Minnesota's educational policy, as Secretary of the Minnesota Educational Association and as editor of this association's publications. In addition, Schulz has served as member of the Board of Regents of the University of Minnesota; of the State Normal Schools; and of the State High School Board.

President Ernst F. Pihlblad of Bethany College (Lindsborg, Kans.) served as a member of the Kansas State Text Book Commission during 1912–16, and of the State Board of Education, 1932–36. In 1936, Pihlblad was elected State Senator and, as such, sponsored the last Teacher's Certification Bill, and was responsible for the reorganization of the State Text Book Commission. Pihlblad is continuing in Kansas an influence which was begun during the days of O. Olsson in the early 'seventies and developed through Carl A. Swensson, who undoubtedly did much to influence the educational policy of the State of Kansas. For a while, during 1899–1903, Frank Nelson, now of Minneapolis, served as State Superintendent of Public Instruction in the State of Kansas. Nelson was also, later, a member of the Kansas State Text Book Commission.

The present State High School Supervisor of the State of Washington, L. O. Swenson, has been State Supervisor since 1928. He has written extensively, and published some twenty volumes of *Courses of Study*. He has been Director of the State Library, chairman of all State curriculum committees, Chairman of the Washington State Theatre under a Rockefeller grant, and Chairman of the State Commission of the Northwest Association of Secondary Schools.

In the State of Nebraska, in addition to the services of W. A. Rosene, Director of Certification, George Walter Rosenlof has exerted an important influence. Since 1934 he has been Director of Secondary Education of the State. Rosenlof is an authority in his field, and is professor of secondary education at the University of Nebraska. His influence, however, has extended beyond the boundaries of the State and, since 1935, he has served as Secretary of the Commission on Secondary Education of the North Central Association. He is contributing editor of the *High School Teacher*, and the author of *Library Facilities of Teacher Training Institutions* and the *Adult's Part in Character Education*. He ranks among the foremost educators in America in the field of secondary education.

J. M. Munson, President of Michigan State Normal College (Ypsilanti), since 1933, is influential in the State of Michigan. During 1905–13, Munson was Superintendent of Schools at Harbor Springs, and during 1913–19 was Deputy State Superintendent of Public Instruction for the State of Michigan. After having served as director of Central Michigan Normal

School, and Editor of *Moderator Topics,* he became President of Northern State Teachers' College, Marquette, Michigan. He held this position until he accepted the presidency of Michigan State Normal College. Munson is directing a progressive and wholesome influence on the State of Michigan's educational policy.

The rise of Miss Agnes Samuelson reads like a saga. It is the story of a rural-school teacher, a city-school teacher, high-school principal, and county superintendent, who finally wins the highest office in the state system of education. In 1927, Miss Samuelson was elected to her present position as Superintendent of Public Instruction in the State of Iowa. Since 1927, Miss Samuelson has made a number of improvements in the public schools of Iowa, and has become recognized as a leader in the field of education throughout the United States. In 1935 this led to her election as President of the National Educational Association. Educational journals testify to her many-sided interests in the field of public education. She is the author of a number of articles in several magazines, and has written many educational monographs. Miss Esther E. Tronstrom, an able assistant of Miss Samuelson, and chief clerk of the Board of Educational Examiners for the State of Iowa, accepted her position at the same time that Miss Samuelson did, in 1927. Her career is similar to that of her chief, Miss Samuelson, and prior to 1927, she served as County Superintendent for two terms.

Besides the contributions of Schulz in the State of Minnesota (already referred to), other educational leaders in that State must be mentioned. Senator Henry N. Benson of the Minnesota legislature sponsored an educational act granting State aid to schools offering courses in manual training and other practical work. Benson was for several terms chairman of the committee on education in the Minnesota senate, a position which at present is held by Ansgar I. Almén. Harry L. Wahlstrand, as Chairman of the committee on education in the lower house of the Minnesota legislature, has played a part in shaping the State's educational policy. S. A. Challman has been Assistant Commissioner of Education during the last twenty-seven years. All plans for the erection of public school buildings in Minnesota must secure the approval of Challman.

Many Swedes have served on the board of education of such large cities as Superior, Rockford, Detroit, Minneapolis, Chicago, and New York. Not long ago, a Swede directed the Board of Education of Superior, Wisconsin, with an iron hand. Professor David F. Swenson of the University of Minnesota has for many years been one of the most influential members of the Board of Education of Minneapolis. Charles S. Peterson was for a long period a valuable member of the Board of Education of the city of Chicago. In 1936, Mayor La Guardia appointed Mrs. Johanna M. Lindlof as a member of the Board of Education of the city of New York. Since she was the only woman on the Board and a former teacher of "reading, writing and arithmetic" for thirty-five years, her appointment received special attention in the press. Many severely criticized the Mayor for his selection, since it was unprecedented in the educational history of the city. Her appointment, in fact, caused wide reverberations.

Within a short time, however, the public recognized the wisdom of La Guardia's choice, and Mrs. Lindlof became known as an efficient and militant educational leader. She visited 150 schools, and addressed more than 100 meetings, in behalf of the Board, during the first year of her tenure. She made use of the radio frequently, in order to express her views on the educational problems of the city. Successfully she urged the Board to provide outdoor playgrounds for children, in the construction of new school buildings or plants. She introduced "movable furniture," to test the belief of progressive educators that a changing environment leads to greater efficiency in the schoolroom.

A number of Swedes have also won fame as directors of child-study associations, educational associations, bureaus of educational research, etc. J. E. Wallace Wallin, now of Wilmington, Delaware, has been director of a number of clinics and bureaus of special education. His particular field of interest has been "handicapped" children. Arthur E. Lindborg organized the Virgin Island Educational Association in 1924. John L. Sten-

AGNES SAMUELSON

STATE SUPERINTENDENT OF PUBLIC INSTRUCTION, IOWA

quist is Director of the Bureau of Educational Research of the public schools of Baltimore. Miss Cora Lee Danielson, Assistant Supervisor of the Education of Exceptional Children, Los Angeles, California, has contributed a number of articles to the *Journal of Educational Psychology*, the *Year Books*, and the *Educational Research Bulletin of Los Angeles City Schools*. She is the author of *A Language Ladder* and *Sentence Vocabulary Test*.

In the field of psychology and educational psychology, Swedes have made important contributions. The first in this field is, undoubtedly, Dean Carl E. Seashore of Iowa. (See the chapters on "Composers" and "Professors.") Educational psychologists throughout the nation have, directly or indirectly, been influenced by him. Among Seashore's students, C. Fritiof Malmberg, of Illinois State Normal University, and H. H. Anderson, who is rapidly making a name for himself at the University of Iowa in the field of "child welfare," should be mentioned. Undoubtedly others, such as Carl I. Erickson of Washington State College, Otto Edward Peterson of Illinois Northern State Teachers' College, and Frans A. Ericsson of Upsala College, have been directly or indirectly influenced by Seashore. Probably this is also true of such eminent psychologists as Vivian Allen Charles Henmon of the University of Wisconsin and Alfred L. Hall-Quest, editor of the Macmillan series on *Supervised Study*.

In the field of elementary and secondary education, in addition to the names already mentioned, the following should be noted: Carl Frithiof Borgeson of New York University, who has written on the school system of Sweden; Rupert Franz Asplund, Editor of *New Mexico Journal of Education*, 1907–19; John W. Wahlquist, Director of Secondary Education at the University of Utah; Carl Gustave Frederick Franzén, professor of secondary education at the University of Indiana; Herbert Theodore Olander of Johnstown Center, Pittsburgh; Charles Joseph Anderson, Dean of the School of Education, University of Wisconsin; Howard Anderson, now of Cornell University; Iwar S. Westerberg of Redland's University, California; Carl M. Hanson of Knox College; C. Emanuel Ekstrom, chairman of the Department of Education in Brown University; Philip Gustaf Johnson of the University of Nebraska; Paul V. Sangren, President of Western State Teachers' College, Michigan; Miss Anne Foberg, training-school Principal in the Connecticut Teachers' College at New Britain; and many others.

The public has become alarmed over the great increase of automobile accidents in our country, and courses in safety education are being introduced in the public schools. George N. Anselm of the University of North Carolina, director of the Curry School at Greensboro, has made an extensive study of the causes of automobile accidents involving children, and is a leader in this comparatively new field.

It is impossible to list the names of all Swedes in the various teachers' colleges. They are too numerous. For instance, at Michigan State Teachers' College, at least five faculty members are of Swedish origin. The same number is found in Illinois State Normal University and Western Illinois State Teachers' College. A large number of Swedes are found in the teachers' colleges of both the Atlantic and Pacific States. These have, however, not made the contributions that the universities have made. There is no question but that E. F. Lindquist, of the University of Iowa, will be generally recognized throughout the nation as a leader in the field of education. He is already an authority in the field of "achievement testing." Elmer T. Peterson, professor of education at the University of Iowa, has traveled extensively throughout the State of Iowa, visiting school boards in an advisory capacity. He is an authority in the field of finance, and is called upon especially for advice in matters dealing with school-building construction.

Many of those prominent in the field of elementary and secondary education have, of course, taught in the public schools. C. J. Anderson was Principal of Galesville High School, Wisconsin, during 1912–19, Superintendent of Stoughton Schools during 1919–20, and Assistant Superintendent of Public Instruction in Wisconsin, from 1920 to 1925. Rudolph D. Lindquist, once a rural-school teacher in Minnesota, became later Vice-Principal of Elko County High School, Nevada.

Eventually he moved to California, and served as supervising Principal of Columbus School at Berkeley, and as research director in the public schools of Oakland. Then he became Assistant Superintendent of Schools, and, finally, President of California State Teachers' College.

In the field of teachers' training, Henry Johnson of Columbia Teachers College deserves special recognition. He has been associated with the Minnesota State Normal School at Moorhead and Southern Illinois State Teachers' College at Charleston. He has for years served as secretary of the Association of History Teachers of the Middle States and Maryland, and was president of this association from 1914 to 1915. During 1911–15 he was chairman of the editorial committee of *History Teacher's Magazine*. He has been a member of the State of New York's committee on history in high schools, since 1916, and has served as member of the National Board of Historical Service for over twenty years.

Johnson has written extensively and contributed to a number of educational journals. He is the author of *The Problem of Adapting History to Children*, published in 1908. Seven years later he published his well-known *The Teaching of History*, which is extensively used as a textbook in "Method Courses" throughout the nation's universities, colleges, and normal schools. In 1932, Johnson published *Introduction to the History of the Social Sciences*. No other Swede has exerted a greater influence on American public schools, with the possible exception of Seashore.

In the field of agricultural education, Carl E. Rosenquist of the University of Nebraska; Dean E. P. Sandsten of Colorado Agricultural College; R. B. Jeppson, the State Supervisor of Agricultural Education, Nevada; Christ Christenson and T. A. Erickson of the College of Agriculture, University of Minnesota, have played an important part. The last named is the founder of the 4-H Clubs of the State of Minnesota, and for about twenty-five years their leader.

Other immigrant groups probably can present as formidable a list of educational leaders as the Swedes. Extensive biographies, containing names of articles and books written by the

Swedish-American leaders mentioned, would have given only a false impression, and have, therefore, largely been omitted. The more important leaders associated with the universities have been mentioned by Professor Adolph B. Benson in his chapter on "Professors." If anyone cares to pursue the study further, plenty of material will be found in the various journals of education published by the many states, and in *Educational Method, Elementary School Journal, American Childhood, American School Board Journal, Occupations, Educational Screen, School and Society, Progressive Education, Educational Review, Journal of Educational Research, Educational Administration and Supervision, Journal of the National Education Association* and similar magazines.

Lawyers

G. AARON YOUNGQUIST

During the administration of President Hoover (1929–33), Mr. Youngquist was Assistant Attorney-General of the United States, in charge of
the division of taxation and prohibition in the Department of Justice,
and in this capacity argued some seventy cases before the Supreme
Court of the United States. Born in Västergötland, Sweden, in 1885,
he was brought to America by his parents, when but two years of age.
Graduating from the St. Paul College of Iowa in 1909, he was admitted
to the bar the same year, and served four years as County Attorney of
Polk County, then as Assistant Attorney-General and later as Attorney-General of Minnesota. From there he went to Washington, and has
now resumed the practice of law in Minneapolis.

THE Swedes are not a litigious people. In Sweden law is
simple and lawyers are few. Perhaps this accounts for
the fact that, in the early annals of this country, we find
relatively few Swedish lawyers.

The identity of the earliest of the Swedish colonists, and of
their immediate descendants who were lawyers, is, with a few
exceptions, unknown. Notable exceptions are John Morton, who
for many years pursued his practice with distinction in Philadelphia, and was a justice of the Supreme Court of Pennsylvania from 1770 to 1774, and Alexander Contee Hanson,
grandson of John Hanson, who practiced law at Annapolis,
Maryland, and served both as Senator and as Representative in
Congress.

Others of more recent years are Thomas F. Bayard, who
served as United States Senator from Delaware—a member of
a family contributing five United States Senators from that
State; George A. Elliott, also from Delaware, and the Paxson,
Yocum, and Rambo families of Pennsylvania. Another is the
Sinnickson family, which produced Clement Sinnickson, a Civil
War captain and Congressman, and a judge in New Jersey,
and, in the present generation, J. Forman Sinnickson, also a
judge. The Keene and the Springer families have likewise produced many lawyers who have practiced, not only in the East,

but in other parts of the country as well. One of the descendants of the latter family is Milton E. Carter of Missouri, who is now assistant to the United States Commissioner of Internal Revenue. Secretary of the Interior, Harold L. Ickes, a lawyer, is a descendant of an old Swedish family, and President Roosevelt, who also practiced law, is a remote descendant of an early Swedish family which settled in New Amsterdam, the present New York.

For the rest, we must turn to the past generation or two. Unfortunately, no source exists which can supply either the names or the achievements of those who have attained prominence at the bar; and, furthermore, only the comparatively recent years mark the rise of the sons and daughters of immigrants from the ranks of farmers and artisans to the professions.

The number of lawyers bearing Swedish names is rapidly growing, however. There are some three hundred of them in the State of Illinois alone, and nearly the same number in Minnesota. Other states, with fewer residents of Swedish blood, likewise have a substantial number, of Swedish blood, at the bar; but certain sections of the country, particularly the South and the Southwest, have virtually none at all. It is likewise true that the number who have attained high distinction before the bar is small. Nevertheless, it may be fairly said that, with the exception of those whose roots have been in American soil for many generations, the record compares favorably with that of any other national group. Distinction in this connection does not mean notoriety. The latter, fortunately, does not seem to be a Swedish tendency.

A mere listing of lawyers of Swedish names, in States like New York, Illinois, Minnesota, and Iowa, would occupy many pages, and probably reach several thousand persons in number. Even the naming of all those who have gained prominence in their local communities would require so much space that this recital must of necessity be limited to only a few.

The Swedes of Illinois have produced a number of lawyers and judges of note. Among those in the first rank was Judge Harry Olson. After a period of preparation in private practice, and as Assistant State's Attorney, he became Chief Justice of the Municipal Court of Chicago in 1906, and held that post until his death. He was responsible for important reforms in judicial administration, and was, during his lifetime, active in organizations concerned with criminology, judicial reform, and child welfare.

Another is George E. Q. Johnson who, though born in Iowa, has spent his active years in Chicago, interrupting his private practice of the law with a five-years' service as United States Attorney, during which he directed and participated in the prosecution, under the Federal income tax laws, of a number of Chicago racketeers and gangsters, among them the notorious "Al" Capone. It is an interesting coincidence that the investigation and prosecution which resulted in the Capone conviction was carried on under the supervision of a Swedish-born Assistant Attorney-General of the United States. Mr. Johnson also served for a short time as United States District Judge before resuming his private practice.

Carl R. Chindblom, another Chicago attorney, served as County Attorney, Master in Chancery of the Circuit Court of Cook County, Referee in Bankruptcy, and for six terms as a Representative in Congress. He has also held important positions in Swedish organizations in this country.

Another is Oscar E. Carlstrom, who, after having been engaged in private practice and served as State's Attorney and as a member of the State Tax Commission, was elected Attorney-General of Illinois, and filled that office with distinction for eight years before returning to private practice in Chicago.

Another interesting example is that of Carl Hjalmar Lundquist who, born and educated as an engineer in Sweden, studied law after coming to this country and is now serving as Assistant Corporation Counsel of Chicago. In addition to an active life at the bar, he has found time for service to innumerable Swedish organizations.

Gustaf Bernhard Anderson, Swedish Vice-Consul in Chicago since 1914, born 1867, is a native of Småland. After being graduated from Harvard he spent the year 1893 at Uppsala University as a student of the Scandinavian languages. Later he decided to study law, which he has practiced in Chicago ever since he was admitted to the bar in 1896.

Minnesota competes with Illinois in its production of lawyers of Swedish birth or descent. One of its outstanding lawyers and public men was John Lind, born in Sweden. In a long and busy life as a lawyer he found time to serve as President of the Board of Regents, as Governor of Minnesota, four terms as Representative in Congress, and, in 1913, as President Wilson's envoy and personal representative to Mexico.

The senior judge, in years of service, in the Minnesota courts is Andrew Holt. After having practiced law for thirteen years he became municipal judge in Minneapolis, then district judge, and in 1911 Associate Justice of the Supreme Court of Minnesota, which office he still fills, after forty-three years of unbroken service as a judge. He stands high in the estimation of the bar for learning and courage.

Another member of the Supreme Court of Minnesota is Harry H. Peterson, who, after having practiced law in St. Paul, became County Attorney, a few years later Attorney-General of Minnesota, and was then elevated to the highest court of the State, on which he still serves.

Several of Minnesota's governors of Swedish birth or descent were lawyers—Adolph Olson Eberhart, who served from 1909 to 1914, and is now practicing in Chicago; Joseph A. A. Burnquist, Minnesota's war Governor, now in Minneapolis; and the late Floyd B. Olson, who, before occupying that office, had practiced law and served as County Attorney in Minneapolis. The present United States Senator from Minnesota, Ernest Lundeen, has been a lawyer in Minneapolis since 1906.

It is interesting to note that the office of Attorney-General which, in Minnesota, had always been regarded as a "Yankee" berth, was from 1929 to 1936 filled three times in succession by men of Swedish antecedents—G. Aaron Youngquist; Henry N. Benson, an attorney of high standing, a former member of the Minnesota Senate, and for many years Chairman of the Board of Trustees of Gustavus Adolphus College; and Harry H. Peterson.

The office of Attorney-General, the highest law office in the gift of a State, seems to have particular appeal to the Swedes. In addition to the experience of Minnesota and Illinois already referred to, that office in the State of Delaware is occupied by P. Warren Green, a descendant of Peter Rambo, one of the earliest Swedes. Clarence V. Beck is Attorney-General of Kansas; Enar K. Matson is Attorney-General of Montana. The late Joseph H. Peterson, who appeared before the Supreme Court of the United States on a number of occasions, served first as Assistant Attorney-General, and then as Attorney-General, of Idaho; and Oscar L. Heltzen served as Assistant Attorney-General and Attorney-General of Rhode Island, as well as its Commissioner of Insurance.

In Wisconsin, Irvine L. Lenroot, who was a United States Senator from that State between 1918 and 1927, was admitted to the bar in 1897. He is of Swedish descent. For six years he was a member of the Wisconsin legislature, and of the House of Representatives in Congress for nine years, before being elected a Senator. He is now a judge of the United States Court of Customs and Patent Appeals in Washington.

Mention should likewise be made of men like Lawrence A. Liljeqvist, a prominent Oregon lawyer who acted as Special Assistant Attorney-General in that State from 1919 to 1936; Albin W. Norblad of Astoria, who served in the State Senate and as Governor of Oregon; Waldemar Seton of Portland, who served both as State and Federal Deputy District Court Attorney and as attorney for the Vice Consulate of Portland, and is a Knight of the Order of Vasa; Eskil C. Carlson of Iowa, who has served as solicitor and as municipal judge of Des Moines, and is now occupied in private practice, and as instructor at Drake University Law School; Axel P. Johnson of Reno, Nevada, who was for some time a member of the faculty of the Westminster Law School at Denver, Colorado, and a member of the legislature of that State, and Herbert L. Emanuelson, who practices law at New Haven, serves as judge in Connecticut, is President of the John Ericsson League, and takes an active part in matters of interest to Swedish-Americans.

Since there is no means available for ascertaining the existence, or the identity of all Swedish lawyers who have gained distinction in their states or communities, the omission of some of them from this short summary must unavoidably occur. Such omissions are not intentional but are due to lack of information. The number is rapidly growing and, judging the future by the performance in the short past during which the country has had lawyers of Swedish ancestry in any considerable number, some of their representatives may in time be expected to take their places in the very front rank of the legal profession.

Public Officials

O. FRITIOF ANDER

For the biography of Dr. Ander, see the chapter on "Public School Educators."

MANY half-truths and misrepresentations have found their way into the writings of those who have deplored the small number of Swedish-Americans in state and national politics. This lament, which has been echoed by a score of writers, is based upon the assumption that few Swedes have achieved political office, either elective or appointive.

It has likewise been maintained that, though the Swedes as voters are seriously interested in politics, they abhor "dirty" political-party machines. Therefore, they do not become professional office seekers, and in one sense are not "politically minded" as far as "practical politics" is concerned. Furthermore, it has been claimed that the Swedes' faithfulness to the Republican party has caused that party to favor other national groups whose political allegiance is more uncertain. Particularly favored by both major parties have been the Germans and the Irish, while the Swedes have had to be satisfied with less than crumbs, as they faithfully sang "hail, hail to the Grand Old Party."

To these, at most, "half-truths" were gradually added misrepresentations by attributing the small number of Swedish public officials to a peculiarly "lofty Swedish mind," a supposed heritage from Sweden which caused them to shun "deceit, cunning, and hypocrisy," the weapons commonly supposed to be used by American politicians. Furthermore, it was claimed that the Swedes were interested in "productive labor," and lacked "political instinct." "*Svensk avundsjuka*," or jealousy, was also said to be an obstacle to the politically ambitious. One writer states: "It is true that politics, as a profession in itself, seldom appeals to a Swede. His training, education, and tradition, as a rule, have been along other lines."

On the other hand, Vilhelm Berger's list of Swedes, prominent in American public life, should cause anyone to be amazed at the large number of those actively engaged in political work and throw overboard any idea to the contrary, or any conception even attributing either success or failure in politics to a "national heritage."

A study of the census of the United States and the distribution of immigrants clearly indicates a correlation between the numbers in the national groups and their representation in politics—a factor which, with rapid Americanization, will become even more evident. In 1930 there were, in the United States, approximately 1,562,700 persons of Swedish descent of the first and second generations. In Minnesota the Swedes constituted almost 11 per cent of the total population, and in Illinois about 3.4 per cent, while Pennsylvania's 46,000 Swedish-Americans and New York's 121,000 constitute less than 1 per cent of the populations of those two States. The geographical distribution of the Swedes may be more effectively represented by saying that about one third of the Swedes in America are to be found in Minnesota and Illinois. The Swedes thus constitute a very small percentage of the entire population in the United States. The widespread distribution of Swedes outside of Minnesota and Illinois, including such States as North Dakota, South Dakota, Nebraska, Kansas, Missouri, Colorado, Montana, California, Oregon, Washington, Iowa, Wisconsin, Michigan, Indiana, Ohio, Pennsylvania, New Jersey, New York, Massachusetts, Connecticut, Rhode Island, Maine, and Texas, has tended to make them a less potent factor in American political life.

Further, it must be stated that only a comparatively small number of Swedes arrived in America before the Civil War. Participation in the war and membership in the military order of the Grand Army of the Republic were almost a prerequisite, after the war, for a successful political career in the North, just as an enlistment in the Confederate Army was a prerequisite for political preferment in the South during the age of hate that followed the war. Colonel Hans Mattson, probably to no small extent, owed his political career in Minnesota to his service in the Union Army.

Then the church organizations of the immigrants, though not opposed to politics and political activities on the part of their members, were steeped in orthodoxy and ultraconservatism, fostering a spirit which did not stimulate a wide outlook and outspoken progressivism or liberalism. But, to place too great a stress on the church as a factor retarding active participation in American politics, would be to ignore the fact that the Swedes, like other immigrants, tended to form their own settlements to which later immigrants flocked. Here they organized their own churches and "social bodies." It was not necessary to seek associations for religious or social reasons outside of the national group. The immigrants may have learned English in a fashion, enough to make themselves understood; beyond that it was unnecessary. They may, also, have subscribed to an American newspaper, even in the early days, but a Swedish-American newspaper satisfied them far better and contained news of greater interest to them. There was a "Little Sweden" in America, filled with all the gossip, sorrows, and joys to make life sufficiently entertaining and varied. American influences may have at times disturbed the idyl, as during state or national election campaigns, but if so, it was far more interesting to listen to campaign orators of one's own race, speaking the language of "heroes" and comparing Lincoln, Grant, Hayes, Garfield, Blaine, Harrison, McKinley, and Theodore Roosevelt with Gustavus Adolphus, not to mention Charles XII; and the identification of the Irish and Catholics with the Democrats caused the Swedes no end of pride in their own allegiance to the Republican party. Anyway, who cared what an American campaign speaker, even a presidential candidate, said, as long as there was an "Uncle Slokum," a "Kalle Swensson," or an Enander!

But soon the Swedes began to clamor for political recognition, though as yet they were unwilling, or unable, to change their own environment. At election time they organized their own "Republican Clubs" as "Lincoln Clubs," "Grant Clubs," and, by 1880, the Swedish-American press was loud in its insistence that Swedes should assert themselves more in politics. Though this press severely criticized the political parties for not selecting Swedes for either elective or appointive offices, the truth hardly justified their outcry. Most of the Swedes, even if some had had university training in Sweden, had few of the qualifications required for political preferment. They were too exclusive; few had mastered the language; few had a legal training. Swedes of even the second generation were taught Swedish before they were taught English. Their colleges and other educational institutions were looked upon as essentially schools for training ministers; and often the very existence of these institutions was precarious. In view of these facts, one is amazed to find that even prior to 1900 a large number of Swedes had been favored with political appointments or elective offices, thus probably causing Professor H. H. Boyesen of Columbia University to write in the 'nineties that the Scandinavians "take as naturally to politics as goslings do to water."

The best-known Swede in American politics before 1900 was John Lind. He was born in Sweden and was the first Swede to be elected to Congress. He was elected in 1886, and reëlected in 1888 and 1890. In 1896 he was the Fusion party nominee for Governor of Minnesota, and in 1898 he was elected, serving as Governor from 1899 to 1901. He was also the first Swede to hold this important office, but the Swedes of strong Republican sentiments never really appreciated Lind, because he had deserted their own party.

Before him the best-known Swede in American politics, prior to 1900, was Col. Hans Mattson, who died in 1893. Mattson, like Lind, was born in Sweden. Three times he had been elected Secretary of State in Minnesota, and he had been an active member of the State Board of Immigration. He had also served as United States Consul-General in India, from 1881 to 1883. His activities as a newspaperman and as a land commissioner, his political career, not to mention his Civil War record, focused the spotlight of attention on Mattson as a successful Swedish politician.

By 1900 a number of other Swedes had been elected to public office in Minnesota. Among them was John Albert Johnson, who later became Governor of Minnesota. Andrew Holt of Minneapolis began his long career on the bench when, in 1894, he was appointed by Governor Knute Nelson as municipal judge.

JOHN LIND, 1854–1930
FIRST GOVERNOR OF MINNESOTA OF SWEDISH
EXTRACTION

In Illinois, the Swedes had to be satisfied with smaller offices. Carl Gustav Linderborg, Swedish-American journalist, was elected to the Illinois legislature in 1874; Peter A. Sundelius, another journalist, was elected to the legislature in 1884, serving three terms in that body. The Swedes attributed to him the unpopular Republican educational legislations by which Governor Altgeld and the Democrats profited, since it was interpreted as hostile to both parochial and private schools. A. W. Berggren of Galesburg was elected State Senator in 1880 and was reëlected in 1884. For a short time, he also served as Superintendent of the State Penitentiary at Joliet. He was regarded as a very successful politician. Frederick Lundin, of "Juniperade" fame, was first elected to the Illinois Senate in 1894, and thus he entered upon a career which was to make him generally known as a shrewd and influential politician.

In Iowa, Nebraska, Kansas, and Massachusetts, Swedes had also been elected to State legislative positions. Among these were C. J. A. Ericson of Iowa, who had arrived in the United States at the age of twelve in 1852. In 1860 he was made postmaster at Ridgeport, and, after having moved to Boone, Iowa, where he became a successful businessman and banker, he was elected successively to both houses of the Iowa legislature. As State Senator he served for ten years. Ericson was one of the few Swedish politicians closely affiliated with the Lutheran church on which he showered liberal gifts. It is estimated that Augustana College and Theological Seminary alone received donations in money and land from Ericson, valued at $100,000.

Charles O. Lobeck, whose Swedish mother was married to a German, began his political career in Nebraska in 1892, when he was elected to the Senate. Eric Johnson, whose Civil War record should have been an asset, was too impatient in clamoring for preferment. Outside of being made journal clerk in the House of Representatives in Springfield in 1871, he failed in his efforts to win political recognition in Illinois. He was not much more successful in Nebraska, to which State he later moved, though he was elected to the Nebraska legislature in 1888, as an Independent. In 1891 he became chief clerk of the House of Representatives at Lincoln, and was reappointed to that position in 1893. His flirtations with Populism were probably no help to him after the movement had declined, even though he returned to the Republican fold.

The Reverend Carl A. Swensson, founder and President of Bethany College at Lindsborg, Kansas, also had more than a "stump" acquaintance with politics, for he served one term in the Kansas legislature. Since he was an active and influential Republican who advocated temperance, some have given Swensson considerable credit for the Kansas temperance legislation which won the State almost "Maine" fame. In Massachusetts, also, the Swedes had begun to stir as the century was turning, electing a member to the Massachusetts lawmaking body.

But the Swedes were not satisfied with these rewards, and were under the impression that they were being discriminated against. As a result of this feeling, a movement gained ground that temporary clubs during election campaigns were insufficient. A stronger organization of a more permanent nature must be founded. During the latter part of 1894, and early part of 1895, the Swedish-American press of Illinois was jubilant over the founding of the Swedish-American Republican League of Illinois.

Among those taking an active part in organizing this League were Edward C. Westman, Will S. Hussander, G. Bernhard Anderson, "Alex" Johnson, Gustav L. Nelson, M. O. Williamson, and Carl R. Chindblom, a graduate of Augustana College, who was then young and filled with enthusiasm. There were banquets, orations, speeches on Lincoln, John Ericsson, and loud praise for Gustavus Adolphus and Charles XII. "Siberian Punch," "Roman Punch," and possibly "Swedish Punch" added punch and joy to the meetings, to which, also, prominent American politicians were invited. Whether or not the League was responsible for M. O. Williamson's election in 1900, as State Treasurer of Illinois, is not known, but he was one of its first members to be elected to office.

Soon similar organizations were formed in other states, and the John Ericsson Republican League of Illinois, as the organization came to be known, undoubtedly did become a factor in at least mid-Western politics. But the election of a larger number of Swedes to political office, after the turn of the century, was more likely due to the fact that the Swedes were gradually losing the earmarks of immigrants. Some who were politically ambitious, yet suffering from an inferiority complex—that of being looked upon as "poor Swedes"—tried to sever their connections with immigrant organizations. In this they were assisted by the narrow nationalistic attitude found in both the church and the social organizations.

This generalization, however, does not hold true in all cases. Some persons, in spite of hostile forces, clung to their immigrant heritages, and yet achieved a measure of success in politics. The outstanding example of this is, undoubtedly, Carl R. Chindblom of Chicago, who has remained in close touch with Swedish-American life. From 1919 to 1933 Chindblom served as a member of the United States Congress, and throughout his career he has remained in close touch with Augustana College, and has been an active member of the Augustana Synod. He was first elected Congressman from Illinois in 1918, and was reëlected six times. His defeat in 1932 may be attributed, in the main, to the general unpopularity of the Hoover Administration, as well as to his own attitude toward prohibition. He is now a referee in bankruptcy in Chicago. In the Federal Government, few men have kept closer contacts with Swedish-Americans than Chindblom. In the state offices, on the other hand, a larger number of occupants have followed Chindblom's example. Many politicians, however, look upon Swedish-American organizations as "foreign"; and their acquaintance with them goes only as far as is politically expedient.

It is, therefore, no surprise that a bill, breathing intense hostility to immigrants, was introduced in the Oregon legislature by a Swede, Albin Walter Norblad, which forbade the publication of newspapers, periodicals, or any other literature in any language other than English. But when one takes account of the spirit of narrow nationalism that prevailed in America during the World War, perhaps the only surprising thing is the fact that Norblad was born in Sweden. This, as well as the fact that, upon Governor Patterson's death in 1929, Norblad became Governor of Oregon, may be attributed to accident.

The number of graduates of Swedish-American colleges who

have attained political offices of importance up to this time has
been very small. These colleges were steeped in Swedish traditions, and fostered an exclusiveness which did not develop successful politicians. Furthermore, there has been a close connection between a legal training and a successful political career,
and, as a rule, these institutions did not offer such a training.
Among the number of "Swedish" governors of Minnesota, only
one, Adolph O. Eberhart, was graduated from a Swedish-American institution of learning.

The twentieth century found the Americanization process in
full swing, and even Swedish-born American citizens felt its
force. Though it tended to sweep away much that was dear to
Swedish-Americans, it brought political success and political
plums, starting a new chapter in Swedish-American political
activities. The age of Enander and Carl Swensson was forever
past, and the John Ericsson Leagues began to decline, or became mere shadows of what they were originally intended to be.
Aggravated by the World War, the feeling of being a "foreigner" became as dreaded as leprosy. It has been pointed out
that Swedes and Scandinavians in general, assimilate rapidly;
and it is, therefore, difficult to state who and what was truly
representative of Swedish-America during and after the World
War. Perhaps it was Norblad, after all, with his Norblad Law.
Perhaps it was "our Magnus Johnson" of the milking contest.
Perhaps it was the stand taken by Ernest Lundeen, when he
opposed the United States' entrance into the World War. Perhaps it was Senator Lenroot, with his few Swedish-American
contacts. Perhaps it was Chindblom, with his feet squarely on
Swedish-American ground, cherishing Swedish-American traditions. Perhaps there was no longer a Swedish-America in the
strictest sense. Perhaps they were all true to Swedish-American
traditions, and represented only degrees of the Americanization
process.

During the first decade and a half of the twentieth century,
a large number of Swedes won minor political offices, and a considerable number, major political recognitions. Andrew Holt
of Minneapolis was elected and reëlected as judge of the local
District Court, and was finally made a member of the Su-

preme Court of Minnesota. In the legal profession few men have received greater recognition than the late Judge Harry Olson of Chicago, who was responsible for the organization, in 1911, of the Branch Court of Domestic Relations; in 1913 of the Morals Branch Court; and in 1914 of the Boys' Branch Court in Chicago. He became one of America's most noted criminologists.

For ten years, from 1927 to 1937, Peter B. Hanson, a native of Hälsingborg, Sweden, served as a justice of the Children's and Domestic Relations Court of the Borough of Brooklyn, New York, whose population exceeds that of any one of thirty states. As a Democrat, he had previously served as counsel to various officials of the co-extensive King's County, and as a district leader. He has now returned to private law practice.

In the field of politics, the State of Minnesota naturally produced the largest number of office holders. John Lind, after having served as Governor of Minnesota from 1899 to 1901, was again elected to Congress in 1902, but on the Democratic ticket; and in 1913 he was appointed by President Woodrow Wilson on the famous Mexican mission. As a Democrat, John Albert Johnson was elected Governor in 1904, and was reëlected in 1906 and 1908. Up to that time only one other man, John S. Pillsbury, had been twice reëlected to the governorship of Minnesota; and Johnson was mentioned as a potential candidate for the presidency of the United States in 1912. But an untimely death cut him off in 1909, and he was succeeded by Adolph Olson Eberhart, a Progressive Republican, who had long been active in State politics. Eberhart was elected in 1910 and reëlected in 1912. Joseph Alfred Arner Burnquist, who had been Lieutenant Governor, succeeded to the governorship in 1915, and was reëlected in 1916 and 1918. In 1906 Charles A. Lindbergh, Sr., was elected to Congress and served five successive terms. Lindbergh gained the reputation of a liberal, and was fearless in his attacks on "money trusts." Sydney Anderson was elected to Congress from Minnesota, in 1910. He was reëlected six times, serving on numerous important committees, especially those dealing with agricultural problems. Anderson's father was Swedish and his mother Norwegian. One of the most able men representing Minnesota, however, is Harold Knutson, who is now serving his twenty-first year as a Congressman. He was generally looked upon, in the heydays of the Republican party, as the "whip" of the House. He is a member of the Ways and Means Committee.

Before the World War, the Swedes outside of Minnesota had made small contributions to the list of officeholders, though they had a number of representatives in various legislatures. Frederick Lundin of Illinois was elected in 1908 as a representative in Congress, and for many years was, as stated before, a force in the Illinois Republican party. Charles O. Lobeck, State Senator since 1892, was elected to Congress in 1910, from Nebraska, and was later reëlected. Peter Norbeck was active in South Dakota politics, both as State Senator and as Lieutenant Governor, and the critical year of 1917 found him Governor. His father, too, was Swedish, and his mother Norwegian. Francis O. Lindquist served one term as Congressman from Michigan, 1913–14. As in the case of Anderson and Norbeck, Lindquist's father was Swedish and his mother Norwegian. George Alfred Carlson was elected Governor of Colorado in 1914. In Massachusetts a number of Swedes were elected to that State's legislative body. In Oregon, Conrad P. Olson was elected to the Oregon legislature in 1912, and had the distinction, in 1914, of being nominated by both the major political parties. In 1916 he was elected to the Oregon Senate.

Of a large number of Swedes in various municipal offices, one of the unique careers had already been started, long before 1917. In 1908 Samuel A. Carlson had been elected Mayor of Jamestown, New York, and he served almost continuously until 1938—believed to be a United States record. Carlson's long tenure was in itself an achievement, and he proved to be a most efficient and progressive administrator, winning acclaim for his many reforms. His most publicized accomplishment was the establishment of Jamestown's municipal power plant. In other "Swedish" cities, just as in Jamestown, Swedes laid the foundations for strong and honest governments, and were breaking records in length of tenure of minor office.

J. Edward Swanstrom, the son of a Swedish clergyman, was

THE LINDBERGHS

(PHOTOGRAPH TAKEN IN 1909, WHEN CHARLES A.
LINDBERGH, SR., 1860–1924, WAS A
MEMBER OF CONGRESS)

President of the Board of Education in the old city of Brooklyn, New York; and, after the consolidation, became President of the Board of Education of the city of New York. In 1901 he was elected President of the Borough of Brooklyn, and served a full two-year term during the administration of Seth Low as Mayor. He died in 1911. Charles S. Peterson was appointed a member of the Chicago Board of Education in 1913, and held various other municipal offices prior to being elected City Treasurer in 1927.

A surprising thing about the active and successful Swedes in politics prior to the World War was the fact that, in many cases, their rewards came through the Democratic party. This may be surprising because the Swedes were generally faithful to the Republican party; but it probably proves that party loyalty does not pay, or that the Democrats were fishing for Swedish votes, and therefore nominated Swedish candidates.

The election of 1912 can be said with safety, however, to have played havoc with political-party allegiance; and the economic unrest that preceded the World War and gave rise to Republican Progressivism, and the Farmer-Labor party in Minnesota also did much to break up solid Republicanism among the Swedes. With the victory, in 1932, of Franklin D. Roosevelt, who claims distant, partly Swedish ancestry, a number of the old-guard Republicans among the Swedes suffered defeat, and new men took their places. Meanwhile, however, many had gained offices during the Harding, Coolidge, and Hoover administrations. Among the new men from Minnesota, in Federal politics after the World War, we find Magnus Johnson, who in 1922 had run on the Farmer-Labor ticket for Governor. Upon the death of Senator Knute Nelson, July 16, 1923, Johnson, as his successor, became a well-known figure in Washington overnight. After the expiration of Nelson's term, which Johnson was filling, many "tall" stories kept him out of national politics until 1933, when he was elected Congressman. On the other hand, it was said that Johnson had been deprived of reëlection by flagrant fraud on the part of the opposition party. In the midst of the election campaign of 1936, Johnson died. He was undoubtedly a much abler man than was generally supposed, in spite of linguistic difficulties which brought him ridicule. On February 16, 1933, Godfrey G. Goodwin died while serving as a Member of Congress, having been elected in 1924, and reëlected to that office until the time of his death. His mother was Swedish. The Farmer-Labor party presents a formidable list of such able men as the recently elected United States Senator Ernest Lundeen, who took the place of Governor Floyd B. Olson on the senatorial ticket, upon the latter's death in 1936. Olson, who was elected Governor of Minnesota in 1930, and twice later reëlected, serving until his death, was of Swedish-Norwegian parentage. Olson was a progressive leader who had won national recognition. Death probably robbed him of a brilliant political future.

In state politics, all the men named took an active part. Joseph Alfred Arner Burnquist continued in office as Governor of Minnesota until 1921. Others who have played a prominent part in Minnesota politics include such persons as Victor Lawson, State Senator. Harry Peterson, Farmer-Laborite, was elected Attorney-General for three terms, and is now a justice of the supreme court. C. J. Swendsén served for years on the Parole Board of Control. The present Lieutenant Governor, Gottfrid Lindsten, is a Farmer-Laborite, and Mike Holm's long career as Secretary of State is unique, in view of the fact that Holm is a Republican, and the State has had a Farmer-Labor Governor for years. Henry N. Benson, another Republican, served as Attorney-General of Minnesota from 1929 to 1932. A. C. Lindholm, the present Secretary of the Parole Board of Control, is also wielding considerable influence in Minnesota politics.

In Illinois, where the Swedes apparently clung more closely to the Republican party than in Minnesota, Carl R. Chindblom was, as noted, consistently reëlected to Congress through the 'twenties. The same State saw the rise of George E. Q. Johnson, the Nemesis of "Al" Capone, as a United States District Attorney of the Northern Illinois District, and for a brief time, from 1929 to 1932, John A. Swanson made the headlines in Illinois newspapers as State's Attorney of Cook County, in connection with his efforts to rid Chicago of its criminals. Oscar Nelson served as State Treasurer for one term in the early 'twenties. Oscar E. Carlstrom, after having served as a member of the State Tax Commission from 1921 to 1925, was elected Attorney-General of Illinois, which position he held for two terms. In the last two elections he has been a candidate for governor in the Republican primaries, but, although he is very capable, was unable to overcome formidable opposition. Several Swedes are now members of the Illinois State legislature, though they are not so numerous as in the Minnesota legislative body. A few have also won political recognition in Iowa.

Wisconsin furnished the United States Senate with a capable man, in the person of Irvine Luther Lenroot who, upon the death of Senator Paul O. Husting in 1918, succeeded him by appointment. In 1920 he was elected Senator and served one term. At the Republican convention it was said he had been slated by the party managers to be Harding's running mate as Vice-President, but was forced out by the coup that nominated Coolidge. He thus came near being Harding's successor as President. In 1929 he was appointed judge of the United States Court of Customs and Patent Appeals, which office he still holds. Adolphus P. Nelson, also of Wisconsin, was a member of the Sixty-sixth and Sixty-seventh Congresses.

In Nebraska, Fred G. Johnson, who had taken an active part in State politics, serving as Lieutenant Governor from 1923 to 1925, and as a member of both legislative houses, was elected to Congress in 1928. Johnson's father was Swedish. John Nathaniel Norton was also very active in State politics, prior to his election to Congress in 1926. As early as 1913, Norton introduced the first proposed constitutional amendment for a unicameral legislature in Nebraska, and advocated this change as a member of the Nebraska Constitutional Convention in 1920. In 1924 he was the Democratic party's nominee for Governor. In 1930 Norton was reëlected to Congress. From 1933 to 1936 he served as a special adviser in the United States Department of Agriculture, and in 1936 was elected a member of Nebraska's first unicameral legislature.

But among these new leaders Peter Norbeck, who has been referred to earlier, was undoubtedly the best known. He was elected United States Senator from South Dakota in 1920, and held that office until his death in 1937, being reëlected in 1926 and in 1932. As a Republican he was of the progressive group.

In Kansas, the Reverend Ernst F. Pihlblad, successor to Carl A. Swensson as President of Bethany College, was elected to the State Senate in 1936 on the Republican ticket, without Democratic opposition.

Since the death of Norbeck, Edwin Carl Johnson of Colorado is, however, among the most prominent and promising politicians. After having served as both Lieutenant Governor and Governor of Colorado, Johnson was elected United States Senator in 1936, with the largest majority ever given anyone in the State. His career reads almost like a fairy tale. A native of Kansas, he migrated to Colorado to save his health, became a rancher and coöperative store manager, and was then sent to the State legislature. The high executive positions followed.

Governor Norblad of Oregon was undoubtedly among the first Swedes to win political recognition on the Pacific coast. The Democratic landslide in 1932 led to the election of Monrad C. Wallgren and Martin F. Smith to Congress—both from the State of Washington. Both were also reëlected in 1934 and in 1936. Smith was the first Democrat elected as a representative from the Third Washington District and, since 1932, has constantly increased his majority vote. He has served as member of the Committee on Rivers and Harbors, the Committee on Pensions, and the Committee on Claims. At present, he is also director of the National Rivers and Harbors Congress. Like Senator Johnson of Colorado, he has not severed his contacts with the Swedish-Americans, but is a member of such organizations as "Runeberg," "Vasa," and the Swedish Baptist Church.

In 1936 another Democrat of Swedish parentage was elected to Congress from the State of Washington; namely, Warren G. Magnuson, a young lawyer of Seattle. Though the Swedes seemingly won many new political honors as a result of the sweeping Democratic landslides since 1932, Frank Carlson of Kansas was elected to Congress on the Republican ticket in 1934, and reëlected in 1936.

In the East the Swedes have made fewer contributions, though a large number of persons distinguished themselves in minor offices. A man who has become prominent, particularly as an archfoe of James M. Curley of Massachusetts, is Eugene C. Hultman, former Police Commissioner of Boston, and later State Commissioner of Parks. Though a number of other persons could be mentioned, the East has contributed only one Swede to Congress; namely, Pehr G. Holmes, who was born in Sweden in 1881. After having served as Mayor of Worcester from 1917 to 1919, he began to take a more intensive interest in State and national politics. In 1930 he was elected to Congress as a Republican from the Fourth Congressional District of Massachusetts, and was reëlected in 1932, 1934, and 1936.

A number of persons have, however, secured other recognition, both in State and Federal Government; and it suffices here to mention only a number of the prominent ones. Mary Anderson, who was born in Sweden, has won national fame. Since 1920 she has been Director of the Women's Bureau of the United States Department of Labor. In 1933 she was appointed by President Roosevelt chairman of the United States delegation to the seventeenth session of the International Labor Conference at Geneva. She has served in her present capacity under four different presidents, representing two different political parties. Katharine Lenroot, the daughter of Judge Lenroot, has been head of the Children's Bureau in Washington since November, 1934. She acted as chairman of the United States delegation to the fifth and sixth Pan-American Child Congresses.

In the United States diplomatic service, too, several men of Swedish extraction have held important posts. Thus Alfred J. Pearson, now Dean of Drake University, Des Moines, Iowa (see the chapter on "Professors") was appointed by President Coolidge in 1924 as American Minister to Poland and the following year to the corresponding post in Finland, which he held until 1930. During the World War and later, Col. Oscar N. Solbert, a high-stand West Point graduate, who had been brought from his birthplace in Sweden to Worcester, Massachusetts, when a child, served as United States Military Attaché, first in the Scandinavian countries and later in London, where he was stationed five years under three different ambassadors. Upon his return he was appointed Presidential Military Aide to President Coolidge and as such escorted the then Prince of Wales, now Duke of Windsor, as his Honorary Aide-de-Camp on his first tour of the United States in 1924. While in London he had made the personal acquaintance and even gained the friendship of the Prince and was therefore able to arrange the details for his trip. In 1926 he served in the same rôle as the official American escort of the Swedish Crown Prince, Gustaf Adolf, and the British-born Crown Princess Louise during their trip through the country. As head of the executive committee of the Swedish American Tercentenary Association and chairman of its board of directors, he has had a guiding hand in the preparations for the forthcoming second visit of the same Swedish royalties and the celebration of the New Sweden Tercentenary itself. As an official member of the royal Swedish party he will again direct their tour in the United States. Privately, he is an executive of the Eastman Kodak Company of Rochester, New York.

Captain Charles H. Thorling of New York is another native of Sweden who served the United States Government as an Assistant Military Attaché in Stockholm during the World War. Educated partly in Stockholm and partly in New York, Philadelphia, and Paris, Captain Thorling entered the first officers' training camp at Plattsburg, New York, in 1917, and from there was assigned, first, to the Army War College in Washington and later to the diplomatic service in Sweden, where he remained until 1919. He then became a career man in the American Foreign Service and was appointed American Vice Consul, first at Rangoon, Burma, and later at Bombay, India, and Singapore in the Straits Settlements. In 1922 he resigned and entered private business in New York. In the American Foreign Service there are several young career men of Swedish ancestry, such as for instance, Eric C. Wendelin, a native of Quincy, Massachusetts, who earned golden opinions as Third Secretary of the American Embassy at Madrid when the Civil War broke out in 1936. When the Ambassador and the higher ranking officials were ordered to leave for France, Mr. Wendelin was left in full charge until the post became untenable because of air raids and shell fire.

The Swedes have made valuable contributions to American political life since the Civil War, and these contributions will, without a doubt, increase with each generation. In a number of states the Swedes and their descendants have held the highest office in the state; namely, that of governor. Others have been lieutenant governors, secretaries of state, state treasurers, attorneys-general, senators, and representatives in state legislatures, and judges of various courts, not to mention the many minor offices held. In the Federal Government we find them as chiefs and assistant chiefs of bureaus, judges of Federal courts, members of the United States Senate and House of Representatives—a real accomplishment for a national group representing less than 2 per cent of the total population. Such persons as John Lind, John A. Johnson, Harry Olson, Irvine Lenroot, Carl R. Chindblom, Samuel A. Carlson, Mary Anderson, Edwin C. Johnson, Ernest Lundeen, Harold Knutson, and others, have served their country well, and have reflected great credit on Americans of Swedish stock.

Doctors

SELMA GIVING AND
DAVID L. TILDERQUIST, M.D.

Mrs. Giving, *nee* Mattson, is a native of the Province of Värmland in Sweden, a graduate of Minnesota College, now closed, and the University of Minnesota with a degree in journalism. After working on a weekly Minnesota newspaper for two years, she spent a year collaborating in the preparation of a medical history of the State, and, after extensive foreign travel with her husband, has been engaged with him in lecturing. Dr. Tilderquist, on the other hand, is a native of Vasa in Minnesota, a graduate of Gustavus Adolphus College, and the University of Minnesota Medical School. After graduate studies in Europe, and Philadelphia, 1910–11, he has specialized in eye, ear, nose, and throat diseases at Duluth, Minnesota.

ANY presentation of the activities of the Swedish people in the United States, in the field of medicine, falls naturally into two divisions, associated with two distinct periods of Swedish immigration—that to the Delaware Valley which started in 1638, and that which began about 1850, and directed itself to the Middle West.

The first Swedish physicians began their labors in the early settlements on the Delaware River. These medical men, who had received their training in Sweden, accompanied the first expeditions of Swedish people to America. They were usually called "barber-surgeons," because at that time the barber's craft was joined with the profession of surgery. To this day, the barber pole stands as a reminder of this age; for then, as now, a striped pole was used as a symbol of the craft. The *filet* around the pole indicated the ribbon used for bandaging the arm in bleeding it, and a basin suspended from the pole was supposed to catch the blood.

The Swedish barber-surgeons were apparently well trained. As early as 1600, the requirements for the study of medicine were very high. Thus the period of preparation covered from four to six years, including "journeyism," which may be comparable to the present system of internship.

One of the earliest of these practitioners among the Swedes in the colonies was Jan Peterson of Alfendolft, who was "barber" to one of the first settlements. A surgeon by the name of Hans Janeke arrived in 1644 on the ship *Fama*. He had been engaged to serve before the ship left Sweden, and had been given 60 D (dalers) for the preparation of his medicine chest.

Perhaps the most prominent of these barber-surgeons was Timon Stidden (also spelled Stedham or Stidham), who sailed from Gothenburg in 1649. Dr. Thomas C. Stellwagen, at one time professor of physiology at the Philadelphia Dental College, in a paper read before the Historical Society of Delaware in 1896, states that the colony of Delaware was very early the home of distinguished disciples of Æsculapius. He mentioned, in particular, "Dr. Tyman Stidham."

Dr. Stidden, who, according to statements made in his will, was born at Hammell, north of Sundsvall, Sweden, apparently had had all his training before he emigrated. In 1656 he was ordered to give "an affidavit of the cure of some soldiers on South River." Once an old man was killed by the Indians, and Timon Stidden was called to examine the body.

A large part of the city of Wilmington, Delaware, is built on land once in the possession of this surgeon. He resided at first at Upland, now Chester, Pennsylvania. A metal case in which he carried his surgical instruments on visits to his patients, authenticated by bearing his name and title engraved upon it, has been preserved by one of his descendants.

Privations, change of climate, and too hard labor caused much illness and suffering among the colonists. In 1647 the Swedish settlers suffered from influenza, the first epidemic of its kind mentioned in American history. For a long time the colonists depended upon European-trained physicians. The young men born in the colonies, who chose medicine as a career, usually studied at such centers as Edinburgh, London, Paris, and Uppsala.

The first diploma given by a medical college in America was granted to John Archer in 1768. Upon this diploma, which hangs on a wall in the College of Physicians and Surgeons in Baltimore, is the signature of Adam Kuhn, professor of *Materia Medica* and botany in the medical department of the Col-

lege of Philadelphia, now the University of Pennsylvania.
Kuhn had been a student in *Materia Medica* and botany, under
the famous Linnæus at Uppsala, who exerted a profound influence upon the gifted pupil. Linnæus named an American
plant, the *Kuhnia eupatorioides*, in honor of Kuhn. Thus,
through Kuhn, who was of German descent, there was exerted
an indirect influence upon early American medicine, by the
great Linnæus of Sweden.

Among the descendants of the Delaware Swedes, there are
several who have gained distinction in medicine; but it is impossible to trace all of them, because of the diffusion of the
Swedes among the general population.

Dr. Alfred Stillé of Philadelphia, 1813–1900, a graduate of
the University of Pennsylvania School of Medicine in 1836,
studied in Paris and, upon his return to the United States,
gained prominence as a teacher, research worker, and writer.
Through his father, Stillé was a direct descendant of Olof
Peterson Stillé of Penningsby Manor, Roslagen, Sweden, who
emigrated to America in 1641. In 1835–36 he was house physician in the Philadelphia Hospital under Dr. W. W. Gerhard
who, in a series of papers published in *Hay's Journal*, first explained the difference between typhus and typhoid fever. According to Sir William Osler, Alfred Stillé played an important part in distinguishing between these two maladies.

After lecturing on pathology and the practice of medicine
before the Philadelphia Association for Medical Instruction,
he was elected in 1854 to the chair of practice in the Pennsylvania Medical College, and in 1864 he took the chair of medicine at the University of Pennsylvania. Stillé was honored for
his distinguished service to medicine by local and national
medical societies. He became the first Secretary of the American Medical Association, and became its President in 1867. His
first important work, entitled *The Elements of General Pathology*, was published in 1848. *Materia Medica and Therapeutics*
and *The National Dispensatory* are two of his larger works.
A monograph on *Cerebro-spinal Meningitis* and one on *Cholera*
are mentioned by Sir William Osler as important.

The name of Dr. Moreton Stillé (1822–55), a younger

brother of Alfred Stillé, is famous in the annals of medical jurisprudence, for it was he who, in collaboration with a contemporary lawyer, Francis Wharton, wrote *A Treatise on Medical Jurisprudence*. This work by a physician and a lawyer working together—the first produced in America on the subject—has been published in several editions.

The dean of American surgeons, William W. Keen, M.D., LL.D., Ph.D., of Philadelphia, was a descendant of Jöran Kyn, who came from Sweden with Governor Johan Printz on the ship *Fama* in 1643. This internationally famed surgeon was born in Philadelphia in 1837. Honorary degrees were conferred upon him by eleven great universities in America and Europe. He was further honored by membership in distinguished American and foreign professional and honorary societies; and he was a recognized leader in many of these. In 1898 he served as President of the American Surgical Association; in 1899, of the American Medical Association; in 1903, of the Congress of American Physicians and Surgeons; and, in 1920, of the International Congress of Surgery in Paris. The Royal Colleges of Surgeons of England, Ireland, and many other countries, made him an honorary foreign member. In 1920 he became an officer of the Order of the Crown of Belgium, and in 1923 of the Legion d'Honneur, France.

His professional career included many important positions. In 1866–75 he conducted the Philadelphia School of Anatomy, and was simultaneously engaged in lecturing at the Jefferson Medical College in Philadelphia. He then became professor of "Artistic Anatomy" at the Pennsylvania Academy of Fine Arts, 1876–89, and professor of surgery at the Women's Medical College, 1884–89. Again he joined the Jefferson Medical College staff, where he was professor of surgery until 1907, and then professor-emeritus until his death on June 7, 1932.

A prolific writer and a brilliant editor, Keen made significant contributions to the literature of his profession. Only a small portion of his work can be mentioned here. Keen's *System of Surgery*, in eight volumes, is a standard work. In the field of medical history he produced *A History of the Philadelphia School of Anatomy* and *Early History of Practical Anatomy*.

He edited a large number of important works, including: *Heath's Practical Anatomy; American Health Primers; Headen's Medical and Surgical Landmarks; Gray's Anatomy;* and *American Textbook of Surgery.* At the age of eighty-four, he wrote a book for the general public, *I Believe in God and in Evolution.*

The medical progress among the Swedish people, during the second period of immigration, has been interwoven with the general medical advance of the country. The Swedes, as such, have at no time established any medical schools, or maintained any separate medical journals, and have organized only a few separate medical societies. The only activity in medicine, into which they have entered as a national group, has been the building and maintaining of hospitals. For this reason any records of accomplishment must, to a large extent, take the form of records of individuals.

One of the first Swedes to gain prominence in medicine during this period was John Arvid Ouchterlony, who was born in Sweden in 1838 and came to America in 1857. After receiving his M.D. degree in 1860, he entered the army in 1861, and the following year was assigned to hospital service in Louisville, Kentucky. His learning and skill soon attracted attention, and, in 1864, he became lecturer on clinical medicine at the University of Louisville. For one year he held this position, together with his work in the army. Late in 1865 he resigned from the Government service and began private practice.

Ouchterlony's brilliant career was marked by many outstanding accomplishments, and he received international recognition. He was one of the founders of the Louisville Medical College in 1876, and in 1878 he accepted the chair of principles and practice of medicine in the Kentucky School of Medicine. In 1882 he resigned to take the chair of principles and practice of medicine and clinical medicine at the University of Louisville, where he remained until his death in 1908.

For the thirty years prior to 1880, there are available, aside from that of Ouchterlony, very few records of Swedish physicians. The immigrants in the West were as yet poor; the country undeveloped; communications were difficult; and there was

little to attract professional men. There is a record of Carl
Petter Tigerhjelm, who arrived at Vasa, Minnesota, about
1867. He was well trained, had several medical diplomas from
Europe, and had practiced medicine in Härjedalen and Jämtland, Sweden, before coming to America.

During the period from 1880 to 1900, Swedish doctors began to appear. Some of them had received their training in the
old countries, and others in the United States. They were welcomed by the Swedish people, who felt a real need of Swedish-
speaking doctors. These early physicians often also became
leaders in church and community life.

A man typical of this period was Dr. John J. Eklund who,
at the age of five, came with his parents from Hälsingland,
Sweden. He studied at Gustavus Adolphus College, St. Peter,
Minnesota, and in 1885 received his medical degree from the
Minnesota College Hospital, which two years later became the
medical department of the State University. He came to Duluth, Minnesota, in 1885, and developed a large medical and
surgical practice. He assisted in establishing and building St.
Luke's Hospital, served as coroner of St. Louis County in
1890–96, was chairman of a relief-fund committee for the
famine in northern Sweden in 1903, chairman of Federal Ex-
emption Board No. 4 during the World War, and held many
other positions of public trust and honor.

Other physicians of this period and type were Drs. Carl J.
Rignell, A. E. Anderson, and Alfred Lind, of Minneapolis,
who were leaders in building the Swedish Hospital of Minneapolis. Drs. Erik Lundholm and Olof Sohlberg took similar
leadership in the building of the Bethesda Hospital in St. Paul.
Dr. Lind, in 1903, presented the first course in hydrotherapy
offered at the University of Minnesota. Dr. A. A. Westeen of
Grand Forks, North Dakota, was another outstanding physician of this period.

Dr. Anders Frick is one of Chicago's foremost Swedish-
American physicians. He was born in Sweden and educated at
Lund University and Karolinska Institutet, Stockholm. He
has practiced in Chicago since 1897, and has taught at Rush
Medical College and at the University of Illinois.

After the opening of the present century, the medical schools in the Middle West developed rapidly into mature institutions; and in this they were influenced by the medical teachers of Europe, to whom American medicine, as a whole, has always acknowledged a deep debt of gratitude. They were stimulated, as well, by the leadership of the older medical schools in the East. In this development the Mayo Clinic, organized in the 'nineties, played no small part. To these institutions young men of Swedish birth or descent came in increasing numbers, and, after graduation, became active in one capacity or another in American medicine.

The following may be mentioned as representative of their respective fields:

Ranked as one of the leading physiologists of the United States, Anton J. Carlson, a member of the faculty of the University of Chicago for thirty-three years, has brought honor to the Swedish people. Born at Svarteborg, Sweden, in 1875, he came to the United States in 1891. He has B.S., A.M., and LL.D. degrees from Augustana College, Rock Island (Illinois), and his Ph.D. degree from Stanford University. He began his brilliant career as assistant in physiology at Stanford in 1902, and as research assistant at the Carnegie Institute in 1903–04. Then he joined the faculty of the University of Chicago in 1904. His research work includes: *Rate of Conduction of the Impulse in Nerves; The Nature of the Heartbeat; Comparative Physiology of the Circulation; Comparative Physiology of the Thyroid and Parathyroid; Physiology of the Alimentary Tract;* and *The Visceral-Sensory Nervous System.* (See also the chapter on "Professors.")

Dr. Harry C. W. S. deBrun was born in Stockholm, Sweden, in 1889. He received his B.S. degree at New York University, his M.D. at Fordham University, and served as interne at Lenox Hill Hospital, in the surgical division. In the World War he took part in active service, first with the Italian and French armies, and then as Chief of a Surgical Team, Evacuation Hospital, for the United States Army. This was a mobile hospital which traveled from front to front, wherever action was most intense. He resigned from the Medical Corps with the rank of lieutenant colonel, whereupon he began private practice in New York City, specializing in bone surgery. Dr. De Brun is a fellow of the American College of Surgeons, associate professor of surgery at the New York Polyclinic Hospital and Medical School, surgeon to the Polyclinic Hospital, associate surgeon to the Swedish Hospital, and consulting bone surgeon to the New York Police Department. In addition, he has written monographs on traumatic surgery, and has a new textbook on the way, entitled *Treatment of Fractures, Dislocations, and Epiphyseal Separations.*

Dr. C. Elmer Carlson, graduate of the University of Oregon Medical School in 1920, is one of the successful young orthopedic surgeons of Portland, Oregon.

Dr. Lester R. Dragstedt, physiologist and professor of surgery at the University of Chicago since 1925, was born at Anaconda, Montana, in 1893. The University of Chicago granted him his Ph.D. in 1920, and Rush Medical his M.D. in 1921. He has written on physiological subjects for medical journals.

In St. Paul, Dr. Robert Earl works in general surgery. Having been graduated from the University of Minnesota with an M.D. in 1896, he later studied in Vienna, and in the New York Post Graduate School and Hospital for Crippled Children.

Dr. Erick Hjalmar East was born in Sweden in 1866. After having been a medical missionary in India from 1901 to 1912, he settled in Portland, Oregon, in 1912, and has continued in general medicine and surgery.

Dr. Otto Knut Olof Folin was, for twenty-seven years (1907 to 1934), a distinguished professor in the medical school at Harvard. Born in Sweden in 1867, he came to the United States in 1882. Acclaimed as a leader in a significantly important branch of biochemistry, he has been internationally recognized by universities and learned societies. (See "Professors.")

Dr. Edward John Engberg, a specialist in nervous and mental diseases since 1914, in St. Paul, was in 1937 made Superintendent of the Faribault State School for the Feeble Minded.

Dr. Carl H. Fornell, born in Värmland, Sweden, in 1887, spent his early childhood in New Sweden, Maine, afterwards moving to Quincy, Massachusetts. He received his A.B. and

M.D. degrees at Harvard University, in 1910 and 1914, respectively, and then served as interne and resident surgeon at Bellevue Hospital, New York City. During the World War, he was Lieutenant in the Medical Corps of the United States Navy. After the War, he became instructor in surgery at the College of Physicians and Surgeons of Columbia University, resigning in 1921 to begin private practice in New York City. Dr. Fornell specializes in eye, ear, nose, and throat work, and has been on the staff of the Manhattan Eye, Ear, Nose and Throat Hospital since 1922. In addition to the publication of articles in connection with his specialty, he has invented several useful surgical instruments.

Dr. Bengt Leopold Hamilton, born at Uppsala, Sweden, in 1892, completed his medical education at the university there, before emigrating. In 1923 he became an instructor at Harvard University, in 1927–30 was associate professor of pediatrics at Johns Hopkins Medical School in Baltimore, and in 1930 he became professor of pediatrics at Chicago University.

Dr. Kristian Gösta Hansson was born in Ystad, Sweden, in 1889. Obtaining his early education in the land of his birth, he later came to this country and received the A.B. and M.D. degrees from Cornell University, whereupon he began private practice in New York City, specializing in physical therapy. Dr. Hansson is clinical instructor in orthopedic surgery at Cornell University Medical College, as well as director of physical therapy at the Hospital for Ruptured and Crippled, and New York Hospital. In addition, he is consultant in physical therapy in other hospitals located in New York City and its surroundings. Dr. Hansson has also contributed numerous articles to the literature of physical therapy, a specialty in which Sweden, as a country, ranks foremost. (See "Gymnastics.")

As professor and head of the department of surgery at the University of Illinois, Dr. Carl Arthur Hedblom held a prominent position. Born at Dayton, Iowa, in 1879, he received his A.B. and M.A. degrees at Colorado College, and his M.D. at Harvard in 1911. For three years, 1913 to 1916, he was professor of surgery at the Harvard Medical School of China at Shanghai. Upon his return to America, he became a fellow in

CARL ARTHUR HEDBLOM, M.D.
1879–1934
SURGEON AND EDUCATOR

surgery at the Mayo Clinic, and in 1919 was placed in charge of the Department of Chest Surgery. In 1920 the Mayo Foundation, in conjunction with the University of Minnesota, granted him a Ph.D. degree in recognition of his pioneering work in this branch. He remained with the Mayo Clinic and Foundation, as a surgeon and associate professor of surgery, until 1924, when he was appointed professor and head of the department of surgery at the University of Wisconsin. In 1926 he went to the University of Illinois, as professor and head of the department of surgery. He was a pioneer in thoracic surgery, having interested himself in this field during its early development. At the time of his death he enjoyed an international reputation in surgery of the chest. He contributed more than a hundred articles to medical literature, most of which dealt with thoracic surgery. His thesis on chronic empyema will remain a classic on this subject. He was the staunchest advocate of the multiple-stage operation for pulmonary tuberculosis, which at the time had much opposition, but which today is universally accepted. His untimely death at the Toronto General Hospital on June 6, 1934, was widely deplored.

Of the many men practicing ophthalmology, otology, rhinology, and laryngology, Dr. Anderson Hilding, of Duluth, deserves mention for his research work. After receiving his M.D. degree at the University of Minnesota in 1919, he served as instructor in pathology there in 1920 and 1921, and in 1929 was granted a Ph.D. degree. From 1930 to 1932, he acted as assistant in medicine and ophthalmology at the Mayo Clinic. He has written articles on the use of iodized oil in nasal sinus disease, on experimental renal insufficiency, the relation of blood pressure to the amount of renal tissue, and on the physiology and pathology of the upper respiratory tract.

Dr. Paul Gustafson of Boston, a brother of the late William Gustafson (see the chapter on "Opera Singers"), was graduated from Harvard College in 1912, and from the Medical School in 1916; whereupon he joined the famous Harvard Medical Unit with the British Expeditionary Forces in France. He returned from France early in 1919, and then worked in various hospitals in New York and Boston, until 1922. Since then he has been engaged in private practice in Boston, specializing in obstetrics, and is a member of the staff of the Boston Lying-in Hospital, as well as the teaching staff of the Harvard Medical School.

Dr. Johannes Hoving was born of Swedish parents in Wiborg, Finland, in 1868, and studied at European schools before coming to the United States in 1903. He now resides in Sweden but, while here, he was active as a lecturer, popular writer, and a leader in many Swedish-American circles.

Dr. Herman M. Johnson of Dawson, Minnesota, was particularly successful in his work as chairman of the committee on public policy and legislation of the State Medical Association, especially in being instrumental in securing passage of the Basic Science Law. In 1926 he was President of the State Association.

Dr. Olof Larsell, professor of anatomy in the Medical School of Oregon University since 1921, is noted for his research work on the nervous system, especially with reference to the comparative anatomy and development of the cerebellum, on which he has published a series of papers in scientific journals. For the past eight years he has carried on experimental studies on the nervous system and on sinus diseases. He has also written a number of papers on the medical history of the Pacific Northwest, and has published biographical sketches of such Swedish anatomists as Olof Rudbeck, Anders Retzius, and Gustaf Retzius. In 1934 he published a translation from the Swedish of the autobiographical notes of J. J. Berzelius. He was born in Rättvik, Sweden, in 1886, and received his Ph.D. from Northwestern University in 1918. (See "Professors.")

Dr. B. Hjalmar Larsson of Detroit, Michigan, was born in Vesterås, Sweden, in 1881. He studied in Sweden and Germany, and then came to America, where he received his M.D. at the University of Michigan Medical School, in 1914. After working for some time as a hospital surgeon, he entered military service during the World War, and went overseas with the American Expeditionary Force. Upon his return he resumed his work in surgery, and has contributed many treatises to medical journals and has made translations from the Swedish.

Nils P. Larsen, Director of Queens Hospital in Honolulu, was born in Stockholm, June 15, 1890, his father, whose name was originally Larsson, being a native of Brunskog, Värmland. At an early age he was brought by his family to the United States, and was graduated from the Cornell Medical College in New York. During the World War he served as a medical officer with the famous One-hundred-sixth Regiment in France, and for bravery under fire, viz. the personal rescue of a soldier who had lain wounded in an exposed position for thirty-six hours, he was decorated with a silver star, and was cited in the general orders of the War Department. After demobilization, he served as instructor at the Cornell Medical College, and later at Bellevue Hospital in New York. Since he took charge of the hospital in Honolulu in 1922, it has been raised in rank from the fourth grade to the first. He has taken a prominent part in many medical congresses, as well as local civic enterprises.

As head physician of the Los Angeles schools, Dr. Sven Richard Lokrantz supervises many doctors, nurses, and dentists. He was born in Sweden in 1892. He has served as consulting surgeon with several hospitals, and has contributed many articles to medical periodicals.

Dr. Fritjof Emil Berge of Los Angeles, California, one of the official surgeons of the Olympic Games in that city in 1932, was born in Sweden, but came to America with his parents when a child. He was brought up on a farm in Wisconsin, and taught in the local public schools before he was graduated from the University of Michigan Medical College. After some private practice at Grand Rapids, he took postgraduate courses at Johns Hopkins University, Baltimore, and the University of Edinburgh, Scotland, and then moved to California. He is a member of the senior staff of the California Hospital.

Dr. F. H. Magney of Duluth is at present a member of the Minnesota State Board of Medical Examiners. He was born in Pierce County, Wisconsin, in 1886, and received his medical training at the University of Minnesota.

Dr. Paul Budd Magnuson, associate professor in the Northwestern Medical School, Chicago, has done original research in bone surgery. He was born in St. Paul, Minnesota, in 1884, and attended, first the University of Minnesota, and then the University of Pennsylvania Medical School. He began his practice in Chicago, and devoted much attention to industrial surgery until 1917, when he entered the Army. Upon his return, he acted as consultant to a number of large industries, and became medical director of the Illinois Industrial Commission.

Among the Oregon practitioners of Swedish extraction may be mentioned Dr. Theodore J. Malmgren of Phoenix. Born in 1871, he has been in general practice there since 1909. He is a graduate of the University of Iowa College of Medicine.

Dr. Carl Ferdinand Nelson, head of the department of physiological chemistry at the University of Kansas, was born at Mörlunda, Sweden, in 1882. He received his Ph.D. at the University of Wisconsin in 1912, and his M.D. at Rush Medical College in 1917.

Dr. George B. Norberg, President of the Kansas City Academy of Medicine, is author of *Golden Rules of Gynecology*. He was born at Bishop Hill, Illinois, in 1872, and was graduated from the University Medical College of Kansas City, Missouri. He was professor of gynecology at his Alma Mater from 1901 to 1905, and later served on the staff of Trinity Lutheran Hospital.

The University of Pennsylvania Hospital and Medical School, the first university in this country to establish a physical-therapy department, selected Dr. Joseph B. Nylin, a native of Sweden, to head its new unit in 1912. He was graduated from the Medical School of the University of Pennsylvania in 1910, and later studied in Stockholm and Vienna.

Dr. Nelse Frederick Ockerblad was born at Staten Island, New York, in 1881, and was graduated from the University of Kansas Medical School in 1916. He has served on the staffs of the Bell Memorial Hospital and St. Luke's Hospital, and as consulting urologist with the Kansas State Penitentiary. He has written numerous articles on urology.

Dr. Rudolph J. E. Oden, born at Ottumwa, Iowa, in 1882, is a member of the Board of Directors of the Augustana Hospital in Chicago, and has been attending surgeon there since 1919. After his graduate work at the University of Pennsylvania,

1912–13, and in Berlin 1913–14, he became attending surgeon at Mercy Hospital, Cadillac, Michigan. During the World War he was in charge of general surgery in U. S. Hospital No. 9, Lakewood, New Jersey, in 1918; U. S. Hospital No. 32, Chicago, in 1919; and was consulting surgeon at the U. S. Marine Hospital in 1919–20.

The rise from the lowly job of a laboratory janitor to that of a widely known research chemist and technician in the Medical School of Cornell University, is the interesting career of Emil Osterberg, who never received a college degree. In 1936 he retired from the Cornell faculty, after thirty years of service. He played an important rôle in the development, in America, of metabolic studies, and has, in collaboration with others, contributed many scientific treatises to professional journals, both native and foreign.

Born in Sweden in 1874, Dr. Louis Ostrom, of Rock Island, came to America early, and received his education here. He had wide teaching experience, before entering his specialized field of medicine, ophthalmology, otology, rhinology, and laryngology. He has served as clinical assistant at the New York Eye and Ear Infirmary, and as attending specialist with the United States Public Health Service. He contributes to medical journals, and is an inventor of surgical instruments.

Dr. Algot Ostrum, born in 1881 in Sweden, was chiefly interested in gymnastics for a long time, but entered Columbia University as a medical student in 1917. He later attended the New York University Medical College and the Boston University School of Medicine. He has served as instructor in orthopedic surgery at New York Post Graduate School and Hospital, and as surgeon at Lincoln Hospital.

Born in Dalsland, Sweden in 1881, Dr. Anders Peterson came to the United States and studied medicine at the University of Southern California and at the Mayo Clinic. In 1916–18, he was clinic instructor at his Alma Mater. His professional activities include membership on the urological staffs of Los Angeles County General Hospital, and Clara Barton Memorial Hospital.

In the field of obstetrics and gynecology the name of Dr.

Reuben Peterson, for a long time professor of obstetrics and
gynecology at the University of Michigan, is a prominent one.
His teaching, writing, and research have won him wide recognition. Born in Boston in 1862, he was educated at Harvard. He
then moved to Michigan, where he became a prominent figure
in medicine. In 1898 he became professor of gynecology at the
Chicago Post Graduate Medical School, and at Rush Medical
College in 1899. In 1901, he joined the faculty of the Medical
School at the University of Michigan. During the World War
he was assigned to Lansing, Michigan, to act as medical aide
to the Governor of the State, when he had complete charge of
the medical draft-board work in the State of Michigan. Being
a prolific writer, Dr. Peterson has contributed much to medical
literature. He is editor of *Obstetrics* and *Peterson's Practice of
Obstetrics*.

Dr. O. T. Roberg is among the outstanding Swedish-American surgeons in Chicago. He is a graduate of Rush Medical
College, 1899, and in 1902 was selected to serve as surgeon-in-
chief of the Swedish Covenant Hospital. In 1919–20 he was
chief of the neurology service at Fort Sheridan.

Dr. David E. Seashore, of Duluth, Minnesota, was born at
Dayton, Iowa, in 1874. He studied medicine at the University
of Iowa and at the University of Minnesota, receiving his M.D.
degree from the latter in 1902.

Dr. Gilbert Seashore, of Minneapolis, first Swedish-American
coroner of Hennepin County, Minnesota, has held this position
continuously since 1909. He was born in 1874, attended Gustavus Adolphus College, and received his M.D. at the University of Minnesota in 1902.

As a neurologist, Dr. Andrew Leonard Skoog of Kansas
City, Missouri, who joined the faculty at the University of
Kansas in 1910, has gained recognition. He was born at Carver,
Minnesota, in 1877. After his graduation from Northwestern
University in 1902, he studied at the University of Vienna, the
University of Paris, and the National Hospital in London. Be-
fore joining the faculty at Kansas, he was physician at the
Woodcraft Hospital, Pueblo, Colorado, and Assistant Super-
intendent of the Kansas State Hospital for Epileptics, at Par-
sons, Kansas.

Dr. Karl Wilhelm Stenström, head of the radium and roentgentherapy departments at the University of Minnesota Hospital, was born in Gothenburg, Sweden, and received his Ph.D. at the University of Lund in 1919. Before coming to Minnesota in 1926, he was a physicist with the State Institute for the Study of Malignant Diseases at Buffalo, New York. His interest centered originally in roentgen-ray spectroscopy and, since he entered the field of biophysics, it has extended to the application of physical knowledge to medical problems, to radiation therapy, to cancer research and treatment, and to improvement of technique, and studies of the effect of radiation on chemical compounds and tissues. He is a member of the Committee of Research and Standardization of the American Radium Society. He has helped develop protective measures for doctors and technicians, against dangerous exposures to roentgen and radium rays.

Dr. Francis G. Swedenburg of Ashland, Oregon, is a graduate of Rush Medical College, 1907. He specializes in surgery. Dr. Karl J. Swenson, born in 1879, a graduate of the University of Pittsburgh School of Medicine in 1908, has been engaged in general practice in Portland, Oregon, since 1910.

Many Swedish-American physicians and surgeons have rendered their most distinguished service as directors and founders of hospitals.

Dr Nels A. Johanson has been connected with the Swedish Hospital of Seattle since its founding in 1908; and he is generally credited with having built up the institution to its present fine standing. In Seattle, the largest medical-technical laboratory is operated by Dr. G. A. Magnusson.

The Emanuel Charity Board, operating Emanuel Hospital of Portland, Oregon, was organized in 1912. It started work in a small frame building accommodating twenty-five patients, but in 1936 it cared for 7,936 patients. The organizer and first superintendent was Reverend C. J. Renhard. Axel M. Green, superintendent since 1917, is responsible for much of the remarkable growth and development of the hospital.

Early in the present century Swedish people came to Denver, Colorado, seeking relief from tuberculosis. Because of the shortage of proper housing facilities for these people, Dr. C. A.

Bundsen, in December, 1904, called a meeting of the leading citizens for the purpose of discussing the building of a sanatorium. The result was the Swedish National Sanatorium in near-by Englewood, Colorado. Dr. Bundsen was born in Sweden in 1872. In recognition of his services, he has been decorated by the King of Sweden with the Order of Vasa. (See the chapter on "Charities and Self-Help.")

The Immanuel Deaconess Institute of Omaha, Nebraska, completed in October, 1937, half a century of distinguished service. The Immanuel Hospital, one of the departments of the Institute, was opened in 1890, and is owned and controlled by the Evangelical Lutheran Augustana Synod. Reverend Emil G. Chinlund is the Director. The Swedish Evangelical Covenant Hospital, established in 1905, is also located in Omaha.

Caring for the mentally defective and the crippled, the Bethphage Inner Mission Association of Axtell, Nebraska, has been in operation since 1913. Dr. C. A. Lönnquist was the superintendent from 1917 to the time of his death in 1937.

The Iowa Lutheran Hospital and the Iowa Lutheran Maternity Hospital, both at Des Moines, are owned and controlled by the Hospital Association of the Iowa Conference of the Augustana Synod.

The need for a Swedish Hospital in Minneapolis early became apparent. The Swedish Hospital Corporation was formed in 1898. An old dwelling house was used as the first hospital. Today it has a capacity of 325 beds and, with its fine buildings and equipment, is a tribute to Swedish enterprise.

Established in 1882, the Bethesda Hospital in St. Paul is owned and controlled by the Minnesota Conference of the Augustana Synod. Dr. Oscar W. Holcomb, Chief-of-staff, has played an important part in its development. He was born in Minnesota in 1877, received his M.D. at Northwestern University in 1905, and came to Bethesda Hospital as a pathologist in 1907.

One of Chicago's leading hospitals, the Augustana Hospital, established in 1884, with E. I. Erickson as present superintendent, is a Swedish enterprise. The Swedish Covenant Hospital, established in 1886, also located in Chicago, is controlled by the Swedish Evangelical Mission.

The contribution to medicine, by the Swedish people in Kansas City and vicinity, centers in Trinity Hospital, formerly known as the Swedish Hospital, founded in 1906 by the Reverend A. W. Lindquist. This institution has grown from small beginnings to be one of the leading hospitals in that great city.

Carl J. Hedin, a native of Värmland, is superintendent of the Bangor State Hospital at Bangor, Maine, a position he has held since 1919. He came to the United States as a boy of fourteen, and is a graduate of the Mount Hermon School in Massachusetts and the Dartmouth Medical College in New Hampshire. During his medical career he has been connected successively with the Massachusetts State Hospital at Tewksbury, the Augusta State Hospital at Augusta, Maine, and the Pownal State School in Maine.

Dr. Carl N. Lindquist, a graduate of Bethany College (Lindsborg, Kansas) and of the University of Kansas Medical School, is President of the staff at Trinity Hospital, where another prominent member of the staff is Dr. Carl A. Jackson, a graduate of the University Medical College in Kansas City in 1897.

The Swedish Hospital Association of Brooklyn, New York, was founded in 1896, and its hospital dedicated in 1906. "Vasa Klubben" took the first steps in its organization; but other Swedish societies aided later. A nurses' training school was added in 1908. Recently a new building has been acquired, and a drive is under way for $250,000 to reconstruct it into a more modern hospital, which it is estimated will be worth $750,000.

Dr. Arthur W. Shaleen is Director of the Memorial Hospital at Hallock, Minnesota. He was born in Lindstrom, Minnesota, in 1878, and was graduated from the University of Minnesota in 1902.

The number of outstanding Swedish-Americans in the field of medicine and the related sciences is too large to be adequately treated in a brief chapter like this one. A few who have gained recognition in their respective fields, by being included in *Who's Who in American Medicine, American Men of Science, Vem är Det* (the Swedish *Who's Who*), and other standard biographical works and medical histories, have been selected. A few men, not so mentioned, have been recommended by their fellow physicians. Many, equally as great as those herein mentioned, have, perhaps, been left out; but that is because it is impossible, in a pioneer effort like this single chapter, to adequately cover the field. Future historians will have the task of evaluating and recording the work of many other men who are now in the midst of making contributions to the field of medicine.

Gymnastics

THEODOR A. MELANDER

Captain Melander is himself one of the leaders in physical education
according to Swedish principles, in the United States. He was born at
Sigtuna in Sweden, and was graduated from the Royal Military Academy in 1889. During his service as an officer in the regular Army, he
went through the Royal Gymnastic Institute, 1893–96, and served for
many years as an instructor in the Army, the Military Institute, and
the Stockholm Fire Department. Captain Melander came to New York
in 1902. His first job was that of physical director for the National
Cash Register Company at Dayton, Ohio, and after working in clubs,
private schools, and the Y.M.C.A. in New York, he became chief instructor and lecturer at the Savage School for Physical Education in
New York City, a post he held for twenty-six years. During the World
War, Captain Melander trained reserve officers for the American Army;
and for many years he was attached to different hospitals for orthopedic work. In 1916 he founded, in New York, the Swedish Institute of
Physiotherapy, partly for corrective work and partly for training of
masseurs and physiotherapy technicians. Close to one hundred students
are graduated each year. Captain Melander has also been active for
many years in various Swedish gymnastic societies in New York and
vicinity.

A T the beginning of the nineteenth century, Sweden was in
a depressed condition. The country's youth had been
sacrificed in disastrous wars; the sister nation, Finland,
had been lost, and the outlook in general was gloomy.

At this time we find a young Swede, Per Henrik Ling, who
for several years had lived in different parts of Europe—especially Denmark—devoting himself to the study of languages,
gymnastics, and sport. On his return to Sweden he realized the
necessity of a national recovery; and his ideas found expression
in the system of gymnastics which he, from then on, made his
life work, and which has given him the name, the "Father of
Swedish Gymnastics." By means of untiring work and perseverance, he worked out a set of exercises for both healthy and
ill persons, arranging the different movements according to
physiological principles. In 1813 he founded and became the

first principal of the Royal Central Gymnastic Institute of Stockholm, from which men and women of different nationalities have since been graduated, later acting as spokesmen for what they had learned and practiced.

The renown which the Swedish system of gymnastics has gained throughout the civilized world ought to be the best proof of its inherent qualities, and the past 125 years can show many ardent and successful advocates for its use in various countries.

As pioneers for the Swedish system of physiotherapy in the United States we find two brothers, the Drs. George and Charles Taylor. The former introduced the Swedish-exercise methods at his hydropathic institute in New York in 1855, and the following year the younger brother made a study trip to London and Stockholm, and, as an expression of his admiration for Ling, he named his own son "Per Henrik Taylor," who also became a physician and who, in his own orthopedic practice, always used the Swedish system.

In the beginning of the 1870's, a Russian medical practitioner by the name of Wischnewetzky, who had studied under Jonas Gustaf Wilhelm Zander, the founder of medicomechanical gymnastics, and others in Stockholm, set up an elaborate medicomechanical institute in New York. This so-called Zander Institute met, in the beginning, with great success but, after having changed ownership several times, gradually died out. Dr. Zander's machines for physiotherapy have been installed in many American hospitals but, probably because of lack of skilled operators, have been relegated to the "rubbish-room."

In the 1880's, two notable pioneers in introducing the Ling System in America, Nils Posse and Claes Enebuske, appeared. Baron Nils Posse, a young army officer who had recently finished his course at the Royal Central Gymnastic Institute, arrived in the United States in 1885, and settled down in Boston, where at first he instructed teachers in the public schools. A Mrs. Hemmenway, known for her philanthropic activities, became keenly interested in the Swedish gymnastics, and, in 1890, founded The Boston Normal School of Gymnastics for the training of instructors in gymnastics, according to the Ling System, Posse becoming one of the chief instructors. One year later, however, Posse founded his own institute, the Posse Gymnasium, from which about thirty instructors were graduated every year. This institute exists to this day, but now goes under the name, Posse-Nissen School of Physical Education, and has a four-year course, both in gymnastics and in physiotherapy. For many years it was excellently conducted by Harry Nissen, who served as its president. Posse was also widely known as an author, and he wrote books about both gymnastics and physiotherapy. His promising career was cut short, however, by his untimely death in 1895.

Dr. Claes Enebuske came to the United States in 1887, after having received instruction from the well-known gymnasts, Colonel Norlander and Professor Hartelius. He began his career by practicing physiotherapy in New York. Later, he likewise became an instructor, both in theory and practice, at the Brooklyn Normal School of Gymnastics; and during summers he taught at Chautauqua in New York State. He was next invited to succeed Posse at the Boston Normal School. At this time Swedish gymnastics were made obligatory in all public schools in Boston, under the direction of a Dr. Hartwell, who, after having taken two courses at the Royal Central Gymnastic Institute in Stockholm, became one of the warmest spokesmen for the Ling System. After Enebuske had received his M.D. degree at Harvard University, he gradually retired from the gymnastics, but left behind him an honored and widely known name.

Enebuske was succeeded at the Boston Normal School by his former assistant, Carl Collin, born in Blekinge in 1864, who was likewise a graduate of the Royal Central Gymnastic Institute in Stockholm. Following in the footsteps of his predecessor, Collin also took a medical degree at Harvard. He remained for more than twenty years at the Boston Normal School and at Wellesley College, whereupon he continued his activity as instructor at the Schools of Physical Education at Battle Creek, Michigan, and in Chicago. After having served the cause of gymnastics well, Dr. Collin retired later to his farm in New Hampshire.

William Skarström, M.D., born in 1869 in Stockholm, succeeded Collin at Wellesley College, where he worked with great success for twenty years, until 1931. Skarström arrived quite young in America and, being an interested and capable gymnast, was employed as instructor at the Y.M.C.A. in New York, and at Pratt Institute in Brooklyn. Skarström was later graduated from the Boston Normal School of Gymnastics, and took his medical degree at Harvard in 1901, whereupon he became instructor at the Groton School, the Massachusetts Institute of Technology, and the Boston Normal School. He was professor of physical education at Columbia University until 1912, when he became connected with Wellesley College. Dr. Skarström was an exceptionally ardent spokesman for the Ling System and, thanks to his personal skill as a gymnast and his quiet ways, he was always extremely popular among his pupils. He has written *Gymnastic Kinesiology* and *Gymnastic Teaching*.

In the beginning of the 1890's, Jakob Bolin arrived in New York as a graduate of Lidbeck's Institute in Stockholm, and from the start became known for the energetic and skilful work which characterized him all through life. Bolin continued Enebuske's work at the Brooklyn Normal School of Gymnastics, and was for many years instructor, lecturer, and principal of the physical department at Chautauqua, where a big building for gymnastics, called "The Bolin Gymnasium," was built according to the Swedish pattern. Pupils from all parts of the country came to this summer institute, and Bolin's great services to Swedish gymnastics made it known and appreciated. He later became instructor at the Savage School for Physical Education in New York, and remained there until 1910, when he became professor of physical education at the University of Utah. Bolin is also known as an author of treatises on gymnastics, and in 1909 he received a prize of 1000 kronor, in Sweden, for his essay, "Vårda Arvet" (Preserve Your Inheritance). He was permitted to work only a few years, among the youth in the West. After an extended illness, he died in 1914.

Hugo Oldenberg, born in Närke in 1868, a graduate of Lidbeck's Institute in Stockholm and the Royal Central Gymnastic Institute, arrived in America in 1893, and for some time managed his own gymnastic institute in Chicago. After studies in

Paris, he became a professor of physical education at the Rush Medical College in Chicago, where he remained until his death in 1919. Oldenberg wrote several treatises on "Massage and Gymnastics in Traumatic Joint-Affections," which attracted wide attention.

Carl Gustaf Carlström, having been graduated from the Royal Central Gymnastic Institute, came to Chicago in 1907 and worked as Oldenberg's assistant. He succeeded Oldenberg at the Rush Medical College. In 1910 Carlström took over Bolin's work at Chautauqua; in 1918 became a member of the faculty of the American College of Physical Education; and in 1923 was appointed its President. He has become known as a distinguished instructor, and is one of the most ardent spokesmen for Swedish gymnastics.

Carl G. Anderson arrived in his youth in Boston, in 1903. He was a graduate of Ullman's Institute in Stockholm, and from the start became known, both as a skilful gymnast and as a pioneer in introducing the Ling System. Having been graduated from the Boston Normal School of Physical Education, he became instructor in the Posse Gymnastic Society, and at the high school at Waltham, Massachusetts. In 1910 he moved to New Jersey, where, under his leadership, Swedish gymnastics were introduced in the Newark high schools, the Newark Athletic Club, and Panzar's College of Physical Education in East Orange. For several years Anderson has been athletic director at the Newark Athletic Club. He has made for himself a still greater reputation as an athlete and trainer in various forms of sports. (See the chapter on "Sports and Sportsmen.")

The West coast, too, can furnish many well-known names, the bearers of which persistently and successfully have spread the knowledge of Ling's great achievement.

Dr. Sven Lokrantz has worked for approximately twenty years in Los Angeles. He was born in 1892 and studied at gymnastic institutes in both Stockholm and London. Thereupon he came to Boston in 1914, and started at once his medical studies at Tufts College, graduating as an M.D. in 1918. Dr. Lokrantz settled in Los Angeles in 1920, where he has become widely known and recognized for his work as organizer and head of the

Department of Health and Hygiene in the local school system —especially for physiotherapy, and the corrective treatment of deformities among the youth. Dr. Lokrantz' organization of school hygiene has made him highly appreciated in the medical world all over America; and he has justly deserved the many expressions of honor which have been bestowed upon him. In 1932 he was chief physician at the Olympic Games. (See the chapter on "Doctors.")

Since 1925 Capt. Fausto Acke has resided in Los Angeles. Born in Sweden in 1896, he was graduated from the Royal Military Academy. Later he served in the Swedish Army as artillery officer for many years, whereupon he took a course at the Royal Central Gymnastic Institute. Acke was an exceptionally skilful gymnast and athlete. He won prizes at the Olympic Games in Antwerp in 1920, and worked hard as a member of the Olympic Committee in Los Angeles, in 1932. In 1922 he worked in Rome as instructor at a military gymnastic institute. Having arrived in America in 1923, he worked for two years in Washington, D.C., then went to Los Angeles. During four years he was an instructor at the Urban Military Academy in Hollywood, and later at the Black Fox Military Institute. Since 1933 Captain Acke has operated his own gymnastic institute.

For many years Dr. A. O. Lindström has been active in gymnastics in San Francisco. He was born in Stockholm in 1863, and studied in both Sweden and England. He came to San Francisco in 1893, and some time later started The Lindström Naturopathic Institute, featuring physiotherapy and massage according to Swedish principles. There is something quite unique in this institute; namely, a large collection of Dr. Zander's gymnastic apparatus. Because of his professional knowledge, his conscientious work, and winning personality, Dr. Lindström is one of the best-known and most-appreciated Swedes on the West coast.

Signe Hagelthorn is a Swedish woman, who has carved for herself a great and enduring name in the annals of physical education in the United States. And many are the schools, colleges, and universities, in various places all over the country, which have benefited from her thorough knowledge and ability as an organizer and instructor. She is justly called "a health crusader." Miss Hagelthorn was born in Värmland, and, as a young girl, went to America to visit relatives in Boston. She immediately took a liking to the new country, and decided to stay and take a course at the Boston Normal School, where she was graduated in 1906. Her greatest desire was now to do something for the growing generation, especially in regard to its bodily well-being. She decided to study at Wellesley College, specializing in physical education.

Signe Hagelthorn's first field of activity was Oshkosh, Wisconsin, where she organized the health and hygiene instruction in the city's schools, opened playgrounds, and led courses for instructors in physical education. In 1910 Miss Hagelthorn became director of physical education at Mills College, Oakland, California, and, later, held a similar post at the University of California, Los Angeles. Afterwards she returned to Oakland and, during three years, opened forty-two playgrounds and organized courses for instructors. She then became instructor and lecturer in the medical faculty of the University of California. San Francisco was next to benefit by Miss Hagelthorn's skill. She remained there for seven years and won admiration and gratitude, especially for her indefatigable work for the crippled children, who suffered in the severe paralysis epidemic in 1917.

In 1925 Miss Hagelthorn was made professor of physical education at New York University, where she remained for seven years. After having visited Sweden, she returned and, since 1935, has held the responsible office of Dean at Adelphi College, situated on Long Island, outside of New York. Dean Hagelthorn can look back with satisfaction upon a great and useful work for physical education in the United States; and at every opportunity she has emphasized the value of the Swedish gymnastic system.

Signe Brunnstrom, born in Stockholm in 1898, was graduated from the Royal Gymnastic Institute in Stockholm in 1919. Her first position was as a teacher in physical education in Chexbres, Switzerland, 1920–21; from there she went to Lucerne and established the Swedish Institute of Physical Therapy

and Physical Education. After seven years of successful work
as Director of this Institute, Miss Brunnstrom came to New
York in October, 1928, and accepted a position in the Physical
Therapy Department of the Hospital for the Ruptured and
Crippled, where her experience and conscientious work are evidenced by the improvement shown in the children under her
care. At the same time, she has acted as instructor and lecturer
in Doctor Hansson's School for physiotherapy technicians in
the same hospital, and was appointed Dean of the School in
1937. Miss Brunnstrom was appointed Director of Physical
Education Activities for Women in 1929, at the Metropolitan
Life Insurance Company in New York. She has taken courses
in the departments of Physical Education at Barnard College
and New York University, and received the degree of M.A. in
1936.

As a medical gymnast and physiotherapist, Gottfried Becker
has made himself known in Greater New York. Becker was born
in Linköping in 1876, and was graduated from Lidbeck's
Gymnastic Institute in Stockholm in 1897, where he later acted
as assistant. At the same time he attended courses at Dr. Arvidson's school, and at Karolinska Institutet. From 1898 to 1901
he practiced in Hamburg, Dresden, Leipzig, and Berlin, where
he was a student of Dr. Thure Brandt, Jr., in "Gynecological
Massage." In 1901 he came to America and settled in Brooklyn, where he established the Becker Institute, which, from a
comparatively small start, has developed into one of the largest
and most modern institutions for physiotherapy. During all
these years, Becker's work has been highly appreciated, both by
the medical profession and the insurance companies, for his conscientious treatment of private patients and compensation cases.

At the end of the nineteenth century Swedish gymnastics
were introduced in several schools for women in the Eastern
States; and the Women's College of Baltimore counts, for example, among its instructors, such women gymnastic directors
as Braun, Gihl, Wallin, and Öberg.

Voluntary gymnastic societies have been organized during
the last five decades in various parts of the country, but in many
cases have ceased, because of lack of good instructors. Massa-

chusetts, with its relatively large Scandinavian population, has been the leader in this respect, and organizations are still active in Boston, Worcester, and Cambridge.

The Swedish Gymnastic Society of New York was very active for twenty-five years under the leadership of Theodor A. Melander and Capt. Birger Cnattingius. As most of its members lived in Brooklyn, a "Svensk Gymnastikförening" was organized there some years ago; and it has many members, both men and women, under the leadership of a young Swedish student and physiotherapist, Kjell Peterson.

At the West Point Military Academy, the so-called German gymnastic system has always been prevalent. At the Naval Academy in Annapolis, the Swedish system was formerly in use, in accordance with the regulations for the English Army and Navy, but has gradually been discarded in favor of "setting up" exercises and athletics.

Institutes for Physical Education have almost completely abandoned "Swedish gymnastics," and these institutes now use only exercises on bar and horse, tumbling, building of pyramids, etc. The few institutes that still use the Ling System to any extent are some military academies and Catholic schools, in which seriousness and discipline prevail.

American youth in general, and especially in the Eastern States, where so many nations are mixed, do not care much for attention and discipline—two things absolutely necessary for the Swedish system. This laxity, sad to say, seems to be prevalent also among the younger generations of Swedish descent. This proves that our health gymnastics, despite hard and time-sacrificing work by many, has not succeeded in establishing itself in the United States. At the same time, however, it is gratifying to see that massage and physiotherapy, according to original Swedish principles, are always in demand, and have gained appreciation from the medical profession as well as from the population in general.

Sports and Sportsmen

GERHARD T. ROOTH

Mr. Rooth, a native of Sweden, is a member of the editorial staff of *Nordstjernan* (North Star), Swedish language weekly of New York. He is also Sports Editor of *The American Swedish Monthly,* and since 1922 New York correspondent of *Idrottsbladet,* Stockholm, Sweden's leading sports newspaper. In his leisure moments he has done much to promote sports among the Swedish-Americans, founding both tennis and bowling clubs. He has also acted as manager for several American athletic teams visiting Sweden and other countries in Europe, and, finally, he writes articles on sports for *The Amateur Athlete,* and other American magazines. As a sports reporter he has covered three Olympics.

UPON the physical welfare of a young nation depends, in large measure, its future destiny. Hardy pioneers and robust settlers are needed in the early days for the great task of building a new country, which requires sound qualities of endurance and determination, industry and adaptability. The glad burden of creating their ideal land, in which they and their fortunate descendants are to dwell, should rest upon vigorous shoulders, that the youthful nation may be well integrated and progress steadily onward. The rising civilization has a firm foundation when its citizens possess rugged physical and mental health. Thus equipped, it moves more surely on toward its goal of greatness.

From Sweden have come many eager colonizers, to take part in developing this mighty country. They have been among those who labored and fought and struggled, to bring out of the vast primeval wilderness, with its wealth of natural resources, a glorious modern America. The Swedes have aided in the immense work, and have made valuable contributions to the national life.

The task was one for which they were adequately fitted, for theirs is a sturdy heritage. In that rigorous northern climate the natives have evolved, by a process of natural selection, strong physiques capable of surviving and wresting a living from the stern environment. There are the long winters and the toils of agriculture with which to cope. Difficulties attend hunting, trapping, and fishing; other industries, like mining and lumbering, have their hazards. But overcoming obstacles is arduous exercise which helps to form sinewy muscles, and inculcates qualities of courage and stamina. Life in Scandinavia has not been soft or easy, and victories over an unyielding nature are hard to win; but the result has been that a hale and disciplined people have emerged, true descendants of the dynamic, adventurous Vikings.

Those early forebears were fine specimens of physical perfection and athletes of the first magnitude. They were expert with bow and arrow, excellent wrestlers, swimmers, and rowers. They could catch a javelin in its flight and could handle a sword with either hand. The old Norse sagas describe feats of running and jumping—"dressed in full war equipment they could jump the length of one man both forwards and backwards." Those splendid Northmen could also follow a horse in full gallop. Ball games were very popular and the ancient tales tell of one called *"knattespeil,"* which was played on the ice, and required much skill.

The children were early taught how to ski, hunt, shoot, row, swim, wrestle, and ride horses. They learned to be fleet of foot and manually dexterous. Games and athletic pursuits trained mind and body, so that faculties grew sharp, and limbs acquired great speed and strength. The Vikings learned to think fast in critical moments, meet danger without fear, and be ever ready for either defence or attack. The fighting instinct was strong, and the purpose of much of their training was the preparation for war. Nor were their skills allowed to dull for lack of practice. But the inherent dauntlessness and fortitude of those tall-statured, hard-muscled warriors became the legacy which they handed down to their posterity.

Descendants of the memorable Norsemen were among the first settlers of America, and came in increasingly larger numbers through the years, as ardent immigrants to a fertile new land. The intrepid Swedish colonizers found in America a wide outlet for their abounding strength, ready hands, and venturesome spirit. In their efforts to tame the virgin forests and build homes for themselves and their families, inborn traits found ample expression. Pioneering struggles further developed the natural assets; in this tremendous country, body and soul could fully expand.

With the physical qualifications which are theirs in, perhaps, special degree, the Scandinavians should be among the leaders in promoting health and participating in athletics. It is in their blood; and so their names should be conspicuous in this field. That such is the case has been apparent during the past seventy-five years, particularly, when sport has truly come into its own; i.e., the game is played for its own sake—for the love of it, for the fun derived, and for the excitement of friendly rivalry.

Before this time, sports had been combined with the more sober business of securing a living and of defending oneself. The hunter was primarily concerned with obtaining game for food and clothing. The sailor earned his livelihood with his boat. The skier propelled himself on his skis, because this was frequently the best means of locomotion over the frozen terrain. The swimmer eluded pursuit in the water. But, in latter years, the pressure of necessity has lessened, and in this machine age sports are engaged in extensively for the pleasure they give, and for their physical and mental advantages. Schools and universities employ athletics to develop the students' bodies and character. Sports foster superb health and teach, also, self-control, precision, coöperation, and good sportsmanship. This twofold training has come to result in well-balanced young men and women being sent out from American schools, to assume the duties of responsible citizenship.

WITH this brief review in mind, the part which Swedes and Swedish-Americans have played in the realm of sport is better understood. True to their Viking traditions, they are drawn to those branches which demand muscular power and sustained force. Their preference in games reflects the inner characteristics, and they like those requiring brawn, stamina, and perseverance. They love the open, the great outdoors; the water and the snow.

We find that the sons of Norse forefathers take part in the same sports in America as are enjoyed in their native land, and also those new ones here for which they are suited. The Swedes make excellent wrestlers, long-distance runners, and cross-country skiers. They take naturally to weight events (javelin, hammer, discus); they make sure marksmen, skilled equestrians, good bicyclists, fine soccer and rugby players. At swimming, sailing, and rowing, they prove adept.

Sweden itself has often produced exceptionally powerful men, possessing that sheer strength which is able to bend iron bars, lift huge weights, make corkscrews out of horseshoes, or drive long nails through wooden planks, with bare hands. The famous ones have exhibited in America, and among them were "Starke Arvid" Larson and Anders Anderson, better known as "Siljansnäs Anders." It is said of the latter that everything he touched broke. He handled big logs in the lumber woods as though they were twigs, and he could hold three people suspended from each arm. Once this giant was a train brakeman, and he literally did break the brakes. When Anders went to America in the 1890's, his parents were happily relieved, because at times he actually did not realize his own strength. Here, however, "Siljansnäs" was regarded with much admiration, as he performed feats which no one else could duplicate, on his tours throughout the country. One of these was to lift five hundred pounds from the ground with one finger.

A sport which requires exceptional physical strength is wrestling, a very old Swedish diversion; and it is natural that Swedish-Americans should be among the foremost in American rings. This strenuous sport is in high esteem and has produced numerous champions.

Perhaps the most outstanding was Hjalmar Lundin (the Swedish "Lion"), who for many years was the undefeated champion in New York and, though he did not have the world-champion title, was always very close to the top. He started out as a strong man with Ringling Brothers, and was one of their attractions as the "Giant," challenging anyone to match his

prowess. One of his exploits was lifting twenty men on a platform, which he placed on his breast. But his real success was
achieved in the wrestling ring, where he was feared and admired. Lundin was the only one who ever won a fall from the
great Frank Gotch, for years world champion. (See his recent
book, *On the Mat and Off*, published by Albert Bonnier in New
York, 1937.)

There have been many others before and after Hjalmar
Lundin. The following were among the best known: Alex Swan-
son; Fritz Hanson; Bobby Bylund; John Berg; John Free-
berg; Hilmer Johnson; Anton Gustafson; John Alexanderson;
Carl "Benny" Benson (American amateur champion); Nils
Remer (Jess Westergard); "Cyclone" Burns-Carlson; Harry
Chelstorp; Edwin Anderson; Cliff Olson; Tor Johnson; Johan
Richthoff (double Olympic champion); Carl G. Anderson
(Olympic prize winner, 1908, and perhaps the first Swede to
win an American championship in wrestling); Clarence Ek-
lund; Harry Larson; "Swede" Ferguson; Theo. Bergquist;
Oscar Nygren, "Roslagsbjörnen."

Boxing does not conform so well to the Swedish temperament
as wrestling, and we find that marked success has not been
achieved in this field, though several Swedes have made good
in the ring. Harry Persson once aspired to the world championship, and had a notable professional career in America. Otto
von Porat, born in Sweden, but brought up in Norway, was
also near the top. Then there have been Nisse Ramm; Oscar
Gardner; Ragnar Holmberg; "Kid" Nelson; A. Kellberg;
Fred Lindström; Arthur Ahl; and John Anderson—all fairly
good boxers. However, this sport is not so well adapted to the
Scandinavian, who prefers the slower pace of wrestling, and
welcomes the call upon his tenacity. The boxer must be fast
and agile, but does not need the muscular force or endurance
of the wrestler.

Tug of war, a favorite Swedish pastime, illustrates our
point well. It requires brawn and staying power in unusual
degree and, being possessed of this combination, the Swedish-
American teams have made formidable opponents. The first
team was organized in 1888, and took part in many contests in

the old Madison Square Garden, New York. Among its members were Erik Hagström, Albert Johnson, Hjalmar Molander, and Hjalmar Gordman. For awhile there was a real tug-of-war fad in America; and then teams were formed all over the country, with the heavy, husky Swedes in greatest demand. One such team from New Britain, Connecticut, was champion of New England for a number of years.

In 1897 there was an exciting world-championship contest, with ten nations taking part in it. The setting was Suttro Baths, the show place of San Francisco at the time. In the finals, Canada and Sweden met, with the former favored to attain the title. To win, either team had to gain five feet and when, after twenty-seven minutes, the Canadian flag fell and the Swedish one flew in victory, it made a thrilling scene according to a witness of the event. His teammates gave "Power" Anderson from Öland, who was the anchor man, most of the credit. Three of them together, it is said, could not move Anderson from one spot, and he was known as the one-man tug-of-war team.

Another sport calling for powerful muscles is weight-lifting, which has been cherished for years by some of the leading Swedish-American athletic clubs. One of these, the Swedish-American Athletic Club of Brooklyn, has been particularly active, and has developed many good lifters. Those who made a name for themselves were: Oscar B. Wahlund (incidentally, inventor of the term, "free-style" wrestling); August W. Johnson (awarded first prize in McFadden's Physical Culture Show, held at the old Madison Square Garden. He was the only one who could raise a 200-lb. dumbbell from the floor at arm's length, over his head); "Calle Sven" Swenson (who placed second in the same show); Gustaf Holmberg; Eric Hagström; Anton Gustafson (Java-Gustaf), and Arvid Anderson.

Renewed interest has recently been taken in this sport, due, perhaps, to improved equipment and a more modern technique in lifting.

The Swedes in America have continued to play their beloved soccer football, a game ideally fitted to the Scandinavian disposition. Wherever they live and build in the United States, they play soccer. In recent years schools and universities have taken it up, and many Swedish names appear on their teams. Indeed, several descendants have been on American Olympic soccer teams.

The Swedish players, especially those who arrived here after the World War, have done much to popularize this biggest of all ball games, which has now assumed international proportions. It has spread out over the globe and is probably played in every country. Each day it wins new supporters in the United States, and provides pleasure for both player and spectator. The game here has seen many Swedish stars, like Herbert "Murren" Carlson, Eric Levin, and "Cairo" Schylander.

A typical Swedish-American branch of soccer is "six-a-side," a variation of the big game itself. This version is a summer game, which of recent years has grown widely in popularity. It is played on a smaller field and in less time, with six players instead of eleven.

Some Americans of Swedish descent have taken to the national game of baseball; and frequently we find their names on the first teams. There have been, for example, Fred Lindstrom (one of the best third basemen the game has known); "Hal" Carlson and "Rube" Walberg, both excellent pitchers with the big leagues. This fact shows that Swedish-Americans can take to a very technical game like baseball. It is, however, rarely played in Sweden and no player born in that country has made the major grade over here. Many youngsters with Swedish names are now coming up in the minor leagues, and already well known are Dahlgren, Erickson, and Wennberg.

The American game of football (rugby) is right in line with the Scandinavian constitution. Consequently, we expect Americans of Swedish parentage to do well in this sport. Names like "Swede" Youngstrom from Dartmouth, "Pug" Lund in Minnesota, "Hunk" Anderson from Notre Dame, come easily to mind. Grantland Rice, the celebrated sports writer, once said: "The teams out West, especially the Minnesota teams, are the most feared of our American teams, solely for the Norse power supplied to them by the huge muscular Swedes with which they are amply staffed." The American form of football requires a great deal of strength and coaches look first for large, husky fellows, when the material for rugby teams is being examined; and so the Swedes, who are generally big and strong, get the first call.

During the past fifty years Swedish-Americans have come to the front in track and field athletics, and have achieved a praiseworthy distinction. Splendid coaches and trainers have enabled them to develop their abilities, so that an improved technique has been added to the natural equipment. Swedes have ever been known as fine runners—particularly long-distance ones, good throwers, jumpers, and hurdlers.

There has been a long row of good marathon runners; and from the list we should like to mention John Svanberg, who is, perhaps, the best known of all Swedish runners. He finished second in the Olympic games in Athens, 1906, and came to America a few years later to turn professional. In his prime, Svanberg defeated everyone of prominence, and came to be looked upon as a first-class athlete, one for the youth of the day to emulate.

Other famed marathoners were: Gösta Ljungström; Thure Johanson; Alex Ahlgren (who is still credited with the world record for the marathon race—2 hours, 24 minutes, 15 seconds); and Fritz Carlson, who won the Boston marathon in 1913.

Coming down on the distance, we find a list of good Swedish runners around six miles, three, and under, some of whom have represented either America or Sweden at Olympic games (the goal of all athletes). There are such well-known names as Edwin Wide, who broke many records during his stay here; Anatole Bolin; Runar Öhman; Hans Schuster; John Eke; and Eric Ny.

A particularly strong group is comprised of those of Swedish birth who received all their training in this country. Among the illustrious ones has been Ernest Hjertberg, the "Flying Swede"—later, an equally celebrated coach. Perhaps his greatest achievement came at the end of his running career when, on New Year's Eve (at 12 midnight), 1899, Hjertberg won the first Race of the Century, in New York City, a widely heralded

victory at the time. Then there was the miler, Oscar F. Hedlund, who represented the United States in the 1908 Olympics;
as did also Frank Danielson and John Lindquist. Other Olympic athletes were Edward Lindberg, Eric Everlund, and the
long-popular discus thrower, Robert Edgren—later sports
writer and cartoonist. (See the chapter on "Journalists.")

The Swedes of America have proved themselves in the field.
Among these have been the Olympic high jumper, Egon R.
Erickson, who jumped for the United States in 1908 and 1912;
Carl Johnson; Eric Erickson; Karl Fryksdahl. Eric Almloef,
who took part in the Olympics of 1912 and 1920, was, both
times, a prize winner.

In later years, youngsters of Swedish ancestry have come to
the fore in these sports, and no doubt some of them will fulfill
the promise they have shown. A shot-putter named Edward
Swenson and a quarter miler, Karl Larson, seem to possess
special merit.

All forms of water sports are favorites with the Scandinavians. They learn to master the water as children, and are adept
at handling boats of all kinds. We may, therefore, expect to
find their names well up in the ranks of expert swimmers and
sailors.

It has been noted that in swimming and diving the Swedish-
American is successful indeed; and here, as in no other sport,
the ladies have come to the fore. To mention a few, there are
Martha Norelius (Olympic champion and holder of many
world records in her prime); Lisa Lindstrom; Svea and Karin
Nilsson; and the diving champions, Marjorie Gestring (who,
at the age of thirteen, won the Olympic title in 1936 for the
United States); and Greta Johanson (also an Olympic champion). Swedish girls' names are numerous on all-American
teams; and they have achieved excellent reputations for themselves.

Prominent among the men, we may mention Arne Borg, the
most famous, who is still a world record-holder at several distances. At his peak Borg made a long-remembered tour of
America. Then there were Charles Norelius (father of Martha); Eric Ericson; Gustaf Wretman; Nils Regnell—and the

divers, Hjalmar Johanson (Olympic champion); Ernst Brandsten; Fred Spongberg (Olympic prize winner); Oscar Dose; and "Stumpen" Eklund. Brandsten, Johanson, and Spongberg became well known as coaches, and their accomplishments in that line will be told farther on.

A noteworthy feat of a Swedish swimmer should, perhaps, be recorded here. It was in the days when the celebrated Channel swimmer, the Englishman, Captain Webb, came to America, after making the first triumphant crossing of the English Channel. A Swede named Sundstrom raced with Captain Webb, from the Battery to Harlem River (Manhattan Island from end to end) and return, winning his race, to the astonishment of the spectators.

In rowing, sailing, and yachting, Swedish-Americans take an important part, perhaps in view of their special fitness for these sports, and an inherited love of the sea. We often find rowers of Swedish extraction on the all-conquering Western crews from Washington State. It has been observed that the big American yachts are sailed by crews which number in the majority, Scandinavians, who are desired for their efficiency, mechanical and navigating ability, strength, and alertness. Those sturdy yachts which have defended the America's cup have, in substantial part, been manned by sailors of Swedish and Norwegian origin, whose seamanship has helped to keep the cup on American shores for eighty-six years. Indeed, the first mate on *Ranger*, the successful defender of America's cup in 1937, was Vilhelm Karstens, a Swede from Norrköping. Three other Swedish sailors, whom Commodore Harold S. Vanderbilt remarked that he would not be without, were Henry Swanson, Hans Peterson, and Henry Ohlin.

A sailing feat in this country, well worth recording, took place in the Olympic Sailing Regatta in Los Angeles, 1932, when the 6-meter *Bissby* from Sweden, sailed by Sven Salén, captured the laurel from a strong competing fleet. The American sailing experts at the time acclaimed Salén as the best sailor to have visited these shores.

The Swedes have been among the pioneers in winter sports in America; and their influence has aided in making the country ski-conscious, of recent years. For them, skiing has been a centuries-old sport. The long winters and abundant snowfall make it a practical necessity in the northland. Every child in northern Sweden learns to ski soon after it can walk, and presently traverses the snow-covered hills with ease.

Following in their forefathers' ski tracks have come the Swedish-Americans, particularly in those northern States of America—Minnesota, Wisconsin, Michigan, the New England States, and the great Northwest. Wherever the Swedes have settled, climate allowing, they have practiced their beloved sport, formed ski clubs, and taught others the healthful exercise. From their numbers have been chosen those who have had the honor to represent the United States at important contests.

Well-known skiers here have been Olle Zetterstrom and Nils Backstrom, members of an American Olympic team, and the jumpers, Robert Palm and "Sig" Steinwall, among others.

The Scandinavian influence has been responsible for a new development in skiing. In some parts of the country, where the snowfall has been insufficient for indulgence in this grand winter recreation, "snow" trains have been arranged to carry large groups of ski enthusiasts farther north, where there is plenty of snow. These excursions have proved immensely popular, and promise to create a greater interest in the time-honored sport of skiing, which is now being taught in American colleges by Swedish-American instructors; while, in the large department stores where the skis are sold, patient salesmen explain to the zealous purchasers how to wax and otherwise care for them.

Other winter sports are in high favor with Scandinavians, whose names have become familiar to the American public, as able exponents of ice and snow feats.

On various occasions the three-time Olympic winner in fancy skating, the late Gillis Grafström, exhibited here, displaying his graceful talent. The Swedish ice princess, Vivi-Ann Hultén, has been well received and admired for her accomplished performance. Her dancing on the ice is sheer delight.

There is a well-known instructor in fancy skating, who has done much to popularize this beautiful art in America—Bror Meyer. For many years he has been teacher to the "four hundred" of American society, and also numbers among his disciples many of America's best fancy skaters. In his amateur days, Meyer won numerous contests alone and, in the pair skating, he and his partner, Emma Bergfelt, were frequently awarded first prizes.

At the end of the last century, the most renowned speed skaters were the Swedish-Americans, John S. Johnson, and the two brothers, John and Eric Lawson, who, singularly enough, were among the country's best bicycle riders as well. In that connection they will again be mentioned.

On the big-league ice-hockey teams we quite often find Swedish names; for this is a very strenuous game and calls for the essential qualities which Swedes possess. No winter sport is unknown to the people from the North, who are at home on snow and ice. They are familiar with all the invigorating pastimes which are possible in cold weather.

We are reminded here of an exhilarating sport which the Swedes have introduced in the West—sailing on ice, individually, and on yachts—which will likely grow in favor with the years, for it provides thrills in abundance.

In the next section we wish to sum up the outstanding achievements of Swedish-Americans in seven or eight other branches, in order to record their attainments in rather diversified lines.

For example, bicycling must needs be mentioned, for this is a very popular sport in Sweden, and with Swedes in America. Around 1890, John S. Johnson, whom we have just named, was the world's champion bicyclist, and considered one of the greatest athletes in the country at that time. He was first heard of in Independence, Iowa, in 1893, when he surprised the populace by riding a mile in 1:56. The world record then was 2:08, so one can appreciate their amazement. In that race Johnson rode against a horse, beating the animal. By 1895 he had twenty-eight world records in different distances. In the winter, when there were no cycling contests, John Johnson took part in ice-skating competition, both in the United States and Canada, scoring numerous triumphs.

Other fine bicyclists were the two Lawson brothers—already

named—John and Eric, "The Terrible Swedes," who were long-distance champions. John's most famous victory was in Chicago, 1895, with over 500 starters in a 25-mile race, when he won with his big bicycle (the front wheel weighed 42 lbs.). Incidentally, he was the inventor of a stationary home-training bicycle (improved models of which are now in general use) and both brothers were 6-day riders of renown. In the Century Race at San Jose, California, 1900, Eric Lawson won the 100-mile race in the then-world-record time of 4½ hours. On ice skates, the Lawson brothers held records from 10 to 50 miles.

Among other good bicyclists may be mentioned Aronson, Lindquist, and Julius. At this point we should tell about a very colorful personality, Tilly Anderson, who was a famous bicycle rider at the end of the nineteenth century. She took part in many men's races and frequently defeated riders of the opposite sex, for she was very fast on the wheels. Tilly Anderson was immensely popular with the crowd; was, indeed, a sensation. Whenever Tilly was riding, the house would be sold out. She gave exhibitions all over the country and was admired for her gay manner, as well as for her skill.

Speaking of John Johnson racing a horse brings to mind the fact that Swedes make excellent horsemen and are keen supporters of equestrian sports. Military teams, sent here from Sweden, have won coveted prizes at exhibitions and have displayed their splendid horsemanship to their American friends. The most distinguished name here is the gallant Count Clarence von Rosen and his Olympic prize-winning son.

Swedish-Americans are known to make good cavalry officers, and the American Army numbers many among its ranks.

Captain C. Westlund, of the American Army, has made a name for himself in polo.

The old bow-and-arrow game is finding a new vogue in America, the pioneer in archery being General Ivor Thord-Gray, of Greenwich, Connecticut, who has formed clubs, and helped to reawaken interest in the venerable sport. He is also an archeologist, explorer, and British Army veteran.

Very widespread is bowling, a diversion esteemed by Swedish-Americans. There are bowling clubs all over the United States, and its popularity continues to grow. The best known among Swedish-American bowlers is Adolf Carlson, in the West. Nels Carlson of Schenectady, New York, is another adept.

At billiards, Charles C. Peterson is known as a "wizard," being an exceptional trick-shot billiard player.

In golf and tennis, not many Swedish-Americans have attained prominence, and perhaps these games do not quite match the Scandinavian makeup. Patty Berg of Minneapolis, however, is a well-known woman golfer, and Karl Schroeder of Stockholm has won two American championship titles at tennis. Many Swedish-Americans now play these two games, and perhaps the future will produce more superior players of Swedish blood.

Much of the Swedish success in sports has been made possible by the support which athletic clubs and other organizations throughout the country have generously given. By their sponsorship, these groups aid the great cause of sport in numerous ways, thus doing a full share to promote health and provide wholesome recreation for their members. The sports clubs become centers of activity for the youth of the nation, who are encouraged to strive for athletic honors. Very often the foundation is laid for worthwhile careers in afterlife. Training rules for success are exacting, and this contributes to careful living and the formation of good habits.

Athletes themselves frequently become instructors, at clubs and at schools, when their days of active competition are over; and several Swedish-Americans have been markedly successful in teaching their art to younger generations. The best known is Ernest Hjertberg, the noted distance runner, whom we have already mentioned. He has been a pioneer in coaching in America, specializing in track and field. Both in the United States and in Sweden, Ernest Hjertberg has had a long and highly successful coaching career. He has trained ninety-two men who have placed in four Olympic games, and has instructed at a number of American universities and athletic clubs. His record is enviable at the New Jersey Athletic Club; Berkeley School; Military Athletic League; Columbia University; Irish-American Athletic Club; New York Athletic Club; and Rice Institute. Mr. Hjertberg was called to Sweden in 1910, to organize Olympic teams; his name is almost legendary there, for Sweden won the 1912 Olympics, largely due to Ernest Hjertberg's efforts. Later he was invited to Holland for the same purpose.

Another well-known instructor is Carl G. Anderson who, in his younger days, was an Olympic wrestler, as previously mentioned, a good soccer player, all-round athlete, and gymnast. He has been coach at Harvard, Rutgers, and the Newark Athletic Club. Mr. Anderson has been with the latter institution for many years, and is also president of the New Jersey Amateur Athletic Union. (See the chapter on "Gymnastics.")

Two other fine coaches who should be mentioned here are Carl Olson of Pittsburgh University, and Oscar M. Hedlund of the Massachusetts Institute of Technology.

Then there are the swimming instructors: Ernst Brandsten (coach at Leland-Stanford University for over twenty years); Fred A. Spongberg and Hjalmar Johanson (a well-known coach on the Pacific coast for many years). The success of American divers during the past quarter-century has been largely due to the training methods introduced by these three men. Their teaching methods have become standardized, and are in general use among most other instructors. They have been responsible for a score of national and Olympic diving champions, men and women, and may well be considered pioneers in their field.

Ernst Brandsten designed a greatly improved springboard, which has been a real boon to divers. It is made from a solid piece of Douglas fir, and is remarkably resilient, so that more intricate dives have been made possible. He also invented a movable fulcrum, which permits each diver to make a perfect adjustment of the springboard for himself.

Mr. Spongberg is assistant athletic director and swimming instructor at the Downtown Athletic Club in New York City, and enjoys an excellent reputation among American boy and girl divers. In 1924, both Spongberg and Brandsten were coaches on the American Olympic swimming team, and saw their divers excel in springboard and platform diving.

Instructors and leaders, sports clubs, and benefactors, are

equally indispensable. In the last-named group belong those fine, public-spirited supporters, like Hans Lagerloef and Charles K. Johansen of New York, who have given of their time to the advancement of sport, and donated prizes in many competitions. With the generous aid which has been bestowed from so many quarters, the future does, indeed, appear bright for the continued growth of health-giving athletics. Now that the value of sport has been universally acknowledged, participation in all branches, and by both sexes, seems destined to spread throughout the nation in ever greater degree. It is possible that, without the Swedish influence, the recognition may have been longer delayed. We believe that Swedish-Americans will keep on contributing their share to the splendid work, for they have the capacity and desire to do so. They will continue, in years to come, to make their influence felt and do their full share in furthering American sports; for theirs is the strength and endurance to carry on.

Inventors

JOHAN LILJENCRANTS

Baron Johan Liljencrants was born and educated in Sweden, where he was commissioned a Second Lieutenant in the Royal Svea Life Guards, in 1906. Four years later he resigned, then pursued postgraduate studies at Princeton University, 1912–13, and obtained the Ph.D. degree at the George Washington University, in psychology and psychiatry, in 1921. Between 1926 and 1936, he was the Editor, successively, of *The Swedish American Trade Journal* and *The American Swedish Monthly*. In the preparation of the present chapter, he has been assisted by members of the John Ericsson Society of New York, particularly its President, E. Theodore I. Thygeson; and from the *Swedish Forum* of western Pennsylvania, he has received valuable suggestions.

INVENTIONS by Swedes and Swedish-Americans contribute, perhaps more than is generally known, to everyday comfort as well as to industrial development in America. Swedes are noted for technological skill; and Sweden has given to the world more than her due share of inventors. During the last decades of the immigration period, she also sent to these shores many well-trained young men, representing a fair quota of inventive talent. A complete survey of the field cannot be attempted in this connection, but a few examples will serve to illustrate what Swedish and Swedish-American inventors have contributed to American life.

The Swedish inventor best known and most honored in America is John Ericsson, not so much, perhaps, because of his mechanical genius and versatility, as because of the great service he was able to render the nation at a critical stage in the Civil War. His "cheesebox on a raft," the *Monitor*, in stopping the formidable *Merrimac* and establishing much-needed naval supremacy for the Union, made him a national hero. As an inventor, however, his accomplishments were many; and the list of his patents, numbering a hundred items, includes a share in the screw propeller, and several more inventions of first magnitude.

Ericsson's forefathers had, for generations, been associated

JOHN ERICSSON, 1803–89

INVENTOR OF THE *MONITOR*

with the iron industry in the Province of Värmland, where he was born at the small foundry estate of Långbanshyttan, on July 31, 1803. His father, Olof Ericsson, had inherited a share in the estate, and his mother was the daughter of its principal owner. The family, however, lost all in the postwar depression of 1809, and, in the following year, Olof Ericsson accepted a position as director of blasting on the Göta Canal, then in course of construction.

At first John received a classical education at the hands of private tutors. On the Canal project, however, he came in contact with mechanical things, which gradually began to absorb his interest. He learned to draw and make models and supplemented his classical studies with mathematics, physics, and mechanics. In these matters he was encouraged and guided by friendly engineer officers. Finally, one day, the Admiral, Count Baltzar von Platen, the planner and builder of the Canal, happened to see his handwork and became so convinced of his talents that he took him under his protection and appointed him a cadet in the Mechanical Corps of the Royal Navy, which was in charge of the Canal construction.

Under Count von Platen's powerful patronage the road to an engineering career lay open before him, but suddenly John Ericsson decided to become a soldier, instead. Over Von Platen's objections, he resigned from the Mechanical Corps and got an ensign's commission in the Jämtland Royal Rifles. There, among other duties, he was assigned to making maps. These were shown to the King of Sweden, Napoleon's former Marshal Bernadotte, who found them so good that he commanded Ericsson to draw maps of his campaigns, for a work to be published in book form, and appointed him a lieutenant. Ericsson now had a royal patron.

While in Jämtland, Ericsson made his first great invention, the caloric engine, of which he completed a working model in 1823. It was based on the principle of the expansion of gases from heat and had two communicating cylinders, one of which enclosed the fire pit. The expanding air and combustion gases moved the piston in that cylinder upwards, compressing the air on top, which in turn acted on the piston in the second cylinder. His main purpose with the caloric engine was to save fuel—the steam engine of those days being very wasteful; and this was done, partly by putting the fire pit within the cylinder and partly by means of a regenerator that absorbed the heat from the exhaust gases and transferred it to the intake air.

On the King's advice, Ericsson went to London in 1826 to exploit his invention. He received excellent introductions through a friend, Count Adolf Eugène von Rosen, and demonstrated his caloric engine before influential people; but, although it worked well, the experts, including Faraday, rejected it on the ground that they saw no reason why it worked. But his royal patron did not abandon him in adversity. A friendly letter from his son, Crown Prince Oscar, arrived in 1827, inclosing a captain's commission—a title of which Ericsson was always proud.

Subsequently Ericsson became associated with John Braithwaite, the head of a mechanical works in England, and a period of intense experimentation now began, during which he brought out such important devices as tubular steam boilers, the surface condenser—of vast importance for the development of the marine engine—and a steam fire engine. At short notice he also built a locomotive, which, in a competition, made better speed than George Stephenson's "Rocket," being much lighter and of better design; but a mishap, due to hasty construction, forced it out of the contest. Later rebuilt, it reached a speed of forty-eight miles per hour, and its performance aided the new movement for passenger railroad transportation.

Ericsson's next great invention was a development of the screw propeller, destined to usher in a new era in ships. The underlying principle may have been known long before; but it had found no practical application until 1836, when Ericsson took out a patent on a rotating propeller. In 1837 he launched a small ship, equipped with two independently acting propellers, which made successful trips on the Thames; but, when it was demonstrated before the Lords of the Admiralty, those experts declared—in spite of what they saw—that it was "impossible for his boat to steer, as the power was in the stern."

This was a new discouragement, but, fortunately, Ericsson at that time came in contact with an American naval officer, Lieutenant Robert P. Stockton, who was interested in constructing ships for the American Navy. Ericsson revealed to him his plans for a new type of warship, built of iron and driven by steam through a propeller. It was a bold plan in a day when naval experts still clung to wooden ships and to sails, paddle wheels being too vulnerable. Stockton made a trip on Ericsson's ship, quickly grasped the advantage of the propeller, and, on the spot, ordered two small iron steamboats equipped with the new device. Both crossed the Atlantic by their own power to the United States, where, later, one of them served on the Delaware-Raritan Canal for thirty years.

Ericsson had found England singularly unreceptive to his ideas, and so, when assurances came from Stockton of an American Government contract for a warship to be designed by him, he did not hesitate. On November 23, 1839, he arrived in New York, where he established an engineering office. He became an American citizen on October 28, 1848, and lived in New York for the rest of his life.

The promised Government order, arriving in 1842, was for an iron frigate of 600 tons, for which Ericsson was commissioned to design hull and engine. In addition, he equipped it with a heavy gun of his own design and with a range finder of his own invention. Named the *Princeton*, the frigate made its maiden voyage in the following year, and won an easy victory in a race with the side-wheeler, the *Great Western*, then considered the finest steamer afloat. Ever since then, the propeller has been rated one of the most important devices of all times.

Seemingly unfair treatment by the Government, however, deterred Ericsson from further dealings with it for many years. Instead, he returned to work on the caloric engine, which he finally perfected in 1854. Because of its great economy, this engine for decades found widespread use in driving pumps, and in small industries in need of a modest power plant—about ten thousand were in use, before its place was taken by internal-combustion engines and electric motors. Besides a fortune, later spent on new experiments, it earned for its inventor the great Rumford gold medal.

At the outbreak of the Crimean War in 1853, Ericsson returned to earlier plans for a turret warship. He hoped to do something to help curb Sweden's old archenemy, Russia. In those days, warships had practically all their guns in broadside, and a great number were required to obtain all-round fire, for which reason the guns had to be light and small. Much maneuvering was also necessary in firing broadsides.

To eliminate these drawbacks, Ericsson constructed a revolving steel turret, containing a single, heavy gun that, by rotating the turret, could be fired in any direction. He made a model of an iron ship, with his turret mounted on deck, and sent it to Emperor Napoleon III, who returned it with his compliments. It then rested in Ericsson's office until after the outbreak of the Civil War, when Ericsson showed it to a caller, Cornelius S. Bushnell, a naval constructor. Largely through the latter's intervention, Ericsson received an order from Washington for such a ship, and within a hundred days, as the order stipulated, he delivered his famous *Monitor* that made history on Hampton Roads, and helped turn the tide of the Civil War. Even more than the *Princeton*, it revolutionized naval warfare—in fact, at one stroke it rendered all then-existing navies obsolete, as the London *Times* at once admitted.

Up to his death (on March 8, 1889), John Ericsson remained busily engaged in experiments and new constructions. Toward the end, he worked on a solar engine for utilizing the heat radiating from the sun. But while he solved the problem in theory and made a working model, the engine was still in the experimental stage when his career closed. In 1890 the United States cruiser, *Baltimore*, brought his body back to Sweden.

Important inventions by Swedes or Swedish-Americans are found in every branch of modern engineering. (See also the chapters on "Engineers" and "Manufacturers.") Modern blasting technique, for example, is based on inventions by Alfred Bernhard Nobel, the prize donor, whose ignitor and dynamite brought previously undreamt-of effectiveness to high explosives. Of old Swedish stock, from the Province of Skåne, Nobel was born in Stockholm in 1833. In his ninth year he followed his father, Emanuel, to St. Petersburg, where the latter had been invited by the Czar to demonstrate submarine mines of his own invention, and where he later established an ordnance factory. In this connection, the elder Nobel, too, experimented

with nitroglycerine, first produced by an Italian, Ascanio So-
brero, in 1847.

Young Alfred Nobel received his main education from private tutors in St. Petersburg. In the early 1850's, he spent two
years in the United States, where he came in contact with John
Ericsson. Later he continued his studies in Paris and finally
returned to St. Petersburg where, with his brothers, he became
employed at his father's munitions works. He devoted himself
especially to the practical application of nitroglycerine. His
first achievement was the "Nobel ignitor," a glass tube containing black powder with a fuse attached, later exchanged by him
for a metal percussion cap containing a mercury salt. The
ignitor caused the full charge of nitroglycerine to explode, and
its introduction marked the foundation of modern blasting
methods.

Returning to Stockholm in 1863, Alfred Nobel continued
work on adapting nitroglycerine to practical uses. He first patented an improved and safe method of manufacturing it in
large quantities. Nitroglycerine, however, in its natural state
is a highly unstable liquid; many explosions occurred in handling it, and seepage from drill holes caused serious accidents.
It was not suited to ordinary blasting. This defect Nobel tried
to remedy, and his efforts resulted in his invention of dynamite.
First he made it by mixing nitroglycerine with pulverized black
powder into a dough that could be transported and used with
reasonable safety; later, in 1867, he exchanged the powder for
infusorial earth, capable of absorbing great quantities of the
liquid.

The invention of dynamite proved epoch-making, because
this explosive in its great effectiveness greatly surpassed black
powder. It not only reduced necessary drilling to a fraction of
what had been formerly required but also permitted operations,
such as tunnel building, on a scale that could not have been
attempted before. Finally, by his invention in 1875 of gelatine
dynamite, a jelly-like substance of great explosive power consisting of nitrocellulose of low nitrogen content dissolved in
nitroglycerine, he perfected his former discoveries.

Nobel founded factories in Sweden and other European countries as well as in the United States. After having lived in Paris since 1873, he moved his residence to San Remo, in 1890, where six years later he died, a bachelor, leaving the vast fortune he had amassed, as a fund for the yearly distribution of prizes to promising young workers in the fields of literature and science, and for the promotion of peace, in which for years he had been actively interested. He had fondly hoped that his high explosives would make war too destructive to be resorted to.

Another Swedish invention in general use in the United States as well as almost everywhere else, is the safety match, and, as is so often the case, the conception, perfection, and practical adaptation of it must be credited to a scientist who had the idea, to a manufacturer who applied it, and to an inventive engineer who designed the machinery for mass production. The scientist in this case was Gustaf Erik Pasch, whose true family name was Berggren, a pupil of Berzelius, the pioneer in chemistry. (See the chapter on "Four Representatives of the Intellect.") In 1844 he received a patent on the idea of removing the poisonous yellow phosphorus from the match head, exchanging it for the far safer brown amorphous phosphorus, and spreading that substance on the side of the box, while making the match head from chemicals that would ignite only by contact with the brown phosphorus on the box. This not only reduced the risk of accidents but also protected the match workers from the dreaded "phossy jaw." In other words, it made matches safe. In 1855 Johan Edward Lundström, who had also studied at the University of Uppsala, began to make matches at Jönköping, his home town in Småland, by automatic machinery, which was later improved and developed by Alexander Lagerman, an engineer and inventor, in whose name there is to this day in Sweden a special fund for giving prizes to other inventors. Automatic mass production made matches cheap, so that everybody could afford to use them. At the first Paris Exposition in 1855, Swedish safety matches were awarded a high prize, which opened the way to the international market.

Two other Swedish devices, in common use in America as well as in other countries, which, on account of the inventor's French-sounding name, are seldom associated with Sweden or Swedish people, are the De Laval cream separator, and the De Laval steam turbine. The former may be said to have been the foundation of modern, large-scale dairying (see the chapter on "Farmers"), while the latter gave new efficiency to steam power. Their inventor, Carl Gustaf Patrick de Laval, was born in the Province of Dalarne in 1845, his father being a Captain in the Swedish Army. Originally French, the family had lived in Sweden for over two hundred years, and had absorbed many new strains. De Laval, a graduate of both the Royal Institute of Technology in Stockholm and the University of Uppsala, constructed, in 1878, his first continuously operating cream separator, which, although since then improved in various ways, became, nevertheless, the foundation of one of Sweden's world industries as well as of manufacturing plants in other countries, including the United States. Similar separators, based on the centrifugal force, are now used in the purification of oils, and the separation of many other mixtures of liquids of different specific gravity, while the extremely speedy "ultra centrifuge," recently constructed by The Svedberg, professor at the University of Uppsala and Nobel Prize winner in 1926, is now used as the latest instrument of science in the study of matter. In the words of the Harvard Tercentenary's doctor's citation for Professor Svedberg in 1936, "it sees beyond the microscope."

As a suitable motor for his separator, De Laval constructed in 1883 his first commercially practical steam turbine, by which he obtained the required high speed almost direct from steam power. Later he added many improvements, one of the most important being the diverging steam nozzle, invented in 1888, and now widely used. It develops a corresponding velocity of the steam for a wide range of pressure drops, without which high efficiency would be impossible. The revolutionizing character of this invention is illustrated by the fact that, although application for an American patent had been filed in 1889, the examiners refused for four years to believe that it would work, and it was not until a De Laval single-stage turbine, fitted with diverging nozzles, was exhibited in operation at the Chicago World's Fair in 1893, that the claims were allowed, and the patent issued.

In the steam-turbine field, De Laval had a competitor in Sir

Charles A. Parsons of England; but the two, working independently and partly on different principles, are credited with having done the pioneering work for modern steam turbines. "The 'simple' type of steam turbine or steam 'windmill,' " says the *Encyclopædia Britannica* (14th ed. XXII, 576), "was first perfected by the great Swedish engineer, Gustav C. P. de Laval after several years of preliminary work. It ranks as a great achievement, inasmuch as within the limitations just described, it is a perfectly practical solution of the problem, worked out, moreover, in days when reliable data on the properties of steam were practically non-existent."

"De Laval's early work in the high pressure and high temperature fields," writes Arvid Peterson of the De Laval Steam Turbine Company of Trenton, New Jersey, "is the more remarkable as the advantages of high steam pressure and high temperatures have only recently been realized and applied in practice." De Laval has to his credit several other inventions in very wide use today, as, for instance, the high pitch-line helical gears, considered an outstanding contribution to the development of the steam turbine, particularly for ship propulsion. By January, 1938, the American De Laval Company at Trenton had delivered to the United States Navy alone, helical gears for a total output of about 4,500,000 H.P. "I believe," adds Mr. Peterson, "that de Laval was also the first to conceive and to develop formulas for the flexible shaft, first introduced in 1884 and today used in modern impulse turbines of great capacities." In 1902, De Laval received the large gold medal of the Swedish Academy of Science. He died in 1913. (For more details about his various contributions, see the article, "A Pioneer in High Pressure Steam," by George H. Gibson, in *Power Magazine* for November 6, 1928.)

In more recent years, a compound-reaction steam turbine has been designed in Sweden by the brothers, Birger and Fredrik Ljungström, who had been employed, successively, by both Nobel and De Laval. In 1908 they launched the Ljungström Steam Turbine Company of Stockholm. Among its products has been a turbine locomotive, noted for both great power capacity and fuel and water economy. It is also equipped with the Ljungström air preheater, a fuel-saving device which is now used in many of the large stationary steam-power plants in the United States and other countries.

Still another versatile Swedish engineer is Sven Gustaf Winquist, inventor of the self-aligning spherical ball bearing, for the exploitation of which the famous "SKF," or "Svenska Kullager Fabriken," was founded in Gothenburg, Sweden, in 1907. It has now an important subsidiary in the United States. (See the chapter on "Manufacturers.") In 1899, Winquist became engineer in charge of operations at the Gamlestadens Textile Works in Gothenburg, and there he became interested in the problem of bearings and the saving of energy by reduction of friction. The self-aligning spherical ball bearing was the result. In 1921, he received an honorary degree from Stevens Institute of Technology at Hoboken, New Jersey, and he is now managing director of the famous Bofors Steel and Munition Works in Sweden.

The recent death, at the age of sixty-eight, of Nils Gustaf Dalén, brought new attention to the paradox that one who had done so much to bring light to both land and sea should himself have been totally blind during the last twenty-five years of his life. Born in the Province of Västergötland, the son of a farmer, he had early to learn the meaning of hard labor. Thanks to the pecuniary help of De Laval and friends in his home village, he was enabled to enroll at the Chalmers Institute of Technology in Gothenburg, which has given by far the greatest number of Swedish-trained engineers to the United States. After having been graduated in 1896, he, too, busied himself with steam turbines and dairy machinery, obtaining several patents on improvements that are still in use. Then, as chief engineer of the Swedish Carbide and Acetylene Company, he became interested in problems of using gas for light.

His principal inventions, now used in nearly all parts of the world, including the United States, are two—the gas accumulator, in which large quantities of gas can be stored safely under compression in relatively small space, and the sun valve, by which beacons and crossroad blinkers are made to operate automatically. The basis of his accumulator is a porous substance, *"aga massan,"* which absorbs acetylene gas under pressure, and it is due to acetylene gas, thus compressed, that the crossroad

blinkers one sees everywhere in America, marked "AGA, Elizabeth, New Jersey," as well as the automatic beacons on the sea-
coasts, can operate for a year at a time, without refilling. After
having thus provided the fuel for continuous automatic lighting, Dalén devised the sun valve, which automatically shuts off
the light at daybreak and turns it on at dusk. It operates on
the principle that of two otherwise similar metal rods, one with
a dark surface absorbs more light, and therefore more heat,
than one with a bright, polished surface. Heat causes expansion, and the inequality in expansion is sufficient to open and
shut a valve as the amount of light varies. Thus the sun valve
is so sensitive that it lights a beacon when the sky is only dark-
ened by clouds or by a solar eclipse. In the British Dominions
it is used on wind indicators, landing lights, and floodlights. In
forty countries of the world, stocks of AGA parts are kept in
readiness. AGA lights have come into use in navigation, transportation by land, and aviation, resulting in an incalculable
saving of human lives.

For this invention, Dalén was awarded the Nobel Prize in
Physics in 1912. Soon after that, he lost his eyesight in an explosion, but, nonetheless, he continued to direct the operations
of the Gas Accumulator Company. On his desk were dozens of
telephones, connecting him directly with every part of the plant.
"These are my eyes," he would say. Before his accident, he
visited the United States several times and always took intense
interest in American technological developments. His latest invention, now also manufactured in the United States, is the
AGA stove, which operates continuously on as little as ten
pounds of coal for twenty-four hours; it has a heat-storage device, or accumulator, that keeps the heat under cooking platters
and ovens constant at all times.

For another household article, in even wider general use in
America, the Electrolux refrigerator, we are indebted to two
inventors trained at the Royal Institute of Technology in
Stockholm and still residents of Sweden. They are Baltzar Carl
von Platen and his roommate and chum at the Institute, Carl
Georg Munters. When about to be graduated from the Institute
in 1922, they cast about for a suitable subject for a graduation
thesis and selected that of artificial refrigeration. While read-

ing the available publications on the subject and conducting experiments for the thesis, they also stumbled upon an application of a phenomenon in physics, according to which, to all appearances, the Electrolux turns "heat into cold." Their discovery became the foundation of a new industry, now well established in the United States, as well as in Sweden. Having no moving parts at all, the refrigerator works in complete silence. For their work the inventors received, in 1925, the Polhem Medal in Sweden and, in 1932, the John Price Wetherill Medal in the United States.

In the field of steam-turbine engineering, several inventors of Swedish birth and training have carried on the work of De Laval, after arriving in the United States. Perhaps the most noteworthy example is the late Oscar Junggren, who was born at Landskrona in 1865. After having been graduated from the Technical School in Malmö four years previously, he came to America in 1889.

"A prolific inventor," said a statement by the General Electric Company of Schenectady, at the time of his death in 1935, "he had some one hundred and thirty patents to his credit, most of which were related to new developments in the steam turbine field. From 1924 to 1932 thirty turbines, each representing a new design and marking an outstanding achievement in the field, were developed under his direction—an average of one new turbine design every four months. During this period not only were turbines of record size developed and put into use, but so many new ideas for improving efficiency were incorporated that at the end more than twice as much electricity could be obtained from the same amount of fuel. The importance of this record is made still more impressive by the fact that according to estimates, nearly half the electric power in the world supplied by steam turbines comes from those manufactured by the General Electric Company under Mr. Junggren's guidance."

He was named an "Associate Edison Pioneer" and in 1931 received the Charles A. Coffin Award as "the designer and creator of large turbine units and especially for his invention of the triple compound turbine, a distinct advance in the art."

The Westinghouse Company also has a Swedish-born and

Swedish-trained engineer and inventor, in charge of the engineering division of its steam-turbine manufacturing plant in Philadelphia. He is Carl Richard Söderberg, born at Ulvöhamn in northern Sweden, in 1895. He was trained at the Chalmers Institute of Technology in Gothenburg and at the Massachusetts Institute of Technology. He joined Westinghouse in 1922. He, too, "has made numerous inventions in connection with steam turbines, particularly those related to devices for balancing very large rotary machinery, spring mountings for machinery subject to vibration, and many features in the design of turbo generator rotors," according to a statement from the Westinghouse Company's office in Pittsburgh. In fact, one of the world's greatest capacity turbines (of 183,000 kw.) for the Philadelphia Electric Company, was built in 1934 under his direction.

Hans P. Dahlstrand, born in 1874, at Bosebo, in the Province of Småland, and a graduate of the Borås Technical School, has been associated, since 1904, with the Allis Chalmers Manufacturing Company of Milwaukee, Wisconsin—a company that also utilizes the Swedish flair for steam-turbine inventions. Dahlstrand has to his credit more than twenty patents on steam-turbine elements, the most important of which relates to cylinder joints and speed governors.

The same company boasts another Swedish-born engineer and inventor, Gustaf L. Kollberg, as manager of its Blower and Compressor Department. He was born in 1878, at Ljusne. He first came to America with his parents, as a small child, but returned at the age of thirteen and attended a technical high school in the Province of Dalarne. He came back to America in 1895 and continued his education in Chicago. He has been associated with the Allis Chalmers Company since 1901 and has participated in the designing and installation of a great number of large triple-expansion and compound-reciprocating pumping engines, built for municipal waterworks in the United States. Some of these machines held the world records for economy for years. He has also designed and built numerous oil-line pumps and pumps for high pressures, covered by several patents.

The Bucyrus-Erie Company of Milwaukee is another large

American concern employing the services of a Swedish engineer and inventor, William Mattsson Bager, born of Swedish parents in Copenhagen, Denmark, but graduated from the Latin School in Lund in 1897, and from the Royal Institute of Technology in Stockholm, as an electrical engineer, in 1900. He emigrated to the United States and, except from 1902 to 1905, has been associated with the same company, of which he now is Vice-President, in charge of sales and engineering. He holds about twenty-eight patents and has others pending. Of those issued "there are four or five that can be considered to be of fundamental importance to the excavating industry inasmuch as they have revolutionized certain phases of excavating machinery construction."

In the metallurgical field, another Swedish specialty, there are so many inventors that it is hopeless to try, even, to list their names. To mention some who might well be called wizards, there are the inventors of the so-called scientific "divining rod," used in the electromagnetic method of locating metal ore, petroleum, and other underground treasures. We refer to Hans Lundberg and Karl Sundberg. Their method is used in the United States as well as other parts of the world, and was first employed in the location of the great gold, silver, and copper deposits at Boliden, Sweden, the finding of which resulted in the growing up of a new industrial community where formerly there was but a barren wilderness. Similar deposits have been discovered by the same "magic" in Lapland and in other parts of Sweden. In Newfoundland, a new lead vein was located at Buchans Mine. Gold deposits have similarly been found in northern Ontario and elsewhere in Canada, so that a new impetus has been given to the search for the earth's hidden riches, giving employment to many men and replenishing the metallic resources of the world.

In the Pittsburgh district, many Swedish-trained engineers and inventors have been identified with the growth of the American steel industry, almost from its beginning. Some of these were the principal engineering collaborators of men like Andrew Carnegie and Charles M. Schwab. A. W. Söderberg, chief mechanical engineer of the Carnegie-Illinois Steel Corporation at the Homestead Steel Works, Munhall, Pennsylvania, "has made several inventions that have benefited the steel industry, principally the Rocking Type Heavy Plate Shear, which eliminates the 'shear bow' or arching of the plate along the cut edge." Ragnar Berg, chief engineer of the Koppers Company, Pittsburgh, is the inventor of a laborsaving device in the coke oven field. He also designed new types of garbage-incinerator furnaces, as well as sewage-disposal plants. Gustav L. Fisk, now a consulting engineer in New York, when chief engineer of the Mesta Machine Company of Pittsburgh, invented numerous modern rolling-mill-machinery units, especially the "Fisk Cooling Bed for Merchant Mill Stock," and another, Martin Hokanson, has many patents on mining machinery and also on refrigerators. Interesting and most valuable inventions and improvements have been made in the handling of metal in molten form. Carl P. Åstrom is the holder of many patents, among which is one on a new type of hot-metal car, of a capacity up to two hundred tons, which makes it possible to keep the metal in molten form for as much as fifteen hours, and to transport it long distances while in that state. To his credit, also, is the invention of a modern cinder car of up to eight hundred cubic feet capacity of liquid slag. The use of this cinder car greatly reduces the cost of removal of such waste products, which really are not wasted, since slag is put to many uses. Johan H. Olson, engineer and inventor, is the holder of patents of still another improved hot-metal car and a so-called "braking mechanism," a compound-air-operated contrivance for retarding and stopping cars. Other well-known contributors to the art of steel fabrication are Casimir von Philp, formerly chief engineer of the Bethlehem Steel Company, whose many inventions aided in improving rolling-mill machinery; Robert Palm, an engineer whose entire life has been given to the construction of open-hearth furnaces and soaking pits; E. W. Michaelson, chief engineer at the Treadwell Company's plant in Easton, Pennsylvania, whose inventions cover rolling mills, coilers, pipe-threading machines, and similar mill machinery; and A. G. Witting, chief engineer of the Illinois Steel Company, known for his valuable contributions to steel-mill equipment. John Brunner, once associated with the Illinois Steel

Company, received, in 1936, the John Ericsson Medal from the American Society of Swedish Engineers, in recognition of his research work in the iron and steel industry, and, particularly, for his perfection of the so-called normalizing steel-treating process, which substantially prolongs the life of railway rails. Hjalmar Carlson of Shrewsbury, Massachusetts, invented new methods of making shells during the War, for which he received, in 1921, the medal of the American Society of Mechanical Engineers and, in 1924, the Holley Medal.

In the American nickel industry, the work of the late Noak Victor Hybinette, born at Falun, Sweden, in 1868, has been of fundamental importance, because of his invention of the electrolytic process for the refining of nickel and its alloying with steel. He, too, was educated in Sweden, and in 1892 he became the general manager of the Oxford Copper Company of Bayonne, New Jersey, which later was absorbed by the great International Nickel Company, of which he became chief metallurgist in 1904. In this capacity, he helped the American nickel production grow from very small beginnings to what it is today. In the fall of 1937, he died at Palermo, Italy.

In the metallurgical field we may also mention the former chief engineer of the Ludlum Steel Company, N. Axel V. Paulson, now associated with the Avesta Steel Works in Sweden, who greatly improved the quality of tool steel.

In all mechanical-precision and mass-production industries, another Swedish name looms large—that of Carl Edward Johansson, widely known as "Precision Johansson," who invented the "Swedish" gauges, due to which the most delicate parts can be made in widely separated plants and then assembled into all types of precision machinery. The blocks are so accurate that, in using them, even the heat of the operator's body has to be allowed for.

Johansson was born in Sweden in 1864. In 1882 he emigrated to America, settling at first in Duluth, Minnesota, where an older brother had preceded him. He worked at several industrial plants in the Northwest and then took a course at the Swedish-American Gustavus Adolphus College at St. Peter, Minnesota. He returned to Sweden and became employed at the rifle works at Eskilstuna, Sweden's "Sheffield," an old head-quarters of fine machine work. On being sent to Germany to inspect the Mauser Rifle Works for the Swedish Government, he began to realize more fully the waste in piece-by-piece construction. He had visions of mass production; but, in order to make that possible, there had to be a uniform standard of measurement, so accurate that all parts made in accordance with it would instantly fit together. For years he worked patiently on this idea, submitting his data to the International Bureau of Weights and Measurements at Paris. When the World War came, he had his reward. To make munitions, it became a vital necessity to have all parts conform to a simple, accurate standard. Among others, the United States Government ordered for its arsenals several sets of the Johansson gauges that had been manufactured at Eskilstuna in Johansson's own plant since 1911; and in 1917, when America joined the War, the Government decreed that the Johansson gauges were to be considered the standard in munition manufacture. In 1918, a subsidiary of the Swedish company was formed in New York, and in 1923, Johansson joined Henry Ford in Dearborn, Michigan, where he has lived ever since, and where he still supervises the production of his gauges, on the understanding that they are not to be withheld from other manufacturers. He has been honored with decorations by both France and Sweden, and in America, in 1932, when he received the John Ericsson Medal from the American Society of Swedish Engineers.

Of other achievements by Swedish-American inventors in the automobile industry, those of Vincent Bendix have had the most marked effect, chiefly because of the Bendix spring, or self-starter clutch, invented by him. In millions of cars this ingenious little metal sleeve has been installed, so that by a mere touch a gasoline motor may be started. Unlike most of the inventors born in Sweden, Bendix did not have the benefit of a technological training, but, like Henry Ford, he tinkered with machinery, bicycles, and motorcycles, until he began to build his own car, which, however, did not make a success. On the other hand, the Bendix spring, the carburetor he later developed, the four-wheel brakes, and other improvements, are

VINCENT BENDIX
INVENTOR AND INDUSTRIALIST

now used in practically all cars. Vincent Bendix was born in 1881 at Moline, Illinois, where his father, John Bendix, a native of Färgeryd in Småland, was a Methodist minister. His mother was born in Östergötland but grew up in Nebraska. Vincent did not take kindly to such formal education as was offered in his native town and, at the age of sixteen, ran away from home, and somehow landed in New York. There he worked as a messenger boy, elevator man in a hospital, private secretary, and railroad machinist. What education he had neglected at home, he tried to make up for by taking night courses in shorthand, telegraphy, and even law. The janitor of the hospital where he ran the elevator is supposed to have introduced him to the mystery of motors and other mechanical things. He then met Glenn Curtiss, who was later a pioneer in aviation, and with him he began to tinker with motorcycles. Next he designed his own car, in which the "Bendix spring," as part of the new self-starter, was introduced. Improvements in the carburetor and the four-wheel brakes followed. Under his guidance the work of many other inventors has been developed, so that the Bendix Development Company is now said to control over 14,000 patents. (For other details about Mr. Bendix, see the chapters on "Aviation" and "Manufacturers.")

Curiously enough, the "Stromberg Carburetor," once known throughout the automobile field, was not invented by Alfred Stromberg himself, but by an employee of the Stromberg Carlson Company—John S. Gullborg, born in Västergötland, in 1863. He had obtained his early training as a mechanic for the Vulcan Match Works at Tidaholm and later at the famous Huskvarna plant in Småland, where he invented an improvement in the manufacture of guns. He came to America in 1886 and in 1898 began the manufacture of telephone instruments, which formed the nucleus of the Swedish-American Telephone Company of Chicago. In 1902 he sold his interest in this concern and joined the Stromberg Carlson firm. The carburetor was completed in 1906 and, to exploit it, the Stromberg Motor Devices Company was formed. While affiliated with this concern, Gullborg made a number of other inventions and improvements on the Company's products. Later, the concern was acquired by Bendix. In 1912 Gullborg completed another invention that became the foundation of another large business, namely, his automatic die-casting machine, on the basis of which the Alemite Die Casting and Manufacturing Company was formed, with Gullborg as president and general manager. Its products, including the famous grease gun for the lubrication of automobiles, are widely used.

Next to the automobile, the radio has most affected life in America in recent years. In this field, too, the Swedish stock has a representative who is recognized as one of the pioneers, if not as a prime inventor, with the rank of a Marconi. He is Ernst Fredrik Verner Alexanderson, consulting engineer of the General Electric Company at Schenectady, New York, and formerly chief engineer of the Radio Corporation of America. Indeed, it was at President Wilson's direct request that the latter company was formed, to preserve, for the United States, the Alexanderson inventions in overseas wireless telegraphy. An offer for its sale to the Marconi Company of England had already been sent by mail, and it was recalled by cable. Close to three hundred United States patents have been issued in Dr. Alexanderson's name. "Descriptions of them would fill a couple of volumes," he says.

Born at Uppsala, Sweden, in 1878, the son of a university professor and a graduate of the Royal Institute of Technology in Stockholm, Alexanderson is still another illustration of the benefit American industry has derived from Swedish technological training. Through his mother, Alexanderson is related to Verner von Heidenstam, the Swedish poet and Nobel Prize winner, which fact may explain his imaginative qualities. After a brief period with the Swedish General Electric Company at Västerås, Alexanderson continued his studies in Germany, and, while there, came across a book called *Alternating Current Phenomena*, by the "wizard" of the American General Electric, the late Charles P. Steinmetz. It so impressed him that, when he emigrated to America in 1902, he went to Schenectady to look up Steinmetz, and through him he got his first job with the General Electric.

"Thanks to the General Electric," he said in a recent testi-

ERNST FREDERIK WERNER
ALEXANDERSON
PIONEER IN WIRELESS, RADIO AND TELEVISION

mony before the Federal Communications Commission, "I have been fortunate enough to have had always enough funds for the work I wished to do."

"Alexanderson has always devoted himself to creative engineering," says a statement by the General Electric Company, "and has shifted his subjects in accordance with the current interest of the times, covering principally railway electrification, high frequency alternators, ship propulsion, radio, television, and power transmission. He worked out a system of regenerative braking by direct current series motors represented in the locomotives of the Chicago, Milwaukee and St. Paul Railroad. He designed the high tension variable-voltage ratio rotary converter used by the New York Edison system, and developed several new methods of operating induction motors at variable speeds, embodied in the design of the electrical equipment for the United States battleship *New Mexico*. A pioneer in television, he developed the first television projector, capable of projecting a picture seven feet square. It was first displayed in a Schenectady theatre in 1930. The directional antenna used in broadcasting to the first Byrd expedition in Little America near the South Pole was designed by him. His invention employing the high power vacuum tube for relaying and modulation is the basis of *all* broadcast transmitters, and his system of tuned radio frequency reception made possible the modern selective receiver, thus solving the problem of interference between numerous transmitting stations."

In other words, it is due to Alexanderson that we can tune in the station wanted on the radio—no small achievement! Among the honors he has received may be mentioned the gold medal of the Institute of Radio Engineers and the John Ericsson Medal of the American Society of Swedish Engineers.

In connection with radio, the names most familiar to the American public are "Stromberg-Carlson," which one sees emblazoned wherever radio sets are sold or advertised. This firm was originally founded in Chicago, to manufacture telephones, by the late Alfred Stromberg and Androv Carlson—both natives of Sweden—in 1894, when they each invested $500 in a partnership. The next year the company incorporated for

$50,000, and in 1901 it was doing more than a million dollars' worth of business. In 1902 it was moved to Rochester, New York, where it is still located.

Alfred Stromberg was born in Stockholm in 1861, and from 1876 to 1885, as an employee of the L. M. Ericsson Company, was one of the pioneers in the telephone industry in Sweden. In the latter year he entered the employ of the Bell Telephone Company in Chicago and made a number of inventions still used by that concern. In 1890 he joined the Chicago Electric Protective Company and then devised what became known as the "Stromberg system" of burglar alarms. Four years later he returned to the telephone-manufacturing field, forming a company with Mr. Carlson (born in the Province of Västergötland in 1854), who had been employed by the Deering Harvester Works, and later by various other concerns, including the Chicago Telephone Company.

Having had over two hundred patents issued in his name, Frank Mossberg of Attleboro, Massachusetts, must be listed as one of the most prolific inventors of Swedish stock in the United States. They cover such subjects as roller bearings, textile machinery, and tools of various kinds. (See the chapter on "Manufacturers.")

In the electrical field there are many Swedish inventors. Sven Robert Bergman, consulting engineer, was formerly in charge of the experimental laboratory of the General Electric Company in Lynn, Massachusetts. He was born in the Province of Skåne, Sweden, in 1877, and was graduated from the Royal Institute of Technology in Stockholm in 1899. He joined the General Electric Company in 1902 and, under its auspices, has developed a number of new types of electric motors, manufactured in large quantities. In 1931, he developed a reinforced high-speed bucket for rayon spinning, capable of making as much as 12,000 revolutions per minute. This invention has eliminated the bursting of such buckets, which used to cause losses to both life and property. In 1915 he received a silver medal at the San Francisco Panama Pacific Exposition, as collaborator in the General Electric exhibits, and in 1934 a certificate of merit from the Charles A. Coffin Foundation for his improvements in rayon-spinning machinery.

The Westinghouse Company of Pittsburgh refers, in its turn, to two engineers of Swedish ancestry at its electric-lamp factory in Bloomfield, New Jersey, who have made notable inventions, Waldemar E. Anderson and Albert Ferdinand Lindstrom. Waldemar E. Anderson, graduate of the Sheffield Scientific School at Yale University, is the "inventor of the Christmas tree indicating lamp," for which the Company's annual award was given him in 1931; and he is the holder of numerous other patents on improvements in incandescent lamps. Albert Ferdinand Lindstrom, born in 1895 at Jamaica, Long Island, is a graduate of Wesleyan University, of the Class of 1917, and received the Company's annual award in 1928 for solving the problem of inside coating of incandescent lamps, which made possible the coloration of bulbs now extensively sold by both the Westinghouse and the General Electric companies.

For the manufacture of electrical control apparatus, more than fifty automatic machines have been invented by Walter S. Freeburg, factory engineer for the Allen-Bradley Company of Milwaukee. He is of Swedish stock, born in 1892 at Lincolnville, Kansas.

In the field of mechanical construction, there are also encountered several Swedish names, such as Carl Gabrielson of Syracuse, New York, chief designer of the L. C. Smith typewriter. Another famous piece of office machinery that is a credit to Swedish inventive versatility is the Sundstrand Adding Machine, now made by the Underwood Elliott Fisher Company at Bridgeport and Hartford, Connecticut. It was invented by two brothers, Gustaf David Sundstrand and Oscar Joseph Sundstrand. They worked together for many years on the adding machine, completing it in 1913, though obtaining their first patent only in 1916. Nine machines were sold in 1914, all made by hand. After 1915 the older brother devoted most of his time to the designing and patenting of machine tools, particularly the "Sundstrand Stub Lathe," still made in Rockford by the Sundstrand Machine Tool Company, while Oscar continued to develop the adding machine, and contrived the still more ingenious accounting and bookkeeping machines now used in many large offices. The Underwood Elliott Fisher Company acquired the Sundstrand adding machine in 1927.

In American transportation there have likewise been several inventors of Swedish ancestry. Carl J. Mellin, born in 1851 at Hagelborg in the Province of Västergötland, not only had charge of the design and construction of the triple-expansion engines for the United States battleship *Texas*, which initiated a new era in ship propulsion, and of the dynamite-gun machinery for the United States cruiser *Vesuvius*, and its turret and gun-operating gear, which was the beginning of machine-controlled firing, but also, as chief engineer of the Richmond Locomotive Works at Richmond, Virginia, designed various kinds of compound locomotives, which so greatly increased the pulling capacity of locomotives that he may be said to have laid the groundwork for a new period in American railroad history. For his new type of locomotive, he received the highest award at the Pan-American Exposition at Buffalo in 1901 and a gold medal at the St. Louis Exposition in 1904. In 1902 he became consulting engineer for the newly formed American Locomotive Company at Schenectady, New York, where he died in 1924.

Another engineer of Swedish stock, whose inventions have materially affected American railroads, is Karl F. Elers, now a consulting engineer of Pittsburgh, but formerly connected with the Westinghouse Company. He has designed various pieces of equipment used by the principal railroads, such as a flexible gear and flexible drive, which have a cushioning effect on the starting and stopping of trains, as well as on the jolts resulting from bad track conditions. This type of gear is also used on most electric locomotives and has helped greatly to reduce operating costs. It has also been found valuable in other kinds of heavy machinery such as that found in steel mills; and it is used for the operation of the locks of the Panama Canal.

Many parts of American-railroad rolling stock have been designed by Charles Lindstrom, for many years connected with the Pennsylvania Railroad, and later chief engineer for the Pressed Steel Car Company. He invented the Lindstrom hand brake, which was made the standard equipment of all Pennsylvania railroad cars, and later introduced on many other roads.

Gustave Fast of Baltimore is the inventor of a system of power-transmission gearing, which was used in the reduction gears connecting the steam turbine with the propellers in the famous eagle boats that the Ford Company built for the United States Navy during the World War. The system has been used in many other instances in which a noiseless, highly efficient power transmission is required. Mr. Fast has also invented a self-aligning coupling, used on steam turbines and in steel mills, where high speeds and great power capacities are required, and also "oil film bearings" and special couplings for Diesel engines. C. W. Larson, one of the pioneer engineers of the General Electric Company, was a noted designer of mining and industrial locomotives. The locomotives now used at the Panama Canal for pulling the ships through the locks are of his design.

Of important influence in certain phases of the cement industry have been the inventions of Karl P. Billner, a native of the Province of Skåne and a graduate of the Chalmers Institute of Gothenburg. First a designer of cement bridges across the Columbia River on the West Coast, he next entered the field of aerocrete, a porous, lightweight mixture for floors, originally developed in Sweden, and then invented "vacuum" concrete, a mixture from which the excess moisture is extracted by means of vacuum pumps. This new type of concrete is now being developed along a number of lines, and may become of considerable importance in future building construction, which bids fair to become the leading industry in the next generation.

A remarkable inventor, so versatile that he may not be classified under any one head, is W. B. Bronander of North Arlington, New Jersey. He was born in 1889 at Lidköping, in the Province of Västergötland, where he also received his early education. After his arrival in this country, in 1907, he completed his studies at the Pratt Institute in Brooklyn. He has to his credit about 150 patents. They cover, among other things, machines for making cigarettes and cigars, and for packing, wrapping, labeling, treasury stamping, etc. Other patents refer to the manufacturing of textiles, such as silk and rayon, and to the weighting, dyeing, and finishing of silk products. Still others represent mechanical-drive movements, self-aligning roller bearings for railroad service, and reduction gearing. Other patents cover the modern opposed-piston-arrangement for Diesel engines, especially as used for aeronautical service. Further, he holds a group of twenty-five patents in the safety-appliance field, such as fire-extinguisher apparatus and, last but not least, the track-joint tester that has done invaluable service in making the roadbed safe for the modern high-speed trains.

Finally, mention should be made of the man whose invention is a product now so widely used that it rivals in popularity the humble, yet indispensable, common button—Gideon Sundbäck, inventor of the zipper fastener. Sundbäck was born on April 24, 1880, in Ödestugu Parish, Province of Småland, Sweden. After preliminary education in Sweden, he studied electrical engineering at the Polytechnical Institute at Bingen on the Rhine, from which he was graduated in 1903. Shortly afterwards he came to this country and was employed, first by the Westinghouse Electric and Manufacturing Company in Pittsburgh, and later, in 1906, by the Automatic Hook and Eye Company, in Hoboken. While in charge of this company's engineering and development work, he improved the slide fastener of those days. After seven years' work he produced, in 1913, a new type of fastener, the present zipper, together with automatic machinery for its manufacture. Basing its prospects on Sundbäck's invention, a new company, the Hookless Fastener Company (since 1937 called Talon Incorporated), was organized. It took over the assets of the former company and then began manufacturing the incomparable zipper. Sundbäck became its chief engineer, with headquarters in Meadville, Pennsylvania. He remained in that capacity until 1925 and is now its consulting engineer, holding also various offices in foreign allied companies.

Engineers

LAWRENCE E. WIDMARK

Mr. Widmark is a native of Hälsingborg in Sweden, and a graduate of the Chalmers Technical Institute of Gothenburg. Since 1916 he has been connected with the Star Electric Motor Company of Bloomfield, New Jersey, and is now its chief engineer. He has made inventions in electric-welding circuits and voltage regulations of alternators, and is the author of a book, *Industrial Autarchy.*

Sources of Engineering Spirit

IT seems that the Scandinavian people, from time immemorial, always have taken a keen interest in Nature and her ways and workings. This interest has not, as a rule, been of the dreamy and contemplative kind, but rather, robust and practical. We find these traits already manifested in the mythology of the North, which even stages Creation as an engineering feat, including the use of laborsaving devices, under the progress of which "the stream that flows from the source of wisdom" is employed to drive a water wheel supplying the needed power.

There are many reasons for this make-up of the national pattern. The goddess of Nature of the North is neither too generous and easy going with her children, so as to raise them to become spoiled weaklings, nor severe and awe-inspiring enough to take away the spirit of enterprise and achievement. The result has been, as observed by Van Loon:

There are countries in which Man has submitted to the dictates of Nature until he has become her abject slave, and there are countries where Man has destroyed Nature so completely that he has lost all touch with that great living mother who forever must be the beginning and end of all things. And finally there are those where Man and Nature have learned to understand and appreciate each other and have agreed to compromise for their mutual benefit. If you want an example of the latter go North and visit the three Scandinavian countries.

Engineering, the art of making Nature your servant or, rather, your friendly collaborator, is especially favored by conditions in a country like Sweden, that knows of little or no servitude or serfdom. In countries where the press of the surplus population forces down the value of man and his labor to the vanishing point, there is scant need of saving human sweat; but where this is not the case, higher and higher value will be put on the services of human beings; and it will be increasingly important to find ways and means of making human effort as effective as possible, through means of tools and machines.

In the history of Sweden, the technical influence is very pronounced. We thus find that participating in a Viking adventure was, to a great extent, a matter of superior naval architecture. Later on, the struggle for national and political freedom was won by the resourcefulness and stamina of the miners and ironmakers of central Sweden. Subsequently, it so happened that the copper and iron industry provided the means behind a military prowess that suddenly lifted Sweden to the position of a leading power in Europe, until she, under Charles XII, learned the lesson that wars do not pay; and, after that, with only brief interruptions, Sweden has been engaged solely in the pursuit of the gentler arts of peace.

The technical inclination of the sons of Sweden, aside from the considerations already taken into account, can also be traced to the high standing of the handicrafts and other forms of industrial arts among the rural population. The peasants, during the long winter and fall evenings, busied themselves with all kinds of useful handicraft; and so a craftsmanship and a form of industry were developed, which were of no mean value or significance. In most European countries, such industries have been subjected to the monopoly of the guilds of the cities, but in a sparsely populated country like Sweden, this system could never be enforced. While most of this craftsmanship was directed toward supplying implements for the home and for agricultural needs, there was also a variety of more or less complicated machinery, to be built for the spinning and weaving done in every homestead. And there was, finally, engineering work of greater scope to be tackled—harnessing the water-power for the driving of plants and sawmills, as well as the spanning of the waterways, by sometimes imposing bridges.

Industries concentrated in cities were, in the earlier days, not of sufficient magnitude to influence very much the making up of national technical conditions. Whatever this city craft amounted to, it suffered a certain German dominance with the rest of the city life. The Walloon craftsmen, also, who were induced to settle in Sweden during the reign of Gustavus Adolphus, had considerable influence on the technical development.

The International Engineer

IF we are thus able to trace the origin and influence of the engineering spirit of the Swedish people through the ages, it seems to be an accepted rule to wait until the middle of the eighteenth century, before recognizing the existence of the individual profession of civil engineering; i.e., nonmilitary engineering. It has been said that it is not possible to give a better definition of its aims and functions than the one contained in the charter of the Institute of Civil Engineers (London, 1828), where civil engineering is described as "the art of directing the great sources of power in Nature for the use and convenience of Man, as the means of production and of traffic in states, both for external and internal trade. . . ."

The Swedish technical men who have left home and homeland, to engage in engineering work all over the globe, fall under the given definition, though they more appropriately could be called "international engineers."

In the world of today, where self-sufficiency and a narrow nationalism are rampant nearly everywhere, the motives that lead up to the business of being an international engineer might well be analyzed and appraised. Is it the lure of gold or other riches that causes a man to leave his native country and spend the rest of his life in some remote part of the globe, enjoying and gloating over an ever-increasing hoard of accumulated wealth? No! It is hardly that. A man, born with the inclination and capacity for solving technical problems, would never be truly satisfied until he reached the proper field of activity for his particular capability. If this were not available in his own country, he had to seek it outside of its border. In all probability, he will thereby do more honor to his native country than if he had stayed at home and languished in surroundings that did not require the very service which he was best able to render.

The Pioneers

THE saga of the Swedes as international engineers starts, significantly enough, with John Ericsson who, in the year 1826, moved to England, and soon became one of the leaders of engineering thought and invention during this time of greatness of English industrial history. During a few hectic years, he turned out invention after invention pertaining to engines, locomotives, steam propulsion, etc.; and in the year 1839 he moved to America, from which time Swedish engineering activities in America can be considered as having had their beginning.

For quite a few years thereafter, the internationally minded Swedish engineer turned to, and stayed in, England. During the years from 1860 to 1875, we note an interesting group consisting of, among others, C. P. Sandberg, instrumental in the development of the international standard for railroad rails; Gjers, collaborator in the great discoveries of Bessemer; H. W. Widmark, chief designer of the Avonside Locomotive Works, which supplied the world with locomotives, and Theodore Nordenfelt, who can be considered the founder of the giant Vickers and Maxim Works.

This general trend of engineering emigration toward England has one notable exception; i.e., the eventful exodus of the Nobel family toward Russia, where it came to influence the oil and high-explosive industries, in a way comparable only to that of the families of Rockefeller and duPont, here in America.

At the beginning and at the end of the above period, two political events had taken place that had a profound influence, not only on the political conditions and issues involved, but also in the world of industry. The one was the Civil War, the other, the Franco-Prussian War.

The Civil War was, in reality, the first modern war; and it is only fair to say that previously the technical weapons used were of a rather innocent nature. Two Swedish engineers, Dahl-

gren and Ericsson, stand as the precursors of the armaments
of modern times. From Dahlgren on, guns became cannon,
from having been merely popguns, and Ericsson inaugurated
a line of design that is still being elaborated upon in the latest
and mightiest of dreadnoughts. The outcome of the war—or
whatever the reason—called great forces of activity to life in
America, and caused her to welcome a European participation
in the development of its enormous resources, in which the
Scandinavian countries were to play a very important part.
While this was going on, the British technical- and commer-
cial-world hegemony started to decline, especially after the ascendancy of the German world-embracing trade, short-lived
though it was. (See "Soldiers and Sailors.")

During the same period Sweden was, in many respects, a pioneer country for modern technical ways and methods. The
Swedish match industry is one of the earliest examples of automatic mass production for a world-wide consumption. The development and organization of the vast industrial empire of
forest industries in Norrland also took place during this time.
The old iron and steel industries provided the testing grounds
for modern methods in iron- and steelmaking. While Sweden
lost her old supremacy in quantity production of iron and steel,
she still retained her position from the quality point of view.

Through these years we find only a sprinkling of Swedish
engineers in America, until the year 1880, but after this time
they make their influence felt throughout all branches of the
American engineering world.

From the Record

IN the present day, engineers of Swedish parentage form such
an integral component of American technical and industrial
life that it would be well-nigh impossible to find a large American concern without the traditional Swedish interlacing in the
technical staff of the organization. To do everyone justice, or
even to try to arrange an adequate record of the varied accomplishments and enterprises involved, would be too great a task
to be attempted in this account. We will, however, make a short
analysis of the branches of engineering which have attracted
most Swedish engineers, and give some orientating illustrations

in connection herewith, while at the same time stressing the fact that the engineering record in its entirety concerns everyone of Swedish parentage who, with brain and hand, slide rule or compass, with or without singular success, but always with loyalty and devotion, has taken part in the engineering work in this, their adopted land. (See the chapter on "Inventors.")

The mining and metallurgical fields, as could be expected, have had a special drawing power on the sons of a land with such pronounced mining and ironmaking traditions as Sweden; and we certainly do find them in the steel, ironmaking, and mining fields, in all capacities, from that of loading organizer or creative metallurgist, down to lesser positions! Among the organizers should be noted Thorsten Berg, picked by Andrew Carnegie as chief engineer for the Homestead Works; and, among the metallurgists, Victor Hybinette, whose discoveries relating to the production of nickel made this radiant metal available for its present extensive use. Hans Lundberg has, in mining proper, transformed the happy-go-lucky methods of prospecting into an exact science, where the exactness of the electric indicator has forever banished the mystery of the divining rod. The late J. E. Fries was for many years the chief engineer of the Tennessee Coal, Iron and Railroad Company, and as such was active in steel making at Birmingham, Alabama.

There is one thing the good Swedes did not have at home— black diamonds. This lack in their resources has, however, made them particularly keen in detecting new ways of saving fuel, or getting the highest possible output from all power installations. Thus we find them as efficient designers of all kinds of power-development plants and related equipment: boilers; engines; pumps; turbines; etc. Especially when it comes to turbines, they do not fail to live up to the great traditions inaugurated by the achievements, in Sweden, of men like De Laval and the brothers Ljungström. As a matter of fact, for the last ten or fifteen years, the leading turbine builders in this country have been of Swedish birth, as witnessed by the names of Junggren, Hans Dahlstrand, and R. Söderberg. Among builders of giant boiler plants, there appears the name of H. J. E. Banck and, as chief engineer for America's largest pump works, another member of the family of De Laval.

Turning to the railroad transportation field, one recalls the name of C. J. Mellin, who was chief engineer of American Locomotive Works, and whose optimistic dictum, "Yes, one will find surprisingly few things that are impossible to do," deserves to stand as a motto for engineering at large.

In the realm of automobilism and aviation, the name of Vincent Bendix, born of Swedish parents, is by far the most remarkable. His story shows the force of a clever idea, simple in itself, but of such a driving power that it is now embodied in practically every motor car on the globe. Mr. Bendix is one of the few inventors who has been fortunate enough to fully enjoy the fruits of his genius, which made him the ruler in a veritable industrial empire, in the automobile and aviation fields.

Is it, perchance, a reminiscence of the military precision and discipline of bygone days that makes Swedes so prominent in the exacting tool and toolmaking-machinery lines? At any rate, they have had a profound influence in the course of this industry in America, and many a Swedish engineer's name stands for products that have become household words of the mechanical industry as, for instance, the names of Sundstrand, Mossberg, and F. W. Hansson. To cap it all, the modern ultraprecision in the mechanical field owes no trifling debt to the ways and methods that were developed in the old Swedish rifle factory at Eskilstuna, Sweden. The master mechanic there, C. E. Johansson, had developed a technique of exactitude that, for years, was something of a visionary mystery, until it finally was accepted by the whole engineering world as a highly practical thing that bids fair to account for the possibility of present-day mass production of interchangeable parts.

The virtues of precision and exactness are, however, of varied importance in different engineering pursuits. There are even phases of engineering where too much accentuation on preciseness would prove detrimental to a successful dealing with the problems under hand. In many respects, successful engineering consists of effecting a judicious approach to exact principles, rather than a blind insistence upon exactitude. It seems that the Swede, by birth and education, has a leaning toward the side of accuracy and definiteness, and that the blending of these qualities with the American spirit, embodying a somewhat cheerful abandon of too strict rules and abstract principles, has tended to produce a type of engineer in whom these features are happily balanced.

America is the land that created electrical engineering. It must, in all fairness, be said that she has given to the rest of the world immensely more in this branch of engineering than she ever received in exchange. Swedish engineers have, however, participated from the early beginning and the name of Jonas Wenström, in Sweden, ranks among the great world pioneers. Over here we note among the first practitioners of the new field, Fred Lundell. E. J. Berg participated in the building of the theoretical structure behind the practical developments of the industry's coming of age. The most renowned names, in later days, are those of E. F. W. Alexanderson, of world-wide fame as an inventor and leader in wireless telegraphy and radio, and David L. Lindquist, known for his achievements in the electric-elevator field which, incidentally, has had so much to do in making possible the bold sky lines of our cities. As guiding spirits of a number of minor independent concerns, Swedish engineers have exerted an influence, on the industry as a whole, that should not be underestimated.

Behind all involved and intrinsic machinery, there lies the faculty of some brains to visualize, grasp, and follow complicated movements by sheer mental processes. This is a rare natural gift, not likely to be developed by studies and schooling. We find a great number of Swedish technical men of this type connected with the development of automatic machinery of various kinds, and with the employment of such automatic movements in the manufacturing of metallic articles. It seems, also, that a certain business acumen follows this kind of technical mind, as a great many independent businesses are owned and managed by these craftsmen. Among such men are noted W. Bronander, C. A. Eck, G. Fast, E. E. Hollander and P. Wiberg.

In chemistry we meet Jean Skoglund, whose contributions to the manufacture of high explosives centered upon the problem of making explosives less dangerous under transportation and, therefore, was of tremendous importance for America's participation in the World War. The name of Emil F. Johnson is connected with the introduction of an effective milk control for the teeming millions of New York City.

The business of dealing with the surface of the earth—civil engineering proper—is probably the oldest branch of engineering activity, and certainly the one that carries the heaviest responsibility. It is rather natural that the individual engineers are, in most cases, completely submerged by the greatness of the work, that requires complete teamwork more than anything else. Now and then there is a name that rises to claim recognition. Such a name is that of John F. Anderson, civil engineer and contractor on a large scale. His busy life spanned all the activities of civil engineering, and his work was of such a recognized value that Congress, by a special act, conferred upon him his citizenship "as if born an American."

Among builders one might also include "builders of building materials," and here we meet J. G. Bergquist, who made over useless slag into cement; B. G. Dahlberg, who caused the reincarnating of the refuse from sugar cane to heat-retaining material used in walls; and also K. P. Billner, known for his revolutionary way of dealing with cement.

We will end our roster of outstanding Swedish engineers with the name of John E. Ericson, who as City Engineer of Chicago was responsible for the modernizing of the water supply system and the construction of freight tunnels.

It would not be fitting to conclude this study of Swedish engineering activities in America without a tribute to, or an expression of recognition of and gratitude for, all that America has offered to and meant for the Swedish engineers who have chosen to make it their home. It has given them a generous welcome in unstinted opportunities, without bias or discrimination. It has shown them the sheer joy and delight that, as a rule, characterizes engineering over here, and a technical spirit, freer from strait-laced conventions than anywhere else in the world. The medal has, of course, its reverse side, and the struggle for existence might, at times, be bitter and hard; but, taken all in all, these Swedes are here, not for mercenary reasons, but because they *feel at home here.*

Architects and Builders

C. THEODORE LARSON

Mr. Larson is a native of Kansas City, Missouri, where his father, Peter Larson, who was born in Sweden, has done much building, having been in charge, among other things, of the construction activities sponsored by the late Col. William R. Nelson, founder of the Kansas City *Star,* as demonstrations of civic progress. He himself is a graduate of Harvard College, Class of 1925, and holds, in addition, the degree of Master in Architecture from the Harvard Graduate School. In 1929, he was awarded the Nelson Robinson, Jr., traveling fellowship, for the study of architecture in northern Europe and the Mediterranean countries. Since that time he has been on the staff of the *Architectural Record* in New York, and is now an editor of that magazine. For some of the material on architects in this chapter, he is indebted to Francis J. Plym of Niles, Michigan, President of the Swedish American Tercentenary Association, who holds a degree in architecture from the University of Illinois, and, for some of the information on builders, to *The Swedish Element in America* (Chicago, 1931).

AMERICAN architecture is much like the American people, an admixture of forces brought together from many different sources, and fused into something that has its own dynamic quality of growth and change. Just as the Swedish immigrants have been absorbed into the American environment, so also have the technical skills, which they brought with them from the old homeland, become part of the American architectural tradition, which expresses itself in the continuous improvement of building technique and the unceasing development of new structural forms, to meet the needs of a rapidly evolving new nation.

This tradition in American architecture traces back, in part, to the Swedes who came to the Delaware Valley in 1638. They found an abundance of timber, and, having been expert woodsmen in their native land, were not slow to make use of this material in building their new houses. Some historians assert that the log cabin, which became the distinctive mark of the American frontier, had its origin in the work of these early Swedes.

As Fiske Kimball, Director of the Pennsylvania Museum of Art in Philadelphia, states in his book, *American Architecture* (1928):

The log house, of horizontal logs notched together at the corners and chinked with clay, which has been ignorantly assumed to have been borrowed from the aborigines by the first settlers, was unknown either to the Indians or to the English colonists. It seems to have been brought in from the Continent by the Swedes of the Delaware, the first settlers from northern Europe, where it was known also by the Swiss and Germans who followed.

The claim, that the Swedes were the first to introduce the log house to this country, has not been fully established, however. There is still some doubt as to priority. But this controversy is beside the point, for the significant contribution of the early Swedes was their skill in using timber. They knew how to fell trees, cut them into logs, square and notch them, and assemble them into dwellings. By comparison, the "English wigwams," as the early chroniclers called the shelters built by the colonists at Jamestown and Plymouth, were frail constructions of slanting poles, covered with brush, reeds, and earth, perhaps over a low wall of stakes and wattle plastered with clay. The superior strength of the dwellings at New Sweden commended itself to the English, and the Swedish technique of building log houses was soon adopted. (This tradition of expertness in carpentry and wood construction continues on to the present day, as shown by the fact that the English, in seeking a solution for their current housing problems, again find inspiration in dwellings developed by Swedish craftsmen. Recently a group of timber houses, designed by Cyril Sjöström, has been erected experimentally by the Ministry of Health on a site in Glasgow. The houses were presented to the Scottish Government by the Swedish Government and the Swedish Coöperative Building Association, jointly.)

Wood was not the only material used by the Swedes in the Delaware colony. Brick or stone for structural walls became quite common; and some of the buildings, notably the churches at Wilmington and Philadelphia, survive to this day. The mansion of Governor Printz on Tinicum Island, in the Delaware

River just below Philadelphia, where the Corinthian Yacht Club is now located, was a two-story affair, perhaps similar to the ancestral home of the Governor, in the province of Småland. Some of the bricks for the fireplace are supposed to have been brought across the Atlantic, and contemporary records describe the house as both ornately decorated and imposing. Built of logs, its interior was fitted with dressed lumber. After a fire it was rebuilt, and, though the structure itself has long since vanished, the foundations have been recently identified by excavations. There are also a few farmhouses in the Delaware region, which date back to the Swedish colonial period.

We have no record of any other specific architectural influence exerted by the Swedish colonists, for these pioneers soon lost cultural contact with their home country, and were merged with the other nationalities in America. However, as workers, and probably as designers, they undoubtedly contributed much to the creation of the domestic architecture we find in the Delaware Valley. Philadelphia, in particular, is rich in late seventeenth-century designs, and it is quite logical that craftsmen, builders, and even architects, of at least mixed-Swedish ancestry, should have participated in this work.

Later immigrants to this country placed even less emphasis on a stylistic architectural tie with the old homeland. Their churches, for instance, seldom suggested Swedish models, whereas the colonial churches on the Delaware did. Although they were usually expert in the use of saws, axes, augers, planes, and chisels, the newcomers were, for the most part, poor, and of little academic training in æsthetics. They were, therefore, hardly conscious of any architectural style, but only of the need for adequate shelter and comfort. It is this realistic attitude toward building, this emphasis on doing the most with the least, which explains, however, the gradual emergence of a truly indigenous and vigorous new American architecture.

The adaptability of the pioneers is shown, also, by the way they built their homes on the prairies west of the Missouri River. Timber, stone, and brick were not easily obtainable. Finding no familiar resources at hand, the settlers, many of whom came from England, Germany, and Russia, as well as the

Scandinavian countries, resorted to the use of sod from the prairies. One turf was placed on top of another, until the desired wall height was obtained. A heavy ridgepole spanned the gables; other poles and, finally, a cover of sod and dirt completed the roof. These sod houses were not only warm in winter, but also cool in summer. Like the early adobe buildings of the Southwest, they endured for at least a generation, or until the settlers prospered enough to afford better homes. There are early Swedish immigrants still living who for years, when they first arrived in the United States, inhabited such structures. In the Rockies and on the Pacific coast, the early Swedes used the customary log houses. In the settlements on the south Pacific coast, they adapted even the Spanish adobe cabin.

The majority of Swedes coming to America, though rich in health and ambition, had to start from humble beginnings. Their first importance in the building field was as carpenters or bricklayers. With an instinct for building, they soon branched out, becoming adept, not only in general construction, but also in fabricating materials and tools for building (see the chapter on "Inventors"). They also became quickly versed in the economics of a new country in which the people had to be self-sustaining. With this social and economic background, it is not surprising that many Swedish immigrants developed into builders of houses, even though they often had had no special training before coming to this country. Gradually some of these became general contractors, responsible for the construction of large building projects.

For these reasons, it is natural that the builders of Swedish descent should have come into prominence, before the architects. It is natural, also, that building constructors, operating on a large scale, should first appear in Chicago, helping rebuild the city after its great fire. The elevator and the use of iron in construction had been introduced in the 'seventies, and these innovations now made possible the progressive development of the tall, towering buildings, which characterize so largely the American architecture of today. Technically, the skyscrapers represent no new principle in design, other than that of piling floor on floor, with the sky as the limit. More significant in the light of future architectural development is the large-scale, organizational procedure which permitted their erection at unprecedented speed, in the most crowded metropolitan areas. In this respect, the Swedish builders have contributed notably to American architecture, while Swedish carpenters and housebuilders are to be found in almost every American community. It is when we turn to Chicago that we find men of Swedish ancestry, who organized companies that have constructed the finest and largest buildings. In fact, for a time they virtually dominated the field.

As a first example, we may take the late Andrew Lanquist, in whose memory a special builders' and manufacturers' room was dedicated at the American Swedish Historical Museum in Philadelphia, on June 27, 1937. Former Congressman Carl R. Chindblom of Illinois said, on that occasion:

In his long career in Chicago, Mr. Lanquist devoted himself almost exclusively to building construction and related interests and became easily the outstanding leader in the large group of building contractors of Swedish birth or descent who are said to have created modern Chicago in the erection of buildings, running from factory plants, skyscrapers and apartment buildings to private houses, bungalows, garages and gasoline stations.

Born in 1856 at Ving, in the province of Västergötland, Sweden, Mr. Lanquist obtained a limited general education, including some knowledge of the English language and also some technical training. He spent his school vacations in work on buildings and during this time he developed into a proficient building mechanic, including the work of brick-laying. For five years prior to 1881 he was employed in the engineering department of the State Railways in Sweden and worked under one Major Franklin, an engineer in the Swedish army, upon a new railroad line from Stockholm to the Norwegian border at Storlien. He himself said that during these years he lived six months on horseback and six months on skis.

At 25 years of age he decided to seek his fortune in the New World, and came to Chicago in 1881. He once said that he arrived in Chicago with $3.00 in his pocket and the following day got a job as bricklayer at 11 cents per hour. He soon obtained employment, however, in building way stations for the Chicago, Western and Indiana Railroad and because of his unusual efficiency he not only received more than the usual compensation but upon showing his understanding of plans and specifications, he was soon appointed foreman or superintendent of construction.

In 1883 he began building operations in Chicago on his own account and in 1904 organized and became president of Lanquist & Illsley Company which soon became known as one of the leading building contracting organizations in Chicago. Among the buildings which were erected under Mr. Lanquist's leadership and superintendence were the Commonwealth Edison Building, the People's Gas Building, the Railway Exchange, the Mallers Building, the Kesner Building, the Majestic, North American and Kimball Buildings, the Y.M.C.A. Hotel, the State Bank Building, the Wrigley Buildings, the Crane Company Building, and the Marshall Field & Company Men's Building, all in Chicago, and the United States Steel Company buildings at Gary, Indiana, where his operations continued from 1906 to 1910. As early as 1891, Mr. Lanquist erected the first *real* skyscraper in Chicago, the Monon Building.

He also erected, outside of Chicago, such outstanding structures as the Marine National Bank Building in Buffalo, the First National Bank and Bell Telephone Company buildings in Milwaukee, the Whitney Building, the Stroh Building, the Real Estate Exchange Building, the Bok Building and the Dime Savings Bank Building in Detroit, the Bell Telephone and the First National Bank buildings in Omaha, the Memphis Trust Building in Memphis, the Bell Telephone Building in Minneapolis, the Allsworth and St. Louis County Court House in Duluth, the Wrigley Field Base Ball Park in Los Angeles, two large buildings for the glass industry in Toledo, and many others. The contracts for these buildings frequently involved amounts of five million to ten million dollars each. In many instances no bond or security was required beyond Mr. Lanquist's personal responsibility.

Associated with Mr. Lanquist at various times were the two brothers Ericsson, Henry and John E., both born at Moheda in the Province of Småland. In addition to being prominent builders of big office structures, banks, theaters, schools, and other public buildings, the brothers have also served as building

commissioners of Chicago, both being appointed by Democratic
mayors; Henry as far back as 1911 by Carter Harrison, and
John E. in 1931, by Anton J. Cermak.

Henry, who was twenty years old when he arrived in Chicago
in 1881, had had some technical as well as practical education
in Stockholm, and, after working as a carpenter in various
Chicago suburbs, became acquainted with Andrew Lanquist
when the latter was still a bricklayer. The next year, 1882, they
formed a partnership, and their first contract was that of re-
modeling an old church, on Polk Street in Chicago, into a terminal for the Chicago, Western Indiana Railroad. Later they
put up schools, apartment houses, office buildings, and factories.
In 1891, they were associated on the Monon Building, the early
Chicago skyscraper. In 1897, they separated, and each found
new partners. Among the important Chicago buildings put up
by Henry Ericsson, or by companies with which he was connected, are, besides the Monon, the Manhattan, the Harvester,
the Gossard, the Twentieth-Century, the Liquid Carbonic, the
Morton, the City Hall Square, the Garland, the Conway, the
Bloom and the Pittsfield buildings, the buildings of the Illinois
Merchants Bank, and the Chicago Trust Company, the Cort
and Roosevelt Theatres, various important factories and warehouses, thirty-six public schools, and hundreds of other structures. Finally, during the World War, the Ericsson Company
built the famous Camp Grant at Rockford, Illinois, which called
for an original outlay of $8,000,000. For six years Mr. Erics-
son served as President of the Building Construction Employers Association, and many other honors, both professional and
civic, have been bestowed on this former Swedish immigrant. He
has, literally, not only seen Chicago grow up but has materially
helped to form its appearance.

His younger brother, John E., came with his parents to the
remote regions of Minnesota, when he was but sixteen years old,
and, after three years of farm work, went to Chicago in 1884,
and began to learn how to lay bricks. Next, he became a foreman and then a superintendent; and in 1902 he formed a
contracting firm with his brother Henry. In 1906 he joined the
Lanquist & Illsey Company, and in 1919 organized his own
firm and continued building construction on a large scale.

Equally widespread have been the operations of Nils Persson Severin, who had had some practical experience as a builder in the Province of Skåne, where he was born in 1861, before he came to Chicago in 1888. Among other things, he had built a Baptist chapel, and a home for himself. Having left his young wife and small son in Sweden, he had another new home ready for them in Chicago, when they arrived the following year. Launching out as a contractor for himself almost immediately, Mr. Severin erected literally hundreds of buildings, including notable private residences in the Chicago suburbs, schools, churches—among others, the $350,000 Presbyterian Church of Evanston, Illinois; the New Haven Junior High School; the Masonic Temple and the Y.M.C.A. Building of the same city; a group of veteran-hospital buildings in Alexandria, Louisiana; the marine hospitals of Seattle, Washington, Portland, Oregon, Walla Walla, Washington, Tupper Lake, New York, Dallas, Texas, Duluth, Minnesota, and Denver, Colorado. Mr. Severin built the post office and customhouse in Honolulu; the Capitol Building in Juneau, Alaska; the $3,000,000 post office in Baltimore, the $1,000,000 post office in Scranton, Pennsylvania; the Federal Building at Toledo, Ohio; the post office building in Springfield, Massachusetts; the $5,000,000 post office building in Boston; the Federal Building at Albuquerque, New Mexico; and, finally, the connecting part of the Arlington Memorial Bridge at Washington, D.C., a $15,000,000 structure. In 1927 his firm obtained the contract for the remodeling of the White House itself, for which only specially qualified firms were allowed to bid. This work Mr. Severin supervised personally, and upon its completion was received, together with his son Alfred, by President Coolidge himself. They had a long chat about the White House and its various structural changes.

Residential development in Chicago a generation ago was stimulated by the skill and energy of Louis M. Nelson, who had come from Värmland, as a small boy, in 1882, and at the age of twenty-three began his career as a building contractor. He built hundreds, and perhaps thousands, of homes in new subdivisions in Chicago suburbs, and developed high-grade commercial property as well. His extensive philanthropy has reached even to his birthplace in Sunne, Värmland, where a children's hospital has been erected, and is being maintained, largely through his efforts, assisted by former residents of Sunne, now living in America.

Many notable Chicago structures, theaters, hotels, banks, apartment houses, as well as private houses, have been built by Eric E. Skoglund, who, like Louis M. Nelson, is a native of central Sweden, the Province of Närke. At the age of nineteen he arrived in Chicago, in 1897, just before the Spanish-American War, when Chicago was on the eve of its greatest expansion. In Sweden, his father had been a stonecutter and, after getting some education in architecture and structural engineering, the son began his career in Chicago, also as a stonecutter. In a few years, however, he was a building contractor, first in partnership with his older brother, and later alone. Among the buildings which he, or his firms, have erected, are the Apollo Theatre; the Illinois Telephone Building; the Lake View Trust and Savings Bank Building; the Sheridan Road Building, containing 130 apartments; the famous Edgewater Beach Hotel, also on Sheridan Road; the Orrington Hotel at Evanston; the Wesley Foundation Building at Champaign, Illinois; and many others.

Another Chicago builder of apartment houses, hotels, and business structures, the total value of which runs into many millions of dollars, is Adolph Lindstrom of Wilmette, Illinois. He is a native of the Province of Västergötland, and came to Chicago in 1901, at the age of seventeen. He is reported to have had in his employ, at various times, as many as ten thousand Swedish carpenters and masons. Among the prominent buildings he has erected are the McCormick Hotel; the DeWitt Apartments; the Whitehall Apartments; and the Chicago *Daily News* building.

Hospitals have been the specialty of the Erik P. Strandbergs, senior and junior, who have also built the Bankers Life Insurance Building and the Cloister Building, containing eighty-four apartments, and the American Swedish Historical Museum at Philadelphia. The list of hospitals includes the New Augustana Hospital in Chicago, and its nurses' home; the St. Luke's Hospital; the Englewood Hospital; the German Deaconess

Hospital; and the Norwegian Deaconess Hospital. Strandberg, senior, was born in the Province of Jämtland and, when he came to Chicago in 1882 at the age of twenty-two, had already had some experience as a carpenter and cabinetmaker. The son was born in Chicago in 1894 and, since 1915, has been his father's partner.

Many educational buildings have been erected by C. E. Carson, a native of the Aaland Islands in the Baltic, which have always been peopled by Swedes, though for the past century or more, belonging politically, first to Russia, and then to Finland. He came to America in 1882 at the age of eighteen and, though a sailor by training, settled on a farm in Iowa. Then he came to Chicago as a builder. Besides several hundreds of smaller structures, he has built ten grammar schools; three high schools; some of the Northwestern University buildings; the Chicago Business College; the Breakers Buildings; the Second Regiment Armory; and the impressive Winnebago County Court House at Rockford, Illinois.

Space permits the mere mention of only a few of the many other Swedish builders in the Chicago area, about whom more details may be found in Volume III of *The Swedish Element in America:* Fred A. Anderson and his brother, Axel W. Anderson, natives of Småland; Hugo Anderson, a "Vestgöte"; Carl E. Erickson, a native of northern Sweden, formerly associated with Adolph Lindstrom; August Theodore Herlin, who hails from the island of Öland; Axel E. Johnson, who was born in central Sweden; Gustaf Lindell, who, like Louis M. Nelson, comes from Sunne, in Värmland, the home town of Selma Lagerlöf; and Hjalmar T. Nystedt, who likewise comes from Värmland.

Although attention has been focused on the builders of Chicago, there are able contractors and builders in Minneapolis, St. Paul, Kansas City, Seattle, San Francisco, Los Angeles, and many smaller cities throughout the United States, whose work should not be overlooked. As a typical representative of the Middle West, outside of Chicago, there is Godfrey G. Swenson of Kansas City, who was born in Vimmerby, a little town in the Province of Småland, in 1876, and who emigrated to

America in 1896, arriving first at Salina, Kansas, but settling permanently in Kansas City the same year. He began his building career as a stone mason, working first as a journeyman, then as foreman and subcontractor and, in 1906, incorporating the Swenson Construction Company, which has completed at least 142 different building projects, including some of the largest structures in Kansas City and the adjacent territory of Oklahoma, as well as in Kansas. In his lifetime Mr. Swenson has seen Kansas City grow from less than 70,000 to over 600,000 inhabitants.

It was a Swede, Andrew H. Peterson, who had charge of the building of the well-known $12,000,000 Palmer House in Chicago; the $14,000,000 General Motors Building in Detroit; the $11,000,000 Union Trust in Cleveland; the large Field Museum; the McGraw-Hill Building in New York; and scores of commercial, financial, educational, and industrial structures in Illinois, Ohio, Pennsylvania, Minnesota, New Jersey, Rhode Island, British Columbia, and Massachusetts. Mr. Peterson was born in East Boston, of parents who came from Sweden, and his latest achievement has been the very successful administration of the P.W.A. in Massachusetts. During the World War he was one of the three executives in charge of construction for the United States Government of Camp Upton, at Yaphank, Long Island; and he was on the executive committee which built the $78,000,000 Powder Plant for the Government at Nitro, West Virginia. His private business connections have been with two of the largest construction companies in the country, the Thompson-Starrett Company and Starrett Brothers & Eken.

In changing the sky line of New York, contractors of Swedish origin have taken a less prominent part than in Chicago. However, they have participated in the details of construction, especially in foundation work, and Swedish hollow-drill steel has been used extensively in excavating the Manhattan bedrock on which these gigantic buildings rest. Many of the steel-construction workers, who think nothing of swinging on a beam nearly a quarter of a mile in the air, are said to be former sailors of Norwegian or Swedish origin, who have had their early training on sailing vessels.

For both economic and social reasons, as already explained, it was natural that the Swedish builders should have come into prominence before the architects. In the last few decades, however, an increasing number of men of Swedish heritage have chosen architecture as their profession. At present, many sons of Swedish immigrants are enrolled in the architectural schools of both the United States and Europe, or are working as draftsmen and designers in large architectural offices, preparatory to setting up their own offices. Some have long since advanced to the top ranks of their profession, and have become distinguished designers. In reviewing the achievements of the past fifty years, and selecting several outstanding representatives, the following are only a few of those deserving mention. Here again, Chicago and the Middle West come first.

The first Swedish architect of note in Illinois, according to the article by the late Col. John A. Nyden, in the second volume of *The Swedish Element in America*, was the late Lars Gustaf Hallberg, born in Sweden in 1844. Before coming to Chicago in 1871, directly after the great fire, he had been educated in both Sweden and England. While his early work consisted, naturally enough, of private houses, apartments, and churches, he was a pioneer in the use of reinforced concrete. In this respect he has been followed by his oldest son, Lawrence G. Hallberg, a graduate of Cornell University, who joined his father in 1910. His specialty has been manufacturing plants, of which the extensive Stewart-Warner Speedometer Company's factory in Chicago is an example.

Another Cornell graduate of Swedish extraction, born in Chicago, is Arthur Hussander, whose chief work has been school buildings. Since his graduation in 1890, he has practiced in Chicago and for many years has served the Chicago Board of Education, designing such noted buildings as the Nicholas Senn High School, the Carter Harrison Technical High School, and the Lindblom High School (named for the late Robert Lindblom, a native of Sweden, who came to America in 1864, and for a generation was prominent in both civics and business (see the chapter on "Businessmen").

As head of the Department of Architecture at the Armour

Institute of Technology in Chicago, Robert C. Ostergren has also had wide experience in the educational field. Mr. Ostergren has been President of the Illinois Society of Architects, and for several years a member of the Board of Examiners of Architects for the State of Illinois. During the World War, he served as an officer in the Hospital Section of the Construction Division of the United States Army.

In Chicago's municipal architecture Eric Edwin Hall, born in 1883 in the Province of Östergötland, is the most prominent. He has designed not only the Criminal Court Building and Jail of Cook County, of which he has been the official architect since 1915, but also the gigantic Chicago Stadium, the Cook County Hospital Buildings, the Juvenile Detention Home, and such private structures as the Spencer Hotel at Marion, Indiana; the Faust Hotel at Rockford, Illinois; the Hotel Wolford at Danville; the Oak Forest Infirmary Buildings; the Harlem State Bank and the Suburban Trust and Savings Bank at Oak Park, Illinois; and, in Chicago itself, such buildings as the Shore Drive Apartments; the Southmoor Hotel; the Crest Hotel; the Envoy Hotel; the Country Club Apartments; and the Lincoln Trust and Savings Bank. Although Mr. Hall had had some technical education when he arrived from Sweden in 1904, at the age of twenty-one, he continued his studies at the Crane Technical High School in Chicago, the Armour Institute of Technology, and the Lewis Institute, while working at the same time as a mechanic in the Bushnell Tool Shop—a creditable achievement.

Another versatile and self-made, if not self-trained, Chicago architect was the late Col. John A. Nyden, from whose pen we have quoted already. Born in 1878 at Moheda in the Province of Småland, he was a fellow townsman of the Ericsson brothers, previously mentioned in this chapter, and, like them, he came to America in his 'teens. While working to support himself, he attended both the Columbian Trade School of Chicago and, later, the scientific and art course at Valparaiso University in Indiana, which he finished in two years. Next he attended the Art Institute in Chicago and the Art School at the University of Illinois, where he was graduated, both as an architect and as

an engineer. In the meantime, he had had some practical experience with the George A. Fuller Construction Company in New
York as a draftsman, and in Chicago with various firms. As
chief draftsman for Arthur Heun, he had charge of the construction of such important buildings as the Illinois Athletic
Club; the New Southern Hotel; and the J. Ogden Armour
residence at Lake Forest.

In 1907 Colonel Nyden started out for himself, and designed
such Chicago hotels as the Admiral, the Commonwealth, the
Melrose, and the Fairfax, and, in Evanston, the Evanshire.
Among the bank buildings of his design are the Builders and
Merchants; the Belmont-Sheffield Trust and Savings; and, in
other fields, the Illinois Stadium of Springfield, Illinois; the
Minnehaha Academy of Minneapolis; the Bethany Old People's
Home of Chicago; and many institutional buildings for the
State of Illinois, which he served as supervising architect in
1926–27. In Philadelphia he designed the American Swedish
Historical Museum, in which he attempted to "express the seventeenth century architecture of Sweden in American Colonial
terms," to use his own words. During the World War he served
as a major in the Quartermaster's Corps, being supervising
officer over forty-two general and debarkation hospitals. In
1923 he passed the tests for colonel, in the Reserve Corps.

Altogether, there are about seventy licensed architects of
Swedish extraction in Illinois, Colonel Nyden observed, which
means one for every three thousand of the estimated Swedish-
American population of the State; whereas the average of all
architects is but one for every six thousand inhabitants.

In New York the architects of Swedish extraction are probably less numerous, or less well known, amidst a greater number
of practitioners. By common consent, the most prominent is
Harrie Thomas Lindeberg, a native of Bayonne, New Jersey,
both of whose parents were born in Stockholm, Sweden. After
studying at the National Academy of Design in New York, he
spent six years in the offices of McKim, Mead & White, whose
work was looked upon as the most distinguished of the time. In
1907 he started his own office. While most of his designs have
been for private houses in various parts of the United States,

he was appointed, in 1933, the architect of the proposed United States Embassy in Moscow, which, owing to political complications, has, so far, not been built. Since then, he has designed a United States Legation at Helsingfors in Finland, which is now under construction; a Legation for Nicaragua, on which costs are being estimated; and a Consulate at Shanghai, the building of which has also been postponed, because of the Japanese invasion of China. Among other buildings he has designed, are North College of Wesleyan University, Middletown, Connecticut; the Onwentsia Club at Lake Forest, Illinois; the Asheville, North Carolina, Country Club; the Astor Memorial Building, Rhinebeck, New York; and private residences for John S. Pillsbury, Minneapolis; Michael M. Van Buren, Newport, Rhode Island; Eugene Dupont, Wilmington, Delaware; James Stillman, Pocantico Hills, New York; Horace Havemeyer, Islip, Long Island; Cameron Morrison, Charlotte, North Carolina; and William Farish, Houston, Texas.

Also practicing in the New York area is Carl William Larson, who attended the Harvard School of Architecture in 1916–19, and later worked as a designer for various architectural firms in Boston and New York. Since 1926 he has been chief designer in the office of the New York State Architect, at Albany. The list of buildings, for the design of which he has been responsible, includes the New York State Office Building in New York City; the Buffalo State Teachers College; the College of Home Economics at Cornell University; and the Plattsburg, Geneseo, and New Paltz State Normal Schools. He has also designed numerous other public buildings, such as hospitals, prisons, barracks, fieldhouses for parks, etc. Both his parents were born in Sweden.

Among college architects, Jens Fredrick Larson of Hanover, New Hampshire, occupies a prominent position. He is a native of Boston, his father having been born in Sweden, and his mother in Denmark. In 1910–12, he attended the Harvard Graduate School of Applied Science; and then worked as a designer, successively, in Montreal, Glasgow, and London. When the World War broke out, he joined the Canadian Field Artillery in France and, in 1916, was transferred to the British

Royal Air Force as Captain. Since the War he has specialized in college, university, and monumental buildings, and, in 1933–35, was the architect for the International House of the University City in Paris, financed by John D. Rockefeller, Jr. Mr. Larson is the architect in charge of the development of the following institutions in the United States: Dartmouth College, New Hampshire; Wabash College, Indiana; Marietta College, Ohio; Colby College, Maine; Washington and Jefferson College, Pennsylvania; Bucknell University, Pennsylvania; the University of Louisville, Kentucky; St. Francis Xavier University, Nova Scotia; and Hastings College, Nebraska. For Colby College he designed the new memorial church, given to it by the late George Horace Lorimer, Editor of the *Saturday Evening Post,* in memory of his father.

Several college buildings have likewise been designed by Harry Johan Carlson, a native of St. Paul, Minnesota, who since 1896 has practiced architecture in Boston. He originally studied at Massachusetts Institute of Technology, and in 1903 became a member of the firm of Coolidge & Carlson, of which he is now the sole partner. He is the architect of the Normal and Latin groups of school buildings in Boston, and has designed dormitories for both Wellesley and Harvard; a chapel for Bates College in Maine; and a library for Hamilton College in New York State. He also built "Dreamwold," the famous private estate of the late Thomas W. Lawson, at Egypt, Massachusetts, which was one of the wonders of its time.

In Milwaukee, Wisconsin, Herbert W. Tullgren, who was born in Chicago in 1889, of mixed Swedish and Norwegian parentage, has been very active for the past twenty-seven years as the designer of a notable list of buildings, ranging from cathedrals and theaters to schools and garages. It includes such structures as the Cathedral for Wisconsin Consistory, Milwaukee; Village Hall, Whitefish Bay, Wisconsin; St. Catherine's Home for Girls, Milwaukee; Methodist Deaconess Home for Girls, Milwaukee; Hotel Duluth, Duluth, Minnesota; Astor Hotel, Milwaukee; Retlaw Hotel, Fond du Lac, Wisconsin; Northland Hotel, Green Bay, Wisconsin; Loraine Hotel, Madison, Wisconsin; Shorecrest Apartment Hotel, Milwaukee; Racine Theatre, Racine, Wisconsin; Downer Theatre, Milwaukee; Sherman Theatre, Milwaukee; Plymouth Junior and Senior High School, Plymouth, Wisconsin; the high school and three graded schools at Whitefish Bay, Wisconsin.

A discussion of the influence of the Swedes on American architecture is incomplete without mention of the renaissance in Swedish architecture, in recent years. American practitioners, in increasing numbers, have been crossing the Atlantic to study the work of men like Ragnar Östberg, Carl Westman, and Ivar Tengbom. The town hall at Stockholm, with its masterful use of brick, has excited much admiration. So, also, have the radically modern buildings of the Stockholm Exposition of 1930, designed by E. C. Asplund, which were extensively publicized by the American architectural journals. More recently, the work of the Swedish Coöperative Wholesale Society architects' office, headed by Eskil Sundahl, has come into prominence, by reason of its logic and efficiency. At the same time the American architects have been visiting Sweden, it should also be observed that Swedish designers have been coming here for inspiration and study; in this instance, architecture can be said to be truly international.

For a complete survey of architectural influences there should also be a discussion of the contribution of Swedish engineers, but space permits only a few brief references to the many important accomplishments in this field of practice. As an outstanding example, there is the work of David L. Lindquist, chief engineer of the Otis Elevator Company, who was born in Stockholm. After a thorough technical education in Sweden and in Germany, he came to the United States in 1902, and has been with Otis ever since. In 1911 he was appointed chief engineer, and has employed so many technical assistants of Swedish origin that it used to be said in New York that an engineer of any nationality had to know Swedish in order to work for Otis.

During his first ten years in America, Mr. Lindquist was engaged in the introduction and development of the gearless-traction electric elevator, which has since become standard for all buildings requiring elevators of high rise and great speed. In fact, it revolutionized the whole system of vertical transportation. During the early part of the World War, he developed the automatic system of self-leveling elevators, which has displaced the old type that had to be adjusted to the floor by hand. In 1922 he introduced the automatic-signal control, which requires the operator only to press a set of buttons. The importance of the elevator in the development of the American skyscraper cannot be overemphasized. The economic height and size of the structure depends largely on the speed and efficiency of its vertical transportation system.

Another engineer of prominence was the late Werner Nygren, president of the firm of heating and ventilation consultants, bearing his name. Born and educated in Sweden, he began his engineering work in Boston in 1898. During his career he designed the heating and ventilating systems for the Woolworth Building; the American Telephone and Telegraph Building; St. Patrick's Cathedral; Hunter College; the R. H. Macy & Co. Store; and the Columbia Presbyterian Medical Center— all in Manhattan; also the Los Angeles Public Library and the Travelers Insurance Building in Hartford, Connecticut. He was a president of the New York Heating Board of Trade and the New York Association of Consulting Engineers, as well as a member of the American Society of Mechanical Engineers.

The various engineering fields—mechanics, power, lighting, acoustics, air conditioning, communication and transportation, and so on—all represent new forces in American architecture, and in all of these can be found specialists who are Swedish in origin or descent. Closely allied with the engineering, are the industrial developments. Here, too, can be found Swedish names, like those of Francis J. Plym, formerly an architect, and now head of the Kawneer Company which manufactures windows, doors, escalators, and store fronts; Charles P. Dahlstrom and the Dahlstrom Metallic Door Company, whose products have been used in such outstanding building projects as Rockefeller Center; Bror G. Dahlberg and the Celotex Company, whose wallboard is familiar to builders all over the world (see the chapter on "Manufacturers" for further mention of these industrialists).

Particularly in the housing field are the industrial develop-

ments—large-scale operations, prefabrication, and innovations
in materials, equipments, and household services—likely to be
more and more important, in the next few decades. The increasing complexity of building requirements and the potentialities
of science and technology imply a rapid industrialization of the
whole field. Experiments in new housing designs, which have
gone on apace during the depression years, are evidence of this
ferment. Here, likewise, can be cited examples of work by Swedish technicians. The October, 1933, issue of the *Architectural
Record* was devoted entirely to a presentation of new house designs by Harrie T. Lindeberg (see earlier mention in this chapter), based on a standard module system deriving from the
cellular-steel-unit construction. Recently, an experimental concrete house was erected in one day near Washington, D.C., by
Karl P. Billner, a Swedish engineer, utilizing the vacuum-con-
crete process which he invented (see the chapter on "Inventors"). Out of technical explorations like these is emerging a
new American architecture, entirely different in appearance,
and even more useful and beneficial. This continuous evolution
of new and better forms is in the true architectural tradition,
and in its development the Swedes in America can lay claim to
an important rôle.

Composers

VICTOR NILSSON

A native of Skåne, and first educated at Gothenburg, Sweden, Dr. Nilsson has been a resident of Minneapolis since 1887, and since 1907 he has been music editor and critic of the Minneapolis *Journal*. For an appreciation of his work in behalf of musical culture in the Middle West, see the chapter on "Journalists."

THE late O. G. Sonneck, famous musicologist, opens his *A Survey of Music in America* with the statement that an American, fairly conversant with musical life in Europe, will find it by far easier to survey acceptably music in Germany, France, or Italy, than music in his own country. Yet he attempted such a survey, but cautiously left alone the earlier periods of American life and history.

John Tasker Howard, whose *Our American Music, Three Hundred Years of It*, is a valuable source of information, finds it regrettable that records of musical life in this country, during the early years of the Southern colonies and of Pennsylvania and of New York, are not as complete as those of New England. It seems to him unfair to dismiss altogether, as some historians have done, certain elements in America's early music, even if they have exerted no obvious influence upon the future of the nation. "The Germans and Swedes who came to the neighborhood of Philadelphia when William Penn first proclaimed his 'glorious new world' and the Moravians who had settled in Bethlehem, enjoyed a musical life far in advance of anything in contemporary New England." This is a good statement, but suffers from a telescopic compression of historic conceptions. As often is done by writers dealing with the history of Delaware and Pennsylvania, Howard places the Germans before the Swedes, whereas the latter were the first to land upon Delaware shores as the first permanent colonizers, coming half a dozen years before Penn was born, and forty-four years before he came across the Atlantic to take his land grant in possession.

Howard is perfectly sound in his argument, that these settle-

ments were established for religious motives and that many of
their beliefs were fanatical. Yet there was not the suspicion that
any kind of music was "the invention of the devil," as was the
case in regard to secular music among the Puritans of that period in New England. Good singing was required and insisted
upon. Howard tells how one Swedish pastor, Reverend Andreas
Sandel, imposed a fine of six shillings on certain members of
his congregation for "untimely singing," which proves that
"timely singing" was in favor.

It was not until 1694 that a German group of priests took
up their dwelling beside the Wissahickon River, eight miles
from Philadelphia. The leader of these so-called hermits was
Johann Kelpius, from Densdorf in Germany. The hermits early
acquired fame as good singers, for in 1700 they were invited
to act as choristers, and furnish instrumental music at the dedication of the new Swedish church, the Gloria Dei Church, at
Wicaco, in what is now a part of Philadelphia. It was the second church of that name on that site, the first having been a
wooden structure erected in 1646. In addition to many instrumental compositions, Kelpius wrote nearly twenty hymns, and
is considered the first composer on the American soil which
afterwards became part of the United States.

Gloria Dei is considered important musically by Howard,
because it may have been the first American house of worship
equipped with an organ. Some authorities believe that Kelpius
brought with him from Germany the organ that was installed
in that church.

Three years later, Justus Falckner, who was the first German minister in this country, was awarded the pastorate of the
Gloria Dei Church. Then the organ was there, and music was
made upon it by a man named Jonas, as regular organist.
Neighboring hermits, or other mystics, played on the viola,
hautboy (oboe), trumpets, and kettledrums, because the Reverend Mr. Falckner favored attractive and civilizing music, as
of wholesome influence upon the wild Indians, and also as a
means to attract Christians of other sects to the church. This
ensemble may have been the first symphonic group, if not in
North America as a whole, at least the first used there for religious purposes.

Next to nothing is known of the music, or musicians, in early Delaware; but the history of Philadelphia is a record of continued struggle with the Quakers. The Friends were opposed to music of any sort, while the settlers of the earlier, Swedish Delaware were evidently fond of it, and called in people of other Protestant sects to help them provide such, both as a civilizing and cultural power. The Quakers also condemned plays, games, lotteries, and dancing.

Gustaf Hesselius, founder of the American school of painting, was born in Sweden in 1682, and died in Philadelphia in 1755. He belonged to the era of universal genius, which, in Sweden, produced the Rudbecks, the Celsiuses, Swedenborg, and Linnæus. Already, in 1742, he was known as the first organ builder, and also as the first maker of spinets and virginals in this country. In the Revolutionary period he was succeeded by John Behrent, by birth either Swedish or German, who, in 1775, lived in Philadelphia, and built what seems to have been the first American piano.

Thus the Swedish people of Delaware-Philadelphia, and the Germans of Pennsylvania, early associated with them, appear to have performed a fundamental and constructive service to music in this country, even during the colonial and Revolutionary epochs. There were no composers reared among them. It could not have been expected from a people of pioneer stock, who lived in steady struggle with a virgin soil, a climate that was trying in its extremes and sudden changes, and with more or less ignorant aborigines—not to mention their fights with the Dutch colonists for the dominion of the land.

Music and musicians in Sweden were not likely to have influenced the Delaware colonists greatly. It is true that in Sweden the folk songs began to be collected during the late sixteenth century, mostly by royal or at least aristocratic people, who, during this late Renaissance or Elizabethan era, possessed exceptional erudition in music, as well as in poetry. King Gustaf Vasa founded Europe's first symphony orchestra, and his sons and successors upon the throne of Sweden were typical princes of the age. His son, King Erik, made a daughter of the people his Queen, and sang to the lute his own poetry, which he himself had set to music. When imprisoned by his brother, King

John, he wrote, in his confinement, ardent and touching psalms, which are still preserved in the hymnbooks of the nation. Some of these, with others of the seventeenth century, may have been brought over to, or by, the Swedish pioneers of Delaware, as well as many of the folk songs.

The art music of Sweden was much too young. Its recognized father, Johan Helmich Roman, was born in Stockholm in 1694, when Bach and Händel were only nine years old, but twelve years after Hesselius had seen the light of day for the first time, in the Province of Dalarne. Roman spent several years in London, shortly after Hesselius had left that city and had gone to America with his preacher-brother. In 1735 Roman began a two years' tour of England, France, and Italy, as a famous violinist; but no Swedish musician in those days ever conceived the idea of visiting the European colonies in faraway America. Hesselius began making the first organs ever built in this country a year before Roman wrote the first of his most celebrated compositions, "Drottningholm musique" for the wedding of Crown Prince Adolf Fredrik of Sweden, to a sister of Frederic the Great in 1744. Roman died in 1758, or three years later than Hesselius.

Musicologists and dictionaries, as well as old newspaper files and prints, seem to know hardly any American composer or musician, born in Sweden or descending from Swedish stock, during the period from the Revolution to the Civil War. Yet there must have been such, perhaps working quietly as orchestra members, organists, pianists, or teachers of some instrument or other. Balzac and Dostoyevski, two of the greatest of literary psychologists of any period, have drawn several pictures of musicians, as quiet, self-forgetting and all-suffering beings of almost angelic sweetness and humility. Perhaps such musicians abounded particularly in this country, between the rise of our Republic and the assassination of Lincoln.

Victor Williams, born in Sweden in 1816, was a well-known teacher in Cincinnati for more than twenty years, and was occupied with music in connection with public schoolwork. But if he composed, his work is not known.

John Nelson Pattison (1842–1905), born in the city of Niagara Falls, New York, toured with Thalberg in Italy, as a pianist. In the neighboring city of Buffalo, there was quite a group of Swedes settled in those days. All Pattison's names have a Swedish flavor, in a rather strong combination, looking suspiciously Swedish. He was the composer of a "Niagara" symphony, a concert overture, a piano concerto, or fantasia, and many piano pieces.

Athwart the luminous vision that is conjured forth by the very name of Niagara, which for the poets of the world has loomed irresistibly inspiring for the space of 250 years, glides the passing shadow of C. J. L. Almquist, the great romantic genius of Sweden. He was the forerunner of the even greater genius of August Strindberg. For some reasons sound enough, while others probably were caused by his overwrought imagination, Almquist, for the last fifteen years of his life, imposed exile upon himself. Nearly all of this "Inferno" period he spent in this country, where he meandered in a manner thoroughly romantic between places as diverse as New Orleans and Niagara. Like Rousseau, also a kindred genius, and August Strindberg, he went deep into music, and tried to create a new simplified art, built upon folk music. His deep interest in this form of music did not forsake him, even during his itinerant existence. His biographer, A. T. Lysander, relates that from America, he sent back, to a friend in Sweden, notations of Indian melodies he had made in the environs of Niagara Falls—a truly musical idea, which many composers of our time have tried to adapt to some phase of their art, among them the greatest of his country, Edward MacDowell.

A quite prolific composer was the late August Hyllested, prominent Chicago pianist, born in Sweden, but of Danish parents, who provided for him a musical education in Copenhagen. After a notable tour of Europe, Hyllested came to this country in 1885, appearing in recitals with symphony orchestras. In 1891, he became Assistant Director of the Chicago Musical College, and, in the same year, was soloist at the Minneapolis music festival of the United Scandinavian Singers, appearing with the festival orchestra in Grieg's piano concerto.

In this connection should be mentioned Gustavus Johnson, born in Hull, England, of Swedish father and English mother, in 1856, the maiden name of the latter, a daughter of Admiral

Lewis Hole of the British Navy, being Henriette Hole. When his father, who was a Stockholm merchant by the name of Peter Johanson, had moved back to his native city, his son received there his education for piano, organ, voice, and composition, completing it at the Royal Academy of Music, under famous teachers like Abraham Mankel, an organist of European fame. Johnson came to Minneapolis in 1875, and at once began to work as organist and pianist there, founding, in 1898, a conservatory of his own, The Johnson School of Music, Oratory and Dramatic Art, as it was later called. As pianist, college musical director, and composer, Johnson was a path-breaker in his adopted State and city. His compositions consisted of a series of bright pieces for the piano, songs, and several smaller ensemble pieces, and a "piano school," with a course in touch formation. These were mostly published at his own expense. His most pretentious work was a piano concerto, performed for the first time in Minneapolis in 1899, with Mrs. Frank Fayette Fletcher, one of his pupils, in the solo part. He died at the age of seventy-six.

John Victor Bergquist is another prominent Minneapolis composer and music pedagogue, of a later generation, and a native son of Minnesota. He was born at St. Peter in 1877. Bergquist, whose father was an organist, first went to school in his native town, but developed into a musician through years of study in Minneapolis, Berlin, and Paris, under the best of teachers, such as Guilmant, to whom he dedicated one of his two organ sonatas. Returning home, he was appointed organist in the Augustana Lutheran Church in Minneapolis, in which position he had also served before he went to Europe. During the years of 1908 to 1912, he taught music at Augustana College in Rock Island, Illinois, but, returning to Minneapolis, he took up the study of public-school music, and created a new branch of instruction in the high schools, by training the young to express themselves individually in music, through the composition of songs or pieces for the piano, and other solo instruments or smaller ensembles, with which, after a series of preliminary elimination, they appeared in final contests, the youthful composers generally appearing personally as soloists, accompanists, or members of the choruses.

Bergquist wrote an oratorio, "Golgatha," to a Swedish text of his own, adapted from the Bible story of Christ, which was first performed in Minneapolis in the year of its composition, 1906, and met with much success; further, a Christmas cantata and a Reformation cantata, both to English texts, the last-mentioned being first performed in Rock Island, later in Minneapolis; and, like his oratorio, it was produced in several other cities and in the East. While his sacred music was held in a conscious simplification of the Händel style and, in this respect, somewhat approached Wennerberg, he used the modern idiom with exceptional success for a piano suite, "Three Characteristic Pieces," inspired by his own children's games and moods. With this he carried off first prize in a contest, arranged in New York by the St. Erik Lodge of the national Swedish-American fraternity, called the Vasa Order. Bergquist died in Minneapolis in February, 1935. His impressive funeral at the Gloria Dei Church in Minneapolis, where he had been the organist, was partly arranged in the form of a sacred concert with music, chosen from the departed composer's own works for organ and mixed choir.

In Stockholm there died, some time in the 1890's, a Swedish composer by the name of August Elfåker, who had taken his name from his birthplace in the Province of Halland, where he first saw the light of day in 1851. After an organist's and musical director's graduation at the Royal Academy of Music in Stockholm, and a few years spent as music teacher at the "Real Gymnasium" in Gothenburg, he came to America in February, 1885, locating in Chicago, where he became director of male choruses and church choirs. Elfåker soon returned to Sweden, and obtained, in Stockholm, an organist's position which he still held at the time of his death. He was the composer of several solo songs and sacred compositions for mixed choir, some having been already printed before he left Sweden. While on the steamer between Glasgow and New York, he worked out the sketch for a symphony which he completed in Chicago, and which he had performed there at least on one occasion.

A similarly short but brilliant career as organist and composer, under two flags interchangingly, was that of Hugo Bedinger, whose father, also an organist and composer, had formed

his name after his birthplace, Beddinge in Skåne. The younger
Bedinger was born in 1876, and was graduated from the Royal
Academy of Stockholm as director of music; and left for America, after having served as assistant organist in various churches
in the Swedish capital. He spent the last few years of the century, mostly as teacher of vocal and instrumental music at
Bethany College in Kansas. He returned to Sweden in 1901,
and played and taught for a while in Hudiksvall; whereupon
he was appointed organist at the cathedral of Vesterås in 1904,
but died only six years later. He wrote a great number of songs
for his wife, who was a singer, and who toured Scandinavia and
the Continent with him; and published some songs set to Swedish, others to German texts. He also published "Belsazar für
Baryton und Orkester"; choruses for mixed voices; piano compositions for violin and piano; cantatas; and other choral works
with orchestra and several marches; one entitled "Welcome to
Sweden"; organ preludes; and male quartets. Posthumous
works of his were the oratorio "Bethania" (1899), and a violin
sonata.

Ivar Glemming, at present violin instructor in the public
schools at Fargo, North Dakota, is a young musician who has
prepared himself exceptionally well for a career as composer.
Born at Glimminge in Skåne, he had studied with excellent
teachers in Sweden, when he came to the United States in 1920,
and had already had one composition "Skånsk Vinterkväll"
("Scanian Winter Eve") published by Elkan & Schildknecht
in Stockholm. For ten years he was a violinist in the Minneapolis Symphony Orchestra. In 1927 Glemming took the degree
of Bachelor of Music at the Bush Conservatory of Music in
Chicago, and in 1934 that of Bachelor of Science at the University of Minnesota. Among his very promising compositions
are "Poem" for orchestra; a suite for reduced orchestra; a
piano sonata and a number of smaller pieces.

A little slender pamphlet, published by Edna Reinbach in
1930, gives more information about the *Music and Musicians
of Kansas* than many a heavy volume of musicology does about
those subjects in older and more populous states. This is of
special importance to the purpose of the present chapter, because the cultural forces gathered at Bethany College of Linds-

borg, making it a Swedish-American center of education, have become famous for their enthusiasm in maintaining the appreciation of Händel by annual music festivals, featuring the performance of "The Messiah" oratorio very much as, in Bethlehem, Pennsylvania, the works of Bach, in Bayreuth, Bavaria, those of Wagner, and in Salzburg, Austria, those of Mozart are being revived at cyclic festivals. The State of Kansas and the entire Southwest have benefited immeasurably by these Bethany Händel feasts, which have brought there many soloists and recitalists of merit, whom otherwise it would never have been their good fortune to hear. For exhaustive information about Bethany College as a whole, the excellent historique given of it by its President, Dr. Ernst F. Pihlblad, in *The Swedish Element in America*, published by the Swedish-American Biographical Society (Vol. I), is urgently referred to. Here will be stated just the biographical information on the leading spirits in the musical profession at Bethany that Miss Reinbach gives.

Hagbard Brase, Conductor of the Bethany Oratorio Society, was born in Sweden in 1877. He has been connected with the college ever since 1900, the year in which he came to America as a graduate from the Royal Academy of Music of Stockholm. He was organist of the society from that year until 1914, and has been its conductor from 1915, and head of the college department of music since 1916. In addition to songs and choruses, Director Brase has composed several works for organ and orchestra. His "Arietta" has been published by A. G. Ogren.

Samuel Thorstenberg, conductor of the Bethany chorus from 1897 until 1909, was largely responsible for the wide renown which the Messiah festivals gained under his inspirational leadership. He was a Kansan himself, born in Saline in 1875, and he made his studies at Bethany, in Stockholm, and in New York. Thorstenberg was also founder and director of the Jamestown Conservatory of Music at Jamestown, New York, in which city he exerted a powerful influence in behalf of Swedish music as well as music in general. He died in the spring of 1938.

Gustaf Fredrik Holmberg is of Swedish birth, and came to America in 1891. He was graduated from Bethany College in 1899, and taught violin and harmony at his Alma Mater until 1903, when he became teacher of music at the School of Fine

Arts in the University of Oklahoma, being six years later appointed its Dean.

Theodor Lindberg is another native musician and composer, who has carried into fruition elsewhere the seeds of art from McPherson County, Kansas, where he was born in 1874, and from Bethany College where his musical education was grounded, though later completed at the Chicago Musical College and in Berlin. He has directed the Bethany orchestra, has been Conductor of the Wichita Symphony Orchestra, and is now President of Wichita College of Music, founded by him in 1906. Besides his fame as orchestra conductor and composer, he is also noted as violinist and author.

Speaking of the Wichita College of Music, Paul Oberg, born in Minneapolis, is organist and choirmaster there. He studied at the University of Minnesota, and the special honors he won with his degree of Bachelor of Music brought him an appointment as organist and piano accompanist of the Minneapolis Symphony Orchestra. In spite of his youth, Oberg has already won considerable fame as organist and pianist and through radio broadcasting. His vacations he has used for studies with Dr. Howard Hanson, Director of the Eastman School of Music in Rochester, New York. These have already brought him the degree of Master of Music from that institute, and they will be continued until the corresponding Doctor's degree has been won.

To return again to the informative Reinbach booklet, Gustaf F. Soderlund, or originally Söderlund, of Lawrence, Kansas, was assistant professor of organ and theory at the University of Kansas, 1919 to 1927. He received his musical instruction principally at Stockholm, and is an organist and composer of works for the piano and orchestra, including "April Song," "Nocturne," and "Minuet" for orchestra.

Minneapolis and Chicago, and many other musical centers, no doubt, owe more than one debt of gratitude to Bethany or Lindsborg (the two are almost identical, in standing for musical culture). But, one debt these two cities owe jointly, because of the fact that the Sundstrom family moved to them from their home in Lindsborg. It first came to Minneapolis, where Ella Sundstrom (Pendleton) and Ebba Sundstrom (Nylander) were developed, respectively, into performers on the piano and the violin, in order, in their turn, to teach others how to master these instruments. Chicago fell in with Minneapolis in this willing indebtedness, when Ebba Sundstrom followed her teacher, Richard Czerwonky, for postgraduate work, to the first-mentioned city; and there, under his guidance, she developed also into an orchestra leader and conductor of one of the world's largest and finest organizations of its kind, the Chicago Woman's Symphony Orchestra.

From all directions young talented musicians of Swedish descent begin to come forth to take active part in the contemporary development of American art life. Dr. Benjamin F. Swalin is one of them. Born in Minneapolis, and of a family in which several members were devoted to music, he began early his studies of the violin. At the age of eighteen he was made a member of the Minneapolis Symphony Orchestra under Emil Oberhoffer, but relinquished this position after two years, to become a student of the celebrated Frank Kneisel for five years, and with the still more famous Leopold Auer for four more. He supplemented this with general and advanced theoretical work at the Institute of Musical Art in New York. During these years Swalin also essayed the task of acquiring a university education. He was graduated from the Columbia University in 1928, and took the Master's degree in English literature at the same institution two years later. The years 1930–33 were devoted to studies in Europe. While there, Swalin completed work for the degree of Doctor of Philosophy at the University of Vienna in 1932, and received artist diplomas, in violin and conducting, from the Staatsakademi für Kunst in the same city. Upon his return to America, Dr. Swalin was appointed to a professorship in the music department of the DePauw University in Indiana. Since the summer of 1935 he has been associated with the University of North Carolina, as violin instructor and lecturer. In both of his academic positions he has conducted the University Symphony Orchestras. Swalin is today one of the best equipped of American violinists, and if he were to give up his academical career, he would shine as a concert artist, combining depth of interpretation with virtuosic brilliancy. It is more likely, however, that he will turn to composition and musicological research.

Arne Oldberg, born in Youngstown, Ohio, 1874, is an American musician of Swedish descent, who, after thorough and varied studies, has risen to become recognized as a composer and musical pedagogue of solidity and distinction. His father was a noted authority on pharmacy, who gave his son a good education in music, begun at Chicago, and carried into completion with work under Leschetitzky in Vienna, and Rheinberger in Munich, embracing the pianistic art as well as that of composition. Since 1899 Oldberg has been professor in these subjects at the Northwestern University at Evanston, Illinois, which is practically part and parcel of Chicago. Alfred Remy writes of him: "As a composer he cultivates not only the classical forms, but their real spirit; his music entirely free from impressionistic tendencies is 'absolute music,' as the term is generally understood; although showing no very striking individuality, it commands respect for its sincerity, warmth and excellent technical workmanship." Oldberg has to his credit two symphonies in F minor and C minor, respectively, both carrying off national prizes. His works have often been represented in North Shore festivals of music, and have been played by the Chicago, Philadelphia, and Minneapolis symphony orchestras, especially his "Paolo and Francesca" overture, which belongs among his best-known compositions, that must by now range into the forties in number, embracing a piano concerto; "Theme and Variations"; a horn concerto; four songs for alto voice with orchestra; "Academic Overture"; "Symphonic Variations"; "June," a rhapsody, all enjoyed in public performance; and, furthermore, a number of chamber-music compositions, foremost among which is a piano quintet; a piano suite; a sonata; "Variations," and smaller pieces for that instrument.

David Nyvall, Jr., born in Minneapolis in 1891, of families of prominent clergymen on both sides, is one of Oldberg's many, and must also be one of his most gifted, pupils. His father, a brilliant historian and a member of the Northwestern University faculty of history, gave his son an education based on music, making him a capable organist, an excellent pianist, and a prolific composer. Most likely there is hardly an American composer of Swedish extraction who began composition as early as he did, or saw his output accepted by as great or as many different publishers. He has written several cantatas of merit, a great number of choruses, solo songs, and piano pieces.

"Tell me your relation to Bach, and I can tell what is your worth as a musician," recently wrote a famous musicologist. Nyvall's relation to Bach is a feeling of profound love and veneration. He has proved it by a series of arrangements of Bach's "Two Part Inventions" for two pianos, which are both ingenious and charming. For a couple of years he taught music in his native town, and then attracted attention by his fine leadership in directing an Elks society glee club and the Minneapolis Symphony Orchestra auxiliary choir of mixed voices. After some years as head of the music department of the University of Idaho, he returned to Chicago, where, after having been brought to prominence and recognition as a director of an a cappella choir of a Chicago high-school glee club, he was put in charge of planning all the music for the public-school system of that city, an enormous task. He is still a young man of whom much could be expected, if he allowed himself entire devotion to composition.

Carl Emil Seashore (originally Sjöstrand) is the name of fame in that part of the musical world which goes more than skin-deep into that art, as well as in the world of science. When students from every part of the country turn to you for information, and when honor scholars seek you from across the seas, to sit at your feet, then, surely, you are a celebrity who is an honor to the land of your birth as well as to that of your adoption. This is the case of Dr. Seashore, who is one of America's foremost authorities on problems in musical psychology, conducting extensive experiments of various kinds within his field of research. He is author of a long series of articles in various leading magazines such as the *Musical Quarterly*, the *Étude*, etc., besides monographs in *Studies in Psychology of the University of Iowa*.

Especially noteworthy seems Dr. Seashore's contribution to the *Musical Quarterly* for January, 1930, upon "The Rôle of Experimental Psychology in the Science and Art of Music." He says therein: "It is with some satisfaction that I attempt to present an array of experimental procedures that during the last quarter of a century has brought this field of investigation from an entirely uncharted condition of chaos into a fairly organized series of scientific approaches to classical knowledge on the subject." He calls his effort, because of limit of time, "merely the barest skeletal classifications of data, points of view and interpretation," but it is, just the same, a masterpiece of an essay.

Seashore is another genius of Swedish extraction who has performed a fundamental and constructive service to this country, similar to that of the first Swedish colonists on the Delaware. If these built better than they knew, Dr. Seashore is, in contrast, a master builder, modestly but fully conscious of his methods and results. (See "Professors.")

Howard Hanson has by now reached a position in American music which any one of his contemporaries may have reason to envy. Burnet C. Tuthill, who has contributed an excellent monograph upon him and his art, considers Hanson one of the finest American composers, conductors, and leaders in music education. For he finds Hanson unquestionably American in his art, in spite of his being removed only one generation from Sweden, the country whose Province of Skåne supplied him, not only with parents, but also with grandparents, all settling in eastern Nebraska in the 'seventies. He was born in the small Swedish Lutheran community of Wahoo, on October 28, 1897, and was brought up to the tunes associated with Martin Luther's simple and austere hymns, the same foundation upon which Bach built his unexcelled organ and chorale constructions, which Hanson likewise considers fundamental to his own compositions.

Having been under his mother's musical instruction in Wahoo, he was, when only seven, brought to the guidance of Professor A. O. Peterson at Luther College, whose ideals centered around Bach, Händel, and Grieg. At fifteen Hanson entered the University School of Music in Lincoln, where American ideas, also, began to predominate in his young life. Then in due time he carried on to New York, and at its Institute of Musical Art he studied piano under James Friskin. Hanson decided to become a composer, in those days considered something very risky, instead of following the ministry which had held some attraction for him. A teaching fellowship took him to North-

HOWARD HANSON
DIRECTOR OF THE EASTMAN SCHOOL OF MUSIC

western University, where the study of acoustics, with music under Peter Ludkin and Arne Oldberg, brought him the degree of Bachelor of Music, when twenty. A year earlier he had become professor of theory and composition at the College of the Pacific, which California institution two years later made him its Dean. He there composed the works which won him the award of the Prix de Rome with a three years' fellowship at the American Academy of Music in the Eternal City. While still living in California, Hanson wrote his first "Nordic" symphony, his first symphonic poems and his, so far, only string quartet. In California, also, began his first performances, and under his own baton, and afterwards he appeared publicly abroad as well as in this country. On such a visit to Rochester, New York, his fate was sealed for a life's work, because then he met for the first time George Eastman, who had just founded the music school, named for him, as an adjunct to the University of Rochester.

Howard Hanson stands for Tuthill, not only as the all-round first American musician of the age, but, also, above all, as an engaging person, friendly and generous of himself to a fault. Such he also appeared in Minneapolis last spring, the dominant figure of attraction in the North Central Music Educators conference, when, under its auspices, he was presented as guest conductor, with the Minneapolis Symphony Orchestra at his disposal. He had built for it an essentially American program, in which four members out of seven were among his own most representative compositions.

Dr. Hanson proved himself an enthusiastic conductor, with the spirit of whom he infused the orchestra. He is no primadonna conductor, but sincere and direct in his interpretations. A sense of humor marked his contact with the audience, explaining things, when necessary, to its present and listening-in contingents, part of the program being broadcast by radio.

The finale from his second symphony began the line of his own compositions. With his "Nordic" and "Pan and the Priest," heard in Minneapolis earlier, Dr. Hanson wholeheartedly impressed as a symphonist. Now he has his third symphony completed. It was first performed on September 19, 1937, and broadcast in an "Everybody's Music Hour," by the Columbia

Broadcasting Company's Composers Foundation, which had ordered it for that purpose from the composer. Hanson has further to his credit four more symphonic poems. The same characteristics as those already familiar to Minneapolis marked the new specimens of his art. He is a blending of North and South, of East and West, a cosmopolitan and an individualist. "There is no extreme 'ism' in his music. It is written by a man who has remained romanticist in the present century," as Tuthill expresses it; a very serious spirit and another, carefree and humoristic, dwelling together in him with fine balancing of their various elements. A New York *Times* reviewer describes Hanson's Third Symphony as polyphonic.

The unique success of Hanson's career has so far been his only opera, "Merry Mount," written by request for the Metropolitan Opera of New York, to a libretto by Richard L. Stokes, dealing with the conflict between New England Puritans and Cavaliers. The New York première in 1932 was brilliant, ending with fifty curtain calls after the last act. Tuthill characterizes it as essentially a choral opera. In the memorable Howard Hanson program in Minneapolis, the love duet from the second opera appeared in orchestral form as a very fine piece of serious composition, while the preludes and dances seemed the most modern things of his output.

"Back to Bach" has of recent years been the hue and cry in every modern camp of music. The unafraidness of Howard Hanson has made a further step into the great past, that of "back to Palestrina." Last March the Eastman School Chorus and Orchestra combined at the Eastman Theatre in Rochester to give the première of the Kyrie, Credo and Gloria from Palestrina's "Pope Marcellus Mass" arranged for orchestra and chorus by the Director himself.

That Dr. Hanson is interested, also, in composers of Swedish origin, is proved by the fact that last season he conducted the Rochester Civic Symphony Orchestra in "Fugue with Choral" for orchestra by Erik W. G. Leidzén. Born in Stockholm in 1894, Leidzén attended school in Copenhagen, but returned later to the city of his birth for a solid musical education at its Royal Conservatory under Hägg, Fryklöf, Ellberg, and Wiklund. He came to America in 1915, and has been constantly active in New York City as teacher, conductor, accompanist, arranger, and composer. For six years he was leader of the Swedish Glee Club of Brooklyn, and has been guest conductor with the Goldman Band and other choral and instrumental organizations, dividing his time at present between the Ernest Williams School of Music, as head of its theoretic department, and free-lancing as editorial writer for G. Schirmer, Carl Fischer, Lee Feist, and other publishers. Leidzén has to his credit numerous compositions, vocal and instrumental, published here and abroad.

Among other deserving composers and musicians are John Theodore Erickson, Mus. D., a former pupil of Dvorak, and student at the American National Conservatory of Music, who is now organist and choirmaster in Gustavus Adolphus Lutheran Church in New York City; Axel W. E. Austin, composer of marches; Tobias Westlin, teacher of music in Brooklyn, New York; Conrad Forsberg, organist of the Fourth Presbyterian Church in New York and director of music at Upsala College; Arvid Samuelson, organist of the Pilgrim Church of Brooklyn, New York; and Per Olsson, a pupil of Alexander Guilmant of Paris, who is organist of Trinity Lutheran Church in Bronx, New York, associate of the American Guild of Organists, and a composer of organ, choral, and orchestral music.

Conclusion

THERE was a span of a hundred years between the first landing of the Swedish colonists on the shores of the Delaware, and the appearance among them of Hesselius as a founder, not only of America's pictorial art but also of her musical artcraft. Two hundred years of silence reigned in the world of American instrumental and compositional music, as far as Swedish influence upon it is concerned. What had happened in this interval? The answer is, of course, the great immigration to the United States by people of the Nordic race. This influx, dating from the middle of the nineteenth century, brought thousands of hardworking and constructively minded folks of the race to which the Swedes belong, and these immigrants were especially encouraged to occupy and cultivate the extensive prairies of the

Middle West. Their offspring in the second and third generations are now found, filling chairs of music in conservatories,
colleges, and universities, both East and West—musicians of
the finest type and of comprehensive energy and influence. The
Swedes have worked well together, or successively, with the
Norwegians, Danes, and Germans, such as the organist Per
Olsson, with Ole Windingstad, the Norwegian symphony conductor of New York; Ebba Sundstrom of Kansas succeeding
Richard Czerwonky, originally of Germany, as symphony conductor in Chicago; Howard Hanson of Nebraska succeeding
Christian Sinding, the Norwegian composer, as leading spirit
of the Eastman School of Music in Rochester, and sharing
symphonic conducting in that city with Fraser Harrison, An-
glo-American; Carl Busch, the Danish composer and conductor, doing work for Kansas City that corresponds admirably
in one branch to what Bethany College has done for Lindsborg
in another; F. Melius Christiansen, the Norwegian and greatest of Bach enthusiasts, rearing scholars and followers of Swedish parentage, for the reviving of a cappella singing, such as
George Hultgren of Minneapolis and Harry William Nordin
of Chicago; Edgar Nelson, Swedish-American, successfully
taking up in that same city choral work after John Örtengren,
who returned to his native Sweden in 1910.

Opera Singers

MARIE SUNDELIUS

Born in Sweden and brought to the United States at the age of nine, Mme Sundelius obtained her entire musical education from American teachers, except for coaching lessons with the prominent Swedish composer, Wilhelm Peterson-Berger, in Stockholm, and Edmond Clement in Paris. At the Metropolitan Opera House she made her debut on November 25, 1916, in "Iphigenia auf Tauris," by Gluck. During the next fifteen years she was a leading soprano, appearing in such rôles as Marguerite in "Faust," Nedda in "Pagliacci," Anna in "Lorelei," Jemmy in "William Tell," Mimi in "Bohème," Sophie in "Der Rosenkavalier," Juliette in "Romeo et Juliette," and Ah Yo in "L'oracolo." She has also sung at the Royal Opera in Stockholm, and with all the leading American orchestras in concert and oratorio, besides at almost innumerable Swedish-American singing festivals. Personally she is one of the most beloved artists. At present she resides in Boston and in the summertime conducts a singing school in Harrison, Maine.

IN preparing a chapter on Swedish opera singers who have appeared from time to time in the United States, one's first thoughts naturally center on Jenny Lind, the most idolized, the most beloved of all the fine artists who made the name of Sweden honored and respected in America. She was the first great singer from Sweden—as a matter of fact, from any foreign country—to tour America; and the tremendous acclaim which greeted her started a personal cult which has not entirely died down, even today.

Several circumstances, no doubt, contributed to the monumental success of her American tour. First, her marvelous voice, her finished art, and her exquisite personality; second, the reports of her triumphs in Europe; third, the curiosity which America, at the time only slightly music-conscious, and unfamiliar with the art of great singing, felt in regard to this new sensation; and, fourth, but not least, the preparations made beforehand by her impressario, Phineas T. Barnum, "the greatest showman of them all."

Jenny Lind arrived in New York on September 1, 1850.

With her were Julius Benedict, composer-conductor, Giovanni Belletti, baritone, and her secretary and cousin, Max Hjortzberg. Present to meet her at the landing was, of course, Barnum. Masses of people crowded the pier and filled the vessels in the North River, all eager to catch a glimpse of the famous visitor. Two triumphal arches had been raised at the pier gates, bearing welcoming greetings to the singer, in gigantic letters of fire. Emerging from under these arches, she traversed the city in Barnum's phaeton, with Barnum at her side, passing through cheering crowds to the Irving House, while handkerchiefs waved from balconies and windows, and flowers rained down on her carriage. All this had been arranged in advance by the astute Barnum.

That night the Swedish singer was given a serenade by the Musical Fund Society, and she appeared on the balcony and bowed her thanks to the serenaders. It was stated at the time, in the New York press, that no foreign visitor, not even anyone of royal rank, had received such a triumphant welcome as did Jenny Lind.

After having looked over all the concert halls available, Jenny Lind selected the Castle Garden—now the Aquarium—for her first concert, which took place on September 11, 1850, before an audience which filled every available seat in the big auditorium. Barnum had conceived the idea of auctioning off the choice seats, before the regular ticket sale. The first seat was sold at the respectable price of $225, a price which, however, was destined to shrink into comparative insignificance before prices obtained in other cities. Thus the first ticket in Boston was auctioned off for the enormous sum of $625; in Providence for $650; in Philadelphia for $625; in New Orleans for $575; and so on.

At her first concert in New York, Jenny Lind was assisted by Belletti, and an orchestra of sixty pieces under the baton of Benedict, who opened the concert with a spirited reading of the overture to Weber's "Oberon." Jenny Lind's first selection was her famous "Casta Diva" aria from "Norma" which brought her a tremendous ovation from the audience. Other numbers on her program were a duet from Rossini's "Il Turco in Italia," sung with Belletti, an aria from Meyerbeer's "The Camp of

JENNY LIND, 1820–87

Silesia" with obbligato by two flutes, the well-known Norwegian Echo Song, which she had to repeat, and "Greeting to America," written especially for the singer by Bayard Taylor, and set to music by Julius Benedict.

The concert was a phenomenal success, the audience wild with enthusiasm, while the press acclaimed Jenny Lind as the greatest artist and the most beautiful and finished singer of her age, at the same time emphasizing her simple, sweet, and lovely appearance. The entire proceeds of that concert—$10,000— she donated to charities.

The day before this first concert, Barnum had suggested a change in his contract with the Swedish singer. The contract originally called for a fee of $1,000 per performance. Now Barnum insisted on raising the fee to $2,000, so sure was he already of the success of the tour. To this she replied: "Mr. Barnum, you have been called the king of humbug; to me you have acted as a perfect gentleman from the minute I met you. I will sing for you as long as you wish in America, yes, anywhere you say."

Between September 11 and 25, Jenny Lind gave six concerts in New York before packed houses. It was said that those concerts produced considerably more than $100,000. She next went to Boston, where she sang in Händel's "Messiah." The press and the public were equally enthusiastic. The famous orator and statesman, Daniel Webster, whom she met during her stay in Boston, declared that he never had heard anything so emotionally beautiful as the rendition of her part in that oratorio.

After additional concerts in New York, Philadelphia, and Washington, where she met President Fillmore, she started on a long tour through the Southern States and Cuba, accompanied by Barnum and her European entourage, all the time giving concerts to extremely enthusiastic houses. In addition to the regularly planned concerts, she gave numerous extra ones for charitable purposes. Christmas was celebrated that year in Charleston. The diva herself had secretly procured and dressed a fine Christmas tree, and the event was observed in a true Swedish manner. And then followed concert after concert throughout the South and West, until, in Philadelphia, she reached her ninety-third appearance. There Barnum, exhausted, asked to be released from the contract. Jenny Lind, herself tired out and in need of rest, readily agreed. But it was not so easy for her to withdraw, as it was for Barnum. New places clamored for her appearance, and there still were many who needed her help. So it happened that she gave forty additional concerts without the assistance of Barnum.

Of her magnificent gifts to charity one contemporary commentator, Charles Rosenberg, had this to say:

Indeed, in New York, Boston, Havana, New Orleans, Charleston, Baltimore and Philadelphia she has given concerts for charity which must have produced more than $60,000. In St. Louis she gave $3,000 to the poor and the same amount in Cincinnati to the different institutions for charity. Certain we are, that while she lives her talents and her genius will constitute the highest of her claims to public admiration, while after her death her genius will be comparatively effaced by the gratitude which will attend the memory of the splendid and boundless benefice.

A slight change had been made in the make-up of the company during May, 1851. Then Julius Benedict, her accompanist and conductor, was called back to London, and was replaced by Otto Goldschmidt, a famous pianist of his age, who had assisted Jenny Lind at many previous concerts in England and Germany. He was a Jew, but adopted the Christian religion at a ceremony at which the Swedish diva, herself, was a witness. The admiration which the two distinguished artists felt for each other soon ripened into love, and on February 5, 1852, they were married in Boston by Bishop Wainwright. For the place of their honeymoon they selected Northampton, Massachusetts, where they spent several months in blissful seclusion.

Then Jenny Lind was ready to bid America farewell. On May 28, 1852, the happy couple sailed from New York for Hamburg, and Jenny Lind's American tour was ended, after more than a year and a half of glorious and unprecedented success.

The next Swedish star to rise on the American horizon was Christina Nilsson. Perhaps Jenny Lind was the bigger personality, but who can tire of reading the vivid life story of the little peasant girl called "*Stina i Snugge*," who, at the early age of seven, sang, and played the violin in the market places, and at village fairs in Småland. It did not take long before the gifted child attracted the attention of well-to-do music lovers, and so, placed in the hands of excellent teachers, first in Sweden and later abroad, started on her glorious career.

On October 27, 1864, we find her in Paris, making her debut as Violetta in Verdi's "Traviata." Triumph upon triumph followed. She was the star preëminent. Ambrose Thomas wrote for her his opera "Hamlet," in which she created the part of Ophelia. In the famous mad scene he included the lovely Swedish folksong, "Neckens polska."

From Paris she went to England, where her success was not less sensational, and from England she started on her first American tour in the year 1870.

To quote her own words:

In September 1870 I saw for the first time the shores of America. I was met out in the bay by a few music-loving Americans and a reception committee who had chartered a small steamer for the purpose. At least 500 persons were at the wharf to greet me— musicians, lyric artists, lovers of music. As soon as we had docked I was the first one to land. I was met here by Mr. Doremus and Mr. Strakosch, my managers, who took me in their carriage to the Claridge Hotel. I was in good health, but had been troubled with seasickness the first days of the voyage. After my arrival at the hotel a deputation from the festival committee called on me to advise me that my countrymen were giving me a serenade in the evening.

That night the Swedish people began to congregate around Germania Hall on Third Avenue. Never before had so many Swedes gathered at one time in the city of New York. The enthusiasm, the joy, the festive spirit were unbounded; were they not gathered to pay their respect to their famous countrywoman, Christina Nilsson? At half-past-ten Chinese lanterns were passed around, and a parade started. The music was rendered by the famous Dodworth's band of New York. The parade marched on Third Avenue to Fourteenth Street, and then Fourth Avenue to the residence of Professor Doremus, where Christina Nilsson was the guest of honor, at a party where the élite of New York City—socially and musically—was assembled to pay her homage. Here we quote the singer again:

At nearly midnight the serenaders arrived and I went to the open window. My appearance called forth tremendous cheers. When the ovation had quieted down, I spoke, I thanked them for the honor bestowed upon me and told them that the joy and happiness they had given me would be remembered as long as I lived. Then the singing began. When the singers started "Hör jag forsens vilda fall" the tears came to my eyes, and when the band played a selection of Swedish folksongs I had the thrill of my life. Among the melodies played was "Näcken han spelar på böljan blå." Oh, what memories it brought to me! It was the first piece I learned to play on the violin. A longing to see my old home came over me. Then, when the band finished its selection with "Du gamla, du fria" the tears burst forth for good—and why not, after all those dear old melodies, so beautifully played! It was one o'clock before the last of the torches was seen in the distance.

The first concert was held in Steinway Hall, which was packed. On the program was, also, the famous violinist Vieuxtemps—but the crowd was waiting for the new Jenny Lind, and at last she appeared. To quote from the New York *Evening Mail:*

As charming as a May morning, her face lights up with a joy she does not try to hide at the sight of thousands of enthusiastic and sympathetic listeners. What a beguiling personage! Her photographs do not do her justice. Her beauty is from within. Every nuance, every little change of mood shows in her expressive face. And what a voice!

The New York *Herald* had this to say:

Never before has there been in Steinway Hall such a gathering. This city has heard all of the world's great artists; tonight the audience came to hear what this Swedish nightingale had to offer. Ophelia's aria from "Hamlet" was electrifying. Her voice can only be compared with Jenny Lind's, it has the same combination of strength and sweetness. When she sang the melody of Händel the public knew no bounds, so pure, so naive, so deep and true was the voice.

Another reviewer likened her voice to a violin's rich tones, combined with the flute's silvery clearness.

Now followed a tour through the United States which lasted two years. There were 261 concerts in all, and 54 cities were visited. During those two years she gave a number of concerts for charity. On November 13, 1870, she gave a concert in aid of the Swedish Lutheran Church in North Bridgewater (now Brockton), Massachusetts. The church realized $2,000 from this concert, and the members were so grateful that they considered naming their church, Christina Church. Instead, Nilsson Street was named after the singer. The program of this concert, as listed below, is interesting, mostly, perhaps, on account of the few appearances of the star herself—quite different from the concert programs of today.

GRAND

SACRED CONCERT

in Aid of the Swedish Lutheran Church
at the
Church of the Disciples (Universalist) North Bridgewater
on Sunday Evening, Nov. 13, 1870

By Mlle

CHRISTINA NILSSON

Assisted by

Mlle Cary, the eminent Contralto
Signor Brignoli, the favorite Tenor
Signor Verger, the distinguished Baritone
Mons. Vieuxtemps, the world renowned Violinist
Signor Bosoni, Pianist

Programme

1. Trio, "Messe Solenelle"   *Rossini*
   Miss CARY, Signor BRIGNOLI and Signor VERGER
2. Ave Maria   *Gounod*
   Mlle NILSSON
   With Violin Obbligato by Mons. VIEUXTEMPS

3. Romance   *Donizetti*
                    Signor BRIGNOLI
4. Aria, "Ah, mon fils"   *Meyerbeer*
                    Miss CARY
5. Reverie, Violin   *Vieuxtemps*
                    Mons. VIEUXTEMPS
6. Cantique, "Les Rameaux"   *Fauré*
                    Signor VERGER
7. Swedish Melodies
                    Mlle NILSSON

After these two years of triumphs, Christina Nilsson returned
to London to be married. The happy bridegroom was Auguste
Rouzaud, and the ceremony took place in the famous Westminster Abbey on July 27, 1872.

The second visit to America came in 1874. From September
until June she sang in 157 concerts. She also sang under the
management of Strakosch at the opera "Elsa and Lucia."
Then, in 1882, we find her in America again, giving concerts
and operatic performances. In this tour she had the assistance
of the Swedish tenor, Theodor Björksten, who remained in this
country, and finally became one of New York's leading singing
teachers.

On October 22, 1883 Mlle Nilsson was chosen to dedicate the
new Metropolitan Opera House at Thirty-ninth Street and
Broadway. The opera was Gounod's "Faust." Her Marguerite
was famous from Paris, where she had sung in the first performance of "Faust" at the Grand Opéra. During this season
she sang such varied rôles as Gioconda, when that Ponchelli
opera had its première, Elvira in "Don Giovanni," Valentine
in "Les Huguenots." At a benefit concert given on April 21,
1884, she sang Bach-Gounod's "Ave Maria" with violin obbligato, played by her co-artist, Marcella Sembrich.

At the end of the season of 1884 she left for Europe, never to
return. But she lived forever in the memory of those who had
been enthralled by the silver and gold in her voice. As one
reviewer wrote: "Her voice was marvelously sweet, brilliant and
even, and she possessed great skill in vocalization. In her acting

she showed great individuality, fine intuition, rare charm and excellent power of expression."

The next Swedish name to appear on the roster of the Metropolitan Opera was that of Johannes Elmblad, who made his debut in December, 1888, as the king in Weber's "Euryanthe." Elmblad was a *basso profundo* of great reputation from many opera stages in Europe, before he arrived in New York. The only appearance, besides his debut, recorded in the annals of the Metropolitan was in January, 1903, when he sang Hunding's rôle in "Die Walküre." In addition to being a great singing actor, he was an excellent stage manager, and was employed as such in New York, for some time in the early part of the century. He died in 1910 at the age of fifty-seven.

In 1893 another famous Swedish opera singer, a worthy successor to Jenny Lind and Christina Nilsson, made her entrance on the Metropolitan stage. She was Sigrid Arnoldson, a daughter and a pupil of the equally famous Swedish opera tenor, Oscar Arnoldson. She had made her operatic debut in Prague in 1885, as Rosina, in Rossini's "Il Barbiere," and had appeared with tremendous success in Sweden, Russia, France, and England, before she joined the Metropolitan cast. Her American debut was made on November 29, 1893, as Baucis, in Gounod's opera, "Philemon et Baucis," where her brilliant silvery coloratura voice and her exquisite stage presence won her instantaneous success. During her one season's stay with the Company, she sang always with enthusiastic reception, such parts as Margueritc in "Faust" and "Les Huguenots," Mignon, Lakmé, Juliette, etc.

One of the greatest opera stars of all time was Olive Fremstad, born in Stockholm, 1870, of a Norwegian father and a Swedish mother. When she was about twelve, her parents emigrated to America and settled in Minneapolis. After vocal studies in this country and in Germany, she started her operatic career in Cologne in 1895. She was already famous all over Europe, when she returned to America to make her memorable debut at the Metropolitan Opera, as Sieglinde in "Die Walküre," on November 25, 1903. For twelve successive seasons she was one of the Metropolitan's greatest attractions.

Her voice was a superb dramatic soprano, her versatility marvelous, equally at home in rôles so strangely varied as those of Brünhilde, Fricka, Isolde, Elsa, Kundry, Tosca, Santuzza, Carmen, and Salome, the last of which she created in this country. This amazingly gifted artist retired in 1914, after an appearance as Elsa in "Lohengrin," and after one of the most extraordinary demonstrations of affection that a singer ever received at the Metropolitan.

Among Swedish opera stars who have conquered America musically, John Forsell surely is entitled to a prominent place. Already a celebrated opera star in Europe, he first came to this country in 1904, as soloist with the Lund University Student Singers, the first Swedish Student Chorus to tour this country. In the season 1909–10 he was a member of the Metropolitan Opera, making his debut on November 19, 1909, as Telramund in "Lohengrin," which brought him enthusiastic acclaim from the audience, as well as unstinted praise from the critics. But the Metropolitan at the time was overloaded with splendid baritones, so that Forsell did not get a fair chance to show his great art. In March, 1910, he sang Figaro in "Il Barbiere," his perhaps most famous part, and Tonio in "Pagliacci." After having concluded his engagement with the Metropolitan in 1910, he was engaged as soloist at the festival given by the American Union of Swedish Singers in New York, and he then made a concert tour through the United States, before returning to Sweden.

In 1910, at one of New York's famous morning musicales, a name, practically unknown to most of the audience, made its first appearance—Julia Claussen. The singer's ship was delayed and, when she arrived in traveling dress at the close of the program, the audience was ready to leave. The tall, stately singer came out on the stage, and as she started her first song, her glorious full voice singing out her command, all the people on their way out stopped and quietly resumed their seats. She sang as many as seven encores before they let her leave the stage. After the concert, she immediately left for Chicago to fill her engagement with the Chicago Opera Company. Her success in the "Windy City" was instantaneous, and was repeated again and again during the five seasons she stayed with the company. During this time she made a coast-to-coast concert tour, singing every day for two months. Traveling in a private car, she enjoyed the company of her two charming daughters, who attended her on this strenuous trip.

In 1917 she was engaged by the Metropolitan Opera Company. She made her debut there on November 23, singing Delilah to Caruso's Samson. During her many years at the Metropolitan she sang all the Wagner contralto and mezzo rôles, as well as the dramatic soprano rôle of Brünhilde in "Die Walküre." Her repertoire also included Carmen, Aczucena in "Il Trovatore," Orpheus, Amneris in "Aïda," etc. Mme Claussen is now teaching voice at the Royal Academy of Music in Stockholm.

At the end of the World War a tall, handsome soldier was given an audition at the Metropolitan Opera, and was immediately engaged. On March 3, 1921, William Gustafson made his debut as Heinrich, in "Lohengrin." His fine physique and sonorous basso voice were well suited to the many kings he impersonated, as King Mark in "Tristan," and the kingly rôles in "Aïda," "Lohengrin," etc. He was, *par preference*, a Wagner singer, and his Hunding, Fafner, etc., are still well remembered. Although born in Boston, he spoke Swedish without an accent. He was a fine linguist, speaking fluently German, Italian, and French. His art was many-sided. Had he not chosen singing, he would have made his mark as a sculptor or an architect, both of which professions he had studied in Europe as well as here. His untimely death in 1931 cut short a fine career.

Karin Branzell made her debut at the Metropolitan as Fricka, on February 4, 1924. Two days later she sang Ortrud in "Lohengrin." On March 5 she sang Brangäne, and on March 17 a dramatic soprano rôle, that of Brünhilde in "Die Walküre." Then she returned to contralto rôles, displaying her versatility by appearing as Amneris in "Aïda," Aczucena in "Il Trovatore," and Delilah, as well as Venus, in "Tannhäuser." Truly a feat in the short time of nine weeks! Her musicianship is as dependable as is her voice and dramatic art.

During the season of 1925–26 an episode of interest occurred at a performance of "Die Walküre" in Brooklyn. Julia Claussen was singing Brünhilde and Branzell, Fricka. During the

second act Claussen lost her voice. Branzell had barely finished
her part of Fricka when she was rushed into the part of Brünhilde while Claussen retired. A similar incident was repeated
later in New York. Kappell, singing Brünhilde, became suddenly indisposed; at an hour's notice Julia Claussen left her
guests at a dinner party at her home, and sang Brünhilde while
Kappell retired.

Branzell's repertoire is extensive. She not only sings and
acts the dramatic and tragic rôles, but can also be light of
touch, as, for instance, in her Magdalena in "Meistersinger,"
and her charming queen in "Schwanda," Jaromir Weinberger's
short-lived opera. Every season brings her back in finer vocal
and dramatic fettle than the preceding one. Anyone who has had
the privilege of listening to "Tristan" these last seasons will
never forget the two beautiful voices of Branzell's Brangäne
and Flagstad's Isolde. The two voices are like interwoven
golden threads, matchless in their beauty of phrase and color.

Branzell is much in demand abroad. Last season Berlin,
Paris, Prague, London were on her itinerary—and, of course,
guest appearances in her beloved Stockholm. To quote her own
words: "I have sung at the Metropolitan since 1924. I love
America and the old opera house at 39th Street and Broadway.
I am always happy to return." Surely we, here in the United
States, are happy to welcome her back.

In 1924 Martin Öhman became a member of the Metropolitan Opera Company for a short season. The New York climate
did not, however, agree with him, and brought harm to his
beautiful tenor voice. For that reason he did not appear to his
best advantage and failed to score the brilliant success which
has been his, both before and after his Metropolitan engagement.

Nanny Larsén-Todsen made her delayed debut at the Metropolitan on January 31, 1925, as Brünhilde in "Götterdämmerung." She was to have sung in "Tristan" on January 15, but
an accident during a rehearsal of "Götterdämmerung" necessi-
tated a postponement. "Grane," the famous Metropolitan horse
and the worry of all Wagner sopranos, stepped on her foot.
Her debut was auspicious. Her ringing, high tones, her mature
art, and her musicianship were always in evidence. During her

two seasons she sang all the Wagnerian rôles, Rachel in "La Juive," Fidelio, Gioconda, etc. The climate of New York never agreed with her either, and after two seasons she left for Europe, where she has been singing ever since, and where she is hailed as one of the greatest Wagner singers of her time. Her modesty, her sincerity, and sympathetic personality are a source of pleasure to those with whom she comes in contact.

January 25, 1931, brought another Swedish dramatic soprano to the Metropolitan stage, in the person of Göta Ljungberg. Her debut as Sieglinde was sensational. Her colorful voice, her attractive personality, her natural talent for the stage, all helped to make her Wagnerian rôle alive. Blond and tall, she looked the goddess she was impersonating. During that first season she replaced Jeritza in many of her rôles. She also sang Isolde and Kundry, and the Brünhildes of the Ring. At the revival of Strauss's "Elektra" on December 3, 1932, Ljungberg sang Chrysothemis. Later in the season she sang Elektra. On January 13, 1934, it fell to Mme Ljungberg's lot to sing and act the much-discussed and taxing opera, Strauss's "Salome." At the première of Howard Hanson's "Merry Mount," on February 10, 1934, she created the part of Marigold.

Since leaving the Metropolitan, Mme Ljungberg has sung with other opera companies throughout the United States. On her many successful concert tours she has carried the message of Swedish song to the American public.

One event of more than passing interest took place on January 16, 1936, when Gertrud Wettergren sang Carmen, in Swedish, on the stage of the Metropolitan. Never before, and probably never again, will that happen. Called on a short notice to substitute for Rosa Ponselle, who was ill, Mme Wettergren was unprepared to sing the part in French, so the powers that be said: "Well, sing it in Swedish." She did, and made a sensational success. Her impersonation, as well as her singing, was called vivid and elegant, full of fire and imagination.

Mme Wettergren had made her debut as Amneris, in "Aïda," on December 26, 1935. In the season of 1936–37, she recreated Delilah. Before joining the Metropolitan in 1936, she was a member of the Chicago Opera Company, one of the brightest stars of that association. Her concert tour was also a success.

In her short one-and-a-half seasons she established herself as an interesting and individual artist; and the whole opera-going public look forward to the return of this fine dramatic singer.

Another Swedish contralto was added to the Metropolitan roster during the 1936–37 season—Kerstin Thorborg, who made her debut as Fricka in "Die Walküre," on December 21, 1936. A fine artist, a beautiful voice, and a dramatic actress of magnificent power. She came to the Metropolitan, after a career on the leading operatic stages in Europe which had been fraught with brilliant successes. When singing Wagnerian rôles at the Covent Garden in 1936, the London *Times's* famous reviewer, Ernest Newman, after praising the clearness and mellowness of her voice, added that he would rank her as "the greatest Wagnerian actress of the present day." In her short stay of two months at the Metropolitan, she made a profound impression. The next season, 1937–38, saw her at the opera again, for she left with a contract for a return engagement.

With that, to the best of my belief, I have mentioned all the Swedish opera stars who (with the exception of only Jenny Lind) have graced the Metropolitan stage. But there has been a number of other Swedish opera singers, who, from time to time, have visited this country on concert tours and thus have introduced Swedish songs and music to America. First among them should be mentioned Carolina Östberg and Carl Fredrik Lundquist ("Lunkan"), two of the brightest stars of the Stockholm opera of their time. They came here as soloists at the first singing festival of the newly organized American Union of Swedish Singers in Chicago, 1893, and gave a number of concerts in various parts of the country in 1893 and 1894. The list of other Swedish artists of note, who have made successful tours in America, includes Anna Hellström-Oscar and her husband, Martin Oscar, both prominent members of the Stockholm opera, Anna Lundberg, Oscar Bergström, and Ernst Henrik Swedelius.

Nor should the many excellent singers of Swedish birth or descent be forgotten, who, even though they have not, so far, reached the goal of the Metropolitan Opera, have made the music of Sweden known and admired in this country. Among them should be mentioned the late Gustaf Holmquist, with his gentle and sympathetic personality, one of the finest baritones of his time and an interpreter of oratorio, second to none; Jenny Norelius and Agnes Staberg Hall whose beautiful soprano voices brought them popular acclaim on numerous concert stages; Greta Torpadie, an exquisite artist, both in vocalism and interpretation, now residing in Gothenburg; Harold Lindau (Aroldo Lindi), a "Helden-tenor" of purest water, acclaimed as "a second Caruso" on many opera stages throughout the world, including the Chicago Opera Company; Lillian Gustafson, graduated from the Jamestown Conservatory, a beautiful singer with a beautiful soprano voice, known and admired through her numerous concerts with leading orchestras in the important Music Festivals in different parts of the country, and many others whose names and life work I cannot at this time recall.

Recorded in the annals of Swedish musical contributions to America should also be the visits of famous Swedish singing societies, such as the Student Choruses of Lund and Stockholm, the Singing Society "De Svenske," all most excellent performers, and the several ladies' ensembles, having made auspicious and highly successful tours through America, such as "The Swedish Ladies' Quartet" in 1876–77, "The Swedish Ladies' Octet" in 1887, and the famous "Düring Ladies' Quintet." And everybody knows what splendid contributions the American Union of Swedish Singers has supplied to the appreciation of Swedish music in America; but I understand that a special chapter will be devoted to that subject.

There have also been many outstanding singing teachers of Swedish birth, who deserve mention in this chapter. Among them might be mentioned, in the first place, Theodore Björksten, who accompanied Christina Nilsson on her last tour in the United States, and remained here as a teacher; and his wife, the late Mme Torpadie, who had a great following as a teacher in New York. Another distinguished singing teacher was Mme Augusta Öhrström-Renard who, in the early 'eighties, was a member of the Royal Opera in Stockholm. After many successful concert tours in Europe and in this country, she settled in 1897 in New York, where she soon gained an enduring reputation as a teacher and musician of the highest order. It may be safely asserted that few Swedish singers have done more to make the American public acquainted with Swedish songs than she, both through her own singing and through the work of her pupils. Mme Renard died in 1921. Among other prominent Swedish singing teachers should be recorded the late Mme de Berg-Löfgren of Boston, formerly a member of the Stockholm opera, and the late Mme Marie Peterson of Worcester.

Samuel Youngquist (Ljungkvist), a native of Skåne and pupil at the Stockholm Conservatory of Music, made his debut at the Royal Theatre in Stockholm in 1913, as Don Jose in "Carmen." As a tenor soloist he is well known in Sweden, Finland, and America. Now located in New York, he is soloist in the Marble Collegiate Church, and vocal teacher at Upsala College. His wife, Helen Lindström Youngquist, an accomplished pianist, is his accompanist.

What is written above does in no manner pretend to be an exhaustive story of what artists of Swedish birth or lineage have done, to enrich the musical life of this country. The material at my disposal has not been very complete, and probably a good many more names should have been included. But the list, as presented above, is nevertheless an impressive one, showing that in music and song, as in so many other fields of cultural endeavor, America owes a great debt of gratitude to the followers of the first Delaware settlers.

The American Union of Swedish Singers

CHARLES K. JOHANSEN

Mr. Johansen is the publisher of *Nordstjernan* in New York, and also Honorary President of the American Union of Swedish Singers.

THE United Scandinavian Singers of America, the predecessor of the American Union of Swedish Singers, was organized in 1886 at a meeting held in New York, to which five choruses of male singers sent delegates, representing societies from Philadelphia, Boston, New York, and Brooklyn. The following year the first singing festival was held in Philadelphia. Captain Charles M. Machold of Philadelphia, a Dane by birth, was the founder of the organization, and its first president. One Norwegian society from Chicago had joined, and partook in the festival.

The union grew fast, and at its second festival, held in Chicago, 1889, the chorus numbered six hundred voices. The third, and last, singing festival was held in Minneapolis, 1891; the United Scandinavian Singers of America had now increased in membership and numbered seven hundred voices.

At this festival a beautiful, costly, embroidered silk banner, donated by Robert Lindblom, then President of the Chicago Board of Trade, had been accepted with enthusiasm. It was to be sung for at each quadrennial festival, and was to be held by the society receiving the majority vote. The Swedish Glee Club of Brooklyn won the trophy, and it has never been sung for since.

During these years the waves of discord raged high between Norway and Sweden, and continued until the peaceful dissolution of the bonds that had tied Sweden and Norway for so many years. The union was dissolved by treaty in Karlstad, Sweden, September 23, 1905, and on October 26, King Oscar II abdicated his Norwegian throne. For many years before this there had been strained relations between the two Scandinavian countries, and the Norwegians and Swedes in the United States were also at loggerheads, while the Danes were neutral. Robert Lindblom was violently pro-Swedish; he even published a daily paper in English in Chicago to promulgate his program—an expensive proposition.

A meeting of delegates of the United Scandinavian Singers of America was held in New York early in 1892. The meeting was tumultuous. The Norwegian delegates refused to have the Lindblom banner sung for at future singing festivals, and they carried the day. Now, too, the Danish delegates were passive. By instructions from their societies, all of the Swedish delegates resigned and, then and there, ended the life of the United Scandinavian Singers of America—ended in disharmony, whereas the members had been wont to sing in harmony.

At the initiative of the Lyran Singing Society of New York, all Swedish singing societies in the United States were called upon to send delegates to a convention which was held in Chicago on Thanksgiving Day, 1892. Then and there the American Union of Swedish Singers was organized. The first board of officers consisted of Magnus Olson, Chicago, President; Gustaf Wicklund, Minneapolis, Vice-President; Dr. Victor Nilsson, Minneapolis, Financial Secretary; Charles K. Johansen, Secretary; Gustaf Hallbom, Chicago, Treasurer, and Professor John R. Örtengren, Director-in-chief.

The first singing festival of the American Union of Swedish Singers was held on "Sweden's Days" at the World's Fair in Chicago, 1893, where the grand chorus and soloists sang repeatedly to enthusiastic audiences of over ten thousand persons. The soloists were Carolina Östberg and C. F. Lundquist ("Lunkan") of the Royal Opera in Stockholm, and Conrad Behrens, formerly of the same opera. Theodore Thomas conducted the orchestra. (See the chapter on "Opera Singers.")

In all, the American Union of Swedish Singers has held ten quadrennial festivals; namely, in Chicago 1893, 1905, 1924, and 1933; New York 1897, 1910, and 1926; in Jamestown 1901; Minneapolis 1914, and Worcester 1924. All have been musical successes and social events.

After the festival in New York, 1897, a chorus of fifty-four singers, under the leadership of Professor John R. Örtengren, set sail from our metropolis and toured Sweden, singing in a number of cities, starting from Gothenburg and finishing in

Stockholm, where they sang at the Exposition and Skansen. King Oscar II invited the members of the chorus to a luncheon in the Royal Palace; His Majesty sang with them. This was the first chorus of Swedish singers from America who ever toured Sweden, and, previously, none from Sweden had ever sung in this country.

In 1910, a chorus of forty-five men from the American Union of Swedish Singers toured Sweden. In 1923 a number of singers, members of this Union, sang in Gothenburg with the Sweden's Singers' Union. The Swedish Glee Club of Chicago toured Sweden under the leadership of William Nordin, for a month following this festival. In 1930, at a singing festival in Stockholm, no less than 104 members of the American Union of Swedish Singers partook, under the leadership of Oscar Ekeberg of Providence. Individual societies, members of the Union, have toured Sweden; the Swedish Glee Club of Brooklyn, Carl Sylvan, Director; and Svithiod and North Star of Chicago, Joel Mossberg, Director.

The American Union of Swedish Singers sang at the unveiling ceremonies of the John Ericsson Monument in Washington, D.C., May 29, 1926. Previous to the unveiling, the chorus serenaded the President of the United States, Calvin Coolidge, at the White House; and thereafter they serenaded Crown Prince Gustaf Adolf, the Crown Princess, and Minister and Mme Wollmar F. Boström at the Swedish Legation.

After the unveiling ceremonies, the six hundred or more singers journeyed to New York. The festival in the metropolis was held two nights at the Metropolitan Opera House. At the second concert, June 1, the guests of honor were the Crown Prince, the Crown Princess, and their suite, Minister Wollmar F. Boström, Consul General Olof H. Lamm, and other distinguished guests.

Crown Prince Gustaf Adolf, who is President of Sweden's Singers' Union, with which the American Union of Swedish Singers is affiliated, made a speech which was received with fervent applause. The chorus sang under the leadership of Ernest Francke, inspired by the presence of their President, and *sångarbroder* ("singers' brother"). The auditorium was crowded. The soloists were Mme Marie Sundelius and Mme

Julia Claussen of the Metropolitan Opera, and Folke Anderson of the Royal Opera in Stockholm. Howard Barlow conducted the orchestra.

As stated, the American Union of Swedish Singers holds festivals quadrennially, and is composed of seventy choruses, with a membership of about 1,500 male voices. Oscar Ekeberg is the Director-in-chief. The Union is divided into four sections, each holding its own festival, usually the second year after the quadrennial festival. The divisions are: Eastern Division (east of Chicago), thirty-two societies; Midwestern Division, twenty choruses; Northwestern Division, ten members; and Pacific Coast Division, eight choruses.

The next quadrennial festival will be held in Philadelphia in 1938, in connection with the Tercentenary celebration of the Swedes' landing on the Delaware. The chorus will also take part in the festivities in Wilmington.

The officers of the American Union of Swedish Singers are:

CHARLES K. JOHANSEN, Honorary President, New York City.

FRED BOLLING, Honorary President, Chicago.

JOHN R. ÖRTENGREN, Honorary Director-in-chief, Stockholm, Sweden.

JOHN HELLBERG, President, New Rochelle, N.Y.

EDWARD E. JOHNSON, First Vice-President, Chicago, Ill.

CARL BRANDT, Vice-President, New Haven, Conn.

P. O. HEDWALL, Vice-President, St. Paul, Minn.

EMIL HOGBERG, Vice-President, San Francisco, Calif.

JOEL S. SÖDERLUND, Secretary, Chicago, Ill.

THEO. HAGSTRÖM, Financial Secretary, Jamestown, N.Y.

J. E. VANSTRÖM, Treasurer, Chicago City, Minn.

OSCAR EKEBERG, Director-in-chief, Conimicut, R.I.

The official organ of the Union is *Musiktidning* ("*Music News*"), published in Chicago, Joel S. Söderlund, Editor.

The above is a brief history of the American Union of Swedish Singers, now with forty-five years in active work. Long live Swedish song in America!

Moving Picture Actors

LEONARD CLAIRMONT

Like most people connected with the moving-picture industry, the Author of this chapter works under an assumed name. His real one is Leonard Asplund, and he was born in Stockholm in 1904, the son of a prominent police official. In Sweden he studied the art of photography, and, on arriving in the United States in 1923, he "made a bee line" for Hollywood. There he worked, first as a portrait photographer, and later as a producer of short films, newsreels, and travelogues, specializing in archeological subjects. He also writes news and magazine articles for both Swedish and American publications.

THE Swedes came early to Hollywood. Practically from the time of the birth of the cinema, they contributed to it high artistry and skilful workmanship. The rapidly rising prosperity of motion pictures inspired the organization, almost at once, of several new concerns, including Kalem, Fox, Biograph, Kleine, World, Imp, Famous Players–Lasky, and many others. These studios had hardly hung out their impressive signs before the pioneering Swedes made their appearance.

Frank Marion, one of the founders of the now historic Kalem Company, humorously put it: "The moving picture entertainment is the coming thing. Every person with the slightest bit of vision is joining our forces. We already have people from every walk of life in this new industry. People of all nations. *Even Swedes.*"

Yes, that was the first advance troupe, not that our fellow Swedes made motion-picture history overnight; but, by their participation, they gained enough prestige to enable the Swedish name to go down in movie annals as an early and honorable one.

Linda Arvidson was the first to try her hand at the new art. That was as early as 1907. She was, at first, just an actress occasionally employed at the old Biograph Company, in its first days of glory. She later became active as a writer, collaborating with that great pioneer, David Wark Griffith. It was, at that time, a perfectly concealed secret that Linda Arvidson was, in fact, none other than Mrs. D. W. Griffith.

The Swedish cavalcade had begun! Anna Q. Nilsson, for some time an artist's model in New York, began her screen career in 1911. From her home in Ystad, she had emigrated to the United States in 1907. Her blond beauty quickly became an attractive drawing card in Westerns and melodramas. Her popularity with the movie-going public proved to be lasting; and it was not until she was thrown off a horse in 1930, and suffered serious injuries, that she gave up her screen work. She is now staging a comeback.

Sigrid Holmquist, another Swedish girl, became a favorite. Winifred Westover, Jane Novak, and Knut Rahmn followed, blazing the same trail. Knut Rahmn still remains in the industry as a well-known photographer. Emory Johnson succeeded as a director in the earlier days of silent pictures. He, too, still lives and works in Hollywood.

Another chapter in the miracle stories of Hollywood has been written by Warner Oland, who became one of the foremost cinema character actors in America. His Charlie Chan pictures are landmarks in motion-picture history. The Chan-Oland combination is noteworthy, in that it has produced the longest and most successful series of feature-length productions of the cinema.

Born at Umeå in northern Sweden in 1880, Johan Verner Ölund came to America with his family, at the age of thirteen, and first settled in Boston. Then, for fourteen years, Warner Oland, as he renamed himself, devoted his energies to the stage, specializing in Ibsen and Shakespearean characters. He also translated Strindberg. (See the chapter on "Authors.") At intervals during this time, he made a few excursions into the then-insignificant movies. His first screen rôle was in support of Theda Bara, in "Jewels of the Madonna." Then followed nearly a hundred more movie assignments.

The "Charlie Chan" character was brought to life on the screen by Warner Oland, in 1931. Pictures based on the Chinese detective character, adapted from the novels of the late Earl Derr Biggers, had been attempted several times without success. Finally, Warner Oland was tested for the part, as his previous

WARNER OLAND

"CHARLIE CHAN"

screen experience had included the portrayal of many Oriental types. By a muscular contraction of his eyelids, and by brushing the ends of his eyebrows up and the ends of his moustache down, he was able, almost without make-up, to look like a genuine Oriental.

Wherever Warner Oland set foot during his recent journey in China and Japan, he was mobbed by admiring fans—a remarkable recognition of his consummate skill as an actor. A high point of flattery has been reached in Shanghai, where a famous Chinese actor stars in pictures in which he imitates Oland's characterizations. While we sometimes say: "Clever—those Chinese!" the Chinese probably say: "Clever—those Swedes!"

Among the directorial top names in the motion-picture field, Victor Seastrom still stands like a monument. Even though he no longer directs American stars, his name has been so permanently etched into the annals of picturemaking, that a reference to great directors is not possible, without mentioning this sturdy pioneer. His sure and steady hand has piloted many actors and actresses into fame and fortune. And who would know more about this intricate business than Seastrom, being an actor of high standard, himself. One of the more clearly defined influences that directors have brought to the screen is the acting tradition. Seastrom is probably our best example. He is at one with the actors and actresses in his cast. He knew—and still knows—what each occasion requires, and he knows whether or not the players are achieving the effect. This great director, true to the best acting tradition, brought to his work what amounted, almost, to genius in interpretation. Before he made his American career, Victor Seastrom acted and directed simultaneously. In pictures such as "At the Stroke of Midnight" and "Mortal Clay," he played the stellar rôle. While in Hollywood he directed such artistic box-office successes as "Name the Man," "He Who Gets Slapped," Lagerlöf's "The Tower of Lies," "The Divine Woman," and "The Wind." Many of the high-salaried stars of today owe their early success to Victor Seastrom. Now he is at home and at ease in his native country, but his name still lives in Hollywood. In Sweden he has recently essayed the title rôle in a new film based on the life of John Ericsson.

In the annals of Swedish actors in Hollywood, 1925 and 1926 turned out to be years of great importance. Then came a second division of the Swedish cavalcade. New blood from the homeland was transfused into the now old and settled Hollywood. Victor Seastrom had already shown the way.

Lars Hanson, at that time spoken of as Sweden's foremost screen actor, arrived with his actress-wife, Karin Molander, at the movie capital of the world, and went to work for the Metro-Goldwyn-Mayer studios. His stay was not extensive, but long enough to enable him to go down in the records as one of the most talented players from abroad. His outstanding pictures were "The Flesh and the Devil," in which he played opposite Greta Garbo, "The Scarlet Letter" with Lillian Gish, and, under Victor Seastrom's direction, "Captain Salvation." Almost overnight his name became as well known in this country as it had been in Sweden; but, even that newly found fame was not sufficient to keep him in Hollywood. Lars Hanson, like Seastrom, returned to the scenes of his earlier triumphs.

Einar Hanson, that likable and popular young fellow, already well known through his many European films, came to Hollywood about the same time. In record time he appeared in more pictures than all the rest of the Swedes put together, and then came sudden death. One summer morning in 1927 he was found pinned underneath the steering wheel of his overturned automobile, on the outskirts of the film metropolis, and a most promising film career came to an abrupt close.

Soon afterwards Nils Asther came, saw, and conquered. He was the type to please feminine admirers, and the producers quickly realized that Asther was especially suited for leading rôles of a more sophisticated nature. Twice he played opposite Greta Garbo, and at other times with other prominent stars. His climb to fame was swift and without many difficulties, but later, through being cast in spiritless and insignificant parts, Nils became weary, and took up his work in Europe again.

Then a new name came to filmland, a name of magic that was destined to become legendary. By almost common consent Greta Garbo was crowned the Queen of the Cinema. Soon after her first triumphs, she became seclusive, and surrounded herself with mystery, thus giving rise to the Garbo myth. She was

GRETA GARBO

called "Duchess of Solitude," "Goddess of Elusiveness," "Enigma," "Swedish Sphinx," and "The Woman Nobody Knows."

Greta Garbo has placed herself in the glare of the most merciless spotlight in the world, and, until she steps out of its penetrating rays, she cannot know the peacefulness and quiet of the dim shadows. Greta Garbo's story is a study in anomalies. Few of the known facts of her life and personality dovetail. It is as though Greta Lovisa Gustafsson, the woman, were one person, and Greta Garbo, the glamorous and elusive motion-picture star, another and different individual, altogether.

Pieced together, the life story of Greta Garbo follows this chronology. She was born September 18, 1905, in Stockholm, in an ordinary tenement house. Her parents were of modest circumstances, and of plain, Swedish, home-owning farmer stock. After a childhood of normal life, she went to work in a department store. But her ambition impelled her to quit the job she needed so badly for the uncertainty of work in the Swedish film studios. For two seasons she studied at the Royal Dramatic Academy to further her education, which has stood her in such good stead ever since. She flung her ambitions to full abandon. The flame all but consumed her entirely. She had no thoughts for anything but her career.

In the spring of 1923 Greta Garbo met the man who was to become the greatest and most driving influence in her life. He was the late Mauritz Stiller. Under his direction Garbo played the part of Countess Elizabeth Dohna in "The Story of Gösta Berling," by Selma Lagerlöf, a picture that won world-wide acclaim. It happened that Louis B. Mayer, vice-president of Metro-Goldwyn-Mayer studio, was traveling in Europe at that time, and heard of the Mauritz Stiller picture and the girl he had named Garbo.

In July, 1925, Greta Garbo left her home in Stockholm for the journey to the United States, leaving Gothenburg on the steamer *Drottningholm*.

In California, at the studio, weeks dragged into months— many months—before she was placed before a camera. Finally they put her to work in her first American picture, "The Torrent," the picture that established Garbo overnight on the screen in America. From that day to this, her popularity has ascended to boundless heights. With Mauritz Stiller by her side during her first year in Hollywood, she felt confident and sure of herself. But later, during the making of "Wild Orchids," she received a cable from Stockholm announcing the death of her great friend and guide, who had originally accompanied her to Hollywood, but who had failed to find a permanent place for himself. To Stiller, Garbo owed her early success, but later the pupil rose above the master. What the name, Greta Garbo, means to the motion-picture industry, the whole world knows. Never before has any screen actress reached the same popularity. And what makes her a special source of pride to her countrymen is the fact that everyone knows that she is Swedish.

Native-born Americans of Swedish descent in the motion-picture business are plentiful and of high standing. Almost every studio on the Coast has one or more under contract, and it is with great pride that I can name them in connection with the Swedish "home-grown variety."

Jean Rogers should head the list, because of her striking beauty and promising future. She has been called the most beautiful natural blond in California. Jean's real name is Elinor Lövgren. She was born in 1915. Her father is from Malmö, her mother from Lund. She has been an actress for many years and, at present, is being groomed for important rôles, with stardom not far away.

Astrid Allwyn is also of Swedish parentage, born in Boston. Her name is becoming more and more known among the second-lead players. At her comparatively tender age, she has participated in approximately forty pictures, which is a more than creditable record for an actress who has been in Hollywood only a few years.

Eric Linden is as Swedish as his own name, although born in New York City. His father, Philip Linden, was once a member of the Royal Opera in Stockholm, which accounts for his ardent interest in dramatics. Ever since he left the DeWitt Clinton High School, there has been nothing but acting for this young man. After two years of schooling at the New York Theatre Guild, he joined the Paris American Stock Company in France, and, after returning to the United States, spent many years on the stage, and in motion-picture work. His place among Hollywood Swedes is not to be forgotten.

Dorothy Peterson, character actress, best known through her outstanding work with the famous Dionne quintuplets, has been in Hollywood since leaving the Broadway playhouses. Moving rapidly from one vivid characterization to another, she has, in a comparatively short space of time, appeared in over sixty pictures. While she will be long remembered for her portrayal of the motherly head nurse in "The Country Doctor" and her later portrayal of the same character in "Reunion," Miss Peterson had, as a matter of fact, long before become established in the public mind as a competent and clever actress. Known on the stage for her versatility and dash, and for the smooth sophistication they implied, she very readily found appreciation of such qualities in Hollywood.

Veda Ann Borg, daughter of an interior decorator in Boston, is also making good progress. Tired of modeling in gown shops, she listened to the voice of inspiration, and left Boston to secure an outstanding position in the movie metropolis. Although still a relative newcomer, she has steadily been moving up into the front lines.

There could hardly be much doubt about Leif Erikson's ancestry. He looks like one of his Viking forefathers, tall and strong, and is endowed with the physique of a true Nordic, including a mane of light-brown hair. He was born in California in 1914, his father being a sea captain in the North Pacific trade. Erikson's first professional appearance was that of a singer. He later toured with Max Reinhardt, and finally landed in the films, in which one of his most recent rôles was that of the dashing "brother" of Greta Garbo in "Conquest." In private life he is the husband of Frances Farmer.

I could mention a whole list of Swedes whose names are quite familiar on the screen. Little thirteen-year-old June Carlson, daughter of a Los Angeles schoolteacher of Swedish birth, is another newcomer. Then there is Shirley Grey, born Agnes Zetterstrand; Ruth Peterson; Greta Granstedt; four-year-old May Carlson; five-year-old Frances Peterson; Evelyn Knapp; Agnes Anderson; Arthur Pierson; Allyn Drake; Gustav Wally (Wallenberg); Henry Hunter (Jacobson), and many more.

They do not all show their Swedish origin in their names, no more than does the writer of this article. But they are all sons and daughters of the Vikings.

Then, of course, we have an ensemble of 50 per cent, or less, Swedes, not all extremely important, but, nevertheless, sufficiently outstanding not to be omitted. Gertrude Niesen, lush-voiced, exotic jazz singer, whose father was Swedish, and mother Russian; Polly Rowles, born to wealth and social prestige; Larry Blake, whose real name is Lorenz Lundberg; Sarah Padden, an old-time Broadway actress, whose mother was of Swedish descent; Myrna Loy, one of whose grandmothers was of the same stock; Gloria Swanson, whose father, an American army captain, was born of Swedish parents in Chicago; Lona André, whose real name was Luana Anderson, her father being Swedish; Anna Sten, born in Russia, of a Russian father and Swedish mother from Poland; Joel McCrea and Moroni Olson—all with enough Swedish blood in their veins to boast about it.

Connected with motion pictures there is another Swedish woman in the film capital, so outstanding that she is practically a part of Hollywood itself. While not strictly an actress, she occupies a unique position. Her name is Olga Celeste, animal trainer and daredevil. She was the first woman to bring her trained jungle cats before the movie camera—and that was way back in the old Selig Zoo days, when "The Adventures of Kathleen" used to keep the movie-goers talking for days.

You may remember that old thriller, in which Kathleen breaks through the green wall of the jungle, and flees in terror across the little clearing, straight at you, and how, a split-second later, from the same gap in the jungle barrier, the lithe, low-leaping form of a great spotted leopard emerges and earnestly takes up the pursuit of the heroine! And then—"Continued next week!"

When the Kathleen Williams picture was being made, Olga Celeste always took the dangerous parts; and she got away with it, to the glorification of Kathleen. And Olga is still doing the very same thing, day after day, in the studios of Hollywood. Twenty-five years of the most exciting job anyone could wish for. Olga is really a woman without fear.

Olga Celeste was born near Lund, in southern Sweden, Knut-

DOROTHY PETERSON

IN "THE COUNTRY DOCTOR"

son being her real name. As a young girl she emigrated to the United States, and soon joined the Madigan Circus, as a bare-back rider. Later, she became associated with the famous "Big Otto," who taught her how to handle wild animals. After a few years of circus life, she finally settled down in Los Angeles, where she is now known as "the leopard woman," daily putting the movie leopards through their routine, and "doubling" for stars in dangerous sequences. There is not a producer nor a di-rector who does not know Olga Celeste.

Actors, actresses, and directors are not all that Sweden has contributed to Hollywood. There is a multitude of motion-pic-ture technicians of all sorts and descriptions—every one of them holding an important part in a great industry that inter-ests the whole world. Many fine cameramen, writers, film edi-tors, instructors, sound engineers, designers, architects, and other skilled craftsmen have grown up with the studios, and be-come men of significance—men whom Hollywood could not do without. To be a Swede in Hollywood has more than once proven to be the key to preferment.

In the field of moving-picture projection, two Swedish names must be mentioned—P. John Berggren of Chicago and A. F. Victor of New York. With the financial support of George K. Spohr of the once-famous Essenay Films, Mr. Berggren con-structed, some years ago, a film camera which took a three-dimensional picture. Gigantic views of Niagara Falls, taken by this camera, were shown in New York studios in the late 1920's, and later at the World's Fair at Chicago. There was, also, a sound film of an operetta taken in New York, showing life-sized figures on a natural-size stage, giving a perfect illusion of depth, as well as of height and width. The screen was so large that it covered the entire proscenium of a theater. Mr. Berg-gren was born in northern Sweden in 1888 and came to America in 1912. As an inventor he has obtained several patents in other fields than that of the cinema. Mr. Victor's work has been in making practical the 16-millimeter educational film, and its pro-jection in homes and schools by apparatus of his own design. He was born in Bollnäs, Hälsingland.

Stage and Radio Performers

HOLGER LUNDBERGH

Holger Lundbergh was born and educated in Stockholm, his father being the late Teodor Lundberg, a noted sculptor, who was head of the Academy of Fine Arts, and his mother, Ellen Lundberg-Nyblom, a poet, novelist, and playwright. For the past ten years Mr. Lundbergh has contributed both verse and prose to American newspapers and periodicals. He lives in New York, and is Assistant Manager of the American-Swedish News Exchange.

MANY Swedes, as has been shown above, have achieved stardom in American films. On the other hand, Broadway luminaries of Swedish blood have been comparatively few. What they have lacked in numbers they have, however, made up for in importance.

Take, for instance, the case of Martha Hedman. Contemporary playgoers have become accustomed to comedies that run for three or four years. They easily forget that there was a time when no "Old Soak," or "Lightning," or "Rain," or "Kiki," or, more recently, "Abie's Irish Rose," broke record upon record of longevity. If they took the trouble of looking back far enough, they would find that the first genuine Broadway perennial was a light, slight, but amusing, piece by the title of "The Boomerang." This play, written by Winchell Smith and Victor Mapes, and produced by David Belasco, ran for 522 consecutive performances in 1915 and 1916 at the Belasco Theatre in New York, after which it enjoyed two extremely lucrative seasons on the road. It was in the leading rôle of the romantic nurse, Virginia Xelva, that the blue-eyed, golden-haired Swedish actress, Martha Hedman, scored an unusual success.

Born in Östersund, Miss Hedman made her stage debut in 1905, at the Alexander Theatre in Helsingfors, under the expert tutelage of Siri von Essen, first wife of August Strindberg, and regarded as one of Scandinavia's foremost actresses. After a few seasons in Finland, during which she played minor rôles, she returned to Sweden, and for three years appeared under the management of Albert Ranft, the country's foremost theatrical entrepreneur.

At twenty-one, she made a pleasure trip to England, with no intention of seeking employment on the London stage. She had, however, made a study of English, and one day she was introduced to the late Charles Frohman, the New York manager. He persuaded her to take the part of Renée de Rould in the Bernstein play, "The Attack," which he was soon to produce in New York. Young and optimistic, Miss Hedman immediately accepted. She first hastened to Paris, where the piece was then playing, to familiarize herself with the part; and thence proceeded to Manhattan. Her American debut took place at the Garrick Theatre on September 12, 1912, to the warm applause of press and public.

There followed a number of other rôles—Blanche Chilworth in "Liberty Hall," Katherine in "Indian Summer," and Lilian Garson in "Half-an-Hour." In the meantime English managers were bidding for her, and in 1913 she went to London, where she made her debut on New Year's Day, 1914, at St. James's Theatre. The vehicle again was "The Attack." In London she was also seen, as Mrs. Guilford in "The Two Virtues," before she returned, after the outbreak of the World War, to New York.

She opened, on October 5, as Anna Swanjen, a Scandinavian rôle, in "The Heart of a Thief," and later went on tour with John Drew as Simone, in "The Prodigal Husband." In 1915 she played Jane Carson, in "The Trap." In many cases she found herself cast in the blood-and-thunder melodramas of the War years, insignificant thrillers that often survived only a few evenings. She used each part, however, to further her stage technique, to widen her scope of interpretation, and, most important of all, to improve upon her English. The result was that, in almost every instance, the youthful and ambitious Swedish actress far outshone the rest of the cast, and lent, even to intolerably weak comedies, a note of distinction and honesty.

Other New York managers were looking at her with eager and envious eyes. One of these was David Belasco who, in the spring of 1915, brought her under his banner. Shrewd and artistic, he cast her in the rôle of Virginia Xelva in the above-mentioned "Boomerang." Supporting her were such first-water Broadway actors as Arthur Byron and Wallace Eddinger. The play opened in Wilmington, Delaware, on April 15, and became an immediate and tremendous success.

The "Boomerang" period of Miss Hedman's career, which lasted more than four years, brought her stardom and a world-wide reputation. She was generally regarded as the handsomest woman on the American stage, and her clothes, hobbies, and favorite dishes were discussed and copied. The simple manner in which she wound her rich golden hair around her head, was imitated by thousands of American girls, and many of New York's beauty salons decreed that the "Hedman Swirl," like the Garbo long bob later on, was the height of fashion.

When the comedy at last made its journey to Cain's Ware-house, Miss Hedman found a great number of attractive parts, in which she appeared with continued success during the following eight years. Among them were Lola in "The Dancer," Diana Trawley in "Three for Diana," Countess Hildegarde in "Forbidden," Jean Oliver in "Hole in the Wall," Marina Duval in "Transplanting Jean," Rosario in "The Romantic Young Thing," Frieda Neilson in "The Woman Who Laughed," and Margaret Lawton in "Persons Unknown."

Toward the end of the 1920's, marriage terminated her remarkably glamorous and successful stage career. Her farewell to the theater was made with a comedy, "What's the Big Idea?" which she wrote in collaboration with her husband, Capt. Henry A. House, before she retired from the footlights, to her Connecticut home.

A success comparable to Miss Martha Hedman's in "The Boomerang," was achieved in the late 1890's by a handsome, dark-haired Swedish singer and actor, Arthur Donaldson. Born in Norsholm, Sweden, he came to the United States when he was fourteen years old, and soon embarked upon a stage career. At first he appeared with various Swedish acting companies, but, after a few years, made his debut with Colonel Duff's celebrated troupe, in an English-speaking part. Later he joined the W. Augustine Daly Company, where he was seen and heard

in more than 350 parts, ranging from classics to modern melodramas and light operas.

It was, however, in the "Prince of Pilsen" that he, almost
overnight, became a star on the American stage, under the able
management of Henry W. Savage. This gay and handsome
extravaganza offered him a part ideally suited to his voice and
temperament. As the dashing, athletic young prince, in a uniform glittering with stars and gold braid, Donaldson created
a character that pleased the eye as much as it charmed the ear.
He immediately became a matinee idol of the first magnitude.
The première of this operetta took place on March 17, 1903,
at the Broadway Theatre, in New York, where it ran uninter-
ruptedly for more than 1,000 times. It was also shown in Boston with similar success, and, altogether, Donaldson appeared
in the part 1,345 times. He is still active on the New York stage.

Among the feminine stage artists, of Swedish birth or extraction, who also won acclaim in the American theatre, was Hilma
Nelson. In the 1890's she appeared with considerable success
in dramas and operettas, such as "Trelawny of the Wells" and
"The Geisha." Her father, L. P. Nelson, was one of the first
managers of the Swedish-speaking stage in the United States.

What Warner Oland has done in the films to develop and
popularize Oriental rôles, Arvid Paulson has done on the
American stage. A native of Skåne, this actor arrived in the
United States as a young man, and in 1916 received his first
important part, Logo, a Japanese, in "The Willow Tree."
Other Oriental interpretations include Quong, the Chinese, in
"Curiosity," and a similar part in "Yellow Jacket." He has
also appeared in several Ibsen plays, and done some radio work,
as well as translations.

Toward the end of the last century almost every large American city boasted at least one troupe of Swedish, or Swedish-
American, players. Some of these groups were highly artistic
and for years presented series of ambitious programs; others,
again, remained small but industrious. Their number was surprisingly large, and their interesting history is told in Volume
IV of *The Swedish Element in America.*

The only American actor of Swedish descent to appear in
three Pulitzer Prize-winning dramas is Glenn Anders. The

plays are Sidney Howard's "They Knew What They Wanted," Hatcher Hughes's "Hell-Bent Fer Heaven," and Eugene O'Neill's "Strange Interlude." The first and the third of these were produced by The Theatre Guild.

Born in Los Angeles in 1890 of a Swedish father, Glenn Anders attended Columbia University in New York, and made his stage debut with a Pacific Coast stock company. He toured for a while with Sothern and Marlowe, and appeared on Broadway in 1919, as Harry Nattles, Jr., in "Just Around the Corner." In the following five years he was seen in a great number of varied rôles, but his first real success came in 1924 with "Hell-Bent Fer Heaven," in which he took the part of Andy Lowry. The same year he duplicated this fine performance in the Guild's production of "They Knew What They Wanted," sharing honors with Richard Bennett and Pauline Lord. Two years later, he acted the same rôle at the St. Martin's Theatre in London. When the English producer, Basil Dean, was looking for a suitable actor to take the difficult part of Lewis Dodd in the dramatization of Margaret Kennedy's "The Constant Nymph," he selected Glenn Anders. The play, with Miss Beatrix Thompson of London in the leading part, opened at the Cort Theatre in New York, and added another fresh laurel to the interpreter of the erratic musician, Dodd.

A much more daring and novel rôle was offered Anders by The Theatre Guild, in 1928, when O'Neill's "Strange Interlude" was produced. The tricky "asides" and, not the least, the unorthodox length of the play, put the young actor to a severe test. However, as Ned Darrell, he gave splendid proofs of his keen insight, sensitiveness, and great dramatic skill.

The years that followed that memorable performance have been filled with a bevy of interpretations, such as Pat Farley in Philip Barry's "Hotel Universe," Nicholas Hay in the same author's "Tomorrow and Tomorrow," and Victor Hallam in "Another Language." Among his most recent appearances have been parts in "If This Be Treason," "Call It A Day," and "Moor Born."

John E. Hazzard, the celebrated stage comedian, can, despite his name, claim Swedish ancestry; his mother was a native of Norrköping. Born in New York in 1881, he made his first professional debut in 1901 in "The Man from Mexico." Unfortunately, too many of the sprightly and topical musical comedies, in which this versatile and talented actor appeared, are long since forgotten. There was, however, a time when such delightful fare as "The Yankee Consul," "The Hurdy Gurdy Girl," "The Girls of Gottenburg," "The Candy Shop," "The Lilac Domino," and "Very Good, Eddie," attracted packed and enthusiastic houses in dozens of American cities.

Of Hazzard's more recent rôles, well remembered by contemporary play-goers, are his irresistibly funny Bob White in Jerome Kern's "The Night Boat," King Home Brew in "Tangerine," Captain Kidd in "A Houseboat on the Styx" (which he wrote in collaboration with W. Kenneth Webb), and his hilarious performances in "The Greenwich Village Follies" and "H. M. S. Pinafore," as well as in Heywood Broun's "Shoot the Works."

In his long and successful career, Mr. Hazzard has also written several volumes of delightful poetry and, in addition to the above-mentioned piece, has sired the comedy, "Nunkie," and collaborated on other plays with Winchell Smith and John Golden.

In later years histrionic talent has also found an outlet on the radio. Numerous are the young men and women with Swedish names—vocalists, actors, comedians—who delight unseen American audiences from coast to coast. In this vast army undoubtedly Edgar Bergen, the ventriloquist, is not only the most famous but the highest paid. His parents came from Hässlcholm, and Edgar was born in Chicago. As early as during his student days at the Northwestern University, he conceived his celebrated "Charlie McCarthy," the snippy, saucy, back-talking dummy, who today is known to millions of radio listeners. For years he has lugged the top-hatted, ungainly figure of "Charlie" from stage to stage, argued with, and cajoled him, listened to his complaints, and given him fatherly words of warning, all to the tune of roaring laughter and thunderous applause. Bergen, whose real name, of course, is Berggren, now performs regularly on the radio, and is at present in Hollywood, where the croaking voice of "Charlie McCarthy" is one of the loudest heard in the film capital.

Painters and Sculptors

OLIVER A. LINDER

For biographical information about Mr. Linder, see the chapter on "Newspapers."

SWEDISH-AMERICAN art is as old as Swedish-American history. The very earliest settlers who came here in the seventeenth century brought with them implements and utensils that were not only artistic in form but elaborately carved, such as spoons, dippers, bowls, snuffboxes, chests, clocks, etc. These settlers also continued the art of wood carving in the colony. The spoons and other implements were made and decorated during the winter months, when they had little else to do. Even their dwellings were said to be artistic and Governor Johan Printz tells us that the carpenter of New Sweden "built a beautiful portal" at the entrance to Fort New Gothenburg on Tinicum Island. This artistic activity continued throughout the history of the colony, and lived on for a century or more.

About two generations after the capture of New Sweden by the Dutch, there arrived in America an artist who had acquired a reputation before coming here. His name was Gustaf Hesselius, and he was a cousin of Emanuel Swedenborg. He had been born in Dalarne in 1682, and probably studied art in Germany and in England. Two of his brothers went to America as pastors of the old Swedish churches on the Delaware, and, as a consequence, he also went to this "new land of promise," where he hoped to gain a wider field, for the exercise of his talents, than could be found in his native land. He arrived here in the beginning of May, 1712, and settled in Philadelphia, where he made the painting of portraits his business; and apparently he was successful at it. For some reasons, possibly because wealthy patrons lived there, he removed to Prince George County, Maryland, where, at the time, he became the most famous portrait painter in the colonies, and eventually acquired a small fortune. While in Maryland he executed the first commission for a public building in this country, an altarpiece for the St.

Barnabas Church, Prince County, Maryland, which was called "The Last Supper." It is one of his best-known works. About 1735 he returned to Philadelphia and bought a residence in the business section of the town, where, together with "an artist from London," he opened a studio.

Gustaf Hesselius was one of the first artists of consequence in America. He greatly influenced the beginnings of American painting. His technique was individual; his handling of colors exceptional; and his ability to grasp the main characteristics of his subjects unusual. The two Indian chiefs, which he painted for Governor John Penn in 1735, are masterpieces of their kind, and show Hesselius, as an artist, to the greatest advantage. His paintings and portraits are scattered far and wide and now command large prices. Two of his canvases are found in the Old Swedes Church in Wilmington. "The Last Supper" is in possession of Mrs. Rose Neel Warrington of Fredericksburg, Virginia; "The Holy Family," once in possession of the American Swedish Historical Museum in Philadelphia, is now in the Academy of Fine Arts in that city; and his portrait of Carl Magnus Wrangel hangs in the church at Sala, Sweden.

Gustaf Hesselius was not only the foremost artist in the colonies of his day, but possibly the most versatile genius in the country at the time. Like his cousin, Emanuel Swedenborg, he tried his hand at the construction of new mechanical contrivances of many kinds, and was a skilful organ builder, having constructed one of the first organs made in America. He died in Philadelphia on May 25, 1755, and was buried in the cemetery of the Old Swedes Church. Some of his descendants are still living, but his name has become extinct.

His son, Johan Hesselius (1728-78), also occupies a conspicuous position in American painting, and a great many canvases from his hand are scattered throughout the East, some of them having been wrongly attributed to his father. Johan Hesselius not only gave the first lessons in painting to Charles Wilson Peale, but also made it possible for the famous American artist and director of museums to go to London, to study the profession in which he was to make a name for himself in American history.

Sixteen years after the death of Johan Hesselius, another

famous Swedish artist came to Philadelphia, Adolph Ulric Wertmüller. In company with his friend, Henry Gahn, he arrived on May 13, 1794. Through his introductions from prominent people in Europe, and thanks to his charming manner and great ability, he soon acquired patrons among persons of influence in Philadelphia; and, before long, he found many customers who wanted their portraits painted. The most famous of these was George Washington. The well-known painting was done in 1795, and presents Washington as an aristocrat, "differing from all of the other portraits of the Father of His Country." The artist made several replicas, as was the custom in those days, when photography was nonexistent.

While in Philadelphia, Wertmüller became acquainted with Elizabeth Henderson, a granddaughter of Gustaf Hesselius, the painter. The acquaintance soon ripened into devotion. In October, 1796, Wertmüller left for Europe to look after his business, to the great sorrow of Miss Henderson and her mother. Before coming to America, Wertmüller had accumulated a considerable fortune in Paris; but this was lost through the Revolution, and he went to Stockholm on a business trip to look after his holdings and investments there. While in Stockholm, he obtained many commissions, and several of his canvases date from this period. He was offered a professorship in the Academy of Fine Arts, but declined, although he seemed determined at times to remain permanently in his native land. His plans were to marry Miss Henderson, and take her to Sweden. His friend Gahn, however, advised him strongly to return to America, "the land of real liberty." For a time, he even had it in mind to establish himself in Hamburg, Germany, and went there in the spring of 1798 to investigate the prospects. But misfortune followed him in Europe. Through the failure of his brother-in-law he lost all his property in Sweden. The political situation of the country also disturbed him and, in the beginning of 1800, we find him on his way back to America. He arrived in Philadelphia in the fall, and remained here for the rest of his life. Having applied for American citizenship, he married Miss Henderson in the spring of 1801. The following year Wertmüller bought an estate, an old Swedish farm, near Naamans Creek on the border between Delaware and Pennsylvania. Here he spent "eight of the happiest and most peaceful years of his life," forgetting his paint brush and his easel, and the brilliant courts of Europe. He died on August 5, 1811, without issue.

Wertmüller lacked imagination and originality, and was an imitative, rather than a creative, painter. Some of his works are rather conventional, especially those of mythological subjects. His portraits, however, are usually of a high order, and show his talent to the best advantage. Some of them are exceptionally good. They are full of life and vigor, and show considerable power of characterization. In many cases, he has caught the very soul of his subject, and has made it glow and live on the canvas "in immortal color." In America he is best known for his Washington portrait. Most of his canvases are in private hands. Originals of Wertmüller are found in the National Museum of Stockholm, in the Academy of Fine Arts, Philadelphia, in the American Swedish Historical Museum, Philadelphia, and in some other places.

It is not particularly surprising that there were few Swedish-American artists before the middle of the last century. The earlier Swedish immigrants coming to America were, in most cases, men who, from necessity or from upbringing, were restricted to physical labor. To rely exclusively on the use of the artist's brush or the sculptor's chisel for daily bread was then, more than now, a highly precarious policy, with little or no prospects of worldly goods or affluence.

As time went on, there came, of course, a steadily increasing number of Swedish immigrants from all classes in the old country, and among the newcomers were also a few artists. During the last seventy years, the number of these has grown so that at present we have a large colony of actors and worshipers at the altar of Art; and among them we find many who are not only locally, but nationally, known. And they exert an influence, individually or collectively, as members of art associations, that is highly beneficial.

In connection with the above, it may not be amiss to quote what a critic wrote in substance a few years ago: With the immigrant settler it took a long time for the appreciation of art to awaken, and this explains why the Swedish-American artists were late in receiving the encouragement from their countrymen, that they should have had. But at last a natural interest in the subject came to life, and at present the artists have certainly nothing to complain of in this respect. This has particularly been the case in the city on the shores of Lake Michigan. Chicago has indeed become the Swedish-American art center.

It has more and more come to be an accepted view that the intellectual training of the young generation is not enough for an all-around education, and that as a result art schools have been added to many of the Swedish-American colleges. Besides, quite a number of the growing generation have taken up art courses at American colleges, where in many cases Swedish-American artists have been engaged as teachers.

The first Swedish-American art exhibition was held in the year 1899, in Lindsborg, Kansas. It was not a great success, as far as the number of participating artists was concerned, for there were only three exhibitors, and two of these, Birger Sandzén and C. G. Lotave, were teachers of art at Bethany College in Lindsborg. The third one was G. N. Malm, fresco painter and decorator, also a resident of Lindsborg.

The first society of Swedish artists in Chicago was organized in 1905, but it did not last long. It was succeeded in 1911 by the Swedish-American Art Association, which was reincorporated in 1920, and now has a membership of 170. These associations were promoted chiefly by Charles S. Peterson and his wife, Mrs. Thyra H. Peterson. Both being inspired by the love of art, they contributed, with unselfish spirit and bountiful hands, to the furtherance of it among the Swedish-Americans, and they deserve the highest credit for their devotion. These associations have arranged for one or two exhibitions every year, with only one or two exceptions, and, in these shows, artists from all over the country have taken part. They have been very successful in fostering a living interest in art, and encouraging the artists to do their best.

Another art association in Chicago is the "Swedish Artists of Chicago," which was organized in 1927. This society has also arranged yearly exhibitions, which have been very successful. The membership is about eighty. There are several smaller organizations in other places.

But the pioneer artist, in what we may call modern Swedish-American history, was an independent who probably did not belong to any Swedish art association. He was Lars Gustaf Sellstedt, sailor and painter, who was born in Sundsvall, 1819, and died in Buffalo, 1911, at the age of ninety-two. By most Swedes he seems to be utterly forgotten, and yet it was he who, of all his countrymen, was first elected to full membership in the National Academy of Design (N.A.). This was in 1875 and he had been elected to associate membership three years before.

At the age of twelve young Sellstedt, with his mother's knowledge, ran away from home, and for several years literally sailed the seven seas. In 1834, he set out for America as a cabin boy. A century ago he joined the United States Navy, where he served three years. He landed in Buffalo in 1842. He had early studied drawing and, as a sailor, had made figures on whales' teeth, and sketched scenes from the seaman's life. After 1845 he was able to devote his chief attention to art and literature. Though a self-made artist, he painted many notables, including Presidents Fillmore and Cleveland. Sellstedt was the principal founder, for twenty-six years Superintending Director, and, from 1876 to 1877, President of the Buffalo Fine Arts Academy. His voluminous and remarkable autobiography, *From Forecastle to Academy, Sailor and Artist*, appeared in 1904, when the author was eighty-five years old; and in 1910, at the age of ninety-one, he published *Art in Buffalo*. The name of Sellstedt—who was also a poet of ability and taste—is unique in Swedish-American history.

Chicago had no Swedish artist before the 'fifties. It was in 1852 that Peter M. Almini, a native of Stockholm, settled in that city. After a couple of years he added to his line of business a department of fresco painting, and soon won a name for himself, both as an artist and as a decorator. He possessed great skill and exquisite taste. He was engaged to do the mural painting in several churches and assembly halls in Chicago and other cities. While he was looked upon, perhaps, chiefly as a commercial artist, he also ranked high as a devotee of pure art. He had made a profound study of ancient and modern art, and stood high in the esteem of his fellow artists. He died in 1890.

Another prominent artist of that time was Henry E. C. Peterson. At the outbreak of the Civil War he had enlisted in the Navy, and served for more than three years. Thereupon he came to Chicago and took up painting as a profession. In his younger days he had studied art in Stockholm. In order to acquire a better art education, he went to Paris, and there studied at the Julien School. After his return he painted, while a resident of Chicago, a great number of portraits. Among those who sat for him was Brigham Young, as well as many bishops and leading men of other churches. He later moved to New York, where he continued to paint prominent people.

Peter Roos, a native of Skåne, was, from 1880 to 1890, engaged as a teacher of drawing at the University of Illinois. He had arrived in 1872 in Boston, and there organized, in 1874, an art school called the Boston Art Academy. In the 'nineties he began to paint landscapes, which were well received.

We pass now to later periods. Not all artists can be named here, as the allotted space for an article of this kind will permit us to let only the best known pass in review. Nor is it safe to make any definite assertion about the relative quality of their work. The present writer certainly will not presume to select among the comparatively large number of prominent Swedish-American artists, those who are greatest in their field. A consensus of opinion in respect to any one cannot be obtained.

It is, however, a conceded fact that Birger Sandzén, as a painter, ranks among the very foremost, and the pronounced characteristics of his work, his powerful style, and intuitive intelligence, in which he is without any threatening rival, place him near the top, or, as many will have it, at the top. Sandzén, who was born in Sweden, 1871, is rated equally high as a painter in oil and as a lithographer, and is nationally, even internationally, known and admired. He is an independent who goes his own way; and the success he has attained speaks well for his individuality. His favorite subjects have for years been the mountainous landscapes in the southwest part of the United States. No one has surpassed him in reproducing the grandeur and strength of peaks, crests, and rugged mountain sides. Sometimes his paintings are visions in form and colors. He is at times a realist, and at other times a dreamer. In his prints one finds the same geniality and a shimmering form. Since 1894, he has been director of the art school at Bethany College, Lindsborg, Kansas.

There are few names of Swedish-American artists so often mentioned in matters pertaining to achievements in art as that of John F. Carlson (born 1875), the landscape painter. His place in the front rank has been assured for a long time, and he is a member of the National Academy. He studied under American artists, and is himself now a master. He was for several years a teacher in the artist colony in Woodstock, New York, and is now head of the school for landscape painting there. He is especially strong as a painter of forest scenes. He believes in freeing the forest interiors from the dark and dreary atmosphere that most artists give to them. His painting is clear, and it breathes happiness and beauty. So many honors have come to him that it would take too much space to enumerate them. In 1936 he won the Altman Prize in New York. (See *The American Swedish Monthly*, May, 1936.)

Knute Heldner, born in 1886 in Småland, arrived in the United States a poor immigrant. Now he is held in general esteem as a landscape painter. It took years of hard work, and a strong determination, to overcome the handicap and win out. He received the first acknowledgment of his ability to handle the brush, when he was given a gold medal at the Minnesota State Exposition, 1914. He has received many prizes and awards since then. The art critics claim for him a many-sidedness that is not often met with. He sometimes comes close to impressionism in his canvases.

As a painter of marines—and especially battle scenes or gatherings of war vessels—Henry Reuterdahl, born in Malmö, 1871, occupies a high place. He was entirely self-educated, but this did not prevent the development of his natural ability.

During the Spanish-American War he was engaged by a magazine, to accompany naval operations and make sketches; and later was in the service of the Navy itself. Thus he became intimately acquainted with what he later chose as his favorite subject. His marines are to be seen in many prominent places. In the National Gallery in Washington hangs the large canvas, "The Battle between *Monitor* and *Merrimac*," and not less than ten marines are in the Naval Academy in Annapolis. Reuterdahl died in 1925.

No one among the Swedish-American artists has met with more success than Charles E. Hallberg, who first saw the light of day in Gothenburg, 1855. He is also a painter of marines, and nothing else; but that is enough. His is a remarkable career, in view of the fact that he, too, is entirely self-made, and did not start to paint until he was forty-five years old. He grew from a janitor on Chicago's west side into one of the foremost Swedish-American marine painters. Because he was a sailor for many years before he arrived in Chicago, 1890, he knows the sea in all its moods. His larger paintings are to be seen in many museums and private homes. There is one, "A Sunny Day on the Atlantic," in the National Museum in Stockholm; two marines in the museum in Gothenburg; and two in the American Swedish Historical Museum in Philadelphia, of which one bears the title, "Before the Battle between *Monitor* and *Merrimac*."

The marines of Leon Lundmark, who was born in Småland in 1875, have long been valued by connoisseurs. He paints the sky and water with a clever technique, and an instinctive sense of color. He appeals not only to the critic but to the average man, as is best evidenced by the wide sale of his works.

A high rank as an artist has, by consensus of opinion, been given to Henry Mattson. There is no doubt that a real genius directs his brush when he paints. It, nevertheless, took him a long time to come into his own, for the reason that, to a great extent, he was untaught and had to feel his way. Born in 1887 in Gothenburg, he came to America in 1906. His indomitable spirit carried him on through years of bad luck; but he kept on and attained success. In his landscapes he does not copy

Nature to the point of tiresomeness. He paints mostly, one may say, from his inner perception of the subject matter. "The only problems he is interested in solving are those arising from his efforts to translate volatile forms of imagination into the reality of paint," one critic says. He has for many years been a member of the Woodstock artist colony, and has been granted many substantial prizes, as, for instance, the Guggenheim Award ($1,800); the Corcoran Prize ($1,000); and third prize ($500) at the International Art Exhibition in Pittsburgh —all in the year 1935. His canvas, "Wings of the Morning," was recently purchased by the Metropolitan Museum of Art.

Portrait painting was the forte of Arvid F. Nyholm's ability as an artist, although he was also a fine portrayer of nature in his landscapes. In 1891 he came to the United States from Stockholm, and located in New York. He resided there for twelve years, and made himself recognized by critics, and admired by the public for his fine work. He was a member of the National Academy of Design. In 1903 he moved his easel to Chicago, and resided there until his death in 1927. He died in the midst of his best and most mature productivity. He was a disciple of Anders Zorn, and his portraits generally followed the methods of his teacher, especially in using clear and distinct colors.

Carl G. Lotave, born in 1872, had studied art in Sweden and France, before coming to America. In 1897 he became a teacher of art in Bethany College. Later he moved to Colorado Springs, where he produced many first class portraits and landscapes. After moving to New York, he won high credit for his portraits of notables, such as Marshal Joffre, King Albert, General Pershing, Venizelos, and Marshal Foch. He was also an illustrator for magazines. He died in 1924, and his dust is entombed on the top of Pike's Peak, Colorado.

One of the finest etchers, as well as colorists, in the United States, is Bror Julius Olson Nordfeldt of Santa Fé, who was born in Sweden, 1878. He came to this country as a young boy, and studied art in Chicago, Paris, and London. He has exhibited in many of the larger art salons, both in America and abroad, and has received numerous awards.

Peculiarly enough, the Chicago dune landscapes have not lured many artists. And yet there is nothing more interesting, or pleasing to see, than the dunes. But it must be admitted that before you have seen them in all their glory with your own eyes, they lack appeal. One Swedish-American artist, who has painted a number of dune landscapes of undeniable excellence, is Gotthilf Ahlman. His paintings possess such appealing color, and the details are so fine, that they have been conceded to come from a master brush.

Few Swedish-American artists have been so well known to their countrymen in America as Olof Grafström (from Medelpad, born 1855), mainly, perhaps, because of his many skilfully painted altarpieces. But his landscapes are well received, too, as they always appeal to the public's inner love of Nature. Grafström was, for several years, instructor in the art school at Bethany College, Lindsborg, Kansas, and later taught in the same capacity at Augustana College. He was unusually accurate in his reproduction of Nature and this, at times, called forth the criticism that he was too meticulous in details. But form and color were always perfect. In the year 1928 he moved to Sweden, where he died March 30, 1933. His daughter, Ruth Grafström of New York, has reached the top round, as a fashion illustrator.

C. F. von Saltza, born in Sweden, 1858, was a noted portrait painter. His work was characterized by a touch of genius, which made his pictures not merely likenesses of persons but real works of art. He was instructor in several art schools after he, in the year 1891, had come to the United States. He was, for a time, in charge of the department of painting at the Museum of Fine Arts in St. Louis. Later he was head of the department of painting at the Art Institute of Chicago. He died in 1905.

A Swedish-born artist, whose work was highly appreciated by both the critics and the public, was Gunnar Widforss. He excelled in water colors, and selected a great number of his subjects in the United States National Parks. One of these paintings, "Three Patriarchs," is owned by the National Museum in Washington. He was awarded first prize at the Scandinavian Artists' Exhibition, 1928, a highly esteemed honor. Several of his reproductions are to be found in European museums. Somewhere midway, between the old and the new school, stands Thomas Hall. He paints the nature of New England with a sure eye and hand, using plenty of color. A. Linus has painted a number of highly creditable canvases. He might be called an all-round artist, and his work has been far above the average. He is a Chicagoan. Carl E. Wallin certainly possesses the nature of an artist, but seemingly a phantastic urge commands his soul, for, too often, he paints scenes with spooky contents. They are always masterfully executed canvases. No one denies that. But he is too closely allied with mysticism. He has, however, also painted landscapes of fine beauty, both as to color and subject.

When Alfred Jansson, born in Värmland, 1863, died in 1931, his death was deeply lamented in wide circles; for he was an artist of considerable ability, and was growing stronger every year. He was an ardent lover of Nature, and his winter landscapes were especially impressive. He could paint snowy ground with a realism that sent cold shivers to the bones of those viewing his canvases; but at the same time they were always decorative.

Henrik F. Hillbom, a native of Uppland, born 1863, now of Wallingford, Connecticut, is a many-sided painter, although landscapes are his specialty. He possesses a sure hand and a fine judgment of color and form. He has studied in London, Paris, and New York, and is also a designer and silversmith.

Oscar Brousse Jacobson, a native of Sweden, came to the United States in 1890, and was educated in the Yale School of the Fine Arts and in Paris. A noted teacher and lecturer, he has, since 1915, been director of the school of art and music at the University of Oklahoma. In 1924 he was Director of the Broadmoor Art Academy in Colorado Springs, and in 1924–25 traveled and painted in the Sahara Desert. He has exhibited his work in Stockholm, and in several cities of the United States. He has served on juries of awards in Kansas and Texas; is a member of art associations, both in America and abroad; and was, in 1931, awarded the gold medal in the Midwest Exhibition by the Kansas City Art Institute.

Among the additions of later years, to the contingent of

Swedish-American artists, Carl Oscar Borg must not be forgotten. He has devoted himself chiefly to etching, in which branch he has become an acknowledged master. He has specialized in sketching Indians in their home surroundings, and is undoubtedly one of the finest in his line. His landscape paintings of the Southwest are of high order. He is now an associate member of the National Academy (see *The American Swedish Monthly* for January, 1935).

August Franzén, born in 1863, noted illustrator and portrait painter of New York, who, among others, has executed an excellent likeness of President Taft, is a member of the National Academy. Other artists, who deserve special mention here, are Carl Eric Lindin (born 1869, in Västmanland), a member of the Woodstock colony of painters; Emil Gelhaar of the Lehigh University faculty; Ava Lagercrantz, portrait painter; David Erickson (born in Motala, 1870, now of Duluth, Minnesota); Herman Södersten of New Haven, Connecticut, portraitist, now deceased; Carl Ringius, landscape and harborscape artist from Hartford, Connecticut, who is now Secretary of the Connecticut Academy of Fine Arts; Oscar Anderson, principal founder and, at present, President of the Gloucester (Massachusetts) Society of Artists; Yngve Soderberg, etcher (see *The American Swedish Monthly*, June, 1936); and Oscar Cesare, well-known cartoonist of the New York *Times*.

Anders Zorn, the great Dalecarlian etcher, painter, and sculptor, had many contacts with American art. It was not only his daring, seemingly facile, technique, that invited imitation. Zorn also was well known personally, because of his frequent visits to the United States. These journeys, which often lasted for months, and took him from coast to coast, brought him intimately together with his American colleagues, upon whom his strong, individual temperament made itself felt.

Zorn first visited here in 1893, when he was Commissioner of the Swedish Art Pavilion at the Chicago World's Fair. Three years later he returned, and in 1900 he came to America for the third time. Two more visits were made, in 1903 and 1911. While in America, a number of prominent persons sat for him.

Among them were President Cleveland, Mrs. Cleveland, President Taft, Vice-President Sherman, Senator Aldrich, Andrew Carnegie, Adolphus Busch, the Potter-Palmers and the Deerings of Chicago, Mrs. Jack Gardner of Boston, and many others. A retrospective exhibit of Zorn's art in America was held from June 8 to July 8, 1925, at the Grand Central Art Gallery in New York. His works are still featured at important art sales.

If this summary of what Swedish-American painters have accomplished could have been extended to take in all those worthy of mention, many pages could have been filled. They have all honestly endeavored to meet the demands of an enlightened public; and the failures have been few.

Among the prominent sculptors who have won popularity and honors, there are several who have received deserved praise from the best critics. They are David Edström, Charles Haag, Karl F. Skoog, Agnes V. Fromén, Carl J. Nilsson, Axel E. Olsson, and, last but far from least, Carl Hallsthammar. There are several of lesser eminence that, perhaps, should be mentioned in this connection, but lack of space forbids. Of the seven sculptors named, it is very hard to pick out the best one, for each artist has shown unusual merits in his productions. And, in a way, they are not rivals—each one has chosen a field for himself.

About the Smålander David Edström's allegorical creations there is no division of opinion. A marked originality, psychology, and deep thought are evident in most of his productions. He is far from being conventional, and often gives himself over to symbolism. But his greatness has not been questioned. He has received many prizes and other tokens of recognition. In 1937 he published his autobiography under the title, *"The Testament of Caliban."* (See the chapter on "Authors.")

Karl F. Skoog showed decided ability as a sculptor. He came to the United States in 1902, and started at once to take lessons in modeling and sculpture. His earliest recognition came in 1910, when he was awarded honorary mention for a statuette at an art exhibition in Providence, Rhode Island. After that time several prizes came to him. In 1920 his Perry Memorial in Malden, Massachusetts, was erected, and in 1922 he won over seven competitors with his model of a War monument for Cambridge, Massachusetts. He was rated very highly as an artist in his line. He died in Boston, June 5, 1933.

Several Swedish-American women have met with appreciable success in sculpture. One of them is Agnes V. Fromén of Chicago. She is a true artist in every sense of the word. Her fountain, "The Well," brought her the Municipal League Prize in 1912, and it is now occupying a place in the Art Museum. She has won first prizes in several exhibitions since then. Her works are characterized by strict conformity to Nature, without any frills, and purity and cheerfulness of conception.

A woman sculptor, not generally known outside her immediate circle of friends as being of Swedish birth, because of her married Italian name, was Hilda K. Lascari. She came to the United States as a child, and took up sculpture at an early age. Mrs. Lascari, in 1926, won the gold medal of the National Academy of Design, by her study of a nude girl. She met an untimely death through accident in 1937.

A successful sculptress is Vicken von Post Totten of Washington, D.C., who was born in Sweden, 1886, and is represented in the Metropolitan Museum of New York. Eleven panels in the Federal Post Office Building of Waterbury, Connecticut, were executed by her. Martha af Ekenstam, born in Malmö, 1880, of Pasadena, California, has specialized in metal work, and in ebony and ivory.

There is no gainsaying that Carl Hallsthammar looms high as an artist. It is generally conceded that he is without any serious competitor in his particular line, wood sculpture; and certainly his place as a leader in that art is assured. The groups that Hallsthammar carves out of wood are always excellent in taste and form. The figures are perfectly natural, and to this more often than not is added a contagious humor. He has also carved groups of Indians, after an extended study of the red man, in his own home in the West. These groups have been rated very highly. A special honor was bestowed upon Hallsthammar in 1936, when he received the highly valued Frank Logan Prize ($500), together with the gold medal for his "Venus Playing Tennis."

Another eminent wood carver is Karl von Rydingsvärd, who emigrated from Stockholm to America in 1883, and has taught his subject of wood sculpture in several institutions, including Teachers College at Columbia University. He has executed a much-admired frieze of twelve scenes from American pioneer life, for the library of Arthur Curtiss James's summer home in Newport, Rhode Island.

One of the best designers of metal tablets in the country is Hugo O. E. Carlborg, of Providence, Rhode Island. He is an instructor in the Rhode Island School of Design.

Born in Blekinge, 1857, Axel Elias Olsson came to Chicago in 1881 and must, therefore, be counted as one of the earlier Swedish-American exponents of art. He had studied exclusively in the old country, and was well versed in the handling of the chisel. But it was not until 1923 that he came to be known in wider circles. At the Columbian Exposition he exhibited two reliefs, representing Spring and Autumn, and also contributed the plastic groups that adorned the Hall of Animal Industry and Machinery, which were given high praise. He made a large number of low reliefs, allegorical, and portrait figures. In 1903 Olsson completed a marble group in high relief, representing Psyche and the Zephyrs, and also a statuette "The Whisper," which met with general appreciation. Olsson had the true artistic temperament, creating his own atmosphere rather than seeking it elsewhere.

Since 1899 Carl J. Nilsson has been a resident of the United States, most of the time living in Chicago. He had done very fine sculptural work in the old country and enjoyed high standing as an artist there. He has accomplished much creditable work here, mostly decorative groups and reliefs. One of the most typical of his productions was a life-size bust of King Oscar II, first exhibited in 1905. He has made several portrait reliefs, of which some are in the American Swedish Historical Museum, Philadelphia.

Charles Haag, born in 1867 in Norrköping, came in 1893 to America, having previously studied sculpture in Sweden, Germany, France, Italy, and Switzerland. He resided the first six years in the Eastern States, and, after that, moved to Winnetka, Illinois, a suburb of Chicago. From childhood used to poverty, he was able to handle this subject in art, with the insight born of experience. His best group is perhaps "Emigrants," in which is impressively told the tragedy of the newcomers. One of his sculptures was the first by a Swedish sculptor accepted by the Metropolitan Museum of New York. He died in 1933.

F. E. Hammargren, sculptor, was born in Örebro in 1892. For several years his home and studio have been in Leonia, New Jersey, where he also conducts an art school. He is represented in the Brooklyn Museum of Art and the Newark Museum of Fine Arts.

Lastly we must mention the most prominent of all living Swedish sculptors, who recently has joined the number of Swedish-American artists; namely, Carl Milles. His fame has for many years been world-wide. When he now has decided to take up his residence in the United States, we hope to be excused for counting him among the many who have brought honor and respect to the Swedish name on this side of the Atlantic. Milles can point to an almost phenomenal production of masterpieces during the forty years that have elapsed, since he exhibited his first sculptural work, "Hylas." His earliest sculptures showed some influence of the taste of the time, but he soon began to show the remarkable independence for which he is now known and respected. Since 1902, when he was awarded a prize for the Sten Sture monument, raised in Västerås, he has won many high awards and honors, both at home and abroad. There are a large number of statues and monuments from his hand erected in Sweden and elsewhere, all portraying an intuitive perception of the inner character of the subject, besides plastic taste. It would crave a full page to enumerate all his works. It is natural and logical that an artist like Milles, who belongs to both Sweden and the United States, and who represents the best cultural interests of both, should be the man to execute the New Sweden Monument on the "Rocks" in Delaware. There could be no better representative of the two countries concerned, no better symbolism or personification of the friendly relationship between the two, than this monument and its creator.

CARL MILLES

It must be admitted that what the Swedish or Swedish-American artists have accomplished from the earliest to the present time, has been to their credit and, what is of even greater weight, has been a very valuable contribution to the art of America—in some cases, of priceless influence. And for these reasons, they occupy, as a whole, an envious place in the esteem of their fellow artists.

Soldiers and Sailors

NILS G. SAHLIN

The author of this chapter served for three and a half years in the
Swedish Navy and, after honorable discharge as a noncommissioned
officer, came to America at the age of twenty-one. He knew no English
then, but prepared for college in two years; graduated from Yale in
another three; and, later, won his doctorate from that university. He
has studied and taught both in Germany and the United States, and
has for several years been a member of the German Department in Yale
University, where he is also a Fellow of Timothy Dwight College. Dr.
Sahlin is Editor-in-chief of the Farrar & Rinehart series of German
texts, and is on the regular staff of the Bureau of University Travel.
Captain Nels A. Nelson, U.S.A. (retired), has done some research work
for this chapter in Washington, and Einar Thulin has collected data on
sea captains in New York.

NATIONS no longer pray for protection against the
ravages of the Northmen. In the course of a thousand
years the warlike character of the Scandinavians has
changed so radically that the world looks upon the northwest
corner of Europe as the home of sense and sanity. While almost
every other nation is torn by foreign or civil strife, by economic
difficulties or clashing political and social philosophies, we are
prone to regard the countries of the North as a fair approach
to Utopia, a place where all problems either have been solved or
are near solution. This attitude is particularly prevalent in regard to Sweden, partly because she has, indeed, pioneered many
a social reform, partly because of the greater amount of publicity which her achievements have received. As the world in
general gradually prostrates itself again before Mars, and
seems inclined to honor might more than right, it is logical to
ask whether the valorous Swedes of yore have become a nation
of bespectacled analysts who, with superbrain and chicken
heart, delve into their own problems.

For 125 years Sweden has had peace—a proud record to most
of us. America has received a significant share of the benefits

accruing from the undisturbed efforts of this period. Young men and women, whose energies were not dissipated by useless wars in the homeland, sought new outlets for their spirit of adventure in the inviting wilderness or surging city life of the United States. Peace at home has not dulled the responsibilities of the Swedes, when confronted with the defense of a righteous cause. Anyone in doubt on this score did not witness the calm courage with which an armed neutrality was maintained during the volcanic days of the World War. Nor have the children of that northern corner of Europe shown any loss of ability in turning from peaceful adventures to those of the battlefield, whenever their adopted country needed them. The muster rolls, as well as the fatality lists, of the major wars that our young republic has waged abound with Swedish names. The fact that their number generally exceeds the proportionate quota expected may be an indication that there is a survival of that warlike spirit, which, as an undercurrent, flows through an apparently calm and undisturbed nation. When Colonel Mattson issued his call for volunteers during the Civil War, he included the belief that "our children and grandchildren will reverently mention our names in days to come." It is the primary purpose of this article to call to the reader's mind a few of the representative men of Swedish birth or descent, who have aided America in times of war.

The first Swedish soldiers and sailors to enlist in an American war were officers who came with the French forces to serve in our War of Independence. Most of these were naval officers. On land, the struggling colonists could, in some measure, compensate for the superior training and equipment of the British, by means of the now famous "Spirit of '76," and their knowledge of the terrain on which the war was fought. But, at sea, they were largely dependent on French aid. People skilled in handling war vessels and conducting naval engagements were as rare as the ships on which to employ them. Hence, it is not surprising that volunteers coming from Sweden, and desirous of enlisting for army service in America, were turned back in considerable numbers, while at the same time the Swedish Ambassador reports a dearth of officers for the naval service. On February 3, 1780, Count de Creutz wrote to his King, Gustavus III, that no more army officers could be placed. But in the French Navy, he says, he could easily find room for fifty more.

Among those who did take part in the battles, both on land and sea, were many men of distinguished merit who either came from Sweden or were of Swedish descent. Interest has recently been revived in a man whose romantic and varied career came to a tragic end in 1810. When this young man appeared in Paris in 1774, he had to his credit a truly Continental education, excellent family connections, and a charming personality. Three years later Axel von Fersen became a colonel in the Royal Suédois—his father's old regiment—and at twenty-one had captured the favor of the French Court and, in particular, that of its Queen. As early as 1778 he made efforts to join the French expeditionary forces in America; and two years later he embarked for these shores with an appointment as first adjutant to Count de Rochambeau, who, with 6,000 French troops, had been sent to aid General Washington. The first year proved rather less exciting than expected, for Rochambeau found himself unable to leave the French fleet, which at that time was blockaded by the British in Narragansett Bay. During this period of relative inactivity, Von Fersen was preferred for a number of secret missions, in connection with the plans and negotiations that concerned the two armies and their leaders, enjoying, as he did, high confidence in both headquarters. In July of 1781 the French forces were finally able to join Washington on the Hudson, and the celebrated march to Yorktown began. Here Von Fersen contributed markedly to the success of the American arms. He was charged to "hurry the troops" and get the French artillery to the scene of action in time. He took active part in the siege, and was present as Cornwallis surrendered, on the nineteenth of October. Count de Creutz writes as follows: "The Duke of Lauzun told me that in all the operations where the fighting was intense, Fersen was present, now in the trenches and now in the midst of the attack, and that he exhibited the most brilliant proofs of valor." Von Fersen left America in December, 1782, and after some audacious adventures during the Revolution in France, including the attempted rescue from the scaffold of Louis XVI and Marie Antoinette, he returned to Sweden. He had been decorated for valor and service, both by his own Government and by France; from Washington he received the coveted Order of the Cincinnati. At the age of forty-six he was appointed *riksmarskalk*, an office which he held until 1810, when, absurdly and unjustly accused of poisoning the King-elect of Sweden, he met a horrible death at the hands of a mob in Stockholm, during the funeral of his alleged victim.

Another less romantic, but most able, Swede who "fought with great bravery during the American War of Independence" was Baron Johan Henric von Fock. He, too, saw action at Yorktown, and "exhibited extraordinary valor and intelligence" in repulsing a vicious cavalry attack by English dragoons. He later resided in England, and died there in 1817.

In December, 1779, four months before Von Fersen set sail for America, a Swedish soldier, who had already covered himself with glory in the American war, returned, badly wounded, to France. Baron Curt von Stedingk was the object of much attention and admiration in Paris, and bore the distinction of being one of the very first volunteers to proceed to the American scene of war. He participated in a number of engagements at such widely separated points as the island of Grenada, southernmost of the Windward Islands in the West Indies, and Savannah, Georgia. The success of the "difficult and violent" attack on the fortress of Grenada (St. George) was in no small measure aided by the talent and courage of Curt von Stedingk, who commanded the central column, and his younger brother Victor—this, according to a letter to De Creutz, from Count d'Estaing, Commander of the French fleet. Grenada was taken, but the siege of Savannah, for which d'Estaing had left the West Indies, was less successful. On the ninth of October, 1779, Curt von Stedingk led the left column in the assault, and was severely wounded in the leg. It was pierced by grapeshot, and the seriousness of the wound was further aggravated by his insistence to continue the fight at the head of his column. He still hobbled about on crutches in Paris during the early part of 1780. In his diary, Stedingk expresses the opinion that "one can not last long in this country because of the heat, fatigue, and oppressiveness of the climate." He spent most of his time in the South, and his observation was correct, but it was the grapeshot at Savannah that ended his American adventure. He never returned, although he had wished and planned to do so; but he continued to distinguish himself both as a soldier and a diplomat. He was the Swedish Ambassador to St. Petersburg, at which Court he was held in high esteem by Catherine II, and was in command of the Swedish troops at the Battle of the Nations at Leipzig, in 1813. When he finished his long and useful life, at the age of ninety and some months, he had, indeed, covered himself with glory and honor. The whole Swedish Army went into mourning for its dead Field Marshal, and the courts of Europe keenly felt the loss of this illustrious and calm arbiter and mediator of many an international European problem. Like Fersen, he was a member of the Cincinnati.

Curt von Stedingk's brother, Victor von Stedingk, referred to above, was a navy officer on the *Robuste* at the capture of Grenada. He returned to America in 1782, after a sojourn in Paris because of ill-health. Later he was repatriated, and eventually rose to the rank of Admiral in the Swedish Navy.

The naval operations before Savannah, about two years after the unsuccessful siege, claimed the life of the brave and able Carl Raab. He died of his wounds on September 6, 1781, at the age of thirty-two.

To the names of Grenada and Savannah are linked not only the names of the Von Stedingks, Fock, and Raab, but also that of Baron Otto Henric Nordenskjöld. Born in Finland (then Swedish) in 1747, he spent a short time in English service, but transferred to France in 1778. He has the distinction of having greatly distressed the defenders of Fort St. George by carrying out an audacious cruise by night below the fortress, while subjecting it to effective bombardment. Both before and after the siege of Savannah, from which he apparently escaped without a scratch, he took part in a number of naval engagements and skirmishes. He was called home for Swedish service in the enforcement of the Armed Neutrality, and, in time, became a Vice-Admiral.

The naval and land battles at Grenada constitute a focal point for Swedish participation in the American War of Independence. It seems that an unusual number of Swedes were assigned to Count d'Estaing's fleet, and had an opportunity to show their mettle in murderous clashes. Lest it be thought that these engagements were "murderous" only in the relative sense, it may, at this point, be well to recollect Curt von Stedingk's description of the naval battle near Grenada.

I had desired to be present at a naval battle [he writes] but I hope with all my heart that I shall never have to be present at another. Whereas land troops require bravery, the personnel of the navy demands heroism. The consequences of a naval battle follow in more rapid succession and are more terrible. The firing is done at pistol range with cannon á 36. Three times I was knocked down by projectiles which crushed or injured ten or twelve men at a time, and it is no exaggeration to say that the deck of our ship was literally covered with blood, brain substance, and mutilated limbs. . . . Six thousand shots were fired on each side; yet we lost only a thousand men. . . .

In addition to those mentioned above as having participated in the struggles at Grenada, we may give brief mention to the following:

Georg K. de Frese won honors there, and is described by Count de Creutz (together with Nordenskjöld; see above) as a man of "real genius" and "superior merit." This officer was already high in the esteem of the French; for he had, two years earlier, saved a French vessel from destruction. Lieutenant[1] S. Gyllenskepp proved his ability and bravery at this bitterly contested point. Peter Monthell, who was an ensign in Count d'Estaing's squadron, was probably also one of the participants. Carl Gustaf Rehbinder, a Roslagen boy and supernumerary lieutenant with Count d'Estaing, was there. We shall mention him later in connection with the naval battle near Dominica. Ensign Jackris Schultén fought at this siege; later in the same year he helped capture two English frigates, and was promoted to Lieutenant. In April, 1782, he fought in another bloody battle near Guadeloupe, but lived to pursue a successful career in the Swedish Navy, after his return home. Another super-

1. It should be borne in mind that the title *"lieutenant de vaisseau,"* here rendered by "lieutenant," was a relatively high rank in the French Navy of the time. It was the highest rank to which a foreigner could be promoted.

numerary officer present at Grenada was Aron Sjöstjerna; he was severely wounded in action.

The greatest naval engagement of the war was the battle of Dominica, usually referred to, in English sources, as the "Battle of the Saints." Here, too, Sweden was well represented. Lieutenant Rehbinder, whom we mentioned above, proved his heroism by giving his life at the age of eighteen in this battle. He had left Sweden at the incredibly early age of fourteen; despite his youth, he is reported as having been commended and respected by the French, both for his knowledge and for his personal qualities. He is said to have taken part in no less than eight general battles, and a romantic report claims that he sought death to clear the family name of a stain caused by a brother. David Gustaf Blessing, fourth officer on one of the French ships, suffered the rest of his life from wounds received on that twelfth day of April, 1782, so disastrous to the French forces. De Creutz makes particular mention of the valor displayed by this officer, and by Henric Johan Nauckhoff.

The latter suffered a severe head injury in the same battle, and returned to France upon recovery. Like so many other Swedish officers, his being wounded was not allowed to prevent his continuing in the battle. Both the captain and the second officer in command, on the ship to which Nauckhoff had been assigned, were shot, and although he could not, as a foreigner, take command of the vessel, it was generally conceded that disaster would have overtaken the ship, if Nauckhoff had not been there to guide the action of the French ensign to whom the charge had passed. Carl Donat Feif apparently was not present in the above-mentioned battle, but had the opportunity to fight in three battles during the years 1780–81 against the same Lord Rodney who commanded the English forces at Dominica. Carl Fredrick Toll was wounded in this engagement, but survived to see Swedish service until his untimely death, at the age of forty, in 1798. We have no definite information to the effect that Lieutenant Carl Frederic von Rajalin took part in the Battle of the Saints. The defeated French squadron was commanded by Admiral de Grasse, and the Admiral himself was taken prisoner by the English. One report states that he was assigned to this squadron, and that he died in 1782 in an explosion. This, however, conflicts with a letter by Count de Creutz which refers to Rajalin's death a year earlier. His older brother, Salomon Mauritz von Rajalin, however, spent about a year fighting in the West Indian waters, and was engaged in at least four major naval battles, including that of Dominica, to which we have linked the above names. It seems that some French officers had not conducted themselves too heroically in this battle, whereas Rajalin had shown great bravery and presence of mind in bringing the vessel on which he was stationed to the aid of a disabled French man-of-war. The reports praise him for his "zeal, courage, *sang-froid,* and power of discernment." Like so many of the Swedish officers who survived the American wars, he rose to great prominence after his return to Sweden. He was for a time Governor of the then Swedish island of St. Barthélemy in the West Indies, was for twenty years Provincial Governor of Gottland, and commanded, as Admiral, the Swedish *skärgårdsflotta,* in the war of 1809 with Russia.

Another locality in which the Swedes added glory and honor to their name was Pensacola, Florida. Nils Bjelke had become a lieutenant in the Swedish Navy at the astonishing age of fifteen, having, *before* that, been a member of the Royal Body Guard. Not quite eighteen years old, he served as a lieutenant during the capture of Pensacola in May, 1781, and was decorated for bravery. Less than a year later he was killed in a naval engagement against the British in East Indian waters, still fighting in the American war on the other side of the world. By one of the startling coincidences of history, this battle was fought on April 12, 1782, on the same date as the Battle of the Saints, which we discussed above. In the West the French lost; in the East they won. In the same battle, another Swedish officer by the name of Lannerstjerna was killed; but he had never fought in American waters.

Another young stripling who ended up as a Swedish admiral was Magnus Daniel Palmquist. He entered French service as an ensign in 1778, aged seventeen, and contributed materially, in May, 1780, to the successful capture of Pensacola. We are not informed about the details, but the report goes that he forced the English to burn three of their own ships in the harbor. Palmquist also had the privilege of sharing in the naval operations preparatory to the battle of Yorktown, at which the English were dealt such a decisive blow by the surrender of Cornwallis. As though these engagements and numerous other skirmishes were not enough, he also participated in the bloody battle of Dominica, mentioned so often above. He survived them all, and served his own land long and well, until his death in 1834.

In comparison with some of the above-mentioned young men who entered military service almost before they had learned to sleep out of a cradle, Magnus Aurivilius Rosén von Rosenstein was a seasoned old tar with a formidable name when he entered the French service at the age of twenty-four. He already had behind him English service (as midshipman), and a captaincy in the Swedish Navy. We have to assume that he conducted himself bravely at Pensacola. The details are lacking, but we do know that not long after his ship had left Florida again, it blew up, after the crew had fought a fire on it for three hours. Nothing daunted and still very much alive, Rosenstein received transfer to another vessel and, four months later, we find him fighting against the English squadron under Admiral Graves, who thereby was prevented from coming to the aid of Cornwallis at Yorktown.

We shall end this account of Swedish officers who took part in the American War of Independence with a brief mention of another outstanding man, Adolph Fredrik Petersen, later ennobled under the name Rosensvärd. The exploits of this Karlskrona boy read like an adventure in fiction. He received a good education; studied at Lund University; and participated in some journeys to Africa and the Mediterranean, before becoming a lieutenant in the Swedish Navy. At the age of twenty-four (1777), he entered French service, like so many of his countrymen who sought adventure and experience. Four years later we find him, too, at Pensacola, Florida. Petersen was to affect a landing with two detachments, and to join the Spanish General de Gálvez. Despite fire from the heavy cannons of the fort that were trained on them, and the stubborn resistance of English troops, Petersen reached his objective, and was put in charge of a brigade of artillery. A few days later he was ordered to take an enemy entrenchment on a hill dominating the

English fortress. This had been attempted earlier, but the attack had been repulsed. Petersen succeeded. Exposed to the gunfire of two forts and one redoubt, he held his position for fourteen hours, until he had had time to "dig himself in." During this time he was wounded, however, receiving a gun bullet in the lower leg, a cannonball wound in the upper leg, and sustaining, in addition, a head injury. Nothing daunted, he kept his wits and his command. When attacked four days later, he had himself *carried* at the head of his artillery, and turned back the enemy. The siege lasted six weeks and ended when one of the English forts blew up; the other was taken by storm. The British capitulated and were taken prisoners on May 8, 1781. As Petersen returned, carried by his soldiers, the whole army saluted him. It has been said that without Petersen and his corps of Irishmen (!) the Spaniards would never have captured Pensacola. It is small wonder that Count de Creutz wrote his King enthusiastically about this man, and Louis XVI himself wrote to Gustavus III extolling Petersen's "exceptional valor, much brilliance, and burning zeal and loyalty." He was decorated and commended on all sides, and later given a peerage by the Swedish King. Upon his return to Sweden in 1783, after service under Admiral de Grasse, he rejoined the Swedish Navy. Rosensvärd died as rear admiral in his native town at the early age of forty-six.

The above sketches have been culled largely from Adolph B. Benson's able and interesting book, *Sweden and the American Revolution*. Professor Benson mentions another score of men who served with the French. Quite a number of other officers (Benson mentions twenty-two) served the American cause in other parts of the world without ever fighting in America proper or in American waters. All of these are worthy of our gratitude and admiration.

Before we leave the War of Independence, however, we must insert a mention of an important contribution made by Dr. Amandus Johnson in *The American Swedish Monthly* of September, 1935. In his article, Dr. Johnson mentions a number of Swedes who served under John Paul Jones, and names seven that were in the crew of the *Bon Homme Richard:* Peter Nolte, Carl Peterson, Daniel Edblom, Peter Björkman, Benjamin

Gartineau (?), Peter Molin, and Oliver (Olle?) Gustafson. In regard to Peter Nolte I quote Dr. Johnson:

"It was Peter Nolte who, crawling out on the yard-arm, helped to execute the orders of John Paul Jones to throw grenades into the hatch of the English vessel [*Serapis*]. The attempt was successful, and one of the grenades fired several dozen cartridges which blew up the hatchway, killing or crippling more than fifty men on the English ship. This put an end to the fight and gave John Paul Jones his greatest victory [September 23, 1779]."

To a Swedish officer by the name of Johan Meijer, Dr. Johnson gives a fairly full account. This man joined Jones's frigate *Ranger* at Nantes (France) as *Volontair d'honneur*, took part in several engagements, and, with an unnamed Swedish sailor, was instrumental in quelling a mutiny. Through these men, John Paul Jones was informed in time to take necessary measures.

The next two wars in American history we can pass over rapidly, especially since little is known about the part that Swedes might have played in them. Few, if any, Swedes participated in the War of 1812. Besides, the descendants of the early Swedish settlers had by this time been so assimilated in the nation that we have difficulty in distinguishing them from other Americans, and the wave of immigration from Sweden was not to begin until some forty years later. We know definitely, however, that there were some Swedish participants in the Mexican War.

In 1839, Gustaf Clemens Hebbe, the owner of an estate in Småland, decided that the undertaking was a failure, and decided to emigrate. He had studied law and was well educated; when he appears next he is employed by the London *Times*. Some time afterward, probably in the early 'forties, he betook himself to the United States. Here he earned the degree of Doctor of Laws and became quite well known as a lecturer. During the Mexican War he was a lieutenant in a regiment of volunteers from Pennsylvania. Hebbe was, indeed, an interesting soldier of fortune, but details as to what he did in the war are lacking. He later stumped for President Pierce, held some Government offices, and then, for unknown reasons, went to

Norway. Here he worked as a free-lance writer and translator, introducing, among others, Emelia Flygare-Carlén to English readers. He died at a ripe old age in 1893. If Hebbe did not add great glory to the record of the Swedes, he is at least a good example of the adventurous, versatile spirit that we so frequently find among them.

Another name that must be mentioned in this connection is that of Capt. Oscar Malmborg. After eight years as an officer in the Swedish Army, he offered his services to the United States in the Mexican War. He served with distinction, and when the Civil War breaks out, we again find him in active service. This brings us to the subject of Swedish participation in this sanguine conflict.

Before 1861, relatively few Swedes had settled in the states of which the Confederacy was composed: the census claims less than one thousand. The records are almost silent on Swedish participants on the Southern side, although there undoubtedly were a few. There are, however, a number of references to August(us) Forsberg, who first appears as a lieutenant in the Fifty-first Virginia Regiment. In the course of time he was promoted to colonel and was, as such, in charge of Forsberg's Brigade, composed of the Forty-fifth, Fiftieth, Fifty-first, and Thirtieth Virginia regiments. In February, 1862, the then lieutenant "rendered very efficient service in rallying and leading the men, and throughout the day distinguished himself for gallantry and acts of daring." In September he is cited for "gallantry, cool bravery, and soldierly bearing." Dr. Ella Loon of Goucher College lists eighteen Swedes besides Forsberg who served the Confederate Armies in various capacities.

The Civil War differed, of course, in many respects from the War of Independence. We have no great influx of Swedish officers seeking adventure and experience in the conflict, but among the soldiers who took the field were Swedish immigrants and Swedish descendants by the thousands. They all filled their place both in the ranks and in positions of command, as a matter of course. They went out there in the firm belief that they were helping to make the United States what it was supposed to be—a free land where all men, white or black, are equal. The price was dear but willingly paid.

Also in contrast to the War of Independence, we find that the part played by the Swedes is by far greater on land than at sea. But Sweden is represented in the naval activities by two men of greater renown than any of those who fought in the Army.

John Ericsson's contribution to human welfare through the invention of the propeller, and the successful encounter of his *Monitor* with the ironclad *Merrimac*, will live in American memories forever. He has been treated more fully under the chapter on inventors in this volume. It remains for us only to point out here that several in the crew of the *Monitor* were Swedish. M. T. Sunstrum was fourth-assistant engineer; among the seamen were Hans Anderson from Gothenburg and one Charles Peterson.

Admiral John Adolph Dahlgren was born in 1809, the son of a Swedish immigrant, who later became Swedish Consul in Philadelphia, the future admiral's native city. He trained for the service from the beginning, and at the age of twenty-two became an officer in the American Navy. From about 1845 he gave most of his time to studies and inventions in artillery construction, and has been treated in the chapter on inventors as the originator of the Dahlgren gun. At the outbreak of the Civil War, Commodore Dahlgren was in command of the Washington Navy Yard. He was promoted to rear admiral in 1862 and, a year later, was put in charge of the Southern Atlantic blockade which involved over ninety ships. Admiral Dahlgren took active part in the conquest of Savannah in 1864, as well as the siege of Charleston in the early part of 1865. Here his flagship was torpedoed and sunk, but Dahlgren escaped. He died in 1870.

More romantic than the relatively calm, practical, and useful life of John A. Dahlgren is that of his son, Col. Ulric Dahlgren. His reckless exploits and sacrificing enthusiasm carried him to the front ranks of the heroes of that day. Just before the battle of Fredericksburg, he distinguished himself on a reconnoitering expedition in November, 1862. The young captain of cavalry, with 150 followers, was unexpectedly attacked by a numerically much superior enemy. They turned to defend themselves, and not only escaped but also brought back prisoners and much needed information. A minor engagement that preceded the battle of Gettysburg netted our hero a bullet through the foot which rendered amputation necessary, and he retired with the rank of colonel. But about March first, 1864, a raid upon Richmond was planned, to free the Northern prisoners of war who were held there. With his old enthusiasm, Colonel Dahlgren asked to be allowed to participate, in spite of his amputated leg. One night he was caught in ambush, however, and he, and about one hundred of his followers, were mowed down on the spot. The mutilated remains of the twenty-two-year-old colonel were interred then and there, but were, after the war, brought to Washington in solemn procession, and then to Philadelphia, where he was accorded a decent burial with full military honors.

In the second volume of *The Swedish Element in America* appears a reprint from Ernst W. Olson's *History of the Swedes of Illinois*. In this excerpt Olson has ably argued the case of Capt. Oscar Malmborg, whose name we have already mentioned in connection with the Mexican War. A man in his prime, Malmborg had just turned forty, when he was asked to help in organizing the Fifty-fifth Illinois Volunteer Regiment. Paradoxically enough, this well-trained and experienced soldier knew too much about military matters and warfare to suit those who had joined with ambitions to become officers but were too green to deserve the distinction. When, to these thwarted ambitions, are added Malmborg's iron discipline, his accent, and quick temper, it can easily be seen that the man who soon was appointed lieutenant colonel of the Fifty-fifth was not a very popular man. But his military ability was proved too often, and the commendations from his superiors too frequent, for posterity to doubt the outstanding zeal, diligence, and devotion of Malmborg.

He led the regiment into numerous battles, mostly successful, displaying most unusual bravery and perseverance. As the opposition to Malmborg had reached such a point that he was not reëlected colonel of the Regiment, General Logan criticized sharply the new colonel-elect and said: "We have been accustomed to look upon the 55th as the best regiment in the army . . ." and indicated that would no longer be the case, with

Malmborg gone. Partly because of impaired health, he resigned in 1864 and, although he again entered active service for a few months in the early part of 1865, his great days as a soldier were over. Before Vicksburg in May, 1863, Colonel Malmborg was wounded twice, first in the right, then in the left eye. The wounds did not prevent him from remaining active in the siege for weeks afterward, but later the injuries affected his eyesight. He returned to Sweden and died, almost completely blind, in Visby, in 1880.

Among the men whose valor and intrepidity have frequently been extolled, the name of Gen. Charles John Stolbrand (Carl Johan Möller) ranks high. He was born in Kristianstad in 1821, and came to the United States in 1851, after long service in the Swedish Army. When the Civil War broke out, he left his home in Chicago, and returned to his old profession. He entered the service as captain in October, 1861, and was promoted to major on the following New Year's Eve. By 1863 he had been assigned to the duties of a brigadier general, though still a major. As there were no vacancies, promotion was not forthcoming, and Stolbrand resigned. General Sherman, however, sent him home by way of Washington and, in a well-known interview with Lincoln himself, he was greeted by the title "General." When attempting to correct Lincoln, he was told he was mistaken—he was not a major—and Stolbrand returned to the Army as a full-fledged general. He participated with distinction in the sieges of Vicksburg and Savannah. In May, 1864, he had the unpleasant experience of being taken prisoner of war by the Confederates. Somehow, he is back again on his own side, still chief of artillery, in October of the same year. He mustered out in January, 1866, and died in 1894 as a plantation owner in Charleston, former enemy territory. Not only was his great contribution to the Union cause recognized and commended here by all his superiors, but the King of Sweden (Charles XV) also rewarded him with the Royal Order of the Sword. Colonel Mattson, whom we shall mention below, was told by General Sherman that "a braver man and a better artillery officer than General Stolbrand could not be found in the entire army." In the book mentioned above, Ernst W. Olson also mentions the names of about a dozen Swedes who served under Stolbrand in his battery.

Among the few men who came directly from Sweden to volunteer for the war, Ernst von Vegesack is, perhaps, the most outstanding. One of the relatively few Swedish officers in the East, he participated in more than a score of major engagements and sieges. Born on Gotland in 1820, he started as captain of the Fifty-eighth Ohio Volunteers, but rose next year to colonel, and was put in charge of the Twentieth New York Volunteers. His innumerable acts of efficiency and valor were crowded into the short space of two years. In 1863 he returned to Sweden, received his commission *in absentia* as brigadier general of the American Army, in 1865, and died at the age of eighty-three in Stockholm. Few foreigners were cited as often as Von Vegesack by their superiors. He was "conspicuous for bold and gallant conduct in actions," "distinguished for efficient service at Hanover Court-House, and gallant and meritorious conduct at the battle of Chickahominy"; showed "calm courage" under fire and "gave an admirable example" to his men; was "particularly gallant" at Antietam Creek; at Hanover Court-House he "was fired at six times, and narrowly escaped with his life"; he is cited for "intelligent and efficient service" repeatedly, etc. His bravery excited general admiration and, as a veteran of such fields as Gaines Mill, Antietam, Fredericksburg, and Gettysburg, he deserved, indeed, the distinguished recognition that he received.

Another worthy Swede, whose name we have seen nowhere except in a pamphlet published about him in 1869, the year of his death, is Karl Blomberg, appearing in the Civil War records as Carlo Blomberg. He arrived in America in 1861 at the age of twenty-eight, and almost immediately joined the First Light Artillery Regiment of New York. He participated as simple soldier in nine major battles and the sieges of Yorktown, Richmond, and Fredericksburg. At the last-mentioned siege he was wounded for the second time, and could not return to service until 1864, when he joined the Sixteenth Heavy Artillery Regiment of New York. After a number of important assignments and commands, he resigned in 1865, and returned to Sweden where, *in absentia*, he received his commission as a major in the American Army the following year.

Brief mention should be made of Joseph E(sbjörn) Osborn, who died as recently as 1932. Osborn was born near Gävle in 1843, and, at the outbreak of the war, both he and his brother Paul took service. The brother fell at Lexington, aged twenty-four. Joseph was in Stolbrand's company, and took part in several sieges. In 1864 he commanded a Negro company, later was in charge of a depot, and left the service in 1866 with a captain's rank. In his long and useful civilian life he distinguished himself as an editor and musician.

Colonel H. Mattson's book, *Minnen*, is well known. His chapter on the Civil War is, of course, pertinent in this connection; and we learn from it not only details about Mattson himself, but also a great deal about his Swedish brothers-in-arms. Hans Mattson was born in Skåne in 1832 and emigrated at the age of nineteen. When the war broke out he was about thirty and had, after various and sundry adventures, managed to study law, and was by then a full-fledged lawyer and county auditor. After publishing his call to the Swedes for volunteers, which we mentioned at the beginning of this article, in *Hemlandet* and English papers, he himself volunteered as a matter of course. He takes occasion to comment on the large number of Swedes who joined the colors, and mentions a number of officers by name. Besides those to whom we have or shall give separate paragraphs, we find such names as the Colonels Steelhammar, Broddy, Elfving, and Brydolf; Captains Arosenius, Eustrom, Stenbeck, Sparrström, Lempke, Charles Johnson, Vanstrum, and Lindberg; Lieutenants Edgren, Liljegren, Johnson, Lindall, Olson, Gustafson, Lundberg, Nyberg, Ackerström, and many others. Mattson entered as a captain and, as such, commanded Company D of the Third Minnesota Regiment. He was promoted to colonel in 1863. Although Mattson's activities were confined mostly to what might be called the "quieter" Western Front, his four years of service were far from lacking in exciting experiences. Modestly Mattson says that his time of service passed "without any incidents of especial interest or importance," but the siege of Vicksburg, and subsequent capitulation, at least, must have been one. According to Mattson's own judgment, it was one of the biggest victories in recent history. A bitter blow related by Colonel Mattson was the surrender of his own regiment on July 13, 1862. After serious sickness in Tennessee, he had been sent home to recuperate, and was just on his way back to join his troops when word came that the regiment had capitulated to General Forrest. Colonel Lester sounds convincing in his report: 450 men surrendered to "about 3000." But Colonel Miller says, a week later, that Colonel Lester was "reported as having been stupid with fear, some complain, cowardly." It is reported that the men had wept when denied the chance to go into action; and the number of the attacking force supposedly was not much more than one half of Lester's estimate. For Mattson, this unfortunate event led to a higher command, since all the officers who had voted for surrender were dishonorably discharged. Mattson took charge of his own regiment (released on parole), the Twelfth Michigan Infantry Regiment, and a battery of artillery. His regiment, while on parole, was free to help against the Indians, who then were on the warpath in western Minnesota.

Colonel Mattson led a life of distinguished public service after the war. He was twice Secretary of State in Minnesota, and in the years 1881–83 he served as American Consul General in Calcutta, India. He died in Minnesota in 1893.

We mentioned Ernst von Vegesack above, as one of the few professional soldiers who came to America with the express purpose of joining the war. Another of these men was Axel Silversparre, born in Strängnäs in 1834, who resigned from the Svea Artillery Regiment and served, at first, under General Freemont in Missouri. In 1861 he formed his own battery (First Illinois Light Artillery, Battery H), composed largely of Swedes. They and their commander distinguished themselves at the battle of Shiloh under General Grant. Early in 1863, however, while stationed in Memphis, Tennessee, Silversparre met with the misfortune of being taken prisoner by a band of bushwhackers. For ten months he endured imprisonment in the Libby prison at Richmond, but finally made good his escape. After various activities as an engineer and draughtsman, he passed away in a soldiers' home in 1906, aged seventy-two, and was buried with full military honors.

Much remains to be investigated in regard to the activities of the Swedes in the Civil War. The usual difficulties are encountered when it comes to identifying the names, especially the Andersons, Johnsons, and Nelsons, and those that have been corrupted or Anglicized. Ernst W. Olson's *History of the Swedes of Illinois* contains a wealth of material for that particular section, but little has been done with the *Official Records of the Union and Confederate Armies*, which abound with interesting and authentic information. Many of the details included above come from these records. We have seen that whole companies were Swedish and, according to Mattson and other writers, large numbers of Swedes were scattered through the various regiments. Mattson's Company D alone contained not less than 156 names, of which all but three or four are unquestionably Swedish. When, to the American-Swedish volunteers, we add not only the second generation and Swedish descendants in general, but also those who came directly from Sweden to participate in the war, it is clear that the Swedish contribution compares favorably with that of any other racial or national group. Olson claims for the Illinois Volunteer Regiments alone, 1,342 Swedes; and credible arguments have been advanced that a larger number volunteered than could normally be expected from their group on a percentual basis.

The Spanish-American War of 1898 lasted a trifle over three months and was, as such, a minor affair. By that time more than a million souls could be included in the Swedish population of the United States, and it is certain that a great many served, both on water and on land. Had the war lasted longer, this number would have been swelled by volunteer companies such as that formed in Chicago by C. Liljenstolpe and A. af Jocknich.

In an investigation carried on by Capt. Nels A. Nelson, it was found that about fifty Swedish-Americans were members of Roosevelt's Rough Riders. He also mentions Charles C. Nathurst, who was born in Malmö and fought in the Spanish-American War as a private. After the war, Nathurst was transferred to the Philippine Constabulary, where he rose rapidly and, in time, became a brigadier general. He resigned in 1932,

with the proud record of having risen from the ranks to one of
the highest positions in the service.

An obscure young fellow of twenty-one from Worcester,
Massachusetts, by the name of George Fried, also served in the
United States Army during the Spanish-American War. He
later learned the ways of the sea, and we shall return to him
in the last part of this chapter.

The World War is beyond the scope of this article. We are
too near to it to have a good perspective, and the tremendous
number of participants makes the sifting of the records, for
Swedish deeds of valor and efficiency, a giant undertaking. It
must be remembered that, when the armistice was signed in
1918, the American Army had more than two million men in
France of whom, obviously, thousands were of Swedish descent.
The compulsion that was inherent in the selective draft also
robs the World War of some of the glory inherent in volunteer-
ing. But, as time goes on, we shall find that gradually a group
of outstanding Swedes will crystallize out of the large number,
as has been the case with the earlier wars.

A LARGE element in Swedish life, since the days of the Vikings,
has been the tradition of the sea. So great a number of the
coast population become sailors, that it seems difficult to find a
ship on which there is not at least one, and even the inland boy
is likely to dream of a future that involves oceans and foreign
lands. The seagoing men of Sweden are willing to concede at
least equality to those of Norway, but to no one else. Hence, we
can reasonably expect that this tradition has been, in some
measure, continued by the Swedish element in America, and,
upon examination, we find that theirs is a proud record indeed.
If the Swedes have retained their valor of old, the thirst for
adventure, and the desire to live dangerously, that we have witnessed among the participants in the American wars, then we
can expect them, in large numbers, to choose the most adventurous of peacetime occupations, the sailor's life. Space does
not permit detailed accounts of any great number of Swedes,
active in the American Merchant Marine; but we can at least
call to mind some typical careers among our sea captains.

When, in 1849, a boy was born in Lysekil and christened Wilhelm Mattson, he was probably destined for the sea, since the great majority of children in that town always have been. At the age of ten he did go to sea; and ships occupied the rest of his life. At the age of eighteen he had rounded the Horn, and was making his first visit to San Francisco. He stayed in 'Frisco and, in three years, had earned his master's papers. His first command was a schooner plying between San Francisco and Puget Sound. Twelve years later, in 1882, we find him as part owner and master of the *Emma Claudina*. He had long been of the opinion that the Hawaiian Islands possessed great trading potentialities. His little 200-ton schooner was the first step in proving this contention, and his idea seemed reasonable enough to gain the confidence of the men who were helping financially. Outward bound, Matson carried general merchandise and returned with raw sugar, pineapples, coffee, and hides.

Five years later a second vessel came under William Matson's control, and ship after ship followed in rapid succession. By 1901 Captain Matson had a fleet of about ten ships and, with associates, he organized the Matson Navigation Company. The future of the organization seemed assured when, in the following year, the transfer from sail to steam was begun and their steamer, *Enterprise*, put into service. Neither the San Francisco fire of 1906 nor the World War seems to have impaired the progress of the company. The roaring 'twenties witnessed great but sound expansion through outright purchase of, or part investment in, other lines, and through extension of the routes covered. The present state of this great company can be glimpsed from an article "Ahoy, Australia! Ahoy, New Zealand!" by Peter B. Kyne in the *Saturday Evening Post* for October 24, 1934. The company today controls thirty-eight freighters and twelve passenger liners, some of which are crack express liners, real greyhounds of the Pacific. Kyne gives much space to the luxury liner *Mariposa*, 632 feet long and with a displacement of 25,885 tons. When we compare this with the *Emma Claudina* (200 tons) it is hard to realize that only fifty years separate the two ships.

But Captain Matson himself was not destined to witness the most spectacular growth of the organization he founded. The man, whom Kyne characterizes when he first sailed the *Emma Claudina*, as "a young viking who became one of the most dynamic and picturesque figures in the history of trans-Pacific shipping," died in 1917. We can get no better characterization of the man than Kyne's; it is firsthand: "I knew him intimately for many years. He was a superb seaman, a lover of fine horses and the best dressed man on the San Francisco waterfront. Like all men who have done great things in the world, he was a dreamer. And it took the biggest ocean in the world to provide enough room for his dreams, for they were always of ships— more and more ships—bigger and bigger ships."

The Matson Navigation Company has had in its employ a number of Swedish seamen. One of their early captains was Charles W. Peterson from Blekinge. Coming to America in 1897, aged sixteen, he sailed on various American ships, then studied navigation through the International Correspondence School, and received his license in 1902. He first entered the Matson employ in 1905 and, with the exception of a short break after the World War, remained in their service until 1925. During the War he joined the Naval Reserve Force, and was given the rank of lieutenant commander. He commanded several Matson Line vessels during the War, and in 1919 brought back from Europe the S.S. *Matsonia*, his old ship, which had served as a troop ship for the A.E.F., and remained in command of her for some time. For more than a decade now, Captain Peterson has been bar pilot for San Francisco.

Senior captain of the Matson Company, and in command of its flagship, is another astonishing Swede, Charles Arthur Berndtson. He was born in Marstrand in 1894, and has followed the sea since he was fifteen. The Matson Line employed him in 1916 as quartermaster and, a year later, on the day the United States entered the World War, Berndtson received his mate's papers. During the War he served on the Matson ship *Wilhelmina*, which made fifteen round trips as a war transport. It was fired at by enemy submarines, but never hit. In the Naval Reserve, Berndtson started as lieutenant, junior grade, but was, within a brief time, promoted to lieutenant commander. In 1921, not yet twenty-seven, he became captain of the *Wilhelmina*, and from then on, while in charge of various other passenger ships, his rise was rapid; and he became one of the most popular skippers on the Pacific. Since 1933 he has been in command of the S.S. *Lurline*. The tradition apparently will be continued, for Captain Berndtson's son is now a midshipman in the United States Navy, and expects to receive his commission in 1940.

Another former captain of the veteran ship *Wilhelmina*, now in command of the express liner *Monterey*, is Capt. E. R. Johansen, born in 1889 in Gothenburg. During the World War Johansen was also in the Naval Reserve, and commanded the U. S. Shipping Board freighter *Mohinkis*. His huge ship, *Monterey*, plies the California-Australia route and the master enjoys a philosophy of life which includes California, single bliss, books, motoring, and flying. It is difficult not to become envious.

Captain Peterson, whom we mentioned above, served for some time with the Dollar Line. On their records we also find several Swedes, among whom we may mention Capt. K. A. Ahlin. In 1924 Captain Ahlin was placed in command of the *President Harrison;* in 1935 of the *President Coolidge;* and is now about seventy years old. Another Dollar Line captain was Fred E. Anderson, born in Gävle in 1866. Since 1920 he commanded not less than ten of their ships, and finally retired in 1935, after fifty-four years on the water. His last command, for four-and-one-half years, was the *President Hoover*, which was shipwrecked off Formosa in December, 1937. The Swedes have luck as well as skill; the captain who met with misfortune does not have a Swedish name. In his day, Captain Anderson had plenty of adventure; effected several rescues; experienced two fires at sea, but never had a serious accident. A hard worker, he was known for his cheerful kindness, justice, and modesty. Captain Anderson revisited his native Sweden in 1937.

Captain E. W. Sundstrom, master of the *Dixie*, Southern Pacific Steamship Lines (Morgan Line), can also present a proud and clear record, after about thirty-five years on the water. He was born in Sweden in 1884.

If we turn away from the merchant marine, we find that Swedes are also trusted and preferred men in yachting. Many have been employed on American cup winners such as the *Reli-*

ance, Defiance, and others. Captain Frank Nolander has been in American yachting since 1899, except for a few years during and shortly after the World War, when he was employed by the U. S. Shipping Board. He is at present in command of a 375-ton auxiliary sailing vessel with which he has made several round-the-world trips. Captain Nolander, born in Bohuslän in 1877, lives in Brooklyn, New York.

When speaking of seafaring Swedes in America, it is impossible to overlook the large number of Klangs engaged in shipping of one kind or another. There are not less than six of them, five captains and one engineer, and all hail from Lysekil, where the father was a fisherman named Johan Simon Klang. Captain Gustaf Klang is at present in charge of Vincent Astor's famous *Nourmahal,* on which the owner combines pleasure with the business of scientific expeditions, and also takes President Roosevelt fishing. Captain Klang was born in 1878, and came to America at the age of twenty. After getting his master's papers he spent some time in the merchant marine, but soon was employed by Howard Gould, as captain of his *Niagara.* He has now been with Mr. Astor for twenty years, and commands his fourth *Nourmahal.* The 3,000-ton luxury yacht has a crew of forty-three, among whose Swedish members we should mention the first mate, Conrad Carlsson, from the seagoing town of Karlskrona. South Sea Island cruises and crossings to Europe and Scandinavia are frequent, and Mr. Astor keeps his captain busy by spending six to seven months a year on the ship.

Gustaf Klang's older brother Victor was born in 1873. Victor Klang enlisted in the American Navy in 1895 and served, during the Spanish-American War, on the cruiser *Columbia.* He was a participant in the West Indies campaign in 1898, and afterward received his service medal. Securing his master's papers in 1901, he joined the lighthouse service, and has now been in Government employ for an aggregate of forty-three years. During the World War, Captain Klang commanded the *Larkspur,* doing patrol and lighthouse duty, as well as minesweeping activities, which brought him a second service medal. Since 1922 he has commanded the *Spruce,* and has, for several years, had the rank of senior captain in the service. Captain Klang plans to retire this year (1938).

Of his two sons, the older, Victor, Jr., is now thirty-five, and a pilot at Sandy Hook; the younger, Eddie, also a sea captain, serves as junior officer on his father's ship. Then there is John Klang, a cousin, former skipper of President Harding's *Pioneer*, now on a large yacht at Long Branch. A nephew of the older Klangs is chief engineer on another ship.

We shall end our all-too-brief account of seafaring Swedes in America with a few words about the man who is, perhaps, the best known of them all. We have already had occasion to refer to George Fried, in connection with the Spanish-American War. Since the great sailor-to-be hailed from the inland city of Worcester, service in the army did not at that time seem illogical. He had, however, already tried to enlist in the Naval Training Station at Newport, but he was found out—he had run away from home, and was only fifteen. Shortly before the turn of the century, he enlisted in the United States Navy and, in five years, advanced to chief quartermaster. During the World War, a period replete with the danger and adventures of submarine warfare, Captain Fried commanded the freighter *Zuidedijak*. In 1922 Fried took his first command of a passenger ship, the *Peninsular State*, later renamed *President Roosevelt*. Beginning with this position, he rapidly rose to international fame, as the man who had an uncanny flair for being in the right place, where he could aid those in distress at sea. His great series of rescues started in 1926 when, with the *President Roosevelt*, he went to the aid of the disabled British freighter *Antinoe*. It was necessary to stand by for three days in mountainous seas, before opportunity came to take the crew of twenty-five off the sinking vessel. His terse but graphic story of this feat astonished the world, and the valiant captain became an honorary reporter of the Associated Press, and was given an inscribed gold watch. The United States Lines also gave him a larger command, the *America*, on which he earlier had been navigation officer.

Three months later, George Fried, now in command of the S.S. *America*, rescued a crew of thirty-two from the sinking Italian freighter *Florida*, in the middle of the Atlantic. The rescuer arrived just as the freighter was about to sink in the huge, raging seas. Not only were tremendous waves breaking

CAPTAIN GEORGE FRIED

SUPERVISING INSPECTOR, BUREAU OF NAVIGATION AND
STEAMBOAT INSPECTION, U. S. DEPARTMENT OF COMMERCE

over both ships, but darkness was setting in. With obstacles apparently insurmountable, Fried, nevertheless, maneuvered his ship into position, and a boat crew commanded by the equally valiant chief officer, Harry Manning, reached the disabled craft and removed the crew. This has become a classic story of the sea. On their return, the rescuers as well as the rescued were tumultuously received in New York. Fried was welcomed by the mayor in the City Hall, and given a scroll and gold medal. Secretary Wilbur sent letters of commendation, and the United States Congress recessed in Captain Fried's honor. The Italian Government presented him with a silver medal.

Captain Fried is a well-deserving member of the Adventurers' Club, and to recount all of his deeds here would lead us too far. On one occasion he altered the course of his ship, the *George Washington*, to save the life of a sick man on a freighter. In 1932 he found and rescued the Atlantic flier Reichers from his sinking plane off Ireland. Two years later he saved five people from a wrecked seaplane. And we still have not mentioned the near-rescues. In 1930, when the Swedish freighter *Ovidia* sank, and the New York *Times* wanted to know about the rescue, Captain Fried radioed pleasantly: "Sorry, *Mauretania* beat me by an hour."

In 1935 Captain Fried became an inspector in the Bureau of Navigation and Steamboat Inspection. After considering his record, it is hard to believe his statement that he welcomed his new duties on *terra firma*. But, in the past four years, Fried has rendered immense contributions to the problem he knows so well —safety at sea. Captain Fried is now (1938) sixty-one years of age, and still has before him a number of years of such invaluable service as only he can give.

Space allotment decrees that this brief sketch come to an end. Some day the records imperfectly outlined above will be presented more fully, and proper attention given to the many we have had to omit.

Aviation

JOHN GOLDSTROM

The writer of this chapter is the author of *A Narrative History of
Aviation,* published by the Macmillan Company in 1930. For more biographical details, see the chapter on "Journalists."

THE winged helmet of the Viking was a symbol prophetic
of today's winged Vikings of the Eighth Sea—infinitely
more vast than all the Seven Seas together. It was inevitable that descendants of the Norsemen of the sagas should
become sailors of the sky, when that became possible. An aircraft wing is a horizontal sail propelled by a wind machine.
Rudder and propeller originally were marine inventions. Erik
Nelson and Charles Rosendahl were sailors before they were
airmen; and it is not unlikely that among the Swedish ancestors
of Charles Lindbergh there were men of the sea, as this is true
of most people of Scandinavian blood.

The number of those of Swedish origin engaged in flying, in
designing, constructing, or servicing aircraft, or in operating
airways, is greatly out of proportion to the numbers of the race
from which they sprang. This is particularly true in the United
States.

Swedes have been pioneers in aeronautics since the attempt of
the Andrée-Strindberg-Fraenkel expedition to reach the North
Pole by balloon, an ill-fated but a trail-blazing venture, which
airmen of other lands have hailed as heroic in the extreme. That
was in 1897, six years before the first airplane flights of the
Wrights. Count Cederström was making cross-country flights
in Europe before the end of the first decade of the present century.

Dr. Victor O. Freeburg, in *Aero Digest*, has recalled that
Salomon A. Andrée first became actively interested in aeronautics when he was in the United States in 1876, as an employee
at the Swedish section of the Centennial Celebration at Philadelphia. A graduate engineer of a technical school in Stockholm, he worked at the Exposition as a janitor, to gain daily

admission. He met an American aeronaut named John Wise, who instructed him in aerial navigation.

A single chapter can take into account only a few of the outstanding figures of Swedish origin or ancestry who have taken historic part as Americans in the development of aviation. The first of historical importance was—and is—Maj. Erik H. Nelson (U. S. Army Air Corps, retired), engineering officer and mainspring of the first of all flights around the world. That was in 1924, three years before the Lindbergh flight to Paris.

He was born in Stockholm on June 12, 1888, the son of Erik Edward Nilsson, engineer; his mother, before her marriage, was Kristina Ahlen. After leaving high school, he studied engineering in the Stockholm Technological Institute, and business methods in Borgar Skolan. He spent the summer of 1905, when he was seventeen, on a training ship, and then went to sea. In the following four years he saw much of the world as a sailor before the mast, in various sailing ships. In the spring of 1909 he decided to come to the United States, and sailed from Hamburg as a passenger on the *President Grant*.

His first work in this country was as a rigger in a shipyard at Greenwich, Connecticut, for about two months, after which he joined the crew of a schooner yacht for the summer and fall. When winter came he went to work for A. T. Demarest & Company in New York City, which was then one of the leading automobile firms there. While testing cars on the old speedway at Mineola, Long Island, he became interested in aviation.

His first aircraft job was as a mechanic for the aviator Victor Vernon, on a Curtiss "F" flying boat, during the winter of 1913–14. Three years later, when the United States went to war, he was employed in the experimental motor department of the Curtiss Aeroplane Company's plant at Buffalo, New York. He tried to enlist for Army aviation in February of that year, but was rejected. He was in his twenty-ninth year, and they wanted youngsters. The Canadians also turned him down. A second attempt to join the American force also failed. Most men would, by this time, have suspected that the Allies had decided to fight the war in the air without his assistance. Not Nelson. He made still another attempt, and in October was accepted. In the following month he was assigned to the ground school at Cornell University, from which, in January, he was sent to Ellington Field, in Texas, for flight training. His advancement was steady, and, when the armistice came, he was in charge of acrobatic flight training. First-class instructors could not be spared for action in France; the younger men were sent over.

Two interesting flights varied the routine of training in the last year of the War. He was engineering officer and a pilot of a flight that photographed the Grand Canyon. Airplanes for the first time flew down into and through the Canyon, a dangerous undertaking. In the summer of that year Nelson was engineering officer, also, of an extensive recruiting flight.

In the September following the armistice, he was assigned to Kelly Field, Texas, to make up the First Bombardment Group, and was made engineering officer of the Twentieth Aero Squadron. In the following May he was sent to Mitchel Field, Long Island, to supervise the engineering, and to fly as engineering officer of the first flight from New York to Nome, Alaska, and return. Four planes flew a total of 11,000 miles, without a forced landing. It was his work on this flight which led to his selection as engineering officer of the first flight around the world. Congress later awarded him the Distinguished Flying Cross.

He first suggested this flight three years before it was actually begun, and was the only man in the expedition who was not a native American. Designated to consult with Donald W. Douglas, designer of the world cruisers, as to changes which had to be made to meet requirements, he recommended, after many conferences, the purchase of a trial plane. After testing it for a few hours over the country around the factory at Santa Monica, California, he flew it east to McCook Field at Dayton, Ohio (home of the Wright brothers), where it was tested as a landplane. It was given trial flights as a seaplane at Langley Field, Virginia, and was finally approved.

Before dawn of April 6, 1924, eight pilots in four planes took off from Sand Point, on Lake Washington, near Seattle. Only two of the four were to complete the historic flight. The plane of the commander, Maj. F. L. Martin, crashed in the mountains of Alaska; another, piloted by Lieut. Leigh Wade,

MAJOR ERIK H. NELSON
PIONEER CIRCUMAVIATOR OF THE U. S. ARMY

was forced down in the North Atlantic. Fortunately no lives were lost. The planes flown by Lieuts. Nelson and Lowell H. Smith successfully completed the first circumaviation of the globe.

The last transoceanic stage of this flight was of special interest to Scandinavians. Along much of the North Atlantic route, by way of Iceland and Greenland to North America, Nelson and his companions flew over the route the Vikings had sailed five centuries before the first transatlantic voyage of Columbus. Three years later, another airman of Swedish blood was to be first to fly, alone and nonstop, eastward across the North Atlantic.

After flying through blizzards and fogs over the North Pacific, blasting winds over Asiatic deserts, and the varying weather of Europe, the world fliers almost came to disaster in dense fogs, and among icebergs, in the North Atlantic. Weather prospects were not good when the planes took off from Kirkwall, North Scotland. The fog became so thick that the planes soon lost sight of one another. Smith and Wade were forced back to Kirkwall. Nelson, with his aide, Lieut. Jack Harding, got through to Iceland. The other fliers rejoined them next day.

The late Brigadier General William Mitchell, then Chief of Operations of the U. S. Army Air Corps, said to the present writer that Nelson had performed one of the greatest flying feats in the history of aviation. When I repeated this to Nelson recently, he laconically said that he and Harding had been merely lucky. The detailed record may be read elsewhere, and the reader may use his own judgment. (This chronicler, who was privileged to write an article forecasting the flight two years before it was made, based on an interview with General Mitchell, flew with the Air Corps escort from Boston to New York.)

Between Greenland and Nova Scotia, and again off the North American coast, the world fliers were forced by fog to fly low among icebergs, dodging in and out among them, sometimes at a speed of a mile-and-a-half a minute.

They were given great public receptions at New York, Washington, and other American cities. President Calvin Coolidge honored them. They were hailed as Magellans of the air. "Other men will fly around the world," said Admiral Robinson, "but never again will anybody fly around it for the first time." They had won a permanent place in history.

By a special act of Congress, Erik Nelson was advanced five hundred files on the promotion list of the Army, was awarded the Distinguished Service Medal, and governmental permission to receive decorations from foreign countries. King Gustaf of Sweden conferred upon him the Royal Order of the Sword, as an expression of the esteem and admiration of the people of his native land. France made him a Chevalier of the Legion of Honor. Japan gave him the Order of the Rising Sun. Tufts College conferred upon him the honorary degree of Master of Science. In 1929, he was made a major in the Air Corps Reserve.

Nelson resigned from the Army in 1928 to become sales manager of the Boeing Aircraft Company of Seattle, where his world flight began and ended. There he became associated with Philip G. Johnson, of Swedish parentage, one of the most important figures in the development of American air transport, especially the United Air Lines. In 1933 Nelson was made vice-president in charge of sales, and a member of the Board of Directors of the Boeing Company, one of the world's foremost manufacturers of both civilian and military planes. Under Johnson and Nelson, it pioneered in the making of high-speed transcontinental transports in the United States. It is now making the world's largest passenger planes. Many of its officials, engineers, and craftsmen are men of Scandinavian blood.

In 1936 Nelson retired from active duty with the Boeing Company, but through encouragement and counsel to younger men, especially aeronautical engineers, he continues to devote time to the development of aviation. Boating, hunting, and fishing, swimming, gardening, and motoring fill the leisure hours of his well-earned rest.

Soon after his retirement from Boeing, Major Nelson was married to Miss Julia Dodge of San Francisco, daughter of the late Commodore and Mrs. Frederick Dodge. They have a beautiful home on the shores of Lake Washington. The summer of 1937 they spent in Sweden, much of the time motoring over the countryside.

Major Nelson is a member of the University Club and the

Washington Athletic Club, both of Seattle; of the Swedish Engineers Club of Chicago; and of the Army and Navy Club of Washington.

Philip G. Johnson, son of Charles S. and Hanna (Gustavson) Johnson, was born November 5, 1894, at Seattle. His father came to the Northwest from Karlstad, Sweden, his mother from Åmål. After leaving the College of Engineering of the University of Washington in 1917, he entered the engineering division of the Boeing Company. He joined the production department the following year, and in 1919 became superintendent. After three years he was made vice-president and general manager, and in 1926 was elected president. Then only thirty-two years old, he was one of the youngest leaders of the industry in the United States. He remained president for seven years, the most important period of the company's development.

During part of this time, from 1931 to 1933, Johnson was president, also, of the Varney Air Lines, Inc., of National Air Transport, and of the United Air Lines, Inc. The latter company, using Boeing planes, was the first transcontinental operator of the air transport of passengers, mail, and freight. These companies have employed a considerable number of executives, engineers, pilots, and mechanicians of Scandinavian blood.

Johnson was a voting trustee of the United Air Lines Transport Corporation from 1934 to 1935, inclusive, after which he retired from all connection with this company. He devoted most of his attention in the following year, and part of the next, to the development of the Kenworth Motor Truck Corporation of Seattle, of which, in 1937, he was still vice-president, as well as a director of the Puget Sound Navigation Company and of the Pacific National Bank, both of Seattle.

In 1937 the Canadian Government procured an appropriation of $5,000,000 from the Dominion Parliament, to provide equipment, organization, and operating expenses for three years, for a new national system of airways. After considering many distinguished men in air transport, on both sides of the Atlantic, the Trans-Canada Air Lines invited Philip Johnson to become vice-president in charge of operations. Not being a Canadian citizen, he could hold no higher office. It would be his task to select planes and other equipment, and technical assistants, and to organize the new airways, designed to connect with the transatlantic service of the British Imperial Airways, then in course of organization, and to become an important part of the Empire system of aviation. The Canadian transcontinental route extends from Vancouver to Montreal, branch lines running northward to Calgary and Edmonton, and southward from Vancouver, Montreal, and other points, to connect with air lines in the United States.

Johnson accepted, made a survey flight across the Dominion, purchased planes in the United States, and, as this is written, is actively engaged in the general organization of the system. Although spending most of his time in Canada, he continues to maintain American citizenship and his residence in Seattle.

The official announcement of his engagement said, in part: "Trans-Canada Air Lines feel that they have secured an executive whose experience with modern air transport will insure to the new project the most prompt and satisfactory development in its difficult initial stages."

Swedish and other Scandinavian blood courses through most of the arteries of the network of airways that spreads over the Americas and extends across the oceans to the rest of the world. In 1929 the Lindbergh Line of the Transcontinental & Western Air became the chief rival of the Johnson-operated United Lines. It was surveyed, and technically organized, by an airman of Swedish paternal ancestry who, for more than a decade, has been one of the most extraordinary figures which aviation has produced.

When the Wright brothers were making their first flights, Charles A. Lindbergh was less than two years old, so that his own growth and development was contemporary with that of the airplane itself. He was born in Detroit on February 4, 1902, the son of a father born in Sweden and a mother of American stock of English, Irish, and French derivation. Before coming to the United States just previous to the American Civil War, his grandfather, Ola Månson, had been a member of the Swedish Parliament. In this country he changed the family name to Lindbergh. He and his wife, Louisa, had brought with them from Stockholm an infant-in-arms, born in 1860, who was to become the first Charles A. Lindbergh, a Congressman from Minnesota.

They settled near Sauk Center, Minnesota, which became the locale of Sinclair Lewis' *Main Street*, of which the Swedish Nobel Prize Committee was to take note two generations later, when it awarded its prize for literature to the author. The first Lindbergh home in America was a log cabin, which other Swedes helped them to erect on a pioneering homestead. (Early days of the Lindberghs in Minnesota have been described by the Reverend C. S. Harrison, in an account published by the Minnesota Historical Society. See also *The Lindberghs* by Dora B. Haines, Vanguard Press, New York 1931.) The son received his first schooling at home, with an occasional short term in country schools. Then he attended Grove Lake Academy, from which he was graduated to enter the University of Michigan. After graduation from its law school, he began practice at Little Falls, Minnesota, where later he was to serve as county attorney. He had married a graduate of the University of Michigan, the daughter of Charles and Evangeline Land, at Detroit, and it was there, also, that their historic son was born. When the infant Charles was less than two months old, he was taken by his parents to a farm near Little Falls. (See the chapter on "Public Officials.")

Charles was four years old when his father was elected to Congress from the Sixth District of Minnesota, which he was to serve for ten years. As the Lindberghs spent winters in Washington and summers in Minnesota, the boy's primary schooling was necessarily irregular, but it was supplemented by tutoring from his parents. He was ten years old when, with his father, he saw his first airplane near Washington, and was fascinated by the brief exhibition flights of the pioneer planes.

After graduation from the Little Falls High School, he studied mechanical engineering, and two years later entered the College of Engineering at the University of Wisconsin. But he was chiefly interested in aviation, and restlessly spent much of his time outdoors, generally on a motorcycle. He left the university after the first half of his sophomore year, and headed for the flying school of the Nebraska Aircraft Corporation at

Lincoln. His first flight as a passenger was with Otto Tim, an instructor. Later Pilot I. O. Biffle, formerly an Army instructor, became his first aviation teacher, and found him an excellent pupil. After some experience at "barnstorming" with various pilots in the Midwest and Southwest, and a course of factory work at Lincoln, which laid the groundwork for his subsequent knowledge of the mechanics and aerodynamics of flight, he enlisted as a cadet at the U. S. Army Air Corps' training school at Brooks Field, near San Antonio, Texas.

That was in March of 1924. In the following September he was among the few students selected to be transferred to the advanced school near-by, at Kelly Field. It was here for the first time that he attracted metropolitan newspaper attention, of which, less than three years later, he was to receive more than any ruler or statesman or any other man in the public eye. As aeronautical editor of the New York *Evening World*, the author of the present chapter happened to write the first article about him early in 1925.

In a copy of the monthly mimeographed U. S. Army Air Corps *News Letter*, intended for circulation among the personnel of the Corps, was found, buried far down and in blurred type, a routine report by the young Cadet Charles A. Lindbergh, recounting his part in a collision between two training planes in the clouds, a mile above Kelly Field. He and Lieut. C. D. McAllister had stepped out of the tangled and locked wreckage of the planes and safely descended by parachute. His report, in easy, clear, and simple language, did not indicate consciousness that he was already making aviation history, for it was the first time that anyone had ever escaped alive from a mid-air collision of aircraft. As there had been no previous news report from Texas—for flying fields give out news of crashes only when there is death or serious injury—the story was worth a column in the *World*, but it was not widely reprinted. The copy of the Air Corps *News Letter*, that went into the wastebasket after it had served its purpose, would be valuable today as a first-edition of Lindbergh's first aviation writing.

In less than an hour Cadet Lindbergh was flying again. After his graduation with honors that year as a second lieutenant in the Reserve Corps, there being no regular flying posts available, he resumed barnstorming, making cross-country flights between exhibitions. Before the end of the year an opportunity came to fly the mail between St. Louis and Chicago for the Robertson Aircraft Corporation, which had won a contract from the Government. While in the employ of this company, he had to make three more parachute jumps to save his life when planes failed him, twice in fog and at night.

On one of these night flights Lindbergh decided that it would hardly be more dangerous to try for the $25,000 prize which Raymond Orteig, proprietor of the Brevoort Hotel in New York, had offered for the first flight between New York and Paris. This decision was made in 1926; but it was not until February of the following year that he was able, with some capital of his own and more provided by St. Louis friends, to purchase a Ryan monoplane, powered with a Wright Whirl-wind motor of 200-horsepower. When the plane was under construction at the San Diego factory he introduced ideas of his own, and named it the "Spirit of St. Louis." After test-flying it himself, he rode it across the continent to New York, making only one stop, overnight at St. Louis. This was the longest cross-country flight he had ever made, and his first across the United States.

When he landed on Curtiss Field, Long Island, Commander Richard E. Byrd and Clarence D. Chamberlin, each with a larger and more powerful plane, were also almost ready to hop off for Paris. Both were already famous, Byrd for his flight to the North Pole, and Chamberlin for record-endurance flights. Compared with them, Lindbergh was an unknown, a tyro regarded as having little or no chance in competition with such aviators. But his one-stop flight across the continent had attracted attention, and the tall, slim, smiling, and businesslike young mail pilot almost instantly became a popular favorite with the crowds at Curtiss Field and the near-by Roosevelt Field, from which take-offs were to be made.

For a week there had been violent weather over the Atlantic. Byrd and Chamberlin were still waiting for better reports, when Lindbergh suddenly decided to take off. Misty rain was falling through fog at dawn of May 20, 1927, when Lindbergh ordered his plane towed to the soggy runway of Roosevelt Field.

At 7:52 o'clock he was off, clearing telephone wires by hardly more than a dozen feet, as veteran pilots turned away, expecting him to crash. Heading toward the Newfoundland Banks and the Atlantic, he soon vanished in the mist, and sailed off into history.

Since then many books and millions of words have been written about Lindbergh. There is room in this chapter for only a summary of his career, the most amazing in modern times, and with which everyone who reads is familiar. After a day and a half of flying, much of the way through rain, fog, sleet, snow, and wind, he landed, after dark of the second night, at Paris—and on the front page of every daily newspaper in the world, as the first man to fly alone, and without stop, across the Atlantic, from the New World to the Old.

When he landed against a misty wind on Le Bourget Field, all Paris rushed to meet him, in a tide of popular acclaim that was to be duplicated in every city he visited, for the next few years, on both sides of the Atlantic. Statesmen joined with the crowds to do him honor. Medals and offers of millions of dollars were showered upon him.

The greatest crowds since the Armistice greeted him at Brussels and London, as well as at Paris. His boyish smile and winning modesty won Europe, as had the personality of no other American before him. Invitations came to him from every European country.

The President of the United States, Calvin Coolidge, sent a warship to bring him home. The demonstrations for him at Washington, where he was greeted by the President and his Cabinet, and later at New York, where millions cheered him, were such as no popular hero has ever known.

Not only was his plane, the *Spirit of St. Louis*, given a place of honor in the National Museum at Washington, but there was established at St. Louis a special museum for the permanent display of decorations and gifts which came to him from all parts of the world.

He refused motion-picture offers and others totaling many millions, and announced that he would continue in aviation. He was made a colonel in the Air Corps Reserve, into which he had graduated as a second lieutenant.

COLONEL CHARLES A. LINDBERGH

The title of his book, *We*, in which he describes in detail his preparation for, and the flight to, Paris was popularly interpreted to mean his plane and himself. It meant more than that, as he indicated in his response, when Charles Evans Hughes, later to become Chief Justice of the Supreme Court, presented to him, on the steps of the Capitol at Washington, the Cross of Honor. He said that credit "should not go to the pilot alone but to American science and genius which had given years of study to the advancement of aeronautics. . . . It was the culmination of twenty years of aeronautical research and the assembling together of all that was practicable and best in American aviation."

A single instance of what he meant has not been generally known. When he landed at Curtiss Field, Brice Goldsborough, maker of navigational instruments for aircraft, examined the instrument board of his plane, and warned him that his magnetic compass might become deranged off the Newfoundland Banks. Lindbergh told him it was the best he could afford. Goldsborough consulted with his associate, Morris M. Titterington, inventor of the earth-inductor compass, an early type of which had guided Nelson and Smith around the world. Their offer to install, without charge, an improved model of this compass (on test flights of which this writer had recently accompanied Titterington, whose apartment he shared) was eagerly accepted. After the flight, Lindbergh credited this compass with the accuracy with which he flew through Atlantic storms such as had cost the lives of other fliers. (Goldsborough afterward was lost in a storm of exceptional violence over the Atlantic; Titterington crashed to his death in the Allegheny Mountains—two of many who have given their lives to advance aviation. Their Pioneer Instrument Company was afterward acquired by Vincent Bendix, an aircraft-accessories manufacturer born of Swedish parents.) (See page 548.)

After his return from Paris, Lindbergh made a flying tour of the United States, visiting every city of importance, and giving to aviation the greatest popular impetus in its history. There followed a "goodwill" flight to Mexico, Central America, and the West Indies. In Mexico he met Anne Morrow, daughter of the American Ambassador, Dwight W. Morrow. Two years later they were married. She accompanied her husband on flights of exploration over lost Mayan cities and elsewhere, and he taught her to fly.

Since then they have made flights together across the North Pacific to China; over the North Atlantic, by way of Greenland and Iceland to Europe, where they visited birthplaces of his ancestors in Sweden; then southward from Europe to Africa; across the South Atlantic to South America; and northward again to the United States. On the transoceanic stages of the latter trip they were making surveys for the Pan-American Airways System.

Most of their flying together has been done since the tragedy of the kidnapping and slaying of their first-born, Charles, in 1932, a crime that shocked the civilized world. Late in 1935 they took their second son, Jon, to England, where they have continued to live, though friends expect them to return to the United States eventually.

In the last few years Colonel Lindbergh has divided his time between aviation and science. In the summer of 1936 he and his wife flew to Copenhagen to attend the International Congress of Cytology, before which Lindbergh demonstrated the "mechanical heart" which he had devised for Dr. Alexis Carrel, Nobel Prize-winning physicist of Rockefeller Institute. Into this mechanical heart went a part of Lindbergh's experience with airplane motors. "The outstanding significance of the apparatus," said Dr. Carrel to the delegates, "is that Lindbergh has succeeded in making a blood serum pulsate. Here is an approach to one of life's great riddles."

In the same month, facing the Berlin Aero Club, in the heart of a Europe preparing for war in the air, he urged that aviation be used as an instrument of peace and for the advancement of civilization. "Aviation," he said, "has brought revolutionary changes to a world already staggering with changes. It is our responsibility to make sure that we do not destroy the very things which we wish to protect."

In 1937 Colonel and Mrs. Lindbergh made a recreational flight from England to India, by way of Egypt. In December of that year they came to the United States on a visit, in the course of which Lindbergh, for Pan-American Airways, invited bids for the construction of a fleet of one hundred passenger-transport planes for transatlantic service. At thirty-six, he continues to be a world figure of unpredictable possibilities.

Another American airman of Swedish parentage, who is of international importance in aeronautics, is Commander Charles E. Rosendahl of the United States Naval Air Station at Lakehurst, New Jersey. As America's foremost commander of great airships, he is also the principal American proponent of lighter-than-air transport across the oceans. Sailor as well as airman, he has a record of extraordinary achievement.

The son of Charles Oscar and Johannah (Johnson) Rosendahl, who in their youth came to this country from Sweden, Commander Rosendahl was born in Chicago on May 15, 1892. Removing to Topeka, Kansas, in his boyhood, he was graduated from grammar school there, and later from high school at Cleburne, Texas. From there he went, in 1910, to the United States Naval Academy at Annapolis, Maryland, graduating as an ensign four years later. Then followed sea duty on board the armored cruiser *West Virginia*, and the cruiser *Cleveland*. In 1917 he was commissioned lieutenant, junior grade.

Just before the American entrance into the World War, he returned to duty on the *West Virginia*, the name of which was changed to the *Huntington*. During most of the War he served in various billets, from watch officer to navigator, on board this ship, which was engaged in convoying troop ships across the Atlantic. Late in the War he went on duty in connection with the fitting out of a new torpedo-boat destroyer which—"unfortunately," he says—was not completed before the armistice. After the War he spent several years on destroyer duty, and in the fall of 1921 returned to the Naval Academy as an instructor.

Early in 1923 the Navy Department issued a call for volunteers to take training for service on board airships. Lieutenant Rosendahl was among the first volunteers, and in April of that year reported for duty at Lakehurst. He qualified as a naval aviator and was assigned as a member of the original crew of the *Shenandoah*, the first of the large rigid dirigibles of the Navy.

Rosendahl was aboard the *Shenandoah* as one of its officers when it crashed in a line squall in Ohio, in 1925. The great airship broke into two parts. Finding himself in one section with a part of the crew, Rosendahl managed to land it safely several miles away. This remarkable demonstration of coolness, courage, and airmanship won him world-wide fame. The present writer happened to be in Germany at the time, on a tour of the European airways, and, in the birthplace of the Zeppelin type of airship he heard expressions of amazement over the unprecedented feat. It marked him for advancement.

In May of the following year, Rosendahl was given command of the *Los Angeles*, which had been built in Germany as a war-reparations ship, and had been flown across the Atlantic by a German crew, headed by Dr. Hugo Eckener. For three years he continued in command of what was then the world's largest dirigible, making transcontinental and other training flights, the first nonstop flight from New York to the Panama Canal, and the only landing of an airship aboard an aircraft carrier, the *Saratoga*. This was the most successful period of the pioneering of large airships in the United States; and it is a notable fact that in the unfortunate record of lighter-than-air craft in this country, no ship commanded by Rosendahl has ever crashed. He is regarded by Dr. Eckener and other German experts as the ablest of American airship commanders and technicians.

At the beginning of 1929, Rosendahl was made commander of naval rigid-airship training and the experimental squadron of the United States Navy, and, after a year, went to the Naval Bureau of Aeronautics, with headquarters at Washington, where he served another year.

Following this he went to Akron, Ohio, with a Navy airship crew, and commanded the trial flights of the new *Akron*. In October of 1931 he became its first commanding officer, and served in that capacity until the following June. Under Navy regulations it was then necessary for him to serve at sea again, and he went aboard the new battleship *West Virginia*. After a year he became navigating officer of the heavy cruiser *Portland*. In June, 1934, he was appointed commanding officer of the Naval Air Station at Lakehurst, and in the following February was promoted to the full rank of commander. He has continued

COMMANDER CHARLES E. ROSENDAHL
OF THE U. S. AIR STATION. EXPERT ON DIRIGIBLES

in charge at Lakehurst, the most important of American airship bases, which has also served as a landing place for the transoceanic Zeppelins from Germany. He was in command of the Station when the *Hindenburg* exploded on May 6, 1937, and helped succor the victims.

Commander Rosendahl has had an extensive experience with the German ships. In connection with the completion and trials of the *Graf Zeppelin*, he was sent to Germany in 1928 as U. S. Naval observer, and made the first North Atlantic crossing in that ship, in October of that year. In August, 1929, he flew around the world in the *Graf Zeppelin*, in the then record time of twenty-one days, the historic first flight of any airship around the world. In August and September of 1936 he made a round-trip crossing of the North Atlantic in the *Hindenburg*, and also a round trip in the same ship across the South Atlantic between Germany and Brazil.

Commander Rosendahl is credited with having done more than any other man for the development of American lighter-than-air flying. There was much criticism, both in Congress and in the press, because of the airship disasters which followed his routine transfer to sea and land duty, the critics contending that his ability and experience should have been continued to be utilized in airship duty. Now, in 1938, as commander at Lakehurst, the most important airship post, he is leader of a movement to restore and expand the American position in the airship field. In this interest he has made a number of appearances at Congressional hearings, has delivered many public addresses and radio broadcasts, and has written numerous magazine articles. He is the author of the authoritative airship book, *Up Ship!* and, in 1938, of a second book, *What About the Airships?* which has evoked high critical appraisal. Commander Rosendahl is a member of the Army and Navy and of the Circumnavigators Club.

Martin Elmer Johnson, flying explorer and naturalist of the American Museum of Natural History, was, like Lindbergh, the son of a man who was born in Stockholm, and in his infancy he had been brought by his parents to the United States. The internationally known motion-picture recorder of wild-animal life in Africa, Borneo, and other parts of the world, was born in Rockford, Illinois, in 1884. In his boyhood the family removed to Lincoln, Nebraska, and then to Independence, Kansas.

In his youth Johnson became interested in photography, and in his 'twenties accompanied Jack London and Mrs. London as a photographer on the famous voyage in the *Snark* to the South Sea Islands. After his marriage to Osa Helen Leighty, at Chanute, Kansas, in 1910, the two spent the remainder of their life together in exploring uncivilized places in many parts of the world. They traveled around the world six times, and in Africa, and elsewhere, used airplanes of their own. Between explorations they lectured and exhibited their motion-picture records of vanishing wild-animal life.

Both insisted that the jungle was safer than civilization for them; and this was tragically proved when Martin Johnson was killed in the crash of a transport plane near Burbank, California, on January 12, 1937. Mrs. Johnson recovered from serious injuries, to carry on her husband's work.

Johnson was the author of *Camera Trails in Africa* and other books, and was a member of the Explorers, Circumnavigators, Travelers, and Authors clubs. F. Trubee Davison, President of the American Museum of Natural History, described his death as "a great loss to natural history and science in general."

Vincent Bendix, automotive inventor, is one of the foremost American manufacturers of aircraft accessories. (See the chapters on "Inventors" and "Manufacturers.") Having acquired wealth in the automotive industry, he began, after the Lindbergh flight to Paris, the acquisition of companies manufacturing aircraft instruments, self-starters, landing-gear, and other accessories, and became president of the Bendix Aviation Corporation, operating in many cities.

The Bendix Trophy, annually awarded to winners of transcontinental airplane speed races under the auspices of the National Air Races, is one of the principal competitive awards in aviation. In 1937 he announced plans for an "aviation city" to bear his name, at Teterboro, New Jersey. The airport there was remodeled, and an aeronautical plant, complete with engineering and laboratory buildings, erected. Bendix is a trustee of the Armour Institute of Technology of Chicago, and a member of the Society of Automotive Engineers.

Among other men of Swedish blood who have achieved out-standing positions in American aviation are:

Charles A. Rheinstrom, who, in December of 1936, was made vice-president and sales manager of the American Airlines, whose transcontinental routes cover 6,970 miles, the largest domestic mileage in the United States; his headquarters are at Chicago.

Captain Ralph Dahlstrom of Alameda, California, one of the pioneer pilots of the transpacific service of the Pan-American Airways System. In the fall of 1936, Captain Dahlstrom piloted a clipper plane, in a flight of press representatives, from California via Honolulu, to the Orient.

Captain Westside T. Larson of the U. S. Army Air Corps, with headquarters at Washington, D.C.; winner of the Mackay Trophy for 1933, in recognition of experimental flights, including blind landings and take-offs, while developing the frontier aerial-defense system of the Air Corps.

Captain Edwin Blom of Alameda, California, who piloted one of the first of the Boeing multimotored transport planes, and was killed in December of 1936 when a Douglas transport of the United Air Lines crashed in a storm of great violence in Rice Canyon, California.

Captain Charles Backman, who came from Rättvik, Sweden, to the United States, in 1925, and was with the Robertson Aircraft Corporation at St. Louis, when Lindbergh left its employ to fly to Paris; pilot on the New York–Chicago division of the American Air Lines.

Miss Clara Johnson, daughter of a father born in Sweden and an American mother of Norwegian descent, is one of the first stewardesses to have flown more than a million miles on transport planes. Her father, born in Malmö, came to the United States when he was nineteen and became a boat builder. Her mother, who was Miss Elsie Ellison, died more than twenty years ago. Miss Johnson was born in San Francisco, where she was graduated from the French Hospital in 1931. In the same year she became a stewardess with United Air Lines, and in 1937 was on duty between Oakland and Seattle.

Flying journalists have a special share in aviation, in that they literally have a bird's-eye view of history in the making, and occasionally are themselves privileged to take part in that making. One of the outstanding men in this field is "Duke" Krantz, whose reportorial and photographic flights for the New York *Daily News*, and its syndicate, have made him widely known.

Aron Fabian Krantz was born in Småland, Sweden, and came to the United States in 1915, when he was nineteen years old, and at first worked on a farm in Illinois. When the United States entered the World War, Krantz was refused admission to the air force, because he had not been naturalized and spoke little English. In 1919 he had taken out citizenship papers, and then enlisted as a private at Kelly Field, Texas. He became a sergeant, but was refused a chance to win a commission in the cadet school (which later graduated Lindbergh), because he could not produce a diploma from an American high school. He left the Army in 1922, and two years later joined Gates' Flying Circus as a stunt performer, thrilling crowds at county fairs. He did not become a pilot himself until 1928, when the circus had disbanded.

Not long afterward, Krantz remained in the air 177 hours, breaking an endurance record which had been set by the very same Army officer who rejected him at Kelly Field. In 1934, the *News*, looking for a pilot who could land a plane anywhere, and fly in any kind of weather, engaged Krantz. Among his better-known feats were the pictures taken of the passenger ship *Morro Castle*, burning at sea off the New Jersey coast.

Manufacturers

BERNARD PETERSON

A native of Glimåkra in the Province of Skåne in Sweden, Mr. Peterson came to Boston in 1891 and, since 1893, has been a member of the editorial staff of the Boston *Evening Transcript,* specializing in recent years in such topics as business, public health, industrial relations, and the conservation of natural resources. In the early part of the century he reported the great textile strikes in Lawrence and Lowell; and during the World War he went to France as a Y.M.C.A. welfare worker, serving the "Wildcat Division" under intense fire. At home he is Secretary of the Eastern Sunday School Association. For some of the material in this chapter he wishes to give credit to *The Swedish Element in America,* published in Chicago by the Swedish American Biographical Society, Charles S. Peterson, President.

TO the least reflective mind it must be evident that, before coming to America, the Swedes could not have existed for so long in a country with such a rigorous climate as that of Sweden, if they had not been resourceful in mind and adept in the use of their hands. In the course of time it is geography that molds the races and when compared, for instance, with the natives of the tropics, or even of southern Europe, the Swedes at once stand out as specially fitted to make their living in the northern parts of the United States. In the early years they were, like the British, Dutch, or French colonists, preeminently farmers, buying their manufactured goods from Europe, or getting along with the simplest equipment made by themselves; but, as native American industries developed, they played their part both as craftsmen and as organizers and executives.

The thing to bear in mind when evaluating this contribution to American civilization is that, while the majority of the Swedes were poorly supplied in goods when they came, and at times could not compete on even terms in trade with the Dutch or the English colonists, they did know how to till the soil and how to provide themselves with tools. Already on their arrival, whether in colonial days or later, some of them were shoemakers, tailors, blacksmiths, carpenters, cabinetmakers, or stone masons. In other words, given the raw materials found in such abundance in the New World, the Swedes were well prepared not only to take care of themselves, but also to provide others with both handmade and machine-made goods.

As a rule the Swedes have preferred to work in either wood or metals, the materials with which they had been familiar at home. What the Swedes have done as carpenters and builders, particularly in such cities as Chicago or as iron riggers on the skyscrapers of New York, will be told in a separate chapter; and it is no accident that three such typical Swedish industrial centers as Jamestown, New York, Rockford, Illinois, and Grand Rapids, Michigan, are famous for their furniture. In the hardware plants of New England there are many highly skilled Swedish mechanics. In this respect the Pratt & Whitney airplane motor factories in Hartford, Connecticut, and the Yale Lock Company's shop in Stamford, are typical. In Waltham, Massachusetts, and Elgin, Illinois, they make watches; in Detroit it is motorcars. Even among the jewelry makers of Rhode Island there are many Swedes, as is also the case in such shoe centers as Brockton and Lynn in Massachusetts.

As to the sum total of the contributions to American industry by these thousands of skilled craftsmen, whether born and educated in Sweden or in the United States, it is impossible to make an estimate. But one needs only to imagine the gaps in the American industrial ranks that would ensue, should all these workers of Swedish ancestry all of a sudden drop out, or the time and expense that would be required to bring up and educate substitutes. In fact, it is a fair question whether American industry would have reached its present level of efficiency and productiveness, had no skilled artisans from Sweden ever come across the Atlantic, or whether corresponding substitutes could have been recruited in any other country. Suppose, for instance, that Sweden, like the Netherlands, had founded a colonial domain of its own in some other part of the world, where its surplus man power and brain power would have had room for free play. What would have been the effect on American life?

As American industry has developed, the Swedish element

has not been content to remain as employees, but has taken the initiative and financial risk to start or develop industries of its own. In almost every section of the country there are manufacturers of Swedish ancestry, and they are so numerous that but to list their names would fill a volume. All that can be done here is to pick out typical examples. In general they fall into two groups, those who have built up industries on the basis of their own inventions, and those who have developed the inventions or organized the technical skill of others—in either case endowing American life with new conveniences and new wealth. On the other hand, there are very few industrialists of Swedish descent whose position is founded on the exploitation of natural resources such as mines or forests, or on purely financial power, acquired either by marriage, inheritance, or speculation. While many of them have been well educated, either here or in Sweden, almost every one is "self-made." In other words, they have started from scratch.

Such Swedish captains of industry have made noteworthy contributions to the economic competency and convenience of American life. Industrial plants of Swedish ownership or origin have grown up in many states, without invading existing markets. They have created new demands with new products, given the American people new conveniences, and brought new activities and better prospects.

Though Swedish people did not come to America in impressive numbers until the big waves of European immigration had rolled in, after the middle of the nineteenth century, they were here in time to compete for the big budding opportunities of industrial development. The great modern inventions were still to come, such as the telephone, the electric light, the automobile, airplane, and radio, each unfolding visions of new fields for production and profit. People of Swedish birth or descent are found in key positions in all these industries, having contributed materially to their development, both mechanically and financially.

Illustrative of these major developments are the Bendix drive which revolutionized the operation of the automobile, the Celotex wall-insulative board, the plastic art that has placed beautiful jewelry within the reach of all classes of people, high-speed winding machinery for the textile and wire industries, abrasives which have speeded and refined mechanical precision, and innumerable inventions around which Swedish manufacturing plants have sprung up.

Take, for instance, the career of Francis J. Plym, the President of the Swedish American Tercentenary Association. Born in the poorest part of Småland and brought, when an infant, to America, where his father had preceded him, he grew up in Aledo, Illinois, which was then in a relatively undeveloped prairie country. He did not become a farmer, however, but developed into a skilled carpenter and cabinetmaker. By working part time he was able to enter schools of higher education, and finally the University of Illinois, from which he was graduated in 1897 with a degree in architecture. After that he studied at the National Academy of Design in New York, and in 1899 set up as a practicing architect at Lincoln, Nebraska, where four years later he married. The same year he moved to Kansas City, Missouri, and, after four years more of architecture, began his career as an inventor and manufacturer which today makes him an employer of thousands of men, chiefly at Niles, Michigan. Personally he had little capital, but he had an idea in which he had faith, and it has more than justified itself. As a practical, working architect, he had had occasion to design the interior of stores and, in that way, came to invent ready-made, hollow-metal store fronts of ornamental design. His first patent had been granted him in 1905, and now he holds a hundred in his own name, and many more jointly with others. Besides the store fronts, he makes architectural fixtures for banks as well as stores, metal-casement windows for ships and lighthouses, parts for automobiles and airplanes, and even escalators, such as those installed in some of the new buildings of Rockefeller Center, in which the Tercentenary Association has its New York headquarters. In the meantime the Kawneer Company, which he founded at Niles, Michigan, a generation ago, has expanded greatly by the acquisition of several other concerns, so that now Mr. Plym directs plants not only at Niles, but in Chicago itself, Chicago Heights, Illinois, and Berkeley, California. At Niles he is also president of the company that publishes the only local daily newspaper. He has

FRANCIS J. PLYM

PRESIDENT AND FOUNDER OF KAWNEER COMPANY
NILES, MICHIGAN

given Niles $100,000 for a hospital, and donated a 67-acre tract for a nine-hole golf course, baseball fields, and other playgrounds. At the University of Illinois, where he had to support himself while getting his own education, he maintains two $1,200 fellowships for postgraduate study in architecture abroad. He has, furthermore, made large donations to Swedish-American colleges, such as Augustana at Rock Island, Illinois, and Bethany at Lindsborg, Kansas, as well as to the American Swedish Historical Museum at Philadelphia. He has even provided his native town of Bäckaby, in Sweden, with an old people's home. He had the energy to earn himself an education; the inventive genius to generate new ideas; and the inborn taste for the beauty of design that characterizes all his products. Out of his brain he has added a new industry to American life.

The same could be said of Mr. Plym's neighbor in Michigan, Emil Tyden of Hastings, whose inventions and industrial products are even more widely used in the American market and also abroad. Chester and Richard Messer, long active in the agricultural business at Hastings, Michigan, and later connected with the Hastings City Bank, were responsible for the starting of Hastings' prosperous industries, by making available the skill and tireless energy of young Tyden, who was destined to bring honor and distinction to his race. It was while on a vacation trip in Colorado that Richard Messer first met Emil Tyden, then working for the Union Pacific Railroad. The latter showed him an automatic self-locking car seal, which he had invented and patented. Mr. Messer induced him to come to Hastings, assuring him of the necessary capital for a factory. It was a long struggle, as Mr. Tyden had to invent and work out the details for special automatic machines, to be used in the manufacture of car seals. With true Viking persistence he stuck to that job, and today the International Seal & Lock Company, which really should be called the Tyden Seal Company, is recognized as an outstanding manufacturing success. It is the largest car-seal factory in the world. For nearly forty years it has manufactured the Tyden self-locking seal, now used exclusively by over 95 per cent of the railroads in the United States, and by railroads all over the world. The principle of the seal, as originally designed, has never been changed.

The factory has a capacity of over 500,000 units a day. In the past thirty-seven years it has produced over 2,250,000,000 seals. The Tyden seal is used also by the Customs departments of the United States and Canada, for sealing cars containing freight in bond. It is used by all express companies and by more than 10,000 large shippers.

To perfect the automatic machines to make seals, Mr. Tyden established a factory in Chicago, the Consolidated Press & Tool Company, which brought out a long line of stamping presses. It later moved to Hastings and passed into new hands. Mr. Tyden also became interested in the Hastings Table Company, and invented and patented a locking device for pedestal dining tables, which put the company on a substantial financial basis. Later he perfected an organization which made the Table Company an outstanding success in the furniture industry. It was through Mr. Tyden's inventive genius, sound business judgment, and backing, that the Viking Corporation and the Hastings Manufacturing Company were established in Hastings. Both of these have become prosperous institutions. During the years of depression the Hastings Manufacturing Company became one of the five largest piston-ring companies in the world, making the only complete line of replacement rings in the industry. Featured among these rings is one whose sensational performance has been given national publicity. By 1937 this new company had overcome all the depression problems and had developed a world-wide business. Numerous other contributions to American industry, notably an automatic sprinkler, known as the Viking, have been made by Mr. Tyden who, with modest reserve, said to the writer: "I have a splendid organization in the enterprizes with which I am connected and they deserve as much credit as I do for whatever success has been obtained."

Phenomenal in its influence on American life has been the work of Vincent Bendix, son of a Swedish clergyman, the Reverend John Bendix of the Swedish Methodist Church in Moline, Illinois. (See the chapter on "Inventors.") After spending some years in New York, he became, in 1907, a salesman for the Holsman Automobile Company in Chicago, and was the first to visualize the principle of self-starting for automobiles. Before his invention of the "Bendix Drive," all motor vehicles had to be cranked by hand, which limited their use to men of dependable muscular development. Bendix made it possible for the women of the country to step into the driver's seat. He built his own car in 1908, but only one feature of it survived the test. That was the Bendix self-starter, which has since been adopted for all makes of automobiles and airplanes, bringing Mr. Bendix his first huge fortune. He has continued to supply the industry with important parts, such as the wheel brakes which also became standard equipment in the United States. His market soon widened to world-wide proportions, and aviation opened new fields for his inventive mind (see the chapter on "Aviation"). He built factories, organized new corporations, consolidated old ones, expanded production, sales, and financing, on huge scales, and spent money lavishly on research work, as well as on philanthropic projects.

Bendix has risen to the top in every field of his choice; as an industrialist, he is the dominant president of the Bendix Aviation Corporation, a holding company that controls thirty-two subsidiaries which manufacture and distribute a hundred essential products for the automotive, aviation, and marine industries. Practically all of his products are manufactured and distributed throughout the entire world. His employees number 12,000 today in this country, and probably 4,000 abroad. His latest venture is an automatic washing and ironing machine.

Two Swedish names, George N. Jeppson of Worcester, Massachusetts, and the late George Berkander of Providence, Rhode Island, are known far and wide in this country and abroad. Their permeating influence over industrial and social development radiates from their respective factories, like spokes that point in all directions. It is the universal use of their products on the market, and the fact that they pioneered in their own fields, that suggest a parallel between the two names.

George Berkander was born in Västergötland, Sweden, in 1879, and died unexpectedly in the fall of 1937. He had come to America with his parents in 1891 and, after trying his hand at a few small jobs, as most ambitious boys would, he caught a vision of an entirely new line of industry and promptly launched his novel venture, which gave the world its first view and apprecia-

tion of plastic jewelry. A few stores in Providence agreed
rather reluctantly to handle the first celluloid products. Demand developed. Inexpensive ornaments, as exquisite in design
as costly jewelry from Paris, were turned out in Berkander's
shop. Its fame spread all over the country. Chain stores procured it and displayed it on their counters, and the business
grew until Mr. Berkander was using fifteen to twenty tons of
celluloid a week. Of bracelets alone his factory was making
145,000 a day, and today Berkander products are sold in practically every store in the country dealing in inexpensive jewelry. Designers in the Berkander plant make over fifty new
designs a day for jewelry, novelties, and favors. One of the
latest ideas led to the harvesting of pine cones on Cape Cod,
for conversion into buttons and brooches. It takes 100,000
bushels of cones a year to fill orders, and when the demand for
these pine-cone novelties begins to wane, they drop from the
production program and the research laboratory has something else for the public. Mr. Berkander was the first to introduce plastic jewelry, both in this country and abroad, and his
enterprise has brought him bounteous reward. The whole world
was quick to follow in Berkander's footsteps, once it had acquired a taste for its inexpensive beauty and the knowledge of
production.

George N. Jeppson of Worcester, Massachusetts, son of an
experienced potter from Sweden, John Jeppson, is continuing
the operation of a world-wide enterprise which his father helped
to organize in 1885. This is the Norton Company of Worcester,
the largest and one of the oldest manufacturers of grinding
wheels, abrasive products, and grinding machines. American
industry had not developed to the point where it could make
very extensive use of abrasives when John Jeppson came to
this country, and the art of preparing abrasives was little understood. But Mr. Jeppson adapted his knowledge of pottery
to it as a new technique. Implements for grinding metal, wood,
and stone, were produced in the little Norton shop. They were
sold to other manufacturers to facilitate other metalwork,
woodwork, and stonework, first in Worcester, then in surrounding territories, and now throughout the world. The business of
Jeppson customers expanded also, because finer products were

GEORGE N. JEPPSON
THE NORTON COMPANY, WORCESTER, MASSACHUSETTS

made with less labor, increasing the demand for abrasives. Young George Jeppson, who came to the factory to work with his father, went later as a student to Stockholm, Sweden, to complete his technical education at the Royal School of Mines. Upon his return to the United States in 1898 he reëntered the service of the Norton Company, for the purpose of learning the business from the ground up. Today he is treasurer and vice-president in charge of production. From the small beginning in a new field, the Norton Company has developed into an international institution with factories and affiliates at Niagara Falls, New York; Wesseling, Germany; Chippawa and Hamilton, Ontario in Canada; Bauxite, Arkansas; La Courneuve, France; Welwyn Garden City, England; Corsico, Italy; Troy, New York; and Littleton, New Hampshire.

Norton abrasives, in various forms, are now used in practically every industry, for rough finishing and precision surfacing, for cutting, cleansing, and polishing. They are used for cutting stones, grinding lenses, and for leveling out humps on railroad rails, for sharpening the lumberman's saw and axe, and the surgeon's knife. They are used in the finishing processes for the delicate works of ladies' watches, and in the production of huge gun-grinding machinery for American battleships. In its production the Norton Company is aided by several thousand employees, largely of Swedish stock. Their loyalty and contentment Mr. Jeppson appraises as a great asset to the corporation; and it is a matter of common knowledge in Worcester that they are treated with the utmost consideration for their economic and social well-being.

In kitchenware utensils there is a distinct Swedish influence. Many housekeepers throughout the country are acquainted with aluminum products sold by the Super Maid Cook Ware Corporation, whose name was changed in 1933 to Advance Aluminum Castings Corporation, with offices in Chicago. E. G. Grundstrom, who was born in Sweden in 1882, and who came to America in 1901, is the chairman of the Board; Roy Wilson, born in Chicago of Swedish parents, is president; and Nils Shoan, born in Sweden in 1884, is secretary and treasurer. Production plants in Chicago and Rockford use 138,000 square feet of factory space. Mr. Shoan and Mr. Grundstrom started this industry in 1917 as the Advance Pattern and Foundry Company and the Super Maid Cook Ware Corporation, introducing various ways of cooking without water, so as to retain all of the food qualities, salts, iron, vitamins, flavors, etc. Hospitals, clubs, and colleges, as well as homes, have adopted the method quite extensively, as shown by the fact that combined sales by Shoan-Grundstrom enterprises amounted to $31,017,-308 in the years from 1919 to 1930, and the sales in 1936 were $2,152,524.

In the paint- and varnish-manufacturing industry, Swedish immigrants have achieved notable success, among them Marcus N. Gustavson, who was born in Löfbo, Småland, in 1875. In 1901 he founded the Diamond Products Company in Chicago, which today has branches in Fargo, Minneapolis, Sioux City, Kansas City, Los Angeles, Marshalltown, Mason City, Long Island City, and New York. It is one of the largest concerns of its kind in the country.

Great advance in design and durability of office furniture was made in 1920 by the Corry-Jamestown Manufacturing Company, organized by David Alfred Hillstrom, who was born in Västergötland, 1877. He came to America in 1900 with a good technical-school foundation, which he extended and completed in this country, and then developed his own business which now reaches into the big offices all over the country. His company specializes in the manufacturing of steel office furniture so extensively adopted for efficiency and fire protection. The Corry-Jamestown Company takes its hyphenated name from the towns in which Hillstrom had worked. It has offices in several important cities, and does business, also, in England, China, Egypt, Scandinavia, and Germany.

Children's furniture has a strong promoter in Carl H. Hedstrom of Gardner, Massachusetts, the chair city of the country. Mr. Hedstrom was born in Dalarne, and is one of the most successful manufacturers in Gardner. He is the founder and head of the Hedstrom Union Company. Baby carriages and gocarts have been his specialty. He started alone in 1911, doing all his own work, and today employs about five hundred workers in Gardner and Fitchburg, Massachusetts; Beacon, New York; and Brattleboro, Vermont.

Had there been a little more of the spirit of venture in Massachusetts capital at the dawn of the automobile industry, the title and affluence which have gone to Henry Ford might have gone to a young Swedish immigrant, Frank Mossberg, who put a twenty-mile-an-hour automobile on the road two or three years ahead of Ford's successful model; and the city of Attleboro might have developed into the nation's motor-industry center. Mossberg spent his borrowed capital on production, built cars that had good speed and could go sixty miles on a single battery charge. His supporters could not be convinced, however, that there was a future for the automobile. They missed their opportunity and young Mossberg, abandoning the automobile, brought other ideas to the front in his fertile mind. He has contributed materially to the modernization and success of the jewelry industry, the tool, machine, and textile industries. One of his inventions revolutionized the process of rolling cigarettes by machinery, and another creation of his brain constitutes an important part of the Underwood typewriter. Mr. Mossberg's first contribution to the mechanical world was in the form of machine-shop tools. He followed with numerous inventions of machinery for the manufacture of jewelry and silverware, especially roller mills fitted with roller bearings. Presses of various kinds were developed, including drop hammers, machines for making finger rings, and methods of making table knives, doorknobs, and handles. From this assortment he proceeded to the production of larger pieces, such as roller-bearing equipment for disappearing gun carriages, and for the Panama Canal operations. Automatic fog signals for ships and lighthouses were invented by Mr. Mossberg; wrenches of all kinds, reels and spools for the wire industry; braider carriers for all kinds of textile braids; machinery for speeding up the textile industry. More than two hundred patents have been obtained in the United States, Canada, Great Britain, France, Belgium, Germany, Sweden, and Russia. His most important patents, considered from the industrial standpoint, are those covering the braider carrier, used by braiding machines nearly everywhere in this country, and quite largely in Europe. Next in importance is probably the roller bearing, developed before any roller bearing was used in connection with power-driven machines, and nobody has as yet improved on the Mossberg type.

In Michigan, destined to be the home of the American automobile industry, a self-taught young Swedish mechanic, Charles Herman Blomstrom, whose parents had come from Svenarum Parish in Småland to Lisbon, Michigan, in 1865, did construct his first "horseless carriage" as early as 1892. In 1900 he constructed another, "a buggy with an engine," and the next year the family moved to Detroit, where the "Blomstrom Motor Car Company" was organized and, until 1905, continued to make a car known as the "Queen." The plant was then one of the largest in Detroit, with an output as high as from "thirty to forty cars a week." (See *The Swedish Element in America*, IV, 31.) "In 1906 the Blomstrom Manufacturing Company was formed," the account continues, "to make a car called the 'Blomstrom,' " a four-cylinder car of relatively large size, whereas the "Queen" had gone through the earlier developments of one-, two-, and four-cylinder engines. Later Mr. Blomstrom helped design such cars as the "Gyroscope," the "Griswold," the "Lion," and the "Rex," all made in Michigan, and the "Frontmobile" in Camden, New Jersey, "the first front drive car built in production lots in the United States," adds Dr. C. E. Hoffsten, author of the chapter quoted above. "Mr. Blomstrom was the inventor of many features in the early automobiles. His death occurred in Detroit in March, 1923," concludes the saga of this Swedish farm boy from Michigan, whose education consisted of the public-school curriculum in his home town, and a correspondence course in mechanical engineering. His "Queen" car now looks no more unsteady than others of that time. "His son, Lowell C. Blomstrom, is now chief engineer of the Federal Mogul Corporation of Detroit, which specializes in bearings."

Aside from the many thousands of mechanics and technicians employed from the start in the American automotive industry, there have been some noted executives. Among these may be cited John Bjorn, a native of Värmland, who from 1916 to 1926 was the general manager of the Nash Motor Works at Kenosha, Wisconsin. Previous to that he had held the same position for the "Jeffery," which was rebaptized the "Nash."

According to *The Swedish Element in America* (III, 322), Bjorn "had been instrumental in inventing the 'clincher tire,' a development which made Jeffery a millionaire." As a youth he had worked on railroad construction in Swedish Lapland, and for the first years after he had emigrated to America in 1890, had been compelled, though well educated, to perform the most menial tasks. Then, in Chicago, he got a job with Gormully & Jeffery, makers of the old-fashioned, high-wheeled bicycles, and with this firm he stayed through the whole bicycle era and into the automobile age. Many of the employees he hired for Nash were Swedes like himself.

Another top-notch position in the automobile world, though his name seldom appears in print, is held by Ernest W. Seaholm, who has been chief engineer for the Cadillac Division of the General Motors Corporation since 1921. During that time he has been responsible for the development of the Cadillac and LaSalle cars. He was born in Lidköping, Sweden, in 1887, and in early childhood came with his parents to Hartford, Connecticut. After graduating from the Mechanic Arts School of Springfield, Massachusetts, he worked as designer for various machine firms, and in 1913 joined the Cadillac Company.

Though no American automobile now on the market is made by a Swedish firm, practically all of the cars have some parts made by Swedes, sometimes far away from Detroit. Some cars are supposed to have as many as forty parts made of Swedish steel, so that the Swedish contribution to the motorcar industry from its beginning merits a special study. In Jamestown, New York, for instance, there is a concern called the Jamestown Metal Equipment Company which makes, among other things, automobile radiators and heaters. In 1937 it delivered over half a million radiators to the various automobile factories, and close to four hundred thousand heaters. Not only is the management Swedish, but about 80 per cent of the workers as well. The president and general manager of this company is Oscar A. Lenna, a native of Hälsingborg, Sweden, where he was born in 1876. His father left for America when the son was a minor, but he soon disappeared from sight. His last letter, written in the early 'eighties, informed his family in Sweden that he was going to California to dig gold, and he was never heard from again. At the age of eighteen the son followed him across the sea. As an orphan at the age of seven, young Oscar had begun to earn his first pennies watching a neighbor's sheep, and how he made his way in America and reached his present position is a romance of rugged individualism, which may not be so common in the future as it has been in the past. It cannot be told in detail here. Suffice it to say that Mr. Lenna did not enter the metal industry until 1914, and that he is neither an inventor nor a practical mechanic himself, but an organizer and leader of other men and also of capital. Both his father and grandfather had had military careers in Sweden. Incidentally, he sells car radiators to the Swedish automobile industry, for, due to his mass-production methods, he is able to overcome transportation costs, import duties, and higher wages as well. "I believe in protective duties to offset differences in wages," he says, "but not to guarantee profits." Mr. Lenna has a guiding hand in two other Jamestown industries, the Jamestown Malleable Iron Company, which makes castings for many purposes, and the Blackstone Manufacturing Company, which makes electric washing machines and ironers. For the past two years the production has been over sixty-five thousand washers and ironers per year.

Jamestown is, of course, the most notable Swedish manufacturing center in the United States, and various kinds of furniture and fixtures, the main output. In the metal trades, the Art Metal Construction Company, founded by the late Earl Fenton, son of a former governor of New York, has been the parent organization. Much of its early success was due to the late Enoch Ohnstrand, who for many years was general manager. He was succeeded by Algot J. E. Larson, who had advanced from the workbench to the post of superintendent, and is now president. Many shares of stock, though never the controlling interest, have been held by men of Swedish ancestry. In its shops many immigrants have been trained in the beginnings of metal construction, and many local industries have been started by former employees. The most noted of these is, perhaps, the Dahlstrom Metallic Door Company, founded in 1904 by the late Charles P. Dahlstrom who had come to Jamestown from Sweden in 1890. While employed by the Art Metal Company, he invented the fireproof metal door which is now used in all parts of the country, particularly in the skyscrapers. For the new Rockefeller Center buildings alone the Dahlstrom Company has delivered over fifty thousand fireproof metal doors. Mr. Dahlstrom died in 1909, but the company is still in the hands of Swedes, Paul N. Anderson being the president and general manager, and Axel G. Dawson the superintendent. Another prominent Jamestown industrialist was the late Karl Peterson, founder and manager of the Crescent Tool Company, whose products are widely used.

In the metal trades there are, of course, industries owned or managed by men of Swedish stock in many localities, particularly in New England and the East in general. In New York City one of the best known is located in the Borough of Brooklyn, the Ericsson Screw Machine Products Company, of which E. Walfrid Ericsson is the president and principal owner. Mr. Ericsson is a native of Värmland and came to America at the age of seventeen—the usual story of a pair of empty hands, a good brain, and an abundance of health and willingness to work. It was with the Western Electric that young Ericsson learned the rudiments of the metal trade and, later, with the National Acme Company, which specializes in screws of all sorts. For this concern Ericsson worked fourteen years, the last eight of which he was chief European salesman. In 1912 he started his own plant, in the management of which his two college trained sons now assist him—a typical American story of progress.

"SKF," symbol for Swedish ball bearings, is a familiar sign and a factor of efficiency and smoothness of operation in factories throughout the United States. (See the chapter on "Inventors.") The SKF Industries in this country is now located in Philadelphia. Connected with it for some time was one of the most imposing figures in Connecticut's industrial life, Bengt N. W. Hanson, who came to America about fifty years ago. It is said of Mr. Hanson that, while he was employed by the well-known firm of the Pratt & Whitney Company, of Hartford, Connecticut, in which he rose to the position of general manager and president, he originated more distinctly new machines for the mechanical industries than all other machine builders in the United States combined. He was responsible for the development of the special rifle-making equipment that the Pratt & Whitney Company furnished to a number of arsenals all over the world, immediately before and during the early part of the World War. In 1915 he was appointed a civilian member of the Machine Gun Board of the War Department. Upon leaving Pratt & Whitney, he became vice-president and general manager of the Colt Patent Firearms Manufacturing Company, where he had charge of gun production during the critical stages of the World War. Through his connection with the Hartford Chamber of Commerce and the Connecticut Chamber of Commerce, Mr. Hanson was instrumental in bringing the SKF ball-bearing industry to the United States, establishing a factory in Hartford, which has now been consolidated with the plant in Philadelphia. The Swedish Ball Bearing Company is one of the largest manufacturers of ball and roller bearings in the world, with thirteen factories, two hundred offices, and fifty-eight subsidiaries. It has sales offices in practically all civilized countries, and in all the large industrial centers of the United States.

In the electrical field the Swedish race is well represented by Albert Ivar Appleton, manufacturer and business executive, who was born in Halland in 1872 and came to the United States as a young man. By 1903 he had established himself, on his own account, as a manufacturer of electrical conduit fittings and specialties, and is now president and treasurer of the Appleton Electric Company. From a modest beginning of two employees, his business has grown greatly, and today employs six hundred people. It has factory buildings in Chicago and a modernly equipped foundry in Wisconsin, operated under the name of the Wisconsin Appleton Company and employing approximately 250 people. Its products are used all over the world. Branch offices are located in numerous large cities, and sales agents have been appointed in practically all foreign countries.

When Oscar Nelson came to America from Sweden, where he had been born in 1879, he brought native ability into play in the carbon-black industry, and became one of its outstanding leaders. Today he is producing two thirds of all carbon black consumed in the United States, and is selling extensively to the manufacturers of rubber. An automobile tire, for instance, contains 10 per cent of carbon black by weight. Ink manufacturers are Mr. Nelson's next-best customers, and most of the makers of paints, crayon, and stove polish have to come to him for their important ingredients. The United Carbon Company, of which Mr. Nelson is president and director, was incorporated in Delaware in 1925, as a consolidation of fifteen companies engaged in the production of carbon black and gasoline. The company dismantled all the carbon-black plants in Kentucky and transferred production to Louisiana, Montana, Utah, and Texas, with general-sales office in Charleston, West Virginia, and branch offices in New York, Akron, Chicago, Trenton, Louisville, Montreal, Toronto, London, and Manchester.

The great motorcycle industry received its first impulses from Carl Oscar Hedstrom, who was born in Småland in 1871, and built the first "Indian" motorcycle in a shop in Springfield, Massachusetts. One of his models may be seen in the Smithsonian Institute. Mr. Hedstrom has been identified with the Hendee Manufacturing Company since 1901, and his "Indian" is now one of the speed chiefs on the highways of America.

In the application of the principle of internal-engine combustion, which is the soul of modern air and highway transportation, the Swedish engineers and mechanics saw a challenge to their natural bent, and they were quick to accept it. They were among the first to build horseless carriages, and turned out good models which met the requirements of the early days, though not surviving in the sharp competition that followed. Such men as Bendix, George William Borg, Adolf Storm of Minneapolis, Stromberg-Carlson, and A. B. Bodine of Wisconsin, have contributed to the phenomenal success of the motor-vehicle industry by supplying vital parts, among them the self-starter, carburetor, clutch, and ignition equipment. The Bodine Manufacturing Company has an automotive division, besides its heating and air-conditioning factories, and supplies parts for the leading cars. Its manufacturing plants are located in Racine, Wisconsin, and La Porte, Indiana. Fractional horsepower motors have been developed since 1905 for a multitude of uses, by the Bodine Electric Company of Chicago, which was organized by Carl D. Bodine and his brother Paul J. Bodine who came to Loomis, Nebraska, in 1886. Some of their early training they acquired in the employ of the Stromberg-Carlson Telephone Company. They manufacture many electrical appliances, but their principal product is the small motor which is used by dentists, in electric clocks, talking-picture machines, electrical-therapy machines, refrigerators, etc., and which is sold all over the world.

Few of the users of the Williams shaving soap are aware of the fact that this is of Swedish origin. The compound was first made by Lorentz August Berg who was born in Stockholm, 1803, and who came to America about 1840. He had studied pharmacy in Sweden and, upon arrival in North Manchester, Connecticut, associated himself with J. W. Williams. Together they started a factory in Glastonbury in 1847.

On the Pacific coast a paper mill, owned and managed by the two Fernstrom brothers, Fritz O. and Erik, at Pomona, California, makes enough paper wrappers for the citrus trade to cover over three billion oranges a year. It was started in 1925, and its capacity is about seven thousand tons of paper annually. Trade-marks are printed for individual customers among fruit growers in Australia, New Zealand, and Mexico, as well as various parts of the United States and the West Indies. Like many other paper mills in the United States, this one uses a considerable amount of Swedish pulp.

Enfrid R. Jacobson, who was born in Gothenburg, 1877, entered the employ of the Straube Piano Company of Chicago in 1898 and, by 1911, he owned the company. He has been president of the Music Industries Chamber of Commerce of America and of the National Piano Manufacturers Association. The Straube piano is in wide distribution and is manufactured in Hammond, Indiana.

In the automatic musical field, both in player pianos and coin-operated phonographs, pioneering work has been done by J. P. Seeburg of Chicago, who came to America in 1886. He was born in Gothenburg in 1871, and there attended the Chalmers Technical School. His firm has also originated the parking meters, and developed automatic ice-cream and soft-drink dispensers, as well as meters used for selling refrigerators.

Herbert Ragnvald Hedman, son of Carl Max Hedman, who

was born in Norrbotten, Sweden, in 1862, is one of the first men in America to commercialize television, but he is also prominent in another field of invention and production, having been associated with his father, who invented the F. & E. Lightning Check Writer and other devices to prevent forgery of signatures. Mr. Hedman is now manufacturing protection devices used by business houses all over the country. Among his devices are the F. & E. Lightning Coin Changer and the F. & E. Sign-O-Meter. Mr. Hedman's financial interests extend also to the Alemite Die Casting Company, of which he is a director, and the Western Television Corporation which manufactures receiving sets and broadcasting apparatus for television.

It is not surprising that the Swedish people in this country should have made some contribution to the cleaning industry; and their outstanding representative in this field is the Magnusson Products Corporation of Brooklyn, New York, which has developed scientific cleaners for every industrial purpose. Edward Magnusson, who was born in Kalmar, Sweden, is the founder and president of this corporation. He developed his first specific cleaning compounds in 1912, and is now supplying nearly every industry in the United States and Canada and some in foreign countries. When but fourteen years old Magnusson left his home at Kalmar in Småland, and became a pantry boy on a ship; and for the next twenty years he literally sailed the seven seas, holding every position available on a boat, except that of master. When he was about to get his captain's certificate, he met a certain girl and decided to become a "landlubber" after all. A cousin had a soap factory in Brooklyn, and there Magnusson learned to make shaving creams and other chemicals. Three years later he had a factory of his own, and in the meantime he had married the girl. Next he lost his business through trickery and became a salesman, among others, for the Oakite Company, at which he was the success a true *Smålänning* ought to be. In this way he learned the needs of various industries for different kinds of cleaning compounds, and on this basis he started, in 1923, his present concern, which makes over 220 specialized compounds for over 300 different industries. While the main plant is still in Brooklyn, there are eighteen warehouses from coast to coast, and a rapidly growing branch in Canada. Like Mr. Lenna of Jamestown, Mr. Magnusson is the organizing kind of industrialist, rather than the engineer or inventor. He has created, nevertheless, a new industry where there was none before, making for a cleaner, brighter world. Mr. Magnusson is vice-president of the Swedish Hospital in Brooklyn, and has found time to do a great deal for it.

Another Swedish-born organizer of an industry where there was none before, and user of materials that previously had gone to waste, is Bror G. Dahlberg of Chicago, president of the Celotex Corporation. Until the end of the World War there was practically no such article on the American market as synthetic wood or special insulation material. Now "celotex" made of "bagasse," or what is left of sugar cane after the sugar has been squeezed out of it, has become a household word, and is even used as a generic term for all kinds of wallboards with insulating effect. It has added warmth and comfort and fuel economy to thousands of American homes; and this is Dahlberg's contribution.

He was born at Kristianstad in the Province of Skåne, Sweden, in 1881, and was brought to America when but a lad of eight. His father was an artist, who had been well off, but had lost his fortune. In America he could not recover it, either in Omaha or in Minneapolis, and when he died about a year later, he left his widow and five little children, all but destitute. At thirteen, Bror had to go to work and, like Vincent Bendix, his first job was that of an elevator boy. Like Bendix, he also learned other things, among them shorthand and typewriting, and some law. But while Bendix became an inventor and automobile pioneer, Dahlberg learned the railroad business, under James J. Hill, on the Great Northern. Next he went into business for himself as a shippers' agent, and then was hired as an executive by a huge Northwestern lumber and paper company. In this connection he observed the gradual destruction of the American forests and foresaw the need of synthetic lumber. This led to the development, under his guidance, of "celotex," which has had many imitators, but which still holds the lead. Like Lenna and Magnusson, Dahlberg is an organizer rather than an inventor or engineer, but he, too, has created a new American industry, where there was none before.

Millions of people all over America have been literally hand in glove with Peter A. Waller of Kewanee, Illinois, a descendant of the Walloons who helped develop Sweden's iron industry, and an immigrant from Gestrikland in 1885, cheerfully paying tribute to him for providing them with excellent canvas working gloves, at popularly low prices. Mr. Waller was seventeen years old when he came to America, and on his first job of consequence, which was in the house-heating industry, he was earning $1.25 a day. When he died, he was president of the Boss Manufacturing Company of Illinois, the largest glove-manufacturing plant of its kind in the country, with fourteen factories in Kansas City; Kewanee, Illinois; Fort Wayne and Lebanon, Indiana; Toledo, Findlay, and Bluffton, Ohio; Brooklyn, New York; and Peoria, Illinois. In partnership with F. N. Lay, Mr. Waller organized this business, placing on the market a new commodity, especially useful to farmers and laborers.

Mr. Waller's philanthropies and contribution to the tone of community life were commensurate with his industrial and financial achievements. Two of his sons were with him in the business, Ellis Julian Waller as vice-president and director, and Harold Everett Waller as an associate and director. The name Waller ranks high in industrial and commercial council, both in American and international business conferences.

This is but a partial list of American manufacturers of Swedish extraction, but it is extensive enough to indicate the great variety of industries in which they have made their mark. Given the Swedish facility for construction and sense of realities, it is probable that in the future there will be more, rather than fewer, such entrepreneurs. It is also a remarkable fact that few of the Swedish born industrialists have, so far, had serious labor troubles.

Businessmen

GUSTAF SUNDELIUS

Mr. Sundelius was born in Sweden, where he attended Uppsala University. He came to the United States in 1900 and, after a business career in Boston, became, in 1920, executive secretary of the Swedish Chamber of Commerce of the United States of America. In 1926 he was appointed Editor of *Nordstjernan,* Swedish-language weekly in New York, and for the past six years he has been attached to the Swedish Vice Consulate in Boston. His wife is Marie Sundelius (see the chapter on "Opera Singers"). For some of the material in this chapter the writer wishes to give credit to *The Swedish Element in America,* Chicago, 1931.

AS a rule, businessmen of any nationality are not self-recording, for, unlike members of the professions or practitioners of the arts, they do most of their work either anonymously or in comparative seclusion. It is, therefore, difficult to arrive at an estimate of their contributions to the growth of civilization in any country. The businessmen of Swedish birth or ancestry in America are no exception. We do know, however, that like those of other racial strains, they have been useful in the distribution of either goods or services, without which modern life could not have been developed, and since the distribution of wealth, rather than the creation of it, seems destined to be the principal task for the future, their rôle is likely to grow in importance. Unfortunately, only a few who have reached more than local importance can be mentioned.

In the New Sweden colony on the Delaware, trade with the Indians and the other settlements was at first a monopoly of the sponsoring company, and the governors themselves were, therefore, the chief traders, as well as military commanders. In other words, the economy was planned and business an official matter. Under such circumstances there was, of necessity, little opportunity for individual enterprise in trade, and no names of outstanding businessmen have come down to us. This situation probably continued unchanged during the few years that New Sweden was under Dutch rule, but, after British dominion had become established over the entire Atlantic seaboard, there came gradually greater opportunity for private business activity. Goods circulated more freely between the various racial groups and settlements.

The first Swedish businessman in America seems to have been one Jonas Nilsson, born about 1621 in the Province of Västergötland, who had come over to New Sweden with Governor Printz in 1643. He served first as a soldier in the garrison of Fort Elfsborg, in what now is the State of New Jersey, or at "Myggenborg," as it was called, on account of the troublesome mosquitoes. Later in life he went into business, building a strong stone house, with walls two feet thick, at Kingsessing, in what is now Philadelphia, where he established a famous trading post, and where he built up an extensive traffic with the Indians. It is recorded that his trading post was the busiest place in New Sweden. Skins were at that time the principal commodities in which deals were made with the Indians. For more details, see *Where Pennsylvania History Began*, by Henry D. Paxson, Philadelphia, 1926. Nilsson died in 1693, leaving seven sons and four daughters. Among lineal descendants of Jonas Nilsson may be mentioned the prominent Philadelphia families— Jones, Chew, and Paxson.

On May 13, 1794, there arrived in Philadelphia, in the company of the painter Ulric Wertmüller, who later made a portrait of George Washington (see the chapter on "Painters and Sculptors"), a young Swedish businessman by the name of Henrik Gahn, who was firmly resolved to make his fortune as a colonizer on a grand scale (see the chapter by Amandus Johnson in *The Swedish Element in America*, IV). They had met in Cadiz where a relative of Gahn was the Swedish Consul General. Before settling down, Gahn made exploration trips through New York and the New England regions, but nothing came of his colonization schemes. Instead, he started a "mercantile" business in New York City, with an American friend named Mumford, and in 1797 became Swedish Consul in New York. Though he married an American woman and became an American citizen as early as 1796, he kept up close contact with Swedish visitors throughout his life. "His descendants are still living in Brooklyn," adds Dr. Johnson.

In 1838 a young man from Sweden was shipwrecked off the coast of Galveston, and his arrival there marks the coming of the first Swedes to Texas. He was Sven Magnus Swenson, born in Barkeryd. Before he left his native land, he had been a clerk in a grocery store in Eksjö, likewise in Småland. Swenson's early training, coupled with a boundless ambition, soon made him a partner in a general store in Columbo, at that time the capital of the Republic of Texas. Anticipating the removal of the seat of government to Austin, he acquired large tracts of lands in and near Austin, and established there a large general store and banking business, in partnership with his uncle Svante Palm, who had arrived from Sweden in 1844. Shortly after that he built the first hotel in Austin, and soon became one of the most important businessmen in the city. When the Civil War broke out, Swenson, with his decided sympathies for the North, became *persona non grata* in Austin and, to save his life, fled to Mexico. At the close of the war he returned to the United States, established a cotton-export business in New Orleans, and later moved to New York, where he founded the important banking house of S. M. Swenson & Sons, which is still located in Wall Street. He died in Brooklyn in 1896, leaving an estate valued at several million dollars. His descendants are very prominent figures in the New York banking world, and they still own an important cattle ranch in Texas. Since 1912 a son, Eric P. Swenson, has been a director of the National City Bank, and from 1921 to 1929 was chairman of the Board.

Thanks to the efforts of S. M. Swenson, a good many Swedes came to Texas in the middle of the nineteenth century, and some of them, showing industry and business acumen, became prominent. Among them was the previously mentioned Svante Palm who, in 1884, was appointed Consul in Texas for Sweden and Norway. Most of his library of thirty thousand volumes was given to the University of Texas. Another of the early settlers who should not be forgotten was Anders Johan Nelson. He arrived in Galveston as a young boy with his parents, in 1854, and grew up to become a large land- and cattle owner, amassing what, for his time, was a great fortune. He was known as

"Rich Nelson," but it is said that he freely extended a helping hand to many early settlers who stood in need of assistance, financially or otherwise.

In Chicago one of the most prominent businessmen and civic leaders a generation ago was the late Robert Lindblom, for whom one of Chicago's largest high schools is named. He had come to America in 1864 when twenty-one years old, and for several years he was a grain dealer in Milwaukee. To Chicago he came in 1877, or soon after the great fire, and there he became a leading figure on the Board of Trade. He was appointed a member of the Chicago Board of Education in 1893, and of the Civil Service Commission in 1898. He was also one of the principal backers of the first World's Fair or Columbian Exposition in 1892–93, subscribing half a million dollars to its guarantee fund—a sum that seemed much larger then than it does now.

Few Swedish-American businessmen are so well and so widely known in this country, as well as in Sweden, as Charles S. Peterson of Chicago. He was born in Värmland in 1873 and came to this country in 1887. He had learned the printing trade early in life, and in that trade he engaged himself, after he had settled in Chicago. In 1899 he organized the Peterson Linotyping Company. Subsequently, he acquired the controlling interest in the Regan Printing House and in the G. K. Steers Company At present he is the Vice President of the Inland Press, one of the largest printing concerns in the country.

Mr. Peterson's commercial career has been a busy and successful one. Yet he has found time to give to other fields of endeavor, for which his extraordinary ability was solicited. He has been a member of the Board of Education of the city of Chicago, and chairman of the Board's Finance Committee, City Treasurer, and City Comptroller, president of the Swedish Club of Chicago, president of the Swedish Choral Club, president of the Swedish National Society, and president of the Swedish Old People's Home. And last, but not least, Mr. Peterson was vice-chairman of the highly successful Century of Progress Exposition in 1932–33. When that undertaking seemed doomed to fade out in its preparatory state, it was his personal efforts that awakened new interest and new initiative. Hence Mr. Peterson may justly be given credit for much of that remarkable achievement.

Many other Swedes have been engaged in the printing business in various parts of the country. In 1937 Sweden was visited by the seventy-one-year-old twin brothers, Louis and Charles Traung, from San Francisco, heads of the Stecher-Traung Lithograph Corporation of that city. They had never before visited Sweden, but said their father, a sea captain who had emigrated in 1848, had married in California and settled down there. He lived to be ninety-four.

In banking, too, several Swedes have attained a certain prominence, especially in the Middle West. Among the best known in Chicago are, perhaps, the late John R. Lindgren and Henry S. Henschen. Lindgren, who died in 1915, was the son of Capt. Charles M. Lindgren, a former sailor, born in Sweden in 1819, who, at the age of fourteen had gone to sea, and in 1849 was one of those who washed for gold in California. To Chicago he came in 1852, and gradually he built up a shipping business on the Great Lakes. The son was born in Chicago in 1855 and, until his father's death in 1879, he was associated with him. He then formed, with Helge A. Haugan, the banking firm, Haugan & Lindgren, which in 1891 became the State Bank of Chicago. From 1893 to his death he represented Sweden as its Vice-Consul.

For thirty years Henry S. Henschen was connected with this firm, rising to part owner, vice-president, and then Swedish Vice-Consul, from 1909 to 1914. Henschen was born in Brooklyn in 1873, his father being William Henschen, a graduate of Uppsala University in Sweden, who later became one of the leading scholars of the Swedish-American section of the Methodist Episcopal Church. In 1920 Henschen resigned from the State Bank of Chicago, and formed his own investment firm, which was taken over in 1927 by the newly formed Congress Trust and Savings Bank, of which Henschen became president. In 1929 he became president of the Chicago Bank of Commerce. He is now retired and lives in Winnetka, Illinois.

Edgar L. Mattson, banker, the son of Col. Hans Mattson (see the chapter on "Soldiers and Sailors") and his wife, was

born in Kristianstad, Sweden, in 1871, during a visit which
that famous couple made to Sweden. He grew up in Minneapolis, where he attended the public schools. At the age of nineteen
he made his first connection with the banking world, obtaining
a position as a bank messenger. Since that time he has been
continuously in banking business, in which he has risen to leading positions in three different institutions. At present he is the
president of Midland National Bank and Trust Company,
Minneapolis. What prominence Mr. Mattson has attained may
be demonstrated by the following data: He is a former president of Minnesota Bankers Association; also of the National
Bank Division, American Bankers Association. He was national
chairman of the American Bankers Association's Committee on
Legislature, president of Minneapolis Clearing House, and
treasurer of Hennepin County Safety Commission. When the
Governor of Minnesota appointed a Commission, in 1923, to
represent the State at the Tercentenary celebration in Gothenburg, Sweden, Mr. Mattson was made its chairman.

Among the businessmen in Jamestown, New York, Charles
A. Okerlind has a place of distinction. He was born in Stockholm, Sweden, in 1865, arrived in this country with his grandparents in 1874, and settled in Brooklyn, New York. He started
his business life at the age of twenty-one with the Cunard
Steamship Company (New York), and remained with that concern for six years. In 1892 he moved to Jamestown, and entered
on his career as a banker and public official. He was city auditor
of Jamestown for ten years and, in the meanwhile, rose in the
banking field, until he was elected president of the American
National Bank of Jamestown in 1915, an office from which he
later resigned. He was a member of the Lighting Commission
of Jamestown from 1900 to 1912, treasurer of the Board of
Education from 1911 to 1913, and director of the Jamestown
Chamber of Commerce from 1912 to 1916. Since 1923 he has
been Vice-Consul for Sweden in Jamestown.

Among the many other American bankers of Swedish descent
there is space left to mention only Hugo A. Anderson, Vice
President of the First National Bank of Chicago, and Ormond
Rambo, Jr., a director of Battles & Company, Inc., investment
and security bankers of Philadelphia. Mr. Rambo is a descend-

ant in direct line from Peter Rambo, one of the original Swedish settlers in the Delaware Valley nearly three hundred years ago. He is also treasurer of both the Swedish Colonial Society and the American Swedish Historical Museum.

Emil O. J. Danielson, since 1933 Vice-Consul for Sweden in Boston, Massachusetts, and president, and chief owner, of the clothing concern of Scott & Company, Ltd., of Boston, was born in Stockholm in 1875, the son of Andreas and Amanda Danielson. When, in 1891, his father decided to wind up his business interests in Sweden, and move his home to America, Emil was a lad of sixteen. The family first went to Kansas, where young Emil attended Lawrence University. Being ready to enter business, he moved in 1894 to Providence, Rhode Island, where he met and married Miss Alma Odén. Having been offered a position with the tailoring firm of Hibbard & Mason in Boston, he moved there a few years later. Not long after that, Scott & Company, Ltd., which, a few years earlier, had been started on a rather elaborate scale by Collins & Fairbanks, as manufacturers and retailers of men's clothing, invited Mr. Danielson to become a member of the firm. He acquired enough stock to become a director in the company, and rose rapidly from one position to another, until he became its president. Under his guidance the now-famous clothing firm has grown steadily and gained customers all over the country. It manufactures its own retail goods. In 1935 the honorary title of Consul of Sweden was conferred on Mr. Danielson.

Another important clothing firm in Boston, F. L. Dunne & Company, located on the second floor of the Boston *Evening Transcript* building, is headed by a native of Sweden, Charles J. Erickson, who was born at Kalmar in the Province of Småland in 1868. He came to New York in 1885 and, forty-seven years ago, became a cutter for Dunne & Company. In 1929 he became part owner and president. For several years he has been chairman of the First District of the National Association of Merchant Tailors of America. In Chicago, Alfred Blomquist, who in 1893, at the age of fifteen, also came from Småland, is now president of the H. M. Stevenson Company, with which he started as a journeyman tailor soon after his arrival. In New

York, too, there are several merchant tailoring firms, managed by Swedes.

A fine example of a young Swedish-born businessman, who has reached the pinnacle of success in the United States, is Walter Hoving. He was born in Stockholm, Sweden, in 1897, son of Dr. Johannes Hoving and his famous actress wife, Helga Rundberg. When the family moved to America and settled in New York, Walter was six years old. He went through the public schools and later entered Brown University, where he was so outstanding in sports that, in 1920, he gained the coveted title of "All American" in football. After his graduation the same year, he entered the commercial field, and held various positions with insurance, import, and export concerns until 1924, when he became connected with the department store of R. H. Macy & Company of New York. There he reached the position of executive vice-president. Then, in 1932, he was chosen vice-president and member of the board of directors of the famous mail-order firm of Montgomery Ward & Company in Chicago. In 1936 his services were sought by the noted department store of Lord & Taylor of New York. He was soon elected chairman of the board of directors and, in 1937, became president. Mr. Hoving is, besides, a director of several other corporations.

Even the briefest sketch of Swedish-American businessmen could not fail to include the name of Charles Walgreen, head of the country-wide chain of drugstores that bear his name. He was born in Knox County, Illinois, of Swedish parents. As a boy he got a job in a shoe factory in Dixon, Illinois. One day something went wrong with the machine he tended, and his hand was badly injured. A friendly doctor who treated his injury took an interest in the lad, and persuaded him to accept an easier job in a drugstore. It is said that young Walgreen did not take a very deep interest in the science of pharmaceutics, but that he saw at once the business possibilities of the trade. With thoroughness he devoted himself to his new duties, determined to give the greatest amount of service to the customers of his employer. It was the strict observance of this business code, coupled with ambition and ability, that soon made him a partner and, eventually, the owner of the store where he had started.

Gradually new stores were acquired, until the Walgreen Drug Store Company today owns and operates 470 stores in 31 different states and 130 cities, with many warehouses scattered over the nation, a dozen ice-cream plants in strategical locations, laboratories, etc. Mr. Walgreen himself says: "My aim is today as it was in the beginning: to give the people the best in the way of drugs and other merchandise in the most cheerful and comfortable stores that can be constructed. Add to this the ideal of courteous, prompt, careful, kindly service, and you have the basis of my business creed."

Everybody knows the Greyhound Lines, but how many know that the founder and president of that bus enterprise was born in Sweden? His name is C. Eric Wickman, and he was born in Dalecarlia in 1887. As a lad of seventeen he emigrated to America, where his first job was in a sawmill in Arizona. Later he moved to Hibbing, Michigan, worked for some time in the iron mines, and subsequently opened a motorcar agency. The mining development around Hibbing was rapid at that time, necessitating rapid transportation of the mine workers, and that gave Wickman the idea of opening a "jitney" service with a secondhand automobile, to and from the mines. From this idea, which proved commercially profitable, he developed a steadily growing transportation business, with tentacles reaching out in every direction, until today the tremendous Greyhound combination of motor coaches traverses the United States from coast to coast, and from Canada to the Gulf of Mexico. Mr. Wickman, as president of the Greyhound Corporation, is today the principal owner and the guiding spirit of a concern which, in 1934, operated a fleet of over 1,900 modern passenger buses itself, and which directs the operations and controls the policies of twelve other Greyhound systems throughout the United States. Today the fleet, commanded by Mr. Wickman, doubtless can count a great many more units.

Prominent in transportation affairs on the Pacific coast is Nelson Kinell, assistant general-passenger agent of the Southern Pacific Railroad Company, since 1920. Born in Sweden, he is the son of the late Reverend A. Kinell, who was one of the pioneer Lutheran ministers in California.

In the nursery and florist business, which is a "natural" to the soil-loving Swedes, several of them have gained both fame and fortune. To Chicago came as early as 1854 one P. S. Peterson, born in 1830 at Nöbbelöf in southern Sweden. From the time he was eleven years old he had had to support himself, and in Chicago he did odd jobs for the first two years. Then, in 1856, he leased a few acres of land which became the Rose Hill Nursery. "At the time of his death in 1903, it occupied five hundred acres and had made its owner a millionaire," wrote Oliver A. Linder in *The Swedish Element in America*, I.

The feat was duplicated in Connecticut by another native of Skåne, the late A. N. Pierson, who arrived at Cromwell in that State in 1870, borrowed money, built a small greenhouse, worked hard, paid bills promptly, and added to the greenhouse as credit developed, so that today it covers 1,156,000 square feet of ground, the largest establishment of its kind in the country under single ownership and management. Many other flower growers and florists' shops in the East were started by Mr. Pierson, who was called the "Rose King of America." He is succeeded in the management by his son, Wallace Pierson, a State Senator for Connecticut.

New Jersey, likewise, has had a prominent florist of Swedish birth, the late John E. Lager, who died October 30, 1937, at the age of seventy-six. For many years he maintained extensive greenhouses at Summit, New Jersey, where he specialized in orchids. At one time he was reported to have sold the world's most valuable orchid plant for $10,000 to a European commercial establishment which, in turn, sold it to Baron Aaron Irmen Lambeau, who kept it in his private hothouse. Before coming to America in the 1890's Mr. Lager studied horticulture in both London and Paris, and later in life he personally led orchid-hunting expeditions to South America. From a plant found in Colombia, he once obtained pure white blooms.[1]

In advertising, too, an indispensable adjunct to business, the Swedes in America are represented by numerous executives, as well as technicians. Of the former there is room to mention only two, the late Alfred W. Erickson who, at the time of his death

1. In this connection it is interesting to note that the dahlia is named after a pupil of Linnæus, Anders Dahl (1751–89), who later became an instructor in medicine and botany at Abo University in Finland.

in 1936, was chairman of the board of the McCann-Erickson Company in New York, and Charles C. Younggren, executive vice-president of the Reincke-Ellis-Younggren-Finn agency in Chicago. Mr. Erickson's father was a Swedish civil engineer, while he himself was born at Farmers Mills, New York, in 1876. Educated in Brooklyn schools, he entered, at the age of twenty-four, the advertising department of the Cleveland Baking Powder Company, later merged with the Royal. In 1900 he became advertising manager for James McCutcheon & Company, the linen store on Fifth Avenue, New York City, and two years later founded his own firm, which was merged with the H. K. McCann Company in 1930.

The New York *Times* said, at his death,

Mr. Erickson was for many years a dominant figure in the American Association of Advertising Agencies, and was one of the organizers of its predecessor group. He was one of the advertising pioneers whose efforts to form advertising agencies into an association and to establish codes of ethics for their guidance were responsible in a large degree for the development of the advertising agency business in this country.

Mr. Erickson was an organizer of the Congoleum Company, which was subsequently merged with the Nairn Linoleum Company to become Congoleum-Nairn, Inc. At his death he was chairman of the board of this company. He was also closely associated with the Bon Ami Company and with the Barrett Company, roof manufacturers.

An ardent supporter and a personal friend of the late Theodore Roosevelt, Mr. Erickson was a trustee of the Roosevelt Memorial Association. During the war he was the American representative of The Stars and Stripes by appointment of General Pershing. He was also business manager of the Vigilantes. He was one of the founders of the Audit Bureau of Circulation. Mr. Erickson founded the Erickson Trust, which owns and operates the Desert Sanatorium of Southern Arizona at Tucson.

Mr. Younggren is a native of Kansas, a former aviation officer in the World War, and a former president of the International Advertising Association. He began his career as the publisher of the *Kansas Farmer* at Topeka, Kansas, and then became advertising and sales manager of the Case Plow Works at Racine, Wisconsin. After the War he went into the advertising-agency business in Milwaukee, and later moved to Chicago. In 1936 he was elected president of the Alpha Delta Sigma, national collegiate-advertising fraternity. His paternal ancestry derives from Sweden via Germany and Canada.

Imports and Importers

VICTOR O. FREEBURG

Dr. Freeburg is Editor of *The American Swedish Monthly,* published
by The Swedish Chamber of Commerce of the United States of America.
(See the chapter on "Journalists.")

T HAT even so small a country as Sweden can profoundly
affect our way of life in America, through inanimate
materials alone, can be illustrated by naming a few examples of imports. It would be almost impossible to find a single
home in this country where the Swedish safety match has not
become a familiar object. This used to be our best-known import from Sweden. And, although we now manufacture such
matches ourselves, the invention itself is an importation. Then
there is the safety razor. How many men in America shave with
it, we cannot guess, but we do know that, when the safety razor
was introduced, the blades were made of Swedish steel, which is
used today by at least thirty American manufacturers of razor
blades. Swedish *knäckebröd,* also known under such names as
"hard bread," "health bread," and "crisp bread," is being
crunched today in thousands of homes throughout the land.
When Americans go to a restaurant, hotel, or club for a meal,
they will sooner or later find themselves at a Swedish *smörgåsbord,* and, however the name may be misspelled or mispro-
nounced, this method of preparing and serving foods has armies
of devotees representing every racial stock.

To tell even a substantial part of the story of American imports of materials, goods, and inventions and other commercial
ideas from Sweden, is at the present moment impossible, because
the facts have not yet been assembled. We may, however, get a
glimpse, here and there, of what that story essentially is.

To begin with, the New Sweden (Delaware) Tercentenary
celebration recalls the fact that it was a foreign-trade enterprise which brought the first Swedish colonists to this country.
But for the lure of money-making in exports and imports, there
would have been no settlement at that time. Although the first
two cargoes unloaded from Swedish ships in America in 1638

consisted principally of manufactured goods bought in Holland, there can be little doubt that Swedish steel had been used in making the axes, hatchets, adzes, and knives which were named, among other things, in the bills of lading. This belief is based on the fact that there were, at that time, close commercial relations between Holland and Sweden, and that, while Holland did not produce iron, Sweden was then the greatest iron-producing country in the world.

Outside of the personal belongings of the colonists, and weapons and ammunition, the first imports from Sweden, as far as we can judge from historical accounts, were the three or four horses brought over in 1640. Hence, it is quite appropriate that a horse is to be immortalized in a bas-relief on the New Sweden monument by Carl Milles. In 1641 two ships brought farming implements, goats, sheep, and cattle, as well as more horses, all of which, judging from the records, were from Sweden. More Swedish goods for the colonists arrived in 1643. These included 250 copper kettles which, even if made in Holland, must have been made of Swedish copper from the famous mine at Falun. This cargo also included blades for a sawmill, and a pair of large millstones. It seems extremely likely, therefore, that the first sawmill and the first gristmill in the Delaware Valley were made possible by Swedish imports.

In 1646 a Swedish ship brought to New Sweden a cargo of goods, apparently of Dutch manufacture, which included 200 adzes, 387 axes, 302 kettles, 774 knives, 264 sharp knives, 432 thimbles, 10,000 fishhooks, and 96 copper chains for ornament. Here, again, the basic materials were doubtless Swedish. These imports, like large quantities of similar imports in earlier years, were mostly exchanged for furs in the Indian trade. The Leni-Lenapes, Minquas, and other natives living near by, doubtless raised their standard of living a bit through the use of these novelties of white fabrication.

Iron and steel have, for centuries, held an honorable position among Sweden's exports to foreign lands, and in America these Swedish raw materials have been of great value in developing our manufactures. The story goes back at least as far as 1648, when a Swedish ship unloaded at Fort Christina, New Sweden, a cargo which included 74 bars of iron and 600 pounds of steel. At that time there were two blacksmith shops in the colony, in which these commodities were speedily forged and hammered into shapes for use by American farmers.

The basic data for the above observations, it should be said here, have been gleaned from Dr. Amandus Johnson's *The Swedish Settlements on the Delaware, 1638–1664.*

After Sweden had lost political control of her colony in the Delaware Valley, immigration from the old country was practically discontinued. During the ensuing century and a quarter few, if any, ships sailed directly from Swedish ports for America. Perhaps there were, nevertheless, some further imports of Swedish goods during early colonial days, but we have no information on the subject.

During the Revolutionary War, however, the colonies managed, in one way or another, to obtain much-needed raw materials from Sweden, as has been shown by Professor Adolph B. Benson in his book, *Sweden and the American Revolution.* As early as 1777, tar and pitch from Stockholm were advertised for sale at Boston. In Providence and Newport, Swedish iron was advertised during 1781 and 1783. Steel, also, was imported. Ships under the Swedish flag were seen in our harbors. "The quite lively trade relations which had developed between Sweden and North America after the outbreak of the war" are referred to by Baron de Hermelin, who came here in 1782 to study commercial possibilities. Early in the same year Benjamin Franklin and the Swedish Ambassador in Paris began negotiations for a "Treaty of Commerce and Amity" between Sweden and the United States, and this was concluded on April 3, 1783, exactly five months before the treaty of peace with England. Thus, Sweden was the first neutral country to recognize our independence.

What happened during the next decades, after the end of the war, cannot be ascertained without considerable special research, but since American manufactures, protected by the Federal Government, were developing rapidly, it seems probable that the imports of iron from Sweden continued in substantial quantities. In fact, it is not improbable that Swedish iron has had a longer continuous history as an American import than any other commodity from any source. In the early 1820's, for instance, our imports of Swedish iron bars averaged about $1,000,000 a year in value. A quarter-century later, in 1845–

46 and 1847–48, to pick years more or less at random, the figures for the same item were around $700,000 a year. At about this time England became a powerful competitor, and, by the middle of the century, she almost monopolized the American market. However, in 1872–73, bar iron from Sweden was valued at more than $2,000,000, as against $2,870,000 worth from England. In 1884–85, partly manufactured iron and steel from Sweden amounted to $2,800,000 in value, as against less than $2,000,000 worth from England. These figures are merely illustrative. It would be tedious to go into further detail. The main point to make here is that iron ready for further manufacture constituted the bulk of American imports from Sweden during the long period from 1648 to about 1912, when wood pulp took the lead.

The import of iron ore from Sweden seems to have begun about 1906, and by 1913 the annual value had risen to nearly a million and a half dollars.

The tremendous growth of the total circulation of our newspapers is the principal factor in creating demand for wood pulp, needed for the manufacture of newsprint and other paper of the less expensive grades. Our purchases of Swedish pulp, starting at about the turn of the century, had passed the quarter-million dollar mark in 1903, after which they grew steadily in volume to nearly $4,400,000 worth in 1914. After the World War the imports of Swedish pulp continued to grow so that, for instance, in 1936 the value was more than $34,000,000.

In spite of heavy pulp imports from Sweden, Finland, Germany, and Canada, the United States has found it profitable to buy newsprint from Sweden. Beginning in a small way just before the War, the imports of Swedish newsprint in 1921 amounted to more than $4,500,000 in value.

Extremely important in American manufacture have been Swedish ball and roller bearings, widely used in automobiles, trains, and other vehicles and machines. These imports, the famous SKF products, beginning with less than $29,000 worth in 1911, rose to a value of about $650,000 in 1929. Since then, the annual values of the imports from Sweden have been much smaller, due to the increased production by the SKF factory in this country.

In the above brief sketch we have concerned ourselves with

raw materials and partly manufactured, or finished, goods brought into this country for use in further manufacture. In the class of goods ready for immediate use which appear on our list of imports from Sweden, the principal items are safety matches, cream separators, glassware, earthenware, hard bread, fish and other food products, surgical instruments, cigar- and cigarette-making machinery, and lighted beacons and buoys. In the case of the Electrolux refrigerators and vacuum cleaners, both Swedish inventions, there are at present no imports, due to their manufacture here. These subjects are discussed elsewhere in this book, in the chapters on manufacturers, inventors, and engineers.

The reader must have noticed that, up to this point, we have not mentioned individuals of Swedish birth or descent living in America and connected with the trade between this country and Sweden. This omission is due to the curious fact that such individuals, if there were any, did not manage to get their names stressed in historical records, until about the beginning of this century.

Heading the list, chronologically, is the name of Alexander Edward Johnson, who died in New York, in 1918, at the age of seventy-eight. He came to this country from Sweden, apparently in 1854 at about the age of fourteen. As land commissioner in Minnesota for a railroad company, he became very active in promoting immigration from Sweden. In 1883 he founded the firm of A. E. Johnson & Company and engaged in the passenger-agency business. At the time of the dissolution of this firm in 1917, it had its main office in New York; and there were branch offices in Chicago, Minneapolis, and elsewhere. The Johnson firm had always been actively interested in steamship traffic, and it became the general agency for the Scandinavian American Line in 1898. In 1905 Johnson was appointed a Swedish Consul in the United States. When The Swedish Chamber of Commerce of the United States of America was founded in 1907, he became its first president.

Another man who will long be remembered for his influence in fostering trade between Sweden and the United States, for his brilliant achievements in other business activities in America, and not least for his magnetic personality, was John Aspegren.

Born in Malmö, Sweden, in 1876, he died in New York in 1924. For a time he was enrolled as a student at Lund University, and later studied at a business college in Hamburg, Germany. After some business experience in Belgium, France, and England, he came to this country in 1899. In the same year he and his brother Adolf, who had preceded him, established the firm of Aspegren & Company, interested primarily in cottonseed oil. He immediately rose to prominence in the councils of the cotton-oil trade. From 1910 to 1912 he was vice-president, and for the next two years president, of the New York Produce Exchange, achieving the double distinction of being the first foreign-born, and the youngest, man to head that organization. We cannot give space to a listing of the numerous other important business and cultural organizations in which he was prominent. In 1907 he and Hans Lagerloef founded the Scandinavian-American Trading Company, New York, interested primarily in the importation of wood pulp. In 1919 he organized the Scandinavian Pulp Agency. Aspegren was one of the founders of The Swedish Chamber of Commerce of the United States of America, succeeding A. E. Johnson as its president in 1916, and holding this position during the next eight years until his death.

It was natural that two men as outstanding as Johnson and Aspegren should have been among the founders and leaders of The Swedish Chamber of Commerce. This organization, the objects of which, according to its bylaws, are: "The fostering, facilitating and protection of Trade, Commerce and other Relations" between Sweden and the United States, came into existence in 1906, and was incorporated early in 1907 under the laws of the State of New York as a non-profit membership corporation. Through expert assistance given to its members and also to innumerable individuals and institutions not connected with it, the Chamber has exerted a tremendous influence, with an effectiveness which has more than once been commented upon in the publications of the United States Government, as well as by numerous beneficiaries and observers. For a survey of this very interesting development, the reader must be referred to the files of the Chamber's annual reports, numerous special publications, including *Twentieth Anniversary Year Book, 1927*, and *Twenty-fifth Anniversary of The Swedish Chamber of Commerce of the United States of America,* 1932, and its periodical, *The American Swedish Monthly,* which, in its earlier issues, was known first as *Bulletin,* and next as *The Swedish-American Trade Journal.*

Discussing the general objects of The Swedish Chamber of Commerce, Oscar G. Marell, who was the Secretary of the Chamber as well as Editor of *The Swedish-American Trade Journal* in 1916–18, returning as the Editor in 1922, and who became the Secretary and General Manager in 1926, says in a recent article:

Although primarily organized to render practical service in trade matters, it has with the years developed into a general office of information, and its assistance is now sought on every conceivable subject, no matter how far removed from commerce and trade. . . . Mainly, of course, the attention of the executive offices is centered on the commercial field.

The initiative in forming this organization was taken by a visiting lawyer from Sweden, Gustaf Thyreen, who in 1906 conferred in New York with those interested. Emil F. Johnson presided at the first general meeting for purposes of organization, and Hans Lagerloef was the secretary. At the first annual meeting, in 1907, the following directors were elected: Adolf Aspegren, John Aspegren, Count J. W. H. Hamilton, Consul Alexander E. Johnson, Axel Josephsson, Kurt M. Lundberg, J. Abraham Ohlsson, Count Henning G. Taube, and Gustaf P. Wern. The only one of that group now remaining on the board of directors is Mr. Hamilton, who renounced his title of nobility upon becoming naturalized. He is now Vice-President and Assistant Treasurer.

In the pulp-importing field a number of names stand out. Hans Lagerloef of New York may be counted as one of the pioneers. Born in 1880 in the Province of Östergötland, he came to this country in 1903, after studies and experience in Germany, France, and England. Here he at first became connected with Aspegren & Company as head of its wood-pulp department. As has been mentioned, he and Mr. Aspegren organized the Scandinavian-American Trading Company in 1907. In 1918 he established the Lagerloef Trading Company, which has been engaged principally in importing wood pulp from Finland. Besides being active in business, he takes a lively interest in social and cultural affairs. Having been active in the preliminaries to the establishment of The Swedish Chamber of Commerce, he served it for a number of years as Secretary, Honorary Secretary, Treasurer, and Vice-President.

Nils R. Johaneson, President of Johaneson, Wales and Sparre, New York, and Treasurer of The Swedish Chamber of Commerce, has been importing Swedish pulp for many years. Born in Stockholm, Mr. Johaneson came to this country in 1912. In 1916 he became connected with the Scandinavian-American Trading Company, and was appointed its Vice-President and manager in 1918, continuing in this position until the end of 1921. In 1922 he founded the firm of which he is now the President. He is Chairman of the Finance Committee of the Swedish American Tercentenary Association. Associated with him is Count Pehr Sparre, son of the Swedish painter, Count Louis Sparre.

A. J. Pagel, President of Pagel, Horton and Company, wood pulp importers, New York, and a vice-president of The Swedish Chamber of Commerce, has also done significant work in the import trade. Born in Sweden, Mr. Pagel began his business career in London in 1908. However, he soon came to America, and studied for a time at the University of Pennsylvania. In 1911 he joined the firm of Price and Pierce, New York, and in 1915 he and George A. Horton established the firm now headed by Mr. Pagel. Both he and Mr. Johaneson have served as president of the Association of American Wood-Pulp Importers. Another importer of pulp, who should be mentioned here is J. A. Miller, Vice-President of Perkins-Goodwin Company, New York.

Among the Swedish-born leading importers of steel from Sweden are N. K. G. Tholand, President of Ekstrand and Tholand, New York, G. Löfberg, President of the Uddeholm Company of America, L. W. Wilkens, President of A. Johnson & Company, New York, and Sixten F. Wollmar, President of SKF Steels, New York. The latter company imports Swedish steel, especially for use in manufacturing ball and roller bearings. In this connection it may be mentioned that Björn G. Prytz, who resigned as chairman of the board of the Swedish Ball Bearing Company (SKF) when this year he became the

Swedish Minister to the Court of St. James's, lived in New York from 1913 to 1917, during which time he conducted the negotiations resulting in combining the operations of the SKF Ball Bearing Company in Hartford, Connecticut, with the Hess-Bright Manufacturing Company in Philadelphia. More recently another Swede, Gustaf Sahlin, organized the American sales and, later, the manufacture of, Electrolux vacuum cleaners in the United States. He left his position as president of Electrolux, Inc., New York, in 1933, to assume the office of Vice-Managing Director of Aktiebolaget Elektrolux, Stockholm. Many of his duties in the American company were taken over by Elon V. Ekman as vice-president and treasurer of Electrolux, Inc., and director of Servel, Inc., in New York. Axel L. Wenner-Gren, head of the Electrolux concern and its various companies, is virtually a commuter between Sweden and the United States. Besides his interests in Electrolux, Inc., and Servel, Inc., the latter being the holder of the American rights to manufacture the Electrolux refrigerator, he also has extensive wood-pulp and other interests. Roy Johnson, Vice-President of the Arenco Machine Company, New York, reports that the cigar- and cigarette-making machines, invented in Sweden, which his company has imported, are now packing between 60 and 70 per cent of all cigarettes and 10 to 12 per cent of all cigars made in America.

All of these men are, or have been, intimately associated with the rapid rise of our import trade from Sweden during the present century. This rise has, of course, been the product of several factors other than the initiative, enterprise, skill, and energy of individuals. But before commenting further, let us look back at the statistics. We find that the first high mark for the value of total imports from Sweden and Norway (these two countries having been bracketed from 1823 to 1902), was reached in 1873, the figure then being more than $2,500,000. Five years later, in 1878, the total had gone down to $137,756, after which it recovered gradually and passed the $3,000,000 mark in 1884. During the rest of the nineteenth century it fluctuated, with a high of more than $4,000,000 in 1893, and never going below $2,500,000. During the first seven years of the present century a good deal of steadiness characterized the imports from Sweden.

The figures for the period 1908 to 1937 are shown in the following table:

Fiscal Years	U. S. Imports from Sweden Dollars	U. S. Exports to Sweden Dollars	Total U. S. Imports Dollars	Total U. S. Exports Dollars
		(Thousands omitted)		
1908–09	4,486	6,731	1,311,920	1,663,011
1909–10	6,830	5,991	1,556,947	1,744,984
1910–11	8,532	7,973	1,527,226	2,049,320
1911–12	9,521	9,451	1,653,264	2,204,322
1912–13	11,174	12,104	1,813,008	2,465,884
1913–14	11,590	14,644	1,893,925	2,364,579
1914–15	11,661	78,273	1,674,169	2,768,589
1915–16	11,846	51,979	2,197,883	4,333,482
1916–17	24,048	44,683	2,659,355	6,290,048
Calendar Years				
1917	18,069	20,467	2,952,467	6,233,512
1918	5,935	15,674	3,031,212	6,149,087
1919	13,722	133,069	3,904,364	7,920,425
1920	31,612	114,889	5,278,481	8,228,016
1921	19,765	37,565	2,509,147	4,485,031
1922	33,350	32,468	3,112,746	3,831,777
1923	36,183	42,402	3,792,065	4,167,493
1924	40,031	42,319	3,609,962	4,590,983
1925	41,033	42,465	4,226,589	4,909,848
1926	44,018	40,854	4,430,888	4,808,660
1927	47,896	44,689	4,184,742	4,865,375
1928	46,086	57,323	4,091,447	5,128,356
1929	52,986	58,704	4,399,361	5,240,995
1930	45,525	44,922	3,060,908	3,843,181
1931	34,271	32,156	2,090,635	2,424,289
1932	24,480	17,457	1,322,774	1,611,016
1933	30,972	18,598	1,449,559	1,674,994
1934	33,949	33,064	1,655,055	2,132,800
1935	41,247	38,216	2,047,485	2,282,874
1936	48,178	43,074	2,422,592	2,455,978
1937	58,567	64,449	3,084,060	3,345,157

While the main reasons for the rise in the volume and value of goods imported from Sweden were the growing demand produced by our own economic expansion, coupled with the growing ability of Sweden to supply goods of high quality at attractive prices, other factors of importance were the better organization of marketing activities, through The General Export Association of Sweden and other Swedish organizations with similar objectives, The Swedish Chamber of Commerce of the United States and, finally, the establishing of regular shipping facilities between Sweden and America.

The regular direct shipping connections have proved especially important. Occasional sailings from Swedish ports to America under Swedish as well as other flags were not uncommon during the nineteenth century up to about 1870. Such vessels, usually full-rigged ships, brigs, or barks, carried both passengers and cargoes. However, with the rapid improvement in steam navigation and England's lead in that field, Swedish goods and passengers came to be carried more and more in British vessels, departing from Liverpool and other English ports. The first attempt to establish a direct line between Sweden and the United States occurred in 1864, according to a statement in Volume IV of *The Swedish Element in America*, when the combined steam- and sailing ship *Ernst Merck*, built in Nyköping, brought "four hundred emigrants destined for the State of Maine, and who, after all kinds of tribulations, finally reached their destination." We do not know the rest of the history of this shipping enterprise. About 1882 the Danish Thingvalla Line seems to have become the real pioneer in direct regular service from Denmark and Norway. The name was changed in 1898 to the Scandinavian American Line. While these facilities served both Swedish passengers and exporters, none of the sailings were direct from Sweden. The same may be said of the Norwegian America Line, started in 1913.

The first direct service on a regular schedule between Swedish and American ports began in September, 1912, with the arrival in Newport News, Virginia, of the S.S. *Texas*, of the Swedish America Mexico Line. The Nordstjernan Steamship Company, known as the Johnson Line, in 1914, established a service between Sweden and ports on the Pacific coast.

In December, 1915, came the inauguration of the direct passenger and cargo service of the Swedish American Line. Today there are no finer liners on the seas than the motorships *Kungsholm* and *Gripsholm*. These, together with the S.S. *Drottningholm*, at present handle the brisk traffic of the line. A new motor liner, the *Stockholm*, is under construction. The old S.S. *Stockholm*, which pioneered in this service, has been sold. This is not the place to expand on the successful service of the Swedish American Line, but tribute must be paid to the significant contribution of this company to the lively development of trade, as well as passenger traffic, between the two countries.

The man who took the initiative in starting the Swedish American Line was William R. Lundgren, of Gothenburg, Sweden, who began discussing the project as early as 1900. Among the Swedes whose interest he gained was Dan Broström, the first president of the Line, and Axel Carlander, his successor. The present head of the Line is Axel Jonsson. On the American end of this development the leading rôle has been played, since the beginning, by G. Hilmer Lundbeck, the American Managing Director of the Line. Mr. Lundbeck's experience in America dates back to 1881, when, as a lad of eleven, he came to Boston from Sweden, where he was born. He began his work in New York in 1893, when Sophus Nielsen and he founded the private banking house of Nielsen & Lundbeck, which has been concerned principally with business between Sweden and the United States. Incidentally, Mr. Lundbeck has been the sole owner of the firm since 1920. He was the natural choice for the position of general passenger agent for the United States and Canada of the Swedish American Line, when it was founded. In 1929 he became the general manager on this side. Mr. Lundbeck was elected a vice-president of The Swedish Chamber of Commerce of the United States in 1916, and, when Mr. Aspegren died in 1924, Mr. Lundbeck succeeded him as president. It is safe to say that of all those who are active in the trade and cultural relations between Sweden and the United States, no one is more widely or more favorably known than Mr. Lundbeck.

Glancing back over the official statistical records of imports from Sweden, one must realize that they are necessarily incomplete. During the nineteenth and early twentieth centuries, a considerable bulk of goods originating in Sweden was first shipped to England, Germany, or some other foreign country, and then forwarded from a way station to America; and it is known that such goods have often been credited to the nation from which the final shipment occurred. Other invisible imports are those brought in as personal property by the immigrants from Sweden. Records indicate that about one and a quarter millions of Swedes have emigrated to this country during the three centuries since the original settlement in the Delaware Valley. One can only guess the total value of the goods which they brought along, but the figure must have run into several millions.

In this connection should also be noted the rôle played by Americans who go to Sweden for a visit. This travel is promoted not only by the Swedish American Line but also by the Swedish Travel Information Bureau, in New York, which was organized in 1921. Heading this organization, which also represents the Swedish State Railways and the Swedish Traffic Association, is Birger Nordholm, who was born in Stockholm and who came to this country in 1918. He reports that the number of American visitors to Sweden, which was some two or three thousand in 1923, rose to well above nine thousand in 1927, and to more than seventeen thousand in 1937. These visitors make a number of purchases in Sweden, including such things as textiles, glassware, porcelain, pewter, provincial costumes, and toys. Assuming that the individual average of such purchases is no more than $25 or $30, certainly a conservative estimate, the total in one year would amount to half a million dollars.

At such American retail stores as W. & J. Sloane, Franklin Simon & Company, Lord & Taylor, R. H. Macy & Company, New York, Marshall Field & Company, Chicago, and Sweden House, New York, which deals exclusively in Swedish imports, and at many others in leading cities, there is a growing business in the sale of Swedish glassware, furniture, ceramics, and textiles. What is more, these goods are accorded the flattery of having a definite influence on American manufactures, some of which are even advertised as being in the Swedish style. Pioneer in importing glassware from Sweden thirty years ago was

G. HILMER LUNDBECK

AMERICAN DIRECTOR OF THE SWEDISH AMERICAN LINE

Brase, Hagbard, 169, 443
Bremer, Fredrika, 85, 95, 96, 124, 241 ff., 283
Brett, Axel, 297
Bring, S. L., 157
Broddy, Colonel, 522
Bronander, W. B., 405, 414
Broström, Dan, 595
Brown, Marie A., 243, 245, 246, 248
Brown, Nils F-son, 189
Brunner, John, 396, 397
Brunnstrom, Signe, 363 ff.
Brydolf, Colonel, 522
Bundsen, Dr. C. A., 353, 354
Burglon, Nora, 217
Burnquist, Joseph Alfred Arner, 318, 329, 332
Butler, Nicholas Murray, 154
Bylund, Bobby, 370

CAMPANIUS, Rev. Johan, 11, 14, 29, 30, 44, 54
Carlander, Axel, 595
Carlborg, Hugo O. E., 503
Carlson, Adolf, 379
Carlson, Androv, 401, 402
Carlson, Anton Julius, 150, 286, 344
Carlson, Burns, 370
Carlson, Dr. C. Elmer, 345
Carlson, Conrad, 124
Carlson, Eskil C., 319
Carlson, Frank, 334
Carlson, Fritz, 373
Carlson, George Alfred, 330
Carlson, "Hal," 372
Carlson, Harry G., 297
Carlson, Harry Johan, 431
Carlson, Herbert "Murren," 372
Carlson, Hjalmar, 397
Carlson, John F., 495
Carlson, June, 479
Carlson, Knute E., 179
Carlson, May, 479
Carlson, Nels, 379
Carlson, Oliver, 213, 224
Carlson, Rev. Peter, 105
Carlson, Samuel A., 217, 330, 337
Carlsson, Conrad, 529
Carlsson, Rev. Erland, 131, 136
Carlström, Carl Gustaf, 361
Carlstrom, Oscar E., 317, 333
Carnegie, Andrew, 164

Carson, C. E., 425
Carter, Milton E., 316
Cawley, F. Stanton, 64
Cederstam, P. A., 104
Cederström, Count, 532
Celeste, Olga (Knutson), 480
Cervin, A. R., 158, 159
Cesare, Oscar, 500
Challman, S. A., 309
Chapman, H. G., 248
de Chary, Pauline, 249
Chelstorp, Harry, 370
Childs, Marquis W., 238
Chindblom, Carl R., 317, 326, 327, 328, 332, 337, 420
Chinlund, Rev. Emil G., 354
Christenson, Christ, 313
Christina, Queen of Sweden, 7, 16, 20, 31, 237, 240
Christopher, Rev., 9, 23
Clairmont, Leonard, 473
Claussen, Julia, 462, 463, 472
Cnattingius, Capt. Birger, 365
Cock, Capt. Lasse, 45
Collin, Dr. Carl, 359
Collin, Rev. Nicholas, 47, 51, 55, 58, 59
Collmodin, Rev., 55
Creutz, Gustaf Filip, Count de, 508

DAHL, Rev. K. G. W., 201
Dahlberg, Bror G., 415, 433, 570
Dahlgren, Adm. John Adolph, 124, 411, 518
Dahlgren, Col. Ulric, 518
Dahlgren, Ulric, 286
Dahlstrand, Hans P., 394, 412
Dahlstrom, Charles P., 433, 564, 565
Dahlstrom, Capt. Ralph, 549
Dalén, Nils Gustaf, 391 ff.
Danielson, Cora Lee, 311
Danielson, Emil O. J., 578
Danielson, Frank, 374
Dawson, Axel G., 565
de Berg-Löfgren, Mme., 468
de Brun, Dr. Harry C. W. S., 344, 345
De Laval, Carl Gustaf Patrik, 89, 389 ff., 412
Dellquest, A. W., 208
Deming, H. C., 243
Denkmann, Frederick C. A., 161
Donaldson, Arthur, 484 ff.

Dose, Oscar, 375
Dowell, Philip, 159
Dragstedt, Dr. Lester R., 345
Drake, Allyn, 479

EARL, Dr. Robert, 345
East, Dr. Erick Hjalmar, 345
Eberhart, Adolph Olson, 166, 318, 328, 329
Eck, C. A., 414
Edblom, Daniel, 515
Edgren, Lieut., 522
Edgren, August Hjalmar, 63, 199, 203, 246, 287
Edgren, Rev. Johan Alexis, 137, 199
Edgren, J. Urban, 597
Edgren, Robert, 236, 374
Edholm, Charlton Lawrence, 214
Edquist, J. A., 159
Edström, Aron, 189, 193
Edström, David, 218, 501
Edwards, Everett E., 75
Eisen, Gustavus A., 216
Ekblad, A. Theodore, 162
Ekblaw, Walter Elmer, 107, 287
Eke, John, 373
Ekeberg, Oscar, 471, 472
Ekeley, John Bernard, 287
Ekenstam, Martha af, 502
Eklund, Clarence, 370
Eklund, Dr. John J., 343
Ekman, Elon V., 592
Ekstrom, C. Emanuel, 297, 311, 312
Elers, Karl F., 404
Elfåker, August, 441
Elfving, Col., 522
Eliason, W. H., 305
Elliott, George A., 315
Elmblad, Johannes, 461
Elmblad, Magnus Henrik, 189, 196
Elmquist, A. Louis, 64, 69, 73, 74, 297
Elswick, Henrick von, 19
Emanuelson, Herbert L., 319
Enander, Johan Alfred, 183, 184, 189, 193, 200, 323, 328
Enard, Einar O., 189
Enebuske, Dr. Claes, 358, 359
Engberg, Carl Christian, 297
Engberg, Dr. Edward John, 345
Engholm, A., 166
Englund, Eric, 75
Engstrand, Agnes, 306

Engstrand, Stuart David, 212
Enwall, Hasse Octavius, 297
Erickson, Alfred W., 581, 582
Erickson, Rev. C. G., 173, 174
Erickson, Carl E., 425
Erickson, Carl I., 311
Erickson, Charles J., 578
Erickson, David, 500
Erickson, E. E., 297
Erickson, E. I., 354
Erickson, Egon R., 374
Erickson, Eric, 374
Erickson, Franklin C., 297
Erickson, John Theodore, 451
Erickson, T. A., 313
Ericson, C. George, 189
Ericson, C. J. A., 160, 325
Ericson, Charles Telford, 214
Ericson, Eric, 374
Ericson, John Ernst, 415
Ericsson, E. Walfrid, 565
Ericsson, Frans A., 173, 174, 311
Ericsson, Henry, 421, 422
Ericsson, John, 124, 240, 326, 382 ff., 410, 411, 475, 518
Ericsson, John E., 421, 422
Erikson, Arthur E., 306
Erikson, Estrid, 597
Erikson, Leif, 479
Esbjörn, Constantin M., 158, 162
Esbjörn, Rev. Lars Paul, 126, 130, 131, 136, 156, 157, 162
Eugen, Prince of Sweden, 218
Eustrom, Capt., 522
Everlund, Eric, 374
Exstrom, Paul E., 306

FABBE, Harry F-son, 189
Fabritius, Rev. Jacob, 46
Falckner, Rev. Justus, 436
Fast, Gustave, 404, 414
Feif, Carl Donat, 512
Ferguson, "Swede," 370
Fernstrom, Erik, 568
Fernstrom, Fritz O., 568
Fersen, Count Axel von, 508 ff.
Field, C., 247
Fielden, F. J., 249
Fisk, Gustav L., 396
Fjellstedt, Rev. Peter, 127, 131
Fleming, Erik, 597
Fleming, Adm. Klas, 8, 10, 13

Flom, George T., 62, 64, 69, 72
Fluviander, Rev..Israel, 11, 30
Flygare-Carlén, Emelie, 243, 251, 517
Foberg, Anne, 312
Fock, Johan Henrie, Baron von, 509
Fogelström, Rev. E. A., 175
Folin, Otto Knut Olof, 287, 288, 345
Fornell, Dr. Carl H., 345, 346
Forsander, Nils, 162
Forsberg, Col. August(us), 517
Forsberg, Conrad, 451
Forsell, John, 462
Foss, Claude William, 135, 162, 237, 244, 246, 248
Franck, H. A., 238
Francke, Ernest, 471
Frank, Tenney, 288
Franklin, Rev. A. W., 105
Franklin, Benjamin, 259, 586
Franzén, August, 500
Franzén, Carl Gustave Frederick, 311
Freden, Gustaf, 297
Fredenholm, Axel, 200
Frederiksen, N. C., 207
Fredin, Karl G., 61, 70, 189
Fredrickson, A. W., 178
Fredrickson, William, 179
Freeberg, John, 370
Freeburg, Victor O., 208, 226, 532, 584
Freeburg, Walter S., 403
Fremstad, Olive, 461
Frese, George K. de, naval officer, 511
Frick, Dr. Anders, 343
Fried, Capt. George, 525, 530
Friedländer, E. A., 242
Fries, Anna E. B., 244
Fries, J. E., 240, 412
Froeberg, Rev. Peter, 172, 173
Fromén, Agnes V., 501, 502
Frycklund, Verne Charles, 303
Frykman, Rev. Nils, 105
Fryksdahl, Karl, 374

GABRIELSON, Carl, 403
Gahn, Henrik, 573
Garbo, Greta (Greta Lovisa Gustafson), 476 ff., 479
Gardner, Oscar, 370
Gartineau, Benjamin, 515
Gelhaar, Emil, 500
Gestring, Marjorie, 374

Girelius, Rev. Lawrence, 41
Giving, Selma, 338
Gjers, C. J., 410
Glemming, Ivar, 442
Glen, James, 280
Glyer, G. A., 303
Goldhuhl, Carlos, 189
Goldschmidt, Otto, 456
Goldstrom, John Gustaf, 226, 227, 532
Goodwin, Godfrey G., 332
Gordman, Hjalmar, 371
Gosse, Edmund, 248
Gould, Chester N., 64, 69
Grafström, Gillis, 376
Grafström, Olof, 160, 169, 498
Grafström, Ruth, 498
Granstedt, Greta, 479
Granville, William Anthony, 288
Green, Axel M., 353
Green, P. Warren, 319
Grey, Shirley (Agnes Zetterstrand), 479
Grimberg, C., 237
Gröndahl, Bror Leonard, 297
Gronwall, Thomas Hakon, 297
Grundstrom, E. G., 559
Gullberg, Elsa, 597
Gullborg, John S., 399, 400
Gullmes, O., 189
Gustaf Adolf, Crown Prince of Sweden, 1, 336, 471
Gustafson, Lieut., 522
Gustafson, Anton, 370
Gustafson, Anton (Java-Gustaf), 371
Gustafson, Axel Ferdinand, 297
Gustafson, Lillian, 467
Gustafson, Oliver, 516
Gustafson, Dr. Paul, 347
Gustafson, Reuben Gilbert, 288
Gustafson, William, 347, 463
Gustav V, King of Sweden, 536
Gustavson, Marcus N., 560
Gyllenhaal, Leonard, 189
Gyllenskepp, Lieut. S., 511

HAAG, Charles, 501, 503
Hagelthorn, Signe, 298, 362, 363
Hagström, Erik, 371
Hagström, Theodore, 472
Haij, Alfred, 189
Hall, Agnes Staberg, 467
Hall, Eric Edwin, 428

Hall, Olof, 216
Hall, Thomas, 499
Hallberg, Charles E., 496
Hallberg, Lars Gustaf, 427
Hallberg, Lawrence G., 427
Hallbom, Gustaf, 470
Hallgren, Mauritz A., 212, 224
Hall-Quest, Alfred L., 311
Hallsthammar, Carl J., 501, 502
Hamilton, Dr. Bengt Leopold Knutsson, 298, 346
Hamilton, Count J. W. H., 590
Hammargren, F. E., 504
Hanson, Alexander Contee, 315
Hanson, Bengt N. W., 565, 566
Hanson, Carl M., 311
Hanson, Einar, 476
Hanson, Fritz, 370
Hanson, Howard, 176, 177, 304, 444, 448 ff., 452, 465
Hanson, John, 3, 315
Hanson, Lars, 476
Hanson, Marcus L., 76
Hanson, Peter B., 329
Hansson, F. W., 413
Hansson, Dr. Kristian Gösta, 346
Hart, Albert Bushnell, 299
Hartman, Johan, 26
Hasselquist, Rev. Tuve Nilsson, 131, 135, 157, 159, 160, 162, 184
Hauberg, Dr. John H., 161
Hauberg, Mrs. John H., 161
Haugan, Helge A., 576
Haugen, Einar, 64, 65
Hazzard, John E., 486, 487
Hebbe, Gustaf Clemens, 243, 249, 516
Hedberg, Axel, 189
Hedblom, Dr. Carl Arthur, 288, 346, 347
Hedenstam, Rev. P. A., 105
Hedin, Axel, 124
Hedin, Dr. Carl J., 355
Hedin, Florence Benedict, 228, 251
Hedin, Naboth, 228, 251
Hedin, Sven, 240
Hedlund, Oscar F., 374
Hedlund, Oscar M., 380
Hedman, Herbert Ragnvald, 568, 569
Hedman, Martha, 482 ff.
Hedstrand, G. F., 189
Hedstrom, Carl H., 560
Hedstrom, Carl Oscar, 567

Hedstrom, Rev. Jonas J., 105, 126
Hedstrom, Rev. Olof Gustaf, 130
Hedwall, P. O., 472
Heldner, Knute, 495
Hellberg, John R., 472
Hellström-Oscar, Anna, 466
Heltzen, Oscar L., 319
Henmon, Vivian Allen Charles, 288, 289, 311
Henschen, Henry S., 576
Henschen, William, 137, 194, 576
Herlin, August Theodore, 425
Hesselius, Gustaf, 43, 437, 438, 451, 488 ff.
Hesselius, Johan, 489
Hildebrand, K., 200
Hilding, Dr. Anderson, 347
Hill, James J., 100, 164, 570
Hill, S. M., 175, 176
Hillberg, John Emanuel, 194
Hillbom, Henrik F., 499
Hille, Einar, 289
Hillstrom, David Alfred, 560
Hjertberg, Ernest, 373, 379, 380
Hjort, Dr. Axel Magnus, 298
Hogberg, Emil, 472
Hogfeldt, Otto, 189
Hokanson, Martin, 396
Holcomb, Martha A. L., 240
Holcomb, Dr. Oscar W., 354
Holcomb, Thomas A. E., 240
Hollander, E. E., 414
Holm, Mike, 332
Holmberg, Gustaf, 371
Holmberg, Gustaf Fredrik, 443
Holmberg, O., 302
Holmberg, Ragnar, 370
Holmes, Rev. Ludvig, 200
Holmes, Pehr G., 335
Holmquist, Gustaf, 179, 466
Holmquist, Peter, 124
Holmquist, Sigrid, 474
Holt, Andrew, 102, 166, 318, 324, 328
Höök, Swen, 19
Hoving, Helga Rundberg, 579
Hoving, Dr. Johannes W. W., 204, 348, 579
Hoving, Walter, 579
Howard, Velma Swanston, 218, 247
Howitt, Mary, 237, 241, 242, 243
Hudde, Andreas, 30
Huebsch, Alfhild, 249

Hultgren, George, 452
Hultman, Eugene C., 335
Hultman, J. A., 179
Hunter, Henry (Jacobson), 479
Hussander, Arthur, 427
Hussander, Will S., 326
Husting, Paul O., 333
Huygen, Hendrick, 7, 9, 19, 21, 22
Hybinette, Noak Victor, 397, 412
Hylander, Clarence, 298
Hyllested, August, 439

ICKES, Harold L., 316

JACKSON, Rev. A., 163, 164
Jackson, Dr. Carl A., 355
Jacobson, E. T., 307
Jacobson, Enfrid R., 568
Jacobson, Oscar Brousse, 499
Janeke, Hans, 339
Janson, Rev. Eric, 126, 130
Janson, Florence Edith, 75, 79, 108 ff., 298
Janssen, Jan, 30
Jansson, Alfred, 499
Jeppson, George N., 557 ff.
Jeppson, R. B., 313
Jocknich, A. af, 524
Johaneson, Nils R., 591
Johansen, Charles K., 189, 381, 469, 470, 472
Johansen, Capt. E. R., 528
Johanson, Greta, 374
Johanson, Hjalmar, 375, 380
Johanson, Dr. Nels A., 353
Johanson, Thure, 373
Johansson, Carl Edward, 397 ff., 413
Johnson, Lieut., 522
Johnson, Albert, 371
Johnson, Albin E., 228, 229
Johnson, Alex., 326
Johnson, Alexander Edward, 588, 590
Johnson, Alexander J., 199
Johnson, Amandus, 5, 26, 27, 37, 52, 53, 72, 76, 77, 515, 516, 573, 586
Johnson, August, 209
Johnson, August W., 371
Johnson, Axel E., 425
Johnson, Axel P., 319
Johnson, Carl, 374
Johnson, Carl Edward, 289

Johnson, Capt. Charles, 522
Johnson, Clara, 549
Johnson, Edward E., 472
Johnson, Edwin Carl, 334, 337
Johnson, Emil F., 414, 415, 590
Johnson, Emory, 474
Johnson, Eric, 194, 325
Johnson, Fred G., 333
Johnson, George E. Q., 317, 332
Johnson, Gustavus, 439
Johnson, Henry, 289, 313
Johnson, Dr. Herman M., 348
Johnson, Hilding, 234, 235
Johnson, Hilmer, 370
Johnson, John Albert, 164, 233, 234, 324, 329, 337
Johnson, John S., 377
Johnson, Magnus, 328, 331
Johnson, Martin Elmer, 547, 548
Johnson, Rev. O. J., 164, 175, 176
Johnson, Philip G., 536 ff.
Johnson, Philip Gustaf, 312
Johnson, Roy, 592
Johnson, Tor, 370
Johnson, W. G., 64
Jönsson, Anders, 31
Jonsson, Axel, 595
Jöranson, Einar, 298
Josephsson, Axel, 590
Judd, F. A., 248
Junggren, Oscar, 393, 412

KALLGREN, Carl Alfred, 227, 298
Kallgren, Everett, 227
Kalm, Peter, 37, 56, 239, 259
Karlstrom, Carl E., 303
Karstens, Vilhelm, 375
Keen, Dr. William W., 341, 342
Kellberg, A., 370
Kelpius, Johann, 436
Key, Ellen, 218, 244
Kieft, Governor, 21
Kilander, K. A., 70
Kinell, Rev. A., 580
Kinell, Nelson, 580
Klang, Capt. Eddie, 530
Klang, Capt. Gustaf, 529
Klang, Johan Simon, 529
Klang, Capt. John, 530
Klang, Capt. Victor, Sr., 529
Klang, Capt. Victor, Jr., 530

Klinckowström, Martin, 125
Kling, Måns Nilsson, 7, 9, 14, 21
Knape, Otto, 189
Knapp, Evelyn, 479
Knudsen, Karoline M., 247
Knudson, Karl, 189
Knutson, Harold, 330, 337
Kollberg, Gustaf L., 394
Kramer, Hans, 13
Krantz, Aron Fabian, 550
Krause, Alexander L., 243
Kronberg, Rev. Sven J., 105, 202
Kuhn, Adam, 339, 340
Kumlien, Thure Ludwig, 78
Kyn, Jöran, 341
Kyne, Peter B., 526

LAGER, John E., 581
Lagercrantz, Ava, 500
Lagergren, Rev. Carl G., 137
Lagerloef, Hans, 381, 589, 590
Lagerlöf, Selma, 65, 218, 243, 245, 250 ff.
Lagerstedt, N. S. W., 301
Lamb, Rev. James Hart, 48
Lamm, Martin, 266
Lamm, Consul General Olof H., 471
Landon, Herman, 215
Lanquist, Andrew, 420 ff.
Lanrin, C. G., 238
Larsell, Olof, 239, 290, 348
Larsen, C., 244
Larsen, Hanna Astrup, 208, 248, 252
Larsen, Dr. Nils P., 349
Larsén-Todsen, Nanny, 464
Larson, Albin V., 303
Larson, Algot J. E., 564
Larson, Arvid, 369
Larson, C. J., 189
Larson, C. Theodore, 416
Larson, C. W., 405
Larson, Carl William, 430
Larson, Emil Leonard, 298
Larson, F. A., 189
Larson, George V., 306
Larson, Gustus Ludwig, 298
Larson, Harry, 370
Larson, Jens Fredrick, 430
Larson, Karl, 374
Larson, Capt. Westside T., 549
Larsson, Dr. B. Hjalmar, 348
Larsson, Gösta, 214

Lascari, Hilda K., 502
Laury, William, 7
Leach, Henry Goddard, 1, 208
Lee, R. E., 249
Leidzén, Erik W. G., 450, 451
Lempke, Capt., 522
Lenna, Oscar A., 563, 564, 570
Lenroot, Irvine Luther, 319, 328, 333, 337
Lenroot, Katharine, 335
Levin, Eric, 372
Lidman, Carl, 301
Liljefors, Bruno, 238
Liljegren, Lieut., 522
Liljencrantz, Baron Johan, 382
Liljengren, J. A., 179
Liljenstolpe, C., 524
Liljequist, Lawrence A., 319
Lilliehöök, Knut, 12
Lilliehöök, Per, 12
Lincoln, Rev. Julius, 59, 73, 140
Lind, Dr. Alfred, 343
Lind, Jenny, 124, 157, 304, 453 ff.
Lind, John, 124, 166, 318, 324, 329, 337
Lind, Samuel Colville, 290
Lindahl, Josua, 159, 171
Lindall, Lieut., 522
Lindau, Harold, 467
Lindberg, Capt., 522
Lindberg, Rev. Conrad E., 162
Lindberg, Edward, 374
Lindberg, Rev. Paul M., 177
Lindberg, Theodor, 444
Lindberg, Walter, 202
Lindbergh, Anne Morrow, 543 ff.
Lindbergh, Charles A., Sr., 223, 329, 539
Lindbergh, Col. Charles A., 124, 218, 532, 538 ff.
Lindblom, Ernst, 194, 195
Lindblom, Robert, 469, 575
Lindborg, Arthur E., 310
Lindeberg, Harrie Thomas, 429, 434
Lindell, Gustaf, 425
Linden, Eric, 478
Linder, Oliver A., 61, 73, 162, 181, 193, 197, 198, 205, 488
Linderborg, Carl Gustav, 189, 325
Lindeström, Peter, 5, 17, 37, 39
Lindgren, Dr. Carl C., 298
Lindgren, Capt. Charles M., 576
Lindgren, John R., 576

Lindgren, Valdemar, 290
Lindholm, A. C., 332
Lindin, Carl Eric, 500
Lindlof, Johanna M., 310
Lindquist, Rev. A. W., 355
Lindquist, Dr. Carl N., 355
Lindquist, David L., 414, 432
Lindquist, E. F., 312
Lindquist, Francis O., 330
Lindquist, John, 374
Lindquist, Rudolph D., 312, 313
Lindsten, Gottfrid, 332
Lindstone, C. E., 189
Lindstrand, Frans Albin, 197
Lindstrom, Dr. A. O., 362
Lindstrom, Adolph, 424, 425
Lindstrom, Albert Ferdinand, 403
Lindstrom, Charles, 404
Lindstrom, Fred, 372
Lindström, Fred, 370
Lindstrom, Lisa, 374
Lindvall, Rev. Carl Axel, 161, 202
Ling, Per Henrik, 240, 357
Linné, Carl von, 124, 239, 240, 254, 258 ff., 340, 581
Linus, A., 499
Litzenberg, Karl, 64
Ljungberg, Göta, 465
Ljungh, Esse W., 189
Ljungström, Birger, 390
Ljungström, Fredrik, 390
Ljungström, Gösta, 373
Lobeck, Charles O., 325, 330
Lock, Rev. Lars, 33, 40, 53
Locock, C. D., 240, 247, 248
Löfberg, G., 591
Lokrantz, Dr. Sven Richard, 349, 361, 362
Lönegren, F. W., 189
Lonegren, Sigfrid K., 597
Longfellow, Henry W., 241, 242, 281, 283
Lönnquist, Rev. Carl Adolph, 201, 354
Lorenzen, Harry, 207
Lotave, Carl G., 492, 497
Louise, Crown Princess of Sweden, 336, 471
Lowell, James Russell, 242
Lowell, Mary, 242
Loy, Myrna, 480
Lucassen, Andreas, 7
Lund, Emil, 180

Lundbeck, G. Hilmer, 595
Lundberg, Lieut., 522
Lundberg, Anna, 466
Lundberg, Ferdinand, 213, 224
Lundberg, Hans, 395, 412
Lundberg, Kurt M., 590
Lundbergh, Holger, 482
Lundeen, Ernest, 318, 328, 332, 337
Lundeen, Col. J. A., 166
Lundell, Fred, 414
Lundgren, Dr. Leonard, 302
Lundgren, William R., 595
Lundholm, Dr. Erik, 343
Lundholm, Oscar Helge, 298
Lundin, Frederick, 325, 330
Lundin, Hjalmar, 369
Lundin, Laura M., 298
Lundmark, Leon, 496
Lundquist, Carl Fredrik, 466, 470
Lundquist, Carl Hjalmar, 317
Lundquist, Gustaf Adolph, 298
Lundström, Johan Edward, 388
Lunnow, Magnus, 189
Lycke, Joachim, 15

MAAS-FJETTERSTRÖM, Märta, 597
MacFarland, Rev. Charles Stedman, 215
Machold, Capt. Charles M., 469
Magney, Clarence R., 166
Magney, Dr. F. H., 349
Magnuson, Dr. Paul Budd, 349
Magnuson, Warren G., 334
Magnusson, Carl Edward, 298
Magnusson, Edward, 569, 570
Magnusson, Dr. G. A., 353
Magny, Rev. J., 166
Malm, Gustaf Nathanael, 203, 492
Malmberg, C. Fritiof, 311
Malmberg, Luther Ansgarius, 298
Malmborg, Capt. Oscar, 517, 519, 520
Malmgren, Dr. Theodore J., 350
Malmquist, Frithiof, 189, 198
Malmsten, Carl, 597
Manning, Harry, 531
Marell, Oscar G., 590
Markham, William, 46
Matson, Enar K., 319
Matson, Capt. Wilhelm (Mattson), 526, 527
Mattson, Edgar L., 576

Mattson, Col. Hans, 102, 196, 232, 322, 324, 507, 520, 522 ff.
Mattson, Henry, 496
Mattson, Rev. P. A., 164
Mattsson, Ernest, 597
Mauritzson, Jules, 73, 74, 162
McCrea, Joel, 480
Meijer, Johan, 516
Mejerberg, C. J., 301
Melander, Axel Leonard, 290
Melander, Capt. Theodor A., 357, 365
Mellander, Rev. Axel, 179
Mellin, Carl J., 404, 413
Messer, Chester, 555
Messer, Richard, 555
Meurling, Emil, 189
Meyer, Bror, 376
Michaelson, E. W., 396
Michelet, Maren, 69, 70
Miller, J. A., 591
Milles, Carl, 36, 504, 585
Minuit, Peter, 67, 121 ff.
Molander, Hjalmar, 371
Molander, Karin, 476
Molin, Peter, 516
Montelius, Oscar, 240
Monthell, Ens. Peter, 511
Morton, John, 3, 149, 315
Mossberg, Frank, 402, 413, 561
Mossberg, Joel, 471
Munson, J. M., 308, 309
Munters, Carl Georg, 392

NATHURST, Gen. Charles C., 524
Nauckhoff, Henric Johan, naval officer, 512
Nelander, Rev. E., 167, 169
Nelson, A. P., 180
Nelson, Adolphus P., 333
Nelson, Anders Johan, 574
Nelson, Dr. Carl Ferdinand, 350
Nelson, Edgar Andrew, 304, 452
Nelson, Elna E., 206
Nelson, Maj. Erik H., 532, 533 ff.
Nelson, Frank, 308
Nelson, Gustav L., 326
Nelson, Helge, 91, 93
Nelson, Hilma, 485
Nelson, Knute, 324, 331
Nelson, L. P., 485
Nelson, Louis M., 423 ff.
Nelson, Milton Nels, 398

Nelson, Capt. Nels A., 506, 524
Nelson, O. N., 204
Nelson, Oscar, 332, 333
Nelson, Oscar, manufacturer, 566, 567
Nelson, Victor Emanuel, 290
Nelson, Victor Folke, 217
Nelson, Col. William R., 416
Nertunius, Matthias, 15
Newbranch, Harvey Ellsworth, 227, 228
Nicolls, Richard, 45
Nielsen, Sophus, 595
Niesen, Gertrude, 480
Nilsson, Anna Q., 474
Nilsson, Carl J., 501, 503
Nilsson, Christina, 238, 304, 456 ff., 467
Nilsson, Rev. F. O., 105
Nilsson, Jonas, 573
Nilsson, Karin, 374
Nilsson, Svea, 374
Nilsson, Victor, 205, 230 ff., 232, 435, 470
Nissen, Harry, 359
Nobel, Alfred Bernhard, 240, 386 ff.
Nolander, Capt. Frank, 529
Nolte, Peter, 515
Norbeck, Peter, 330, 333, 334
Norberg, Dr. George B., 350
Norblad, Albin Walter, 319, 327, 328, 334
Nordenfelt, Theodore, 410
Nordenskjöld, Adolph, 240
Nordenskjöld, Otto Henric, Baron, 510
Nordfeldt, Bror Julius Olson, 497
Nordholm, Birger, 596
Nordin, Harry William, 452
Nordin, William, 471
Nordling, Rev. J. E., 175
Norelius, Charles, 374
Norelius, Rev. Eric, 105, 145, 162, 163
Norelius, Jenny, 467
Norelius, Martha, 374
Norlin, George, 291
Norman, Carl Gustaf, 194, 195
Norton, John Nathaniel, 333
Novak, Jane, 474
Noyd, Rev. Martin, 175
Ny, Eric, 373
Nyberg, Lieut., 522
Nyden, Col. John A., 427, 428, 429

Nygren, Oscar ("Roslagsbjörnen"), 370
Nygren, Werner, 433
Nyholm, Arvid F., 497
Nylander, Ebba Sundstrom, 179, 444, 445, 452
Nylander, Dr. Victor Theodore, 298
Nylin, Dr. Joseph B., 350
Nyquist, J. P., 164
Nystedt, Hjalmar T., 425
Nystrom, Paul Henry, 291
Nyvall, Rev. David, 137, 178, 202
Nyvall, David, Jr., 446, 447

OBERG, Erik, 225, 226
Oberg, Paul, 444
Öbom, A. G., 183
Ockerblad, Dr. Nelse Frederick, 350
Oden, Dr. Rudolph J. E., 350
Oestlund, O. W., 159
Ohlin, Henry, 375
Ohlson, Rev. Algoth, 179
Ohlsson, J. Abraham, 590
Öhman, Martin, 464
Öhman, Runar, 373
Ohnstrand, Enoch, 564
Öhrström-Renard, Augusta, 467, 468
Okerlind, Charles A., 577
Oland, Edith, 217, 247
Oland, Warner, 217, 247, 474, 485
Olander, Herbert Theodore, 311
Oldberg, Arne, 446, 449
Oldenberg, Hugo, 360, 361
Olson, Lieut., 522
Olson, Alexander, 189
Olson, Axel Ragnar, 298
Olson, Carl, 380
Olson, Cliff, 370
Olson, Conrad P., 330
Olson, Emery Evans, 291
Olson, Ernst W., 74, 154, 180, 189, 194, 195, 244, 519, 520, 524
Olson, Floyd B., 318, 332
Olson, Harry, 316, 317, 329, 337
Olson, Johan H., 396
Olson, John, 175
Olson, Julius E., 69
Olson, Kenneth E., 232, 233
Olson, Magnus, 470
Olson, Moroni, 480
Olson, N. P., 233
Olson, Wallace, 307

Olsson, Anna, 209
Olsson, Anna (Aina), 203, 204
Olsson, Axel Elias, 501, 503
Olsson, Göran, 8
Olsson, Rev. Olof, 160, 168, 308
Olsson, Per, 451, 452
O'Neill, Eugene, 247
Örtengren, John R., 452, 470, 472
Osborn, Joseph E(sbjörn), 522
Oscar II, King of Sweden, 469, 471
Oscar, Martin, 466
Östberg, Carolina, 466, 470
Östberg, Ragnar, 432
Osterberg, Emil, 351
Ostergren, Robert C., 428
Ostlund, Clarence, 306
Ostrom, Dr. Louis, 351
Ostrum, Dr. Algot, 351
Ouchterlony, Dr. John Arvid, 292, 342
Oxenstierna, Axel, Chancellor, 6, 13, 16, 23
Oxenstierna, Eric, 16

PADDEN, Sarah, 480
Pagel, A. J., 591
Palm, Robert, 376, 396
Palm, Svante, 574
Palmer, Eric, 223
Palmer, George M., 223
Palmer, Gilbert, 307
Palmquist, Rev. Gustaf, 126
Palmquist, Magnus Daniel, naval officer, 513
Palmstierna, C. F., 237
Pamp, Fredrich E., 179
Papegoja, Johan, 11 ff., 20, 31
Pasch, Gustaf Erik, 388
Pattison, John Nelson, 438
Paulson, Arvid, 485
Paulson, N. Axel V., 397
Paxson, Henry D., 73, 573
Pearson, Alfred John, 292, 335
Pearson, Irving F., 205
Pearson, P. H., 217
Peel, Roy V., 298
Pendleton, Ella Sundstrom, 444
Penn, William, 2, 28, 29, 33, 34, 43, 45, 46, 54, 76, 435
Perce, Elbert, 243
Percival, Dr. James Gates, 260
Person, Johan, 183, 194, 199
Persson, Harry, 370

Petersen, Adolph Fredrik, naval offi- cer (Rosensvärd), 514, 515
Peterson, Dr. Anders, 351
Peterson, Andrew H., 426
Peterson, Arvid, 390
Peterson, Bernard, 551
Peterson, Carl, 515
Peterson, Carl Frederik, 189, 194, 195 ff.
Peterson, Charles, 518
Peterson, Charles C., 379
Peterson, Charles S., 310, 331, 492, 551, 575, 576
Peterson, Capt. Charles W., 527, 528
Peterson, Conrad, 58, 73
Peterson, Dorothy, 479
Peterson, Elmer T., 215, 225
Peterson, Elmer T., educator, 312
Peterson, Elmer W., 229
Peterson, Enoch, 189
Peterson, Frances, 479
Peterson, Rev. Frank, 105
Peterson, Dr. Frederick, 215, 216, 248, 292
Peterson, Frithiof (Röl Gording), 179
Peterson, Hans, 375
Peterson, Harry H., 318, 332
Peterson, Henry E. C., 494
Peterson, Ivar, 189
Peterson, Jan, 339
Peterson, Joseph H., 319
Peterson, Karl, 565
Peterson, Kjell, 365
Peterson, Marie, 468
Peterson, Olof August, 298
Peterson, Otto Edward, 311
Peterson, P. S., 581
Peterson, Dr. Reuben, 351, 352
Peterson, Ruth, 479
Peterson, Thyra H. (Mrs. Chas. S. Peterson), 492
Peterson, William Harold, 292, 293
Petri, Rev. Carl J., 158
Philp, Casimir von, 396
Pierson, A. N., 581
Pierson, Arthur, 479
Pierson, Wallace, 581
Pihlblad, Rev. Ernst F., 168, 170, 307, 308, 334, 443
Platen, Baltzar Carl von, 392
Plym, Francis J., 416, 433, 554, 555
Porat, Otto von, 370

Posse, Baron Nils, 358
Princell, Rev. John G., 133
Printz, Johan, Governor, 10 ff., 23 ff., 36, 39, 42, 44, 49, 52, 53, 76, 341, 417, 488
Prytz, Björn G., 591

R AAB, Carl, 510
Rahmn, Knut, 474
Rajalin, Lieut. Carl Frederic von, 512, 513
Rajalin, Salomon Mauritz von, naval officer, 513
Rambo, Ezekiel, 48
Rambo, Ormond, Jr., 577
Rambo, Peter, 319, 578
Ramm, Nisse, 370
Regnell, Nils, 374
Rehbinder, Lieut. Carl Gustaf, 511, 512
Rehnstrand, Vera C., 306
Remer, Nils, 370
Renard, Fred O., 597
Renhard, Rev. C. J., 353
Reuterdahl, Arvid, 298
Reuterdahl, Henry, 495
Rheinstrom, Charles A., 549
Richthoff, Johan, 370
Ridder, Peter Hollender, 8, 9, 11, 22, 23
Rignell, Dr. Carl J., 343
Ringius, Carl, 500
Rising, Johan, 17 ff., 28, 31, 32, 37, 39, 42, 53, 76
Roak, Rev. John, 47
Roberg, Dr. O. T., 352
Roberts, Rev. William, 48
Rogers, Jean (Elinor Lövgren), 478
Roman, Johan Helmich, 438
Romell, Lars Gunnar Torgny, 299
Roos, Måns Herman, 189, 196
Roos, Peter, 494
Roosevelt, Theodore, 188, 524
Roosval, J., 238
Rooth, Gerhard T., 189, 366
Rosen, Count Clarence von, 378
Rosendahl, Comm. Charles E., 532, 545 ff.
Rosene, W. A., 308
Rosenlof, George Walter, 308
Rosenquist, Carl E., 313

Rosén von Rosenstein, Magnus Aurivilius, naval officer, 514
Rosewall, Oscar Waldemar, 299
Rossby, Carl Gustaf Arvid, 293
Rothery, Agnes, 238
Rothstein, Dr. Thor Christian, 299
Rouzaud, Auguste, Count de Miranda, 460
Rowles, Polly, 480
Rudberus, Johan, 15
Rudman, Rev. Andreas, 40, 46, 47, 54, 78
Runbeck, Margaret Lee, 217
Rydberg, Per Axel, 176, 293
Rydberg, Victor, 191
Ryden, Rev. Ernest Edwin, 207
Ryden, George Herbert, 35, 293
Rydingsvärd, Karl von, 503

SAHLIN, Gustaf, 591
Sahlin, Nils G., 506
Salén, Sven, 375
Saltza, C. F. von, 498
Samuel, H. B., 247
Samuelson, Agnes, 309
Samuelson, Arvid, 451
Sandahl, Charles Fredrick, 180
Sandberg, C. P., 410
Sandburg, Carl, 209, 210, 211, 234
Sandel, Rev. Andreas, 436
Sandelin, Jacob Evertssen, 7
Sandsten, E. P., 313
Sandström, Flora, 217
Sandzén, Birger, 169, 492, 494
Sangren, Paul V., 312
Scheele, Bishop Gezelius von, 162
Schecle De Vere, Maximilian, 283
Schleussner, Ellie, 247
Schmidt, Emanuel, 199, 200
Schmidt, Nathaniel (Anderson), 293, 294
Schön, Anders, 189, 193
Schroeder, Karl, 379
Schuch, Edward, 201
Schultén, Lieut. Jackris, 511
Schulz, C. S., 307, 309
Schuster, Hans, 373
Schylander, "Cairo," 372
Seaholm, Ernest W., 563
Seashore, Rev. A. T., 176, 177
Seashore, Carl Emil, 166, 294, 311, 447, 448

Seashore, Dr. David E., 352
Seashore, Dr. Gilbert, 352
Seashore, Robert H., 299
Seastrom, Victor, 475
Seeburg, J. P., 568
Sellin, Johan Thorsten, 74, 294
Sellstedt, Lars Gustaf, 493
Seton, Waldemar, 319
Settergren, Anna C., 244
Severin, Nils Persson, 423
Shaleen, Dr. Arthur W., 355
Shaw, Clement B., 240, 245, 246
Sheldon, James A., 306
Shoan, Nils, 559
Silversparre, Axel, 523
Sinnickson, Clement, 315
Sinnickson, J. Forman, 315
Siwertz, Sigfrid, 249
Sjöblom, Rev. P., 166
Sjöstjerna, Lieut. Aron, 512
Sjöström, Cyril, 417
Sjöström, Rev. Gustaf, 194
Skarström, Dr. William, 302, 359, 360
Skoglund, Eric E., 414, 424
Skoglund, Jean, 414
Skogsbergh, Rev. E. August, 105, 138, 178
Skoog, Dr. Andrew Leonard, 352
Skoog, Karl F., 501
Skute, Sven, 17
Smith, C. A., 100, 104, 160, 170
Smith, H. L., 166
Smith, Martin F., 334
Soderberg, A. W., 395
Söderberg, Carl Richard, 394, 412
Soderberg, Yngve, 500
Söderblom, Archbishop Nathan, 93, 134, 161, 179
Soderlund, Gustaf F., 444
Söderlund, Joel S., 472
Södersten, Herman, 500
Söderström, Alfred, 198
Sohlberg, Dr. Olof, 343
Solbert, Col. Oscar N., 335, 336
Sparre, Count Pehr, 591
Sparrström, Capt., 522
Spiring, Peter, 12, 15
Spongberg, Fred A., 374, 380
Springer, Carl, 46, 54
Stedingk, Curt von, Baron, 509 ff.
Stedingk, Victor von, 509, 510
Steelhammar, Col., 522

Sten, Anna, 480
Stenbeck, Capt., 522
Stenquist, John L., 310, 311
Stenström, Karl Wilhelm, 299, 353
Stephenson, George M., 75, 79, 126
Stidden, Timon (Tyman Stidham), 15, 339
Stillé, Dr. Alfred, 340
Stillé, Charles Janeway, 299
Stillé, Dr. Moreton, 340, 341
Stillé, Olof Peterson, 340
Stiller, Mauritz, 477, 478
Stockenström, Herman, 189
Stolbrand, Gen. Charles John, 520, 521
Stolpe, Gustav, 160
Stomberg, Andrew Adin, 64, 67, 69, 73, 92, 294, 295
Stork, Charles Wharton, 247, 248
Storm, Adolph, 567
Strandberg, Erik P., Sr., 424
Strandberg, Erik P., Jr., 424
Strindberg, August, 246 ff., 251, 439
Stromberg, Alfred, 399, 401, 402
Stromberg, Gustaf Benjamin, 299
Strömberg, Oscar Leonard, 203
Strömgren, Bengt, 299
Strong, William, 240
Sturtevant, A. M., 69
Stuyvesant, Peter, 31 ff., 37, 39
Sundahl, Eskil, 432
Sundbäck, Gideon, 406
Sundbärg, Gustav, 108
Sundberg, Karl, 395
Sundelius, Gustaf, 572
Sundelius, Marie, 453, 471, 572
Sundelius, Peter A., 194, 325
Sundstrand, Gustaf David, 403
Sundstrand, Oscar Joseph, 403
Sundstrom, Ebba (Nylander), 179, 444, 445, 452
Sundstrom, Ella (Pendleton), 444
Sundstrom, Capt. E. W., 528
Sundstrum, M. T., 518
Sundwall, John, 295, 302
Svanberg, John, 373
Svanström, R., 237
Svedberg, The, 3, 389
Swalin, Benjamin F., 445
Swan, Gustaf N., 162, 205, 207, 251
Swanson, Alex, 370
Swanson, Gloria, 480

Swanson, Henry, 375
Swanson, John A., 332
Swanson, J. Harold, 227
Swanson, Neil Harmon, 212, 224
Swanson, Roy W., 219
Swanstrom, J. Edward, 330, 331
Swärd, Axel August, 200
Swärd, Rev. P. J., 166
Swedelius, Ernst Henrik, 466
Swedenborg, Emanuel, 239, 247, 254, 262 ff., 279 ff., 488, 489
Swedenburg, Dr. Francis G., 353
Swendsén, C. J., 332
Swenson, Andreas, 46
Swenson, "Calle Sven," 371
Swenson, David Ferdinand, 253, 295, 310
Swenson, Edgar, 189
Swenson, Edward, 374
Swenson, Eric P., 574
Swenson, Godfrey G., 425
Swenson, Dr. Karl J., 353
Swenson, L. O., 308
Swenson, Ole, 46
Swenson, Sven Magnus, 574
Swenson, Swen, 46
Swensson, Rev. Carl Aaron, 137, 158, 167, 168, 169, 170, 194, 201, 203, 308, 323, 326, 328
Swensson, Mrs. Carl, 169
Sylvan, Carl, 471

TAUBE, Count Henning G., 590
Taylor, Bayard, 238, 241, 455
Taylor, Dr. Charles, 358
Taylor, Dr. George, 358
Taylor, Per Henrik, 358
Tegnér, Esaias, 240, 241
Tegnier, A., 247
Tengbom, Ivar, 432
Tholand, N. K. G., 591
Thomas, Calvin, 63
Thomas, W. W., 169, 245
Thorborg, Kerstin, 466
Thord-Gray, Gen. Ivor, 378
Thoreau, Henry D., 259, 281
Thorling, Capt. Charles H., 336
Thorson, Andrew, 164
Thorson, Nelson T., 189
Thorson, P. O., 207
Thorstenberg, Samuel, 443

Thulin, Einar, 506
Thurstone, Louis Leon, 295
Thygeson, E. Theodore I., 382
Thyreen, Gustaf, 590
Tigerhjelm, Dr. Carl Petter, 343
Tilderquist, Dr. David L., 338
Tofft, Andrew, 189
Toll, Carl Fredrick, naval officer, 512
Tomasson, Martin, 26
Torell, Rev. J., 175
Torkillus, Rev. Reorus, 8, 22, 23, 37, 38, 41, 52, 54
Torpadie, Greta, 467
Torpadie, Mme. (Mrs. Björksten), 467
Totten, Vicken von Post, 502
Tranberg, Rev. Peter, 37, 41
Traung, Charles, 576
Traung, Louis, 576
Troil, Uno von, 55
Tronstrom, Esther E., 309
Trulson, Anton M., 189
Trybom, J. H., 303
Tullgren, Herbert W., 431
Tyck, Röther, 26
Tyden, Emil, 555, 556

UDDEN, Johan August, 159, 167, 170, 171, 283, 295
Uhler, J. P., 166
Unonius, Rev. Gustaf, 78, 126, 129
Uppvall, Axel Johan, 52, 64, 73, 74, 295, 296
Urban, Rev. Joseph T., 51
Usselinx, Willem, 5, 6

VAN DYCK, Gregorius, 8, 22
Vanström, J. E., 472
Vanstrum, Capt., 522
Vegesack, Gen. Ernest von, 521, 523
Veld, Henry, 160
Venon, J. H., 597
Vestling, Axel Ebenezer, 296
Vickner, Edwin Johan Vallentin, 64, 73, 296
Victor, A. F., 481

WAERNER, Ninian, 197, 198, 199
Wahlin, Gustaf Eric, 299
Wahlin, Hugo Bernard, 299
Wahlquist, John W., 311
Wahlstrand, Harry L., 209

Wahlstrom, L. W., 303
Wahlstrom, Rev. Matthias, 158, 164
Wahlund, Oscar B., 371
Walberg, "Rube," 372
Waldenström, Rev. Paul Peter, 133, 138, 157, 177
Walgreen, Charles, 579, 580
Wallberg, Emil, 161
Wallberg, Marie, 161
Wallen, Theodore Clifford (Ted), 220 ff., 228
Wallenius, Rev. Carl G., 137
Waller, Peter A., 571
Wallgren, Abian Anders, 235, 236
Wallgren, Monrad C., 334
Wallin, Carl E., 499
Wallin, Ivan E., 296
Wallin, Johan Ludwig, 230, 231, 232
Wallin, John Edward Wallace, 159, 296, 310
Wally, Gustav (Wallenberg), 479
Warn, William Axel, 221 ff., 228
Weidner, Revere F., 162
Wendelin, Eric C., 336
Wendell, C. A., 244
Wenner-Gren, Axel L., 592
Wenström, Jonas, 414
Wern, Gustaf P., 590
Wertmüller, Adolph Ulric, 43, 490 ff., 573
Westeen, Dr. A. A., 343
Westerberg, Iwar S., 311
Westergren, Elizabeth Clarke, 247
Westlin, Tobias, 451
Westlund, Capt. C., 378
Westman, Carl, 432
Westman, Edward C., 326
Westover, Winifred, 474
Wettergren, Gertrud, 465
Whitman, Walt, 242, 264
Wiberg, P., 414
Wicklund, Gustaf, 198, 199, 470
Wicklund, Joseph Waldemar, 306
Wickman, C. Eric, 580
Wickman, Gunnar, 189
Wide, Edwin, 373
Widforss, Gunnar, 498
Widmark, H. W., 410
Widmark, Lawrence E., 407
Wieselgren, Rev. Peter, 127, 131
Wilkens, L. W., 591

William, Hereditary Prince of Sweden, 240, 249
Williams, Victor, 438
Williamson, A. W., 162
Williamson, M. O., 326
Wilson, Roy, 559
Wingquist, Sven Gustaf, 391
Wise, John, 533
Witting, A. G., 396
Wollmar, Sixten F., 591
Wrangel, Rev. Carl Magnus von, 47, 48, 58
Wretman, Gustaf, 374

YOUNGERT, Rev. Sven Gustaf, 162, 174
Younggren, Charles C., 582
Youngquist, G. Aaron, 315, 318
Youngquist, Helen Lindström, 468
Youngquist (Ljungkvist), Samuel, 468

ZANDER, Dr. Jonas Gustaf Wilhelm, 358
Zetterstrom, Olle, 376
Ziegler, F. J., 247
Zilliacus, Konni, 194, 195
Zorn, Anders, 218, 238, 500